Don 6. ✓ **W9-CDA-742**

Billy the Kid

By Elizabeth Fackler from Tom Doherty Associates

Backtrail
Billy the Kid: The Legend of El Chivato
Blood Kin

Billy the Kid

The Legend of El Chivato

Elizabeth Fackler

A Tom Doherty Associates Book   New York

This is a work of fiction. All the characters and events portrayed in this novel are either fictitious or are used fictitiously.

BILLY THE KID: THE LEGEND OF EL CHIVATO

A Forge® Book
Published by Tom Doherty Associates, Inc.
175 Fifth Avenue
New York, N.Y. 10010

Forge® is a registered trademark of Tom Doherty Associates, Inc.

Library of Congress Cataloging-in-Publication Data

Fackler, Elizabeth.
    Billy the Kid : the legend of El Chivato / Elizabeth
Fackler.
        p. cm.
    "A Tom Doherty Associates book."
    ISBN 0-312-85559-1
    1. Billy, the Kid—Fiction. 2. Southwest,
New—History—1848—Fiction. 3. Outlaws—West
(U.S.)—Fiction. I. Title.
PS3556.A28B53   1995
813'.54—dc20   95-12768
                                    CIP

First edition: August 1995

Printed in the United States of America

0 9 8 7 6 5 4 3 2 1

To
John Henry Tunstall,
Alexander McSween,
Richard Brewer, Frank McNab,
Harvey Morris, Vicente Romero, Francisco Zamora,
Tom O'Folliard, Charles Bowdre,
and William H. Bonney,
this book is respectfully dedicated.

I never liked the Kid and I didn't approve of his career, but he wasn't as bad as they made him out to be.

Sue McSween

. . . confess over him all the iniquities of the children of Israel, and all their transgressions in all their sins, putting them upon the head of the goat, and . . . send him away by the hand of a fit man into the wilderness. . . .

Leviticus 16:21

Billy, they don't like you to be so free.

Bob Dylan

Billy
the Kid

1

SILVER CITY, NEW MEXICO TERRITORY
September 1874

Blood is what he remembered, a lacy embroidery of blood on her handkerchiefs. Henry would wash them in the cauldron, boiling them with lye, pour the red water into the creek and rinse them clean, then boil them again with starch. He would pin them dripping on the line to dry stiff in the last ripple of wind, so he would have to dampen them again to iron them. He would try to iron away the stiffness and make them soft again, but it would take his mother's blood to do that.

Two events approached, filling him with dread: at the end of summer, he would start school; and soon, maybe even before the first day of autumn, his mother would die. At fourteen, he hadn't been to school in five years. He had never been without a mother.

When she first proposed coming to the Southwest, she had said the climate would make her well. That was why he agreed to her marriage, because the man would give them a home where Henry's mother could heal. Henry figured he could get along with just about anyone, and a country-bumpkin farmer would be putty in the hands of a streetwise kid from New York City. Within an hour of meeting the man—his mother, too, seeing him for the first time—they'd gone directly to the church where Henry and his brother and a couple who were friends with the man had witnessed the exchange of vows. The vows were obedience and service, but Henry hadn't made them. In sickness till death, is what he remembered.

William Antrim was the man's name, though everyone called him Uncle Billy. Tall and stout, he could knock a boy down with one sudden swipe of his clublike hand. A miner, it turned out, neither a farmer nor a property owner, but a laborer and tenant. He was shy and awkward around women, which wasn't surprising since he'd mail-ordered a wife with galloping consumption and two nearly grown sons.

Henry couldn't figure the man's motive, but he admired the way everyone liked Uncle Billy: how the younger children ran laughing to hug his legs, the women always gave him the biggest slice of pie, and the men threw their arms across his shoulder as they walked back to the woodpile to smoke pipes and talk weather until called for supper. Uncle Billy seemed charmed. In his otherwise amiable eyes, only Henry ever saw hatred.

Their house was unpainted wood facing Main Street, which was usually wet with runoff from the mountains. In the tiny mining village, everyone knew who the newcomers were as soon as they arrived. Some of the other kids had grown up on the frontier and mastered things Henry hadn't yet tried. Like surviving in the mountains alone. Riding a horse until it became an extension of your will. Shooting a gun until you could pick off a bottle thrown in the air and watch it explode in a thousand fragments of sunlight. Henry had a lot to learn, but he didn't figure it would happen in a classroom. The only attraction school held for him was the vaudeville show the children put on for Halloween.

Henry thought he was a natural for the stage. He wanted to hold people in rapt attention. The streets of New York had taught him how to weasel in and out of places he had no right to be, how to pilfer a living if he didn't make it home for a few days. Now Uncle Billy was showing him how to charm his way to a supper table; only Uncle Billy was a bumbling gelding and Henry knew he could flirt, too, and be welcomed for more than a meal. So sometimes he followed Uncle Billy and watched him from a distance, how he handled himself and how gladly people greeted him, and Henry learned how it was done. The rest of his time he spent with his mother.

Her room was a small wooden tomb, nearly filled with her featherbed, the two baskets, a small chest of drawers, and the trunk she'd brought from Ireland. She had come across alone from Dublin, having walked three days to reach the port. On her immigration papers her profession was listed as "servant" and her age as seventeen. Her name was Katherine McCarty and her sons bore the same name. They were five years apart, Joseph first, born in St. Mary's Hospital, father listed as unknown though he wasn't. When Henry Michael was born at home, the father registered him simply as a male child born to Katherine and Henry McCarty, who were unmarried, but the certificate didn't mention that.

Katherine had sent it to Uncle Billy as proof of a previous marriage, saying the father of her boys had died in the War of Rebellion serving the Union, and her other papers, the certificate of Joe's birth and the marriage itself, had been lost in a fire. Suspecting Uncle Billy knew the truth, she often wondered why he would take on the responsibility of a sick wife and two boys. But as time went on and she came to know his goodness, she realized he'd simply needed someone to receive it.

Yet his goodness couldn't make her well. She continued to weaken with each painful spasm of her lungs. The fine clean air of New Mexico made no difference. Because of the factory she'd worked in for ten years, twelve hours a day, six days a week, she was infected with death. Her lingering degeneration infected Henry with hatred for the father who refused to help after giving her two bastard sons. In her heart, Katherine admired Henry for hating his father, but her illness left no strength to champion such violent emotions. It had required all of her fortitude to find someone to finish raising her boys.

Katherine knew Joe would get along. He was a steady hand, with no more ambition and less fight than a mule who'd been harnessed for forty years. Henry was different. Irreverent and disrespectful, he acted as if life were half-adventure, half-joke. She blamed his father for that. From him Henry had learned the protection shirking responsibility gave to a person. When Henry was in trouble, it was the Children's Aid Society who came to her rescue. They arranged her marriage with Uncle Billy as part of their Adoption and Foster Homes program. Ship the kid out, was their theory, make a man of him in the West.

Katherine had hopes along the same line. And Henry was doing all right. But he didn't trust her new husband, she could see that by the way he kept to the perimeter of any room they shared. When she asked Uncle Billy to do his best for Henry after she was gone, he answered that he could do no more, so she knew he'd already given up. She pleaded with him to grant the boy more patience, explaining again how thirteen was a hard age to accept a man becoming his father overnight.

Uncle Billy said, "It din't hurt Josie none. He's steady as a rock."

She thought poor Joe was boring as a rock, too, and it was Henry's happiness she longed for. "They're different," she said.

"Aye, that Henry is," he replied, spitting tobacco juice into the basket of soiled handkerchiefs. "Suspect a strong strap was needed when he was younger. Too late now. He's slick, like butter in your fingers. You can track him down, have him within arm's reach, and he still gets away. Don't know, Mrs. Antrim, can't make no promises about that one." She nodded and patted his hand. "Just do your best, Billy," she said, her heart aching for Henry.

He was there when she died. After sweating in the sun washing handkerchiefs, then ironing them in the heat of the kitchen, he brought them to her as a gift. She smiled as she watched him, so proud and eager for the world to be a place of fun and laughter, good times and congratulations, refusing to see life was mostly suffering and hard work till you died.

Yet how could she fault him, coming in with a basket of laundry he'd labored hard and long to bring her? That was something Uncle Billy hadn't learned: it wasn't that Henry didn't work, only that he chose his own tasks. To tell him to do the dishes would send him out on the streets for hours, yet if you kept quiet, he would do them by choice. If you let him pick his own way, he often surprised you with his solicitude. Like taking it on himself to wash her linen.

"There's a bonny lad," she said, then covered her mouth as she coughed.

He sat on the edge of her bed, holding the basket proudly in his lap. When she coughed again, he set it on the floor and handed her a clean handkerchief. She tried to thank him but the cough stifled her voice with a flood of blood, soaking the fresh handkerchief and falling in lacy tendrils onto the quilt. Henry dabbed at it worriedly, then exchanged the soiled cloth for a clean one. When the surge came again, he knew it was the hemorrhage the doctor had foretold. In useless denial, Henry tried to blot the blood away, but finally he gave up and held his mother close, feeling her blood spew like vomit down the front of his shirt until she was still.

When he laid her down, he had to look away from the agony left on her face. Then he picked up a fresh handkerchief and began to clean her. "Ma, you're a mess," he joked, then sobbed, then shook his head. "Can't let 'em see you like this. Gotta go out pretty, ain't that right, Ma?"

He took water from the pitcher and washed her face, shaped her mouth into a becoming, noncommittal line, and arranged her hair so it lay gracefully on the pillow. Removing the soiled quilt, he covered her with the blanket from his own bed, then stood looking at his work. Silence rang in the room, making him realize this was the first time he could remember not hearing his mother cough.

He tried to be glad she was at peace, tried briefly to believe in her heaven, but couldn't accomplish either. Her laughter had been stolen, her wit, her love, her friendship—if by anyone, then by God. Henry couldn't accept a God so cruel in the way He dealt out death. Death should be an arrow through the heart or a bullet to the brain; it shouldn't linger.

In the lonely silence, Henry felt anger like a razor slicing his perception: if this was the end of the game, no one could win. The only thing within your control was the method of death, your only freedom lay in shaping it to your liking. "Life may have me by the balls," he half-laughed, "but I get to choose which bed I get fucked in." Then, feeling bad for cursing in front of her, he said, "I'm sorry, Ma."

When Uncle Billy came home, he found Henry burning the bloody quilt and handkerchiefs in the backyard. The boy wouldn't look at him and Uncle Billy didn't say anything as he walked into the house and looked at the body of his wife. Knowing the boy had cleaned his mother and arranged her the way he wanted, Uncle Billy felt a sorrowful relief. Now her suffering was over, and maybe he and the boys could get on together. He walked back out on the porch and watched Henry by the fire.

He was a small boy; for all his wily ways, he wasn't much bigger than a girl. And he had a pleasant face except for his crooked teeth giving an edge to his smile, and his pale eyes so restive they made you nervous. But if Henry could trust someone to be there for him, not always at work or sick as his mother had been, but someone strong and able to help, maybe then his restlessness would go away. Walking toward the boy, Uncle Billy pulled from his pocket a carving knife he'd bought for himself earlier that morning. Silently he offered it to Henry.

He hesitated. Calculating, Uncle Billy thought. Nothing was ever simple with Henry. "Go on, take it," Uncle Billy said. "Want you to know I'm still your kin. You ain't no orphan."

Henry took the knife and slipped it into his pocket as if daring Uncle Billy to get it back. "Thanks," he said.

Uncle Billy harrumphed with embarrassment. "I'm gonna see the undertaker. Fetch your brother, will you?"

"Sure," Henry said, then smiled almost as if they were pals.

Uncle Billy scurried away from the discomfort he felt under the boy's scrutiny. Looking back from the bridge across Main Street, he saw Henry hadn't moved.

When Uncle Billy returned, he half-expected the boy to still be there, but the fire was barely smoldering in the deserted yard. As he stood wondering if he should fetch Joe or trust Henry to do it, the neighbor's five-year-old daughter ran into the yard and giggled with joy at seeing Uncle Billy. She was wearing a red gingham dress and her hair was curled in long dark ringlets falling from a red ribbon. When she ran on bare feet through the dusty yard to give him a hug, he bent and returned her hug with more vigor than usual. "You look so purty, Elisa Mae," he said. "Where you going all dressed up?"

She laughed. "A birthday party! Is Henry ready? He's s'posed to walk me."

"Henry won't be going," he said sadly. "His mama died today. Go on home and tell your folks and they'll let somebody else walk you, all right, now?"

She nodded, uncomprehending. "Have you seen my kitten?" she asked. "I have to catch my kitten first."

"No," he said, standing up and looking for it.

She ran around the house and disappeared. When he heard a wail of grief, he ran after her then stopped, arrested with shock to see Henry kneeling over the bloody corpse of the kitten.

Henry had thought it a good joke. The kitten was innocent, hadn't hurt even a mouse yet, so it was like his mother. As for right, Henry had the right if God did. God gave him the means and showed him an example of His botched handiwork, and Henry meant to show Him how it was done.

You catch them unsuspecting some bright and sunny day, slip up behind and caress them, then gently pull their head back and slit their throat. To make sure there's no unnecessary suffering, you slash the knife through a joint between vertebrae until you've beheaded the poor sucker and he's definitely feeling no pain.

There was blood everywhere, just as with his mother; but unlike with his mother, someone was screaming. Looking up at Elisa Mae's face, Henry felt sick. He hadn't known it was her kitten. It was just there and alive. Seeing the hatred in Uncle Billy's eyes, Henry sneered. "What'd you expect me to do with a knife?"

He watched Uncle Billy lift the sobbing child and walk away fast. Swamped with loneliness, Henry closed his eyes and vomited on the corpse of the kitten, puking up the bitter rejection he'd always received from men. Wiping his mouth with the back of his hand, he vowed never again to let himself ache with the sorrows of life, neither his own nor anyone else's. From here on he would laugh at all pain, just as he did now at the defiled corpse the child had loved. After a while he gathered the pieces, carried them into the forest, and buried them deep. He buried the knife, too, then he went back and waited on the porch for his brother to come home for supper.

Years later, when William Antrim told this story to reporters, he always finished by declaring the boy was born bad. But history doesn't record what Uncle Billy thought of the Kid taking his name.

2

ON THE SANTA FE TRAIL
Early March, 1875

The fire raged in her circle of stones, built with the first dry wood they had come across in days. After shivering inside her woolen cloak for what seemed like forever, she stood dangerously close to the flames and spread her shawl like wings to catch the heat. Anyone watching would have admired how the light shimmered on the auburn curls of her hair, danced along the graceful curves of her hips, and threw a benign glow on her strong-featured face, sliced by a smile of contentment.

For a moment she was lost to her surroundings as the power of her will sealed the world away. She floated in anticipation, visualizing a future of opulence when she would reign as social regent of whatever town her husband chose. In the new territory of ungathered wealth, their destiny would be grand.

As she opened her eyes on the flat expanse of the Staked Plain, the sounds of the night reclaimed her attention. Loudest was the wind in the canvas of the wagons, the sporadic slap punctuating the murmur of voices amid the clatter of activities and the occasional whinny from horses grazing on the brown grass of winter. Away from the camp, the wilderness stretched unbroken in every direction. For a moment, staring into its vast emptiness, she felt desolate. Then she shook her head and knotted her shawl high to free her hands for making supper.

She busied herself mixing biscuit dough, peeling potatoes, and sawing off strips of the dried beef which must be simmered for hours before becoming tender. Hoisting the bucket to the spigot on the barrel, she braced her arm beneath the weight of falling water, then emptied the bucket into the pot beside the fire, lifted the blackened pot over the flames, and hung it on the hook to heat. Into the water went the shredded beef and chunks of potatoes and her last onion. She rolled the biscuit dough, shaped it in the skillet and set it aside, then spooned coffee into the coffeepot, filled it, too, from the bucket, and placed it on a rock near the fire. With the remaining water she washed her face and smoothed her hair before setting the crude table with the metal utensils she'd hated daily on their journey from Atchison. Looking up, she saw her husband and another man approaching along the line of wagons.

The two men were nearly the same height, but next to the stranger's swarthiness, the pallor of Alexander McSween seemed—to his wife—

noble in its delicacy. His high forehead, edged by straight black hair, gave evidence of an intellect undenied by his solemn, darkly glistening eyes. His gentle mouth was draped by a wiry moustache whose corners fell below his chin, and his black suit and four-in-hand tie, limp with dust against his white shirt, completed the visage of a gentleman of refinement.

She had been his wife for barely a year. Despite his ineptitude in his conjugal duties, she was passionately in love, believing his superior intellect would create the wealth both of them coveted. His education in law made him wily, and his divinity studies gilded him with moral rectitude, a combination she thought unbeatable. Knowing faults that made her flinch during courtship would be unbearable in marriage, she felt justified in having waited twenty-seven years to accept a husband. Spinsterhood wasn't as bad as serving an inferior man, not to the mind of Susan Ellen Homer. Now Mrs. Alexander McSween, wife of the soon-to-be-famous barrister.

Mac touched the back of her waist as he smiled down at her, having missed her in the few minutes they'd been apart. He felt proud, too, that supper was so efficiently begun, the table ready and the aromas around a wilderness campfire reminiscent of home. Introducing his companion, he said, "Sue, this is Miguel Otero, an attorney in Santa Fe. He's been telling me of a highly interesting town in the southern mountains. I've invited him to dinner, do we have enough?"

"Surely," she replied with a smile to their guest. He was as dark as an Indian, yet wore a suit and presented a civilized demeanor. "Please sit down, Mr. Otero. Dinner will be a while, I'm afraid."

As they settled in the chairs placed around the fire, Mac said, "Would you be so kind, Mr. Otero, as to tell my wife what you've been saying about La Placita."

"La Placita," Sue murmured. "What a cute name."

"It was what the original settlers called their town," Otero explained, betraying only a modest accent. "La Placita del Rio Bonito. It means little plaza of the pretty river. The name has recently been changed, however, in honor of your fallen president."

"Do you mean Lincoln?" Sue asked, impressed with his elocution.

"Yes, señora," he answered. "The town and the county are both named Lincoln now."

"Señora?" she echoed. "Is that Spanish?"

He nodded. "Do you like it?"

"I think I do," she said, camouflaging a blush by leaning forward to stir the stew and hide her face in its steam.

"You will hear it often," Otero said, "if you choose to live among us. We are, most of us, of Mexican descent."

"If they're as charming as you, Mr. Otero," she replied, "I'm sure we'll get along just fine."

Mac said with enthusiasm, "They have no legal advisor, Sue. In the entire county, there is not one practicing attorney!"

Her heart beat rapidly in anticipation. "How many people live in this town of Lincoln?" she asked their guest.

"Five hundred, more or less, if you include the outlying regions. Farms are spread all along the river valleys, with the town near the center of a natural pass in the mountains. They rise close on either side and afford a plentitude of fresh water as well as timber, so the area has attracted settlers of both your race and mine since the army returned to Fort Stanton after your war."

"Mostly farmers, you say?" Mac asked.

"In the mountains, yes. Cattle ranchers down along the Pecos. And of course, stores and mills and the usual sporting houses to serve them. The army is there, as I said, and I mustn't fail to mention the Mescaleros."

"Who are they?" Sue asked with a laugh, the name striking her funny.

"Apaches," Otero answered.

Sue felt the frivolity slip from her face, but Otero smiled kindly.

"They're peaceful," he reassured her, "remaining on their reservation and accepting what's given. Now and then one or two will make trouble, but the soldiers keep them under control, more or less." He smiled wryly. "Despite its natural beauty, I don't wish to give the impression that Lincoln is a Garden of Eden. It is still the frontier and violence is not unusual. With the coming of law," he nodded toward his host, "life will change. I believe, sir, that you would do well there."

"It sounds perfect," Mac agreed. "In thirty years, we'll be the old aristocracy."

Otero's smile was indulgent. "You will find life in the territory demands a price of great humility. For those families who survive to the next century, it will indeed be the El Dorado of which you spoke."

"The next century," Sue said, looking fondly at her husband. "We'll be aged by then."

"And respectably rich," Mac said, then added with chagrin, "God willing, of course."

3

SILVER CITY
September 1875

No one knew his real name but everyone called him Sombrero Jack. The hat had long ago been trampled by too many hooves in too many gutters and finally gone the way of a bad loan, but the name endured. Maybe because anyone speaking of him needed something to lighten the occasion.

The women of Silver City thought him a miserable failure, a drunk and a beggar, procurer of tawdry pleasures and corruptor of youth. To the men, he was the butt of obvious pranks and a good sport if the joke was followed by whiskey. To the scruffy boys idling on the streets, he was an opportunity.

Silver City was a small town and everyone knew the source of merchandise offered surreptitiously at back doors. Some bought, others wouldn't. Consumable produce was easiest because the evidence soon disappeared. Recognizable stuff was the worst; people shied away from buying something whose ownership might be challenged. So when Sombrero Jack stole the bundle of clothing off the delivery cart of Charlie Sun and Sam Chung's Celestial Laundry, he knew he'd have to hide the clothes until he could ride over to Chloride Flats and sell them there. With the bundle under his arm, he scurried into the thickets south of Main Street.

There was a kid living on this side of town who hung around the saloons a lot. Jack had seen a hunger in the boy's eyes and knew he was ripe, young enough to take orders from a drunk yet old enough to carry them out. Hurrying to hide his booty before Sheriff Whitehall came looking, Sombrero Jack snuck through the trees and stood behind Mrs. Brown's boardinghouse, staring through the open back door into the kitchen. Henry was there, washing dishes. Jack grunted in sympathy, thinking he was doing the lad a favor by teaching him a better way to pay his keep than women's work.

When Jack whistled long and low, the kid glanced out the door but didn't break his rhythm of soaping the plates and laying them carefully into the basin of rinse water. The old man whistled again, this time putting a little trill on it. Though Jack knew Henry couldn't see, looking out from the light as he was, the kid stared straight at him, then stepped through the door into the yard, drying his hands on a towel. He hung it on the doorknob and walked cautiously away from the light.

He's a canny un', the old man thought, the way he don't say nothing but jus' come out quiet to see what's what. "Over here," Jack whispered.

Henry quickly looked back at the house, then ducked into the deeper darkness beneath the trees with a grin of anticipation. "You got something for me?"

"Don't be so damn eager," Jack growled. "I ain't sure ya can handle this un'."

"I did all right last time," Henry answered with a smile.

"Yeah, yeah," the old man muttered grudgingly. "But this time ya gotta sit on something right tight for a coupla days."

"I can do that. What is it?"

Jack thrust the bundle of laundry into his hands.

"Clothes?" Henry asked skeptically.

"Folks gotta have duds, ain't they? I'll sell 'em over to Chloride."

"I don't know," the kid said, making as if to give the bundle back. "This is awful big to hide."

"Give ya yer choice of shirts," Sombrero Jack offered. "That un' yer wearing looks 'bout wore out."

Henry thought a minute. "Tell you what. I can put half of 'em in my trunk, I'll hide half for you."

"Not fer a whole shirt, ya won't," the old man growled.

Henry hunkered down and opened the bundle, separating the shirts from the long johns. Rolling the shirts into a thick wad, he grinned at Sombrero Jack. "I won't take the fanciest one. When you want 'em back?"

Jack felt he'd been outdone. Henry had the best stuff and he still had a problem. "Ya got two-bits I can borry?"

"If I had two-bits," Henry answered with a laugh, "I wouldn't be working for you."

"Ah, ya smart-ass kid. You'll never work for nobody better. Now ya hide that stuff good and I'll be back in a night or two and collect 'em."

"Don't take too long," Henry warned, then walked back toward the light. Sneaking up sideways on the door to peer in from the edge, he saw the kitchen was empty but another stack of dirty dishes sat on the counter. That meant Mrs. Brown had been in while he was gone. She likely wouldn't return in the next few minutes, so he thought he had a good chance of getting to his room without being seen. Quickly crossing the kitchen, he had just turned the corner to climb the stairs when he saw Mrs. Brown descending.

"Here you are," she pronounced. "I thought you'd run off before finishing your chores. What do you have there?" She came down the stairs with her skirts billowing out behind her, a pretty woman whose face was soft and pink even when she scolded.

This time, however, Henry knew she would be more than angry; her sense of civic duty would demand he right this wrong somehow; and he felt certain he wouldn't care for the repercussions of the next few minutes.

Sarah Brown stopped on the stair above him and looked into his face with a frown of hurt disapproval. "What is this, Henry? Where did you get these?"

"I found 'em," he answered with false exuberance. "Jus' now on the back step. Someone must've left 'em there."

Her frown deepened. "I thought you had more respect than to tell me a lie, Henry Antrim. Turn around, young man. We'll have to fetch the sheriff."

When she said that about the sheriff, Henry turned back and blocked her passage. "You ain't really?" he asked, looking down at her now that they were level on the landing.

"What do you think I should do?" she answered primly.

"Forget you seen me," he suggested with a shrug. "It ain't your concern."

"This is my house," she said. "Your father placed you in my care."

"Stepfather," he muttered, turning away and dropping the wad of shirts on the kitchen table. He saw the collar of a green one he wanted.

"Uncle Billy's as concerned about you as if he were your father," she replied. "He promised your mother he'd take care of you."

"He ain't my kin," Henry stated.

"I'm afraid he won't agree when he sees his name in the newspaper for you having been arrested." She stepped to the door of the hall and called down to the dining room for her husband.

After a moment, John Brown came in dabbing a napkin at his mouth as he stared at Henry with contempt. Sarah had told him the boy was her charge and she would mete out any punishment needed. Which meant a tongue-lashing when anyone with eyes could see Henry enjoyed her scoldings, his appreciation near enough to being sexual to make her husband uncomfortable. "What is it, Mrs. Brown?" he asked gruffly.

"Henry has stolen these shirts," she said, looking at the boy. "I want you to fetch Sheriff Whitehall."

John Brown couldn't resist a smile. "Wise course of action, Mrs. Brown. I'll go right away."

Walking toward the door, he snickered at Henry. Henry gave him the finger where Mrs. Brown couldn't see, but John Brown saw it. "The sheriff, then," he said, and was gone.

"I'm very disappointed in you, Henry," Mrs. Brown said. "Think of how ashamed your mother would be."

"Leave her outta this," he said flatly.

"I hardly can. Just because she isn't here doesn't mean she doesn't care what happens to you, doesn't suffer when you do wrong. I can only hope you learn your lesson this time, that's why I'm going to plead for the maximum penalty. This is a small crime, the punishment will be light at worst. But you must understand, Henry, that it will not behoove you to continue with lawlessness. Eventually you'll learn that society is stronger and more important than you. You must bow before its rules because they're right, they come from the Bible. You know the Ten Commandments. Thou shalt not steal."

"I didn't steal 'em," Henry protested.

"Thou shalt not bear false witness. Oh, Henry, on top of everything, don't lie to me."

"I ain't. I didn't steal 'em."

"Then where did you get them?"

"I told you. I found 'em on the back step. Maybe somebody'll come looking for 'em."

"I'm sure you wish they would, but we both know they won't. You may finish the dishes while we're waiting for the sheriff."

"No," Henry said.

"Horrors to heaven!" she cried, as close to profanity as he'd ever heard her come. "Henry Antrim, you'll do as you're told."

"I ain't," he said, pulling out a chair and sitting down. The shirts were right in front of him. Wanting the green one, he stood up and began unbuttoning his shirt.

"What are you doing?" she asked in dismay.

"Nothing," he said, pulling his shirt off and taking the time to fold it, knowing his half-nakedness would kill her hand. He buried his shirt among the others and pulled out the green one, shaking it loose and sticking his arms into the sleeves.

Sarah Brown sighed. "I'm afraid you're incorrigible, Henry."

"I don't know that word," he said, grinning at her as he buttoned his new shirt.

"It means you're hopeless," she answered, then turned away as he opened his trousers to tuck in the tails.

Henry closed his pants and sat down still grinning. "Gotta go out pretty, is what I always say."

She stared at him a long moment, then said in a low voice of defeat, "Don't come back."

"I see," he said amiably. "This shirt ain't a present, it's a bribe. Seems like presents are always like that. Uncle Billy gave me a knife once but it was a bribe, too. Know what I did with it? I buried it. Don't think I'll bury your shirt, though. I kinda like it."

"I didn't give you that shirt."

"Sure you did. Or you will. By not saying nothing when your husband comes back with the sheriff."

"What makes you think I'll do that?"

Henry smiled, sliding low in his chair. " 'Cause we like each other, and you don't want to send me away in a wore-out shirt."

"You won't need a shirt in prison," she replied tartly. "They give you striped uniforms to wear."

"They won't send me to prison," he scoffed. "The territory ain't even got one."

"Well, at least to jail. Not more than a year, though, I don't imagine." Seeing his grin of disbelief, her face softened with pity, but she said, "This is serious, Henry. It's not a joke."

When they heard the front door open and the heavy footsteps coming down the hall, he watched her face harden into indifference. Reluctantly turning his eyes on the sheriff, a man who'd whipped him a few months earlier for stealing butter, Henry knew mercy was not his fate.

Sheriff Harvey Whitehall had no patience with boys like Henry, seeing them as future adversaries who became more dangerous with age. The sheriff's usual discipline was quick and brutal. He himself had been weaned by a strong arm wielding a fast belt and could see no harm done. It was the boys who grew up under a woman's hand who needed the cockiness beat out of them by a superior force. Trouble was, there came a point when a boy looked at the world so cockeyed no amount of punishment would set him straight. The only thing you could do with a brat like that was come down hard and hope he left your jurisdiction before he became vicious. Arresting Henry Antrim called for such a course of action, and the sheriff felt smug.

Henry followed without resistance, carrying the shirts and not looking back at the boardinghouse he'd called home for nearly a year. The sheriff gripped his arm hard, but Henry didn't say anything, didn't twist or squirm to get away. He was almost sixteen and had spent most of his life successfully getting away. Now he was caught and felt curious to see what happened next. Thinking he'd been wasting time this last year and needed something to shake him loose, he decided becoming a pariah to the people who held him here seemed a sure bet of a way out.

The sheriff's office was a one-room building with two cells partitioned by iron bars. Three prisoners reclined on the jailhouse bunks. The one alone in his cell rolled over to watch as the sheriff came in with Henry. Deputy Moorehead sat with his feet on the desk, picking his teeth with a straw.

"Git your feet off my desk!" Whitehall bawled to the deputy, who complied meekly. "Here, boy, put the evidence on the desk now."

Henry dropped the shirts and rubbed his numb arm until the sheriff ordered him to stand in the far corner. Henry obeyed warily.

"Write this down," Whitehall told his deputy. "This here's Henry Antrim, used to be McCarty. Was found in possession of some clothes not belonging to him." Belligerently, he approached the boy. "How'd you come by them clothes, Henry?"

"I found 'em," Henry answered.

Whitehall slapped him hard. "Tell me the truth now," he said, slapping him again. "I'll stop hitting you when you do." He struck him twice more, using his fist this time as he said, "Sombrero Jack give 'em to you, didn't he?"

Henry crumpled beneath the blows, shielding himself only by raising his arms, but Whitehall's fist crashed through again and again.

Breathing hard, the sheriff retreated and stood glaring at the kid from a distance. "You get all that, Moorehead?" Whitehall growled.

"Sombrero Jack give 'em to me," the deputy pretended to read from his notes.

"Your partner left town, that's how we know he done it," Whitehall told Henry. "Wasn't real nice of him to go off leaving you holding the bag. Shows what friends like him are worth, don't it?" Advancing toward the boy with his fists ready for action, Whitehall bellowed, "Don't it, boy?"

The kid spit blood on the floor and answered thickly, "Ain't got no friend name Sombrero Jack."

"Ah, lock him up," the sheriff said, ending the interrogation with a wave of his arm.

Moorehead moved slowly to take down the big ring of keys, then helped the kid to his feet. Feeling how heavily Henry leaned on him as they crossed the few steps to the cell door, the deputy felt sorry for the boy. The sheriff seemed to hate Henry Antrim and always roughed him up hard. Any fool could see the approach wasn't working if correction was wanted. But Moorehead had been deputy long enough to know Whitehall was a bully, and smart-alecky kids were his perfect victims because they fought back without a prayer of winning.

Moorehead figured the sheriff kept his blade sharp on punks so he could be ready to do his real job, which was capturing felons. The system worked well because it guaranteed a new crop of felons always coming along, young criminals essentially trained by law officers like Whitehall. Moorehead opened the cell door and let go of Henry's arm, watching the kid stumble without outside support. The deputy reached out to help him, but the kid made it alone across to the bunk where he sat holding his head in his hands.

In that moment and all that night, Henry was filled with an immense regret that he'd allowed himself to be caught.

The next morning in court, he wasn't able to muster a smile until John Brown came in. And then it was only because the man was such a puffed-up banty rooster he was naturally amusing. Brown wallowed in righteousness, painting a long-winded picture of his wife laboring fruitlessly to right this young man who'd gone astray, and how the ungrateful lout repaid her generosity by using her home to harbor stolen goods. Eventually even Justice Givens grew bored with the redundancy of Brown's narration and cut it off, then looked at Henry. "Stand up, my boy," the judge said, his voice so stern Henry knew he was in for it.

The judge cleared his throat and intoned, "I find you guilty of theft and complicity to theft, Henry Antrim, and sentence you to one year in the county jail, with the stipulation that after three months of good behavior you be released on probation, and the further condition that within that probationary period you not be brought before this court on any other charge. If you are, you will be remanded to serve the remainder of the year's sentence plus whatever sentence you incur on the new charge. Do you understand, Henry?"

"Yes, sir," he answered without emotion.

"I remand you, then, into the custody of Sheriff Whitehall to serve your sentence. Good luck, lad."

Henry snorted. "Under the sheriff's hand, I'll surely need it."

"You had a gentle hand under my wife," Brown sneered, "and it didn't do you any good."

"Maybe what I need is no hand at all," Henry answered quietly.

"That ain't what you're gonna get," the sheriff retorted, grabbing Henry by the scruff of his neck and hauling him from the room to the sound of laughter.

Twisting to alleviate the pain pinching his neck, Henry saw a lanky half-Mexican kid watching from the back of the courtroom, and the sight of Manuel Taylor from Chloride Flats relieved Henry's mind.

As soon as they were outside, the sheriff shifted his hold to Henry's arm. Despite the pain at the back of his neck, the world looked a lot better to Henry than it had en route to the courthouse. Now he knew he wasn't alone, and he felt grateful when the sheriff pushed him into the cell with no more rough stuff. Glad to simply lie on his bunk, Henry waited for Manuel to rescue him.

In the long shadows of late afternoon, Henry heard a whistle from outside. Glancing through the bars into the office to see Moorehead asleep with his feet on the desk, Henry stood up and looked out the window at the face of his friend. Manuel put a finger to his lips, silencing Henry's greeting.

"Listen quickly," Manuel said. "I know the man who built this jail and he told me the chimney has no flue. If you can get them to let you stay in the office tonight, I'll drop a rope down and pull you up. Can you do it?"

Henry looked around as he thought. His eyes came to rest on the hunched back of his napping cellmate. "Yeah, I got a plan," he whispered. "When Whitey and the deputy go to dinner."

Manuel nodded and disappeared. Henry lay back on his bunk, mentally rehearsing his plan. After a few minutes the deputy yawned and stretched, then stood up and started tidying the office in anticipation of the sheriff's return. He had just lit the lamp when Whitehall came in asking if he was ready to go to supper.

"Sheriff," Henry called, feigning a note of fear in his voice. "Don't leave me alone in here."

"What'cha bellyaching about?" Whitehall asked gruffly.

"This fellow," Henry said, jerking a thumb at his cellmate. "I think he's been in here too long. He's powerful lonely."

"You little punk!" the unjustly accused snarled, lunging for him.

"Here now!" Whitehall yelled. Grabbing the keys from the wall, he unlocked the cell and yanked Henry out. Still holding him, the sheriff glowered at the other man and relocked the cell. Then pursing his mouth as though he would spit, he looked at Henry. "You best be good, kid," the sheriff warned. "Or I'll leave you be next time." He jerked his head at the deputy and they left together, locking the outside door and taking the keys with them.

Henry grinned apologetically at his cellmate. "Sorry, old man, but I gotta get outta here. I don't care for the housekeeping."

"You ain't going nowhere," the man snarled. "You're locked in, same as us."

All three of the prisoners were watching now, the other two with more sympathy. One of them asked, "How you gonna do it, kid?"

"I'm gonna play Santa Claus," Henry said with a laugh. He stepped over to the hearth and looked up the chimney. "Hey, *amigo,* you there?"

"*Sí, cállate,*" the whisper echoed back.

Henry listened to the slither of the rope bouncing off the sides of the chimney as it fell, then grinned at his audience.

"Adiós," he said, grabbing the end of the rope and crawling up the sooty passage. On the roof, he climbed out under a moonless sky into the welcoming embrace of a friend. Within hours, Henry had left Silver City behind, running without a dime in his pocket but knowing a great wealth of freedom beckoned from the far horizon.

4

SANTA FE
November 1876

Alex McSween always stayed at Herlow's Hotel when in Santa Fe. Since his law practice took him all over the territory, his trips away from home were frequent and usually longer than he cared for, but it couldn't be helped. Ambitious to supplant Major Murphy as representative to the territorial legislature, Mac needed friends in all the remote population centers: not only the litigants he successfully defended, but also newspaper editors, ranchers, merchants, and politicians, whose support was essential.

John Chisum had become his major client, supplanting Murphy & Company to the satisfaction of both Mac and Sue. She liked Chisum, almost too much in Mac's eyes. There were times when he felt jealous at the sound of her laughter so enthusiastically bestowed on another man's jokes. But Sue had never given Mac cause to doubt her fidelity; it was simply that he worried about her lack of companionship. If there had been another man in Lincoln with an American wife, his mind would be eased immensely, especially as this trip promised to be a long one.

He was en route to New York to expedite settlement of the Fritz estate. The insurance company had declared bankruptcy and gone into receivership, leaving Mac no hope of collecting full value for the heirs. But despite that, he was anticipating his journey with pleasure. He planned to stop off in Missouri on his return and invite his brother-in-law to join his law practice in Lincoln. Although David Shield was a sour malcontent on whom Mac wasted little affection, Shield was an able attorney and Mac's business showed promise of supporting a partner. His real reason for offering the arrangement, however, was that David would bring his family, thereby reuniting Sue with her favorite sister. In the meantime, John Chisum had promised to invite Sue to his ranch for some of the time Mac was gone, and Bill Brady had said he'd call on her when in Lincoln, so Mac had to content himself knowing she was safe at home.

Santa Fe was a squat town made up of monotonous rows of low adobe buildings lining the dirt streets. White-clad Pueblo men and women displayed their produce—blue corn, orange squash, native herbs, and glossy black pots—spread on blankets beneath the portals. Before them walked every description of frontiersman: buckskin-clad buffalo hunters reeking of slaughter, weathered teamsters, roughly clothed range riders, and merchants in suits ten years out of style. Mingling among them were the Mexicans, though the term was a misnomer because they were descendants of the original Spanish conquistadores. Small in stature compared to the Americans, the Mexicans conducted business warily with their conquerors while the Indians watched with wisely fatalistic eyes, as if waiting to see who would vanquish the Americans.

During his stay, Mac planned to visit the Presbyterian Missionry and express again his desire for a minister to be sent to Lincoln. By planting seeds, he could nurture his community as he liked. The Mexicans, of course, would always be Roman Catholic, a religion he considered little better than the heathen beliefs of the Indians, but the newly arriving Americans would turn to whatever Protestant church was established, and Mac was determined it would be Presbyterian.

He also had an afternoon appointment with Abe Spiegelberg. To settle an unpaid bill, the merchant was pressing a claim for part of the Fritz estate, which Mac intended to deny. The day after that, he was to join a small group driving a wagon north to the railhead at Trinidad. So he had two evenings free in the capital and he hoped to further his contacts, always attentive to his ambitions.

As he walked through the falling dusk toward Herlow's Hotel, the air was crisp with the chill of impending winter. Mac's overcoat was worn thin—he intended to buy a new one in New York—and his valise was heavy with the legal papers required of his profession. Weary with the fatigue of his journey and the weight of his luggage, he threaded his way among the unruly crowd on San Francisco Street, deferring to anyone's right to precede him and conducting himself in all ways as a gentleman expecting only that the world let him go about his business in peace. Preoccupied as he was with his thoughts, he looked up just in time to avoid a collision in front of the hotel. Before him stood a tall, well-built young man smiling at him from between tawny side whiskers.

"Pardon me," Mac apologized.

"Good evening," the young man replied with an English accent.

"Ah, a Britisher," Mac said, pleased.

"From London. And you, sir?"

"Of Scottish descent, but I hail from Nova Scotia."

"I've spent time in Victoria."

"How did you find it?"

"Wet," he said with an easy laugh.

Mac smiled, noticing the Englishman's split-tailed riding coat was of an especially fine wool. "If you mind the damp," Mac said, "you've come to the right place. The high desert is usually as dry as a bone."

Shots rang out on the plaza a block away, followed by a rebel yell of unleashed pleasure.

"And noisy," the Englishman replied, laughing again. Then, as if apologetic for possibly having given offense by speaking ill of the city, he asked, "Are you stopping at Herlow's?"

"Yes," Mac answered. "And you?"

"I have been for several weeks. It's a decent enough place to lodge, but I pick my teeth at the Exchange. Would you care to join me for dinner?"

Mac felt pleased with the unexpected invitation. "I'd be delighted," he said. "Allow me a moment to freshen up. I've been traveling for three days."

"Take your time," the Englishman said with an amused smile. "I enjoy watching these galoots parade about."

They both looked at the rowdy revelers packing the street in front of them. Nearly every man wore a pistol balanced by a knife on his belt as he caroused wildly, shouting inanities and shooting into the air at whim.

"I've enjoyed the Grand Tour of Europe," the Englishman said, "lived for two years in British Columbia, and traveled extensively in California, but I've never been in a place as wild and wide open as your New Mexico Territory." He smiled at Mac. "I find the atmosphere bracing."

Mac laughed and excused himself. As he checked in at the desk, and then while washing in the basin in his room, he pondered the Englishman's presence in Santa Fe. The man was obviously monied. If looking to invest in land, he might be induced to come to Lincoln. Although his religion was probably Church of England, his breeding and education would be an asset to the community, a magnet even, attracting other investors of the best class.

Mac shook the dust from his coat and tie, put on a clean shirt and slicked his hair back with water, then inspected himself in the mirror, recognizing that his wardrobe had fallen into sorry shape. It was a natural development, he supposed, when most of his associates dressed in clothing suitable for branding cattle; but seeing the Englishman had made Mac realize how lax he'd become. Steeling himself against feelings of inferiority, he walked down the dimly lit adobe hall, through the low, dark lobby, and out into the cool night to join his new acquaintance.

The Englishman turned with a smile and extended his hand. "John Tunstall, sir."

"Alexander McSween," Mac replied, shaking the proffered hand and noting that it was as soft as a woman's.

The two men turned east toward the plaza. Across the square, the Palace of the Governors was dark except for a single lighted window in the east end.

"I called at the Palace when I first arrived," Tunstall said with annoyance. "I have a letter of introduction to the governor but he's away for now. Isn't that just my luck?"

"I don't know, is it?" Mac asked.

Tunstall laughed. "Not usually. You said you've only now arrived. Where was it you came from?"

"Lincoln," Mac said.

"And your profession?"

"I'm an attorney at law," he answered with pride.

"Ah," Tunstall said.

They stopped at the corner of the Santa Fe Trail and waited for a packtrain of burros carrying firewood to pass. "Excellent wood," Tunstall said with enthusiasm. "Lovely perfume it puts in the air, don't you think?"

"Piñon, yes," Mac replied. "It's native to the mountains around Lincoln, too."

"Where exactly is that, sir?"

"Between the Capitan and Sacramento mountains, in the southern part of the territory."

"Mountains, you say? Not good rangeland?"

"On the contrary. It's such excellent range that down along the Pecos, John Chisum's herd alone numbers eighty thousand."

The last of the burros passed. As they stepped carefully across the street, Tunstall said, "I wish I had a letter of introduction to Chisum. I'd very much like to meet the man."

"He's famous for his hospitality," Mac replied, opening the front door of the Exchange Hotel, "so you hardly need rely on such formality. I know him well."

"Do you?" Tunstall asked with interest.

They didn't speak again until they'd entered the cavernous dining room and found an empty table among the exclusively male dinner crowd. Despite the crush, a waiter immediately appeared to take their orders. After he'd gone, Mac asked, "Are you interested in the cattle business, Mr. Tunstall?"

"Keenly," the Englishman answered. "I've spent the last two months on various forays into the countryside with an eye to finding suitable range. As a lawyer, wouldn't you say this business of Spanish land grants complicates the issue of ownership?"

"Yes, title to land is a sore spot in the territory just now, so many conflicting claims exist. But the law is clear and those who follow its stipulations will prevail in the end." He paused before saying, "The territory is on the very cusp of civilization. Everything is wide open, but with the air of an animal that suspects it's trapped but can't yet see the enclosure. Those who ally themselves with the future will come out of the transition very well."

"When I was in California," Tunstall agreed, "I saw what happens when the cusp has passed. Land is outrageously expensive, near twenty dollars an acre in some parts."

"You don't say!"

"It's true. And only those who bought when it was cheap can make a profit running cattle. That is precisely what attracts me to New Mexico. It hasn't happened here yet. The economic boom is on the horizon and now is the time to invest heavily."

"Yes," Mac murmured, barely able to contain his excitement. "I believe it would behoove you to make the acquaintance of John Chisum. He has amassed a fortune with minimal investment by simply running his cattle on open land. The scheme is near perfect."

Tunstall shook his head. "The men who did that in California were gradually squeezed out by those who held title to the land." He looked up at the waiter delivering their dinners, then smiled at Mac and said, "I intend to stick a long time to the place I choose."

As they ate, Mac studied Tunstall. From his elocution to the way he handled his cutlery and the adept control of his curious gaze as he studied the room, the Englishman was obviously the product of high society. Such a man was rare on the frontier. Coveting him as a friend and associate, Mac asked, "Is there a family to be the recipient of your success?"

Tunstall nodded. "I have my parents to provide for in their old age. Indeed, it's my father's capital I'm investing. I have a sister I'm very close to, and two younger ones I scarcely know, having left England when they were still in the nursery."

"And will they eventually be joining you?" Mac asked.

Tunstall laughed softly. "I doubt my aged parents could adjust to life on the frontier. They're quite spoiled in London. No, once I have my enterprise running smoothly in the hands of an able manager, I intend to spend half of each year there with them. Have you been to England?"

"I haven't had the pleasure. I am, however, en route to New York. I only regret my wife couldn't accompany me. She's a cultured person and misses society painfully."

"I fear I've yet to discover," Tunstall said with a smile begging forbearance, "what exactly it is, other than descendants, a wife provides her husband. I mean, of course, besides the domestic services a man can as easily hire done."

Mac smiled in return. "I field such forthright questions from only one other person: my wife. And that is the quality exactly, sir. A wife is a confidante and advisor from whom no secrets are kept and no flaws hidden. After dealing with the chicanery of plaintiffs and defendants all day, her honesty is a soothing comfort."

"You must be blessed with an exceptional woman."

"I am. But one such exists for every man."

Tunstall laughed. "I have yet to evince the slightest interest in marriage. I will say women come in handy when one wishes to dance at a ball, but other than that I could spend my life in the company of men and not feel the loss."

Mac laid his knife and fork in the center of his plate in imitation of the Englishman. The meal had certainly been more pleasant than the fare served at Herlow's, but the price was well beyond his budget. Even so, he determined to pay the check for both, considering it seed money with the promise of high yield.

Tunstall caught a waiter's attention and gestured for more coffee. In a moment the man was there, refilling their cups and placing a fresh pitcher of cream on the table before removing the empty plates and leaving the check. Both Mac and Tunstall reached for it simultaneously.

"Allow me, sir," Mac said.

"Nonsense, I invited you," Tunstall said, flicking the check from beneath Mac's fingertips then leaving it, as if forgotten, beside the cream. "Tell me, Mr. McSween, if you were to meet a man of means looking for good range to invest in, would you advise him to consider Lincoln County?"

"I would say he could do no better for himself. On the whole, I know of no other place as wholesome in its natural state." He sipped his coffee thoughtfully. "However, I don't wish to mislead you into thinking there would be no opposition to your aspirations in our county. Civilized it is not, but the fringe of civilization is there, the bad along with the good. They won't give way easily."

"I understand your point," Tunstall replied. "I believe I can give them a run for their money."

* * *

John Henry Tunstall was twenty-three years old and in the enviable position of having been sent abroad to make his family's fortune. He had been impressed with Alexander McSween and intrigued by his description of Lincoln County. The very next morning, Tunstall asked the owner of Herlow's if he knew anything of McSween's character.

"A capital gentleman," the innkeeper replied, his face beaming approval. "Mr. McSween has a reputation in the territory as an expensive lawyer who delivers with acquittals. One can't do better than that in the field of law."

"Indeed," Tunstall murmured.

"He has some powerful clients, too. None other than Jinglebob John Chisum, for one. You've heard of him?"

"Yes, I have."

"McSween's top drawer. Used to be a preacher, they say, and he's honest as a good woman's face."

Tunstall bid the innkeeper good day and walked through the low, dark lobby to the street, intent on breakfast. Propped against the door was a man lying on a moth-eaten blanket to catch the sun, his clothing the shabbiest Tunstall had seen since the slums of London. As he walked past, the man looked up and said, "I wish I could sweat."

"If you would run a mile in the road," Tunstall answered, smiling down at him, "I assure you it will happen."

"I can barely walk," the man whined. "I suffered sunstroke two days ago and am just now regaining my strength."

"I beg your pardon," Tunstall said, feeling badly that he'd made fun of the convalescent. "Have you seen a doctor?"

The man's gaze wandered over Tunstall's frame, taking in his tailored clothes and leather boots. "I appreciate your concern, my friend," the man said, "but I shan't need a physician. I've been so afflicted before and need only to replenish the liquids in my body."

"Good day, then, sir," Tunstall said, turning away and heading for the Exchange. As soon as he was out of earshot, he let loose a burst of laughter so loud that the people on the street turned to observe him with curiosity. He gave them apologetic smiles and continued on through the plaza, chuckling because the ragged man with his erudite speech struck him as absurdly funny. Just as he found a quality of amusement about McSween, the provincial lawyer who took life so earnestly.

When he arrived back at Herlow's, Tunstall asked the innkeeper if he knew of anyone who might be making the trip to Lincoln. Directed to a livery up the street, Tunstall was informed a Juan Patrón intended to depart the next day. Tunstall left a message with the stableman, giving his name and local address and asking that Patrón contact him. Then he walked back to Herlow's, intending to retire to his room and write a letter home. The ragged man was standing in front of the hotel.

"Well now, old fellow," Tunstall greeted him, though the man was in fact close to his own age. "You're looking considerably more chipper."

"Yes, I believe I've shaken myself of the worst of the malady, thank you kindly," the man replied.

"John Tunstall," he said, extending his hand.

"Robert Widenmann," the man responded.

They were near the same height, though Widenmann outweighed Tunstall, making him think the man's diet hadn't suffered the deprivation evidenced by his attire. With shock, Tunstall noted that Widenmann wore no socks beneath his dilapidated shoes.

"Are you going toward the plaza?" Tunstall asked. "I'll walk with you, if you are."

"Delighted, sir," Widenmann replied. "Lying around has atrophied my muscles."

"I like to stay active myself," Tunstall said as they set off. Slowing his gait to match the lethargy brought on by the other's illness, Tunstall asked, "Isn't it amazing to find an entire city built of mud? I find it absolutely marvelous to contemplate, if not to live in."

"You don't care for adobe?" Widenmann asked.

"The rooms are quite dark, don't you find? And then, there seems to be a film of dust on everything. Or perhaps the housekeeping is not what I'm accustomed to."

"I'm sure not. Personally, I admire the ingenuity of a people who use indigenous building materials. The Spanish here have done it with some grace, though I allow it's a crude sense of symmetry. The Moors were much more accomplished. But they had centuries of civilization to perfect their craft. The Egyptians were truly astounding. When I saw the pyramids of their ancient kings, I was carried away in rapture contemplating the immense labor required before our modern knowledge of fulcrums and leverage, to say nothing of the steam engine."

"You've traveled in Africa?" Tunstall asked eagerly.

"While I was studying in Germany."

Tunstall laughed with surprise. *"Sprechen Sie Deutsch,* then?"

"I hope I still remember," Widenmann replied in perfect High German. "It's been too long since I've used it regularly."

"The same is true of me, though I doubt my accent can match yours," Tunstall continued in the foreign tongue. "Imagine finding someone here who speaks German!"

"There are a few others," Widenmann said. "Straub and the Spiegelberg brothers and their families. They're Jews, however."

"And you are a devout Christian," Tunstall answered, tongue-in-cheek.

"I'm an atheist," Widenmann stated. "The world is simply what we see."

"A mind after mine in all respects," Tunstall said. Then in French, "Do you also speak the civilized language of the world?"

"*Ouí. Y también español. Usted?*"

"I'm afraid you've lost me on that one, but it would be of benefit if I'm to settle here." As they passed in front of La Parroquia, he thought the crumbling cathedral of the conquistadores looked melancholy with the melting snow turning its yard to mud.

"Are you considering settling in the territory?" Widenmann asked.

"I like it a great deal, and just last night I heard of a section that sounds perfect: Lincoln County. Do you know of it?"

"I hear it's a rough place controlled by a Major Lawrence Gustav Murphy, who I also hear is ruthless and rather perverse."

"From what I've heard of the man, he sounds like the territory's evil dragon waiting to be slain."

"His own dissipation will do that job. Whether soon enough depends, I suppose, on whether one's under his heel or in his employ." Widenmann stopped before a small cantina. "I feel the need of a dram of whiskey. Would you care to join me?"

Tunstall was intrigued. "I'm not a drinking man, but I'll be pleased to keep you company."

The threshold was built up a foot off the ground, and the passage was so low both men had to duck as they entered the building. The room was snug and dim, lit only by a rustic chandelier, and furnished with a billiards table occupying half the floor space. The other half was filled by a bar facing the few tables.

Widenmann walked directly to the bar and bellied up comfortably. Tunstall followed and turned his back to lean on his elbows as he surveyed the room. Two boys were playing pool, watched by half a dozen men, all slight and dark, dressed in the crude garments of laborers.

Widenmann asked, "What will you have to drink?"

Turning around to smile at the portly barkeep, Tunstall asked with faint hope, "I don't suppose you have any tea?"

"*Sí, hay hierbabuena. Le quiere Usted?*"

"It's a local variety of mint," Widenmann explained.

"Sounds delicious. Yes, please. *Sí,*" Tunstall said, remembering that much Spanish.

"I don't often drink spirits myself," Widenmann felt the need to say, "but my blood is thin after my illness."

"Of course," Tunstall replied. "My prime objection is not the spirit itself but the company it requires you to keep. My beloved mother is worried I'll get myself killed over here, but I've written her carefully explaining that those prone to getting shot meet one of two conditions: they frequent drinking establishments where men wearing pistols become unruly, or they stick their nose into politics. Neither of them do I intend to do, ergo I'll not be shot."

"You're frequenting a drinking establishment now," Widenmann teased. "I hope my influence won't lead to your demise."

"I'm sure it shan't. After all, it's still morning, and I don't expect these fellows to get rowdy anytime soon, do you?"

"I doubt if they get rowdy even in bed with their wives," Widenmann muttered.

Tunstall laughed. "I like you. If I find Lincoln meets my satisfaction, why don't you come down and stay awhile? That is, if your business isn't pressing just now."

"My business is nil," he answered. Smiling at the barkeep bringing the tea, Widenmann raised his empty glass to request a refill. "I've traveled the world over and still haven't found a place to settle. Who knows? Perhaps your Lincoln Town will finally be it."

"We sometimes fall upon decisions quite fortuitously," Tunstall agreed, sipping his tea. "This is excellent," he pronounced, smiling warmly at his friend. "Tell me, do you have any knowledge of a gentleman by the name of Juan Patrón? I'm considering accompanying him south tomorrow."

"Wasn't he shot last year over some altercation in Lincoln?"

"I don't know. Do you think he might be dangerous?"

"Why don't you ask Lawyer McSween? They traveled north together, I hear."

"You seem to know a great deal," Tunstall said with admiration.

"I keep my wits about me," Widenmann replied dryly. "It's necessary in this country."

5

To Tunstall's delight, McSween not only recommended Patrón but offered to introduce them. Over tea in the empty lobby of Herlow's Hotel well after midnight, McSween explained that since Juan Patrón had been educated at Notre Dame, he was an astute observer of territorial politics and could offer Tunstall an insider's view on business in the county.

Early the next morning, congratulating himself on his luck, Tunstall accompanied the lawyer to the meeting place of all travelers in Santa Fe, the riverbank. Wagons were parked beneath the cottonwoods and the smoke of breakfast fires was fragrant on the air. Among the somnolent bustle of men half-awake, McSween found Juan Patrón in lively conversation with Saturnino Baca. After introducing Tunstall and ascertaining that Patrón was happy to have another traveling companion, Mac readied his own departure.

As he climbed aboard the wagon bound for Trinidad, he called back to Tunstall, "Be sure you call on Mrs. McSween when you're in Lincoln."

Tunstall promised he would, then turned still smiling to Patrón. The man was short and dark, dressed as a gentleman, his left leg hanging nearly useless beside a crutch. Despite his infirmity, his knowledge of their destination made him the perfect guide in Tunstall's estimation. Unfortunately, the Englishman had no way of anticipating Patrón's ineptitude with horses.

He had two scrawny nags and a buggy that creaked almost beyond endurance. Flogging the poor beasts the first few miles, he then let them walk, already lathered, while he held the reins so slack that changing course required him to either poke his hands into Tunstall's face or tilt perilously over the side of the buggy.

For Tunstall, who was adept at handling spirited horses, Patrón's clumsiness was torture to witness. Holding his tongue made him so cross that by the time they reached their first stop, he felt tempted to mount his saddle horse and go on alone. Watching Patrón stumble out of the wagon prevented him. After all, the man's original companions had gone ahead, believing Patrón was accompanied by Tunstall. He determined to make light of the situation but it wasn't easy.

They were camped in a grove of trees with a pitifully small fire throwing feeble shadows on the pines overhead. The ground was crusted with snow, and dinner was nothing more than a cold snack because they had expected to make it to someone's cabin by dark but the inferior horses had been unable to travel farther.

Tunstall rolled himself in his blanket and wrapped himself with the melancholy comfort of self-pity. As he often did in low moments, he looked up to console himself with the thought that the same stars shone on his family in London. But the sky overhead was thick with a congestion of clouds threatening snow.

In the morning, they discovered one of the horses had wandered off. Tunstall had hobbled them himself and couldn't understand it, though on reflection he admitted, to himself only, that he had left the rope loose because he had no suspicion the animal was capable of going far. Four hours were required to find it, another half hour to catch it, and an hour to find Patrón and the buggy again. At midday they finally set off on the second leg of their journey.

Patrón was moody and disinclined to talk, so the afternoon passed in silence. By dusk they reached what should have been their previous overnight stop. A wiry old man emerged from a hut beneath a lone cottonwood and watched them come. Seeing the chimney smoke wafting due south like a pale banner beneath the clouds, Tunstall thought it the most inviting sight he could remember. Numbly he let the old man take the horses, then he followed Patrón inside. They made straight for the hearth and stood before it, silently soaking in the fire's warmth.

Presently the old man came in. When he muttered a string of words, Tunstall couldn't pick out one he understood. Patrón appeared not to have heard, lost in private meditation as he stared into the flames. To the old man, Tunstall said, "I beg your pardon?"

"Yabe wanton grub?" he asked again.

"Yes," Patrón answered, recalled from his reverie. "Anything that's hot."

"Aye, esaculd un," the geezer said, retreating to his huge black stove and banging a kettle in place.

"What did he say?" Tunstall whispered to Patrón.

"He said it's cold," Patrón said, turning his face to the fire again.

"And before that?" Tunstall asked.

Patrón shot him an amused look. "He asked if we wanted something to eat."

"How strange," Tunstall said. "Was it English?"

Patrón shrugged. "I suppose it was once. Now it's the speech of an illiterate hermit without any teeth."

Tunstall laughed despite himself.

They waited in the hut for five hours, allowing the horses time to rest after digesting their feed. Then from the moment the men walked out into the icy wind of the already cold night and Patrón picked up the reins, Tunstall's torture began again. He was glad to see the poorer horse somewhat recovered, but that was small comfort beside the spectacle of Patrón's driving, though Tunstall was loath to call it that. Holding the reins was what the man was doing.

Into the darkness of a moonless prairie they traveled, following the river until the road veered east toward distant mountains. At the base of those mountains was to be their next stop, a full day's journey for good horses intelligently used. Tunstall fought despair at the prospect of spending another night in the cold. The day dragged by, each unnecessary careen of the carriage or stumble of the horses infuriating him almost to the point of breaking his gentleman's reserve of silence and taking control. He thought he might have done so at the beginning, but now he was so disgruntled he couldn't trust himself to make the offer with courtesy.

Finally, long after dusk, they drove into the yard of the station and stabled their horses themselves. The house was dark, and only after Patrón repeatedly pounded on the door was his call answered by a gruff voice demanding to know what he wanted. When Patrón identified himself, the door was opened by a grizzled old man who seemed less than happy. Immediately, Patrón asked about Baca. The old man shook his head, saying Baca had left six hours before. This seemed to upset Patrón, but Tunstall was in no mood to take on anyone else's worries. He shook his blankets out near the fire and crawled in without supper, consoling himself with the thought that the next day would see their arrival in Lincoln.

He was to be disappointed. When the sun had risen enough to shine its warmth into the canyon they were traveling through, Tunstall turned to Patrón with an eager smile and said he was glad they would reach their destination by nightfall.

"I'm afraid not," Patrón said. "We'll make Jicarilla Station, if all goes well."

Tunstall's heart sank. "What is this station like? Will we be camping again?"

"No, we'll have a roof over our heads and a fire to roast our boots on," Patrón answered in a sympathetic tone. He gave Tunstall an apologetic look and said, "I'm sorry I've been in a foul mood. I wanted badly to catch up with Baca and now it looks as though he's deliberately kept ahead of us."

"Why would he do that?" Tunstall asked, thinking it would take no effort to stay ahead of Patrón's poor horses and inept driving.

"There's an indictment against me," Patrón said, "and I need Baca's help to have it expunged."

"An unjust indictment?" Tunstall asked. He wondered if it involved the shooting Widenmann had mentioned in Santa Fe.

"Yes. It's a long story." Patrón sighed. "Do you wish to hear it?"

"We seem to have a long road ahead of us," Tunstall said with an encouraging smile.

Still Patrón hesitated. Finally he sighed again, then said, "Last September, John Riley, a local rancher, shot and killed two Mexican boys, claiming they'd stolen a couple of horses and some rifles from his ranch. The way Riley told the story, one of the boys had already left for Mesilla when the theft was discovered. The other confessed and told Riley which route his friend had taken. Riley left the first boy tied up in the corral like an animal and rode in pursuit of the other. When caught, the boy resisted and Riley shot and killed him. Then he returned to the boy left in the corral, put him on a horse, and was taking him to Fort Stanton, supposedly to have him confined in the guardhouse to await trial, when the boy tried to escape and Riley shot and killed him, too. Then he came into town and reported the killings to Major Murphy, who is probate judge.

"As the court clerk, I was in the office at the time, and I heard Riley's account of what happened. I didn't believe it, so I investigated on my own. The facts were that Riley had abused these boys for a long time. No one believed they were thieves, and the consensus was that the killings occurred merely because they were Mexicans and Riley thought he could get away with it."

"Did he get away with it?" Tunstall asked softly.

Patrón nodded. "I gathered a posse and rode out to his ranch. We found the first boy hadn't been killed on the trail at all but was lying dead on the grounds. Riley hadn't even disposed of the body and the season was hot, so the corpse was beginning to stink. The men in my posse were fighting mad and I restrained them with difficulty, intending to take Riley into custody and try him according to law. We buried the boy and were about to leave with our prisoner when a troop of cavalry arrived. Since the soldiers are here to protect the lives and property of Americans only, we knew they wouldn't aid our cause. Angry as we were, we mounted our horses and were riding away when Riley shot me in the back."

"The cowardly bastard!" Tunstall exclaimed.

"Yes," Patrón answered, flicking the reins uselessly. "At first I thought I'd been shot in the leg. I felt a numbness all down my thigh. But the bullet had penetrated just left of my spine and lodged barely beneath the skin of my stomach. The posse were all my friends and wanted to take me home. The army officer, however, placed me under arrest and took me to Fort Stanton. That probably saved my life. The surgeon removed the bullet and kept me in the hospital until I recovered. Everyone predicted I would die, but I didn't. I have only this game leg to remind me of the price of law and order, a price which must be paid even in defeat. Riley swore out a deposition accusing me of assault with intent to murder. McSween says the indictment won't hold up in court and for that reason will never be served, but I don't care to have it hanging over my head for the rest of my life."

"No, surely not," Tunstall replied, filled with new admiration for the man who was so inept with horses.

"So that's why I was trying hard to catch Baca," Patrón finished.

"I'm sorry," Tunstall said. "If I hadn't happened along, you would have had the entire journey to present your case."

"He probably would have found some other excuse to leave me behind. I know he won't go against Murphy, but I want to make him say it to my face."

"What does Murphy have to do with it?"

"Riley works for him and wouldn't have gotten off if he didn't. When Murphy pulls the strings, nearly everyone in the county dances like puppets. Our friend McSween is among the few Americans who has refused his protection."

"I like McSween."

"So do I. But sometimes I worry for his safety. He doesn't wear a gun and thinks that protects him."

"And you don't agree?"

Patrón shook his head. "Anyone who'd shoot a man in the back wouldn't have the scruples to first ascertain whether or not he's armed."

"No, I suppose not," Tunstall murmured.

As they continued their journey, he questioned Patrón further. Listening to his answers, Tunstall privately decided the unfortunate incident was due to a minor form of race war. Though he was sorry Patrón had suffered unjustly, Tunstall felt that, as an Englishman, he would be above the territory's contentious factions.

The next day the sky was bright with a warm sun. Refreshed and replenished after their night at Jicarilla, they drove the last miles to the town of Lincoln, which Patrón still called by its old name of Placita.

As they neared the village, Patrón advised, "Don't mistake the bustle of election day for a common occurrence. The town is the epitome of sleepy, except when violence erupts, and that's sporadic and quickly over."

"And what of the election?" Tunstall asked. "Do you expect success for your party?"

Patrón shook his head. "Last year our candidate was assassinated, so there were no contenders for the honor this year. The election will fall to The House by default.

"The House?" Tunstall innocently inquired.

Just then they came around a bend in the road and saw a huge, two-story building looming to their right. "Murphy and Company's Big Store," Patrón said, "otherwise known as headquarters for The House."

They passed another building on the left, this one a low, whitewashed adobe with a crude fence around the yard and two towering deciduous trees, bare now in autumn. A sign announced it was the Wortley Hotel. "A hotel?" Tunstall asked with pleasant surprise.

"Also belonging to Murphy," Patrón answered. "Usually housing men in his employ."

The adjacent corral held two dozen horses, scruffy but well fed. "He must have a large payroll," Tunstall remarked.

"Some people say you can follow his money into half the pockets of this county, and the other half are empty," Patrón said with a wry smile.

They drove by a tower of crumbling stone which Patrón called *el torreón*, explaining that it had been built by the early settlers as a haven against marauding Apaches. The rest of the town consisted of small adobe homes. To a few of these were attached one-room stores holding what Tunstall thought must be meager inventories.

Horses were tied to every available fence rail and tree and milled about in every corral, their owners sitting on benches under the portals or gathered in dry sunny spots affording a clump of rocks to put their feet on as they leaned on their knees, presumably talking politics.

The road was a pleasant curve beneath the bare trees. Near the hotel, Tunstall had seen mostly American men, all armed with pistols and many with rifles, a surly, rough-looking lot. But as he and Patrón proceeded through town, Mexicans seemed predominant, the occasional American standing taller than most of the men around him. All of them wore guns; Tunstall could spot no exception.

He felt he had found the true frontier at last. Here was the toughest little spot in America, and Tunstall intended to carve his niche out of it and become wealthy in the process. He was quivering with excitement when he stepped down from the buggy and felt the soil of Lincoln beneath his boots for the first time. As Patrón excused himself to his electoral duties, Tunstall happily set off to assess the community.

Near the Patrón home was the Montaño store. Tunstall walked inside and took a cursory inventory of their goods: food staples in tins, a few common pieces of hardware and harness, a large supply of ammunition beneath a glass counter, which also displayed several used pistols. The proprietor was a balding man with a shiny pate and luxuriant black moustache. "May I help you, señor?"

Tunstall introduced himself and said he was visiting with Juan Patrón. He bought a two-penny peppermint stick to show his goodwill, then stepped back onto the street.

Next door, attached to the same building, was a cantina. Thinking he might find some more native tea, Tunstall ducked his head and entered the low, dim room. The floor was dirt and the only light came from tallow candles stuck into sconces hung on the adobe walls, each with its odorous stalactite suspended perilously beneath it. Señor Montaño emerged from behind a cloth curtain covering a door.

"We meet again," Tunstall said with a laugh. "I was hoping to find some tea." The truth was he found the saloon gloomy and wanted only to escape into the sunshine again. But Montaño answered, *"Sí, hay hierbabuena.* Would you like some?"

Tunstall noted the odd mixture of the two languages. *"Sí, por favor,"* he replied.

Montaño disappeared, and Tunstall leaned on his elbows with his back to the bar as he peered around the room. At the far end, nearly hidden in shadow, stood a man. He was an American, young and curious, watching him.

"Good afternoon," Tunstall offered pleasantly. "I didn't see you at first."

"That's the idea," he answered.

"You were expecting someone?" Tunstall asked, puzzled.

"I'm always expecting trouble. That way I ain't never surprised."

"A prudent course," Tunstall said unhappily, turning to Montaño bringing his tea. It was served in a large earthenware cup with the saucer balanced on top as a lid. Tunstall thanked the proprietor, hoping he would stay, but Montaño smiled silently and returned to the store side of his establishment. Tunstall looked again at the man in the corner. "Did you come to town for the election?" he asked.

"What's it to you?" the man wanted to know.

"My name's John Tunstall," he said, eager to allay suspicion. "I'm here visiting with Juan Patrón, who's busy now with the duties of his office, and I was merely trying to pass the time. I meant no offense."

"You talk funny," the man said with a nasal twang.

"Not when I'm home," Tunstall replied. "There I talk like everyone else."

"Where's that?" the man asked, stepping forward into what passed for light. Lean and dirty with dark hair and a drooping dark moustache, he was a few inches shorter than Tunstall, who thought the thin face might have been handsome if adorned with a happier expression. Wearing a gunbelt around his hips and a *bandolera* of cartridges across his chest, the man was drinking whiskey.

"London," Tunstall answered. Seeing no reaction, he added, "England. The United Kingdom?"

"Oh yeah," the man said. "One of them we beat in our War of Independence."

Tunstall sipped his tea. "Yes, that's true," he finally said.

"What're you doing here now?" the man asked.

"What's it to you?" Tunstall threw back.

The man laughed. "Hey, that's all right. Goddamn, a real Englishman, not a used-to-be one. We got a lot of used-to-be people around here." He laughed again. "And you're drinking tea to boot!"

"Tea to boot?" Tunstall asked.

The man grinned. "Name's Charlie Bowdre," he said, extending his hand. "I got a farm jus' west of here. Tunstall, did you say?"

He looked at the grubby paw and hesitated a second before taking it. "John Tunstall," he said, quickly retrieving his hand and wiping it surreptitiously on his pantleg before lifting his cup again.

"You oughta get yourself a gun," Bowdre advised in a friendly tone.

"Why's that?" Tunstall asked, keenly aware of the weight of his Colt's in his pocket.

"No matter what else a man has, it's his gun keeps him alive in this part of the country."

"Men walk around shooting each other with impunity, do they?"

"I don't know that fancy word but shootings happen reg'lar around here. Why, Ham Mills once shot and kilt a Mexican jus' for calling him a gringo."

"What's a gringo?"

"It's a bad name Mexicans have for us. They don't like Americans much, most of us anyway."

"I can't imagine why," Tunstall said. Seeing Bowdre frown, he asked, "So calling an American a gringo is rather like calling a Frenchman a frog?"

Bowdre's frown deepened. "I don't know about that. But Ham Mills, after he kilt the Mexican, he rode into town and yelled Sheriff Baca onto the street and then sat there on his horse and demanded to see the man who could arrest him!" Bowdre laughed with apparent admiration.

"So this Ham Mills is rather bad medicine," Tunstall answered, trying to gain a footing in the conversation.

"Not a bit of it," Bowdre objected. "There weren't a better man in the county than Ham Mills. He had a temper and was fast to let it loose, but he was a crack shot and never crippled. I don't believe the men he kilt felt a thing. And something else, I truly believe Ham was sorry for it after."

Tunstall studied the dark, tumultuous eyes for a long moment, then dropped his gaze and sipped his tea, thinking Bowdre was on the edge of control. He claimed to be a farmer yet was drinking in a saloon on the first sunny day in a week, which showed a definite lack of enterprise. Guessing he'd fallen on bad luck and was being broken under the pressure, Tunstall finished his tea, dropped a nickel on the counter, and picked up his hat. "Pleasure to have met you," he offered politely on his way out.

"Get yourself a gun," Bowdre called as his parting shot.

Tunstall laughed with relief to be back in the sunshine. He walked down the street chuckling in anticipation of writing to his family about Bowdre. How amusing they'd find the story, so totally different from their genteel lives in London. As he threaded his way through the knots of men, he returned their curious stares with friendly smiles but received none in return. Halfway through town he saw a whitewashed post with a sign announcing the residence of A. A. McSween, and he remembered his promise to call on the lawyer's wife.

6

The house was surprisingly modest to Tunstall's eyes, barely large enough to accommodate two rooms of meager proportions. Like everything else in town it was built of adobe, with deep-set window frames painted a charming chalky blue. Also blue, the door was open so he was looking at its inside as he approached.

No pretense of horticulture graced the lawn. Except for the path to the door, laid with flat stones elevated above the mud, the yard was decorated only with native shrub brush, dripping with melted snow. The door was so low, Tunstall felt absurd knocking as he stared at the lintel level with his eyes, as if he were visiting a gnome or a leprechaun. The copper-colored taffeta skirt which soon filled the doorway seemed to belong to a fairy, the way it billowed below such a tiny waist.

He bent down and looked into the pertly pretty face beneath an auburn flounce of curls. Taking off his hat, he said, "John Tunstall, madam, from London, England. I made the acquaintance of Mr. McSween while in Santa Fe and he bid me call on Mrs. McSween. Do I have the pleasure of addressing the lady?"

Sue wanted to purr with pleasure at the sight and sound of this handsome, fashionably clad gentleman at her door. "You do, sir," she replied, giving him the tiniest of curtsies. "Please, come in."

The room was as small as Tunstall had expected, yet arranged with an artistic flair. He took in a Turkish rug and a mahogany horsehair settee before noticing two men standing in the shadow of the near wall. He bowed formally to them as his hostess seated herself on the settee.

"Mr. Tunstall," she said softly, "allow me to introduce two of my husband's associates. Richard Brewer." She paused to allow the handshake and subtle scrutiny to pass between them, then said, "And George Coe. Both local ranchers. Please sit down, gentlemen, before I crimp my neck looking up at you. Here, Mr. Tunstall," she directed with a lift of her hand, "take this chair. Tell me, did you find Mr. McSween in good health?"

Tunstall sat in the needlepoint bow-backed chair she had indicated. "Indeed, madam. He seemed in high spirits, though he spoke several times of his regret that you were unable to accompany him."

"Ummm," she said, her brown eyes darkening for just a second. "Would you like some coffee or cocoa, Mr. Tunstall?"

He looked across at Brewer and Coe. They both possessed a wholesome appearance, though Brewer was the more handsome. Tall and muscular, he was dark, with the rich eyes of a poet. Coe was blond and on the gangly side, with a hungry hollow to his cheeks that Tunstall associated with the lower class. He smiled pleasantly at both of them, noting they held fancy china cups like eggs balanced on their knees, and told his hostess he would enjoy either beverage, whichever was easiest.

To his surprise, she raised her voice and called for someone named Sebrian. After a moment, a fencepost of a black man came into the room. Dressed in a faded black suit and a brick-red shirt, he was obviously as surprised to see Tunstall as the Englishman was to see him. With difficulty, Sebrian shifted his gaze to his mistress and asked, "Yes'm?"

"Coffee, please, for Mr. Tunstall," she said, sharing an amused smile with Brewer and Coe. When Sebrian had left, she leaned forward and said confidentially to Tunstall, "Excuse me for having to shout to fetch him. I have a silver bell, but he says he isn't a slave any longer and doesn't have to answer to bells, that I'm to call him by his name." She smiled and leaned back. "He's such an excellent servant, I do as he asks."

"A small compromise for so great a benefit," Tunstall answered. He thought he detected snickers from Brewer and Coe, but when he looked at them they were smiling in a friendly manner. "Did Mrs. McSween say you were ranchers?"

"I don't know, did she?" Brewer asked, throwing her a teasing look. "She might as well have. We are. And you?"

"I hope to be soon," Tunstall said eagerly, warming to the subject. "I've been in the territory two months now, looking for the right range. Mr. McSween suggested I come to Lincoln and see what the countryside offers. He praised the county highly, and so far, I must say I like what I see."

Sebrian returned carrying another delicate cup on a wooden tray. His age was close to fifty, and that he had been trained in service was evident in the graceful way he bowed as he offered the cup. Tunstall rewarded such finesse with an appreciative smile which Sebrian received with a slow blink. After politely sipping his coffee, Tunstall asked Mrs. McSween, "How do you find life in this village, madam? It seems to hold an endless bounty of charming surprises."

This time he heard definite laughter from Brewer and Coe.

"I beg your pardon?" Tunstall asked with good humor. "Did I say something funny?"

"Everything you say sounds funny," Coe replied baldly.

"George Coe!" Sue scolded. "Forgive these country bumpkins, Mr. Tunstall. They've never heard an English accent before."

"It's the truth and we mean no offense," Brewer apologized. "We're also kind of feeling our oats, being in town and all."

"I understand," Tunstall said smoothly. "Do you work your spreads alone?"

"Pretty much," Brewer replied with a solemn nod.

"Except for the long arm of Murphy," Coe joked, bumping against Brewer as he laughed, making Brewer laugh too.

Sue silently begged forgiveness with her eyes, and it was then that Tunstall realized the men were inebriated. His smile told her he understood the situation perfectly, and rather than censoring her for having two drunken cowboys in her parlor, he credited it to election day.

Again Sue wanted to purr at the delicious subtlety of his demeanor. He was alive with the nuances of society, with a knowledge and perspective that could only come from having known a world vastly more complex than the simpletons in Lincoln could imagine. Having established this silent understanding of their superiority, Sue turned her attention on their entertainment. "Continue with the story you were telling, George," she invited in a honeyed tone.

His blue eyes full of fun, he looked straight at Tunstall when he said, "Nah, I got a better story." Shifting his gaze to Sue, he asked, "You remember that old feller, Tom King, who worked for me awhile back?"

"I don't believe so," Sue answered, pretending to think. She knew the story well and wasn't pleased with the choice.

Leaning forward, his eyes on the Englishman's, Coe explained in an earnest tone, "It was when I was alone at the ranch for a spell. My cousin had gone out to the prairie to cut hay and I was left behind to harvest the 'taters. Well, that ain't no easy job and I needed help to get it done, so when this feller come through looking for work I figured I'd found myself the right hand. He was an old forty-niner, come back as broke as he went out, but he was tough and a good strong worker and everything was fine 'tween us, except for one thing."

Having caught his audience, Coe took a long swallow of coffee. He set the cup and saucer carefully on the floor beside his chair, then resettled himself. "This feller," he continued, "had a bad habit. I don't know what he thought he was doing, but he'd come up to a person and jab his finger into your backside real hard, scare the bejesus outta you. He called it goosing, and after he done it, he'd laugh like it was jus' the funniest thing he'd ever seen, the way you'd jumped and all. I warned him his goosing would get him in trouble sooner'n not, but he didn't listen." Coe paused to rest an ankle of his dusty boot across his knee.

"We was getting along real good with the 'taters when it come around to Sattiday night and there was a *baile* here in town. That's the Mex word for a dance, they call 'em *bailes*. Tom King and I rode in to attend the dance, and we were having a good time till, sure 'nough, he mosied up to a pretty native belle and goosed her behind. She like to scream to call the cows home, and the cowboy who was dancing with her, he was madder'n spit. It was all I could do to get Tom King through the door without that cowboy beating his stars out. That was a long, miserable ride home on account I was so mad at him for cutting our evening short like he had.

"Well, the next day we was working in the 'tater field when this cowboy come riding up. I ask this cowboy, I says, 'What's the trouble now?' And he says, 'Ain't none of yourn 'less you want some of it.' I said I surely didn't, and I stood there and watched him pull his Winchester from his scabbard and shoot Tom King down like a crow on a post, putting an end to his goosing forevermore."

Tunstall looked at each of their faces, searching for a hint that it was a joke and the punch line was yet to come.

Finally, delivering the line that finished the tale, Sue said, "I was at that dance, and I remember that cowboy. It was Ham Mills, wasn't it, who was killed last summer in Seven Rivers?"

"Yes'm," Coe said to her, then to the Englishman, "There's more'n one kind of climate to consider when you're looking at range, Mr. Tunstall."

"I appreciate your point," he replied slowly. "Yet you and Mr. Brewer seem like desirable neighbors."

Coe was nonplussed by the compliment, and it was Dick Brewer who spoke next. "There's plenty of good men in this county, sir, who would welcome you among us. I'd offer you help myself but you can't have a better advisor than Mac. If you do decide to settle here, I'm sure we'll be seeing more of you." He stood up. "We'll call again tomorrow, Sue, after the election is over."

"Please do," she said, standing, too, and walking them to the door. They gave Tunstall parting nods and were gone. Sue returned with a smile, the delight she felt at having Tunstall to herself shining from her eyes. "Pray, sit down," she murmured. "I'm so glad you thought to call."

The rustle of her taffeta skirt as she crossed the room took Tunstall back to a hundred English drawing rooms where elegant young ladies had plied him with the fluid cadence of artful conversation. While enduring those interludes, he'd always felt impatient to be free from such artifice, but after experiencing the democratic parlors of America, he appreciated the benefit of having been raised within the strictures of courteous protocol.

He could smile comfortably at this married woman whose acquaintance had been his for less than an hour, certain she would understand him because she'd been raised within the same strictures. As she resettled herself upon the settee, he said, "I'm amazed to find such a lady as yourself in this village, though Mr. McSween did say he was blessed with an exceptional woman as his wife. I can see now he was speaking with more than a husband's hyperbole."

"Thank you, Mr. Tunstall," Sue replied, moving into the far corner of the settee to increase the distance between them. At the same time she gave him an apologetic smile which he returned with a forgiving one, both of them acknowledging that their being alone required the utmost propriety.

"I'm glad I had the opportunity to meet Mr. Brewer and Mr. Coe," he began on safe ground. "They seem upstanding chaps."

"Oh yes, they're that," Sue agreed with a laugh. "But don't pay any attention to the story George told."

"Wasn't it true?"

"Yes, it was," she answered forthrightly. "But his intentions were to frighten you."

"Why would he wish to do that?"

She hesitated a moment. "How much do you know about Lincoln County, Mr. Tunstall?"

"Very little, actually. But I like what I've seen. It's a growing community already claiming some cultured citizens, and the land I saw coming in was excellently provided with forage. All in all, it seems to hold promise as a place to invest."

"And you plan on ranching?"

"Yes," he replied proudly. "I intend to secure an appropriate tract of land and start with young animals because they yield the highest return." He laughed at himself. "I shan't bore you with the details of my scheme, but I have it all worked out to the pound and acre. It only remains to find the place."

"I know I speak for my husband and many people here when I say we'd be delighted to have you among us. But I wonder if you understand the realities of the beef market on the frontier."

"And what do you know of the beef market, Mrs. McSween?" he asked, unable to avoid a patronizing tone.

"There is only one," she answered, her eyes pleading that he listen before judging her. "The government contract to feed the Indians. It's administered by the command at Fort Stanton and is awarded on a yearly basis through a process of sealed bids. Whoever owns the contract owns the market. It's the same with farm commodities. For a decade, those contracts have been in the hands of Murphy and Company, more commonly called The House."

"I see," Tunstall said. "What does Chisum do with his herds? Surely the Mescaleros don't number so many?"

"Chisum drives his cattle to the railheads in Kansas or to the San Carlos Agency in Arizona, a difficult undertaking for even an experienced stockman. As to the number of Mescaleros, on their first accounting, which wasn't given until October of '71, Murphy and Company claimed credit for feeding a few more than five hundred Indians. In their second accounting, done in April of the next year, they claimed to have fed thirteen hundred. According to their third account, the number was nearly two thousand. By March of '73, their books claimed the Mescalero population had grown to two thousand six hundred and eighty individuals. Finally someone in Washington City noticed the figures and sent a letter to President Grant, remarking the rate of increase defied comparison even with rabbits and mice!" Her laughter was a surprise, deep and husky from her throat.

Tunstall laughed too. "And what happened?"

"Murphy was thrown off the fort, but not only because of that— other irregularities were found. So The House moved its store to town and barely missed a step. Since they own the government contracts, everyone else is limited to the production of goods with no control over prices. Twenty years ago, these Mexicans were peons. Their habits haven't changed much in the interim. They live so deeply in debt, their children will be struggling to free themselves. The Americans who came here right after the War walked into a system of serfdom left behind by the Spanish and took it on, adjusting the fit where necessary. Now they're all together, from Murphy and Dolan here, to District Attorney Rynerson in Mesilla, all the way to the U.S. attorney in Santa Fe, Tom Catron. They're all tentacles of what they call the Santa Fe Ring, and they've staked a claim on the economy of the entire territory."

"They call themselves a ring?" Tunstall asked, amused.

"It's the current term." She smiled coquettishly. "I've heard them called names less delicate."

"And they've been in power ten years?"

"Yes, since right after the War."

"That seems a short time, but then again a long time on the frontier. Things are changing rapidly and there's always room for new blood. It keeps the economy vigorous."

"Yes," Sue agreed. "And the railroads are coming farther west every day. In a few years the entire national market will be open to the ranchers. I believe that's when the territory's wealth will be realized." She laughed self-consciously. "My husband disagrees. He says new fortunes are made at managerial levels, that it's the machinations of the courts and the legislature that bestow real wealth."

"I think there's truth to both viewpoints," Tunstall said diplomatically. And then, less adroitly, "Is this a topic you discuss often between yourselves?"

Sue blushed. "I find it amusing to watch the evolution of an economy so simply analyzed. It's an intellectual game in a place which offers very little stimulus. As a lady, of course, I am barred from participation. Our position in the economy is in my husband's hands." She paused to risk a smile before saying, "I bow to the discretion of his judgment."

"How very admirable," Tunstall said sincerely.

Sue laughed. "Will you be staying long in Lincoln, Mr. Tunstall?"

"It depends upon my decision as to the suitability of the range. If I decide favorably, I'll return to Santa Fe, make the necessary financial arrangements, and be back in early December."

"Mac and I are having a Christmas party on the third Saturday," she said happily. "John Chisum will be among our guests. I hope you'll do us the honor of attending."

"I shall be delighted," he answered. Then, noticing the sun had disappeared from her door and the afternoon was nearly gone, he made his apologies. "I'm afraid I must be getting back for dinner with my host."

"Of course," she said, rising and giving him her hand. "Do call again, Mr. Tunstall."

"I feel almost certain I shall," he replied.

7

ARIZONA TERRITORY
December 1876

William Whelan, foreman of the Hooker Ranch in the Sulphur Springs Valley of southeastern Arizona, stood on the porch of the big house and watched the kid unloading the wagon that had just arrived laden with special delicacies for Christmas dinner.

The kid was pondering a keg of molasses. The keg weighed fifty pounds and its girth was too big to get a good grip on. He tried to tip it over with his hands but the keg wouldn't budge, so he sat on the edge of the wagon and pushed it over with his feet. The keg thudded onto the bed and began to roll, rumbling like thunder. The kid watched it a second too long.

He propelled himself over the side of the wagon, vaulting on his arm to hit the dust running. The keg was just teetering off the lip of the wagon when he stuck his arms underneath to catch it. But his footing was off. Watching from the porch, Whelan knew the kid didn't have a chance. The keg struck his chest and knocked him backward. He was quick, though, ducking out of the way the instant before the keg hit the ground.

Its wood cracked, sharp as the retort from a rifle, jerking Whelan down the steps and across the yard before the echo died. "That's three dollars and fifty cents of molasses feeding the dust," he growled, glaring at the kid.

Henry crouched on the other side of the keg and rolled it toward Whelan until the crack was on top. The foreman had to step back out of the way, then they both stood there watching the flow of fragrant black molasses ooze to a stop. Whelan looked at the kid. "You should've lifted the keg, not dropped it."

"Reckon," Henry said. "Was kinda heavy, though."

Whelan nodded. "You *sure* you're sixteen?"

The kid shook his head with a playful smile, revealing his crossed incisors. "I jus' turned seventeen, Mr. Whelan."

"You look fourteen," he retorted. "And I don't think you're even as strong as that. I gotta let you go, Henry. I'm sorry about it, but there just ain't anything you can do for me."

Henry nodded without surprise. "Will you pay me my wages?"

"Can't do that neither," Whelan said. "We've fed and bunked you a month and that's more'n your labor's been worth."

Henry turned away so fast a dust devil rose from beneath his shoes. City shoes, Whelan thought to himself. How could the kid expect to work on a ranch without boots? He sighed deeply. "You oughta get yourself a job in town, Henry. You're smart and know your letters and ciphers. You'll do better working in a store."

Henry nodded again, still not looking at the foreman. "Thing of it is, I don't like being inside all day."

Whelan could understand that, and he felt bad for the kid. "You got any money a'tall?"

"Yeah, I got ten, twelve bucks," Henry boasted.

"You best be on your way, then," Whelan said. "I'm sorry, Henry."

"Me, too," Henry said, extending his hand with a grin. "Been nice knowing you, Mr. Whelan. Maybe we'll see each other around now and then."

"Prob'ly," the foreman said, shaking hands. "Good luck to you."

"Thanks," the kid said, turning away and ambling across the yard as if he hadn't a care in the world.

Whelan watched after him a moment, wondering if the kid wasn't a simpleton as well as a weakling, the way nothing ever seemed to get under his skin. The foreman shifted his gaze to a horseman riding into view, then recognized his blue cavalry uniform and forgot about Henry, wondering if the soldier brought news of marauding Apaches.

Henry waved to the soldier as he rode by. When he tipped his hat without breaking the gait of his horse, Henry turned around and stared into the cavalryman's retreating dustcloud. Thinking he would rather ride than walk to town, Henry watched from a distance as the soldier swung down and tied his mount to the corral fence, then walked with the foreman toward the big house. Henry stood there watching for several minutes after they'd disappeared inside, then he sprinted for the horse.

Before he got there, he slowed down so as not to spook the animal. Coaxing softly, he untied the reins and leapt into the saddle, then ambled the horse out of the yard to keep its hooves quiet in the thick dust. When he was a good distance down the trail, he turned cross-country, leaned low into the mane and kicked in his heels, galloping north toward Eureka Springs.

The horse was branded with a huge U.S. on its hip and Henry knew he couldn't sell it anywhere near Camp Grant. But up in Globe City he might find a buyer. Might even get as much as the ten bucks he'd lied to Whelan about having. The exchange seemed just: ten bucks for a month's work. That it came from the coffers of the army instead of the

Hooker Ranch didn't bother Henry. He'd get what was due him, that's the way he figured it.

Just south of Eureka, he saw a fellow he knew sitting by the side of the road. They'd met in Atkins Saloon near Camp Grant only the week before and they'd gotten along, though John Mackie was ten years older than Henry. As the kid reined to a stop in front of him, Mackie stood up. "You got yourself a nice piece of contraband there," he said with an insinuating smile.

Henry shrugged. "Jus' a ride to me."

"Where you going?" Mackie asked, eyeing the horse's broad back behind the saddle.

"Globe," Henry said.

"Would you give me a ride to Pueblo Viejo on your way?"

"Ain't on the way," Henry said. "It's clear the other direction, and closer to Grant, too."

"I know a fella in Viejo will trade you that horse for one with a dif'-rent brand."

"Will he pay me cash for it?" Henry asked, interested.

"Maybe." Mackie grinned. "It's closer'n Globe, too."

Henry laughed. "Looks like I'm going to Viejo." He kicked the stirrup free so Mackie could swing up behind, then reined the horse east.

After a while, Mackie said, "Thought you was working for the Hooker Ranch."

"Got fired," Henry said.

"What for?" Mackie asked.

"Dropping a keg of molasses."

"Did you get to slurp any of it up 'fore it soaked in?"

Henry shook his head. "The foreman was right there chewing me out, so I didn't get a chance."

"How'd you come by the horse?"

"It got there the same time I was leaving," Henry said, "and the coincidence seemed too strong to let pass."

"This horse'll bring twenty-five, thirty dollars," Mackie gloated.

"That much? I was hoping for ten."

"Will you buy me supper if I get you more'n fifteen?"

"Sure," Henry said. "I can double whatever I get at the monte tables quick enough."

"It's a good thing you got a knack with cards," Mackie teased. "It don't appear you can hold a job."

"Maybe not," Henry retorted. "But your getting kicked outta the cavalry was jus' plain dumb."

"I din't cotton to fighting Apaches," Mackie replied.

"I've done it," Henry said.

"Yeah, well, it ain't the same being under orders. You gotta do what they say when you can see plain you'll die if you do. Even if you don't, them uniforms are wool, and after you build up a good sweat they itch you to death."

Henry looked down at Mackie's foot hanging by the horse's belly. "Trade you my shoes for them army-issue boots."

"Reckon my feet are bigger'n yours," Mackie said pleasantly, as if he'd do it otherwise. "If we get a good price for this horse, you can buy yourself some boots. Them heels'll give you a coupla inches and maybe folks won't think you're so puny."

Henry spun around and punched Mackie hard enough to knock him off the horse, then dived after him, landing on his chest and knocking the wind out of his lungs. Mackie gasped for breath and came back flailing hard with his fists. They rolled across a patch of devil's claw that ripped their shirts and into a pit of loose sand thrown from a huge ant hole. Henry came out on top, pinning Mackie's shoulders with his knees.

"Who's puny?" Henry taunted.

Mackie looked at the angry ants rushing to attack. "Nobody!" he cried.

Henry laughed and leapt to his feet. Mackie jumped up to brush sand and ants off his clothes, then looked at the kid. "You li'l sonofabitch," he jeered. "Where's your goddamned horse?"

Henry spun around and saw the horse was gone. "Sonofabitch!" he yelled. "Straight to the fort and a belly full of hay, the lucky sucker."

"Want to go pay it a visit?" Mackie teased.

Without a reply, Henry started walking toward the town that served the fort, thinking maybe he could get into a crap game with the two-bits he had and win enough to sit down at a monte table. Mackie followed along.

It was midnight when they hobbled into town on blistered feet. They stood in the alley behind Atkins' Saloon, listening to the music and laughter from inside as they considered their next move. Henry was hungry more than anything right then, but if he spent his two-bits on food he wouldn't have a stake to get into any kind of game. A quarter wasn't much of an ante anyway. The only ones likely to take it were urchins, and they had all found their beds for the night. Henry was considering doing the same and begging breakfast in the morning when he saw a man come out of the saloon.

"Hey, mister," Henry called. "You int'rested in a small game of chance?"

The man stopped and looked him over, studied Mackie a moment, then took a few steps closer. "What'd you have in mind, son?"

"Flip you a quarter, double or nothing," Henry said.

"Do you have a quarter?" the man asked doubtfully.

Henry dug it out of his pocket and held it up to the light. "I'll flip and you call. Okay?"

"Go ahead," the man said.

"Can I see your quarter first?" Henry asked with a friendly smile.

The man laughed, pulled a handful of change from his pocket, selected a coin and returned the rest. "I'm ready," he said.

Henry tossed the two-bits high into the black sky, watching it catch light as it spun.

"Heads," the man said.

It fell with a soft thunk. They all huddled over it, leaning with their hands on their knees in the dimly lit alley. Lady Liberty shone from the dust. The man laughed as he picked her up.

Henry watched the coin disappear inside the winner's pocket where it clinked against others as it fell, then he laughed, meeting the man's eyes. "Maybe my luck'll be better next time."

"Anytime, kid," the man said, walking away.

"Shit," Mackie said. "What're you gonna do now?"

"You ask too many questions and never have no answers," Henry muttered, looking at the door of the saloon.

"Least I got a quarter," Mackie said. "That's more'n you."

Henry turned around with a smile. "Stake me to a game and I'll pay you back with in'trest."

"You'll lose it like you did t'other."

"I've never lost twice in a row," Henry boasted. "Lady Luck likes me."

"Couldn't prove it by me," Mackie said.

"Earlier you were saying how I got a knack with cards," Henry reminded him.

"Maybe I was, and maybe you do," Mackie argued. "But anyone looking at you would think Lady Luck don't care nothing 'bout being in your vicinity."

"She often travels incognito," Henry answered.

"What's that mean?"

"She likes to go about disguised," Henry said. "How about that quarter? You gonna lend it to me?"

"Where'd you learn that word?"

"From a book," Henry said. "Don'cha ever read?"

"Nope," Mackie replied. "I ain't wasting my eyesight on words some fool with nothing better to do writes in a book."

"You got something better to do?" Henry asked with sarcasm.

"Yeah," Mackie said. Then looking at the trash-littered alley behind the adobe saloon, he laughed with chagrin. "Most of the time."

"Lend me that quarter and we can get something to eat," Henry coaxed. "How's that sound for a pastime?"

"Fulfilling," Mackie said. "But I ain't got a quarter, Henry. I was lying to you."

Henry assessed him, wondering which line was the lie. It seemed by the time a man was pushing thirty he ought to have his life arranged at least to the point that he ate regular, but here Mackie was, tagging along with a kid with no credit to his name at all. "I'll mosey in and see if I can't hustle something," Henry said. "If not, I'll jus' plain beg it, which I can still do, but you're too old to beg, John." Walking toward the saloon, Henry didn't look back, feeling embarrassed for Mackie.

The saloon was a low, rectangular room lit with kerosene lanterns. Several scarred tables filled the space between the bar and the raw adobe wall, and half a dozen men sat at the tables over games of chance. Atkins was behind the bar. At the far end was a man Henry didn't like, a blacksmith by the name of Windy Cahill. Beyond him, by the front door, was the piano where an old man banged out a gay tune. Henry danced in the doorway a moment, then moved with the beat as he ambled to the bar and waited for Atkins to come over. The proprietor had bushy eyebrows beneath a bald pate, oily and iridescent in the irregular light thrown from the lanterns. "What'cha want?" he asked indifferently, knowing Henry rarely had money.

"Was wondering, Mr. Atkins," Henry asked politely, "if you have any chores needing to be done?"

"Not in the middle of the night, I don't," the saloonkeeper answered testily. "Come back in the morning and I'll pay you a dime to scrub out the spittoons."

Henry looked at the four cuspidors nearly full of phlegm and tobacco juice. Hoping he could double the dime and pay Atkins back without doing the work, Henry gave the man his best smile. "Will you pay me first?"

"Hell, no!" Atkins retorted.

Henry's smile didn't waver. "Will you loan me a dime, then, so I can get into a game and earn enough to buy supper and pay you back too?"

Atkins shook his head.

"I'll give you a dime," Cahill said from the dark end of the bar.

Knowing there was a sharp hook attached to the offer, Henry didn't figure he was in any position to turn it down. "What for?" he asked.

Cahill fished into his vest pocket and dug out a dime, then quietly laid it on the bar a foot in front of him. "All you gotta do," he teased, "is come get it."

Henry looked at the dime shining in the light, then at the bulk of the man behind it. Cahill outweighed Henry by a hundred pounds, and the blacksmith's swing was twice as long as Henry's and driven by twice as much muscle. Henry looked at the dime again, knowing his strongest asset was speed. If he feinted one direction then darted back, he might be able to grab the dime without getting hit. He was pretty sure he'd end up with it, whatever else happened, and once in possession of the coin, he could outrun the big ox, no sweat.

In a taunting maneuver, Cahill turned his back to the bar. Henry ducked low to the big man's left. When Cahill swung and missed, Henry darted under the blacksmith's arm and hit the bar to vault over it. The dime was right under Henry's nose but he was using both hands for leverage, his feet sailing through the air. In another second he'd be behind the bar and could grab the dime as his hands followed through, then sprint for the door. But Cahill caught Henry's feet and he fell flat on his face. Quick as a snake, his tongue licked out and claimed the dime.

Cahill dragged Henry back across the bar, took hold of his belt from behind, and threw him toward the door. Landing on his hands and knees, he stayed there a minute, letting his head clear and trying to listen through the jeering laughter for Cahill coming to give him more. Suddenly Henry became aware of blood gushing from his nose. When he shook his head, the blood went flying to spatter on the floor in a lacy pattern that knelled a memory of a gentle love he'd once known. Then the memory was muffled by the heavy footsteps of the blacksmith approaching across the dirt floor. Henry tried to gain his feet but the longing he felt for the love he'd lost dragged at his speed and he wasn't quick enough.

Cahill picked up Henry again and threw him into the darkness of the alley. When his back hit the ground, he swallowed the dime. Rolling over fast, he coughed as he gained his hands and knees, then he forced himself to puke, hoping to see the dime. But it didn't come up with the froth of blood.

Mackie emerged from the shadows and hunkered down close. "Reckon you're getting too old to beg, too, kid," he said with sympathy. "Let me look at you."

Henry settled cross-legged in front of his friend and tried to wipe the blood away before showing his face, but when he dragged his sleeve across the end of his nose, pain screamed inside him like a hundred thousand losses of love. "Yow!" Henry said, gingerly touching his nose.

"Let me see," Mackie said, taking hold of Henry's chin and forcing his head up. "Your nose is broke."

Henry was sucking air through his mouth. He wiped the blood away again, this time more gently. "Sonofabitch," he gurgled through the blood.

"Come on down to the crick," Mackie said, standing up and extending a hand to help.

Henry ignored the hand. He pulled himself to his feet and stumbled toward the creek on his own. Once there, he lay on his belly and submerged his face in the cool, flowing water. He stayed under as long as he could, then came up sucking air. Sitting on the wet sand, he carefully touched his nose, then said again, "Sonofabitch."

"Don't s'pose you got any money," Mackie said.

"Swallowed it," Henry said.

"How much?" Mackie asked eagerly.

"Dime," he said.

"Well, you can eat tomorrow," Mackie said, "after you shit."

Henry snorted, then held his head against the pain he'd shot through his nose. He sat there listening to his blood drip onto the sand between his knees, remembering his mother's blood on the quilt when she'd died, how it had scattered in that delicate, lacy pattern so out of sorts with what was happening. When his nose finally stopped bleeding, he looked up at the stars in the black sky. They twinkled and winked as if teasing him, and Henry laughed, then sprang to his feet and started walking out of town.

Mackie caught up with him. "Where you going?"

"Peloncillo Mountains," Henry said.

"On foot?" Mackie asked with disbelief.

"I'll be crawling when I get there," Henry predicted.

"What's there?" Mackie asked, puzzled.

"A man I used to know," Henry said. "He was married to my mother once, and I figure he might lend a hand."

"You mean he's your pa?"

Henry shook his head. "Jus' an old man once claimed me as kin. Reckon I'll go find out if he still believes it."

"Reckon I'll stay here," Mackie said.

"Suit yourself," Henry answered, not breaking his stride as he left Mackie behind.

Henry kept walking north, following the stage road between Globe and Silver City. Since coming to Arizona, he'd often wondered how his brother was doing back in New Mexico, and just recently he'd heard William Antrim was prospecting in the Peloncillos. Henry hadn't thought the information was worth much, but he'd tucked away the details of the location in case he changed his mind. Hungry and sore with a broken nose, he had run out of choices.

Truth be told, Henry was having a hard time keeping himself. He'd had three jobs in Arizona and been fired from two; the first because he hadn't the strength to handle the eight-horse teams hauling logs down from the mountains, and the second because he'd dropped a keg of molasses. The job he'd been able to keep was washing dishes for a restaurant in Globe. It only paid two dollars a week while taking up twelve hours of every day, and Henry thought it was a poor way to pass time. He was a fair hand with cards but never had enough capital to get into a worthwhile game. What he needed was a stake. If he could pull together twenty bucks, he could ride his losses and gradually increase his winnings until he could make a respectable living for himself. Buy some new clothes and those boots he'd been wanting so long, maybe even a pistol so bullies like Cahill wouldn't find him such easy prey.

In his attempts to get by in the world, Henry had never done any mining. The idea of spending daylight hours underground gave him the willies. But he figured if he could stick a winter with his stepfather, come spring he'd have himself a stake and wouldn't have to ask anyone for anything, ever again.

After walking two days on no more nourishment than a bowl of beans begged from the lady at the stage station the day before, Henry felt his hopes fade as he stood at the edge of Antrim's camp. The claim consisted of a tunnel dug out of the mountain and a tent to sleep in, and the poverty made it clear Antrim wouldn't have any money to share. He had to have food, though, and Henry felt weak with hunger.

"Howdy-do!" he called into the apparently empty camp.

His voice echoed off the mountains towering all around, then died into a silence that gradually filled with birdsong again. He crossed the clearing and lifted the flap of the tent. Inside were hundred-pound bags of flour and beans, smaller bags of sugar and coffee, and a slab of jerky hanging from the beam. He dropped the flap and looked around the camp again, then at the gaping hole of the tunnel leading into the mountain. With dread, he approached the mine.

The tunnel was pitch black and he didn't like leaving the sunshine behind. It was cold, too, and he shivered in his shirt, damp with sweat from hiking in the sun. Ahead he heard a pick working methodically. Its impacts loosened trickles of dust to fall on Henry's head as he walked toward the sound. When he turned a corner, he saw the light from a lantern a hundred feet ahead. He stopped and watched his stepfather swinging the pick to dislodge a boulder from the wall of dirt. The big man's sweaty face gleamed in the lamplight, his expression gnarled with strain. Finally he staggered back away from the boulder and glared at it, breathing hard.

"Howdy, Uncle Billy," Henry said softly.

William Antrim whirled around, staring as fiercely as he had glared at the boulder. He hacked a gob of phlegm from his throat, turned his head and spit into the darkness, then looked back at Henry without a trace of welcome. "What'cha doing here, Henry?"

"Come to see how you're getting along," he answered cheerfully. "Thought you might need a hand through the winter."

"You give up stealing laundry?" Antrim asked with sarcasm.

"I never stole no laundry," Henry said, his hope diminishing in the face of the old man's scorn.

"How'd you get your nose broke?"

Henry wanted to touch his nose, which was still sore, but he kept his hands at his sides. "Fell off a horse," he said.

"What'd you do, steal a horse, then get throwed?" Antrim snickered. "You ain't even a good crim'nal, Henry."

"I ain't no criminal a'tall," he answered guardedly. "I jus' come 'cause I thought we had something in common, and maybe we could help each other out."

"S'pose you got in more trouble with the law," Antrim grumbled, "and that's why you're here. S'pose you think my claim's a good place to lay low. Ain't that it?"

Henry shook his head. "Thought we could help each other out, is all," he said again.

Antrim looked him up and down. "You ain't growed much."

Henry shrugged.

"Push that there wheelbarrow out to the yard and we'll talk about it," Antrim said.

Henry looked at the wheelbarrow loaded with rocks. Even at his best it was doubtful he could move it, but worn out and hungry he didn't have much of a chance. He picked up a handful of dust and rubbed it between his palms, then took hold of the handles and steeled himself a moment before he hefted the stanchions off the ground. He pushed hard but the wheels didn't turn. Sweat popped out on his forehead as he strained against the weight. Finally he had to set the stanchions down again.

When he looked at Antrim, the big man's grin made Henry mad. He took another deep breath, hefted the handles, and threw his weight against the wheels. They turned and he kept pushing, weaving an erratic path through the tunnel. After what seemed like a mile, he reached the turn and saw sunlight beckoning ahead. It gave him something to aim for, and he hit a good stride. When he felt the sun's warmth on his back, he dropped the load and grinned up at the sky in self-congratulation.

From behind him, Antrim said, "You can dump the rocks into that ravine over yonder."

Henry looked across the dirt a hundred yards to the edge of the ravine, then back at his stepfather. "Don't think I can, Uncle Billy," he replied pleasantly. "My inner man's 'bout played out."

"So it's vittles you're wanting," Antrim jeered.

"Would be obliged," Henry said.

"Ain't got none to spare," Antrim announced. "Jus' enough to see me through winter, and it took all my funds to get that. Ain't got nothing for you, Henry. But thanks for stopping by to push my barrow outta the tunnel."

Henry stared at him hard. "You talk like you hate me," he said, puzzled.

"You ain't worth hating," Antrim answered. "I jus' don't want nothing to do with you. If that ain't clear enough, I'll say it plain: Get out."

Henry took a step back, momentarily bewildered. Managing a smile, he said, "Best of luck to you, Uncle Billy. I think you're gonna need it." Then he turned and walked away as if he had somewhere to go.

As soon as he was hidden in the trees, Henry climbed higher up the slope of the mountain until he had a good view of Antrim's camp. He watched the old man trundle the empty wheelbarrow back toward the hole of the tunnel, then stop and look around suspiciously. After a few minutes, he pushed the wheelbarrow into the mine. Henry waited a few minutes more, then sprinted down the hill, into the camp and inside the tent. Spying an empty gunnysack, he tossed in a tin of biscuits, a crock of honey, and some strips he tore off the slab of jerky. After peeking back through the flap to be certain he was still alone, Henry sauntered from the tent and out of the clearing, heading west toward Pinal Creek.

In a clearing milky with moonlight, he dropped belly-down over the stream and drank deeply of the cool mountain water. An owl hooted nearby. Henry sat up and studied the forest until he spotted the bird in the highest branch of the tallest tree on the other side of the creek. "Whoo-whoo," Henry called across the gently rippling stream, silver in the moonlight.

"Whoo-whoo," the owl answered, making Henry laugh.

He leaned against a boulder and held the gunnysack upside down until the jerky, biscuits, and honey fell out. Opening the crock, he used his finger as a scoop and dribbled honey onto a biscuit, licked his finger, and popped the bread into his mouth.

He ate all six biscuits, each one drenched with honey. Even so, there was some left in the crock and he scooped out more with his fingers and licked it as it ran down his hand to his wrist. Completely satiated, he tossed the crock deep into the forest, smiling as he thought of the happiness of the critter who found it. He leaned over the creek and cleaned the sticky residue from his hands, then lowered his face and drank deeply.

"Whoo-whoo," the owl called.

Henry stood up and hooted back. He folded a strip of the jerky into his mouth, put the rest in his pants pocket, and started walking northwest again, back toward Globe and that dishwashing job.

By morning he'd descended from the mountains and was on the prairie beneath a gray sky threatening snow. The stage road cut across the land with deeply gouged furrows that had been dug during the last thaw but were frozen now. Henry didn't have a coat and the winter wind sliced through his shirt. Hugging himself for warmth as he walked, he kept within the deepest rut because it afforded some protection from the gusts. When he saw riders ahead, he stopped and watched them come, hoping for help. Even when he could see they were soldiers, he still didn't run, having forgotten about the horse he'd stolen from the Hooker Ranch.

The three cavalrymen reined up in a circle surrounding him. "Who are you?" one of them asked.

Henry took a moment to puzzle over the hostile reception. "Who's asking?" he finally answered.

"Private Charles Smith of the Sixth Cavalry, Camp Grant," the man barked. "Ain't you Kid Antrim?"

"My name's Henry Antrim," he conceded.

"We got a warrant for your arrest," one of the other soldiers crowed.

"What for?" Henry asked, suddenly remembering the horse.

Smith said, "Stealing my mount, you little punk! Did you think we wouldn't figure it was you?"

Henry lifted his hands as if baffled. "I ain't got no horse."

"You sold it then," Smith accused.

Henry laughed. "I ain't got but a dime on me."

"Then you lost the money gambling or spent it on sin," Smith said. "We're taking you back to Grant."

"You gonna let me ride?" Henry asked hopefully, thinking at least he'd be warm and fed in the stockade.

"Hell, no!" Smith retorted. He swung down and reached into his saddlepockets for a length of rope.

Henry turned to run, but the other two soldiers were suddenly pointing pistols at him. With sinking spirits, he faced Smith coming forward with the rope. Smith tied Henry's hands together in front of him, then remounted and started off at a leisurely pace toward the fort. Henry walked lagging behind, each tug of the rope tightening it more.

The soldiers rode comfortably in their wool uniforms, felt hats, and leather gloves. Henry shivered in his shirtsleeves, his head bare in the wind. His shoes were about worn through, and the frozen ruts of the road felt like corrugated iron, making the bottoms of his feet throb as if they were two solid bruises. He kept watching the soldiers on their horses, promising himself that as soon as he got loose, the first thing he'd buy, after boots, would be a mount so he could cross the country like a man.

The sky was crowded with stars by the time Henry was shoved unceremoniously into the black pit of the guardhouse. He stayed awake just long enough to determine he was alone, then groped in the dark until he found a blanket, rolled himself up like a papoose, and fell asleep.

Awakening to the smell of baking bread, he felt his stomach contract with hunger. He opened his eyes to see he was in a small room built of wood planks stuck into a rock and mortar foundation. The ceiling was thatch and so low he could touch it when he stood up. He had to use both hands because they were still tied together, but the stretch felt good so he did it again. Along the top of the walls was an open space for ventilation, the air coming through sharply cold. The sunlight, though, shone so cheerfully from the blue sky that it made Henry smile. He walked across to the door and pressed his face close to peer through a crack at the parade ground in front of him.

Henry had been inside the fort before. He knew that behind the guardhouse was the sutler's store. With any luck a horse would be tied to the hitching rail. He figured he could borrow the horse. If he let it loose once he got away, it would wander home again. The point of actual thievery came when you sold the property in question, at least that's how Henry saw it. Anything less than profit was just borrowing from a neighbor, and they were all neighbors out here on the frontier. The trouble was, though Henry wanted to be everyone's friend, not many people wanted to be his.

He paced the floor, trying to ignore the growls of hunger from his stomach, then went back and pressed his face against the crack in the door again. Soldiers were moving around now. When he saw some come out of the commissary mining their mouths with toothpicks, Henry felt tempted to yell out, "Don't the army feed its prisoners?" But he kept quiet. He'd heard stories about soldiers being punished with bullwhips, and he knew he didn't want any of that.

Finally a young soldier not much older than Henry opened the door. Henry blinked into the sudden glare of full sun, then smiled at the tray of breakfast in the soldier's hands. Taking the tray, Henry hunkered down on the floor, digging into the fatback and eggs and hot bread with melted butter. There was a mug of coffee, too, and even a shaker of salt. He studied that salt as he shoveled eggs into his mouth, then looked up and smiled at the soldier who was watching him with bored curiosity.

"You must've been hungry," the soldier said.

Henry nodded, setting the tray aside. "You been in the territory long?" he asked pleasantly.

The soldier shook his head. "Only a week."

"Where you from?"

"Indianapolis."

"Where's that?"

"Indiana," the soldier said, as if Henry should know.

"Never been there," he said. "There goes a good-looking mare, don'cha think?"

When the soldier turned around to watch the horse being led by, Henry emptied the salt into the palm of his hand. He stood up. "Reckon I could go out back now?"

The young soldier blushed. "Couldn't rightly refuse such a request," he answered stiffly, gesturing for Henry to precede him out the door.

The latrine was halfway between the stockade and the sutler's low adobe. Three horses were tied in front of the store, so with any luck Henry figured he'd have his choice. He smiled over his shoulder at the cavalry boy following him. "Bet this is dif'rent from Indianapolis, ain't it?"

"Sure is," the soldier said, casting his gaze around the thick tangles of orange buffalo squash growing among the spiny mesquite.

The instant he raised his eyes again, Henry threw the salt in the soldier's face. The soldier shouted in pain as Henry ran for the closest horse. Yanking the reins free, he threw one across the far side of the horse's neck, then leapt up to grab the horn with both hands, being as they were still tied together. He pulled himself into the saddle, spinning the horse in a half-rear and kicking in the worn-out heels of his city shoes.

He heard yelling at first, then only the happy cadence of the horse's hooves on the sandy soil. For a while he ran the horse hard, then slowed it to a fast trot, cutting distance north toward Globe. When he could see the lights of the city on the horizon, he stopped and swung down. He was about to slap the horse home when it occurred to him to check the saddlepockets. Telling himself they might hold food that would spoil if not eaten right away, he opened the closest pocket and rummaged blindly inside. His fingers touched the hard, cold steel of a knife, and he smiled.

The blade was a good six inches long and he had no trouble cutting the rope off his hands. He threw it far into the desert, laughing as he heard critters scurry away from the disturbance. When the horse bobbed its head and whinnied, Henry heard the clink of coins settling deeper into the saddlepocket. Sliding the knife behind his belt, he held his hand over the booty and told the horse, "Whatever I get, I'll call it severance pay from the cavalry."

He pulled a coin out and laughed to see a Gold Eagle, American currency worth ten dollars. "Guess my luck jus' took a turn up," he told the horse, slapping it away from him. "Hope yours does the same," he called after it, then stood watching until it disappeared in the darkness.

He turned around and started walking toward the lights of the city, laughing as he called ahead, "Beware, all you monte dealers and shysters of slick cards. Kid Antrim done found himself a stake."

8

Lincoln Town

On a cold Saturday evening in December, John Tunstall was walking east on Lincoln's only street toward the McSweens' Christmas party. Dressed in his best suit of fine gray wool and a black cloak heavy enough for the moors, he strode quickly across the newly fallen snow. Smoke hung like a fog, blue and sweet with piñon, undulating past the lighted windows of the adobe homes as Tunstall thrust his fists deeply into the pockets of his jacket, one hand holding the metal of his revolver to warm against his skin.

He had spent nearly a year looking for the perfect land and had finally found it. The next step was to pinpoint the exact location and make an offer. That, of course, required money, and John's father wanted the land chosen before sending funds. It took six weeks to carry a letter between Santa Fe and London, enough time to stall a deal. But that was the situation, and there was nothing John could do but find the land and proceed.

Eager to discuss the possibilities with Mac, Tunstall hoped they could spend a few moments alone in the evening ahead. He had seen the lawyer only briefly since his return to Lincoln, and even those few minutes had been sandwiched between waiting petitioners. The crush of Mac's business had impressed Tunstall. He'd left the office thinking he'd found himself an excellent advisor, and that everything was falling into place.

The *torreón* loomed ahead, a black void inside its crumbling circle of stones. As Tunstall passed its gaping gun slots, his ears detected an absolute silence that was so comforting he stopped and stood a moment, letting his eyes plumb the depths of darkness inside the tower. Built as a haven from Apaches, it was an edifice less than thirty years old yet already obsolete. Beyond it the frozen river made no sound, in the trees overhead the wind was motionless, the animals were silent in their distant stables, the people inaudible behind their snug adobe walls. Alone with a relic ignored or forgotten by everyone except children playing ghostly games with bones, John Tunstall suddenly felt heavy with loneliness, as if his cloak were drenched with sorrow.

A powerful homesickness possessed him. Suddenly he wanted to kiss his sister Emily and wish her a merry Christmas, to tell her everything he had seen and learned in America, and to hear her wise and affectionate advice. But she was half a world away and there was nothing he could do about it.

He was caught standing in the shadow of a ruin, caught in a silence so profound he felt suspended in time. As he studied the stone refuge built for a need no longer alive, he thought about history being beyond anyone's power to change, and that perhaps the future too was ordained by rhythms already established. Tunstall was not a religious man, and his thoughts turned not on a deity controlling the universe, but on an impersonal and uncaring thrust of events, casting its shadow on his endeavors just as the *torreón* lay a darkness about itself that he sheltered within, cold and unmoving, as if turned to the very stones in whose shadow he stood.

Softly, as if from a recollected dream, he heard a piano pealing forth a carol. He looked toward the music and saw the McSween home, its flat roof outlined with glowing lanterns for the festivities of the season. He hummed along with a few bars of "O Come, All Ye Faithful," then laughed with pleasure that Mrs. McSween had a piano and knew how to play. Thinking Christmas wouldn't be so lonely after all, he chided himself for standing in the snow freezing his feet when a few yards away he was expected in a warm room full of convivial people.

Mac opened the door in response to Tunstall's knock, and John was hit by a flood of warm air fragrant with hot spiced cider and scented

candles. The lawyer's normally pale complexion was flushed with pleasure as he welcomed his guest. After hanging Tunstall's cloak on a hook
by the door, Mac squired John into the center of the small parlor.

First to greet him was Sue, rising from the piano bench in a dove
gray evening gown scooped low enough to show a scattering of freckles
across the pleasing curves of her breasts. Her earrings were tiny golden
bells that sang prettily when she moved. Bowing to kiss her hand, he
caught a whiff of her perfume, as sweetly sultry as a hothouse of tropical
flowers. "Mrs. McSween," he murmured, looking down into her shining
eyes, amber in the candlelight.

She took his arm and led him around the room, though it was only a
few steps, introducing her other guests. The man who came first, whose
presence Tunstall had felt even while greeting his host and hostess, was
John Chisum. Over fifty, he was wiry and weathered, his steel-gray hair
emphasizing the blue of his crystal-sharp eyes. His hand was rough, his
grip like iron. Beneath a stiff, black moustache, he smiled with the ease
of a man who spent a great deal of his time laughing. In the brief moment they held each other's gaze, Tunstall was impressed but not surprised with the visage of the reputed Cattle King of the Pecos; he looked
like a man who successfully inflicted his will on the world.

Seated beside him was a young girl, perhaps fifteen, in a red velvet
dress. Her brown hair was thin, twisted atop her head in a skimpy bun,
and her face was narrow and pinched. Sue introduced her as Lily Casey.
Tunstall remembered it was her father who had been assassinated after
the political convention the year before, and in a surge of compassion he
forgave her homeliness. Standing beside her was Dick Brewer. Tunstall
shook his hand as if they were already friends. Last was his former host,
Juan Patrón, whom he did count as a friend.

Tunstall declined a chair, preferring to stand by the fire a moment
longer. Mac stood by the table filling a cup with cider as the others settled back in their seats. Chisum broke the silence. "I suspect, Mr. Tunstall," he said with a heavy Texas drawl, "that Lincoln is a far cry from
London."

Tunstall smiled. "Indeed, sir. But that's not to say which I prefer."

"You like this country, then," the old rancher said.

"I truly believe it's the prettiest place I've seen, and I've traveled extensively." He accepted the cup of cider from Mac with a nod of thanks,
then turned back to Chisum. "You yourself, sir, are evidence that it's
excellent range for cattle, which is my intended enterprise." He sipped
the cider, aware of the Texan's scrutiny.

Chisum nodded, as if in approval. "Mac's told me you're interested in investing in Lincoln County and asked for my help to sway you in the right decision." Chisum laughed gently, looking at the lawyer. "I call him an empire builder, but he says that's an insult."

Mac shook his head with a good-natured smile. "I'm a man of God building a Christian community."

Chisum chuckled. "Call it Christian or call it commerce, what you're doing is building a ring to challenge the Democrats in Santa Fe. I've dabbled enough in politics to know that however much you coat it with sugar, government's money and nobody gets up from the table with clean hands."

"Amen," Brewer muttered.

Seeing that Mac felt uncomfortable with the turn of the conversation, Tunstall quickly said, "I'm sure that's true. But as a servant of the British Crown, I have no intention of imposing myself into local politics. My sole aim is to establish an enterprise in cattle."

"Uh-huh," Chisum drawled. "Well, I wouldn't want you going into such a venture on any notion gathered from dime novels, so I'll tell a tale of how cattle ranching runs in this neck of the woods." He paused, then said, "If you want to hear it."

"Very much," Tunstall murmured, settling onto an ottoman near Mrs. McSween. The sweep of her skirt reminded him of his sister, who had often sat and listened to him discuss business with their father.

"Okay," Chisum said. "Not long ago, five hundred of my cows were driven to El Paso without my having a say in it. Me and my ramrod, Jim Highsaw, tracked 'em there and learned who bought 'em from who. One of those second who's was a fellow name of Dick Smith. Me and Highsaw drove the herd home, then mosied down to Seven Rivers and found Smith with incriminating evidence on the Beckwith Ranch. When the thief went for his gun, Highsaw shot and killed him. He was acquitted, of course, on the grounds of self-defense while in the act of replevin."

"What does *replevin* mean?" Tunstall asked.

"Replevin," Mac explained, "is the act of repossessing stolen goods with the understanding that ownership will be decided in the courts, and if the decision goes against you, the goods will be returned. It's involved in ninety percent of my cases."

"Is rustling that common of a problem?" Tunstall asked.

Everyone else burst into laughter. With good humor, Tunstall watched them enjoy the joke at his expense while he waited for an explanation. When quiet was again restored, Mac said with a smile of commiseration for Tunstall's ignorance, "One could almost say rustling's the major economic activity of the county."

Slowly, Tunstall said, "You make it sound like a veritable den of thieves."

"It is," Chisum agreed. "But for the most part, they're more a nuisance than anything else. There's only one big enough to do any real damage."

"Are you referring to Major Murphy?" Tunstall asked.

Chisum nodded. "Do you know him?"

"I don't," he answered, glancing at Juan Patrón, "but whenever someone mentions any trouble in Lincoln County, his name always comes up. An unsavory reputation for a man to have."

"An unsavory man," Sue said quietly.

Tunstall looked at her, then at Lily, who was glaring up at Chisum with a defiance that almost made her pretty. Turning to Mac, Tunstall said impulsively, "Dolan offered to sell me Fairview. I wanted to discuss it with you first, of course, but he made it sound very attractive." He looked back at the old rancher. "Do you know the land, sir?"

"It's good," Chisum grunted. "Plenty of grama grass, which is a natural strain of hay that grows 'round here, good forage for cattle or horses, and the spread has a natural spring, purty as a picture. Can't say anything against the land."

Tunstall shifted uneasily to Mac. "What do you think?"

Mac sniffed and settled more deeply in his chair, lacing his fingers across the front of his vest. "I'm afraid Major Murphy has no deed to Fairview. Neither he nor Mr. Dolan are legally entitled to collect any monies from the land whatsoever. They may sell their improvements, but the land remains in public domain."

"You mean it's not for sale at all?" Tunstall asked.

Mac shook his head. "Not until land has been surveyed by the government can claims be made through the Homestead Act. Meanwhile, squatter's rights are all there is. The land is yours as long as you hold it, and until a claim is filed."

"I see," Tunstall murmured, disappointed.

"Don't worry," Sue consoled. "The county is scheduled to be surveyed soon." Then she stood up, asking in a sprightly voice as she moved to the piano, "How about some carols?"

"Yes, wonderful!" Tunstall said, grateful to put an end to the serious discussion. "I heard you playing on my way over here, and it was the most delightful surprise to anticipate music as an accoutrement to the evening."

Chisum's laugh boomed through the room. "I'm not sure what it is you said, but if it's music you want, I'll play along with my fiddle, if you like."

"I'd be honored, sir," Tunstall said, extending his arm to Lily and escorting her to the piano.

He held her waist as they all sang "Silent Night," he and Mac and Brewer and Patrón harmonizing beneath the melody carried by Lily, while Chisum's violin rose with passion above them all.

The next morning, Tunstall awoke in his room in the Wortley Hotel to see the sun was bright in a blue sky, promising a splendid day for a ride. The party had been fun and he felt privileged to have as his advisors an able attorney and the undisputed cattle king of the territory. At the end of the evening, he'd received an invitation from Dick Brewer to visit his ranch, and Tunstall was looking forward both to seeing the land and to deepening their acquaintance. Believing himself ushered into his new venture with the best of friends, he ate a hearty breakfast in celebration of his luck.

Just as he was finishing, Jimmie Dolan walked through the door of the hotel's dining room. A short man—Tunstall estimated Dolan's height couldn't be more than two or three inches above five feet—he had a ruddy complexion, icy blue eyes, and blond hair already receding despite his young age, which Tunstall calculated to be near his own.

Dolan stopped at Tunstall's table and smiled as he asked, "Mind if I join you?"

"Please do," Tunstall replied, covering his dislike with a coolly polite demeanor.

With a jerk of his head, Dolan told the boy to clear the table, waited until he was through before sitting down, then muttered a command in Spanish, again waiting for the boy to return with a fresh pot of coffee. He left it on the table, and Dolan filled Tunstall's cup, then his own. "It's good to see you back in Lincoln," he said stiffly.

"Thank you," Tunstall answered.

"Have you given any thought to Fairview?" Dolan asked, lifting his cup and watching Tunstall over the rim as he drank.

Tunstall nodded. "I have, and regret to say I'm no longer interested."

A muscle twitched in Dolan's upper lip as he carefully replaced his cup in its saucer. "Why's that?"

"I've been advised against it," Tunstall said.

Dolan looked down, as if afraid of revealing something he would rather keep hidden. "I'd ask who your advisors are," he said, raising his eyes, "but I already know."

"Are their opinions of Fairview so famous?" Tunstall teased.

"I know you were at McSween's last night," Dolan answered with a snide smile. "It isn't hard to figure your advisors are the same men who were also there."

"How astute. I commend you," Tunstall said.

Dolan frowned, then put forth a salesman's smile. "There's other property available. Maybe I can interest you in another spread."

"No, thanks," Tunstall said. "I don't feel the need of more advice at this time." He watched the other man's face become mottled with anger.

"You're making a grave mistake," Dolan warned. "McSween is a turncoat, out for himself."

"And who are you out for, Mr. Dolan?" Tunstall asked coldly.

"Myself," he admitted. "But I don't put my hands in a friend's pocket when he's not looking. You trust McSween and you best watch your wallet real close."

Tunstall felt offended for his friend. "It is infamy, sir, to accuse a man of theft behind his back! If you were a gentleman, you'd say these falsehoods to his face or not at all. Even if by some unlikely circumstance your accusations were true, I doubt I'd put my trust in your opinions." He stood up.

Dolan laughed. "You'll be back," he crowed. "Poorer but wiser, you'll see I'm right."

9

Tunstall repressed a shiver of revulsion as he strode from the dining room. Waiting for the hostler to bring his horse, he looked up the street of Lincoln and tried to appreciate again the beauty of the provincial village. But a cold wind had risen and the street seemed stark now.

Tunstall thanked the hostler, mounted his horse, and reined it around to head east. He spurred it into a trot and posted through town, his horse's hooves clattering loudly on the frozen ground. When he'd cleared the last hut, the road wound into a forest with mountains towering on both sides. He found the trail as easily as Brewer had predicted, and followed it up to the crest, then down alongside Eagle Creek toward the Hondo River.

At the junction of the two waterways, Brewer was already waiting, grinning a welcome as he watched Tunstall approach. The rancher rode a large roan standing about the same hands as Tunstall's bay, so when they fell in step beside each other, they were carried along on an even keel. After crossing the river, they turned west beside the Hondo's white-water, rushing between banks jagged with broken ice refracting the sunlight into a myriad of rainbows. The wind carried the fresh smell of pines, and the fog of the horses' breath preceded their progress through the forest.

Tunstall looked across at Brewer, admiring the symmetry of his face beneath a morning stubble of black whiskers, the square planes of his cheekbones, his finely shaped nose, the etched clarity of his mouth. His dark hair hid his ears and fell below the collar of his coat, and his eyes were deeply set and a soft brown, alive with intelligence. Tunstall thought him a fine specimen of a man, obviously of good breeding. In his easygoing manner, he started Brewer talking about himself.

"I came out here in '74," Brewer began. "Right after what they're calling the Horrell War."

"Is that when Juan Patrón's father was killed?" Tunstall asked.

Brewer nodded. "The way I understand it, the Mexicans finally ran the Horrells back to Texas and I happened along during a lull in hostilities, you might say. These mountains struck me as about the prettiest place I'd seen, and I'm from Wisconsin, so that's saying a lot." He gave Tunstall a quizzical look. "You know where Wisconsin is?"

"Near the northern Great Lakes, isn't it?" he answered, pleased with himself.

"Yes, and green as velvet, full of crystal clear lakes so blue they hurt your eyes. It's good dairy land. That's what my folks did, dairy farming. I liked it a lot and probably would've stayed and taken over when they got on, but something intervened."

Tunstall kept quiet though he was bitten with curiosity.

Brewer reined his horse to a stop. "See that knob of bare rocks up there?" he asked, standing in his stirrups as he pointed. "My land starts on a line running through those rocks up from the Hondo here, over to another pile of rocks with iron in them so they're kind of reddish, then west to Pine Ridge and back to the river. Five hundred acres." He settled back in his saddle with satisfaction.

"Heavily timbered," Tunstall observed.

"It opens up further down. That's where I had my crops in. Corn and barley, last year. Probably the same again this, though I'm getting more into running cattle than I had. They can be sold off bit by bit if you need funds before harvest." He rubbed the stubble on his chin. "I left Wisconsin because of a woman," he said, not looking at Tunstall. "I courted her hard and she led me to believe she loved me, then up and married this other fellow without warning. He was my neighbor and I would've had to watch her get fat with his children and then old under his husbandry, and I didn't think I could stand it. I knew I didn't want to, so I came West where I wouldn't have to see her anymore."

"Sounds wise," Tunstall murmured.

Brewer shook his head. "I bought this land from Murphy, and I was satisfied with the price by Wisconsin standards, but I found out later I paid half again too much. To get started, I opened an account at the Big Store and they let me have supplies on credit until I made my first harvest. You probably know what I'm going to say, but damn if I saw it coming. When I sold them my harvest, it didn't equal what I owed, so I started my second year in the hole." He chuckled in self-deprecation. "Next harvest was the same thing, only the hole was considerably deeper. I made up my mind not to buy from Murphy anymore and nearly starved last winter, going all the way to Seven Rivers for what I couldn't do without. But it didn't make any difference. The House stuck so much interest on my account, I was still sliding fast. So I went to see Mac, trying to figure some way out. You know what he told me?"

Tunstall shook his head.

"The same thing he told you last night. Murphy didn't own my land, never had any right to collect any monies from it at all. I'd been paying him two whole years for nothing."

"I'm surprised you didn't kill the man!" Tunstall exclaimed.

Brewer threw him a worried look. "I considered it," he said slowly. "But I'd rather stay alive and outlast him."

He turned his horse onto a trail that cut away from the river. When Tunstall had caught up, Brewer said, "Murphy's never alone. You have to go through Dolan and Riley to get at him. Both of them have proved several times they're not above murder. They act as witnesses for each other and testify it was self-defense and get acquitted. Mac convinced me to fight The House legally. He says they're fossils, and if we live according to the law we'll beat them just by surviving while they go under. He's a brilliant man. I have the greatest admiration for Alex McSween."

"Yes, he impressed me, too," Tunstall answered as he ducked a low-hanging pine bough bouncing in the wind. "How did he handle your case?"

Brewer looked a little sheepish. "He bought my note from Murphy. It was hard, letting him do it. But I finally saw it was better to be beholden to Mac than under Murphy's heel. I'm paying him back best I can, and he's getting interest, I made sure of that, but only two percent and not the eighteen Murphy was charging."

"Eighteen percent?" Tunstall asked, astounded.

"Yes, sir. I tell you, my account was growing faster in Murphy's books than the number of Mescaleros he was charging the government to feed, and that was downright miraculous!"

"I heard about it," Tunstall said with a laugh.

"Well, I'm out from under him and I'm glad. But he doesn't waste any affection on me, and he downright hates Mac. Mac used to work for The House, you know. And Murphy and Dolan can't stand it that he knows their secrets and now is set up in opposition."

"Is he actively opposing The House?" Tunstall asked.

"Oh yeah, no doubt. Not right out in the open, but like he helped me, he helps others as best he can. He's not a wealthy man. But what he's doing is creating a backlash, a kind of underground current that's getting out from under Murphy's crippling debt and able to stand free and oppose him. Chisum's in on it, too. He hates the Santa Fe Ring. There's been bad blood between them a long time because he doesn't see how they have the right to take control of the whole damned territory. He can be right ornery sometimes. I know I wouldn't want him for an enemy."

"No," Tunstall agreed. "But then I hadn't anticipated enemies at all."

"It's part of the deal if you settle here," Brewer warned. "In Murphy's eyes, you're either under him or against him, there's no neutral ground. Sometimes I think he sees the whole world as an army and he's commander in chief. A pompous old bastard. Have you met him?"

Tunstall smiled. "I haven't had the pleasure."

"You will. If you stay. There's my home, be it ever so humble."

Tunstall looked ahead to where the trail opened into a wide valley, cleared and ready for spring planting. Beneath a large cottonwood was a small adobe house, and beyond it was an adobe barn large enough to accommodate fifteen animals at most. A vegetable garden had been laid out in between, its scarecrow looking forlorn with frost glistening in the crevices of its rags. Tunstall and Brewer rode directly into the stable and tended to their horses' needs.

Tunstall noted that the barn was solid, and that the tools and harness were in good repair and organized neatly. The stalls were covered with fresh straw, and a sweet smell came from the wild wheat stored loose in the loft. He felt akin to this man who had come West alone and established his notion of order on a corner of the world.

After the blazing sunlight of the winter day, the cabin was dark and chilled. There were two windows, but the adobe walls were three feet thick and the light was diluted through the distance. When Brewer lit a kerosene lantern hanging over the table, the room sprang into relief. As he knelt to start a fire, Tunstall looked around.

The floor was dirt, the walls mud, the roof thatch above a herringbone pattern of latillas. The earthen hearth was built into a corner with a sloping chimney to radiate heat. Tunstall had seen kiva fireplaces in

Santa Fe and approved the excellence of the design, marveling that the English had never devised such a hearth.

"Sit down," Brewer said over his shoulder. "This'll be going in a minute and we'll have some coffee."

"An excellent prospect," Tunstall answered, pulling one of the crude wooden chairs out from beneath the matching table.

He was facing the door and saw a shotgun cradled above the lintel. Propped behind the door was a Winchester. Fifty-pound bags of black beans and cornmeal leaned in a corner, chiles hung in strings from the latillas, and a slab of jerky was suspended from a viga. Shifting his gaze to the small store of foodstuffs in tins and sacks on shelves against the wall, he saw a can of coffee and a burlap bag of sugar, which pleased Tunstall because he liked his coffee sweet. He watched Brewer pour water from a bucket into a kettle and swing it on the tripod over the flames.

"Now," he said, wiping his hands on his trousers as he stood up. "How about a little milk?"

"You have milk?" Tunstall asked with delight.

Brewer laughed. "I have an entire cow. Be right back." He strode quickly out the door and was gone.

Tunstall turned around to survey the rest of the room. Behind him were two rope-mattress beds covered with dark woolen blankets tucked tight. A wooden crate had been pushed into the corner between the headboards. On top of the crate, a candle had been inserted into the mouth of a bottle encrusted with dripped wax. Next to it lay a book which Tunstall guessed from its size to be a Bible. One of the beds had several boxes of cartridges scattered across the blanket. On pegs above it hung a bridle, two braided horsehair lariats, and a framed oval portrait of a young couple in wedding clothes several decades out of fashion. Tunstall guessed them to be his host's parents, which Brewer confirmed when he came back carrying a tin pail half full of frothy warm milk.

The two men put their boots up on the earthen bench around the hearth and savored their sweetened *cafe con leche*. Before the repast was over, they had agreed Tunstall would stay on and start learning firsthand the business of ranching while looking for his own land. They shook hands as fast friends, then Brewer went to his fields while Tunstall rode back to Lincoln to gather his belongings.

A month passed before Tunstall found his land, a fine spread of rolling meadows interspersed with pine-covered mountains along the Rio Feliz, southeast of Brewer's place. When he told Brewer about it that night at supper, Brewer knew the exact location.

"That piece is part of the Casey spread," he said, sopping grease from his plate with a crust of biscuit.

Tunstall felt crestfallen. "It's claimed, then?"

"No, it isn't," Brewer said, leaning back and belching softly. "Casey didn't live long enough to file a claim."

"Then it's available," Tunstall said, his enthusiasm returning.

"Some folks won't like you taking it, though. Remember that little girl with Chisum at Mac's party? Belongs to her family."

"Why don't they claim it?" Tunstall asked.

"They got another spread down on the Hondo below Coe's farm, a store and mill and all. With her husband gone, Mrs. Casey can't keep both places going. Gossip has it the widow's pinched for money and having her debts called."

"I dislike causing her more grief," Tunstall confessed. "But if I don't claim that land, won't someone else?"

"It's a plum waiting to be picked," Brewer agreed.

"I want it," Tunstall said with determination. "I'm going into Lincoln tomorrow and see Mac about filing on it."

"I'll stand behind you," Brewer promised without hesitation. "I'm just warning you that the Caseys are friendly with the Seven Rivers bunch and they're apt to take offense at your claiming that land. They already don't like Chisum, though they feed off his herds. I doubt if there's a cow in the county whose ancestors didn't wear Chisum's brand."

"I'm confused," Tunstall admitted. "If what you say is true, what was Lily doing at the party?"

"Chisum and her daddy knew each other in Texas before coming out here. But the Seven Rivers bunch are the Caseys' neighbors, and small ranchers like Lily's father was. I'm sure Mrs. Casey doesn't bear a grudge against Chisum—Lily's keeping company with the old man is proof of that—but the others do."

"Why?"

"Chisum's big, got a lot of cows. The others are little. That's about all there is to it."

"And is Lily really keeping company with Chisum, in the sense of courting?"

Brewer shrugged. "Chisum's an old bachelor, and it's doubtful he'll take a bride so late in life. But then again, he's always been fond of Lily and I'm not one to second-guess a man when it comes to romance. The Caseys surely need a strong man in the family. All three of Lily's brothers are sickly. I'd rather they join up with Chisum than the Seven Rivers men, I'll say that. They're a mean bunch when they get riled."

Tunstall thought a moment. "Seems to me," he finally said, "no matter where I decide to settle, someone's not going to like it. The only thing to do in such a situation is exactly what I want, or as near as I can come. I want that land, and I'll do my best to get it."

Brewer grinned and stood up. "That calls for a drink," he said, pulling a jug from the shelf and returning to fill their cups with whiskey. He raised his in a toast. "To the Englishman," he said, his eyes full of fun. "May his cows thrive in peace."

Tunstall stood up to return the toast. They both drank deeply, and Tunstall had to fight against coughing the raw whiskey back up.

Brewer laughed. "This will taste like mother's milk to you after a while," he said, resuming his seat. "What's your plan for stock?"

Tunstall sat down and eagerly outlined his conceptualization of the perfect cattle ranch. They sipped at their cups and let their imaginations run with the alcohol, projecting their fortunes for decades forward, counting on a continually increasing market with never a recession or bust. In their schemes everything fell into place, and late in the night when they fell silent and looked at each other across the table littered with charts of cow poundage and profit to the hundredth of a penny, sketches of corral and stable layouts around the main house, and bunkhouses large enough to accommodate twenty hands, they smiled at each other, acknowledging their optimism.

Tunstall laughed. "I like you. We think alike. When I get my spread, will you act as my foreman?"

"I'd love to," Brewer said, "but I have my own spread."

"I'll be a working owner. I just need an advisor with your experience. You'd still have time for your own place, and a salary besides."

Brewer didn't have to think about it twice. "It's a deal," he said, reaching across their scribbled fantasies to shake hands with his new boss.

In the light of the dying fire, the two ranchers stumbled to their beds and a slightly drunken sleep. Only once in the night did Brewer wake and think about what was to come. The Jones boys would be the ones to watch. Marion Turner and the Beckwiths and Bob Olinger, who was spoiling for a fight half the time anyway. Of one thing Brewer felt certain: before all the titles to land were indisputably legal, the citizens of Lincoln County were in for some bloodletting. He hoped the Englishman knew how to handle a gun.

10

Early the next morning, Tunstall rode into town and called on Mac in his office. The lawyer was glad to see him and made room in his busy schedule for a professional consultation.

"Before we get down to business," Mac said with a smug smile, "I want to tell you that in lieu of a debt owed me by The House, I've just received the deed to five acres in the center of town. The property includes their old store building, which I intend to renovate into a home large enough to accommodate Sue and myself, as well as an additional wing for the family of my new partner, David Shield, whom I expect to arrive soon."

Enthusiastically, Tunstall congratulated him on the acquisition, then added, "Mrs. McSween will no doubt be pleased."

The lawyer smiled again, acknowledging his pleasure that Tunstall seemed as fond of Sue as she was of him. Then he dropped personal subjects and discussed the methods of filing a land claim. "Pursuant to impending congressional ratification of the Desert Land Act," Mac said, "you can file on six hundred and forty acres of loosely classified desert and, by planting trees and other conservatory vegetation, gain title for the insignificant amount of twenty-five cents an acre." Nodding at Tunstall's obvious excitement, Mac added, "Much of the land along the Feliz and Peñasco qualify under the Act." He paused before saying, "Of course, citizenship is required, and it's not my impression you wish to relinquish your English allegiance."

Momentarily chastened, Tunstall replied, "I hadn't contemplated anything so drastic."

The seconds ticked by while each man assessed the other. Finally Mac said, "You could have other parties file in their names, with you providing the funds and holding quitclaim deeds against their interests. Does that sound desirable?"

"Highly," Tunstall pronounced. "I knew you wouldn't have told me all this without a way of getting around the legal stipulations."

Mac shrugged. "As long as the men filing the claims are compensated for their involvement, I see no harm in skirting the law on such a technicality. You'd have to choose men you trust, of course, and have the money ready at the time they stake their claims."

Tunstall winced, then related his problem with securing funds quickly. The lawyer came back with an offer to advance the money.

"You have such amounts free for use?" Tunstall asked in surprise.

"At the moment," Mac answered, beaming with generosity. "And I can think of no better purpose than assisting you."

Tunstall smiled at his benefactor. "If you'll also be good enough to loan me stationery and pen, I'll write London immediately and set the wheels in motion so as not to delay repaying you."

Mac offered Tunstall his desk and left him alone to write his letter in private. Quickly calculating the amount he would need for the purchase of the range he wanted, Tunstall wrote his father requesting thirty-two hundred pounds be remitted to his bank account in St. Louis. At the current exchange rate he was asking for sixteen thousand dollars, but he didn't flinch at the large amount, knowing he would soon need more to buy cattle. When he had finished, he found Mac in the saloon which also served as his waiting room. With an excited handshake, Tunstall left the lawyer to post his letter.

Robert Widenmann was leaning against the hitching rail in front of the Big Store, feeling out of place. He had purchased new apparel before leaving Santa Fe and was dressed in the rough clothing of a frontiersman, which was an improvement due to its new condition but not what he was accustomed to wearing. He considered himself a gentleman down on his luck, and had come to Lincoln on the off chance he might encounter the Englishman. But after having spent a night and the better part of a morning in the town, he hadn't caught a glimpse of the man he had come hoping to find.

Suddenly Tunstall strode up and took hold of Widenmann's shoulders, turning him so they faced each other as the Englishman laughed an exuberant greeting. "So you came!" he said happily. "I can't tell you how glad I am."

Widenmann felt pleased with the warm reception, but replied dryly, "I wasn't certain you were still here. I only came because I'd heard so much about the place, I decided to see it before leaving the territory."

Tunstall's happy expression faded. "You can't be serious. You'll tarry a time with me, I hope. Or do you have pressing engagements elsewhere?"

Widenmann smiled. "No engagements, just a lethargy due to lack of enterprise. It's time I got involved in something or other."

"Then stay and help me with my ranch!" Tunstall exclaimed. "I've found the land and am just now going to post a letter requesting funds. Your assistance would be a great asset to my endeavors, and I'd be delighted to have your company."

"Perhaps," Widenmann replied, feigning hesitation. The truth was he had left Santa Fe owing Herlow money and his traveling funds were nearly depleted, so he wasn't inclined to reject any invitation. Yet he didn't wish to appear too eager.

"Come, my man," Tunstall argued affably, "at least stay long enough to allow me to show you the site of my adventures."

"I can do that," Widenmann conceded, as if sacrificing his own plans for the sake of friendship.

"Excellent!" Tunstall rejoined. "Wait for me, won't you? I shan't be a minute."

Widenmann watched the Englishman skip up the stairs to post his letter inside the Big Store. Dolan was standing in the doorway.

"So you've found yourself a spread," the little man said in a sarcastic tone.

Tunstall seemed amused. "Are you in the habit of eavesdropping?"

Dolan shrugged. "Seems to me a conversation held on a street is a public event."

As Tunstall walked on into the store without replying, Dolan assessed Widenmann with apparent hostility. Widenmann gave him a smile which wasn't returned, though Dolan walked directly by him, crossing the street to the Wortley. Tunstall came back and they both watched Dolan disappear inside the hotel's dining room.

"He doesn't seem to like you much," Widenmann said.

"No," Tunstall agreed. "When I first came, he tried to sell me a ranch which I was advised against taking, and now he seems to bear a grudge because of it. A childish way to conduct business."

"I've heard he can be a dangerous enemy," Widenmann said quietly.

Tunstall grinned. "I find it difficult to fear such a little man." They both laughed at Dolan's diminutive stature. "I have so much to tell you," Tunstall continued effusively, starting for the other end of town. "Have you a horse?"

Widenmann shook his head.

"I'll borrow one for today. Tomorrow we can return it and you can ride one of Dick's until we find a suitable mount. Good horses are hard to come by here."

"I'm sure," Widenmann murmured. "Who's Dick?"

"Richard Brewer. I've been staying on his ranch while I looked for my own. He's a capital chap and won't mind another guest, although there are only two beds. I'm afraid one of us will have to sleep on the floor."

"I'm not unaccustomed to sleeping on floors," Widenmann offered.

"Good," Tunstall replied with a laugh. "The house on my range is little more than a hut so we'll both be sleeping on the floor there. How are you at cooking, Mr. Widenmann?"

"Better than most," he answered immodestly. "If we're going to be sharing quarters, you should call me Rob. All my friends do."

"John is my given name," Tunstall said. "I hope you can see your way to staying indefinitely. I have other friends here, but they're all involved in their own enterprises, and I can't tell you how glad I'd be to have a companion in my daily business."

Widenmann could scarcely believe his good fortune. "Maybe you won't like my cooking," he suggested.

Tunstall laughed. "Then I'll hire a cook. Wait until you see my spread! If we leave right now, we can ride out there and be back at Brewer's for supper. How does that sound?"

"Fine," Widenmann answered. "Do you suppose we could find a gentle horse in this town? I'm not an expert rider, I'm afraid."

"We'll change that," Tunstall said.

Jimmie Dolan watched them from just inside the Wortley's front door, wondering which piece of land Tunstall had chosen. He had hoped the Englishman would flounder without the assistance of The House, but it appeared Tunstall was well on his way to achieving his ends. Dolan recrossed the street and entered the store, soon to be all his, needing merely Murphy's signature on the bill of sale.

The clerk was waiting on a customer as Dolan walked behind the counter and directly to the mailbox. He opened it without hesitation and removed Tunstall's letter, carried it back to his office, closed the door, and held the envelope over a kettle spouting steam to loosen the seal. When he had removed the pages he sat down at his desk and laid them flat before him.

He frowned at seeing McSween's letterhead, thinking the Englishman had lost no time allying himself with the wrong element. Noting with consternation the amount of money Tunstall had at his disposal, Dolan sneered, thinking tall men had life too easy. He snickered at the choice of land, knowing the Englishman was stepping on the toes of the men from Seven Rivers, then read the paragraph in which the writer analyzed the condition of doing business in the territory: "Everything in New Mexico that pays at all is worked by a ring; there is the Indian ring, the army ring, the political ring, the legal ring, the Roman Catholic ring, the cattle ring, the horsethieves ring, and half a dozen others. To make things stick it is necessary to either get into a ring or make one for yourself. My ring is forming itself faster than I had hoped, and in such a way that I will get the finest plum of the lot."

Dolan curled his lip in anger, muttering, "We'll see, Englishman, which plum you get." Then he replaced the letter, resealed the envelope, and returned it to the mailbox. Walking out, he crossed to the stable behind the Wortley to get his horse, then rode to Fairview to consult with his mentor, knowing Murphy would share a bottle of whiskey with his advice.

By the end of April, John Tunstall had moved to his ranch on the Rio Feliz. The river flowed fresh and fast, swollen with the winter snow melting in the mountains, and the trees growing along its banks burst forth with buds as if overrun with anticipation. While the cottonwoods released their silken seeds to float lazily on the gentle breezes, Tunstall and Widenmann established residence in the hut.

Their partnership had been loosely defined as an exchange of services for funds, neither item being specified, and both men felt comfortable with the arrangement. Tunstall decided the next step was to hire a cook and a boy to run errands so he could put his mind to hatching his empire. On Brewer's recommendation, he hired Godfrey Gauss, an old ne'er-do-well who was competent in the kitchen, and Fred Waite, who wasn't a boy but a year older than Tunstall and a fair hand with a gun. Half Choctaw Indian, Waite was thick and muscular, with a sweeping black moustache.

The four men set about enlarging their quarters, mixing the adobe bricks and laying the walls themselves. A bunkhouse was built, and a second room was added to the hut. Brewer often rode over and paid them a visit, and sometimes George Coe came too, bringing his fiddle. Then the hut would reverberate with the thud of bootheels pounding its foundations as the men clogged in the kitchen.

The morning after one such evening, when Brewer and Coe had left long after midnight, Tunstall put on a clean shirt and the same trousers he'd worn the day before. Sitting down again to tug on his boots, he looked across the room at Widenmann, who was just pulling himself from sleep.

"Rouse yourself, my friend," Tunstall said with a laugh. "We're going into town."

"What for?" Widenmann asked reluctantly.

"Casey's cattle are being auctioned this afternoon. Mac thinks if I bid five dollars a head they'll be mine. It's a cheap way to pick up a herd."

"Yes," Widenmann agreed, shaking off his lethargy and starting to dress. "I've heard Casey knew something about breeding stock."

They rode at a leisurely pace, side by side where the trail permitted, talking freely. They had already analyzed the economic realities in the county and devised a plan of attack: While waiting for his cattle to mature, Tunstall would corner the market in corn, buying the county's entire harvest. That way, even if he didn't get the government contract up for bid in September, whoever did would have to buy from him, and he could charge whatever he wanted. Now he returned to the subject of opening a store, an endeavor for which Widenmann didn't share his enthusiasm.

"It'll be a strong asset," Tunstall argued, not for the first time, "to have a place of business where we can conduct this brokerage and offer merchandise on credit against crops. The profit we make on the goods will increase our margin on the corn."

"Yes," Widenmann mused unhappily. "But won't Dolan be sour when you open a store that competes with his?"

"No doubt," Tunstall agreed.

Widenmann held on to his saddle as the horses skittered down the bank and across the knee-high current of the Hondo. The trail on the other side was narrow, winding its ascent through dense forest along Eagle Creek, so the two men didn't speak again until they were on the road into Lincoln.

"I think it's an excellent idea," Tunstall said with a confident smile. "Once we have cattle on the range, there won't be much to do but sit and watch them grow. A store will give us a bigger stake in everything that's happening, a headquarters in the hub, so to speak. I'm going to ask Mac to come in with us."

"You put a lot of trust in him," Widenmann said carefully.

"Don't worry," Tunstall answered with a smile. "I've arranged it so he can't slide back on me one iota without hurting himself."

"You're a wily cuss," Widenmann said with admiration.

"It's the only way to do business, my boy," Tunstall replied.

Sue McSween's business was caring for her husband. That entailed a myriad of tasks which challenged her dexterity and patience but never her intellect. Her passionate interest in politics could be expressed only in the sugary solicitude of parlor repartee and earnest consultations with her husband in the privacy of their chambers.

They disagreed on many points. Mac's religion had firmly entrenched in his mind the belief that all men were intrinsically good and it was the world that led them astray. Sue was more cynical. She saw the world ruled by evil men who successfully inflicted their perversions on everyone else. To fight evil, she argued, you must return its methods until it succumbed to its own poison. Mac scoffed at such a remedy, saying in such a case everyone would be corrupted. His solution lay in establishing guidelines so that men, of their own volition, would choose good for its obvious merits. At this point in their discussion he always smiled with indulgent patience, remarking that her thoughts were turning in the right direction but impaling themselves on flawed logic.

Early in their marriage, Sue had fought his patronizing dismissal of her opinions. She'd given up after recognizing that Mac measured himself against her intellectual inferiority. To combat that would require a destruction of the man he was, a fate she would no more wish on him than on herself. He *was* her in the world, and it behooved her to contribute to his strength, not effect his demise.

So she was trapped. She shopped, ran the house, saw to it that his laundry was done as he liked and their meals served for his pleasure. It was also her duty to be always gracious to his many clients, so she dressed and carried herself with the same poise as if she were in society. Sue felt restless more than anything else. None of the women around her enjoyed the pleasures of an intellectually stimulating conversation, and the men she talked with were all associates of her husband, so not people she could confide in without reservation. John Tunstall alone met her on equal ground.

She vicariously enjoyed the development of his ranch, plotting in her mind how she would proceed if given such an opportunity, and it was exactly as he was doing. She envied him immensely. His brotherly acceptance of her as a confidante compensated for her advisory role and strengthened their friendship until he was nearly equal to Mac in her thoughts.

Expecting the Englishman's visit, Sue had gone out early to buy more sugar at Montaño's store. She had walked to the western edge of town and bought a pound of butter and a quart of cream from Berta's farm, then stopped by Luciana's and bought a kilo of fresh tortillas. With her purchases in her shopping basket slung on her arm, she used her free hand to hold the skirts of her lilac dress out of the mud. Her burgundy shawl was knotted across her breasts, her lilac bonnet held atop her curls by ribbons tied beneath her chin.

The strong, cold wind threatened to unperch her bonnet and whipped her skirt against her body immodestly as she approached the Big Store. Its warm respite tempted her but she decided against stopping, wanting to hurry the last quarter mile home so that she might have time to tidy her attire before her company arrived. In front of the store she recognized Dolan's bay gelding and Sheriff Brady's sorrel stallion, a flashy red horse with flaxen mane and tail. She wondered briefly why the sheriff was in from his ranch so early, then her thoughts returned to her culinary preparations.

Yesterday she had cooked a pot of posole, the hominy stew spiced with chile. She had baked two apple pies and was planning a soufflé to be made at the last moment. She loved surprising John with unexpected dishes, and Mac's pride in her skills added to her pleasure. While congratulating herself on how compatible the three of them were, she suddenly frowned, remembering they were four now because Rob Widenmann was always with John.

Sue found Rob pleasant enough, and was glad John had an intelligent companion on his ranch. Mac, however, was unhappy with Widenmann's inclusion in their circle, though he held his tongue except when alone with Sue. Then he confessed to a suspicion of the man being untrustworthy, and dangerous because of it.

As Sue walked in front of the steps leading up to the Big Store, she was thinking Mac's worry was excessive. Widenmann was little more than a valet, and had scant power to influence Tunstall. Then she looked up and collided with Jimmie Dolan.

His eyes seared into hers with such malevolent hatred that she was struck dumb with shock. Thrown off-balance by the impact of their collision, she stood in an awkward posture, arrested by the ferocity in his eyes and the contempt they seemed to unequivocally attribute to her. Finally she found her tongue. "I beg your pardon," she murmured.

He sneered and muttered beneath his breath, then yanked his horse's reins free from the hitching rail and jabbed himself into the saddle, digging his spurs into the horse's flanks so it leapt to a gallop. Sue watched after him a moment, listening to the hoofbeats of his horse reverberate through the quiet town until they were lost. Trembling now, she heard the door open behind her and turned to see Sheriff Brady pulling on his gloves as he came down the steps.

"What's happened?" she asked.

Brady's face was clouded with a disgust he couldn't quite erase, though it was evident he was striving to appear calm. "Dolan was acquitted on self-defense," the sheriff said tersely. "There was a witness."

Still trembling, she asked, "Whom did he kill?"

"A Mexican working for him. The boy pulled a knife. There was a witness, like I said."

"Who was it?" Sue demanded.

"Hiraldo Jaramillo. I'm sure you didn't know him."

Tears stung her eyes. "I did know him, Sheriff. He cut wood for us last summer."

Brady suddenly looked old.

Sue's rancor rose, and she added bitterly, "If all the men Jimmie Dolan claimed to have killed in self-defense truly attacked him, the verdict should be suicide, Sheriff, not justifiable homicide."

Brady stared at her a long moment, then said gruffly, "You're upset, Mrs. McSween. Would you like me to escort you home?"

"Please don't," she replied in a huff. "I'm particular about whom I'm seen with." She stepped around him and hurried away.

The wind froze the tears on her face. Her nose was running and she hadn't a hand free to wipe it, so she stopped beneath a cottonwood near the arroyo. Looking down at the river's thin crust of ice, she shivered as though she would never be warm again.

She remembered Hiraldo Jaramillo as she had last seen him, chopping wood in the sunny yard behind her home. He had been so young, not yet twenty, and had stripped to his waist in the heat, his chest glistening with sweat as he worked. Sue sat in her dark bedroom and watched. She hadn't meant to. Having gone in to retrieve some thread from her old sewing basket, she pulled it out from beneath the bed and sat down to rummage through the basket's contents. When she found the thread and closed the basket, she looked up and saw Hiraldo swinging the axe as he quartered logs, his muscles rippling rhythmically, his belly flat with a dark line of hair disappearing into his trousers, his buttocks outlined round and hard, his black hair flying out behind him like a rooster's crown. "Oh my," she'd whispered, and sat there admiring him for longer than she would ever admit.

Brady came trotting his sorrel up the street, looking straight at her. She could see from his face that her grief didn't sit well with him, and her anger turned to pity for the sheriff. Wiping her nose, she picked up her basket and hurried home. Inside her snugly safe house, she collapsed in a chair, hugging her basket. She was still there when Mac came home.

He stood before her with concern on his face as she told him about Hiraldo Jaramillo and her encounter with Dolan and Brady. But she was unable to explain how terrified she had felt seeing the hatred in Dolan's eyes. When she tried, Mac reminded her that Tunstall was expected at any moment.

She had forgotten the purpose of her foray into the cold wind. Raising a hand to touch her hair, she found it disarrayed beneath her crooked bonnet. Mac smiled with encouragement. She handed him the basket and walked resolutely into the bedroom and closed the door.

Slowly she removed her bonnet and replaced it in its box, tied the ribbons and pushed the box back atop her chiffonier. She sat down before her dressing table, looked at the chaos of her hair, and began removing pins, taking it all down to begin anew, knowing it would require half an hour and she would be late greeting their guests.

She heard them arrive and listened to their masculine voices booming through the adobe walls. Smoothing the tail of her hair within the bouffant she had built around her face, she listened to Mac explain that she would be joining them shortly. John asked after her health, which struck her tenderly, as wounded as she was feeling, and she listened with a rueful smile as Mac assured them she was fine.

Meeting her own eyes in the mirror, she confessed a doubt. She couldn't inure herself to the repeated news of murder. Each report struck like an axe deeper into her reservoir of stamina. She felt vulnerable, but Mac had lately become so preoccupied with business he seemed to expect only a performance of elegant grace from her. Today, however, her audience was John, and she had a rapport with the Englishman. She could be herself with him, knowing Mac approved because Tunstall did.

She tucked the ends of her hair inside her bouffant, feeling satisfied that her coiffure was arranged as she wanted it. Then she stood up and changed her attire, taking pleasure in the spring green dress she had altered from its old style, deleting fullness from the skirt and pulling it behind her hips to fall in scallops over a bustle. As she admired her reflection in the mirror, she didn't delude herself that she was beautiful, but she considered herself a handsome woman.

Feeling pleased with her appearance, she was just turning to join the men when she heard Tunstall say the word "mercantile." Sue smiled, wondering what new avenue John had discovered for his energy. Then she stopped cold as she listened to him enthusiastically describe his plan to open a store to compete with Dolan's.

Her knees trembled as she crossed the room. The men rose at her entrance and remained standing in silence, their greetings dying on their tongues as they looked at her face. In a low voice resonant with conviction, she said, "Dolan will kill you if you do this."

Mac moved solicitously to her side. "Do what, darling?" he asked in a light tone. "You sounded so serious, it gave me a chill."

"It should," she replied, meeting John's eyes. "You're courting disaster if you oppose Dolan."

"I'm sure you're right," Tunstall answered with a playful laugh. "But any enterprise in this county must compete with The House. Please sit down, Sue, and tell us why you're so spooked."

She sat down, but it was Mac who explained about the death of Hiraldo Jaramillo, adding that Sue had been frightened by Dolan's visage of violence.

"Should I be less frightened," she asked, "when he smiles?"

"Decidedly not," Widenmann said. "Mrs. McSween has made an accurate assessment, in my opinion. The ill will of Dolan and Company shouldn't be considered insignificant."

"No," Tunstall agreed. "But neither should we let them stifle our ambitions. It's a free country and a free market. What do you say, Mac? I still haven't heard your thoughts."

Mac sat down beside Sue, his demeanor one of protection. "I cannot totally discount my wife's fears," he said softly, "but I believe they are exaggerated."

Sue looked at the floor, embarrassed at being so easily dismissed. She felt Tunstall's sympathy from across the room but couldn't raise her eyes for fear of belittling her husband.

Mac continued, "I only wonder if a store would engender enough profit to make it worth the risk."

"There is another aspect to this venture," Tunstall said. "We could operate a bank as adjunct to the store. Issue our own scrip and control absolutely the flow of our funds. I've already approached Chisum and he's agreed to be president, though he insists on being a figurehead only. His name would appear on the stationery and he would offer assets to back us, but otherwise he'd remain uninvolved. You, Mac, would be the logical choice for treasurer, overseer of the legality of our operation, and I would be the cashier, dealing with the bread and butter of exchange. What do you say?"

Sue looked up, admiring the ease with which Tunstall bestowed the realization of dreams. She knew her husband would accept, all trepidation regarding the store swamped by the prestige of a bank.

Mac confirmed her expectation when he said, "I accept the honor, sir. We'll triumph over the pernicious elements in this county and make it a God-fearing, righteous community!"

Tunstall chuckled. "We'll run it at a righteous profit, at any rate."

Sue rose to her feet and excused herself, murmuring only that she must see about lunch. In the kitchen, she found Sebrian stirring the posole on the stove. As she set about cracking eggs for her soufflé, she asked without looking at her servant, "Did you hear what they're planning now?"

"Yes'm," he answered.

"All Mac thinks of is winning converts to Christ," she muttered, whipping the eggs with vengeance. "And Tunstall only considers his profits. What will it take to wake them up?"

"I don't know, Mrs. Mac," Sebrian whispered, "but I'd feel a whole lot better if we had some guns on our side."

11

"We gotta get some money," Mackie told the kid. "I ain't eaten since yesterday."

"Thought you had ten dollars," Henry answered, sitting down in the shade of the arroyo to pull off his boots. He'd stolen them from a peddler's wagon and they were too small.

"Lost it at monte," Mackie said.

Henry snorted. "Seems to me you oughta eat 'fore you gamble."

Mackie watched the kid pop a blister on his heel, then tear the loose skin off. "Whaddaya say we hit the store again?"

"My feet are a mess," Henry said. "I can't be carrying no saddle clear over to Globe."

"Why don'cha go barefoot?"

The kid gave him a withering look. "I'd rather have blisters than cactus barbs in my toes."

"You oughta get yourself some new boots," Mackie said.

"Yeah, and you oughta get some supper," Henry replied, "but we ain't got a dime 'tween us."

"When'd you eat last?"

"This morning."

"Where at?"

"Mrs. Hollister's."

"What'd she feed you?"

"Poontang." The kid grinned.

Mackie laughed. "Din't you get no food outta her a'tall?"

"Piece of pie, but I snitched it on my way out." He pulled his boots back on, wincing when he stood up.

Mackie watched him limp down the arroyo. "Where you going?"

"The store," he said.

"What for?"

The kid turned around and walked backward as he grinned, flashing his crossed incisors with charm. "Figure I'll take the horse and the saddle too."

"They'll put you in the hoosegow!" Mackie yelled.

Henry shrugged and kept walking.

Mackie ran down the arroyo and tackled him, both of them rolling across the sand. The kid didn't fight, just let himself get pinned by Mackie's knees on his shoulders. Mackie glowered down at him. "You want to go to jail?"

The kid smiled real slow. "They'll give us supper," he said.

"Send you to Yuma and chain you in a hole!" Mackie retorted.

"Yeah? Like I'm pinned now?"

"Yeah!"

The kid brought his knee up sharp into Mackie's butt and flipped him off. Jumping to his feet, Henry laughed, dancing around with his dukes up.

Mackie wanted to rub his butt but wouldn't give Henry the satisfaction. Pulling himself to his feet, he charged the kid, hitting him head on and propelling him into the wall of the arroyo. They wrestled and fell, rolling in the sand with flailing fists, then the kid came out on top, his nose bleeding as he pinned Mackie to the ground. Henry laughed and stood up. Wiping his nose on his sleeve, he started walking down the arroyo again. "You coming?" he yelled back.

The Camp Grant store sat alone on a barren plot of ground, and the light falling through the open door shone on two cavalry horses tethered with long ropes leading inside the store. When Henry hunkered in the shadows to study the situation, Mackie squatted down beside him and said, "Looks like they think there's thieves in the vicinity."

"There's thieves," the kid said, giving him a grin, "and then there's coyotes."

Mackie snorted. "How you gonna get them horses?"

"I'm studying it." After a minute he said, "Go on in and talk to the soldier boys, keep their attention awhile."

"How long?"

The kid shrugged. "Five minutes. I'll meet you back at the arroyo."

"You gonna rummage their saddlepockets?"

"You'll find out," he said. "Get going."

Henry watched Mackie walk across the yard and through the door, then he snuck after him. He could hear the voices from inside, too muffled for him to catch the words, but all he needed was the sound to tell him the soldiers were occupied. He crept up on the closest horse and murmured softly to calm the animal as he pulled his knife from his pocket, unfolded the blade, and carefully cut the rope off the bridle. Re-tying the rope to the hitching rail, he moved to the second horse and did the same, then quietly led the horses away.

When he was clear of the light, he leapt onto one of the horses and eased it across the soft sand, leading the other. Only after he was out of a six-gun's range did he kick the horses into a trot, heading for the arroyo.

Mackie found the kid sitting with his bare feet stuck up on a boulder to catch the evening breeze, the horses tied to palo verde roots protruding from the bank.

"Goddamn!" Mackie said with a laugh. "I sure was tickled to come outta there and see them ropes holding the hitching rail in place. I bet them soldiers are gonna feel real proud they din't let that rail run off."

Henry laughed, sitting up to pull on his boots. "Let's go over to Globe and see what we can get."

A week later, Henry was back in Camp Grant with a secondhand Colt's .41 stuck in his belt and five bucks in his pocket. As he sauntered into Atkins Saloon, he stopped in the door a moment to study the opportunities. Sitting at the farthest table was a man Henry knew to be a poor gambler. Between him and the game, however, stood Windy Cahill. The blacksmith leaned against the bar, eyeing Henry with malevolence.

Henry knew he'd have to fight the big man sooner or later, but he wasn't anxious to have his nose broken again. Warily, he strolled deeper into the saloon. He was watching Cahill's eyes, looking for that glint of energy that usually preceded action, so didn't notice the blacksmith's foot come out in front of him. Henry tripped over it, sprawling facedown on the floor and sliding to bump the top of his head against a chair.

He picked himself up and faced Cahill, hesitating only long enough to throw the man off-guard before leaping the distance and flailing his fists into the blacksmith's soft gut. Cahill grabbed the front of Henry's shirt and threw him against the wall.

Henry slid to the floor shaking his head, his vision so blurred that he couldn't focus on the huge man coming at him again. Staggering to his feet, Henry flaunted his fists. "I'm warning you to stay away from me, you goddamned sonofabitch!" he yelled.

Cahill stopped just out of range and laughed. "You little pimp. You ought not to swear at yer betters."

Henry snorted. "I don't see no better in front of me."

Cahill stepped closer and slapped him, then backed out of range again. "You blind?" he growled.

Henry leapt, the force of his jump knocking the big man down. They scuffled on the floor but Cahill had him pinned in no time. He slapped Henry's face, slamming his head onto the wooden floor. Grinning, Cahill jeered, "What're you gonna do now, prick?"

Henry pulled his pistol and shot him.

Cahill's mouth opened in surprise. He managed to heft his bulk to his feet, his huge hands clutching his belly as blood poured through his fingers, then he took a couple of steps back and sat down hard.

Henry scrambled up off the floor. Glancing around at the other men staring in shock, he ran. A tall bay was tied to the hitching rail. Henry took the horse and tore out of there, galloping north, around the mountains.

Remembering the surprise on the bully's face, Henry laughed with pleasure. He hoped that bullet pained Cahill's belly a long time, and he figured Ol' Windy would think twice next time he considered picking on someone he thought was defenseless. Wishing he could stick around and enjoy the new respect he'd won with the fight, Henry knew he'd better make himself scarce. He kept the horse moving fast toward the New Mexico border.

The moon would be full when it rose over the mountains, making it easy for a posse to spot him on the flat plateau, so he pushed the horse hard. Knowing he had a long stretch ahead, he cut north around the Pinaleños to cross the San Simon Valley toward the Pinos Altos. He was headed for those mountains because nestled on their southern slope was Silver City, where his brother still lived.

Henry had been gone two years and he figured there must be some kind of limitation on how long the law bothered about stolen laundry. Of course, he'd changed in two years. He stood five feet eight now, was still slender at a hundred and thirty pounds or so, and his skin was darkened from practicing with his pistol in the sun. He reckoned his face had changed some too, but not enough. His crooked front teeth would prevent him from walking the streets of Silver with a smile as long as Whitehall was sheriff.

Henry was nearly broke, however, and there was only one person in the world he could borrow money from: his brother Joe. Henry figured, the position he was in, it wouldn't be smart to filch what he needed, though he considered it more admirable to take than to ask. He'd never asked for anything, and the only two things he'd been given were a pocketknife he'd buried and a green shirt he'd ruined crawling up a chimney escaping jail.

He felt happy as he watched the moon rising over the mountains, looking big enough to crush him. Yet it rose higher and smaller until it was a white disk etched in the star-studded sky. Twisting like a ribbon in front of him, the road seemed wide open all the way to the ends of the earth. Henry settled the horse into an easy gait and sang softly as they loped across the sleeping valley, then both of them concentrated on the ascent into the mountains, urged on by the sweet smell of pine carried on the breeze.

It took him three days to reach Silver. In a saloon, he was told Joe was

living in Georgetown, in the house behind the store painted red, and
Henry lost no time riding over there. Near the house was a dense thicket
of brush big enough to hide the horse. Henry tied it to a black elder tree
and snuck inside.

His brother's house wasn't much better than a cabin. The walls were
rough wood, the floor bare planks. The only decorations were two portraits in faded velvet frames, one of their mother and the other of Henry
when he was seven. He stood there and looked at them a long time.

He had been fourteen when his mother died. He'd thought then that
she was beautiful. Now his eye was better educated to the qualities of
feminine beauty and he could see she'd been pretty, that once her cheek
had bloomed with health and her eyes sparkled with pleasure at being
alive, and that was enough. He laughed at the picture of himself as a
child, wondering who would ever think that sweet-looking kid could
turn into the scruffy no-account he'd become. He thought his fate was
funny, not sealed but still fluid, forming as he searched for someone to
be. He felt optimistic and was enjoying himself, qualities whose persis-
tence surprised his brother as much as the sight of Henry cooking supper
when Joe came in from work.

Joe stopped stock still, seeing his brother stirring a pot on the stove.
It had been two years since Henry left, but they were brothers and Joe
always figured Henry would be back, unless he got himself killed. Now
here he was, skinny as ever but a mite taller. His nose had been broken
but he was still wearing that cocky grin Joe remembered so fondly.
"Goddamn," Joe said, opening his arms for a hug.

They embraced warmly, then stood back embarrassed, telling each
other they looked good several times over.

"You made dinner," Joe said, seeing the pistol on the table as he sat
down. "I'm tired, let me tell you. And starved. Is it ready?"

Henry carried bowls of stew and the skillet of cornbread over to the
table. He slid the gun aside with his elbow to set the food down, then
pulled out a chair and dug in.

"We gotta have that thing on the table while we eat?" Joe asked,
nodding toward the gun.

"Does it bother you?" Henry asked in reply, sticking the pistol in his
belt again.

"Get a man in trouble, like as not," Joe said.

"Or out of it," Henry answered, shoveling through his stew, then
leaning back and belching. "I was hungry."

"Where you been?" Joe asked, slowly raising another spoonful to his
mouth.

"Arizona," Henry said. "Camp Grant last."

Joe methodically chewed the tough cornbread, then asked, "What were you doing?"

"Dif'rent things. Drove a log team a coupla times. Had a job washing dishes once." Henry laughed. "Not much future in that, though."

"I could get you a job at the mine," Joe offered.

"No thanks," Henry was quick to reply. "I like the sunshine too much."

Joe mopped his bowl with a crust of the bread before he looked up and said, "Ain't much sunshine in prison, what I hear. Nor at the end of a rope, neither."

Henry's laughter was smooth. "Don't worry, I ain't going either place."

"Glad to hear it," Joe said. "How long you gonna stay?"

"Thing of it is, I'm broke," Henry said, "and I was hoping you could lend me a little traveling money."

Joe stood up, took a coffee can from the shelf, and set it on the table. "Take what you need," he said. "You're my brother."

Henry opened the can and saw maybe fifty dollars in silver and gold coins and a small wad of territorial scrip. He took out a twenty-dollar double eagle and closed the can. "Thanks. I gotta be going." He stood up. "Know where I can get a horse?"

"Ain't you got one?"

Henry grinned. "Yeah, but it ain't mine."

"I'll come out with you," Joe said, laying his arm across Henry's shoulders and walking him out to the thicket. In the darkness he said, "Don't know when I'll see you again, but hope it's before never. You remember how Mama used to call us her bonny boys? How proud she'd look?"

"Yeah," Henry said, untying the reins from around the black elder tree.

"We're all that's left of her," Joe said. "Us being brothers. It's the last little piece of her alive."

Henry stepped into the saddle and held his hand down to his brother. "You been taking care of her grave?" he asked.

"Yeah," Joe said as they shook hands.

"That's all that's left of Mama, Joe," Henry said. "See you next time."

He spurred the horse away, thinking Joe was a good old soul but he'd been beat from the cradle, somehow; he'd seemed old even as a child. Henry shook his head and caught the road south toward Fort Cummings.

The next afternoon he spotted some men camped beneath a large cottonwood by the edge of the road. He stopped and let them look him over good before he slowly ambled closer.

"Howdy," he called to the shapes he could just make out in the shade.

"Howdy yerself," a gruff voice called back. "What d'ya want?"

"I was looking for some comp'ny," Henry answered, "but don't guess yours is what I had in mind. I'll jus' mosey on, if you got no objections."

"Wait up," a younger, happier voice called. "We're not all that sour. Come on in and sit a spell."

Henry dismounted and led his horse over to where the others were picketed. Tying his reins so he could yank them free fast, he walked into the cavern of shade beneath the tree. It took a minute for his eyes to adjust, then he saw five men sprawled on blankets as if they'd been camped there all day. One of them stood up and offered his hand. He was smaller than Henry, the blue of his eyes bright in the gloom, his hand tight and hard. "Name's Jesse Evans," he said. "The boys here call me Captain."

"That so?" Henry asked, noting they hadn't made a fire. "Is this a troop or something?"

"You might say that," Jesse answered with a laugh. "The sour one who growled you is Buck Morton. That long drink of water is Tom Hill, or sometimes Johnson. The ugly cuss is Frank Baker, and the one that's left is Jim McDaniels."

"Henry Antrim," he said.

"Is that your gun?" Jesse nodded toward the pistol in Henry's belt.

"Yeah," he said.

"Can I see it?"

"It's a Colt's forty-one," Henry said. "I'm sure you've seen one before."

Jesse laughed. "Hey, that's all right. Sit down. You want a drink? Morton, where's that bottle you've been hogging?"

Henry sat down cross-legged in the dirt. He accepted the bottle and raised it to his mouth but only pretended to swallow, then passed it back to Evans.

"What's your game?" Jesse asked.

"Ain't got one at the moment," Henry answered, keeping his eyes on all the men.

"You a green mountain boy jus' down from the hills?" the Captain teased.

"Not exactly," Henry said.

Hill, sometimes Johnson, grumbled in a low voice, "I read in the newspaper about a Kid Antrim killed a blacksmith over in Camp Grant. Man name of Cahill. You that Antrim?"

Henry was glad it was dark and they couldn't see him hit by the news that Cahill was dead. It felt thick and ugly and it took him a minute to wipe it clear. "It's a big world," was all he said.

Jesse laughed. "Here, have another drink, kid. We was jus' fixing to head into Apache Tejoe for supper. Care to join us?"

Henry shrugged. "Guess that'd be all right."

He rode beside Jesse in front of the others, feeling uncomfortable with them at his back. As they entered the settlement, people watched them ride by. Tradesmen kept their eyes riveted on the heavily armed men coming into town, and women with shawls over their heads took steps deeper into the shadows to watch furtively. Henry muttered to Jesse, "They don't seem to like you much."

"We're known," Jesse crowed. "They call us the *Banditti.*"

"That's Mex for little bandits, ain't it?"

Jesse shrugged with a grin. "I can't help what the people call us, *amigo.*"

They dismounted in front of a *tendejón.* When they walked in, all the other customers got up and left. Jesse laughed and said, "We always get the best service."

"Let's sit over here," Henry suggested, pulling a chair out from under a table for two.

Jesse looked at his men, then sat down across from Henry. "I take it you don't like their comp'ny," Jesse said softly.

Henry shrugged. He hadn't needed to be told they were bandits. The number of guns each man sported and the quality of their horses were evidence enough. Add to that the fact that they had been camped without a fire and then ushered into town on a wave of fear, and Henry had the picture plain. But he guessed he was an outlaw now, too, so when Jesse invited him to join them, Henry accepted.

He rode with the Banditti for six weeks, making forays into Lincoln County to steal stock, then herd them across the Tularosa Valley to Shedd's Ranch. It seemed like a game to Henry, running off horses or cattle in the dead of night then collecting hard cash for what essentially was little more than taking a ride. As the junior member of the gang, he wasn't making much money, but he had to admit it was an easy life.

In early September, they rode into the Hondo Valley, to a pretty little homestead with half a dozen horses and a matched pair of gray mules in the corral. Since there was nobody home, it was simple to open the gate and herd the animals out, then through the mountains, down

Tularosa Canyon, and across the white sands. When they arrived at Shedd's, two men were sitting in the shade waiting. One of them was a ruddy runt whose face looked mean despite his smile.

Henry sat his horse with the other Banditti while Jesse went over and talked awhile. Money changed hands and Jesse came back with a grin, then they rode up to Apache Tejoe. When they were relaxing at their favorite *tendejón,* Henry asked Jesse who the runt was.

"Jimmie Dolan," he answered. "And he's only a runt by looking. He owns Lincoln County." Jesse refilled his glass with whiskey and pushed the bottle toward Henry, then noticed he hadn't touched what he had. "Ain't you drinking?"

Henry shook his head. "Got a tic in my stomach and it don't feel right. Who owned them horses and mules?"

Jesse grinned. "Some Englishman that's put a burr under Dolan's tail. Jimmie's trying to drive him outta the county."

"You like Dolan?" Henry asked.

"Nah, he's a shithead." Jesse drank his whiskey and pulled Henry's glass over in front of him. "Pays good, though, and I kinda admire his style."

"How can you admire a man you don't like?"

Jesse shrugged. "I don't have to like a man to do business with him."

"Why don't you like him?" Henry prodded.

Jesse hesitated before saying, "He buggers men."

Henry laughed. "You mean he don't like poontang?"

"Oh, he likes it well enough. What he does with men is something else, is all. Murphy's the one started it. He was thrown off Fort Stanton for his unnatural acts, and the way Jimmie tells it, to join their organization a man's gotta bend over to prove his loyalty."

Henry stared at him a moment, then said, "If Dolan tries to bother me, I'll give it back with the barrel of my gun."

"You best watch your step," Jesse warned. "Nobody crosses Jimmie and lives to crow about it."

Henry had no intention of crossing Dolan. Except for the Banditti's midnight forays, he stayed clear of Lincoln County. Mariano Barela, the sheriff of Doña Ana, was on Dolan's payroll, so there was no threat of arrest. Everything seemed like a high adventure and Henry thought maybe he'd found his niche. He figured after he'd proved himself a little more he'd get a bigger cut of the take, and he enjoyed riding with Jesse. His captaincy was loose, allowing the men to do pretty much as they pleased as far as Henry could see. But he soon learned that wasn't exactly right.

Late in September, Jesse sent Henry with two stolen horses to Sheriff Barela's ranch to pay him off. As Henry was getting ready to leave, he spotted a pretty chestnut mare grazing in a field, and he complimented Barela on the horse. The sheriff said her name was Cashaw and that he won money on her at the races. Henry liked the looks of the mare, so on his way out he took her.

When he returned to the outlaws' camp riding a better horse than the one he'd left with, Jesse asked where he got the mare. Henry laughed as he dismounted and told him, but Jesse didn't see the joke.

"You sonofabitch!" he yelled. "What the hell you think you're doing?"

"Improving the quality of my mount," Henry replied, taking a step away from Jesse's anger.

"Barela's gonna raise holy hell when he finds out you took her!"

Henry shrugged. "We can handle holy hell, can't we?"

"You don't understand the game," Jesse said direly. "Barela's looking the other way on our account. It don't behoove us to go against him."

"I ain't against him," Henry said. "I'm for myself."

"You're s'posed to be riding for me and Dolan."

"I don't like Dolan much. And I figure I deserve what I want."

"You gotta take the horse back," Jesse said.

"I ain't gonna," Henry answered.

Jesse met his eyes for a long moment. Finally he said, "Then you best light out and don't come 'round no more."

"Suits me," Henry said. "I'm tired of this sport anyway."

"Huh. What'cha gonna do?"

"Maybe I'll get a job riding for Chisum. I met his foreman over in Arizona and we liked each other."

"You best go, then, 'fore the others come back. And you best get rid of that horse, too, 'cause without Dolan's protection, Barela's gonna come down on you hard."

"I won't be in his county and he won't be able to touch me." Henry swung onto the mare and smiled as he held a hand down to shake with Jesse. "See you around, *amigo.*"

Jesse laughed. "If you stay alive," he said, shaking hands.

Henry rode away, thinking about what he'd done. He recognized that Jesse was right and Barela would be pissed. But when he thought about the weeks he'd spent with the Banditti, and how no one seemed to welcome them except men who profited by their thefts, Henry decided he was better off on his own. He liked to move among friends, not turn the world into enemies.

Letting the mare stretch her legs toward San Agustín Pass, he felt happy. He'd head over to the Pecos and see if the famous ol' Jinglebob John was hiring. Henry figured he could ride herd if he had to. He was at least as smart as a cow.

12

The route across the Guadalupes was shorter but more dangerous. Most travelers were wary of the Mescaleros and climbed Tularosa Canyon into the Sacramento Mountains, then followed the Ruidoso to where it merged with the Hondo, which ran down to the Pecos. Henry had heard about that way, and of the new towns springing up along the rivers. But being too broke to enjoy the comforts of a town, he decided to risk a skirmish with Apaches.

Eager to get over the mountains and scout out his next adventure, he felt lucky, traveling the whole first day without seeing any sign of Apaches. He was certain that whatever he found down by the Pecos would suit him fine.

He slept under an evergreen with the comfortable sound of the mare munching grass nearby, then woke up and pissed over a ravine into a virgin valley pink with sunrise. As he ambled higher into the mountains, the ascent became so steep he was forced to dismount and lead the mare up the rocky cliffs. Both of them were sweating by the time they crested the peak.

When he stopped to rest, he spotted a spring in the canyon below, too narrow for a horse. The water was blue and deep, shining in the sun, and his canteen was almost empty. He tied the mare to a tree and climbed down, carefully picking his way in his awkward boots. On the canyon floor he lay on his belly and dunked his face in the pool, enjoying the clear cold sweetness of high mountain water.

He was admiring the reflection of the puffy clouds in the calming pool when an Apache warrior suddenly appeared on the cliff above. Henry flattened himself into the shadow of the canyon, watching the Apache slowly turn and look at the spot where he had been drinking only seconds before. Pulling his pistol, Henry held his breath and waited.

The Indian disappeared behind the rim and Henry let himself breathe again. He waited until he was pretty sure the Apache had gone before climbing back up the cliff. The mare wasn't there. Henry hadn't expected to see her, but he had hoped. That left him two-bits, his gun with five cartridges in the chambers, and a canteen of water. He turned east and started walking down the Pecos side of the Guadalupes.

In no time, his boots gave him blisters. He stopped and waited for dark, hoping his feet would do better in the cool night. It was a vain hope, but he decided it was a good idea to travel at night in case more Apaches crossed his path. In the heat of day, he slept hidden under clusters of scrub brush.

When he woke up at sunset and tried to tug off his boots to let his feet air out before tramping on, he discovered his boots were stuck. He could smell blood and the rot of fungus coming from inside, so he gave up getting them off and sat studying the valley below, trying to spot the river. The green mountains descended into a pale desert shimmering pink all the way to the horizon with no hint of water.

He wondered if he had been misinformed and the Pecos was just a myth, like those fairy tales of castles and kings he'd read as a child. River or not, he had to get food and help for his feet. He pushed on, following an arroyo that widened as it went down. He figured the stream was a dependable source of water and the chances were good a homesteader lived somewhere along its flow.

The canyon was dark and deep, banked by cliffs blocking his view of the land. After walking all night he couldn't tell if he was making any progress at all. The arroyo didn't change much. It was wide with flat white stones protruding from the sand. Pools of water had collected here and there, some of them a man's arm span across and knee deep. But the stream that had dug the bed was barely a trickle now, and in some places it disappeared altogether.

The sand was bleached pale. Even the driftwood was white, collected against the cliffs which rose against the sky in stripes of faded pink. He stopped when he found a bush big enough to shade him from the sun, but resting didn't make his feet feel any better so he never tarried long. Once he thought he saw Cahill laughing at him just ahead. When Henry picked up a rock and threw it square into Cahill's ugly mouth, the bully changed into Uncle Billy coming at him with a belt. Then it was Henry who laughed, because Uncle Billy had never once been able to get close enough to hit him with that belt.

"Yeah, come on, motherfucker," Henry taunted, "and I'll give you what I gave Cahill." He even pulled his gun, but Uncle Billy suddenly vanished. Henry puzzled at the emptiness, then realized he was seeing visions out of hunger. He shook his head and continued his painful trek down the arroyo.

Finally the slope was barely perceptible and he figured he was close to the desert floor. He walked through a darkness lit only by stars, stumbling over rocks jutting into his path like enemies. Laughing ruefully, he decided he'd be easy pickings right then. He was nearly as defenseless as he'd been in jail in Silver City, with no hope of a friend to pull him out because he was a stranger here. Knowing that if he didn't keep moving he'd die in this arroyo and be nothing but bones bleached in the sun, he limped on.

Suddenly the southern cliff rose in a towering bluff against the dawn sky, throwing the arroyo into deeper shadow. The canyon swung north against the massive wall of rock, and in the crook of the curve, Henry thought he saw a homestead.

Clumsily, on his tortured stumps of feet, he stumbled closer until he was sure he saw a house, its chimney cold. The graying light was just enough that he could make out a corral with horses watching him. One of them nickered and he stopped, hidden behind a lacy mesquite tree as he studied the house. The door opened a crack and the barrel of a rifle caught the last of the starlight. Then he heard a woman's voice, trying hard to be gruff: "Come on out."

Henry took a few steps from behind the tree but his feet quit and he went down. She was beside him in a moment, smelling of lemon soap like a memory of his mother. "Here now," she said gently, helping him up though she was tiny, supporting him with her arm around his waist as she led him inside and set him in a chair in front of the hearth. He almost thought she was another mirage, or maybe he was dead and his mother was welcoming him into heaven.

She started a fire and in the brightness of its blaze he saw she was a stranger, though a beautiful one. Her dark hair fell in glossy curls over the luminous white of her wrapper, and her milky complexion was so perfect he felt tempted to touch her cheek but hadn't even the strength to raise his hand. She brought a basin of warm water and washed his face.

"You've been walking, haven't you," she said, looking at his torn boots with blood seeping through.

"Yes, ma'am," he managed to answer.

"A goodly ways," she said, kneeling to tug at one of his boots. He lurched with pain and she stopped. "We're going to have to cut them off," she said. "Your feet won't heal without air."

He nodded numbly and watched her fetch a pair of large shears, then cut through the leather and peel it away from his raw flesh. When she was done, she washed his feet without a flinch of distaste, then took the basin away and returned with a cup of milk.

"I don't like milk," he said.

"How long has it been since you've eaten?" she asked, lifting the cup to his mouth.

He sipped at the frothy white stuff. It felt good in his stomach and he drank it down. "Can I have more?"

She laughed. "In a while," she said. "Don't worry about your boots. My son has a pair he's outgrown I think will just fit you. Those you had were much too small."

"You're a good woman," he mumbled, admiring her in the glow of the fire. "What's your name?"

"Mrs. Heiskell Jones," she said. "And yours?"

She was like his mother, and he wanted to tell her he had been good. But when he opened his mouth he said his name was Billy, like his mother's husband, and once it was out he couldn't take it back, so he said, "Billy Bonney."

"Well, Billy Bonney," Mrs. Jones said. "Off to bed with you."

"I can sleep here," he said.

"You'll sleep better in a bed. Besides, do you think I want you underfoot all morning? My family'll be up for breakfast soon, and the Caseys are here, too."

He let her lead him into a bed fragrant with her lemon scent where he fell deeply asleep, dreaming of his mother.

It was three o'clock in the afternoon and Lily Casey figured it was time for the stranger to be waking up. She had been told a boy had wandered in last night, his feet all torn up from walking over the Guadalupes. That was a foolish thing to do, and she wanted to see anyone so stupid as to walk through Mescalero country.

She wasn't in a great mood to begin with. All the boys had ridden over to see John Jones's herd, as if his cows were any different from anyone else's. She hadn't wanted to go. No one needed to think she was disappointed at being left behind with her mother and Mrs. Jones and sweet little Minnie who never had a thing to say for herself. They were all working in the kitchen. When Lily had opened her mouth to complain just once, her mother told her to skedaddle. Which meant Lily didn't have a blessed thing to do but sit on the boulder in the front yard and count horseflies buzzing around the dung in the corral. There were fifteen.

When he came hobbling through the door, leaning on everything available and blinking in the bright sun, she studied him freely. He wouldn't ever be a tall man, she knew that from his bones. His feet were small and childish-looking, horribly blistered and rubbed raw, just beginning to scab over. In a spurt of compassion, she said, "You can sit here." Getting up off the rock, she moved a few steps away.

He was wearing borrowed clothes that were much too big, the pantlegs folded high to give his wounds air, the shirtsleeves rolled up above his wrists. He looked like a scarecrow, his tight belt making the trousers puff out around his hips. A gun was stuck in his belt. She watched him stop wincing as he sat down, and she thought he wasn't unattractive when his face wasn't all pinched up with pain.

"Heard your name's Billy Bonney," she said.

"Who told you that?" he asked with a smile, showing his crooked teeth.

They were no worse than others she'd seen. "That's what you told Ma'am Jones last night, ain't it?"

"Yeah," he said.

But she didn't believe it was right. Not that she cared. She knew lots of men who had changed their names. "I'm Lily Casey," she said, wishing he had asked.

He studied her a moment, apparently not impressed with what he saw. She knew she was considered homely, and her mother had often told her that a sour expression didn't improve anything. Self-consciously, Lily looked down at her slender body in the loose brown dress barely covering her ankles over her dusty bare feet.

"You live here?" Billy asked.

She shook her head. "My ma's taking us back to Texas where we have kin. She says we'll be more civilized, go to school and all."

"Yeah? You like school?"

"I liked it when Mr. Upson taught us at the mill. Ashmund Upson. He's postmaster at Roswell now. D'ya know him?"

"Never been to Roswell," Billy answered.

She could hear the flies buzzing in the corral behind her. Finally she asked, "You ever been to Texas?"

"Nope," he said.

Hearing horses, they both turned around to see nine riders coming down the arroyo.

"It's my brothers and the Jones boys," Lily said.

Billy watched them trot their horses smartly, reining them to a stop in front of the corral. There were ten boys ranging in age from maybe five years to young manhood, the littlest tyke being carried in the saddle in front of the oldest, who swung down and lifted the child to his feet, eyeing Billy.

All the boys looked at him curiously as they led their horses inside the corral and unsaddled. The smallest child was led toward the house by one a few years older who wore a bandage over his right eye. Another had a crippled leg he half-dragged along as he carried his saddle into the barn. The corral was full of milling horses now, snorting dust and shaking off sweat from where the blankets had been hot under the saddles.

Billy watched the boys disperse in different directions, the younger ones yelling in play as they ran up the arroyo, the older ones returning to chores. The young man who had looked at him so intently came back through the horses and climbed over the fence without using the gate. He was tall and lean, with blue eyes and the wispy blond fuzz of a new beard. His tan hat was round as a bowler on top, its brim curled up evenly front to back.

"That there's John Jones," Lily said. And when he had come close, "This is Billy Bonney." As if she owned him somehow because she knew his name.

"Don't get up," John said, extending his hand. "Heard you had yourself a hike."

"More'n I bargained for," Billy admitted.

"Lily, go on to the house and fetch us some cider," John said, flopping his long, loose body against the fence.

She glared at him a moment before stomping away.

Billy watched her leave, then said, "She's ripe for a comeuppance."

John laughed. "She's got a chip 'cause her pa was killed two years ago and they're pulling out and going back to Texas. She'd rather stay here."

"So would I, from what I've heard of Texas."

"What've you heard?"

"That they feud a lot and hate Mexicans." Billy looked up at the bluff, pale rust in the afternoon sun. "This land around here seems real nice."

"If you stick around, I'll show you my spread further up the mountain."

"Don't plan on traveling soon," Billy said, looking at his feet.

"No, I reckon not." They were silent a minute, then John asked, "You any good with that gun?"

"Fair," Billy answered, meeting the blue eyes with a challenge.

John laughed. "Want to try some?"

"Sure. I'm a little short on cartridges, though. Lost 'em with my horse."

"What do you have?"

"Colt's forty-one."

"I'll rustle some up. We got more guns than cows around here."

He loped across the rocky yard, passing Lily carrying a tray with a pitcher and three glasses. Standing up to let her set it on the boulder, Billy stared down at his toes.

"They're a real mess," she said, holding out a glass of cider.

He took it and thanked her, then leaned against the fence. "Sorry to hear about your pa," he said.

A tremor of grief ran across her face.

"You must've been about the same age I was when my ma died," Billy said. "I never knew my pa."

"How awful," she said. They stood in silence, sipping at the sweet cider. Then Lily looked up. "Here comes my ma."

"Mrs. Casey," Billy said, meeting the stern eyes of a stout woman.

"Billy Bonney, I hear. Pleased to meet'cha," Mrs. Casey said, her frown belying her words. "Come along, Lily, I need you in the house."

"Yes'm," Lily said, trading quick grins with Billy as she followed her mother away from him.

John came back and they shot cans for a while, both of them trying to outdo the other and never quite making it. Then John brought a horse from the corral and rode it bareback in a circle while Billy threw squash in the air and John shot it in flight. Billy got on the horse and trotted around the circle and hit one more squash than John had. He was just beginning to feel good when Ma'am Jones came storming down the steps and across the yard, fussing like a riled hen.

"How dare you shoot at my squash!" she scolded. "I babied that squash all summer and it's a sin to waste food." She began gathering the pieces of orange pulp in her apron.

John and Billy looked at each other sheepishly. "We're sorry, Ma," John said, helping her gather the shattered squash. "We was just having fun."

"It's food, John Jones," she said, unrelenting. "I hope I've taught my children the value of food. Lord knows we've done without enough of it plenty of times."

Billy slid off the horse, wincing as his feet hit the ground, and hobbled over to help.

"Look, Ma," John said, dropping the fragments he'd gathered into her apron. "You can still use it. We just sort of chopped it up for you."

She looked at Billy, standing sideways on his feet as he tried to brush dirt off the wet squash, and she laughed. "I hope you don't mind a little lead in your food," she said, teasing and not angry anymore, taking the pieces from his hand and turning back to the house.

They watched her go. "We best make amends if we want to enjoy our supper," John said.

Billy waited while John put the horse up, then they headed toward the house.

With all the boys and men, they were twelve at the table. The two girls, Lily Casey and Minnie Jones, who was fifteen and shy, carried the food from the kitchen where Ma'am Jones and Mrs. Casey worked. Billy sat at one end next to John, who faced his father at the other end. Heiskell was a slight man to have spawned so many sons. He had a long dark beard that hung over the front of his shirt like a bib, and friendly blue eyes. Billy had to say the whole Jones clan were about the most hospitable folks he'd come across. When the patriarch bowed his head and intoned a long, solemn grace, Billy took the opportunity to look around.

John Jones had his eyes closed and his head bowed, either participating in the prayer or doing a good job of pretending. Across from Billy sat John's brother Jim. At nineteen, he was two years younger than John. Next to Jim was Bill Jones, who Billy guessed to be close to his own age, seventeen. Tom Jones looked to be about sixteen. He sat next to Lily's younger brothers, Will and John, both of whom seemed sickly. Next to Billy was Lily's older brother, Add, who was maybe seventeen but small, his left leg crippled. Sammie Jones was about six; he'd fallen the day before and now wore a bandage over his cut eye. He sat between Add and Frank Jones, who was only five. Frank was the tyke John had carried in the saddle that afternoon. Next to him was a toddler named Nib, who was teething. To keep him quiet, John had unloaded his six-shooter and given it to the child, who now sat happily chewing on the metal as he watched Billy smile at him. The tiny toothless mouth broke into a grin around the barrel of the gun.

Behind Nib's highchair stood the women, their heads bowed in prayer. Minnie Jones was a beauty. With a body as slight as her mother's, she also shared her milky white skin and lustrous dark hair, which was worn in braids wound around her head. Both Ma'am and Minnie Jones looked angelic to Billy, the clarity of their complexions seeming to reflect the sanctity of their souls, and he admired Heiskell for achieving what Billy believed was the only real value on earth: a hearth made sacred by the purity of wife and daughter. Women like Ma'am and Minnie weren't common, though. Most matrons were as cumbersome and ungainly as Mrs. Casey, their daughters as homely and sour as Lily.

Yet Billy had enjoyed what he'd seen of Lily's cantankerous spirit. If she let him, he would lay with her in the forest and walk away without regret. But as he sat there watching the gathering say grace, he knew he'd kill the man who did that to Minnie. He also knew Minnie would never consent to accompany the likes of him; she'd save herself for a man like Heiskell, who didn't even wear a gun. Billy didn't expect to ever sit at the head of such a table, as John Jones one day would. It was a legacy handed down by a father.

Billy didn't need proof of that, but he got it anyway. Late the next morning he and John and Lily rode over to the mesa where the Casey herd and wagons were. The Caseys' ramrod was a tough-looking man named Abneth McCabe. While he and John sat talking supplies and weather, Billy edged his borrowed horse over to take a better look at the remuda. He spotted Barela's chestnut mare and laughed out loud.

Lily reined up close, looking almost pretty with excitement, her eyes sparkling and her cheeks flushed. "What's so funny?" she asked.

"Oh, nothing," Billy answered. "Where'd your ma get that flashy mare?"

"Traded Mr. McCullum two steers for her."

"Think she'd sell her to me?"

"No, she's my brother Add's horse. He wouldn't let her."

"That's a lot of horse for a little kid," Billy said.

"Look who's talking," she retorted. "You're no more'n a kid yourself."

"Why don'cha come walking in the woods with me tonight and find out," he said softly.

" 'Cause you can't walk, for one reason. If I need a reason, which I don't." She yanked her horse around and trotted back to John and McCabe, who were still discussing business with solemn faces.

After a while Mrs. Casey came ambling along on a sorry old mount. Billy watched her talk with McCabe a moment, then the ramrod rode off with John, leaving Lily and Mrs. Casey alone. Deciding to try for Barela's mare, Billy nudged the horse he'd borrowed from John over between the mother and daughter.

Knowing he could make a deal with John, Billy said, "I was wondering, Mrs. Casey, if you'd trade me that chestnut mare for this horse I'm riding now."

Mrs. Casey replied in a voice as cold as ice, "That horse you're sitting has a Chisum brand, and I know from John Chisum himself that he never sells a horse wearing his brand. How dare you offer to trade me a stolen horse!"

Billy looked at the chestnut. "That mare of yours is stolen," he said. "I should know, I took her myself."

Lily's laughter was high and shrill until she looked at her mother, then she quieted down fast.

"I knew you for a rascal the minute I laid eyes on you," Mrs. Casey bit off. "It's 'cause of your kind coming into this county that I'm taking my fam'ly back to Texas. And I'm taking that mare, too, Mr. Bonney. If she's missing, I'll know where to look." She jerked her horse around and headed toward the trail to the house, calling back sternly, "Come along, Lily."

The graceless bulk of Mrs. Casey's body was emphasized by her awkward posture in the sidesaddle, and her plain face was made homelier by her scowl, crusted so hard with the will to achieve the trip ahead that anyone could see she was quaking inside with fear of failure. Billy felt sorry for her. He looked over at Lily. "I hear McCabe's a good man," he said, swinging his horse around to fall in step beside her as she followed her mother. "He'll get you through."

"I know that," she retorted. "I don't need any encouragement from the likes of you."

"No, I've noticed," he answered with a smile. "Where'd you get so much spit, Lily?"

"I was brought up to hold my own," she said, not looking at him.

"You're doing that and then some. Think you'll ever be able to enjoy the submissive pleasures of being a wife?"

Her eyes glinted hard. "You'll never know, Billy Bonney. It'll take more man than you'll ever be to find out."

"Yeah?" he asked easily, enjoying the nip and tuck of her emotions. "You ever met one seemed likely?"

"Yes, I have," she said. "I met one this morning."

"What's his name? Maybe I know him."

She peered down her nose at the impossibility. "Robert Olinger," she said.

"I'll look forward to meeting him," Billy said. "I'd like to see a man able to impress a girl so hard to please."

"There's lot of men I admire. Just 'cause you're not one of 'em doesn't mean there's anything wrong with me."

"Who else?" he asked amiably.

"John Chisum," she said without hesitation. "My father, though he's no longer alive. Ash Upson, Abneth McCabe, Uncle John's brothers, James and Pitzer Chisum. The Beckwith boys and Marion Turner. I even admire John Jones once in a while, but he's got too high an opinion of himself to really be any good."

"That's quite a list," Billy said. "I had a hunch John would show up in it somewhere."

"Don't tell him, Billy," she pleaded, suddenly embarrassed.

"I don't think he needs to hear it from me," Billy answered.

She blushed, then said angrily, "It don't matter anyway, not about him *or* Bob Olinger. We're leaving tomorrow for Texas." She kicked her horse to catch up with her mother, and rode beside her the rest of the way back to the house.

After supper that night, John took Billy into Seven Rivers to have some fun. They tied their horses in front of the Seven Sevens Saloon and walked inside. The front area was reserved for drinking and the gaming

tables were in back, the two rooms separated by a narrow staircase leading up to the brothel.

Billy sat toying with his drink, watching a game at the other end of
the room while John talked to the bartender about the girls available
upstairs. He came back, refilled his glass, and took a healthy swig of
Pike's Magnolia whiskey before grinning at Billy. "Three *señoritas* and a
half-breed Apache," John announced. "Not one of 'em over sixteen. This
is the best house in Seven Rivers and that's talking about a populated
field."

"Sounds expensive," Billy said.

"Five bucks," John agreed. Leaning close, he whispered, "It's high
'cause they're fresh. Frenchie only keeps girls new to the profession."

"Tell you the truth," Billy admitted, "I only got two-bits. But if
you'll loan me five dollars, I'll sit in on a game and make enough to pay
you back and join the festivities, too."

"The party's on me," John said with a laugh.

Billy shook his head. "If I can't get my women free, I'd jus' as soon
pay for 'em myself."

"Okay," John conceded, surprised at the sudden coolness in his
friend. He took a five-dollar gold piece from his pocket and tossed it
over. "You'll be playing with Duarte and Spidel, they're pros."

"So'm I," Billy said, standing up.

"You didn't finish your drink," John said, nodding at the full glass
left on the table.

"Gotta keep sharp if I'm to win," Billy answered, then ambled down
to the gaming end of the room.

John watched him go, puzzled by his friend's intensity when he
thought they'd come to town to let loose and have a good time. He finished the abandoned drink and took the bottle over to watch the game,
leaning against the wall beneath the stairs and nipping regularly at the
whiskey while Billy played for an hour, staying about even.

Duarte seemed bored with the low-stake game, but Spidel was obviously enjoying watching Billy's hands faster than lightning lay out the
bull and mare and turn the gate, rake in or relinquish the winnings, and
slap slap slap slap, the next deal was out, the gate hovering, waiting for
the bet. From his drunken lethargy, John marveled at his friend's energy,
gradually recognizing that leaving the table a winner was just as important to Billy as branding a steer or breaking a horse was to him. It was
like Billy saw the world cockeyed: what was fun was work, and what
should have been work was an occasional diversion.

When Billy had ten dollars in front of him, John went over and laid a
hand on his shoulder. Billy stiffened under the touch, and John pulled

his hand back, smiling an apology. "Looks like you made enough to buy a ticket to paradise," he said.

Billy shook his head. "Think I'll sit in a few more hands."

"You'd rather play cards than fuck a woman?" John asked in slurred surprise.

"Yeah, I would," Billy answered. "Don't jinx my luck."

John backed off. "I'll just go ahead upstairs," he said softly.

"Good idea," Billy said. "Give her one for me."

John laughed and turned away, thinking maybe Billy was a virgin and too shy to admit it. It had taken John a few tries to go through with it the first time, too. He leaned heavily on the bar. "Give me one of the girls that ain't been used yet tonight."

"Five bucks," Frenchie said. He watched John pull a coin from his pocket and lay it on the bar, then picked it up and slipped it into his own pocket. "Girls get to keep their tips," he said. "Number Four, on your left."

As John climbed the stairs, he looked down at Billy and saw a newcomer had joined the game. John knew him to be a poor gambler and thought Billy's luck had just taken a turn up. When he saw the girl behind the door, he was pleased with his own luck as well.

By the time he came back down, Billy had thirty dollars on the table in front of him and the game was over, though two men still sat there talking with him. One of them was Frank Baker, whom John had recognized earlier, and the other was Buck Morton. They both worked for Dolan so were all right in John's book. As he approached, Billy looked up and said, "These fellows have jus' offered me a job, what d'ya think of that?"

"Doing what?" John asked, nodding at the men as he sat down.

"We're driving a herd up to Stanton and need an extra hand," Baker said with a friendly smile. "That's all there is to it."

"Pays twenty bucks," Billy crowed. "And all I can win playing monte."

"You still riding that scrubby excuse for a horse you had in Mesilla?" Morton growled.

Billy smiled at John. "He has a pleasant manner, don'cha think?" Then he said to Morton, "No, I lost that prize to a band of Apaches. I was way up in the Guadalupes and decided not to argue. I'm riding a horse borrowed from John here. It'll make the trip."

"Hell," John said. "You got enough money there to buy that horse three times over."

Billy knew he was being offered a bargain but he had to turn it down. "I got another need for this money," he said in a voice which didn't encourage argument.

Early the next morning, before riding out with Morton and Baker, Billy bought himself a brand-new Colt's .41 Lightning Action, a belt and holster with a keeper strap to hold the pistol snug, and five boxes of cartridges because he planned to do a lot of practicing. His thirty dollars were sixteen-fifty short, but he told the storekeep he was a friend of John Jones and the man gave him credit.

Strapping the gunbelt around his middle, Billy felt he'd gained an edge on the men around him. He was still broke and riding a borrowed horse, but he was coming up in the world and the gun proved it. He even had a job, and it tickled him to be finally making a legitimate living. With the twenty he earned from the drive, he could gamble in the Seven Sevens again and double his money. Then he'd be on a roll and he could think about getting himself a better horse.

He soon discovered, however, that legitimate work was no fun. The mountains were pretty and Billy enjoyed the crispness of the air as they left the valley behind, but the damn cows were never doing what they were supposed to and he got tired of chasing their shitty butts back into the herd. At night the other men were too tired to play monte, which amazed Billy. He could play it in his sleep, it was so simple. But all they wanted to do was sit around the fire and pass the bottle.

When they were drunk, their conversation turned to bravado boasting and confessions of gore. Billy listened, all ears, to these older men who had been outlaws with Jesse Evans and were now riding herd peaceably. When they'd met him in Apache Tejoe, he'd been Henry Antrim, but now they accepted him as Billy Bonney without batting an eye. Sharing a secret made him feel like one of them. Just as he knew they were part of the Banditti, but if John Jones didn't know it, Billy wouldn't tell him. Every man made his own way and was judged by how the cards fell around him. And there were no redeals, just a new game every time you turned around.

Some of those games were no fun at all. The morning they delivered the herd to Fort Stanton, Morton paid Billy off with a ten-dollar gold piece.

"Wait a minute," Billy protested. "You said twenty."

Morton shrugged. "We didn't get the price we expected. Everybody shares the loss on a drive and that's your new cut. Sorry, kid, but we all took less."

Knowing he was lying, Billy calculated his odds of going against Morton and Baker both and had to admit he'd been beat. He pocketed his gold piece and backed away to mount his horse, looking down at the men with hatred. "You'll be sorry you cheated me," he said. "I won't forget it." Then he reined the horse around and let it go, galloping back down the mountain to his friend John Jones.

Billy rode hard for the first few miles, burning with humiliation. It wasn't the money so much as the ease with which they'd taken it, lying flat to his face after treating him like a friend. He promised himself he'd get even. More than that, he'd cut a wider swath from here on out to make sure people knew he wasn't a man to be trifled with. They might call him a kid, but in their balls they'd know better.

Lily Casey was in the stable when he rode in. He looked at her with disgust and said, "I thought you'd be halfway to Texas by now."

"Howdy to you, too," she sassed back, watching him ride his horse into the stall before getting off. She could tell he was angry. She noticed his new gun, too, and she wasn't surprised. Young as she was, she'd seen it before: as soon as a boy bought himself a fancy gun, he was prime for any chance to use it.

Meeting his eyes as he came out of the stall, she had to fight feeling afraid. "What happened?" she asked in a motherly tone. She'd learned Billy usually opened up if she pretended she was Ma'am Jones and coated her voice with solicitude.

"Nothing," he said, throwing his saddle across the rack and hanging the bridle on the horn.

"See you have a new gun," Lily said softly. "Looks like a nice one."

He walked straight at her as if he would plow her down. "What's it to you, Lily Casey?" he snapped, breezing on past her and out of the barn. He stopped just beyond the door and turned around. "How come you ain't in Texas, anyway?"

"We have to gather up some more cows," she answered, starting to follow him. But when she got outside he was halfway around the bend in the arroyo. "Where you going?" she shouted.

"Swimming," he shouted back.

That meant skinny-dipping, which meant she couldn't go.

When John rode in a few minutes later and asked if she'd seen Billy, she told him he'd gone swimming, which was crazy this late in the day because the water would be like ice with the arroyo catching early shade as it did. But stupid John Jones went off to go swimming, too.

John and Billy hunkered down beside the creek and watched the water ripple by in the fading light while Billy told of being cheated and help-less to do anything about it. He cursed Morton and Baker every way he knew how, plotting revenge with the cold lucidity of murder. John let him talk, telling himself that in time Billy would forget about the ten dollars and the whole thing would blow over.

After they had sat in silence awhile, John rolled a cigarette and nudged Billy, offering it to him. Billy shook his head and looked away. John chuckled, lighting it for himself and blowing smoke out over the rocky water. "Look, kid," he said, "I know of a farmer who needs a hand through the winter. You int'rested in being a farm boy awhile?"

"Does it pay better'n herding?" Billy asked bitterly.

"No, but the company's a hell of a lot better. George Coe, way up on the Hondo."

"Mountains, huh?"

"And a warm bed and hot food all winter. George plays a sweet fiddle, too."

"I like music," Billy said. "Yeah, that might be all right."

13

The man whom people in Lincoln County called the Englishman was in St. Louis to buy merchandise for his store when he received a letter from his sister that would change the course of his actions regarding those people.

He mulled over the shock for a few days, then wrote Emily a reply. Because of the concerned tone of her letter, he was forced to remonstrate that he was not heartbroken by the news of her engagement, but that he well understood the deepest regard a brother felt for a sister could not compare with the love received from a husband. Privately, John told himself he'd been a fool not to see it coming. Emily was intelligent and beautiful, and from what she had written, her fiancé seemed worthy.

After posting his reply, John made haste to return to his life on the frontier. He'd had his fill of manicured city parks sequestered within crowded streets noisy with the jabbering of trade and the cacophony of commerce. Craving the quiet of the mountains and the company of trusted friends, he arranged for his goods to be freighted to Santa Fe. Then he traveled to Trinidad by rail, and bought himself a horse to carry him deep into New Mexico.

In Las Vegas, however, he awoke one morning to discover he had contracted smallpox. Incapacitated for three weeks, he lay in bed delirious with fever. When he had recovered sufficiently to put pen to paper, he wrote his parents of his returning health. Assuring them he would survive to provide for their old age, he added that, in the unlikely event of his untimely demise, he had arranged his affairs so they could recover his property without losing a farthing.

He then ordered a bath and waited until he was submerged in the water, feeling its heat shrink the scabs of pox on his body, before he opened Emily's letter and read it for the second time. Each word knelled as if he were hearing her voice as she poured out her sympathy for how distressfully she knew the announcement of her engagement would strike him. He felt healed by her kindness, and finally fully accepted that her marriage had been inevitable.

Folding the letter, he tossed it across the room to land on the desk near his satchel. His name was embossed in the leather, along with the year his father had given him the satchel: 1869. John had been sixteen then, beginning his first apprenticeship in a brokerage in Cheapside. Now it seemed the gift had defined him as a merchant, because after coming to the frontier ostensibly to raise cattle, he had opened a store.

It had been John's inordinate love for Emily that impelled their father to send him to America. John had accepted his banishment only because, in his heart, he had believed Emily would eventually join him. Now he knew it would never happen, not in the sense he had wished.

The pleasure of his anticipated success was diminished. No longer craving the time when he would enjoy its bounty, he now determined to jump feet-first into the fray that was business-as-usual in Lincoln County. He decided he would push his luck to the hilt, and garner a few thrills along with his profits.

When the doctor advised him to wait another week before traveling, Tunstall wrote Mac in Lincoln, relating the details of his illness and the name of the hotel where he was staying. A few days later, he received a wire from Brewer saying Jesse Evans had stolen four of his horses and his matched pair of mules. Despite the doctor's advice, Tunstall was on his way south before the hour was out.

He met his goods in Santa Fe and accompanied the wagons on their journey to Lincoln. They were heavy with freight and bogged down often on the muddy roads, so it was after dark on the fifth day when they finally pulled into town.

Mac came out of his new home next to the store, his dinner napkin still tucked into the collar of his shirt. The lawyer made a ceremony of unlocking the door and ushering Tunstall into the store for the first time. Though he was tired and still weak from his illness, he had to laugh, thinking Mac looked silly being pompous wearing a napkin. Tunstall scratched his whiskers a moment, wondering what had possessed him to start this venture, then told himself it would all look better in the morning.

As the freighters unloaded the goods willy-nilly about the store, Tunstall walked around. Behind the counter was a small storage room. The west end of the building contained a private office for Mac, and the east end had been partitioned off to form Tunstall's quarters: three rooms with windows facing the corral, the street, and the alley between.

"It's fine, Mac," he said, because the lawyer was obviously waiting for a verdict. "I'm glad to see you've fixed me a bed. I'm dead tired and want only some dinner and sleep. But, tell me, what about Brewer and the horses?"

"He's gone after them," Mac answered guardedly. "Brady went with them at the last minute, but it was Dick who got the posse together."

Tunstall nodded and sat numbly on the bed. "He's a capital sport," he said weakly.

"He's been looking after your interests as if they were his own," Mac said, finally noticing the napkin and removing it. "Widenmann, too. He's been staying at your ranch since the store was finished. And Brewer hired a new man, Middleton, to help out. I authorized the salary. Five dollars a day, but Brewer says he's worth it."

"Good lord! Does he turn water to wine?"

Mac smiled. "If you find the arrangement not to your liking, you can always discontinue it. Shall I send Sebrian down to Wortley's and have your supper sent up? You do look done in. I'd invite you home, but I'm afraid Sue would talk your ear off and it would be hours before you could escape."

"Thank you," Tunstall said, feeling better about Mac again.

Alone, he sat immobile on his bed until the clumping of the workmen had ceased and the wagons were driven off, noisily clanking their now empty beds. Then he walked from his chamber to take another look around. The store hovered in silence, pregnant with profit. He walked behind the counter and stared at the front door, imagining how he would feel once he was actually open for business.

Sam Corbet brought his dinner. He was a tall, dark man with deeply hollow cheeks that made him look perpetually sad. Having last seen him clerking at the Big Store, Tunstall asked in lieu of a greeting, "What are you doing running meals for Wortley?"

Corbet shrugged. "I didn't care to work for Dolan, so I quit. This was all I could find to fill in."

Tunstall took the tray and set it on the counter, then reached into his pocket for a silver dollar. Tossing it to the man, he asked, "Would you like to clerk for me?"

Corbet's dark eyes flashed in surprise. "What're you paying?" he asked.

"What did Murphy pay?"

"Twenty a month."

Tunstall knew Corbet was inflating the amount by five dollars, but he said, "I'll match it and give you a room in the back. That way, when I'm out on the Feliz, someone will always be here. What do you say?"

"I'll give you good service for twenty-five, Mr. Tunstall," Corbet answered. "Anyone working for you is asking for trouble, and I believe that amount is my due."

"Trouble from whom?" Tunstall laughed, pulling the napkin off his dinner and digging in with relish.

Obviously uncomfortable, Corbet said, "Dolan's fixin' to run you out of business. I don't guess that comes as any surprise."

"What Dolan's 'fixin' to do,' " Tunstall said around a mouthful of chicken pie, "is of no consequence to me. Or to you as my clerk. We can take a little huffing and puffing, can't we?"

"Yes, sir. I can take a lot of that."

"Good," Tunstall said, wiping his mouth. "Can you start early tomorrow? I'd like to open as soon as possible."

"At twenty-five, sir?"

"Agreed. But I'll get it out of you, Sam, you can be certain of that."

"Yes, sir," Corbet said. "Goodnight, then."

Tunstall watched him cross to the door, then called at the last minute, "Corbet, old chap, Mac tells me I'm employing a man by the name of Middleton. Do you know him?"

"Only by sight, Mr. Tunstall," Corbet replied. "He's a gunman, supposed to be the best in the county. You don't need to doubt Dick's choice, sir. He got the best in Middleton."

"Yes, thank you," Tunstall said, leaning back against the wall in his solitude again. Finishing his dinner, he wondered why Brewer thought a gunman was necessary.

Tunstall extinguished the lanterns and carried a candle back to his bed. Its comforts were too inviting for him to worry long. As he stripped to his long johns and snuffed the candle, he thought it was expensive to go on the warpath. Five dollars a day, indeed. Wouldn't his father be amazed to hear that!

He slept fitfully, dreaming of a tremendous thunderstorm. In his dream, he was running down a London street that was strangely deserted. He knew his beloved Emily was alone in the garden, and he wanted so badly to find her and take her inside by the fire. But just as he reached the gate, he saw her with another man who held his cloak over her shoulders as they walked away together. Tunstall stood outside the gate with thunder crashing overhead, his face wet with tears.

Mud fell into his mouth. The taste of dirt woke him as a clump of roof fell into his face, followed by a trickle of water. When lightning cracked, illuminating a hole in the ceiling above him, he blinked in surprise. Then the thunder jolted him wide awake. He sprang up and pulled his bed out from under the leak. Dreading what he would find, he lit the candle and walked into the main room of the store.

He didn't have to see; he could hear the water dripping on the crates of goods. Hurrying to light all the lanterns and yank the boxes out of danger, he thought he was done a dozen times, then spotted a new leak. At one point he realized he was moving in front of the windows of a brightly lit room wearing only his long johns, and he thought he must look a fool as he scuttled boxes back and forth under the leaky roof of his new building.

After a while, he broke even with the roof and could stand for long minutes resting against the counter until a new leak developed. He dealt with it and rested before another appeared. The lightning was faint now, the thunder like a lullaby rolling in the distance. He watched the roof a few minutes more, but when his eyes refused to stay open, he conceded he might as well sleep comfortably in bed rather than standing at the counter. He blew out the lanterns and carried the candle back to his room.

Wearily, he climbed into his blankets only to discover they were wet. They had been soaked while he slept, causing his dream of running through rain. With a curse, he tore them off, picked up the candle, and walked back into the store to pry open a box of blankets. Snatching one off the top, he returned to his room, rolled himself in the first pilferage of his profits, and fell fast asleep.

In the morning, he was awakened by Sam Corbet knocking on the front door. Tunstall rolled over and tried to forget he had asked the man to show up early. Finally he forced himself out of the covers and into his clothes, then stomped across the sunlit store to open the door for his clerk.

Looking past him to see the puddles of standing water and the wet spots on the ceiling, Corbet said, "Oh."

"Indeed," Tunstall said with foul humor. "I feel I did my duty last night, Sam. I leave it in your hands." He returned to his room for his valise and walked back across the store, turning at the door to say, "And for God's sake, get someone to fix the roof." Then he walked out and continued on to the McSween home, approaching the open back door.

Sebrian was cooking in the kitchen. He looked up in surprise to see the Englishman knocking like a beggar. He rather looked like one, too, Sebrian thought, the way his whiskers were grown and his clothes all spattered with mud. "Come in, Mr. Tunstall," Sebrian said. "What're you doing using the back door?"

"I feel too uncouth to enter at the front," Tunstall said, embarrassed before the man's meticulous attire. "May I say, Sebrian, I've always admired that red shirt. I bought one like it for you in St. Louis." He rummaged in his valise and pulled out a crumpled paper package wrapped with string. "I hope you'll accept it from someone rather disreputable-looking at the moment," Tunstall said with a smile.

"Why, thank you, sir," Sebrian said. "You're a gentleman no matter how dirty you get."

Tunstall laughed. "Is Mac still about?"

"No, sir, he left for the office already. I'll fetch Mrs. Mac. She's over visiting with Mrs. Shield. Did you know we got another fam'ly in the other wing?"

"I remember Mac mentioning it," he answered, although he'd forgotten until that moment.

"Mrs. Mac's sister," Sebrian said. "Her husband's working with Mr. Mac in the law office. I'll fetch Mrs. Mac. She'll laugh to see you looking like you do."

"Thanks," Tunstall ruefully called after him.

In a moment, Sue swept in wearing her lilac dress. She was almost running in her hurry, but when she saw him, she abruptly stopped. "Well, John Tunstall," she said from a distance. "I'd welcome you home with a hug but for fear of soiling my frock."

"My loss, madam," he said, bowing. "I'm sorry to present myself at your door in this state, but that's precisely why I'm here: to seek a remedy. Could I trouble you for a bath and the laundering of my garments?"

She dimpled her cheeks in a smile. "I find it impossible in all good conscience to refuse such a humble request. I'll ask Sebrian to set you up in the kitchen. He'll ensure your privacy, too, though I must say my sister has heard your name so often she's anxious to lay eyes on you." With a saucy laugh, Sue swept her skirts out of the room.

An hour later, Tunstall had a wagon loaded with the goods Chisum had ordered from St. Louis. Leaving Corbet in charge, he set off toward Chisum's ranch at Bosque Grande, feeling healthy again for the first time in weeks.

It was a brisk October day, and the fields were a fresh, bright green beneath the red and yellow trees. When he saw a large group of riders approaching, it never entered his mind to consider them a threat. As the group neared, he counted fifteen men, and he thought it unusual for so many to be traveling together. Suspecting it might be the posse, he searched the faces until he spotted Dick Brewer.

Tunstall stopped in the road as Brewer kicked his obviously tired mount into a trot to come abreast of the wagon. "Good to see you, Dick," Tunstall said, reaching up to shake his hand. "How'd you do catching the thieves?"

Dick nodded at the posse. "There they are."

Tunstall looked and saw four men with their hands tied behind their backs. Three of them wore sullen expressions, but the fourth, the young one with bright blue eyes, grinned under Tunstall's scrutiny.

"Tom Hill's on the left," Brewer said. "Frank Baker and George Davis on the right. The other one's their captain, Jesse Evans."

"Pleased to meet'cha, Englishman," Jesse called. "I've heard your name connected to words you wouldn't like."

"I'm sure," Tunstall called back. "Did you know it was my stock you were stealing?"

"They got the wrong boys," Jesse said. "We was getting laid in Seven Rivers when you lost your fine pair of matched gray mules."

"You know they were matched though you weren't there?" Tunstall scoffed. "I'd say you're a liar, sir, as well as a thief."

Jesse laughed. "Where you come from, they call a thief 'sir'? I think I might go there."

Tunstall snorted at the notion of this scruffy outlaw in London. "You'd be incarcerated wherever you go, I'm sure."

"I ain't incarcerated now," Jesse said.

"You will be right quick," Sheriff Brady interjected. He turned his horse and jerked his head for the posse to follow. "You coming, Brewer?"

Quickly Tunstall said, "Ride with me to Chisum's, Dick. We have a lot to talk about."

"You're right about that," Brewer answered, then said to Brady, "No, you go on."

The posse was already moving when Jesse called back, "Hey, Englishman, you got any whiskey on you?"

"Not a dram," Tunstall shouted. "But I'll soak you in jail, if you like."

"It's a deal. Don't go back on me now," the outlaw warned just before disappearing into the forest.

Brewer looked at Tunstall curiously. "You know what you're doing, befriending that cutthroat?"

"It doesn't behoove me to have him as an enemy," Tunstall replied. "Are you going to ride over there or in the wagon?"

"Over here so we can stay friends. I'm ripe as a dead skunk."

Tunstall smiled. "Ripe or not, I'm glad to see you. Did you have any trouble catching those rascals?"

Brewer nudged his horse into pace alongside the wagon. "When I first discovered the animals gone, I took up the trail and tracked them to Shedd's Ranch over in the Organs. I could see the horses and mules plain as day in the corral, but Evans had four men with him. When I demanded the animals, he offered to give me mine but said he'd keep yours. I told him to go to hell. He laughed and said he had orders to kill you and Mac on sight, and wouldn't let up till Mac gives in on the lawsuit."

"He actually threatened to kill us?"

"Aw, he's all bluff and swagger, a thief and not much more."

"So you left him at Shedd's?"

"Yeah, I rode on into Mesilla and tried to get the sheriff to raise a posse, but Barela's afraid of the Boys and wouldn't do it. Coming back I ran into Widenmann on the road, riding hell-bent to find me."

"How's Rob doing?"

"He was after scalps that day, I'll tell you. Had himself appointed a deputy U.S. marshal just to go after Evans, on account of a federal warrant against the Boys for stealing horses from the Mescaleros. It seemed a good idea, not having to fetch a badge every time you want to defend your property. So I had Squire Wilson make me a deputy constable, gathered up a posse of men I could trust, and took off after the thieves."

"What about Sheriff Brady?"

"He came at the last minute, saying he wanted to make it legal, but it already was because I'd been deputized. Brady's against us, John. I hate to say it because it sure isn't any good luck charm, but he's lock stock with Dolan right down the line."

"Did the Boys give up without a fight?" Tunstall asked.

"Hell, no. We cornered them in a *choza* down on Beckwith's range. They shot it out awhile, but we had them stockaded and they knew it, so eventually they gave up. Evans walked right over to me and said he didn't know how he'd missed as he had me in his sights three times with a clear shot and never hit. He's a cool one, I swear. Wasn't even sweating when he surrendered."

"Good lord, Dick!" Tunstall exclaimed.

"Aw, I wasn't hurt. I'll tell you one thing, though. The Boys'll get out of jail sure as fate. Brady'll see to it they get loose. You mark my words."

"I hope you're wrong," Tunstall said. "Tell me about this lawsuit Mac is supposed to desist from."

"He can explain it better than I can."

"Middleton, then. Why did you hire a gunman for the exorbitant wage of five dollars a day?"

"He's worth it." Brewer bristled. "I wouldn't have hired him if I didn't think so."

"Don't get ruffled," Tunstall placated. "Just tell me why we need him."

"I've caught Dolan's men scouting out your herd. I tell them to vamoose when I see them and they do, but they always come back. I figured a little show of force would let them know how far we're willing to go to protect our investment."

"I don't want anyone hurt," Tunstall said.

"Neither do I," Brewer agreed. "But what if they shoot at us? Isn't it better to be ready, or even better, to discourage them from shooting in the first place?"

"I like the discouragement angle," Tunstall said. "How's everything at the ranch? Is Rob there now?"

"Was when I left. Waite's still there, and he's made friends with a fellow who was staying the winter with George Coe. Kid named Billy Bonney. He was with Waite when I left."

"Is he a gunman, too?" Tunstall asked, feeling discouraged.

"He can hold his own," Brewer answered. "Or help us hold ours, maybe. Anyway, he speaks Mexican, and I thought that'd be a help to you. Listen, John, I'm gonna head back. I haven't seen my own spread for over a week."

"All right," Tunstall said, extending his hand. "Thanks for your help, Dick. I'll see you when I get back."

Brewer nodded, shaking with him, then he laughed. "We can figure everything out over a jug of whiskey. It worked before."

"It did, indeed," Tunstall said, remembering that night as he drove on alone. Feeling worried that Brewer was taking Dolan's threats seriously, Tunstall conceded having a show of force on their side couldn't hurt. But he didn't intend to resort to violence. He didn't believe it would come to that.

14

The jail in Lincoln was built along the lines of a *choza,* which was a dwelling half-submerged beneath the ground and framed with saplings stood upright in trenches. To ensure the integrity of the jail, the entire room had been submerged and could be entered only through a hatch in the floor of the hut above. Without windows, the dungeon was damp, attractive to rodents and reptiles, and so disheartening that even as hard a man as Sheriff Brady took pity on his prisoners and allowed them out in the sun once a day.

As Tunstall drove his wagon into town after his trip to the Pecos, he passed by the jail and saw the Boys were out for exercise. The sheriff stood with a rifle in the crook of his arm as he leaned against the wall of the hut, watching them loitering beneath the trees.

"Well, if it ain't the Englishman," Jesse called from where he squatted against a rock. "You bring that whiskey you promised?"

"Not yet," Tunstall called back from his wagon. "I've just now returned. I'll bring it by later, if you like."

"You do that," Jesse said. "Course, we'll be back in the hole by then. Maybe you'll have to bring it down."

"That might be arranged," Tunstall replied carefully.

"I'll make it worth your while," Jesse promised.

Brady stood up straight and said gruffly, "That's enough jabbering. Let's go, boys."

The men moved awkwardly in their shackles to line up and climb down the ladder. Their captain was the last to leave. He grinned back at Tunstall and said, "Don't forget that whiskey." Then he winked just before his head disappeared below the wooden hatch.

Tunstall clucked his team forward, thinking the jail was too severe a punishment for pilfering half a dozen horses and two mules. Ahead he saw Squire Wilson, the village buffoon, beaming with news he was obviously bursting to impart. Tunstall thought him a fool worthy of Shakespeare, being both justice of the peace and the most muddle-brained man in town. The previous year, Wilson had found one man innocent of committing a murder, and a second man guilty of being the first man's accomplice. How anyone could pull such a quixotic justice out of the evidence and lawbooks defied logic. But befuddled or not, except for Major Murphy, who was probate judge but never seen in town, and Sheriff Brady, who kept the town quiet and let the county be damned, Squire Wilson was the only law in Lincoln.

His round pink face aglow with idiot humor, Wilson barely waited for Tunstall to pull his team to a stop before crowing, "Well, Englishman, they seem bound to drive you out of the country."

"How's that?" Tunstall asked, his smile fading.

"All your cattle are run off and probably in Texas by now," the pudgy little man announced. He started to say more, but Tunstall slapped his team into a fast trot toward his store.

It was brightly lit in the rapidly falling dusk, Corbet visible behind the counter inside. When Tunstall walked in and saw the goods neatly arranged, the fire in the stove glowing warm, and his clerk coming forward to greet him, he felt a flicker of pride at his accomplishment.

"I fixed up your office, Mr. Tunstall," Corbet said. "Let me know if you want anything different."

"Thank you, Sam, I'm sure it'll be fine," he said. "See to the team, will you? I'll be next door with Mac."

"Yes, sir," Corbet said.

Without going to his rooms or even seeing his office, Tunstall walked straight to Mac's house, knocking on the front door this time.

Sue opened it, her face miserable with concern. "Come in, John," she said. "We've been expecting you."

Mac was in the parlor before the fire. Tunstall turned around with surprise as Sue left them alone, then he sat down in the chair opposite Mac and asked helplessly, "What's happened?"

"It appears the Widow Casey decided to take her cattle back to Texas after all," Mac answered.

"The thieving hag!" Tunstall exclaimed, half-rising to his feet. Then he remembered himself and settled back in the chair, his fists on his thighs.

"Brewer's gone after them," Mac said. "If he doesn't catch them before they cross the Texas line, however, it will take months to institute replevin and it's doubtful you'll recover as much as half the herd."

"She has her gall," Tunstall muttered.

"I'm sure she's twisted it so it seems right in her mind. Ellen Casey is a good woman, just desperately trying to take care of her family after the murder of her husband."

"I've heard all about the murder of her husband," Tunstall retorted, "but I didn't do it. I bought those cattle at public auction. They're mine." He stopped and caught his breath, then sighed. "Do you think Brewer has a chance of retrieving them?"

"If it's humanly possible, he'll do it. He'd barely returned when we caught wind of what was happening. I had Squire Wilson draw up the replevin papers while Brewer changed horses, and he left again without even stopping to eat. Middleton went along. It's my guess they won't come home empty-handed."

Tunstall sighed again. "I'm fortunate to have Brewer. And he was right to hire Middleton, I admit that. But, good lord, it's like I have a private army in the field!"

Mac smiled. "Two men is hardly an army."

"There's another one now. Brewer told me when we met on the road. Billy Bonney, do you know him?"

Mac shook his head.

"He's a friend of George Coe's."

"Then he must be all right. You made a good choice in hiring Corbet."

"Thanks. Did you know Chisum has sold his herds?"

Mac leaned back and folded his hands across his vest, then nodded.

"Why didn't you tell me? When I offered you the position in the bank and told you Chisum had agreed to be president, why didn't you tell me then?"

Softly, Mac said, "You had already made the agreement between yourselves and I didn't wish to intrude. Also, I was bound by confidentiality, as I am with you, John. I don't discuss your private affairs with anyone but you."

"You're right," Tunstall conceded. "It's just that so much has happened since I've been back. Everything's tense. My God, what am I saying? Everything's being stolen! And one of the first things I learned from Brewer is that the sheriff is against us. How can an officer of the law be for or against anyone? Brewer made it sound like a terrible liability, as I'm sure it would be, but the law is neutral, Mac. You and I know that."

"Yes, and that's our advantage. Let them roar and howl all they want. It's only noise, nuisance, and dust. I happen to know The House is about to go under. Dolan took out a mortgage to buy Murphy's interest and now can't make the payment. That's why he wants to get his hands on the Fritz policy so badly."

"Is that the lawsuit Jesse Evans referred to when he threatened us?"

"Yes."

"What is it, Mac? Is it serious?"

"Not at all. It's a ten-thousand-dollar life insurance policy that has been reduced to less than four after expenses of collection. I've already filed it in court and am waiting only for their direction as to who receives the proceeds."

"Then what does Dolan have to do with it?"

"He's claiming Fritz was in debt to The House and therefore the proceeds are his. But as he won't allow anyone to audit his books, I denied the claim. The Spiegelberg Brothers in Santa Fe also claim the proceeds for a debt. Mrs. Scholand and Charles Fritz claim them as his brother and sister, though he has other relatives in Germany. I presented my arguments for the benefit of all the heirs, which is the correct distribution when the deceased dies intestate, but frankly, it's become such a jumble of ill will, I don't care who gets the money. The case is to be concluded in the January session, and I've left instructions with my partner to follow the court's order, whatever it may be. He has full power to act in my absence."

"Where are you going?" Tunstall asked, astonished.

Mac smiled. "Sue and I are going to New York in December with John Chisum." He leaned forward and spoke more softly, "It's for Sue's benefit. She's become quite upset with all the doings lately and needs a change."

Tunstall mulled this over then said, "I'm sure things will be back to normal before you leave."

"No doubt," Mac said. "The store looks impressive, don't you think?"

"Yes, Corbet's done well. Did he fix the roof?"

Mac chuckled. "You should have called me. We both could have pushed boxes in our underwear."

Tunstall felt himself blush. "I must have looked a fool. But who saw me and didn't offer to help?"

"The man who laid the roof," Mac answered with a smile. "He came over this morning, without being summoned, and did the repairs for free."

"He should do them for free!" Tunstall said indignantly, then added in a pacified tone, "But he was right not to help. I might have drowned him in one of his own puddles."

The two men laughed before the cozy fire. Tunstall could smell supper cooking, and he felt guilty for being so comfortable while Brewer was out in the cold chasing his cows halfway to Texas. But when Mac invited him to stay for dinner, Tunstall accepted. Tomorrow he would ride to his ranch, see Widenmann and meet this new fellow who was working for him, then wait there for Brewer's return. Not knowing when he'd be back in Lincoln, Tunstall wanted to see Sue before he left, hoping he could replace her bleak expression of concern with the laughter of the sprightly spitfire he had admired only a few days before.

When the Shield family joined them for dinner, Tunstall felt embarrassed that he hadn't changed from his traveling clothes. Even though Mac was also at the end of his day, he looked crisp and neat. Tunstall remembered that when they'd first met, he'd thought the lawyer's attire was shoddy. Now he wondered if Mac had improved his wardrobe or if he himself was slipping to the dowdiness of the frontier. He felt uncomfortable all through dinner, a mood which wasn't eased by the stilted conversation among the others.

David Shield was obviously cowed by his brother-in-law, which was ludicrous beside Mac's gentle demeanor, and Tunstall found it difficult to fathom that Eliza Shield was Sue's sister. But gradually he saw a few similarities surface. Both women had a slow way of smiling with just the corners of their mouths, an attribute he found particularly pleasing on Sue. It was attractive on Eliza, too, and he began to detect a glimmer of the woman Sue might have been if she had married a stooge like David Shield and borne him five children in rapid succession.

The girls were all blond as cherubs, scrubbed clean and wearing their Sunday best. Tunstall felt humbled that these people had dressed up to meet him while he hadn't bothered to so much as wash. During grace he felt so vile he almost left the table. But his manners held him afloat and he drifted through the vapid currents of small talk with little more than impatience for it to end.

He was pleased when, immediately after the meal, the Shields bid goodnight and took their daughters home. Mac excused himself to accompany them, saying he needed to consult with his partner. Tunstall and Sue smiled at each other across the now quiet dining room they shared alone.

"Please sit down, John," she pleaded, carrying the silver coffeepot to his end of the table. "Have another cup and talk with me a moment."

"Gladly," he said holding her chair, the one Mac had occupied only moments before. Tunstall resumed his seat as she filled his cup and the air between them became heavy with the fragrance of rich coffee.

"Mac tells me you haven't been well," he said.

"Oh Mac," she scoffed. "That's his explanation for everything. God knows I'm trying, John." Her voice tightened with suppressed tears and she looked away.

"What is it that's upset you?" he asked gently.

She pulled a lace handkerchief from her sleeve and dabbed at her eyes. When she spoke, her voice trembled with anger as her words tumbled out. "Minor occurrences that I'm all wrought up over, that's how Mac describes them. Trivial events like having men shoot into my home, disrupting Sunday dinner. Chisum was here and they were looking for him, but I dislike it so when dinner is interrupted, don't you? And then there was the time Sheriff Brady saw me crying on the street because I'd just learned a boy who'd worked for us and was so alive, so brown and strong, had been killed by that monster Dolan who still walks free. And you know how a lady hates for anyone to see her crying publicly on the street, as if she has no breeding at all. You have no idea the slurs and innuendoes I endure. Mac says if I conduct myself as a lady I'll be treated as one, but doesn't a lady have the right to stroll along the river on a hot August afternoon? And if she meets someone who's also there, isn't she allowed to speak with him and share a moment of kindness, there in the shade along the river, a woman whose husband is busy and whose home has been invaded by the sounds of carpentry next door? The next day that cretin Long hissed at me in the street. In the hearing of everyone, he asked if I'd kiss him down by the river as I had Cisco Gomez. And that's not the worst, John. They've threatened to kill Mac. Juan Patrón told me. He said I should convince Mac to carry a gun, or at least hire a body-guard. But Mac says God is his protection." She stopped and looked away, embarrassed. "Listen to how I've run on. Goodness, and I haven't even asked about you. How was St. Louis?"

"Fine," he answered slowly, agreeing with her husband as to her state of mind. "You'll enjoy it on your way through to New York."

"So he told you about our trip," she said without emotion.

"Yes, I think it's an excellent idea. You two have held the fort here for a while. Now it's my turn."

She looked at him helplessly. "Do you know what it takes to fight these men, John?"

He chuckled. "I grew up in a boys' school in England. They're pretty rough at times."

"Be serious!" she cried. Lifting the tiny handkerchief again, she wiped her nose. "I'm sorry," she said. "It's just so wearying to be treated as a child, as if I can't see what's happening better than Mac. Because I'm a fighter, John, and Mac isn't. He thinks everyone is good. He told me he can foresee the day when Dolan will eat at our table as our friend. Dolan! I'd puke in that man's face before I'd serve him at any table!"

"Goodness, Sue, you're beside yourself," Tunstall said, restraining a smile. "If that dinner party ever comes off, be certain I'm not invited."

She looked lost a moment, then laughed. "Oh John, you're good for me. I can speak my mind to you, you're the only one who listens. But do you hear me, John?" She clutched at his hand. "Do you believe Dolan is dangerous?"

"Mac just told me The House is nearly bankrupt and Dolan's already skirting ruin. All we have to do is wait him out, operate in a legal man-ner and watch The House dissolve of its own incompetence."

She sighed. "You make it sound so simple. Maybe you're right. And maybe Mac is, too. If he wasn't always quoting Job, maybe I could be-lieve him. Do you know what he said the other night? 'The things my soul refused to touch are as my sorrowful meat.' Could you live with someone who goes around spouting quotations like that?"

"I have," Tunstall said with a laugh. "My mother is fond of quips from the Bible, though she's more apt to quote the New Testament. And Widenmann is so pompous, at times I think he's spouting scripture when he isn't. Have you seen him? Is he well?"

"He was here," she said. "It's amazing how you collect men willing to give their all for you."

"You exaggerate," he scoffed.

"Look at Dick Brewer, if Widenmann isn't enough. And Sebrian is certainly your ally since you brought him that red shirt." She smiled coquettishly. "If I was single, John Tunstall, I'd think you were up to no good, giving presents to my servant. Since I'm married, I'll have the audacity to ask why you didn't bring me one."

"But I did," he said, standing up. "I'll fetch it from the store."

"Let me go with you!" she cried. Then, collecting herself, she said in a calmer tone, "Allow me, please."

"My pleasure, madam," he answered, offering his arm.

It was cold outside. She hadn't brought her shawl and huddled against him in the wind as they crossed the short distance between the house and the store. Corbet was still at his post, much to Tunstall's discomfort, watching him come in with the lawyer's wife on his arm. "For heaven's sake," Tunstall said. "Go home, Sam."

"I am home, sir," the clerk replied. "I live in the back."

"Oh, yes." Tunstall looked at Sue, shivering still. He led her over to the wood stove and sat her in a chair. Turning around to find the clerk still watching them, Tunstall said, "Well, close up, Sam."

"Yes, sir," Corbet said, walking across and starting to lock the doors.

"I'll do that," Tunstall said.

"Yes, sir," Corbet replied, blowing out the lamps in the front half of the store, then returning to ring the cash register open and begin counting the money.

"I'll take care of that, too," Tunstall said impatiently. "You're off duty, Sam. On your own."

Corbet looked at him a moment, then put the money back in the till and closed the drawer. "Yes, sir," he said again, and walked around the counter to his room, quietly closing the door.

Tunstall stared after him. "I feel like I've punished the chap and sent him to bed without dinner," he said, rubbing his chin.

Sue laughed fondly. "The benevolent despot. Have you forgotten my present?"

"I had," he admitted. "Are you quite warm now?"

"Yes, cozy," she said.

"Do you think I should tell Mac where you are?"

"I think he'll guess when he sees we're both gone, don't you?"

"Ummm," Tunstall said, wondering what had possessed him to send Corbet away.

"You enjoy keeping a lady waiting," Sue teased.

"I'll only be a moment," he said, crossing to his rooms and retrieving the small jeweler's box from his valise. He wondered now if it was appropriate, though at the time it had seemed the perfect choice. He also wondered what Mac would think of the expensive gift, and then why he hadn't contemplated these complications before. "To hell with it," he concluded. "She's waiting for a gift and I have nothing else suitable for a lady." With that resolve, he carried the tiny box across the store and presented it gallantly.

"Oh my," she cooed. "I love presents that come in velvet boxes." She looked up at him with shining eyes. "Whatever it is, I'll treasure it always."

"Open it, silly goose. You may not even like it."

Carefully she opened the box. "Oh, it's beautiful!" she whispered, lifting the gold locket to dangle on its long chain. "Oh, I love it, John. Thank you." She rose and stood on tiptoe to kiss his cheek. "It's lovely, thank you. I must run and show Mac." She laughed. "See you tomorrow, then?"

"Decidedly," he said. "Let me walk you."

But she was already gone. He followed her out and watched as she ran, with her skirts flying girlishly, to slip inside her front door without looking back.

15

In the morning, Tunstall rode into the mountains alone. Even at the lower elevations the grass was withered brown in the November sun. He felt melancholy, hardly knowing what to expect of his ranch with the cattle gone and Brewer off in pursuit. Somehow the absence of those two seemed the loss of any pretense of a ranch. It was only a house on some land sporting employees, one of whom Tunstall hadn't even met. He encouraged himself with the fact that Widenmann was there.

Spurring his horse the last few miles, Tunstall stopped on the crest overlooking his home to see a boy riding in circles around the yard. He rode bareback with one leg thrown across the horse's withers, his body hanging beside its shoulder like a Comanche or a monkey, Tunstall wasn't sure which, while he shot under the horse's neck at cans on the fence. With each circle of the horse, a can fell, and a second later the noise of the gun reached Tunstall's ears, distinct from the echoes filling the valley.

As Tunstall ambled closer, he saw Fred Waite resetting the cans, so he guessed the boy on the horse must be the new employee. Seeing Tunstall lope across the last stretch of meadow, the two ceased their game and watched his approach, the boy still sitting the horse. He was scruffily dressed, though his face was pleasant, his pale blue eyes sharp with intelligence.

Tunstall reined to a stop but didn't step down. "Afternoon, Fred," he said with a smile. "Who's this?"

"Billy Bonney, Mr. Tunstall. He's a friend of mine." Fred looked up at the boy. "This here's our boss, Billy."

He grinned, revealing his crooked teeth. "Pleased to meet'cha."

"I see you're a good shot," Tunstall said.

"I do all right," Billy answered. "Course, it's easy when you got a friend setting up the targets nice and neat."

"Not as easy as taking aim at a man?" Tunstall asked, hoping for some innocence from the boy.

Billy swung his leg over his horse's neck and slid to the ground, so he was looking up at Tunstall when he said, "I wouldn't know. I ain't never done that."

"My God," Tunstall quipped, "there is innocence left in paradise." He stepped down and shook Billy's hand. "Good to have you with us," he said, then shook hands with Waite. "Nice to see you, Fred. Put my horse up, will you?"

"Sure, Mr. Tunstall," Fred answered, taking the reins.

"And no more target practice today, eh?" Tunstall said. "I've keenly looked forward to some peace and quiet." Turning toward the house, he saw Widenmann standing in the door. "Rob," he called fondly. "You sonofabitch."

Widenmann laughed. "In the flesh, what's left of it. Did you see Brewer?"

"Yes, and he's out again, poor devil," Tunstall said, shaking his friend's hand. "I'm glad someone's here keeping the home fires warm." He walked into the house and looked around. "Just as rustic as I remembered," Tunstall said happily. "It's good to be back."

"Would you like some tea?" Rob asked.

"Starting right in waiting on me, are you? Well, I shan't stop you." Tunstall sat down before the fire and pulled off his boots. "What do you think of our new recruit? Sort of a scruffy-looking fellow, isn't he?"

"Just down on his money," Widenmann answered from the kitchen. "I was pretty scruffy when you took me in."

Tunstall laughed. "You haven't changed all that much under my influence. I'll see if I can't do better with the boy."

"Don't call him a boy," Widenmann warned. "Billy used to ride with Jesse Evans and parted on not the best of terms, so he doesn't like being referred to as one of the Boys any way you phrase it."

"Hmm," Tunstall said. "I wonder if he'd have any influence toward retrieving my mules. Call him in here, will you?"

Widenmann went to the door and leaned out. "Billy," he yelled. "The boss wants to see you."

Tunstall waited, warming his feet before the fire, until the boy who didn't like to be called one came in. He accepted a chair but declined anything to drink, even whiskey, which impressed Tunstall. "I've heard it said you rode with Jesse Evans. Is that true?"

Billy looked hard at Widenmann delivering Tunstall's cup of tea, then he met Tunstall's eyes and smiled before he said, "I met the man in Apache Tejoe, is all."

"Would you say you were friends?" Tunstall asked.

Billy thought a minute. "Why don'cha tell me what you want, Mr. Tunstall, and I'll let you know if I can do it."

"All right," Tunstall said, glad for the bald approach. "I want the mules he took from me. I was wondering if you could induce him to return them."

"You mean give 'em back?"

"Yes," Tunstall said, sipping his tea.

"I doubt it," Billy said. "He ain't my brother or nothing."

"I see," Tunstall said, disappointed.

"I could steal your mules back," Billy said with an insouciant grin.

Tunstall studied his crooked teeth a moment, then looked into the laughing blue eyes and smiled. "I think we'll leave it to the law, Billy."

"Huh!" he said. "That's a sure road to hell."

"I beg your pardon?"

"Sorry, Mr. Tunstall," he apologized smoothly. "Didn't mean to swear at you. It's jus' that in my experience, to leave something to the law is to mess it up completely."

"I'll consider your opinion," Tunstall said. "That's all, you may go." He watched him walk out, then exchanged wry smiles with Widenmann. "Are we paying him five dollars a day, too?"

"No, he's working for room and board," Rob answered. "He wasn't ever hired, actually. He simply moved over from Coe's. And I can't really say he's working. He's just sort of here, like a congenial guest, you might say."

"Yes, well, we'll change that. I can see the ship has drifted loose without its captain."

Three days later, after receiving news that Brewer had replevined the herd and was coming home, Tunstall and Widenmann rode into Lincoln. The day was bright with a cold wind whipping the last of the leaves against the knees of their horses, which the men kept at a vigorous trot, preventing conversation. When they'd scuttled down the trail to the Lincoln road, they kicked their horses into a canter and only slowed again when they rounded the curve into town. The houses were closed snug against the wind, their chimneys billowing smoke.

Tunstall leaned from his saddle to open the gate to the corral behind the store, then he and Widenmann rode directly into the stable and left their horses in the windless warmth of its shelter. Corbet looked up as they came through the back door, eyeing his boss with an expression of wary anticipation.

"Have you heard from Brewer, Mr. Tunstall?" Corbet asked.

Tunstall assured him the herd had been replevined, then gestured toward his companion. "Do you know Rob Widenmann?"

"Yes, sir," Corbet answered with studied indifference.

"Good. You're to follow his instructions as if they were my own." He smiled playfully at Rob. "Unless, of course, I specifically countermand them."

"Yes, sir," Corbet said again.

"Have another bed brought into my room sometime today, will you? Rob will be staying with me. And bring the books you've set up to my office. He can watch the store while you and I come to an agreement on an accounting system. But first, I've just remembered a call I've promised to make." They both watched him move to the shelf of whiskey and slip a bottle of Double Anchor into his pocket. "See you later," Tunstall said, walking out and heading east toward the jail.

The four prisoners were in the yard, stomping their feet to keep warm but still preferring the sunshine to the dungeon. Jesse Evans spotted him right off. "Well, if it ain't the Englishman, come to bring us our whiskey!"

Tunstall looked at Brady to be certain there was no objection before handing the bottle to Evans. The other outlaws came to life, edging closer as Jesse slowly yanked the cork and drained off a fifth of the liquor without stopping. He wiped his mouth with his sleeve, his eyes not leaving Tunstall, and extended the bottle to whoever got it first.

Tunstall laughed. "You seem an intelligent bloke, Jesse. What are you doing spending time locked in a hole?"

Jesse hacked up a gob of spit and propelled it toward the sheriff, barely missing him. "I'm taking a holiday," he answered, smiling at Tunstall. "Resting my eyes from too much sun. I hear it can addle your brain."

"I think your brain's already addled," Tunstall said bluntly. "There may be no hope for those degenerates you travel with, but you're young and smart enough to do better."

Jesse smiled. "You tickle me."

"How so?" Tunstall asked.

"You bring whiskey and talk like we're friends, but you're really jus' begging to get your mules back."

"I've never begged for anything!" Tunstall retorted. "You'll rot in hell and the mules too before that happens!"

Jesse laughed. "What if I offered to trade your mules for helping me escape?"

Tunstall looked at Brady, then back at Evans. "To make such an offer in front of the sheriff denies your sincerity."

"Oh ho!" Jesse howled. "You disappoint me, Englishman. Now I know the whole world's on the take."

"That's enough," Brady growled, stepping forward and flaunting his rifle. "Back in the hole."

Tunstall watched the prisoners line up to climb down the ladder. This time Jesse didn't wink or offer a parting wisecrack, and Tunstall guessed the dungeon was taking the salt out of even him. Court wasn't due to be held until January, and for the Boys to spend another two months of increasingly inclement weather in the hovel of a jail seemed inhumane.

Several hours later, Mac came out of his office with Juan Patrón. Walking Patrón to the front of the store, Mac bid him good evening, closed the door against the cold wind, then turned and asked Corbet, "Is Mr. Tunstall about?"

"In his office, sir," Corbet answered.

Mac walked across and looked through the Englishman's open door. Tunstall was lounging with his feet on his desk, which was cluttered with the remains of a supper from Wortley's, while Widenmann reclined on the settee like a pampered profligate.

"Come in, Mac," Tunstall said. "I'd offer you something to eat but I'm afraid we've consumed every crumb."

"Thanks, I have dinner waiting," Mac said, then smiled. "One of the conveniences of a home nearby."

"A home meaning a wife, and a charming one, too," Tunstall said. "We poor bachelors must suffice with Wortley's."

"I have learned something of interest about the prisoners," Mac said, glancing at Widenmann, who was collecting the dirty dishes.

"Ask Sam to return those," Tunstall told him. "Then come back. I want you to hear this, Rob."

Mac settled onto the settee and waited until Widenmann had returned and closed the door, then he told them both what he'd learned from Juan Patrón: Pantaleón Gallegos had been seen carrying saws and chisels from the Big Store into the jail. As territorial representative, Patrón had confronted Sheriff Brady with the news, and Brady had promised he'd see to it.

Tunstall listened in silence, then asked, "Do you think he will?"

"Yes," Mac answered. "I know him well. He's not a bad man, and will do his duty when it's so clearly pointed out to him."

"It would be grounds for impeachment if he didn't!" Tunstall exclaimed.

Mac laughed gently. "Impeachment may be a reality in Parliament, my friend, but the best we can do is wait for the next election and vote our own candidate into office."

"That doesn't help us at the moment," Tunstall mused. "Damn! All I want are my mules back."

"Corbet told me you had good news from Brewer," Mac said.

"Yes, let's hope this new development turns out as well." He felt suddenly aware of an ague growing in his head. "I think I'll turn in," he apologized. "I fear I've caught a cold."

"Bad luck with winter coming on," Mac sympathized. "Lemon vapor is the best remedy."

"I know just the thing," Widenmann said. "I'll make you a toddy."

"Yes, a toddy, Rob, by all means," Tunstall answered. "I'll sip it under the covers."

"I remember," Widenmann said, disappearing into the kitchen between Tunstall's office and bedroom.

Mac stood up. "Goodnight, then," he said, leaving quickly. As he walked back to his own office, he felt apprehensive about Widenmann. The man possessed less scruples than judgment, in Mac's opinion, and he worried about his influence over Tunstall.

16

Tulles Patrón touched Billy's crooked teeth with her tongue, then giggled, meeting his eyes. "I like them," she said.

"Why?"

"They show your soul," she answered, lying back and stretching her arms high over her head, one of them ending in an atrophied hand. "We are the same," she said, not looking at him now. "Our souls are so bad our bodies grew crooked."

"What makes you think I'm bad?" he asked, pulling the blanket down to reveal her breasts in the milky patch of moonlight falling through the window of the stable.

"You are here with me," she said. "Is that not proof enough?"

"Any man in his right mind would be here if he could," he murmured, kissing the breast closest to him.

"No, Bilito," she crooned. "Few men would risk making my brother mad. He is a representative in the legislature, you know, and a man of great power."

"Oh, I've heard there's been more'n one to take the risk," Billy teased.

She laughed. "See how bad you are! If you were good, you would believe me when I say you are the only man I have ever loved."

"I believe you," he said. "Only I didn't think we were talking about love."

She sighed, turning to snuggle her face into his chest. "Since I first see you, I love you, but I know you have another girl. Her name is Angelita and she lives on Eagle Creek."

"How do you know?"

"She told me. She said she has found a great love who fills her heart with happiness."

"Did she say that?"

"Yes, and more about being filled in other places too. She was an innocent girl, Bilito. With me, you are not the first or the last, but with Angelita I think you will break her heart."

"No, I won't."

"You will marry her?"

He laughed. "I ain't gonna do that either."

"It's one or the other, Bilito. You are younger than me. When you are older, you will see I am right."

"I see it now," he said. "You're right here." He leaned low to kiss her breast. "And here," he said, sliding his mouth down the soft curve of her belly. "And here," he whispered in the warmth between her legs.

She giggled. "That tickles."

"Does it?" he asked, touching her with his tongue.

"Let's do it again," she whispered.

"Why not? I got all night."

The barn door opened, flooding the stalls below with moonlight. "Tulles?" Juan Patrón shouted sternly.

They lay still and silent in the loft.

"I know you're here," Patrón said. "Come back to the house."

"He sounds like a father, no?" she whispered to Billy.

"Pretty close," he agreed.

"Tulles!"

"*Sí, hermano. Ya voy,*" she called sweetly.

Billy laughed.

"Who is with you now?" Patrón asked with subdued anger. "Pantaleón Gallegos again?"

"No, it's me," Billy said, sliding over to the edge to look down on him.

Patrón met his eyes for a long moment before saying, "I cannot allow this, Billy."

"No, I reckon not," he answered with a smile.

Tulles sat down beside him, her dress on now as she combed her fingers through her long black hair. "Why are you such a pill, Juan?"

"Someday our mother will discover what you're doing," he answered, "and it will break her heart."

She laughed. "We were just talking about broken hearts, weren't we, Billy?"

"Among other things," he said.

"Come down now," Patrón said.

Tulles sighed deeply. "I suppose I must," she said to Billy. "Will you come see me again next time you're in town?"

"Don't see why not."

She leaned close to whisper. "Be good to Angelita." Then she was gone with a flounce of her skirt over the edge of the loft.

He listened to her jumping her good hand down the ladder, then the soft footsteps of her walking away with her brother. They left the barn door open, and Billy closed it on his way out.

His horse was waiting in the meadow below the mountains, though it wasn't really his horse. It belonged to John Jones, as did the saddle and bridle. The only things Billy owned were his clothes and his gun, but on the whole, he thought he was doing pretty well. Although his finances hadn't increased since he'd quit the Banditti, he had friends and a snug place to spend the winter. He couldn't see why a man would want more. Well, maybe a better coat, he thought, shivering as he tightened the cinch. He swung onto his borrowed horse and ambled through the trees toward the trail to Eagle Creek.

Trotting down the other side of the mountain, he passed the trail to Angelita's house without stopping. She would be asleep, and anyway, he never visited her and Tulles on the same night. They were different in his mind, and he saved Angelita for special times when he felt clean. Remembering Tulles' teasing, he tried on the idea of marrying Angelita, but Billy couldn't see it. He liked his life the way it was.

He turned up the Hondo and rode past George Coe's spread, then Dick Brewer's, both houses dark and the yards peaceful in the moonlight. He could knock on either door and be welcomed with a meal and warm bed. The same was true for lots of other places now, too. Folks just seemed to like having him around, and it was a kick for Billy. He rarely had any money, but he helped with chores and made his hosts laugh more often than not. They were grateful for that.

As he turned his horse up Pajarito Canyon, he thought about Tunstall, then grinned as he remembered the Englishman asking for help to retrieve his mules. If Tunstall knew Billy had helped Jesse steal those mules, that conversation might've been a little different. But he didn't, and that gave Billy a kick, too, knowing something a man as educated as Tunstall didn't. It made them equals despite the difference in their stations, and Billy looked forward to the Englishman's next visit to the ranch.

Ahead he heard voices, which was unusual in the wee hours of night. Billy stopped and honed his attention on the darkness in front of him. He could catch mumbled words on the breeze, the snort and shuffle of horses, a clink now and then from their trappings, nothing more. Billy nudged his mount forward to slowly approach the riders.

The first man he saw was Jesse Evans. He was standing in a puddle of moonlight fixing his saddle, or trying to. The cinch seemed to be broken. His friends were hidden under the trees, still mounted. Billy picked up their animal wariness the same moment they detected him. "Howdy," he said softly to Jesse.

Jesse wheeled around, his hand close to the gun on his hip, then grinned. "God bless, if ain't the newfangled Billy Bonney materializing like a ghost!"

Billy leaned from his saddle to shake hands. "The sheriff let you out for a ride?" he teased.

"Yeah, but he gave me a busted saddle, so I don't guess he expects me to go far."

"What's the matter with it?"

"Cinch is broke," Jesse said.

Billy swung down and walked over to take a look. "It's been cut," he said.

"No shit." Jesse laughed. "We filched it from the Englishman's stable. You s'pose someone was hoping he'd have an accident?"

"Maybe they knew you'd steal it," Billy said, pulling his knife and notching holes in the strap on both sides of the break. He cut a conch string off the saddle and tied the two ends together. "That'll hold a few hours," he said, "if you don't get in a pinch."

"Goddamn, kid," Jesse said. "I owe you one for sure."

Billy walked back to mount his horse, then watched Jesse test the cinch before trying his weight in the stirrup. The saddle stayed and he swung on, gathering his reins as he grinned at Billy. "Why don'cha ride along a ways? You're going our direction, ain't you?"

"Reckon," Billy said, letting his horse fall in step. The other men rode ahead. Billy could see them clearly now. Tom Hill, Frank Baker, and George Davis were in front. Behind them were Willie Mote, who was one of Murphy's bodyguards, and Pantaleón Gallegos, with whom Billy had Tulles in common. Billy smiled at Jesse and said, "Quiet bunch you're with tonight."

"That's why I asked you along," he answered. "Damn! it feels good to be outta that hole."

"I bet."

"What'cha been doing with yourself, kid? Heard you're staying at the Englishman's."

"You heard right."

"Do you like him?"

"Only met him once." Billy laughed. "You know what he asked me?"

Jesse shook his head.

"If I could get them mules back we stole."

"What'd you tell him?" Jesse asked with a crafty smile.

"I told him I didn't have no influence in your direction."

Jesse laughed. "Don't it get boring laying around a ranch all the time?"

"It's more int'resting than being locked in a hole in the ground."

"No argument there. That goddamned Sheriff Brady was s'posed to let us out, but he never did. I swear I can't tell which side he's on. Sometimes he bends the law and sometimes he don't, and I don't relish being caught on the end he don't.''

"Maybe you should change sides. You might find you like it over here.''

Jesse didn't smile. *"Are* you over there, kid?''

Billy looked all around himself. "Looks like it to me.''

But Jesse was solemn. "Are you really working for Tunstall, or jus' milking him?''

"I ain't doing either one. Me and the Englishman are friends.''

"That highfalutin foreigner cozying up to a country boy? You're dreaming if you think he ain't milking you.''

"What've I got to milk?''

"You're wearing it on your hip,'' Jesse said.

Davis reined his horse back beside them and whispered, "Some Mexicans up ahead skinning a deer.''

"I prob'ly know 'em,'' Billy said. "Why don'cha let me go first, so they don't get scared and pull a gun on you.''

Jesse grinned. "On us, you mean.''

"Reckon,'' Billy said, spurring his horse to trot past the men and come out in the clearing on top of the canyon. Dawn was just breaking, the sky rosy pink to the east, still a deep blue studded with stars to the west. In front of him Francisco Trujillo and his nine-year-old brother Juan stood up from the carcass of a yearling buck.

"Buenos días," Billy said. "Looks like your family's gonna eat good for a spell.''

Francisco wiped his bloody hands on his trousers. "Where are you going so early, *chivato?*'' he asked, using the colloquial Spanish word for kid.

"Home,'' he said. "Been visiting my girl.''

"Ah *sí?*'' Francisco chuckled. "It must have been a good visit to last so long.''

"Yeah, it was. But I met up with a group of *hombres* who are coming along behind me now. I rode ahead to warn you.''

"Of what?'' Francisco whispered, his eyes riveted on the mouth of the canyon.

"To let whatever happens slide,'' Billy answered softly. "If they take something from you, I'll make it up.''

Meeting Billy's eyes, Francisco nodded. "Juan,'' he said, holding his arm for the boy to stand close as they both watched the riders emerge from the canyon.

"Well, lookee here!'' Jesse jeered, reining his horse almost on top of the Trujillos. They took a step back and Jesse laughed. "Got yourself a nice fat buck, don'cha?"

"*Sí, señor,*" Francisco murmured.

Jesse looked around until he spotted their horses tethered a hundred yards away. "*Chico,*" he said to the boy. "Run fetch that bay for me, will you?"

Juan looked up at his brother, who nodded, then whispered in Spanish, "When you get close, run into the forest and hide."

Billy watched the boy trot toward the horses. When he was almost there, Billy spurred after him, reached down and picked him up. "I can't let you do that, Juan," he said. "These fellows are *hombres malos.* If you cross 'em, they might hurt Francisco. You don't want that, do you?"

The boy shook his head.

"I'm gonna let you down, and you're gonna lead the horse back to the man who asked for it. *¿Entiendes?*"

"*Sí,*" the boy whispered.

"*Andale,*" Billy said. To make it look good, he drew his pistol and kept the boy covered as they walked back to the men.

Jesse laughed. "Now that's what I call service." He swung off and pulled the saddle from his horse, dumped it on the grass beside the dead deer, and took the saddle off the bay. "It's a fair trade," he said, yanking the cinch tight. "Or will be when you get that one mended." He swung onto his horse again. "*Gracias, amigos,*" he said, reining away.

Billy sat and watched the other men follow Jesse until they'd all disappeared in the forest. Then he looked down at Francisco. "Good riddance, eh?"

"*¡Sí!* I thought they would take the horse and the deer and everything."

"Not so bad then. I'll get you a saddle next time one falls in my lap."

Francisco warned, "Make sure it doesn't hit you in the head on its way down, *chivato.*"

Billy laughed, turning his horse toward home.

17

Tunstall awoke in his store with a splitting headache and his head stuffed up to feel the size of a boulder. Someone was pounding on the outside door, trying to rouse him. He looked at Widenmann, peering from beneath the blankets in his bed across the room.

"Shall I go?" Rob asked, not moving.

"It's undoubtedly me they want," Tunstall answered, throwing his covers off and feeling the cold blast him awake. "You can stoke the fire," he said crossly as he thrust his legs into his trousers, which were frozen stiff.

Whoever was outside pounded again. Tunstall stuck his head out the door of his room and called, "I'm coming. Don't break the bloody door down."

"They can't," Rob said, crouching before the stove in his long johns to stir the coals with a poker. "You ordered them built with a plate of steel between the planks. The window shutters, too, don't you remember?"

"With this headache, I can barely remember my name," he muttered, tucking in his shirt and reaching for his boots. "Where the devil is Corbet?" he said, stomping into them. Grabbing his jacket, he shrugged it on as he strode heavily across the store to fling open the door.

Squire Wilson stood before him, his face nearly as red as his serape. "Wake up, Englishman," he gasped. "The Boys have escaped and are over at Brewer's ranch. They've been firing at each other since daybreak, and I've just received word that Brewer's been killed!"

"God, no," Tunstall moaned, taking a step away.

"You best do something!" Wilson exhorted, turning his barrel body and running back across the street toward his home.

Forgetting to close the door, Tunstall ran across to Mac's. Now it was Tunstall's turn to pound with the cold rage of righteousness. Mac opened the door still in his nightshirt, his shins like ivory stakes above his slippers. "The Boys have killed Dick," Tunstall said. "Wilson just told me."

Mac grabbed Tunstall's arm and pulled him inside, past the closed door behind which Sue slept, and on into the kitchen close to the stove. After stoking up the fire, Mac said in a calm, courtroom voice, "Tell me the details."

"Wilson came pounding on my door," Tunstall explained. "The Boys have escaped. They must have gone straight to Dick's, he must have just gotten back. God, Mac, if Dick's been killed, I'll never forgive myself."

"Nonsense, you're not responsible for the acts of Jesse Evans. Besides, the key word is 'if.' Let's take this one step at a time. First, we must ascertain that the prisoners have in fact escaped."

"Yes, you're right," Tunstall mumbled. "I'm afraid I'm ill."

"I can see that. Go back to bed. I'll investigate the situation."

"You'll let me know," Tunstall pleaded, "as soon as you've learned anything?"

"Certainly. Now go get yourself warm and doctored up. I suspect this will be a long day."

Mac watched his friend leave, then returned to his bedroom. Sue was awake, huddling under the covers. With obvious trepidation, she asked, "What is it, Mac? Bad news?"

"Good morning, sweetheart," he said with mock cheer. He bent and kissed her cheek, then hurried to dress. "It's been reported that the Boys have escaped. I'm going to see the sheriff."

"I hope they keep riding and never come back," she said, snuggling deeper under the blankets.

"That would be the best solution," he agreed, scurrying out before the news of Brewer's death could cross his lips.

Even in his overcoat and scarf, the cold was piercing. He whispered a prayer as he walked, the vapor from his breath rising and disappearing with his words. When he reached Room 4 of the Wortley, it was his turn to pound and wait.

Brady opened the door in his long johns, his forty-five aimed at Mac's heart. "What d'ya want, McSween?" he growled, his breath foul with whiskey.

"Your prisoners have escaped, Sheriff," Mac announced.

"You're full of crap. One of my deputies would've told me. Go away." He started to close the door.

Mac held out a gloved hand to stop it. "I was informed of the escape by Squire Wilson, who is an officially appointed officer of the court."

"Let me tell you this, McSween," Brady said. "If the Boys are gone, then it's too late for me to stop them now, aint it? If they're not gone, then I don't have any reason to go traipsing up there in my underwear to find out. My advice to you is go home and let me deal with it."

"Deal with it as you did yesterday?" Mac taunted.

Brady sighed. "I'll look into it, Mac," he said wearily.

"Do your duty, Bill. It's all that's required of you."

"My duty's getting downright repetitious lately," Brady bellowed with renewed belligerence. "I arrested the Boys once and I'll be damned if I'll do it again. Here on out, I intend to look after my own interests."

"I'm afraid that position isn't compatible with an officer of the law," Mac replied.

For a moment Brady looked honestly into Mac's eyes, then he warned, "Don't expect anything from me."

"My expectations are not your concern, Sheriff. The safety of the citizens is. Will you investigate the situation at the jail?"

"Yes!" he bawled, making Mac retreat before his breath.

"Good," he said, continuing to move once he'd begun. "I expect a report in my office, delivered personally," he called back.

"Your expectations ain't my concern!" Brady yelled, slamming the door.

Mac chuckled at the man's surly humor, then braced himself for the freezing walk to the jail at the other end of town. Even from a distance he could see the prisoners were gone. The top hinge was broken off the door, so it hung at an angle, and gunnysacks spilling rocks were scattered on the ground before it. The hut was empty, the jailor absent, the hatch open to the dark chill of the dungeon. With a heavy heart, Mac walked back to Tunstall's.

He was in the front room, pacing the floor. Stopping abruptly when Mac came in, Tunstall queried, "Is it true? Are the prisoners gone?"

"Yes, I've just been to the jail. Brady has promised to investigate, but we can't rely on him to help Brewer."

"I'll ride out there," Tunstall said, turning to Corbet. "Saddle my bay, will you, Sam? And put my Winchester in the boot?"

"Yes, sir," Sam said, taking his coat and going out the back.

Tunstall blew his nose, then stuffed the handkerchief into his pocket just as Brady came through the front door.

He slammed it hard. "You're right, they're gone," he said to Mac. "I'm here to find out what the Englishman knows about it."

"I beg your pardon?" Tunstall asked.

"I heard you yesterday," Brady said, taking a few steps closer. "Evans offered to give your mules back if you helped him escape. Did you think I wouldn't be suspicious when the very next day the Boys're gone?"

"If you heard that much, Sheriff," Tunstall replied stiffly, "then you also heard me reject his offer."

"It's a mighty strong coincidence," Brady growled, "and I'm saying you helped 'em vamoose."

Tunstall laughed in his face. "That's ludicrous, Sheriff."

Brady's hand fell to the butt of his pistol.

Mac stepped between them. "He's unarmed," he told Brady.

Brady snarled and lifted his hand, taking a step back. "I won't shoot you now, Englishman, but you got a day of reckoning coming." He whirled and stomped out, leaving the door open behind him.

Tunstall sighed, leaning heavily against the counter. "Thank you, Mac, but I'm not unarmed. I always carry a forty-five in my coat."

Mac looked at him in surprise. "I didn't know that," he murmured.

Corbet came in, saw the open door, and crossed the room to close it before saying, "Your horse is ready in the stable, sir. Shall I bring it out?"

"Please," Tunstall said. He smiled weakly at Mac, then followed Corbet into the cold.

The ride to Brewer's ranch was the most miserable of Tunstall's life. Despite the bright sun in the blue sky, the air was freezing, and his mind was full of dread for what he'd find at the end of his journey.

As soon as he turned up the Hondo, he saw smoke coming from the vicinity of Brewer's ranch. It billowed wispily from two separate sources, not conflagrations but not ordinary chimney smoke either. Tunstall spurred his horse the last distance and reined in at the edge of the clearing to see a pile of hay smoldering in the yard. Raising his eyes, he saw that a missing brick from the chimney distorted the kitchen smoke to curl along the roof. Cautiously, he kicked his horse to approach the house. "Hello," he called. "Anyone about?"

The door opened and two men he hadn't seen before stepped out. They were of equal height, one wiry with dark hair worn rather long, the other thickly muscular and fair. "You must be Tunstall," the dark one said with a grin.

"Yes. Who are you?"

"Doc Scurlock, and this here's Frank McNab. We helped Dick get your herd back. He's up at your spread now."

"Are you certain? Is he safe?"

Scurlock laughed. "He was when we left him yesterday."

"We had a report in town that the Boys were here," Tunstall said.

"They were," the blond McNab answered with a Texas drawl. "Invited themselves in for breakfast. Being as they were heavily armed, we decided not to argue. Jesse Evans left you a message: said you're square with him now and he won't steal any more of your stock."

"The devil he did," Tunstall snorted.

Scurlock laughed. "The Devil may have done it, but it's as good as having a private treaty with the Apaches."

"Keep it to yourselves, will you?" Tunstall petitioned. "Their escape is no doing of mine and I don't want it thought so in the county."

When both men nodded, Tunstall reined his horse around to leave, then turned back. "Why is the hay burning?"

"One of the Boys wondered if the powder burn off his gun would be enough to ignite it," McNab said. "It was."

Tunstall still felt confused. "You sure Brewer's all right? He wasn't even here when the Boys came?"

"He's over at your ranch, prob'ly drinking your whiskey and soaking in your tub," Scurlock said.

Tunstall smiled. "A capital idea. I've caught an ague and it sounds like a good remedy. Would that be your advice as a doctor?"

"I ain't," Scurlock answered. "Just a bit of a vet, so stuck with the handle. But it's good advice anyway."

Tunstall nodded and turned his horse toward home, pushing harder than he should. As he wound along the old Indian trail climbing through Pajarito Canyon, he hoped the news about Brewer was true.

His horse was lathered after the climb and he was forced to travel no faster than a trot to let the animal recover. But when he had a sneezing fit which was so violent it frightened the horse, Tunstall couldn't tend his nose and control his mount, too, so he gave the horse its head, allowing it to gallop the rest of the way to reach the comfort of the stable.

Billy was there, rubbing down a gray mare that was due to foal. After watching Tunstall ride in and dismount, Billy walked across and closed the barn door against the cold, then watched from there as Tunstall stood leaning against the side of his horse, which was lathered and blowing hard. "You all right?" Billy asked.

Tunstall looked over his shoulder at the boy standing just inside the door. "No, I'm afraid I'm ill," Tunstall said. "Will you take care of my horse? I rode him rather hard."

"I can do that. You want me to help you to the house?"

"That won't be necessary," he said, standing up straight and untying his satchel. He walked toward Billy, who smiled with encouragement, and Tunstall suddenly felt affection for the boy because of his crooked teeth. They seemed an Achilles' heel somehow, as if giving a contradictory edge to the apparent innocence in his blue eyes. "Come inside when you've finished," Tunstall said. "We should get to know each other if you're going to be around."

"All right," Billy replied, wary now.

Tunstall laughed. "Why does that put you on guard?"

The boy's eyes were sharp. "You can read people pretty good, can't you, Mr. Tunstall?"

"Yes, and you didn't answer my question. Never mind, I'll see you in a few minutes." Walking out of the barn, he heard the door close behind him.

The house was fifty yards of icy air away. Tunstall kept his gaze on the fat billows of smoke bouncing out of the chimney with the promise of warmth. When he went inside, they were all there: Brewer with his stocking feet near the fire, Old Man Gauss cooking supper at the stove, Waite and another man with a dozen Winchesters spread on the table, two of which they were in the process of cleaning. Brewer stood up and came forward, grinning.

"Thank God," Tunstall said, dropping his satchel and shaking his friend's hand. "We heard you'd been killed!"

Brewer laughed. "By who? The Widow Casey?"

"No, Jesse Evans and his Boys. But it doesn't matter. Damn! it's good to see you, Dick."

"It's mutual," Brewer said. "We had a time, I'll tell you. Caught them just ten miles this side of Texas."

"I want to hear all about it," Tunstall said, then he sneezed and had to blow his nose.

"You best sit by the fire," Brewer said. "Pisser of a time to catch cold, at the beginning of winter like this."

"It's good just to be inside," Tunstall answered, taking a bottle of whiskey from his satchel. "Brought your favorite," he teased, "in case we had to drink it at your wake."

Brewer laughed. "You sonofabitch." He grabbed Tunstall in a hug. They held on tight a moment, then slapped each other's back and broke apart.

Tunstall turned away and saw Billy watching from where he stood just inside the door.

Brewer said, "Drinks're on the house." He pulled the cork, took a swig, and passed the bottle to Tunstall.

"To the best foreman and friend a man could have," Tunstall said, raising a toast to Brewer.

"Here, here," everyone said as Tunstall drank. He held the bottle toward Billy, then turned back to his satchel for a clean handkerchief. Watching the boy out of the corner of his eye, he saw him make a pretense of sipping, then pass the whiskey to Waite, who drank deeply. Waite gave the bottle to the other man, who was older and thick around the middle, his small eyes so black they glinted.

"You must be Middleton," Tunstall said.

"John Middleton, sir," he said, shifting the bottle to his left hand and extending his right.

Tunstall shook with him, thinking he was paying five dollars a day for the talents of the hand he held.

Middleton seemed to follow his thoughts. He raised the bottle and said, "To your health," before he took a swig and passed the bottle to Gauss in the kitchen.

Tunstall looked at all the rifles on the table. "These look new," he said.

"I noticed a crate of them in your store," Brewer explained, "so I took the liberty of arming the men. It was decisive when we came to the showdown. Widow Casey's men all had single-action and didn't stand a chance against these repeaters. I got them all back," he added at the end.

Realizing he could no longer sell them as new, Tunstall looked at

Brewer and said in a bewildered tone, "We didn't anticipate these costs in our plans, did we, Dick?"

All the men laughed as if he'd made a joke. Tunstall let it pass, suddenly too tired to be sociable. He moved woodenly to sit in front of the fire, hearing Brewer tell Gauss to hurry up supper. But Tunstall fell asleep before it was served.

A fit of coughing woke him. He thought himself alone, then heard a noise from the kitchen. Turning in his chair, he saw Billy pouring hot water from the kettle into a cup. "I'm glad you're still here," Tunstall said softly.

The boy carried the cup to the table and added a generous shot of whiskey. "Made you a toddy," he answered, bringing it over. "It'll cut the scum in your throat and help you sleep."

"Thank you," Tunstall murmured, ignoring the reason but accepting the remedy. He raised it to his nose and inhaled deeply. "It smells of juniper."

"I mashed some of the berries and put their juice in," Billy explained, sitting on a stool near the hearth. "Learned the recipe from Ma'am Jones. Course, I added the whiskey part."

"That surprises me," Tunstall said, "since you don't indulge in spirits. I watched earlier when you took the bottle but only pretended to drink. Why was that?"

"I didn't want to insult Dick by not drinking his toast," Billy said.

"So you don't drink at all? I've noticed it before."

Billy shrugged. "I don't find it suits me."

"Fair enough," Tunstall said, feeling the toddy suited him fine. He pulled his lap robe higher on his chest and smiled fondly at his companion. "I'm not sleepy at all. Will you stay with me until I am?"

"If you like," Billy said.

Tunstall sighed, remembering back over the day. "Did you know Jesse Evans and the Boys escaped jail?"

Billy stood up to stir the fire and add another log. "Don't surprise me none," he answered, settling back on his stool. "He's got a lot of friends, I hear."

"I've heard you're one of them."

"We talked about that," Billy reminded him. "Meeting a man ain't being friends."

"I'd like to be your friend," Tunstall said. "Do you think that's possible?"

A calculating wariness shone in the boy's eyes. "You mean you'd like me to be your friend," he said, his voice tinged with sarcasm.

"What do you mean?" Tunstall asked.

"Usually when someone announces they want to do something for you, it's the other way around."

"I see," Tunstall said. "Then I should assume, because you made me this toddy, you expect something in return?"

"No, 'cause I didn't ask to make the toddy. I seen you needed one and did it. You're drinking it, that's all I wanted."

"And why is my comfort your concern?"

Billy shrugged. "It ain't."

"Come now," Tunstall teased. "Is it so difficult to admit you like me?"

"It ain't hard," the boy replied. "But it don't mean much. I once killed a man I liked."

"Ah," Tunstall said, sipping his toddy. "So you lied when you said you'd never shot a man."

"No, this fellow died from a knife wound to his throat."

"You cut his throat?" Tunstall whispered.

"I stabbed him, that's jus' where the knife hit. You were asking about my not drinking and I'll tell you the truth: I was drunk and it made me stupid. I grabbed a knife and hit him."

Tunstall sniffed. "What had he done to make you so angry?"

"I'll try to break it down for you. This all happened in," he smiled as he hesitated, then said, "Indianapolis. I'd had a few run-ins with the law, you know how coppers are always looking for someone to bother. So the child welfare lady arranged a marriage between my mother and a man who would adopt me and my brother, and we was to come West and live with this man. My friend and I were drinking on the street one Saturday night. We had two girls with us, and my brother was there, too. My friend started in on us leaving and how we shouldn't do it. Then he said it'd be like prostituting my mother, letting her marry this man as a way to get away from my problems with the law. I couldn't stand to hear it, Mr. Tunstall. That's all I can say about it. I ran into this cheese shop we was standing in front of, grabbed a knife, and ran back out and told my friend to apologize for what he'd said about my mother. He laughed at me, and I struck him. I ran away and they never found out I'd done it, so we came West and everything turned out the same, except I decided against drinking."

Tunstall mulled this over for a moment as he stared into the fire, then he smiled playfully, meeting Billy's eyes. "It makes a good story to say you committed murder in defense of your mother's honor."

Billy grinned. "You like a good story, don'cha, Mr. Tunstall?"

He laughed. "Indeed. I'm glad you're with us, Billy. Everyone else is so earnest, I find your levity refreshing. And your toddy did the trick, gruesome story of murder by cheeseknife notwithstanding. I'm off to bed." He stood up and smiled at the frontier urchin. "See you in the morning."

Billy nodded and watched him disappear into the other room. Then he walked out into the cold night and stood a moment on the stoop. As he looked at the stars, he was thinking his life had definitely taken a turn up if John Tunstall was his friend.

18

Hendry Brown followed Jimmie Dolan into Tunstall's store and waited just inside the door while his boss approached Corbet at the counter. Only nineteen years old, Hendry had come to Lincoln County because he heard they were hiring guns. He prided himself on his abilities as a shooter. A slender man with blue eyes and a close-cropped blond moustache curling over the corners of his mouth, he was lucky with the ladies when he had money to buy one. Not having money meant he didn't get his ashes raked regularly enough, and that put him in a mean mood.

Looking through the window of Tunstall's store at the mud in the road, he told himself the foul weather was the only thing keeping him in Lincoln. Come spring, he'd ride down to the Pecos and get a job with Chisum's outfit. Jesse Evans had once ridden for Chisum, and Hendry figured if that scoundrel could do it, he could too. The truth was, he felt sick to death of Dolan. Before much longer, Dolan would see it and realize a bodyguard who hated him wasn't much use.

Hendry watched Corbet listen to Dolan's request, then walk across to knock on the door of the Englishman's office. Tunstall came out looking amused. Hendry couldn't see a gun on him, though he felt certain there was one under the counter.

Tunstall walked behind it, then asked, "What can I do for you, Mr. Dolan?"

Jimmie laid a check on the counter. "I want to cash this. It's written on the First National in Santa Fe."

The Englishman didn't even look at the piece of paper. "I'm afraid that's impossible," he said, smooth as glass.

"Why?" Dolan growled. "You're a bank, aren't you?"

"Yes, but I refuse to honor your check," Tunstall replied. "You'll have to go elsewhere."

"You mind telling me why?" Dolan asked gruffly, spreading his feet to straddle more space.

"I don't believe there's any money behind it," Tunstall answered.

Hendry Brown smiled. He had suspected Dolan was broke, the way he was always late with the payroll. Dolan didn't know it yet, but Brown had just quit.

Dolan muttered an inarticulate curse, grabbed his check and stomped out. "Come on, Brown," he snapped.

Hendry let him go through the door, then looked back at the Englishman and laughed before saying, "I told him you wouldn't do it." The Englishman laughed too, as if they were friends.

Hendry followed Dolan out and up the street, watching the runt strut. When they got back to the Big Store, Hendry asked for his wages.

"What the shit!" Dolan snarled, turning on him, then blanching as he remembered who he was talking to. He retreated behind the counter for the cash box and counted fifty dollars. "Take it and get out," he said.

Brown looked at the bills spread on the counter. "You're fifty short."

"It's all you're goddamned worth!" the little man bellowed. "Where were you just now? Why weren't you up there shoving it in their faces, huh? That's what you're paid for, Brown, the leverage of fear. You haven't been doing that for some time now, so I'm paying you half wages for half a job. Now get the fuck out."

Hendry stuffed the money in his pocket, not taking his eyes off Dolan. "You make any more enemies," Hendry said, "you're gonna die of spite."

"Aw, get outta here. I'll die a contented old man, but you'll never work in Lincoln County again." He put his cash box under his arm, walked back to his office, and slammed the door.

Hendry followed him, enjoying the fear that flashed beneath Dolan's surprise. "Look, Jimmie," Hendry said, backing the man around the desk until he was pinned against the wall. "I just want the rest of my money."

Dolan's eyes were as mean as a fighting cock's. "I'm gonna kill Tunstall," he said. "You up for that?"

Brown stepped back in disgust. "No, I ain't."

As if the conclusion were obvious, Dolan said lightly, "Then get out."

"I'll get my money one way or the other," Hendry warned.

"Let's make it the other," Jimmie answered.

Hendry craved to shoot the man right then, but he didn't relish the prospect of being hung. Hendry wasn't stupid, just limited in his approach to life. He walked directly from Dolan's store to Tunstall & Company and applied for a job. The Englishman wasn't there, so he talked to Widenmann. Corbet watched from behind the counter.

"What are your qualifications?" Widenmann asked.

"I'm good with a gun," Hendry said, "and I hate Dolan."

Widenmann frowned. "Weren't you just in here with him?"

"Yeah, and I just quit 'cause I don't care to work for him. He short-changed my wages, too."

Widenmann turned to Corbet. "What do you think, Sam? You know this man better than I."

Corbet disliked Widenmann's including him in the decision. He certainly couldn't say to the gunman's face that he was disreputable and without a conscience. Yet if he recommended him, Widenmann could tell Tunstall he'd hired Brown on Corbet's advice. He struggled to find a neutral phrase. "I believe what he says," he finally muttered.

"Okay," Widenmann said. "Go on out to Brewer's and tell him I said to put you up. You know where his spread is?"

"More or less," Hendry answered. "You ain't said what you're paying."

"Three dollars a day," Widenmann said, as if it were his money.

Hendry looked at Corbet. "He got the power to set this deal?"

Corbet nodded unhappily.

"You're paying Middleton five," Hendry said to Widenmann.

"That's gossip. Good lord, man, we'd be broke paying wages like that."

"Dolan's got the Boys with him. I think you're gonna need my gun, and five dollars a day is cheap for your life."

Corbet winced when Widenmann said, "All right, make it five. Go on out to Brewer's until we send for you."

Sam Corbet watched Widenmann return to Tunstall's office to sit at Tunstall's desk, and he thought the Englishman couldn't have chosen an assistant more different in manner or integrity. But Corbet was a faithful underling who wouldn't presume to criticize his employer without invitation, so when Tunstall returned an hour later, Corbet said nothing about Hendry Brown, though he wanted to. He greeted the Englishman as usual and watched him enter his office and close the door to hear however Widenmann chose to explain, or not, Corbet didn't know.

Widenmann said nothing about hiring another gunman that day. He rose from the desk when the Englishman entered, helped him with his coat, then left the room to make some tea while Tunstall read his mail. When Widenmann returned with the tea, he saw his friend frowning at a letter that had come just that morning from McSween in Las Vegas.

"Bad news?" Widenmann asked, setting the cup on the desk and trying to read over the Englishman's shoulder.

Tunstall closed the letter and stared out the window a moment. Then he looked up and said, "Mac's been arrested."

"My God! For what?"

"Embezzlement of the Fritz policy," Tunstall said with a puzzled tone. "They're holding him in jail in Las Vegas."

"Damn that Dolan! The Santa Fe Ring's behind this."

"He assured me there was no problem with that lawsuit."

"Apparently he was mistaken," Widenmann crowed.

"Yes," Tunstall said, thinking that if Dolan could reach through Santa Fe to effect the arrest in Vegas, that meant the Ring had the territorial courts in its power. And if the courts were allies of The House, Mac was in for a bitter battle. Tunstall sipped his tea thoughtfully, then opened his account books.

Widenmann left the room, returning a moment later to refill Tunstall's cup with more tea. Tunstall looked up from his ledgers and handed him a check, saying, "Look at this, Rob."

The check, written by McSween the previous August in the amount of fifteen hundred forty-five dollars and thirteen cents, was made out to William Brady, Sheriff and Ex Officio Tax Collector of Lincoln County. Widenmann turned it over. It had been endorsed by William Brady and cosigned by Dolan's second-in-command, Johnny Riley, with a final endorsement by Underwood and Nash, a known dealer in stolen cattle.

Slowly Widenmann said, "They used this check to buy cattle to fill their government contract." His emotion rising, he exclaimed, "The gall, the cheek, the assumption they wouldn't be detected! It's astounding."

"Indeed," Tunstall said with a nervous smile. "And perhaps just the thing to knock them out of the ring for good, if you'll excuse my pun."

"This is evidence!" Rob cried. "The governor reported in his yearly address that Lincoln County was behind in its taxes. This check proves why!"

Tunstall leaned back and put his feet on the desk. "I think we've got them, Rob, old boy. The question is, what are we going to do with this piece of evidence? We should wait for Mac before making any moves, don't you agree?"

"Absolutely not!" Widenmann said. "We should write a letter to the editor of the *Independent,* sticking it to Dolan and Brady in the public press. Then by the time Mac returns and goes before the judge, they'll be discredited and the whole affair will be laughed out of court."

Tunstall nodded. "I think you're right. This knowledge made public can't but help Mac's case." He sat up straight and pulled out a sheet of letterhead, then lifted his quill from the inkwell.

Tunstall was a fluid writer and the letter took him no time at all. When he was finished, he read it to Rob:

> Office of John H. Tunstall
> Lincoln, Lincoln Co., N.M.
> January 18, 1878

Editor of the Independent:

Sheriff Brady, as the records of this county show, collected over twenty-five hundred dollars in territorial taxes. Of this sum, Alex. A. McSween, Esq., paid him over fifteen hundred dollars by cheque on the First National Bank of Santa Fe, August 23, 1877. Said cheque was presented for payment by John H. Riley of the firm of J. J. Dolan & Co. to Underwood and Nash for cattle. Thus passed away over fifteen hundred dollars belonging to the Territory of New Mexico. With the exception of thirty-nine dollars, all the taxes of Lincoln County for 1877 were promptly paid when due. Let not Lincoln County suffer for the delinquency of one, two, or three men. By the exercise of proper vigilance the tax payer can readily ascertain what has become of that he has paid for the implied protection of the commonwealth. It is not only his privilege but his duty. A delinquent tax payer is bad; a delinquent tax collector is worse.

> J.H.T.

"Excellent!" Rob congratulated him. "The perfect touch of civic indignation. You're a poet, John."

"Thank you," he said, folding the letter and sliding it into an envelope. He dropped it on his desk, then stared at it pensively.

Rob reached across and picked it up. "I'll take it to Mesilla myself and deliver it to Colonel Fountain personally."

Tunstall rubbed the stubble on his chin as he looked out the window. Everything had happened in a whirlwind and the calming shadows of late afternoon made him hesitate. "Maybe we should wait for Mac. About the letter, I mean. The crime's so blatant, it could be a trap."

"How?" Widenmann scoffed. "The Ring slipped up. This check was supposed to be lost and they probably intended to issue a duplicate if we noticed. Somebody made a mistake. Let me take your letter to Mesilla so we can stick it to them now, when we'll benefit Mac as well as get Dolan and Brady."

"All right," Tunstall said. "How long will you be gone?"

"A week or so. It's a three-day ride to Mesilla. Go on out to the ranch if you get lonely."

"No, I'll wait in town for Mac," he said.

"I'll be back before he is," Rob predicted.

Left alone, Tunstall felt the days between mailing the letter and Mac's return stretching like an eon of empty time, so he took Widenmann's advice and rode out to the Feliz after all.

The morning was sunny but bitterly cold. When he crested the hill overlooking his home, smoke from the chimney was the only evidence anyone was there. The corral was empty, and he guessed the men were all out tending his herd, which had grown to over five hundred head under Brewer's able management.

Old Man Gauss was probably alone in the house, and Tunstall felt disappointed. Gauss was rather taciturn and not much of an intellect when he did talk. Tunstall trotted across the yard and dismounted before the stable, leading his horse inside to the warm respite from the wind.

As he pulled his saddle off and turned to hang it up, he saw Billy Bonney in the door of the mare's stall, holding a curry comb. "Hello, Billy," Tunstall said, glad for his company. "Did she foal yet?"

"Last night," Billy answered with a grin. "Got yourself a stallion if you don't cut him."

Tunstall pulled the bridle off his horse, slapped it into a stall, and walked across to see the newest addition to his empire. It was a spindly-legged bay colt, watching its owner curiously. "Looks like a decent chap," Tunstall said, "but not good enough to breed."

Billy laughed. "No sense dealing with your horse's horniness on top of your own," he said, returning to currying the mare.

Tunstall watched the gentle rhythm of the boy's hands smoothing the mare's coat behind the comb. "You're good with horses, aren't you, Billy," he said.

"I like 'em," he answered. "They're a lot like women, you know. Most of 'em are so used to spurs and Spanish bits, you give 'em a gentle touch and they'll do anything for you, run till their heart bursts if you ask 'em to."

"That's something I wouldn't ask of anyone," Tunstall said.

"I wouldn't want to," Billy said, "but it's good to know it's there if you need it."

Letting his gaze drop to the gun Billy wore, Tunstall remembered him shooting cans from the fence as he rode like a Comanche, hanging off the horse's side and firing under its neck to hit every can he aimed at. "There's a fight brewing in town," Tunstall said, "and I'd like to know you're on my side. But before you give me an answer, you should know we may be going up against Jesse Evans."

Billy laughed. "Ol' Jess gets around, don't he."

"I'm not sure what will happen, Billy," Tunstall said. "We've struck Dolan a blow that will hit hard, and I'd be a fool not to take precautions. If it becomes necessary, I intend to exhibit a display of force."

Billy smiled. "I'll stand with you, Mr. Tunstall, till I have reason otherwise."

"Fair enough," Tunstall said. "Why don't you take the mare when she's on her oats? I like my men to be well mounted."

"This mare?"

"Yes. Don't you like her?"

"Yeah, I do! She's got a lot of spirit."

"She's yours."

Billy looked at him hard. "You mean you're giving me this mare?"

"The mare and an outfit to ride her, so you can return what you're using to your friend John Jones. What do you think he'll do, Billy? Will he side with Dolan if pushed?"

"You'll have to ask John," Billy said. "Did you mean it about the mare?"

"Yes," Tunstall said, wondering if the boy had never received a gift. He seemed astonished, almost speechless, which was amusing because he was usually so glib.

Deciding to leave him to enjoy his good fortune before dinner, Tunstall started for the door and saw the crate of Winchesters that Brewer had borrowed to replevin the cattle. He turned back and said, "Help yourself to one of these rifles, too, Billy. They're only slightly used." He laughed at the naked amazement on the boy's face. "Don't look so surprised," Tunstall said. "It's Christmas, isn't it?"

Billy watched the barn door close, then slowly walked toward the crate of rifles. He could scarcely believe the Englishman had given him a horse and outfit easily worth a hundred dollars, plus a fifty-dollar gun. Stunned by his luck, Billy knelt beside the crate for a long moment, then slowly he reached out and touched one of the rifles.

The metal was cold but he savored the curve of the barrel, running his fingertips up to the sight at the end, then back to the bridge and finally to the comforting wood of the stock. His palm covered the grip as he lifted the gun from the box, hefting the weapon for weight. Turning with a grin to face his new horse, he brandished the Winchester high in the air, then lowered it to his shoulder and sighted down the barrel. He dropped his arm and held the rifle along his leg, then brought the gun up fast, cocking it in motion, ready to trigger a live shell by the time his eye was looking through the sight. He lowered the rifle again, then tossed it toward the rafters, high into the slanted sunbeams falling through the windows near the roof, caught the rifle and cocked it, his finger on the trigger and his eye through the sight. He tossed it again, higher, so it spun in the air but still came down in firing position, his finger on the trigger, his eye on the sight. Again and again he tossed the Winchester, each time catching it ready for action. By the time the supper bell rang, the weapon was warm with his heat.

Tunstall stayed on his ranch through the first weeks of January, waiting for news of Mac's return. The winter was a bitterly cold one in the mountains of Lincoln County, and the rheumatism Tunstall had had since childhood caused him to suffer the aches of an old man. From where he sat bundled in a blanket before the fire, he watched with envy as Billy and Fred came and went with the limber freedom of youth.

The two had established a friendship that was a marvel to Tunstall, who was familiar with the camaraderie of friendship. He was also a student of the interplay of power, and he noticed that Fred followed Billy's lead on nearly everything, though he was six years older than Billy.

One night when they were alone in the house, Tunstall called Fred over to the fire and asked him to sit down for a minute. He scrutinized Fred's half-Indian face, taking in the placid brown eyes and relaxed posture of a man who didn't worry about much of anything. "How long have you known Billy?" Tunstall asked, as if casually.

"Jus' since he came here," Fred answered without hesitation.

"Did you meet him at George Coe's?" Tunstall asked.

"No, sir. I met him in San Patricio, at a *baile* there."

"Do you like to dance?"

Fred grinned between the wings of his dark moustache. "I like doing jus' about anything with señoritas."

Tunstall laughed. "And what of your ambitions, Fred? What do you plan on doing with your life?"

Fred looked puzzled a minute, chewing on one end of his moustache. "I'm doing it, pretty much," he answered. "Not to say things won't change. Billy said something about maybe farming up on the Peñasco. That might work out."

"Maybe you should consider raising horses," Tunstall said. "I could back you on a ranch, supply the capital while you and Billy stake a claim under the Desert Land Act. Does that sound interesting?"

"I'll say!" Then more somberly, "I'd have to ask Billy, a'course."

Tunstall nodded. "You like Billy a great deal. Can you tell me why?"

Fred looked into the fire and thought a moment. Finally he said, "Everything's important with Billy. When I'm with him, nothing's ever boring or disappointing."

"That's quite a gift," Tunstall conceded. "What do you know of his past?"

Fred's face closed. "You'll have to ask Billy about that."

Tunstall smiled. "Your loyalty is admirable, Fred. Billy's lucky having you for a friend."

"I think it's the other way around," he said.

"How so?"

"Well, I'll tell you a story, if you'd like to hear it."

"Very much," Tunstall murmured.

"Did you hear about Frank Freeman shooting the colored soldier in Wortley's?"

"Yes, I did."

"Well, Freeman was a friend of George Coe's. Not to say George approved of what Freeman had done, but he was a friend, and when he came to George's farm asking for food, George fed him. Coupla days later, Sheriff Brady and a troop of cavalry rode into George's farm and arrested him for having harbored a fugitive. Took him back to Lincoln the long way, and it was raining and George was riding bareback with his feet tied 'neath the horse's belly. He suffered bad on that trip. So he lost any loyalty he'd had for Brady. Anyway, the story I was wanting to tell you come about 'cause of what happened to George.

"We was all in Lincoln at a *baile,* me and Billy and George and George's cousin, Frank Coe, and Frank's partner, Ab Saunders. We'd all ridden in together. Jake Mathews was there, too. He's tight with Brady, and to tell you the truth, the Mexican folks who was having the dance didn't want Mathews there, but he walked in and made himself at home. None of the señoritas would dance with him though, so he was standing along the side of the room, jus' watching. Billy, he was dancing with Tulles Patrón—you know Juan's oldest sister? Billy was dancing with Tulles, and he starts spinning her round and round the room, making a wider and wider circle, coming close to Mathews. And Mathews, he starts backing up and flattening himself against the wall till there ain't no more room. But Billy, the next time he come around, he like to step on Mathews' toes, then he made a quick little circle and come back and did it again. Mathews' face got real red, but he knew he didn't hold a candle of a chance to rebuke Billy since the room was full of his friends. So finally Mathews sidled out the door and made for his horse. Billy followed him.

"Now, you know, we all leave our guns at the door for these *bailes.*

And Billy, when he went out, he picked his up, and jus' as Mathews was about to step into his stirrup, Billy shot his hat off. Mathews had his gun on now too, but he didn't use it, not with all of us standing behind Billy like we was. So Mathews he goes over to pick up his hat, and jus' when his fingers are about to touch it, Billy shoots it again and it goes flying. Mathews was downright mad. The hat looked to be new and I don't imagine he wanted any airholes in it. But he still didn't say nothing, he jus' walked over to pick it up, and sure 'nough, Billy shot it again. We was all laughing to beat the band, and Billy, he was grinning, but Mathews was plumb disgusted. I guess he figured with six bullet holes in it the hat was a loss anyhow, 'cause he caught his horse and rode outta there, leaving the hat behind. Billy wore it the rest of the night, and he looked comical, with the crown all slanted down to one side and the six little holes neat and tidy." Fred stopped to laugh. "He's a kick, Billy is. But more'n that." He leaned closer to Tunstall and said softly, "Even though Mathews knew Billy was only funning, he couldn't help notice Billy's skill with a six-gun." He leaned back with the contented smile of a satisfied man.

"I'm sure," Tunstall said. "Although, if he had missed by an inch when shooting off the hat, Mathews would be dead."

"Billy don't miss," Fred crowed. "I've seen him shoot snowbirds off a fence from a galloping horse and hit three outta four. Standing on his own feet with a clear view, Billy don't miss."

Tunstall smiled. "And Jake Mathews knows that now."

"The whole county prob'ly knows it," Fred agreed. "Is that what you were angling for, Mr. Tunstall?"

"What do you mean?"

"Billy told me you asked him to fight for you. I figure you've been puzzling over whether he'll be any good."

"I don't believe it will go that far," Tunstall said quickly.

Fred nodded. "Reckon we're all hoping that. But whatever happens, Mr. Tunstall, me and Billy are behind you."

"Thank you," Tunstall said. "I guess that's what I was angling to hear, Fred."

"Can I go then?" he asked, standing up.

Tunstall nodded, then watched him walk out, thinking the story about Billy revealed a quixotic twist to the boy's character. Since he had acted to redress a friend's grievance rather than his own, there was a touch of heroics in what he had done. But Jake Mathews was a deputy sheriff, so Billy had also displayed a reckless rebellion that made Tunstall feel uneasy. He found it enigmatic that the frontier urchin camouflaged his threats behind laughter. The combination of humor with lethal skill gave an eerie undercurrent to the boy's charm, and the only reassurance Tunstall could claim was that his enemies would find it as unsettling as he did. He concluded his thoughts by being glad Billy was on his side.

19

Mac arrived back in Lincoln the day after Tunstall's letter was published in the Mesilla *Independent,* though no one in town had seen the issue yet. Introducing the stout, dark man who accompanied him as Deputy Sheriff Adolph Barrier from Las Vegas, Mac explained he had been released into Barrier's custody until his scheduled court appearance in Mesilla.

Tunstall wanted desperately to have a private conversation with Mac, but the deputy wouldn't allow the lawyer out of his sight. They compromised by talking in Tunstall's office, leaving the door open so Barrier had a clear view of his ward. Tunstall sat behind the desk, leaning on his elbows to be closer to Mac, who sat in a chair alongside the desk as they spoke quietly.

After listening to Mac express his concern for his wife's safety and his anger at being called to court on a trumped-up charge, Tunstall told him of the letter to the *Independent.* Seeing Mac's response written on his face, Tunstall murmured, "You don't approve."

"I think you were hasty," Mac said. "Do you have a copy of the letter?"

"I don't," Tunstall had to answer.

"Well, fortunately you sent it to Fountain. He's a friend of mine and we can trust him not to alter it in any way, but damn! John, I wish you'd waited."

Tunstall fell back in his chair with dismay. "Isn't the check evidence to hang them?"

"Not alone. We'd have to know an equal amount was actually missing from the taxes Brady paid in. The check could have been used merely as a convenient transfer of funds with no intent to defraud."

"What about the governor's statement that the county is delinquent?"

"That was a fortnight ago. Are you certain Brady's delinquent now? I don't doubt they're defrauding every contract they have an interest in, but they wouldn't leave themselves open for so obvious an accusation."

Tunstall felt miserable. "What's to be done, Mac?"

"I would write a retraction. But knowing Fountain, he won't print it. He likes to keep things stirred up and has a bitter hatred for Jesse Evans and consequently Dolan, who protects him. I'm afraid there's nothing to be done now except ride out the storm. I'm glad Sue isn't here."

"Yes, you were wise to send her on East. What do you think Dolan will do?"

"You know him as well as I, John. He's capable of anything."

"But broke. You said the bank was about to foreclose."

"Apparently he came up with the money and stalled."

"Our fifteen hundred dollars!"

"It's slander if we can't prove it."

Tunstall felt chastened. "I'm going to have to think this out, aren't I, Mac? I can't apologize to that rascal. And anyway, I don't believe I was wrong, not in my heart."

"Then hold to that righteousness," Mac advised. "It'll keep you on course."

So John Tunstall wore a rigid suit of self-justification when he accompanied Mac to Mesilla. It didn't fit and he felt ill at ease, knowing he'd made a mistake but unable to admit it, not with the fat hitting the fire.

David Shield and Squire Wilson accompanied them to testify on Mac's behalf. They made slow progress, meandering down the mountains through the Tularosa Canyon, stopping the night at La Luz, crossing the white sands to spend the second night on the eastern slope of the Organ Mountains, then climbing San Agustín Pass and descending into the Rio Grande Valley to Mesilla.

Judge Bristol held the hearing in his home. A balding man with huge, piercing eyes, he had a cold and his illness made him cross. The district attorney was a tall, immaculately attired gentleman by the name of Colonel Rynerson. Tunstall took one look at him and knew Mac's opposition was no bureaucrat wet behind the ears.

The best Mac could plead from the judge was a delay to allow the probate court judge and territorial representative in Lincoln to testify on his behalf. Bristol continued the case until the April term of court and set bail at eight thousand dollars. When Rynerson objected, Bristol closed court by authorizing the district attorney to accept McSween's bond and release him accordingly. Bristol then excused himself and Mac was left to deal with Rynerson.

"I can give you a personal bond," Mac said, "on my property and my practice."

"Not acceptable," Rynerson said.

"I'm known in Lincoln County, Colonel," Mac argued. "Mr. Wilson, will you tell the district attorney I'm worth what I'm offering."

"Easily that much, sir," Squire Wilson said cheerfully.

"I, also, can attest to that," David Shield volunteered.

"Not acceptable," Rynerson said. "You tried to abscond once, and I have little doubt you'll try it again. I'll accept only cash as your bail."

"This is preposterous," Tunstall exploded, stepping from the corner and entering the fray. "I'll guarantee Mac's bail, but John Chisum himself couldn't raise eight thousand in cash on a moment's notice."

Rynerson smiled. "I'll accept your check, Mr. Tunstall, but don't expect to get it back. Your friend will never appear in court voluntarily."

"I know McSween to be an honest man," Tunstall replied. "Which is more than I can say of you."

"You're evidently fond of publicizing your opinions," the district attorney answered. "I hope you don't write a letter to the *Independent* saying *I'm* a crook."

"You're changing the subject," Tunstall retorted. "Mac's bail is outrageous and you know it."

"Nevertheless," Rynerson said, "the judge left it at my discretion. My duty is to assure this man's appearance in court."

"I will be there," Mac said in a gentle voice. "I am innocent of these charges and the grand jury will see it clearly. It's you who hope I'm not there, Colonel, because you don't have a case."

Seeing Mac's words hit home, Tunstall whipped out his checkbook and wrote a check for the full amount on his account in St. Louis.

Rynerson looked it over and handed it back. "Not acceptable. The funds are out of the territory and may not exist, for all we know."

"You swine," Tunstall muttered.

Mac laid a restraining hand on his arm. "What's to be done, Colonel, since you refuse to accept any bond I offer?"

Rynerson turned to Barrier. "Deputy, you are to deliver this man to the custody of Sheriff Brady in Lincoln to be held for the April term of court. Are you capable of doing your duty?"

It was evident Barrier didn't like Rynerson, but he answered, "Yes, sir, I can do it."

"Good." Rynerson smiled at McSween. "See you in court, counselor."

Before leaving Mesilla, Tunstall sent a letter to St. Louis to release the funds to his Santa Fe account, but the transfer would take weeks to effect. And if the eight thousand was actually withdrawn, his balance would be almost nil. Suddenly everything was in jeopardy. He was so close to the edge, the profits from his store would have to meet next month's payroll.

On their return trip to Lincoln, Tunstall and Mac rode beside each other the whole first day, talking the subject to the ground. Each reassured the other that they were in the right and when it came to court it would be an easy victory. Until then they had to stay calm. Dolan was known for provoking his enemies into violence, and they were determined to wait it out, abide by the law, and achieve justice in the courts.

They camped the first night at Shedd's Ranch on the eastern end of San Agustín Pass. None of the others knew anything about tending horses, so Tunstall took it on himself. Returning to the fire just as two men approached the camp, Tunstall watched them with a curiosity that changed to alert attention when he recognized Jesse Evans and Frank Baker.

Jesse stopped a few yards in front of Tunstall and asked with a grin, "Did you happen to see Jimmie Dolan on the road from Mesilla?" When Tunstall shook his head, Jesse shifted his gaze to the men sitting around the fire.

David Shield nervously answered, "I understood from Rynerson that he wasn't to leave until tomorrow."

Baker guffawed. "We've always found Jimmie to be punctual. He said he'd be here tonight and I'm sure he will. Ain't you, Jesse?"

"Oh yeah," Jesse said. "He ain't real happy with you, Englishman. You know that, don't you?"

"The feeling is mutual," Tunstall replied.

Jesse laughed. "I like you, but that don't mean nothing."

"Doesn't it?"

"Believe it, Englishman," Jesse said, turning and walking away, followed by Baker.

"Who in heaven's name were they?" Barrier asked.

Tunstall sighed, dropping onto his blankets. "Jesse Evans, captain of the local Banditti, and Frank Baker, his illustrious lieutenant. They escaped jail in November and have been creating havoc ever since. And before, too, I might add."

"They've threatened to kill us," Shield said.

"Not you," Mac responded sternly. "They haven't threatened you, David, and won't harm you or your family."

"We could've been killed when those men after Chisum shot up your house!" Shield cried. "Just being associated with you is dangerous." He looked around, obviously ashamed of his outburst, then rolled himself in his blankets and turned his back.

"Appears you're right about the situation down here, McSween," Deputy Barrier said. "I'm beginning to doubt what I should do."

"Hold on to that doubt, my friend," Mac answered. "It's all I ask."

In the morning, they were standing around the fire finishing their coffee after a breakfast of cold biscuits when Jimmie Dolan and Jesse

Evans came around the corner of Shedd's corral. Tunstall dumped the rest of his coffee and dropped the cup on the sand, sliding his hand into his pocket to hold his pistol. The other campers all turned as the two men approached, Shield and Wilson stepping back out of danger, Mac standing close beside Tunstall, Barrier watching with a sharp eye.

Dolan stopped fifteen feet away and spread his legs to straddle more ground. Jesse was right behind and a little to his left, grinning happily. Both men were armed with pistols and Winchesters. Jesse rested the butt of his rifle against his hip. Dolan clutched his in his fist hanging by his knee.

He squared off in front of Tunstall and growled, "Are you ready to fight and settle our differences?"

"I beg your pardon?" Tunstall asked.

"I'm calling you out to fight!" Dolan snarled.

"What is he saying?" Tunstall asked Mac. Then turning back to Dolan with a friendly smile, "Are you challenging me to a duel?"

"You cowardly sonofabitch!" Dolan yelled, jerking his rifle to his shoulder and squinting down the sight. "You gonna fight me or not?"

"Stop it!" Barrier shouted, stepping between them. "I'm a deputy sheriff and you'll hang if you shoot me. Now I suggest you and your friend go about your way."

Dolan glared down the barrel of his rifle. Then with a snort of disgust, he lowered the gun and stalked away. After taking a few steps, he wheeled back and yelled, "You won't fight me today, you damned coward, but I'll get you soon." He tromped on further, then turned again. "Next time you write the *Independent,* say I'm with the Boys!" He stomped behind the corral and disappeared, his grinning cohort right behind.

"Who was that?" Barrier asked.

"Jimmie Dolan," Mac said sadly, his face pale. "Thank you, Mr. Barrier, for intervening."

Barrier looked puzzled. "Why doesn't Sheriff Brady arrest Jesse Evans, if he's escaped jail?"

"Would you?" David Shield asked, gathering the coffee cups.

Squire Wilson giggled as he kicked sand into the fire.

Tunstall and Mac didn't talk much the second day of their journey, both of them dissecting the problem before them and keeping their thoughts to themselves. Mac's solutions turned on intricacies of law and the finer points of courtroom rebuttal. Tunstall's moved toward a more primal defense. When they neared Fort Stanton, he left the party and cut across the mountains to confer with Brewer.

Brewer had been mending harness in the barn when he heard a rider approach. He put his work aside and opened the door to see the Englishman. Welcoming him in, Brewer closed the door against the cold, then returned to his task. Tunstall tied his horse to a stall, flopped down on a bag of feed, and watched as Brewer whipped a big needle around the torn seam of a leather strap. Finally Tunstall asked, "Did you hear that Mac was arrested?"

Brewer nodded, his eyes on his work.

"We've just come from Mesilla. Rynerson set his bond at eight thousand dollars, then refused to accept anything but cash."

Brewer looked up. "That's a lot of money."

"I've sent for it, but until then Mac's to be turned over to Brady and put in jail. I can't let that happen, Dick."

"Will you go against the law?"

"Damn it, man, the law is corrupt! And I can't let them hold Mac in that hole, completely at their mercy."

"It'll mean a fight," Brewer said, laying the harness aside.

"We have Middleton, Waite, and Bonney with us."

"Hendry Brown, don't forget him."

"I thought he worked for Dolan?"

"He did until a little while ago," Brewer answered, surprised Tunstall didn't know Brown was on his payroll. "He quit Dolan and Widenmann hired him, then sent him out here. He's up at the house right now."

"Rob didn't mention it. That makes four, seven with you and me and Rob. He's a deputy U.S. marshal, so we have the law on our side, too."

"Squire Wilson commissioned me a deputy constable when I went after Evans. That holds till taken back, I guess."

"Will we be enough?" Tunstall asked.

"I can ride out and see who else'll stand with us," Brewer suggested. "Doc Scurlock for sure. Frank McNab, Charlie Bowdre. Maybe the Coes. If you're not too particular about your recruits, I could probably gather fifty men if I had a week."

"And Dolan?"

"That many, maybe more."

They were silent a moment, then Tunstall said, "My God, Dick, what are we contemplating? It sounds like war."

"If it comes to that, I'm behind you," Brewer said.

"Thanks," Tunstall said, "but I'd hate to see anyone hurt on my account."

"You can't fight Dolan and the Boys alone. I wouldn't have anything without you and Mac, so I'll risk what I have and that's my choice. It'll be worth it to have a part in taking Dolan down." He looked toward the door of the barn. "Rider coming fast."

They both listened to the hoofbeats galloping toward them. When Brewer opened the door, Widenmann surged in with a cold gust of wind. He dropped from his horse and shouted frantically, "They've attached the store!"

"What the devil do you mean?" Tunstall demanded.

"Brady took possession of it, the keys and everything. He's got deputies in there taking inventory."

"On what grounds?"

"Mrs. Scholand swore out a complaint against Mac for full value of the Fritz estate. That's what Dolan was doing in Mesilla: getting her to sign the writ. So Brady attached the store to secure bond until it's settled in court."

"You can't be serious!" Tunstall exclaimed. "Mac doesn't own anything in the store."

"I told Brady that. He said everyone knows you're partners. He said you can stay open and keep your half of the profits, but there won't be any. Nobody'll come in with an armed guard there."

Looking at Brewer, Tunstall said, "It's on. You take that ride we spoke of and meet me in town." He turned to Widenmann. "Get over to the Feliz as fast as you can and bring the men into Lincoln. I'll want them nearby through this."

"What are you going to do?" Widenmann asked.

"I'm going in and raise hell," Tunstall said. "They've overstepped their bounds this time and they're sure as Satan going to hear about it."

Tunstall led his horse into the cold wind of the fading afternoon and rode hard for town. Seething with anger at the audacity of Dolan and Brady, he framed in his mind the exact epithets he would hurl in their faces. But when he walked into his store, no one was there but Corbet and a deputy asleep by the stove. "Where's Mac?" Tunstall asked his clerk.

"At home," Corbet answered unhappily.

Tunstall sighed with relief. "Not in jail at least."

"Barrier refused to surrender him. Said he didn't believe Mr. Mac's life would be worth a hoot if he did. It was a battle for a while here, sir. Brady made a joke right in front of Barrier, saying Mr. Mac may have had fun accusing him of defaulting on the taxes, but he wouldn't default on breaking Mr. Mac's spirit once he got him in jail. It was an ugly scene, sir."

Tunstall groaned with regret. "Take care of my horse, will you, Sam?" he asked. Then he turned away and walked over to Mac's house.

With Deputy Barrier and Sebrian, they had a grim supper in the dining room, then sat in silence before the hearth. At nine o'clock a knock sounded on the door, making them all look at each other in the light of the fire.

"Open it, Sebrian," Mac said softly.

Sebrian stood up and crossed to the door. Hesitating a moment, he opened it a crack, then stood back and opened it wide. "It's Mr. Widenmann," he called with relief.

Widenmann came into the room followed by John Middleton, Fred Waite, Billy Bonney, and Hendry Brown. As Mac watched the heavily armed men enter his parlor, he murmured, "The things my soul refused to touch are as my sorrowful meat."

"Where's Dick?" Widenmann asked tactlessly.

Tunstall looked at Mac when he said, "Out gathering more men."

"It doesn't have to come to this," the lawyer said.

"I'm afraid it already has," Tunstall replied. "Don't worry, we shan't strike the first blow. But neither will we turn the other cheek."

In the early light of dawn, Deputy Barrier left for Stanton with McSween. As Tunstall watched them ride away, he approved of the deputy's decision to take his prisoner to the fort and ask the military to hold him. Returning inside the house, he waited with his men in the parlor for news of the sheriff's arrival at the store.

Widenmann kept up such a vitriolic demand for justice that Tunstall finally asked him to be quiet. From where he stood leaning against the closed keys of the piano, Billy laughed. Widenmann looked at him, then quickly turned away. Middleton sat paring his nails with a Bowie knife at the dining room table. Fred was in the kitchen helping Sebrian clean up after breakfast. Hendry Brown was outside watching for the sheriff. At eight o'clock he came in and reported, "Brady's there."

"All right," Tunstall said, feeling the weight of his revolver in his pocket as he stood up. "Middleton, you and Brown stay outside. Rob, I want you, Billy, and Fred to come in with me. Fetch Fred out of the kitchen, will you, Billy?"

Billy walked down the hall and came back with an embarrassed Waite drying his hands on his pants.

Tunstall smiled. "Do you think we can look mean, pulling this off? You don't smell like soap suds, do you, Fred?"

Fred's face turned red. "No, sir, Mr. Tunstall," he said, resetting his gunbelt on his hip.

Tunstall looked at Billy's grin. "Of course, if they happen to look at Billy, his smile will scare them to death."

"Whatever works," the boy answered, picking up his new Winchester.

Tunstall led his small troop the short distance to his store. Middleton and Brown stayed behind outside the door, and Billy and Fred stopped just inside. Widenmann accompanied Tunstall across the wooden floor toward Brady, who stood with his back to them, talking with a deputy.

"Look here, Sheriff," Tunstall demanded. "What is the meaning of this?"

Brady turned to face him with a sneer. "I've got a court order to attach the property of McSween. That's what I've done."

"This store is mine alone," Tunstall argued. "How dare you attach my property for a debt of McSween's!"

"You're partners, aint you?"

"Not legally. We had talked of drawing up an agreement eventually."

"That's good enough for me," the sheriff answered, turning away.

Tunstall had to restrain himself from yanking the man back. "It's not good enough for the law, Sheriff. You'll be held to account for this high-handed affair." He glanced at the half-dozen deputies leaning against his merchandise. "This is an illegal attachment," Tunstall warned.

One of the deputies, Jim Longwell, asked nervously, "Why don't you let the courts settle it, then? Nobody wants to get hurt here."

"Good lord, man!" Tunstall exploded. "Haven't I just seen how prejudiced Bristol and Rynerson are?"

Longwell shrugged. "Take it to a higher court."

"I wouldn't get justice there, either," Tunstall retorted. "The judiciary are the most despicable of all the pawns in the Santa Fe Ring!"

"You're quick to make accusations, Englishman," Brady snarled. "You keep it up and we'll throw you in the pokey along with your lawyer friend."

"On what charge?"

"Interfering with a law officer doing his duty! The fact is, I've got a civil attachment ordering me to confiscate property belonging to McSween in the amount of ten thousand dollars. I've done that, and I'm going to hold the property until I get papers telling me to do otherwise. You get the papers, Englishman, I'll clear out of your store. It's a nuisance to me to have to everlastingly deal with the squabbles you and McSween raise. This was a quiet county before you two came."

"Oh yes," Tunstall mocked, "no one but the Mescaleros and the Horrells to disturb the peace."

"Where were you when we got rid of 'em? You didn't earn the right to rule this county, Tunstall. You're a newcomer. You seem to have forgotten that."

"I didn't realize I needed a pedigree," he quipped. "I thought this was America."

"This here's Lincoln County and I'm the law!"

"I see." Tunstall thought a moment. "May I retrieve my personal possessions from my office?"

"No," Brady said, squaring off in front of him. The deputies all stood up straight.

Tunstall felt Billy and Fred tense behind him. "Surely my private papers are of no value to anyone but myself," he argued.

"That's for the court to decide," Brady answered. "The store and all its contents are confiscated till then."

Billy cocked his Winchester.

"I don't want anyone hurt," Tunstall said quickly, "so I'll abide by your travesty, Sheriff. But I warn you, you'll regret this."

"Are you threatening me?"

"Indeed."

"I can't order you out," Brady growled. "But you're not to interfere with me or any of my men. I'll arrest you if you do."

Widenmann stepped up. "I'm a deputy U.S. marshal," he said snidely. "I outrank you, Sheriff."

"Your commission only holds for federal indictments!" Brady shouted. "I'm a deputy U.S. marshal myself and you don't outrank shit, Widenmann."

Tunstall edged between them. "Surely, Sheriff, you'll let me take the horses I have in the corral. You can't believe they belong to the store."

"No, you can have them," he muttered, eyeing Widenmann with venom.

"Come along, Rob," Tunstall said, turning on his heel and walking toward Billy and Fred still by the door. Fred looked tense, but Billy was smiling, the butt of his cocked Winchester resting on his hip. Hearing Widenmann following behind, Tunstall could feel the angry eyes of the sheriff and the sad eyes of Corbet on his back.

Outside, Tunstall faced his men. "Rob, you take Hendry, Fred, and Billy, and drive those horses to the ranch, then come by Dick's and see if he's back yet. Middleton, you stay with me."

"What are you going to do?" Rob asked.

"Try to raise the money to get rid of this damn attachment," Tunstall answered impatiently. "If I'm not at Mac's, I'll be with Juan Patrón."

He didn't wait for an answer but strode angrily away, Middleton close behind.

Patrón ushered them into his parlor and listened to Tunstall's request for assistance in raising the bond.

"I'd be happy to help," Patrón said, "but Florencio Gonzales, who just been appointed probate judge, received instructions not to accept any bond from Mac in lieu of cash. I'm afraid we'll have to endure the situation until the April term of court."

"That's nearly two months," Tunstall argued. "It's intolerable."

"What's the alternative?" Patrón asked softly, casting a quick glance at Middleton. "I'm thinking of the people, John. The county is ready to explode. All the men need is an incident to set it off. For the sake of peace, handle this through the courts. Bristol will be sitting here in Lincoln, not Mesilla. The grand jury will be made up of local men. You'll win if you don't resort to violence. Believe me, I've been fighting The House a long time. Isn't it better to lose a few months' profit than the lives of the men around you?"

"You're right," Tunstall conceded with a sigh. "I admire you immensely, Juan, and bow to your advice. Though it will be bitter having Brady's men underfoot for two bloody months."

"Perhaps it will be resolved peaceably before then. As I understand it, all Mac has to do is deposit the ten thousand in a neutral bank account so the court may decide who it belongs to."

"But that's merely the civil attachment. There's also the eight thousand dollars' bail. I can't come up with both amounts. Besides, Mac has been charged with a crime and feels honor bound to clear his name."

"I can understand that," Patrón answered. "Dolan still has an indictment against me he could yank at any time. But once Mac is cleared, Dolan won't have a leg to stand on. He'll have lost. That's a day worth waiting for, isn't it?"

Tunstall sighed again, then stood up. "Thanks for helping me see things clearly, Juan. I'll do my best to abide by your advice."

With his gunman in tow, Tunstall returned to his store. He didn't speak to Brady or the deputies, but took Corbet into his office and amended their bookkeeping to accommodate the new arrangement. "We're going to work with it, Sam," he said. "We're going to wait them out and survive."

"Yes, sir," Corbet answered with approval.

Tunstall slept poorly that night. As he tossed and turned between fits of sleep, he wondered what sort of quarters Mac had been given at

Stanton, consoling himself that, however humble, any room at the fort would be a vast improvement over the jail.

He was discovering it took more grit than he'd realized to be an overlord like Chisum. If you weren't willing to use any means to win, you lost by default. Tunstall didn't want to lose, but he had enough scruples that neither did he wish to send men into war over a mercantile enterprise. He tried to adopt the placid patience of Patrón, who had been fighting this battle all his life and now, when it was almost won, could wait a few more months to see his enemy defeated. Tunstall recognized Patrón was right: a confrontation like this could easily turn into a bloody vendetta. Hadn't he already sent Brewer out to gather an army?

Only after tossing for hours was he finally able to find sleep. He dreamt he saw the men he employed—John Middleton and Fred Waite, Hendry Brown and Billy Bonney—all carrying guns and following Dick Brewer on horses through the mountains. Tunstall wanted so badly to go with them. But though he yelled to catch their attention, they never heard him, and in his dream he couldn't move.

20

The next day, Widenmann came galloping into town with Billy and Fred to tell Tunstall there was a posse at the ranch threatening to attach the cattle. Widenmann had stalled their leader, Jake Mathews, until he could ride in and confer with Tunstall.

Tunstall listened with growing exasperation as Widenmann told him that Dolan had recruited twenty gunmen under Buck Morton who were waiting at a neighboring ranch, ready to join the posse if needed. Succumbing to the emotion of Widenmann's tirade, Tunstall felt swamped with fierce indignation at being pushed so hard by Dolan. Yet he remembered Patrón's advice. Cutting Widenmann off with a curt demand to make him some tea, Tunstall sat at his desk, struggling to squelch his rage. When he heard shouting from the store, he lurched to his feet and hurried out to investigate. "What the devil's all the ruckus?" he asked Corbet.

Sam nodded at the street outside. "The kid won't let Wortley bring the deputy's supper in."

Tunstall had to restrain a smile as he watched Billy extending his Winchester to block the innkeeper from the door. Jack Long, who had been standing guard inside, had gone out to argue. Tunstall heard him say, "You're spoiling for a game, punk."

Shifting his rifle to his left hand, Billy backed into the street with a smile. "Turn loose now, you sonofabitch," he said softly. "I'll give you a game."

"Get Rob," Tunstall said over his shoulder, already moving through the door. "Here, now, Billy," he called sternly. When he was close to the boy, Tunstall murmured, "Don't waste your talents. I need you for more important prey." The boy's eyes gleamed with appreciation of the compliment.

"Whatever you want, Mr. Tunstall," he said. "I'll stick by you, come hell or a flood of blood."

Tunstall felt queasy at the solemnity of the boy's vow. When Widenmann came out, Tunstall jerked his head for Rob and Billy to follow, then led them into the corral behind the store. "Take Billy and Fred out to the ranch," he told Rob, though he couldn't stop throwing glances at the boy, marveling at the cool way he'd challenged Dolan's henchman. "Allow the posse to attach the cattle only if they leave them on my range. If they try to take them, ride fast and let me know." He looked directly at Billy when he said, "I don't want anyone hurt if we can help it." Then he told Widenmann, "Get going, I'll join you directly."

Tunstall watched them walk toward the stable to saddle their horses, then went back inside to tell Corbet he was leaving to visit Chisum and would return to the Feliz.

His ride to the Pecos was a waste of time. Chisum was still in Las Vegas, and his brother Pitzer declined to enter the fray to any degree. Bitterly disappointed, Tunstall returned on his long, lonely ride into the mountains. He forced himself to dismiss Chisum from his plans, cynically laughing at himself for expecting anything from the crafty old rancher.

It was dark when he finally arrived home. Brewer was there. As they sat late by the fire discussing the situation, only once did Tunstall betray the bitterness he felt for Chisum. Watching Billy come into the kitchen and help himself to another piece of pie, Tunstall told Brewer, "I was counting on Chisum's backing, but now when it's needed, the wily old cuss is nowhere around."

"Didn't he leave orders," Brewer asked, "to supply men at your request?"

"He told me he would," Tunstall answered. "But according to his brother, they don't want any part of the feud. That's the word he used. Damn it, Dick! Neither Mac nor I would have butted up against Dolan without believing Chisum was behind us."

"I know it," Brewer said. "But there's nothing to do now but follow it through."

Seeing Billy watching from the kitchen, Tunstall asked, "What do you think of the high and mighty Cattle King of the Pecos, Billy?"

Billy shook his head. "I heard a lot of dirt about Chisum from John Jones, but nothing strikes me colder than a man going back on his word."

Tunstall nodded. "I feel the same," he said.

In the morning, Tunstall gathered his men around him. Including the three drovers taken on as his herd had grown, there were now ten men in his employ. They all watched attentively as he explained the situation.

"We're going to abide by the law," Tunstall said. "They may round up the herd to cut out any cattle they can prove belong to Mac, but we know there aren't any. Don't let them take the cattle and offer me replevin. If they try that, let me know immediately. I'll take five men to herd the horses Brady already exempted from attachment back to Lincoln. Gauss, load up a wagon with enough food to last a week. Fred, you drive the team. We'll stay at Mac's." He looked back at Gauss. "I'm leaving you in charge. Keep the men out watching the cattle around the clock, and send a rider in to report to me if anything happens."

The old man nodded and got busy loading the wagon. When the small herd of horses had been gathered, and Fred had started the team toward the road to Lincoln, Gauss watched Tunstall and his men herding the horses toward Pajarito Canyon. Tunstall looked back at his ranch, seeming forlorn with the empty corral and the wispy thread of smoke from the chimney above the old man standing alone in the door of the hut.

With Billy and Hendry on either side, and Brewer and Middleton on drag, Tunstall and Widenmann rode in front of the herd of horses as point. Widenmann was still fuming over the posse trying to attach the cattle.

Tunstall soon grew weary of his friend's spiel. "Never mind," he said with fatigue. "The hardest thing is to do nothing, and that's what we'll do. They'll hang themselves, wait and see."

"Jesse Evans was with them," Widenmann said.

"With the posse?" Tunstall laughed. "How ridiculously absurd."

"You wouldn't have thought so if you'd been there. He knows I have a warrant for his arrest, and he sassed right up to my face, asking when I would serve it. 'Anytime you're ready, make your move,' he said, grinning with his hand so close to his gun it was hot."

"What did you say back?" Tunstall asked unhappily.

"I said when I was ready to arrest him, he'd be the first to know. I was scared, I'll tell you. It's his eyes. They're so bright—like a mad-man's—you know he's capable of anything."

Tunstall smiled. "Maybe everyone overestimates Jesse. Billy's not afraid of him."

"Hell, I'm afraid of Billy, too," Widenmann murmured.

Just then Billy yelled from behind, "Hey, look at the turkeys! Can we shoot some and have Sebrian cook 'em up for supper, Mr. Tunstall?"

"You may if you can," he answered with a laugh, twisting in his saddle to smile back at the boy.

Billy drew his pistol and spurred his horse after the birds. Shooting one's head off, he leaned low to grab the carcass from the ground, then held it high, dripping blood, for Tunstall to see.

Tunstall grinned and turned away, realizing the last few weeks had left his men tense with dammed-up aggression. Pulling his Winchester, he handed it to Widenmann. "Why don't you join them?"

"Will you come?" he asked eagerly.

"No, I'll stay with the herd," Tunstall said.

He watched Widenmann leap into the melee of horses darting this way and that as the men chased the shiny dark birds. A few of the turkeys lumbered into the air and attempted to fly. The smart ones stayed on the ground, ducking hoofs.

Tunstall trotted along with the herd, which had picked up speed at the noise of the guns. Following the old Indian trail down Pajarito Canyon toward Lincoln, Tunstall felt very much the boss, the man in control. When he heard horses galloping from behind, he turned around to see Jesse Evans, Frank Baker, and Buck Morton riding hard to overtake him. Tunstall reined up and waited. When they had come close and their horses were prancing to a stop, Tunstall asked pleasantly, "Are you with the posse?"

"You might say that," Jesse answered, pulling his pistol.

For one brief instant, John Tunstall knew he had misjudged the corruption of his enemies. He saw it clearly now, too late. As death belched from the barrel of Jesse's gun, Tunstall's last thought was chagrin at his own naïveté.

Billy had watched Tunstall rein around and trot after the herd, moving at a good clip down the arroyo. They would be in Lincoln in a few hours. Sebrian would cook up a turkey dinner, and later, Billy might slip off and visit Tulles on the sly. He laughed as he took aim at another bird, then frowned, thinking he heard thunder. With a sharp recoil of attention, he realized it was the rumble of many horses cresting the ridge. He whirled around to catch sight of Tunstall, but the Englishman had disappeared down the canyon.

Bullets started pinging around the men just as Widenmann yelped, "Posse!"

"I'll get Tunstall," Middleton grunted, digging in his spurs and galloping down the arroyo.

"Take cover!" Brewer shouted, spurring his horse toward an outcrop of rocks.

Billy followed Brewer with Hendry and Widenmann, all of them jumping off and bellying over their Winchesters aimed at the posse galloping down the slope just out of range. Middleton came barreling back across the meadow through heavy fire. He gained the rocks and swung off to join the others as bullets kicked up dust in his path. Through a crevice in the rocks, Billy watched three riders break free of the posse and hightail it down the canyon. The posse retreated into the cover of the trees, leaving the forest seemingly deserted.

Suddenly two shots rang out, then another, followed by the agonized scream of a horse. Then there was only the snorting and shuffling of the posse's mounts as they left, camouflaged in the deepening shadows. Birds started to sing again, their happy melody jarring into the gloom of Billy's numbing apprehension. His eyes scanned the forest, his finger on the trigger of the rifle the Englishman had given him.

Finally Middleton said what they all knew to be true. "They killed Tunstall."

Brewer's voice spurred them to action. "We have to warn Mac."

Billy sprang onto his gray mare and waited for the others. Widenmann was already starting down the hill when Hendry Brown asked, "What about Tunstall?"

Widenmann stopped and looked down to where the Englishman had last been seen. The sun had slid behind the peaks and twilight filled the canyon, the shadows in the forest already dark. "They could have left snipers to pick us off," Widenmann whined. "We should ride into town and send a wagon back in daylight."

"Let's go," Brewer said, urging his horse past Widenmann to take the lead.

Billy considered staying behind and tending the corpse of his friend, but there was bound to be a fight in Lincoln, and more than anything, he wanted to be in it.

Blood dripping from a severed throat. Shiny dark bird, wings limp, feet kicking, head shot to hell. The Englishman grinning congratulations then turning away, alone, unarmed, even his rifle loaned to a friend. Shot down by Jesse Evans, laughing, no doubt. Ticket to hell is what Jesse was gonna get. Sure shot on the whistle of Billy's bullet.

Little gray mare swift and sure. Hooves striking with vengeance. The men ahead using whips, he only lying into her mane, letting it sting his face for a reason to cry. Creak of leather, slap of reins, the men silent cauldrons of murder. Riding behind so they wouldn't see his face. Had to pull it together, crease it into iron, smother the hurt with a joke so he could laugh when he spit at Jesse's soul falling into hell.

On the road to Stanton, Widenmann yanked his horse to a stop and barked out orders: "Dick, you and the others go into town and wait for us. I'll take Billy and tell Mac."

Brewer looked at Billy. "That okay with you?"

Billy nodded, feeling numb. When Widenmann reined his tired horse toward the fort and kicked it into a gallop again, Billy fell in behind, though he regretted agreeing to follow him. There was sure to be a fight in Lincoln, but here he was riding with a coward to tell a pacifist their friend had been murdered. Fools, both of them. Hadn't John Tunstall just proved what the law got you?

As they trotted into the fort, officers glared at Billy's Winchester. He kept it in his hand. The county was at war. He knew it even if they were still ignorant. He also knew where he stood, which wasn't a place he'd chosen to fight from but where he'd found friends. He carried the Winchester the slain man had given him into the room where the lawyer was.

McSween had been writing a letter to his wife while Barrier smoked his pipe before the fire. Mac looked up as Rob and Billy came in without knocking. Widenmann looked ill, the kid clutched a rifle. Slowly Mac rose to his feet.

"They've killed John!" Widenmann gasped.

"No," Mac whispered.

"We saw them! It was Jesse Evans and . . ."

"Morton and Baker," Billy said. "Hindman, Hill, and Roberts were with 'em, along with about fifteen others."

"My God!" Mac moaned, sinking to his knees and hiding his face in his hands. Into his anguish, Billy's voice cut deep.

"We best do something about it," the kid said.

Mac leaned his weight on the table and pulled himself up. "Yes," he murmured, wiping a hand across his face as if he could erase the horror. "Yes," he said again, looking at Barrier. "I must go to Lincoln."

"All right," the deputy said, his pipe cold in his hand.

"I'll get your horses," Billy said. "Where are they?"

The lawyer was staring at the fire and Widenmann looked lost. It was Barrier who said, "The stable's to the right. A hostler'll be there. He knows."

Billy felt better outside in the cold. To his way of thinking, there wasn't room in life for sorrow, only action.

The hostler didn't waste time getting the horses. Billy led them back to the quarters and opened the lawyer's door, watching the three grim faces file past him. He followed along, feeling scorn for their clumsy, inept pace.

It was close to midnight when they reached Lincoln. As they rode past the darkened Big Store, Billy felt eyes in every window, though no one was visible. From the center of town, he heard a droning rumble. They rounded the bend and saw the street in front of Tunstall's store crowded with riders. Light from the windows shone on the faces of fifty men ready to fight.

In the shock of apprehension, McSween stopped. An army stood waiting to avenge Tunstall's death, looking to the lawyer for leadership, not knowing he was paralyzed by his aversion to war. Billy nudged his horse up alongside and said softly, "Mr. Mac, all you gotta do is get through 'em to the house."

Mac nodded and followed the kid's lead. Before them was the home Sue had decorated with such loving attention. But when Mac walked into the parlor, she wasn't there. Only Sebrian solicitously taking his coat, Dick Brewer with red eyes, and two more gunmen, Middleton and Brown, with grim, hard faces. Mac sat down heavily before the fire and looked at Brewer. "Tell me how it happened," Mac petitioned.

"We were bringing the horses Brady exempted back to town," Brewer began slowly, as if trying to put it together for himself. "Tunstall thought they'd be safer here. He didn't want anyone hurt, Mac. Those were nearly his last words."

"We were following the old Indian trail through Pajarito Canyon," Widenmann interrupted. "We'd just crested the ridge when this flock of turkeys flew up right in front of us. We left him alone when we went after the birds."

"And then the posse came down on top of us," Brewer said. "Middleton was nearest to Tunstall. He yelled for John to follow us as we took cover."

"The posse was firing at us!" Widenmann cried. "There was no matter of presenting a warrant to make an arrest. They rode up shooting at us!"

"When they found Tunstall," Brewer said, "it got real quiet. Then we heard shots and knew they'd killed him."

"Where is he?" Mac asked.

"We were worried you'd be next," Widenmann said. "We rode fast to tell you what happened."

Mac looked at him hard. "You loved him, yet left his body in the mountains alone?"

No one answered, remembering the lonely sloping meadow where the Englishman lay abandoned.

Mac looked at Sebrian. "Will you go to Newcomb's? Ask him to help find the body and bring it to town? They won't hurt you. If I send one of these men, it might be otherwise."

"I understand, Mr. Mac," Sebrian answered, his face dark with sorrow. "I was mighty fond of Mr. Tunstall, and I'll do it, sir."

"Thank you," Mac said, staring into the fire. Finally he looked up and saw the kid by the door. "I believe I saw Atanacio Martínez outside. Call him in, Billy, will you?"

Billy slipped out and spotted the constable in the quiet crowd of men still sitting their horses. *"Oye,* Atanacio, *ven acá, por favor."*

The constable dismounted, his face full of misery. Billy motioned him through the door and followed him into the parlor.

"Ah, Martínez," Mac said, standing up. "I have witnesses here to the murder of John Tunstall. They wish to swear out affidavits in order to have Squire Wilson issue warrants for the murderers' arrest."

Martínez looked around the room cagily. "I am greatly distressed for the killing of the Englishman," he said. "We all are, all of us outside. But we came before that. We came because he," he nodded at Widenmann, "and Señor Brewer came to our houses and asked us to fight against Dolan and the Banditti. This we will do and proudly, in the name of John Tunstall and all the men The House has killed. An eye for an eye, the Bible says, and so we believe. Kill the men of The House and we will have peace again."

"John Tunstall wouldn't want that," Mac said quickly. "These men were witnesses to his murder. With warrants, we can arrest and hang the killers in the name of the law. Without warrants we're a mob, and our violence will be as hideous as theirs."

Martínez considered. "Who are the men you wish warrants against?"

"Jesse Evans, Buck Morton, and Frank Baker for starters," Billy said.

Martínez looked over his shoulder at the kid, then back at McSween. "You already have warrants for those men. He has them," thrusting his chin at Widenmann.

"Those are for larceny," Mac argued. "We want warrants for murder against all the men in the posse. Also Sheriff Brady, who is legally responsible."

Martínez balked. "You expect me to arrest Sheriff Brady?"

Billy pulled his pistol and nudged it into the constable's back. "I'll kill you if you don't," the kid murmured.

"Here now!" Mac said, hurrying forward to take the arm of Martínez and lead him to the table. Providing the constable with paper and pen, Mac said sternly, "We're ready to give our affidavits."

First Dick Brewer, then John Middleton, and finally Billy Bonney stood before the constable and gave sworn statements as to what had happened in the gloomy canyon some seven hours before. Mac listened as the story was told three times, each man describing events from a slightly different vantage point, yet each tale culminating with the terrible deed.

Mac tried to imagine what Tunstall had been thinking as he faced Jesse Evans alone. Doubting that John had suffered any apprehension of being murdered, Mac suspected he may even have surrendered his weapon in the belief they wouldn't harm him simply because they promised not to. John Tunstall would not have resisted a legal posse. Yet evidently he had planned to react with force, because he'd sent Widenmann and Brewer about the countryside in search of warriors.

Aware of the sudden silence, Mac looked up from the fire and studied the faces around him. They would be formidable fighters, but Mac was not a general. His skills at aggression were honed to procedures of law. He could fight only by manipulating the threads of legal machinery outside the Ring's control: Justice of the Peace Squire Wilson, and Constable of the First Precinct Atanacio Martínez. They were his only tools and he was free to use them only by the grace of Deputy Sheriff Barrier, who courageously refused to surrender him to Brady.

But though McSween would not fight, had in fact agreed to a clause that invalidated his life insurance if he picked up a weapon, he understood that he needed the protection of these men to remain alive. He met the eyes of Brewer and spoke softly: "Go outside, will you, Dick? Choose the men you wish to have behind you and send the rest home. Thank them for coming. Tell them we hope they'll carry our cause in their hearts and help us when God gives them the choice."

The men in the room had been waiting for his decision. Now that it was made, the lethargy of grief gave way to the anticipation of action as they listened to the sounds of Brewer's selection filtering through the open door. Brewer came back inside followed by Frank McNab, Doc Scurlock, Big Jim Finlay, George and Frank Coe, Charlie Bowdre, Francisco Trujillo, Hijenio Salazar, and Martín Chavez.

Watching them find places to stand in the elegant parlor of his wife, seeing the pistols on each man's hip, the *bandoleras* of ammunition across their chests and the rifles held in crooked elbows or resting on the floor beside dusty, bespurred boots, Mac felt doomed. A passage from Job returned to his memory and he repeated in his mind the words of the ancient martyr: I was not in safety, neither had I rest, neither was I quiet; yet trouble came.

Slowly Mac stood up to address his men. "Gentlemen," he began in his best courtroom diction, "when the laws of a community have been perverted, it is necessary for its citizens to band together and reassert the virtue of justice. This is traditional in a democratic country, where the private citizen is inherently equal with officers of the law except for a piece of paper. A warrant is justification for detention; an indictment is justification for trial. There was no warrant extant on John Tunstall, therefore the fact that the men who shot him down wore badges and were part of an official posse does not make their murder legal. With the depositions we have made tonight, we shall secure warrants for the killers. Squire Wilson will issue them legally from his precinct court, and Constable Martínez will serve them legally wearing a badge of authority. We, gentlemen, shall become the law of Lincoln long enough to thwart the perversion of legality that exists now. We will call ourselves 'Regulators,' because that will be our aim: to regulate justice back on its true course, to regulate lawbreakers whether they wear a badge or not. And, this is most important, gentlemen, to regulate the violence that threatens to engulf us in a veritable sea of blood, to channel that violence, which is born of righteous wrath over the murder of our friend, to regulate our revenge within procedure of law, so that we will succeed in bringing our enemies to account for their crime, and not fall ourselves into the pit they have dug, the sham of justice that exists here now."

Fifteen voices clamored assent and vowed fidelity to the cause. Constable Martínez called for silence, asked them all to raise their right hands, and swore them in as deputies legally sanctioned under the powers of the precinct court.

Suddenly the air was festive. Some men met each other's eyes and laughed because they were lawmen, others nodded at each other in recognition of their righteous intent, while still others shook hands with vows of loyalty unto death. Mac watched with approval of his success in aligning them in concerted action, noting that only Deputy Barrier seemed ill at ease.

The candles had long since burned down and not been replaced, their loss not even noticed. In the flickering light of only the fire in the hearth, Mac said, "We must try to sleep. As many of you as wish to do so may stay here. Those of you who choose to sleep elsewhere, please return early in the morning. We must move quickly on the warrants."

Slowly he pulled his watch from the pocket of his vest, opened it and stared into its face for a long moment. "It's nearly dawn now," he said. "Meet here again in three hours."

He turned away, too exhausted to hear another word. Alone in his room, Mac sank onto his knees and spent the three hours in prayer. He prayed for wisdom in the days ahead, caution in all his endeavors, and justice for his murdered friend.

21

For a man of McSween's deep religious persuasion, the prayer was more refreshing than any fitful hours of sleep he might have found. In the gray light of dawn, he opened his bedroom door on a snoring Barrier. The deputy woke with a start, stared wide-eyed at Mac for a moment, then scuttled out of his way.

Mac went into the parlor where Brewer, Middleton, Widenmann, and Brown were asleep in bedrolls on the carpet. The men's muffled snoring ceased abruptly when a knock sounded on the front door. The ensuing silence was punctuated with the metallic cocking of weapons drawn from under blankets. Mac met Brewer's eyes and said, "An assassin wouldn't bother to knock."

Winding his way through the men, Mac crossed the room to open the door. Juan Patrón stood outside, his face seamed with sorrow. The two friends exchanged condolences in a shared moment of silence, then Mac gestured for Patrón to come in.

"Let's go to the kitchen," Mac said softly, forging a path through the men with rifles and pistols now conspicuous on their blankets. As Mac entered the small room between the parlor and the kitchen, he could hear the voices of Fred Waite and Billy Bonney, apparently making breakfast. In the sanctuary that would have been a nursery if God had graced Sue with children, Mac stopped and met Patrón's eyes.

"This doesn't look good," the legislator warned.

"I didn't create the situation, Juan," Mac pleaded softly.

"But this is war," Patrón whispered. "Many men will die."

"Not if we act fast," Mac answered, taking the depositions from his pocket and handing them to Patrón. "These are sworn statements from eyewitnesses to Tunstall's murder. Through Wilson we'll issue a warrant and arrest the killers ourselves. We are the machinery of justice now. You, as territorial representative, must give us your sanction."

Patrón scanned the pages. "Constable Martínez took them?"

"Yes, and deputized the men in my parlor. We have fifteen deputies behind us, Juan, all legally sworn officers of the precinct court."

Handing the papers back, Patrón said hesitantly, "It might work."

"It has to," Mac argued. "Or there will be war."

Deputy Barrier joined them in the tiny room, his badge shining in the dim light.

"Let's go to Wilson now," Patrón said, "before Dolan gets there."

Mac replaced the depositions in his pocket and continued into the kitchen. "Good morning, Fred, Billy," he said. "If anyone asks, we'll be at Squire Wilson's."

"Don'cha want Fred and me to go with you?" Billy asked.

Mac looked at Barrier, who nodded. "All right," Mac answered. "Be quick."

The two went back into the parlor. In a moment, Middleton came out, carrying one boot. "You don't want I should go, Mr. Mac?" he asked, looking comical and half-awake.

"No, I don't need an army. We won't be long."

When Widenmann came out, looking comparatively spiffy with his hair wetted down and both boots on, Mac said, "Ah, Rob, I have something for you to do."

Widenmann's face lit up with gratitude and he followed Mac, Patrón, and Barrier into the backyard. Billy and Fred were right behind, wearing hats and coats now.

Mac turned to Widenmann. "As a federal officer, the command at Stanton is legally bound to provide troops at your request. I want you to ride over there and go directly to Purington. Tell him you're a deputy U.S. marshal with warrants for the Boys. Throw your office around, demand cooperation. Then bring the troops back here. By that time, we should have the warrants for murder, but even if not, you can arrest most of the principals for larceny and hold them until we do."

"I understand," Widenmann answered.

As he hurried toward the corral, Mac and Patrón, accompanied by Barrier, Waite, and Bonney, walked across the street and into the meadow toward Squire Wilson's house.

It was a tiny, two-room adobe, its wooden shutters closed tight. Mac had to knock loudly for a long time before the justice of the peace opened the door. Begrudgingly, Wilson asked them into his parlor. It was dark and cold.

"I'm sorry about the Englishman," he said to Mac. "But he had plenty of warning what Dolan was fixin' to do. I see you have guns behind you. That's smart. John Tunstall would be alive today if he'd worn a gun, but he never . . ."

Mac cut him off. "I have sworn statements by eyewitnesses to his murder. I want warrants issued."

"It wasn't murder," the justice hedged. "It was a posse as I understand it, and he resisted 'em."

"It was murder, Mr. Wilson," Mac stated. "I want warrants written against the killers."

Wilson looked at Patrón. "Do you support this, Mr. Representative?"

"Yes," Patrón said. "We must take the law out of their hands by acting now."

"Against Brady?" Wilson cried. "Against Dolan and the Banditti and Rynerson and the Santa Fe Ring? Are you both crazy?"

"We have evidence to hang them all," Mac answered with resolve.

Behind him, Billy said, "And we're gonna do it."

Mac turned and looked at Billy, feeling as if the kid were a half-wild horse continually in need of a tight rein. Turning back to Squire Wilson, Mac said again, "We're going to do it through the law. You are going to issue the warrants."

In a wheedling tone, Wilson said, "I can't issue a warrant for murder without a coroner's jury coming to that verdict. You know that, Mr. Mac. Where's the body?"

"It'll be along soon," Mac said. "Assemble a jury to meet at Tunstall's store. Don't shirk your duty."

Wilson looked at the kid, then at Patrón, before saying to Mac, "I'll gather a jury. You show me a body and an autopsy report."

Suddenly struck with an incongruous realization, Mac turned to Patrón. "Will you help in the selection of the jury? I've just remembered. This is terrible, Juan, but the Ealys are due to arrive today."

"Who are the Ealys?" Patrón asked.

"The Presbyterian missionary I requested be sent. He and his family are to start a church and school here."

Patrón stared at Mac for a long moment, then finally said, "He can give the service at John's funeral."

Mac nodded, painfully accepting that Tunstall was truly dead and would have to be buried. "I'll be at home," he mumbled.

Turning away, he walked back across the meadow. The town appeared empty except for himself, his two gunmen, and the deputy sheriff shadowing his heels. The silence of the street was hideous, the fear palpable around the shuttered homes.

Mac sequestered himself in his bedroom and sat at Sue's delicate desk to write a letter to John's father in London. After sitting numbly for several moments, he began: *Would to God I could in some way that would not pierce and wound your heart tell you that your son John is dead!*

He discontinued his efforts when Widenmann returned with a detachment of cavalry. Mac let him take the Regulators along as they searched the Big Store for Evans, Morton, Baker, and Hill under authority of the old warrants for larceny. Mac stayed home, keeping Hendry Brown and Billy Bonney with him. The first because of his recent connection with the opposition; the latter because Mac wanted to hold him under rein. Waiting in his parlor, he sat before the fire and prayed for Widenmann's wisdom. It was a quality the man had yet to evince, but Mac believed within God's infinite powers even Widenmann could acquire it.

Dick Brewer came back first. He stood staring pensively into the fire so long, Mac finally asked, "Did you make any arrests?"

Brewer shook his head. "They weren't around, though we could smell their stench so strong, we knew they'd just left."

"I'm glad you were there. I don't trust Rob."

Brewer snorted. "I'd as soon trust a snake not to bite me, but he got the store back. I'll give him that."

"What do you mean?" Mac asked, eager for good news.

"After we searched Dolan's place, Widenmann brought the whole bunch of us down to Tunstall's. When Brady's deputies saw us walk in with twenty-five soldiers sitting their horses outside, they vamoosed real quick."

Mac sighed. "It's something, at least." Realizing he could put the Ealys in Tunstall's rooms, he said, "Someone will have to clear out John's personal effects, and send them to his family."

"I think you should do it," Brewer said.

Mac nodded, then rose and walked out his front door. He had forgotten about Hendry and Billy and Barrier. When he heard them fall in step behind him, he glanced back. Hendry and Billy looked so young, so wholesome if not for their weapons. Mac continued on course, not believing peace could come from violence.

The store was open, Corbet glum behind the counter. Mac nodded to him, then walked to the stove and rubbed his hands together over its warmth as he looked around at the Regulators.

Middleton, Fred Waite, and Big Jim Finlay were standing guard at the windows. The Mexicans lounged near the back door. The Coe cousins and Frank McNab stood in a row leaning against bolts of cloth, and Doc Scurlock was talking softly in a corner with Charlie Bowdre. Mac sighed again, then walked into Tunstall's office to confront Widenmann alone.

"I'll take care of John's things, Rob," Mac said gently.

"He left me executor," Widenmann crowed. "It's my duty."

Mac blinked in surprise. "Do you have the document?"

Widenmann produced the paper from a drawer. Mac perused the paper quickly and dropped it on the desk. "This is simply power of attorney. It's neither a will nor any annotation to one naming you executor of his estate."

"I don't believe you," Widenmann said. "I've already written his father. I'll take care of everything."

Mac let the accusation that he was lying pass. "Should I trust you, Rob, to do the job honestly and fairly?"

"You can depend on it, Mac. I'll do right by John."

Mac was impressed with his sincerity. "I shan't obstruct you until I receive official word from John's father. In the meantime, I wonder if you could pack up John's belongings? A Presbyterian minister and his family are due to arrive today, and I'd like to quarter them in these rooms."

"Here?" Widenmann whispered.

"I'm afraid I have nowhere else," Mac explained.

"But these rooms belong to John!"

"Yes," Mac answered, losing patience, "and I'm sure you were hoping to stay here indefinitely, but it's not to be. As sole surviving partner in the construction of this building and an officer of the Bank of Lincoln, I insist you vacate these rooms."

"Where am I to go?"

"You can sleep in my parlor with the others, at least until Mrs. McSween returns."

"So I'm to be turned out," Widenmann pouted.

"Don't be so fawning!" Mac exploded. "It may have worked with John but it sickens me. You're a leech, Widenmann. I'm not worried you'll attach yourself to me because I have no wealth. But please, spare me your complaints because your provider is no longer here to care for you." He spun on his heel and walked out. As he left the store, Barrier and Billy Bonney and Fred Waite fell in behind.

Outside, he saw the Ealys approaching in their humble wagon. Although he'd never met them, Mac knew instantly who they were. The dour, bearded man in his dark frock coat had the pious look of someone certain of his own salvation. With him were two women, also clad plainly in black, and two small girls in brown homespun dresses. The wagon stopped and they all stared as Mac approached.

"Reverend Ealy?" he asked, trying to arrange a smile of welcome on his face.

"McSween?" the man demanded, his voice angry.

"Yes," he answered, hesitant now.

Ealy looked past him at Bonney and Waite and the deputy. Mac didn't have to follow the minister's eyes to know it was the guns that alarmed him. "I'm afraid," Mac said, "you've come at a difficult time. My close friend and business associate was murdered yesterday."

Understanding softened the missionary's face. "That explains why we were searched coming into town. They haven't found the man who did it yet?"

"Searched?" Mac asked, astounded. "By who?"

"Some men in front of that big building down there. When I stopped to inquire as to the location of your home, they promptly searched our belongings. For guns, they said." He stopped and looked again at the men behind McSween.

"I'm afraid you've come to what the Bible calls stony ground," Mac said. He looked at the women and children, then back to Ealy. "Perhaps we could speak privately?"

Ealy stared a moment before handing the reins to his wife and stepping down. Mac guided him to the *torreón,* then turned to gaze back up the street while they talked.

Barrier, Waite, and Bonney were between them and the wagon, standing with the nonchalance of men accustomed to holding guns for long periods of time. "I'm afraid, Reverend Ealy . . . ," Mac began.

"It's doctor," Ealy interrupted. "Besides being a doctor of divinity, I am one of medical science as well. The Presbytery determined that Lincoln was without medical service except for the surgeon at Fort Stanton. A Dr. Appel, I believe. I'm sure he can't be bothered with the common ailments that befall women and children."

"Yes," Mac said, almost laughing at the man's naive expectation of normalcy in Lincoln. "Do you have any experience with gunshot wounds?"

Ealy took a long moment to answer. "I served in the War of Rebellion," he finally said. "Am I correct in gaining the impression this town is in a state of anarchy?"

"I bow to your astute assessment, Doctor," Mac said, grateful that at least Ealy was not dense. "My friend, John Tunstall, a fine man of unblemished character, was murdered yesterday. When I heard the news, I returned to town at once and found an army gathered to avenge his death. It has been only with the greatest difficulty that I've managed to disperse and control them. The unfortunate circumstance is that our sheriff is one of the men responsible for the murder. I am striving my utmost to keep peace and pursue justice. So far I have succeeded, but for how long or to what extent only God knows. If you, sir, wish to remove your loved ones to a safer location, I would blame you not at all, and would, myself, write to the Presbytery explaining why now is not the best time to open a church in Lincoln."

"On the contrary, Mr. McSween, it would appear that the good people of Lincoln need God very much just now."

"I welcome you, then," Mac said, feeling less alone. "I will give you the particulars when we have an hour to ourselves. For now, let's settle your family into their quarters. I'm afraid they'll have to stay with my brother-in-law for the moment. He also has daughters, so the young girls will have companions." He took the missionary's arm and was about to lead him back to his family when Fred Waite said, "Here come Sebrian and Newcomb, Mr. Mac."

He could hear the wagon coming behind him. Suddenly aware he was clutching the missionary's arm, Mac couldn't bring himself to let go, feeling he must hold to someone when facing John's body for the first time.

Sebrian and Newcomb were grim as the wagon rumbled to a stop. There in the bed, Mac saw the long, still bundle wrapped in brown blankets littered with thistles. He looked at Sebrian, near tears. "Take him on into the store, will you, please?" he managed to say.

Sebrian answered, "Mr. Mac, they beat his head in."

"My God," Mac moaned, turning away. "Go along now," he mumbled over his shoulder. "I'll join you in a moment."

He waited until he heard the wagon move and stop again, then he looked up and saw Billy Bonney holding the gate open. Mac watched, forlorn, as the wagon went on into the corral and turned out of sight.

It was Ealy who spoke next. "Let's settle my family in their rooms and then look at your friend, shall we?"

"Of course," Mac answered, dabbing quickly at his eyes.

Ealy helped the women and children from the wagon. He introduced his wife and daughters, and a Miss Susan Gates, who was to teach in the new school. Greeting them as graciously as he could, Mac neither saw their faces nor registered their names. He could think only of the long inert form of his friend lying so still in the wagon.

Before him lay another chore. He walked to his brother-in-law's wing of the house and knocked on the door. David himself answered it.

He said only, "I was afraid, Mac."

"Don't trouble yourself," he murmured with compassion. "You have a family to protect." He introduced Dr. and Mrs. Ealy, then said, "I must presume upon you to take the women and children into your home for the time being. Eventually they can stay in John's rooms. Poor boy, he has no more use for them."

"All right," Shield said. Turning into the house, he called his wife. "Eliza?"

As Shield introduced her to the newcomers and explained they would be staying for a time, Mac watched slight resemblances to Sue flicker across Eliza's face. They made him miss his own wife with a sharp sting of loss. Finally Eliza smiled and took the travelers into her home. Shield remained standing in the open door. "Are you coming in, Mac?" he asked in a neutral tone.

"No, they've just brought John's body. I'll speak with you later." He turned and led Ealy back toward the store.

Inside, it was silent except for the soft clatter of the wooden shutters being closed by Corbet. All of the Regulators were there, their faces frozen, their bodies rigid. The blanket-clad bundle lay on the counter. Dick Brewer stood behind it, his face contorted with grief.

The shutters closed one by one, thudding together with a quiet metallic snap as the latches caught, darkening the room, shutting out the cold sunlight and the street and people of Lincoln. Mac stood in the middle of the floor, unable to bring himself to look at the blanket on the counter. He let his eyes rove around the room, seeing Widenmann nearly overcome in the door to John's office, Billy Bonney leaning against the wall with his hat pulled low over his eyes, John Middleton chewing nervously at his moustache, though surely he had seen death many times.

The light continued to be shut out, Corbet's quiet footsteps the only sound between the closing of another shutter and the further growth of darkness. Charlie Bowdre moved across the room, his footsteps loud, to stand by Billy. George Coe's long angular face was vibrant with anger. His cousin was staring at the floor. Trujillo and Salazar had their eyes riveted on the body. Chavez wet his lips with his tongue. Then the last shutter closed, leaving them all in twilight.

Corbet's footsteps echoed as he crossed to the center of the room and raised the wick on the lantern. With Dr. Ealy at his side, Mac approached his friend.

Widenmann joined them. Mac didn't look at him but met Brewer's eyes across the counter. Slowly, as gently as if the blankets sheltered a frightened child, Dr. Ealy lifted the corners and unwrapped the corpse. Mac and Dick and Rob let groans of horror escape at the sight of John Tunstall.

The wound in his chest had saturated his coat with blood. Another bullet had entered just below his right eye and, on exit, had taken a large piece of his skull with it. Yet that was not the most terrible: his head had been badly beaten and crushed. Mac looked away in despair. Rob leaned heavily on the cash register making dry retching sounds. Dick sobbed out, "The bastards!" and turned around to lean against the shelves of elixirs behind him.

"They shot his horse, too," Sebrian said tearfully. "They laid Mr. Tunstall out beside it neat and tidy, and put his hat under the horse's head like they was making fun of killing him." He stopped, tears running down his cheeks. "It turn my blood cold to see how they done him."

Only a grim silence answered his words. Then, one by one, the Regulators started filing past the body. Mac moved to the chair by the stove and sat down heavily, watching the solemn parade of mourners.

Groans and curses punctuated the silence, filled otherwise only by the shuffling of boots and quiet jangling of spurs. Middleton grunted, McNab shook his head, Doc Scurlock let escape a cry of dismay, Charlie Bowdre's lip snarled in silent disgust. Hendry Brown made a spitting sound as he walked past, the Mexicans muttered curses in Spanish, and Big Jim Finlay whispered, "Goddamn sonsofbitches." Tears ran down the cheeks of Fred Waite, and the Coes looked at each other with an enviable intimacy of sharing.

Billy Bonney finally pulled himself away from the wall and walked toward the body, fixing his hat only at the last moment so his face was hidden as he crossed the room. He stood staring down at the Englishman for several long moments. Then he said softly, "I'll kill 'em all. I swear it."

The door opened, flooding the room with sunlight. At first only a silhouette could be seen against the glare, then Juan Patrón limped in and closed the door. From that distance, he stared at the battered and bloodied face of the slain man. After several long moments he said, "The coroner's jury is ready. Dr. Appel's to perform the autopsy. Brady's paying him a hundred dollars to do it, though the money's from Dolan, of course."

"A hundred dollars!" Ealy scoffed. "That's ten times the usual fee. It's robbery."

"No," Mac replied with fatigue, forcing himself to his feet. "It's bribery, Dr. Ealy."

"Doctor?" Patrón asked.

Mac introduced them.

"He can assist with the autopsy," Patrón said. "We'll make our own report."

Mac turned to Ealy. "Will you help us?"

"I would consider it, as all duties I assume, a service to God. This man has obviously met with vicious battering, and the perpetrators must be brought to justice."

"You see," Mac said to the room at large. "We shall prevail, gentlemen, through the law." He could feel doubt in their minds, but also that they were waiting to give his method a chance. When he looked for Billy, however, the kid was nowhere to be seen. Mac could only assume he had left in the blinding glare of Patrón's entrance.

"Cover the body again, will you, Dick?" Mac asked, moving toward Fred Waite. Dick complied without hesitation as the other men moved away, muttering among themselves. Mac touched the sleeve of Waite's coat. "Go outside and find Billy, will you, Fred?" he asked softly. "Bring him back if you can."

Fred nodded and crossed quickly to slip out the back door. He stood blinking in the bright sunlight until he spotted Billy sitting on the far wall of the corral, facing the river. Quietly Fred approached. When he was a few steps away, he stopped and said, "Kid?"

Billy didn't turn around. "What're you doing out here, Fred?"

"Mr. Mac sent me to look for you."

"You found me."

Fred thought a minute. "You want I should leave you be?"

Billy turned around and gave him a small smile. "If you're gonna stay, why don'cha come over here? It's hard talking to somebody behind me."

Fred climbed onto the adobe wall a few feet away from Billy and looked down into the rusty winter colors filling the valley, the mountain pale with rocks rising beyond the river into a bright blue sky. "It don't make sense," Fred said.

"What's that?" Billy asked.

"This place is so pretty," Fred said, not looking at him. "The land, the sky, the water. It don't make sense that it can be so mean and vicious at the same time."

"You got any smoke?" Billy asked.

"Yeah," Fred answered. He fumbled in his pocket and pulled out his makings. But when he tried to roll the cigarette, his hands shook so he couldn't keep the tobacco in the paper.

With a patient smile, Billy took the makings and started over. Fred watched as he deftly rolled a cigarette and offered it back to him. He took it and watched Billy roll another. "I didn't know you used tobacco," Fred finally said.

"I don't much," Billy said, striking a match and lighting their smokes.

"You sure rolled 'em good. Took me a long time to learn to do it that well."

Billy shrugged. "I'm good with my hands."

"Good with a gun," Fred said, before he knew he would.

"So?" Billy asked, smiling and showing his crooked teeth through the smoke.

"Did you mean it, what you said in there?"

"What do you think?"

Fred looked down at the river, icy in the winter sun. "There must've been twenty of 'em, Billy. You gonna kill 'em all?"

"No, jus' the three. Evans, Morton, and Baker. They're the ones kicked his head in like that."

"And Dolan?"

"Jimmie Dolan ain't shit to me," the kid said, his voice calm. "It's like in a game of monte: it don't matter who the bank is, I play the hand. All that talk about money, like Brown and Middleton are always spouting, don't matter to me. It's the hand. Jesse Evans dealt it, I'm gonna play it back with Jesse. I don't care who's backing who or whose side bet wins or loses. It's my game and I'll play it."

Carefully Fred asked, "Why is it your game, Billy? I want to see justice done too, but I'm hoping Mr. Mac's way wins out and we don't have to do any killing."

"I ain't got faith in Mr. Mac's way," Billy answered. "But I'll go along with it till I see an opportunity otherwise. Is that what he sent you to find out?"

"You make me sound like a spy!"

"If you were, you wouldn't be my friend." Billy smiled, jumping down from the wall. "Want to go back inside now?"

"Yeah," Fred said, jumping down to follow him.

Mac felt relieved to see them return. Having heard of the kid's challenge of the deputy outside Tunstall's store, he considered Billy the least predictable and most independent of the men assembled. Not entirely glad to have the kid on his side, Mac ended his thoughts on the subject as his friend John Tunstall had once ended his: by being grateful Billy wasn't among his enemies.

22

When the time came for Atanacio Martínez to select men to help arrest the sheriff, he chose Billy Bonney and his friend Fred Waite. Bonney because the kid had *mucho cojones,* and Waite because he would follow the kid without hesitation. Having heard rumors that the kid had a killing in his past, Martínez had lost any doubt of their veracity when he felt the kid's pistol poking into his back.

Martínez was a constable. He knew men who bluffed, raised hell to stir up a smokescreen to hide their cowardice, or overestimated their abilities and trapped themselves in their own havoc. A keen desire for survival had also taught him to recognize the men who did none of those things but came at you with a deadly calm, and he put Billy Bonney in that category. The kid hadn't jabbed his pistol into the constable's back; he'd nudged it with a gentle yet undeniable pressure. And his voice had been soft when he'd uttered his threat, intended to be heard only by the man who needed to hear it, not an audience across the room.

So when Martínez stopped outside the door of Squire Wilson's house to give his men instructions, it was the kid he looked at. They were on a fool's errand, in the constable's opinion, and his only goal was to come out alive. His hope for actually making the arrests was nil.

Brady and Dolan weren't alone inside the Big Store. By the congestion of horses in Wortley's corral, Martínez guessed they had at least twenty men with them. He reasoned that if he had chosen to go with all of the Regulators they would likely be shot down before they ever got inside, whereas three men was a delegation small enough to make Dolan's men feel safe. Billy Bonney tipped the scale just enough to let them know if they tried anything stupid, some of them would die.

Martínez looked at the kid, whose eyes were dancing in anticipation, and said sternly, "We'll fire only in defense." He shifted his gaze to Waite, who nodded, then looked back at Billy. "We have a warrant for six men. They're the only ones we can legally take. If the sheriff tries to stop us, we'll have to arrest him, too, for obstructing a peace officer. I'd like to do it without getting killed."

Billy grinned. "That's the ticket."

"*Pinche*," the constable swore, impatient with the kid's levity.

"*Chingada las madres de esos hombres malos,*" Billy replied.

Martínez laughed. The kid could swear like a Mexican, and he liked that. "*Andale, pues,*" he said, turning and starting down the empty street toward The House. He adjusted his gunbelt as he walked, sliding his forty-five in and out of its holster a couple of times to make sure it would be there without a hitch.

Mac was at home, waiting with Brewer and the other Regulators for the return of the constable and his men. Dr. Ealy and Frank Coe were embalming the body. Sebrian Bates was digging the grave.

Squire Wilson had worked from a copy of the autopsy report presented by Juan Patrón, so its integrity couldn't be doubted even though its contents were blatantly biased. Dr. Appel had described two wounds on the corpse, the one to the chest enough to topple the man from his horse, the one to the head instantaneously fatal. He had specifically declared that no violence had been done to the deceased other than those

194   Elizabeth Fackler

wounds, adding with excessive redundance that no part of the body had been mutilated. Attributing the severe fracture of the skull to a thinness caused by venereal disease, he had officially blemished the character of a man beyond defense. Dr. Ealy had written his own, contrary opinion in his diary. It was not official, but at least the truth had been recorded.

The coroner's verdict stated that "John Tunstall came to his death on the 18th day of February, 1878, by means of diverse bullets shot and sent forth out of and from deadly weapons, then and there held by the men whose names are herewith written." Squire Wilson had issued the warrant with a shaking hand, fearful of the consequences but bound by duty. McSween knew his law.

When the three men reached the Big Store and Martínez paused a moment at the bottom of the steps, Billy smiled at the constable's hesitation, then gave Fred a playful grin. Fred didn't smile back.

"Let's go," Martínez said.

Their footsteps were loud, the jangle of their spurs too shrill somehow. When Martínez opened the door, Billy felt the expected blast of warmth carrying the fragrance of dry goods, but only after he had crossed the threshold did he realize it was the silence that was wrong. A split second later he saw two dozen rifles and pistols aimed at him and his friends.

Brady stood with one boot on a crate, his hand on his knee only inches from his revolver. Dolan leaned against the counter, his ankles crossed and his arms folded. They were both smiling, surrounded by a firing squad. Billy cursed silently.

"You fellas come to buy candy?" Brady taunted.

Martínez took a deep breath and held up the warrant he carried. "I've come to make arrests, Sheriff. I ask your assistance in the performance of my duty."

Brady guffawed. "Who taught you to speak them words, Atanacio? I'd bet my last dollar they're straight from the mouth of McSween."

Spotting Jesse Evans smirking in a corner, Billy took a step to the side so he'd have a clear line when the shooting started. Their eyes met, and Jesse's smile grew friendlier. Billy's eyes didn't change. When Jesse realized he was facing a mortal enemy, his smile became brittle.

Martínez's voice was a shade too high when he said, "I have a warrant for the arrest of six men in this room."

"Who might they be?" Brady mocked.

Martínez rattled the warrant open to read the names, but he wasn't quick enough.

"Jesse Evans," Billy said. "Frank Baker, Buck Morton, Tom Hill, George Hindman, and Buckshot Roberts."

Brady looked at him hard. "Who the hell are you?"

"Goes by the name of Billy Bonney," Jesse snickered.

Brady turned back to the constable. "I want you outta here, Martínez. Go tell McSween his plan didn't work."

Atanacio took a step forward. "I am constable of the First Precinct and I came to serve a warrant issued from my court. If you try to stop me, I will arrest you, too."

"Bull*shit* you will! *You're* under arrest, all three of you! Somebody get their guns."

The rifles were already aimed and cocked, the hammers on the pistols suddenly drawn back with warning. Billy hated every man in the room because they all stood for Tunstall's murder. Wanting to blaze away with his Winchester until he was cut down, he watched Martínez raise his hands in the air, then cast his gaze sideways and saw Fred's go up, too.

"It's suicide, Billy," Fred whispered.

Over his shoulder, Atanacio said, *"Hay un otro día, chivato."*

Slowly Billy relinquished his purpose and raised his hands. As Atanacio had said, there would be another day. Feeling his pistol lifted from its holster, he turned to see Jesse handling it with familiarity.

"Good balance," Jesse said. "Bet it shoots real straight, don't it, kid?"

Billy figured he had a chance to get his Winchester into position and shoot Evans before someone shot him.

Jesse grinned. "I'll take that rifle." Reaching up to grab the barrel, he slid the gun from Billy's hand. "Pity we couldn't be friends," Jesse said with a wink, carrying the weapons to Brady.

Billy watched his Winchester being laid on the counter. The rifle meant a lot to him, and he meant to get it back. He looked at Brady. "What are we under arrest for?"

"Creating a public nuisance," the sheriff answered. Looking straight at him, Brady growled, "Handcuff 'em."

It was bear-mauled George Hindman who came up behind Billy, the metal shackles clanking loudly. "Put yer hands behind yer back," the deputy ordered.

Billy did it, holding to his hunger for revenge as the only force strong enough to prevent his instant attack. Fred obviously felt no happier at having his wrists shackled behind his back. He and Billy looked at each other and managed to share a silent message of mutual encouragement. When Hindman approached Martínez, Brady stopped him.

"Not him. It ain't right, one lawman arresting another, not where I come from." He looked at Hindman. "Take some men and escort the prisoners to jail. Atanacio can stay here with me."

Martínez turned and murmured to his men in Spanish, "Don't worry that you'll be there long."

The jail was a hole cold as a grave, the air damp and foul with the stench of a slop bucket that had been emptied but never washed. The darkness was absolute, a yawning pit in front of his eyes, a void of unknown shape or substance. Billy stood in a silence ominous with rage at being trapped by his enemies. Then, in the interest of preserving his sanity, he laughed.

"You ain't got a match, have you, Fred?" he asked as casually as if they were walking down the street.

Fred dug out his makings, extracted a wooden match from the bundle, and struck it against the sole of his boot.

The room was twenty feet square and all dirt. In the walls, nubs of candles protruded from niches dug out of the earth.

Billy exulted under his breath, "Sonofabitch!"

Fred complained, "They could've told us they were there."

The match burnt his fingers and he dropped it, crossed in the darkness to the nearest candle, and struck another match to grace the hole with a dim flickering light.

Billy grinned and asked, "Want to play some monte?"

Half a mile away, Tunstall's grave was ready in the empty lot east of his store. The mourners were gathered under a bright winter sun that teased them with warmth while the cold wind permeated their clothes like slivers of ice. The few Mexican women who had dared to attend were swaddled in black rebozos covering their hair and falling halfway down the sweep of their dark skirts. They stood holding rosaries in gloved hands, their fingers praying for peace.

The men were huddled inside coats tucked behind pistols worn on their hips. Their elbows cradled rifles, their hands stuck deep in their pockets because they had sacrificed the comfort of gloves in the interest of getting their finger on a trigger at hairsplitting notice. All of the Mexican men who lived in the village were there. All of the men who had waited in front of the slain man's store to avenge his death were gathered again, their bitterness softened by the ritual of sorrow before them.

The pallbearers were Brewer, Widenmann, and George and Frank Coe. They were followed by McSween taking the place of family. Dr. Ealy carried his Bible close to his breast as he marched in the solemn procession. Behind him came Miss Gates, who wore a black veil concealing her face. Sue's piano had been moved to the graveside and Mrs. Ealy played a hymn. The music was soft and melancholy falling on the mourners as they all stood in silence, the wind whipping their clothes as they watched John Tunstall lowered into his grave. The pallbearers stepped back, turning away to hide their faces from the crowd.

Susan Gates watched from behind her veil. At twenty-two, she was considered an old maid, yet she was vibrantly alive and the company of so many men passionate with emotion fascinated her. They stood straight as Indians, their faces brown from living outdoors, virile with the fire of anger behind the agony in their eyes, vulnerable because the pain was so poorly disguised despite their efforts.

One of the pallbearers especially held her attention. She had noticed him before because he was nearly always with McSween. She'd managed to overhear the lawyer call him Dick, and later she'd heard Brewer attached to it, so she knew his name, but she doubted that he'd even noticed a single woman had arrived with the new minister.

She let her gaze roam across the faces, protected by her black veil. She had always disliked wearing it, believing the emblem of deep mourning in deference to someone she hadn't known made her a professional mourner, a role too morbid for her taste. Dr. Ealy insisted, however, saying it decorated his services with dignity. Today, for the first time, she felt glad of its protection because it allowed her to examine the men without seeming rude.

Few of them were listening to the eulogy. After each sentence, Ealy would stop and a short, round man ridiculously named Squire Wilson— if Susan had heard correctly—translated the sermon into Spanish, his squeaky voice calling across to the earnest faces of the Mexicans. They hung on each syllable as if truth could be found in the words of a holy man. Perhaps it could, Susan thought, but she had yet to meet a holy man. Still, their sincerity touched her.

The Americans looked mostly at the ground. Occasionally one's eyes would lock on the grave with evident disbelief, then a stony resolve would harden his face as he looked away. Sometimes, when they did this, she saw them touch their weapons.

Fred Waite, the young man she'd recognized as having some Choctaw blood, wasn't among the mourners. Knowing a few words of the Choctaw language, she had spoken them quietly in the kitchen the night before. He seemed as shocked as if she were a ghost. Then he laughed and looked at his friend Billy, who had a pleasing smile despite his crooked teeth. Billy made her feel at ease, maybe because he seemed so simple and kind, his eyes always laughing as if he were a child who could see no great wrong in the world.

Fred Waite's eyes were solemn with the knowledge of injustice. As if coaxing a wild animal, she gently repeated the Choctaw greeting. Fred wiped his hands on his trousers before responding. Then he and Billy had gone back to the parlor, leaving her without knowing if her gesture was welcome. She had looked forward to seeing Fred again this morning, but neither he nor his friendly companion was there.

Reverend Ealy's eulogy finished on a crescendo of anguish, and Squire Wilson squeaked an anticlimactic mimicry that would have been funny to a happier congregation. Here they listened in silence, then bowed their heads when Ealy raised his hands and voiced a prayer for the redemption of the beloved departed and the reassuring hope, nay certitude, that he would one day be reunited with his family in heaven.

Mrs. Ealy began playing "Nearer My God to Thee" as Mr. McSween led the mourners to file past and drop clods of earth onto the coffin. When he turned to leave, he walked straight toward Susan Gates, his face so crumpled with grief she longed to comfort him. Following him into his home, she took his overcoat and removed her veil and cloak, then hung them by the door. Her long black veil was the only emblem of mourning in the room.

Facing him where he stood with his back to the fire, she asked, "Is there anything I might do for you, Mr. McSween?"

He shook his head. "I regret that your arrival has come at such a difficult time."

"You mustn't trouble yourself about us," she replied. "We do God's work wherever we are."

He studied her a moment, as if finally really seeing her, then said, "You seem a capable woman, Miss Gates. I hope the days ahead are not too hard on you."

"I worked for two years among the refugees in the Indian Nation," she answered. "The shame of their poverty and humiliation was torturous to bear, yet I was able to act effectively in many individual cases. Whatever challenges Lincoln holds, I shall rise to serve God among the people. So I ask again, Mr. McSween, is there anything I can do now?"

He sighed. "There is to be a meeting here shortly. If you could serve coffee, it would be a blessing to all. It's so cold, the men will need something to warm themselves."

"How many will be attending?" she asked, expecting him to say half a dozen, more or less.

"Near thirty, I believe," he said. "Coffee, and perhaps some biscuits and marmalade. Poor John, no one's organized a proper wake. Though he was highly respected, I don't want you to think otherwise."

"I can see the men's regard for him in their grief," she murmured. "I'll start the coffee, if they're expected soon."

"Yes, immediately." He sighed again. "And Miss Gates, a prayer for the reign of reason would not be out of order."

She smiled and left for the kitchen. Standing over the stove was the tall Negro, Sebrian Bates. He wiped tears from his eyes as she came in, eclipsing his sorrow behind a mask of professional demeanor. Susan crossed the room and touched his arm. "I'm sorry, Sebrian, for the loss of your friend."

"Thank you, ma'am," he sniffed. "I started the coffee and biscuits. Mr. Mac expects a lot of men and I expect 'em, too. I expect a lot more than Mr. Mac does."

"What do you mean?" she asked. "More guests?"

"No, ma'am. Don't mind me. I'm used to sharing my 'pinions with Mrs. Mac. I surely wish she was here. Mr. Mac depends on her mightily."

"Where is she?" Susan asked, tying an apron around her waist.

"She went back East last Christmas. Living in Lincoln got to be hard on her nerves."

When Susan looked at him with sudden understanding, Sebrian nodded as if satisfied that he'd imparted a message she deserved to hear.

" 'Scuse me," he said. "I've got to cover the grave now the service is over."

She watched him go, felt the blast of cold as he pulled the door closed against the wind, then was left alone in the kitchen with the hiss of simmering coffee and the soft fluttering of the flames in the stove. Hearing the men begin to arrive, she found a tray and set out cups and saucers, knowing she would need two or three trips to carry enough. She lifted the tray, balanced it on one arm, took the coffeepot in her other hand, and entered the parlor.

At the threshold she nearly stopped at the sight of thirty rifles stacked by the door. She swallowed hard and carried the coffee and cups to the table, set them down, and escaped back to the kitchen.

She had no time to be frightened, even though her heart was pounding as she pulled biscuits from the oven and piled them on a platter. She placed the platter on the large breadboard, along with crocks of marmalade, knives, and as many more cups as she could find, and carried the load into the dining room.

A Mexican was speaking in Spanish, softly yet with power behind his words. She guessed from his air of authority that he held an official position in the community. As she stood at the table arranging the food and cutlery, men began to come over and hold their cups, expectant of service. She lifted the pot and poured the steaming, fragrant coffee, listening to their murmurs of thanks but noticing that seldom did they raise their eyes to her face. When the man had finished his speech in Spanish, he sat down and another Mexican used a crutch to pull himself to his feet. He spoke softly in Spanish a moment, then continued in English.

"Florencio has suggested," he said, "that we send a committee to Sheriff Brady asking what he intends to do about arresting the killers of Tunstall."

A tall, blond man stepped forward. He couldn't have been much over twenty, but his voice was strong when he said, "Ask him why he's holding the kid and Waite in jail, too!"

Dick Brewer said, "I'll be on the committee. I want to hear his answer."

Instantly receiving the attention of everyone, though he spoke softly, McSween said, "I don't think that would be wise, Dick. You were too close to Tunstall, and I think Brady would see your presence as a threat. We should send neutral parties, men who aren't allied with either side but seek the peace of the town for its citizens. Florencio, as probate judge, I think you should go."

The man with the crutch quickly translated McSween's words, and the older man nodded, his eyes sharp on the lawyer.

"Who else?" Widenmann asked eagerly. "Should I go, as a deputy marshal?"

"No," McSween said. "We don't want lawmen but citizens, representatives of the people. José Montaño would be a good choice, along with Isaac Ellis, as merchants, and John Newcomb would be a good representative of the small ranchers in the valley. I think they should be enough and they're peaceable men, Brady won't molest them."

Susan returned to the kitchen, relieved to find Sebrian slicing wedges off a smoked hank of ham. The men were hungry and the biscuits had disappeared before all had been fed. While she and Sebrian pulled together a dinner for thirty men, she wanted to ask many questions, but she held her tongue and worked with all her energy. At least she had learned why Fred and his friend Billy hadn't attended the funeral. They were in jail; but she didn't know why or for how long.

When she returned to the parlor to collect the dirty cups, the committee had already left. McSween sat before the hearth, gazing deeply into the fire. Dick Brewer was beside him, staring at the floor. The rest of the men stood scattered about the room, grumbling softly with discontent as Susan gathered the dishes on the breadboard again. When she finished, the young blond man who had spoken earlier came over and lifted the heavily laden board. She smiled her gratitude, then carried the empty coffeepot as she preceded him into the kitchen.

Introducing himself as George Coe, he said he liked it better in there, and he stayed to help her and Sebrian with supper. When the food was ready, Sebrian carried the platter of smoked pork and several bowls of boiled potatoes crooked in his arm, Susan lifted the Dutch oven of pinto beans and a plate stacked with more biscuits, and George hefted the breadboard laden with clean dishes and silverware.

At first the men were shy of approaching the table, but once they began, they cleared it of food as if it were the first they'd seen in days. Standing nearby and watching it disappear, Susan looked up at Sebrian and whispered, "Will we have enough?"

"Ain't nothing else in the kitchen," he answered. "Fred Waite brung a wagon of s'pplies from Mr. Tunstall's ranch, but that was to feed five men no more'n a week, not thirty three times a day. Don't know what to do 'cept ask Mr. Mac."

"What about the store? Can we borrow foodstuffs off the shelves?"

Sebrian sighed. "All that b'longs to Mr. Tunstall's fam'ly in London, I reckon. But we'll take it 'fore Dolan does. He's already got Mr. Tunstall's cattle. Claimed it was for the 'tachment but they'll end up filling his gov'ment contract."

She appraised him. "You know a great deal, don't you, Sebrian?"

He didn't smile as she expected. "Tell you the truth, Miss Gates, I don't like what I know. I wish I didn't know nothing, and that's a fact." He went back into the kitchen, and after a moment she heard him washing dishes.

As she gathered the dirty plates and cups strewn about the room, she noticed neither Dick Brewer nor Mr. McSween had eaten, but both held empty cups. When she returned from taking the dishes into the kitchen, she brought the pot and poured them fresh coffee.

Brewer finally acknowledged her presence, studying her face a moment before meeting her eyes. He thanked her with surprise in his voice, and she fought against blushing. His hair was uncombed from the wind, but he wore a respectable frock coat and a clean white shirt. His handsome face was so pleasing, the hurt in his dark eyes so touching, she had to struggle to control her response. Quickly she moved away. Setting the coffeepot on the table, she arranged the few remaining scraps of food on a single platter and quietly stacked the empty serving dishes. She was just finishing when the citizens committee returned.

It was evident from their faces that they hadn't fared well. They removed their coats by the door and then came forward to be near the fire. McSween and Brewer stood up, so they were six in the center of the room, the others standing around the perimeter in postures of suddenly resumed alertness.

Isaac Ellis spoke first, the bald Mexican named José Montaño translating his words like a soft echo into Spanish. "He was arrogant and crude," Ellis spat out. "When we asked why he'd arrested Bonney and Waite and was holding Martínez, he said: 'Because I have the power.'"

"Brady said that?" McSween whispered.

"His exact words," Ellis replied.

The men grumbled as Susan retreated to the kitchen door. She couldn't bring herself to leave, even though she could hear Sebrian working and knew she should help. After a moment, he came to stand behind her and she felt better.

"What'd he say about arresting the killers of Tunstall?" Brewer demanded.

Ellis shook his head. "He said Tunstall was killed resisting a legal posse, and the men are exempt from prosecution because they were acting in the line of duty."

A murmur of outrage filled the room.

"Jesse Evans!" Widenmann cried. "A known outlaw riding with a posse?"

"Brady had an answer for that, too," Ellis said. "He showed us a letter he'd written to Jake Mathews stating specifically he wasn't to allow any outlaws to go along."

Mac sat down heavily and stared into the fire, thinking if Sheriff Brady was the law in Lincoln, the county was under the heel of a tyrant and democracy had ceased to exist. Looking helplessly at the angry men crowding his parlor, Mac felt desperate. Just then Atanacio Martínez came through the door, and in the person of the constable, Mac saw his only link with justice.

Martínez walked directly to Mac and spoke softly, though everyone heard him. "Brady forgot I have a key to the jail. When he let me go, I walked down there and found it unguarded, so I let our men out. They're coming here but along the river so no one will see them. Dolan has his men scurrying every which way."

"Doing what?" Mac asked with dread.

"Riley's left for Mesilla to get alias warrants to arrest you again and Barrier for obstruction of justice. Brady sent a man to Stanton for troops to help make the arrests. After the soldiers have returned to the fort and you're in jail, Dolan's given orders for Jesse Evans to do his part."

"They'll kill him," someone said.

Agreement echoed around the room: "Kill him." "Get him when he's in jail." "Never see daylight again." "Kill him sure."

Mac looked at Barrier, who seemed confused, then turned to Brewer and said, "I am innocent of any crime."

"We know that, Mac," Dick said. "But you better make yourself scarce. If we resist Brady when he's backed by federal troops, they'll call it insurrection. If they don't shoot us, they'll hang us. You have to stay

out of their way until court in April. We have to trust we'll set everything right then."

Mac sighed, thankful for Brewer's insight. "Where shall I go?"

"Why not Chisum's?"

He shook his head. "I shan't go so far from home."

Everyone stared at his sudden obstinacy. "I am innocent," he stated
to the room at large. "I am being driven from my home, but I shan't go
far, and I shall return." He looked at Brewer. "Is there someplace in the
mountains nearby where I would be safe?"

Brewer scanned the crowd. "Salazar, you know the country around
here better'n anyone."

"I can take you," Hijenio said eagerly, addressing his words to Mac.
"We can stay with my family and friends, always moving. They will
never find us."

Mac looked at the young man willing to risk his life to protect him.
"Thank you," he said, humbled by such generosity. "Allow me some
time to collect a few things."

"Be quick, Mac," Brewer warned. "Sam, see to his horse, will you?"

Mac went into his bedroom, packed some warm clothing in his valise
and nestled his Bible on top, then walked back into the parlor, taking
Brewer aside for a few final words.

"Court is only six weeks away," Mac said. "I will find justice before
the grand jury."

Brewer nodded. "But by the time they hand down indictments forcing Brady to act, Tunstall's killers will be long gone. So it's up to us to
catch 'em before they leave the country."

"Be cautious," Mac advised. "In all your endeavors seek arrests, not
executions. Promise me, Dick."

"I'll do my best," he answered.

The door opened and the Kid and Fred Waite came in. They were
given a heroes' reception by the assembly. When the noisy hurrahs had
quieted down, the two looked across at Brewer. Dick grinned at them,
then rearranged his face into a solemn expression when he turned back to
Mac.

Mac realized again how ill he was cut out to be a fighter. These men
felt Tunstall's death as deeply as he did, yet the contemplation of action
made them jovial. For the next six weeks they would clash with Dolan's
men, and Mac had no doubt lives would be lost. His eyes sought out
Patrón in the crowd. They looked at each other with the sullen knowledge that his prediction of war had come true.

Sadly, Mac looked back at Brewer. "Walk out with me, will you, Dick?"

"Sure," he said, lifting the valise.

As Mac put on his overcoat, many of the men murmured expressions of sympathy. Others reached out to shake his hand as if for the last time as he left them behind. When he walked with Brewer into the cold wind, Barrier and Salazar were already mounted and waiting.

Mac touched Brewer's arm. "Remember, Dick, without leadership these men will become a mob. As their leader, you must strive for peace. Promise me."

"I'll do my best," Brewer said again.

Mac sighed, mounted his horse, and followed Barrier and Hijenio Salazar into hiding.

Brewer watched them leave, then returned to the kitchen and saw George Coe flirting with the new schoolteacher. Brewer gave George a smile before asking Sebrian, "Is there anything left to eat?"

"A little, Mr. Brewer," he said. "Sit down and I'll fix you a plate."

Frank McNab came in, followed by John Middleton and Hendry Brown, who stood leaning against the wall while McNab sat down across from Brewer. "So what'll we do now, Dick?" McNab asked.

"I'm thinking on it," he answered, nodding his thanks as Sebrian set a plate of food in front of him.

Hendry said, "My bet is they've gone to Dolan's cow camp on the Pecos."

The Kid came in with Fred Waite. "Who has?" Billy asked.

"Morton, Baker, and Hill," Hendry answered.

Billy laughed. "Let's go get 'em!"

Brewer looked at the men waiting to hear his decision. Brown had worked for Dolan and was probably right, plus Brewer couldn't see any advantage to waiting in Lincoln for Brady to make the first move. "We'll ride at dawn," Dick said.

23

When they left the next morning, the Regulators were nine strong: Brewer, McNab, Middleton, Bonney, Waite, Brown, Scurlock, Bowdre, and Finlay. All except McNab were motivated merely by justice. McNab, a stock detective, was equally interested in breaking the rustling ring that operated at the instigation of The House; he held authority from cattlemen's associations in Texas to act on their behalf. Brewer was a deputy constable. He carried a warrant issued by Justice of the

Peace Wilson, and the Regulators had all been deputized, so they were legally sanctioned in their purpose.

As they rode down the mountains toward the Pecos Valley, Brewer assessed his men. Middleton was on the dark side of thirty and had the deadliest reputation. The others were in their early twenties, except for the Kid and Hendry Brown, who were eighteen and nineteen. They were all good shooters and expert horsemen, but most were shy of experience. McNab was a professional manhunter, and Brewer saw him as his strongest ally in effecting arrests over executions. Big Jim Finlay was a herder and could be counted on to go along, but Doc Scurlock and Hendry Brown had reputations as able gunmen, so Brewer expected them to be more independent.

Bowdre was a little of both and hot-tempered. Since coming to the county he had developed a rabid hatred of the rich, who took everything for themselves and left the little guy barely enough to survive. Brewer could appreciate the sentiment but didn't think rabid hatred made for a good ally. He also felt wary of the Kid. No one doubted his courage or his skill with weapons, but he was resistant to command. Fred Waite was a follower. His only liability was his close friendship with the Kid. Fred would follow Billy if it came to a choice, and Brewer knew it was imperative that his men act as a unit.

They camped in the mountains and slept well in the cold night air. The next morning, their horses were fresh and the men sharp when they crested a butte overlooking Dolan's cow camp. Despite the chill, no smoke came from the chimney of the *jacal,* making Brewer suspect they had missed the men they were seeking. The corral held fifty head of Tunstall's cattle, however, and he figured the Regulators could at least replevin some of the lost herd.

Suddenly three horses bolted from the lean-to stable at a dead run. Brewer recognized Morton and Baker in the lead. He spurred his horse after them, the Regulators right behind, galloping down the sloping cliff in pursuit.

The prairie was cut with narrow arroyos the horses leapt in stride, the thud of so many hooves loud on the rocky soil. Only the creak of leather and slap of reins voiced the men's unity as they cut distance between their prey. For miles they rode at a dead gallop, their horses dripping lather that blew back in the men's faces, the grunts of the animals more persistent with each leap. Ahead a horse dropped. It was the man no one knew or wanted, and the Regulators thundered past him with no regard for his escape.

The horses under Morton and Baker were stumbling. Brewer silently congratulated John Tunstall for insisting his men be well mounted.

Baker's horse went down. Morton wheeled his with the last of its wind and it fell to its knees. Both men dove for a shallow arroyo, pulling their pistols as they rolled into its shelter.

Brewer stopped the Regulators out of range. As the posse milled around in the noise of tired horses snorting dust, he shouted, "I've got a warrant for your arrest. If you surrender, you won't be harmed."

Morton's horse regained its feet but stood with its head down, wind-blown and wheezing. Baker's horse was dead from a burst heart, blood trickling from its nostrils into the sand. The horses of the posse stomped and shook the dust out of their ears, jangling their bridles.

Finally Morton called back, "You give your word we won't be harmed?"

"I do," Brewer answered.

The two men warily rose to their feet, then stepped out of the arroyo with their hands in the air, their guns left behind.

"Move real slow," Brewer said.

They did, approaching the posse with caution, obviously not trusting Brewer's word. When they were near, Billy Bonney spurred his horse to nearly run them down. He grinned from atop his saucy gray mare, his gun in his hand.

"I told you boys you'd regret cheating me," the Kid said, pulling the hammer of his pistol back with his thumb. "I ain't gonna kill you for that, though. I'm gonna kill you for John Tunstall."

"We're not killing anybody!" Brewer barked.

His thumb still on the hammer, Billy looked sideways at Brewer. "Aw, come on, Dick, they deserve it sure as hell."

The other Regulators clamored agreement.

"Stop it!" Brewer shouted. "Mac said to do by the law and that's what we're doing."

Everyone but the Kid backed down.

Brewer said sternly, "I'm just as sorry as you they surrendered. I'd have rather shot them fair. But to kill them now would be an execution, and we ain't the power to do that."

"I got the power right in my hand," the Kid answered, giving the prisoners a smile that made Baker cry out, "For God's sake, Brewer!"

Softly Dick said, "Put your gun away, Kid." Brewer knew the quiet order asserted his leadership, clear for all rational minds to understand. If Billy disobeyed he became a renegade outside any man's control. Brewer watched to see which way the Kid fell.

Billy gave in with a laugh, grinning down at Morton and Baker. "You're lucky today. But if you try to escape, you can be sure the first bullet that hits will be mine."

"Mine will be right behind it," Brewer said, letting himself breathe again.

He put the prisoners on Waite's big bay. Fred rode behind Billy. Feeling victorious, the posse joked about watching Tunstall's killers hang, goading their captives with brutal fun as they ambled toward Chisum's ranch to spend the night.

Seventeen-year-old Sallie Chisum was the lady of the house at her Uncle John's ranch. She had come from Texas with her father, Jim Chisum, a year earlier to be hostess for the Cattle King of the Pecos' commodious hospitality. Her uncle had recently returned from Las Vegas full of cynical humor over the machinations of the Santa Fe Ring, but it was all politics to her, distant and slightly absurd, something she had learned to disregard long ago. No man ever listened to her opinions anyway. She ran the house, graced the table with frivolity, and enjoyed riding the range and flirting with the cowboys, protected by being John Chisum's niece.

She had heard of the troubles in the mountains, and though she'd met John Tunstall and felt sorry for his death, all that seemed far removed from life in the valley. So she was surprised one night when a posse with prisoners stopped to share her uncle's hospitality. Surprised, too, at the manner in which he greeted their leader, a handsome man by the name of Dick Brewer.

Uncle John seemed to know all the men in the posse, and to approve the capture of their prisoners with more than civic applause. Throughout dinner, Sallie listened to the men talk. One of them said Dolan had recruited John Kinney, the worst ruffian on the Rio Grande, and that Kinney had brought twenty more of the border riffraff with him. When Brewer explained McSween was in hiding, hoping for victory in the courts, Sallie saw her uncle shake his head.

Appalled, she returned to the kitchen and prepared trays of supper which she carried to the prisoners, under guard in a back bedroom. Two men held rifles at the open door: the half-Indian named Fred Waite, and Billy Bonney, who was so young everyone called him the Kid. She smiled at them and asked softly, "The prisoners are allowed to eat, aren't they?"

The Indian put his rifle down and took the trays in. She looked past him to the prisoners, who seemed so miserable it tore at her heart. Then she looked at the Kid and saw how coldly his eyes rested on the captives. "You hate them, don't you," she murmured.

"Yes, ma'am," he said.

"Because you think they killed Tunstall?"

"I seen 'em do it."

Only after Fred had come back and picked up his rifle did Billy look at the girl standing beside him. She was taller than he was, her hair the golden color of autumn wheat, the line of her mouth turned down with concern. She watched his eyes change from steel gray to a pale blue, and with his smile all trace of animosity disappeared from his face.

"Are you John Chisum's daughter?" he asked, his voice playful.

"His niece," she answered curtly. "I've heard of these men. They own small ranches down by Seven Rivers and I don't believe they're capable of murder."

Billy just smiled. It was Fred Waite who said, "Your opinion don't change the facts."

Sallie looked at him angrily, but he was watching the prisoners. When Frank Baker met her eyes, her heart went out to him. "Are you all right? Is there anything I can do for you?"

"I'm afraid we won't reach Lincoln alive," he said. "Could you bring me some paper so I could write my brother in Virginia? I'd like to let him know how I died."

She had to bite her lip against crying. "Of course," she answered, hurrying off to comply with his wish.

Before going to bed that night, she crept down the hall to her uncle's room and knocked on his door. When the old rancher growled for whoever it was to come in and be quick about it, she slipped inside and closed the door, leaning against it as she smiled at her uncle in his bedroll on the floor. John Chisum had spent forty years sleeping on the ground and so far had successfully resisted her efforts to put him in a bed. Sallie studied the familiar, weatherbeaten face of the man she had known all her life as a fountain of kindness and generosity.

"I hope you're not in the habit of visiting men in their bedrooms," he grumbled, sitting up in his faded red long johns, the blanket pulled high enough to cover his lap.

"Only my favorite uncle," she teased.

"What's so important," he asked in a gentler tone, "that couldn't wait till morning?"

"It's about the prisoners," she said carefully.

He frowned.

"Mr. Baker told me he didn't think they'd reach Lincoln alive."

"When did you talk to 'em?" he accused gruffly.

"I took them their supper," she replied with defiance.

He watched her, annoyed for a moment, then his face softened. "They mean something to you?"

"If I said I loved them, would it save their lives?"

"I'd lynch 'em here in the yard!" he bellowed. "They're Seven Rivers scum, Sallie, and I don't like you taking their part."

"They're small ranchers," she retorted, "struggling to get a start, as you once did."

He glared at her a moment, then smiled. "I s'pose it seems so to you, raised as you were in a more civilized section of the country. But those men run Dolan's cow camp, which means they steal my stock and then The House sells 'em to the gov'ment to feed the Indians. I owned that contract once, now it's just my cows're involved. Those men are also directly responsible for the murder of John Tunstall, they're the ones pulled the trigger. You think they should go unpunished for that?"

"Have they been tried in a court of law?"

"There were eyewitnesses who saw 'em among the men who gunned him down. Tunstall didn't have a chance. I should've advised him better, I reckon. He was like you: too ingrained with rules of law. McSween's the same. He's doomed sure as Tunstall."

"Why don't you stop it?" she cried. "Surely you could do something!"

"Like what?" he drawled.

"You could send some men with them," Sallie suggested, "to make sure they aren't murdered on the way to Lincoln."

"I wouldn't consider it murder but justice!" he retorted. "Brewer's wearing a badge, carrying a warrant. I agree with him and wish Morton and Baker hadn't been taken alive." He sighed. "Just to show I'm listening and do care," he said in a kinder tone, "I'll send McCloskey along. He's a Dolan partisan, though he's trying to play both sides and there's nothing I hate more'n a turncoat. But if they kill the prisoners, they'll have to shoot him first. That would be murder flat out and I don't think they'll do it. Does that satisfy you, Miss Sallie?"

"Yes," she said, although she was thinking one man was hardly a guarantee of protection, and she'd also noted he was sending a man he didn't like anyway. But she knew it was all he would give, so she thanked him and left.

She went out on the veranda and sat in the swing, staring through the bare cottonwoods into the black, winter sky. The night was cold and she hugged herself beneath her thick shawl, disliking her uncle for the first time in her life. After a moment she became aware she wasn't alone. She jerked around to see Billy Bonney standing in the corner of the porch, watching her. "You should've told me you were there," she accused.

"I didn't reckon you'd stay, it's so cold out," he answered pleasantly.

"What're you doing here?"

"Waiting."

"For what?"

"Tomorrow," he said, his smile showing his crooked teeth.

"Come here and sit down," she said boldly, surprising herself.

He laughed soft and deep in his throat, and the sound pleased her. When he gestured at the empty space on the swing to ask if she really meant for him to sit so near, she pulled the fringe of her shawl out of his way. The swing creaked softly as he braced a dusty boot against the railing to move them in a rocking motion, his spur gleaming in the starlight.

"You're the one the men call the Kid," she said.

He laughed softly again. "I'm sure they call me a lot of other things they'd never say in front of a lady."

She turned slightly to face him, her knees drawn up protectively close to her breasts. "I'm no lady," she said. "Just a girl who hates to see men kill each other."

"That shouldn't worry you none," the Kid said gently. "Death is a law of nature, we didn't invent it." He reached across and touched her cheek. "Laws of nature jus' have their own way about 'em," he murmured, leaning closer.

She knew he was going to kiss her, that she had invited it by declaring herself not a lady. She didn't care. She even wanted him to in defiance of her Uncle John, who was so powerful yet did nothing. In her anger, she believed the Kid was more of a man than the Cattle King of the Pecos. At least the Kid acted his conscience. Even if he did things she didn't approve, she admired his taking a hand when events teetered on chaos. So she leaned forward to welcome the Kid's kiss, and its gentleness was all the more enticing because she knew he had death in his heart.

The next morning he gave no indication of the liberties she had allowed him, and for that she felt grateful. He did meet her eyes and tip his hat just before the posse rode out. She rewarded his delicacy with a small smile of invitation to visit again, then turned to see Uncle John watching her.

He chuckled and shook his head. "You best watch your step with that one, Sallie. If any of 'em kill your friends Baker and Morton, it's apt to be him."

She stared at the retreating posse, picking out the prisoners riding in the middle. "Why do you say that?"

"Call it a frontiersman's intuition," he answered, raising his arm for one final wave to Brewer, who rode behind the others as if wanting to keep them in line.

Brewer waved back at the old rancher and his willowy slip of a niece. Dick had seen her and the Kid kissing on the porch swing. It was something he'd never mention but which he thought about, how casual Billy was with the ladies. He was always watching for an opening, and damn if he didn't always take it when it came.

The Kid wasn't much to look at and didn't own a nickel. Tunstall had given him his horse and outfit, even the Winchester he'd lost to Brady. Yet Billy acted as if life were easy. He even came out of that hole of a jail in Lincoln laughing about how much he'd won from Fred playing monte. As if it were all the same: lock him in a hole or let him kiss a pretty girl in the starlight, he came out with his eyes dancing as if life were a joke.

Even yesterday when he'd held his cocked pistol on Morton and Baker, he was having fun. Brewer suspected the Kid could have pulled the trigger and watched them die, then turned around and talked about some green chile enchiladas some little señorita in San Patricio had cooked for him special. It wasn't that he was cold. Brewer knew him well enough to appreciate the warmth of his regard, but the Kid could be deadly with a smile. There was something disquieting about that.

The men rode ahead of Brewer in relaxed boredom. They were going into Roswell to let Baker post a letter. Everyone knew nothing would happen between here and there, even the new man Chisum had sent along, McCloskey. It was on the lonely stretch into the mountains where trouble was likely. Brewer wished again that Morton and Baker hadn't surrendered and he didn't have to protect them all the way back to Lincoln.

He felt slightly stupid anyway, following Mac's instructions and returning them for trial. That meant handing them over to Brady, and Brewer couldn't see Morton and Baker staying in jail any longer than Jesse Evans had. So it was a fool's errand he was on, one that would probably demand he risk his life to save men he'd gladly see dead.

Roswell had begun as a general store and sporting house built by two brothers named Van Smith who had come down from Santa Fe for the purpose of starting a town. Choosing the confluence of the Hondo and Pecos rivers, they named their settlement after their father. A dozen or so families had moved in, another saloon opened, a blacksmith set up shop, and before long there were several small stores competing with the brothers. When they had a falling out over the competition and shot at each other, the one took the other to Las Vegas to get him patched up, and they never returned. Virgil Christie ran the store now, and Ash Upson had secured the position of postmaster, which paid just enough to keep him in drink.

It seemed everyone knew Ash. He'd arrived in the county with the Jones family way back in '66, and Brewer met him when he'd been the schoolteacher at Casey's Mill. Ash was also a journalist who sporadically sent articles of local events to the Las Vegas *Optic*. His stories were a source of amusement to the people he wrote about because he embroidered and just plain invented anything he thought would improve their flavor.

Standing on the portal of the general store, Ash watched the twelve men trot up the street and swing their horses to a stop in front of him. He coughed up phlegm, trying to clear the scum of a night of heavy drinking from his mouth as he looked them over, noting right away that Morton and Baker had their hands tied. Then he saw the constable's badge on Brewer's coat. Ash spit off to the side, shifted his furred tongue around in his mouth a minute, and said, "You boys're up early."

"Come to post a letter," Brewer said.

Ash let his eyes drift around all the guns. "Must be powerful important."

"It'll most likely be my last," Baker said, extending an envelope.

Ash stepped into the street to take it. The paper was soft with sweat, and when he looked into the prisoner's eyes, Ash saw fear. Stepping back under the shade of the portal, he asked Brewer, "These boys under arrest?"

"We're taking 'em back to Lincoln," Brewer said, "to stand trial for killing Tunstall."

"Uh-huh," Ash grunted. "Looks like your posse's all friends of the Englishman's."

"We're the only ones willing to do it," Brewer answered. "Brady chose to sit out the dance."

Billy was straightening the mane of his mare, combing it to lie smooth on one side of her neck. He was only half-listening to Brewer and the postmaster, some old geezer full of his own juice. Letting his gaze wander the wide dirt street, Billy remembered telling Lily Casey he'd never been to Roswell. Now here he was, but he couldn't say much for it. Then he noticed a new store of raw lumber whose sign said it belonged to Marion Turner and John Jones, Props. Billy grinned and turned his horse to amble over.

John Jones had heard the posse ride in and was just finishing with a customer before going out to investigate. He buckled on his gunbelt, then stepped into the street still settling it on his hip, so he was touching his weapon when he saw Billy Bonney sitting a pretty gray mare right in front of him. The Kid threw up his hands in mock surrender.

John laughed, moving in long strides to reach up and shake hands. "I ain't seen you since you left to be a farmboy."

"I graduated since then," Billy said.

John looked behind him to the posse. "You with them?" he asked, suddenly somber.

Billy nodded.

"Why?" John asked, incredulous.

"They killed Tunstall," Billy answered. "I've sworn to get all the men who did."

"Jesus Christ, Billy," John said. "I almost went along when they came recruiting men, but I had personal business to get done." He stopped and the two friends assessed each other for a long moment. "More'n likely," John said, "I will be with 'em next time."

Billy laughed. "Well, come shooting, *compadre.*"

John laughed, too, but with less joy. "Sonofabitch, Billy. I don't like going against you."

"Then don't fight for Dolan."

"I ain't! I'm fighting Chisum and I'll stand alongside the Devil himself if I have to. I can't believe you're taking his side!"

"Chisum ain't nothing but a supply of ammunition to me," Billy said with a smile. "Though he's got a pretty niece who made me feel I'd be welcome if I went back."

"Sallie Chisum's got a burr under her tail," John replied, then laughed, this time for real. "Goddamn, it's good to see you."

The posse started moving off and Billy leaned down to shake hands with his friend. "Don't get in front of me, John, and I won't have to shoot you."

"I'll try, Billy," he answered. "I don't want to shoot you, either." He hesitated, then said, "I prob'ly shouldn't say this, but rumor has it Dolan's sending some men to make sure you don't reach Lincoln." He shrugged, then laughed. "What the hell, think I'll sit this one out, too."

"Thanks," Billy said. "Say hello to your folks for me." Then he spurred his horse to overtake Brewer, who was riding at the rear of the posse.

Brewer had seen the Kid talking to John Jones, and he figured Billy would catch up soon enough. He didn't expect him to come at a gallop and rein his mare so close she slid in the dust as if roping a cow. Brewer's horse shied, and he had to grab the horn to keep his seat. The Kid was laughing but Brewer frowned, then listened with appreciation to the news of a planned ambush. "Good work," he said. "We'll take the Agua Negra trail and avoid them. Ride up front and tell McNab."

The Kid clucked to his mare and she was off like a gray streak of wind around the posse. Brewer thought Tunstall must have liked Billy to give him such a good horse, especially as there weren't many things in life the Englishman had appreciated more.

Brewer suddenly missed Tunstall with a renewed sense of loss. He wondered if he'd feel better if he went ahead and killed the prisoners, if satisfying his craving for revenge would quiet the pain he felt every time he remembered how Tunstall had died. Brewer knew only one thing: if Dolan's men tried a rescue, Morton and Baker would be the first shot.

When they took the north trail through Agua Negra Canyon, Baker looked back with panic. Brewer just stared, wanting him to stink with fear before it was over. Which meant, if he was successful, delivering both of the prisoners alive to Brady, who would eventually release them. Later, Brewer blamed his ambivalence for what happened.

He had let himself drift so far behind that the posse was out of sight in a switchback on the trail. Billy and Fred were in front with McNab. Scurlock, Finlay, and Bowdre rode around and between the prisoners. Middleton was behind them with McCloskey, whom he knew from before, and Hendry Brown brought up the rear, being the last man to disappear around the bend out of Brewer's sight.

There was a fork in the trail, a northeast route toward the upper Pecos and Fort Sumner. Three hundred yards past the junction, the cut-off made a hairpin jag behind the wall of the canyon, affording protection to anyone fleeing. Morton saw it as his last chance. He slowed his horse to be nearer McCloskey, then waited until Middleton's horse snorted to cover his voice as he muttered, "I'm gonna make a break. Gimme yer gun."

McCloskey quickly calculated his chances of convincing the posse that Morton had stolen his gun. He figured the odds were pretty low, and that Morton and Baker wouldn't make it behind the cliff anyway, so why stick his neck out? "Don't be a fool," he warned. "Wait for Lincoln."

"You're the fool if you think we'll see Lincoln alive," Morton growled.

Both Morton and McCloskey had forgotten Hendry Brown rode behind them. At the turnoff, Morton grabbed for McCloskey's gun. McCloskey didn't stop him because he was dead. Morton felt hot blood spray on his hand as he turned to see Hendry Brown's forty-four aimed at his heart. Morton dug in his spurs and tore down the east trail. Baker yanked his horse right behind, gaining a hundred yards of freedom before eight pistols fired and dropped the fleeing men dead in the sand.

An instant later, Brewer galloped around the bend to see the posse holding their smoking guns, their horses stomping and churning in fright. He saw McCloskey dead on the ground nearly beneath the hooves of his horse, and Morton and Baker dead two hundred yards from the canyon wall. "What the hell happened?" he demanded. "Goddamn, I leave you alone two seconds and they're dead! Who shot McCloskey? Let's start with that."

"I did," Hendry Brown answered, holstering his pistol and looking at Brewer with arrogance. "He gave Morton his gun."

"Then they made a break for it," Middleton said, "and we all shot 'em."

Brewer watched them putting their guns away and calming their horses until they all sat like schoolboys awaiting his verdict. "Is that true?" he asked. "You all shot 'em?"

The men nodded, watching him.

Brewer turned his horse and trotted across to the bodies of Morton and Baker. For a long moment, he looked down at their blood flooding the sand, the bullet holes ugly in their coats. They both lay facedown, as dead as they were ever going to get.

Discovering he did feel better that John Tunstall's death was avenged, Dick Brewer pulled his own pistol and fired a bullet into the back of Buck Morton, then Frank Baker, taking pleasure in the pure justice of the act. He turned his horse and looked at his men. "We all shot 'em," he said. "That's all we'll ever say about it."

As he rejoined them, the men moved their horses out of his way with deference, waiting in a respectful silence for his instructions. His voice was so soft they had to strain to hear. "We best not all go into town after this," Brewer said. "I'll go on alone and find Mac. You ride over to San Patricio and spread out. I'll be along directly."

He looked at McCloskey sprawled faceup, his dead eyes open to the sky. "There's a sheepherder lives near here," Brewer said. "I'll pay him to bury the bodies. Let's move." He turned his horse and rode away by himself.

The men watched until he was out of sight, then reined their horses around to file past McCloskey's body. For some, seeing a man shot dead was a familiar sight. They rode by as if the corpse were no more than a rock to be circumvented. Those who had never seen the reality feasted their eyes on the gruesome truth.

Billy watched Hendry Brown ride by without looking. Billy looked, feeling a macabre compassion that the sucker had pissed his pants. But he was more interested in Hendry.

Billy had seen it happen. He had been turned in his saddle looking behind when Morton pulled McCloskey's gun. McCloskey raised his arm to get out of the way, not stop him. The next thing Billy saw was the flash from Hendry's gun. He never did see him draw it. Then McCloskey's blood sprayed all over Morton, and the prisoners ran.

Knowing they could pick them off easily, the posse had taken their time, aiming square for the spot they wanted. Billy laughed, remembering the precision of the action. He urged his horse to overtake Hendry, then reached across and slapped him on the back. "I seen what you did and it was mighty clean," Billy said with a grin.

"You would've done the same," Hendry said, a tight smile beneath his thin blond moustache.

"Yeah, but I ain't, least not yet, jus' shot a man flat out like that. You have, I seen you do it."

Hendry frowned, suddenly not sure the Kid was paying him a compliment.

Billy grinned, leaning close as if he were about to ask something important. "You like green chile enchiladas?"

Hendry thought he was joking. Then he remembered Billy saying the enchiladas weren't the only thing hot in that kitchen. "I've been craving some for a long time," he said.

"I know the sweetest señorita," Billy said, "and damn if she ain't got a pretty sister."

Fred Waite usually got the sister. Riding right behind, he said, "She ain't so pretty."

Billy laughed and beckoned him closer, which was all Fred wanted. He knew Billy would find another sister somewhere.

24

Dick Brewer rode into the mountains alone, wishing he could go directly to his farm. The Coes were watching it for him, but they both had their own spreads and any attention given his was bound to be minimal. Brewer hadn't focused his entire energy on his own endeavors since meeting Tunstall. John had had a charisma that made men want to help him, knowing they were receiving more than a fair return.

With Tunstall's death something had died in Brewer, too. The part of his mind that formerly held a strong belief in moral virtue was now crowded with a cynical hatred for the corrupters. He found, however, that the satisfaction of shooting two of Tunstall's killers had evaporated, leaving a bigger need to be filled. The awareness that he was consumed with vengeance cast his thoughts into a despair threatening to hold him in its depths forever. The only solution he could see was action: kill as Tunstall had been killed, kill the men who made it happen. Only then could he find the man he'd been before.

Hijenio Salazar, riding the trail toward him, saw the change. Though never quick with a joke, there had been an easy grace about Brewer, a sense that he was centered in his purpose and so in a position to give help and comfort. Now his face wore a habitual scowl, his eyes sharp for potential attack or defense. Hijenio guessed it was the same with himself, suddenly turned into the hunted by guiding McSween from sanctuary to sanctuary.

He was searching for the Regulators to let them know McSween was no longer in hiding. The governor had come to Lincoln and Mac had returned home to gain an audience. Leaving him with Barrier, Hijenio had ridden toward the Pecos in hopes of joining his *compadres* in action. He was as surprised to see Brewer alone as Dick was to see Hijenio without Mac.

They sat their horses and exchanged news. Hijenio was sorry he had missed out on the killing, but happy he could return to his home in San Patricio. When they parted, Brewer rode on toward Lincoln with renewed hope. If Governor Axtell had decided to take a hand in the state of war in Lincoln County, maybe justice would return and they could all go back to farming and pondering the complexities of women.

In the shadows of dusk, he rode into the stable behind Tunstall's store. He took his time about settling his horse in for the night, giving it an extra scoop of grain then checking over its hoofs. The stable was warm with the body heat of half a dozen horses, all watching lazily as Brewer hung up his outfit and walked back into the cold, shutting the door and laying the latch securely.

The sunset was crimson as he walked toward Mac's house, deliberately not looking at the store. He went in through Mac's back door without knocking and saw Sebrian and Deputy Barrier and the new schoolteacher cooking together. They all stopped and stared at him so long he realized he was dirty and windblown from the trail. But he merely asked Sebrian if Mac was around.

"Yes, sir, he's in the parlor," Sebrian answered solemnly.

Brewer nodded at the others, then strode on into the parlor where he found Mac sitting morosely before the fire. The lawyer didn't get up as they stared at each other for a long moment. Finally Brewer said, "I got bad news, Mac."

McSween sighed and stood up, extending his hand. "Sit down and warm yourself. I have coffee here, would you like some?"

"Thanks," Brewer said, taking the smaller chair he knew belonged to Sue. As he sat watching her husband pour a cup of coffee and hand it to him, he wondered if she was ever coming home.

Mac leaned back and folded his hands across the front of his vest. "Now, what is it?" he asked kindly.

Brewer sipped his coffee, then told Mac that they'd found Morton and Baker at Dolan's cow camp, had captured them, and gone to Chisum's for the night, and that Chisum had sent McCloskey along when they left. Brewer stopped and drank deeply of the coffee, then set the cup aside. Mac was watching him, waiting to hear the rest.

"We went through Roswell," Brewer continued, "to let Baker mail a letter to his brother, and the Kid learned Dolan had sent men to intercept us. So we took the Agua Negra trail to avoid 'em. Morton must've thought we went that way to murder him and Baker where we wouldn't likely be seen, not as likely as on the Lincoln road anyway. It all happened so fast, Mac, there was no question of stopping it. Morton got McCloskey's gun and shot him. He and Baker took off, and we all put bullets in their backs."

The fire crackled in the silence. Then Mac asked, "They're dead?"

"McCloskey, too. I had a sheepherder bury 'em."

Mac leaned forward and hid his face in his hands.

"They were shot while trying to escape," Brewer pointed out. "It was legal, Mac." When the lawyer didn't answer, Dick added, "I wish I could say I'm sorry, but they deserved what they got."

Mac looked up, his face contorted with anguish. "The governor was here in town, did you know that?"

"I heard," Brewer said, looking into the fire.

"He wouldn't see me," Mac said.

Brewer looked back at him hard. "Flat out refused?"

Mac nodded. "When Juan Patrón tried, he had to speak to him on the street. A territorial representative! Even he couldn't get an appointment and had to accost the man publicly. Do you know what Axtell said?"

Brewer shook his head.

"He said he'd heard all about the situation and didn't care to discuss it further. Dolan was with him at the time."

"So the Ring's got him, too," Brewer muttered.

"And us," Mac said. "I'm afraid. I came home because I've done nothing wrong, Dick. I've committed no crime yet I've been living like a fugitive, shunted from *jacal* to *jacal,* sleeping in a bed with five or six

children. I feel so loathsome, as if I haven't the right to share the innocence of their sleep. And why? I've done nothing that I should hide!"

"I know that, Mac."

"Axtell issued a proclamation. He declared Justice of the Peace Wilson's appointment to be illegal and all his acts in office void. He declared
Brady the only law in the county."

"What does that mean?"

"That you're neither a constable, nor your men deputies. Your warrant is invalid and your actions outside the law."

Brewer felt the whole force of his character yank him to his feet.
"Fine," he uttered. "If they've made outlaws of us, they're gonna see the
meanest damn killers in creation."

McSween was on his feet before him. "Don't be rash! You have everything to lose."

"What have I got?" Brewer shouted. "Brady can fucking hang me for
murder!"

"Please, Dick," Mac said. "There's a lady in the house."

"Don't worry, I'm leaving," he muttered, turning to pick up his
coat.

"Where will you go?"

"To tell my men they're outlaws," he answered, jabbing his arms in
and closing the buttons. "What're you gonna do?"

"Meet me at Chisum's in a week. Take a circuitous route and keep
your men out of trouble. Can you do that, Dick? Help me to avoid more
killing on either side?"

"I'll do my best, Mac. But a man can only be hung once. The men
already got that on their heads for killing Morton and Baker. I don't
expect 'em to be cautious."

"Can we disperse them? Send them away, each in a different direction, until things calm down?"

"Lincoln's our home. None of us are leaving."

"Can't you induce them?"

"No," Dick stated flatly. "All I can do is try and hold 'em together so
we act as a unit. That's the most control they'll take. I'll get 'em to Chisum's. I can promise that much."

"Good," Mac said. His face brightened. "Mrs. McSween will be
there. She's coming home, God protect her."

Brewer thought she'd picked a poor time to return. "I'll look forward
to seeing her," he said. "Will you be safe, getting there?"

"I think so," Mac answered, shaking his hand. "God be with you,
Dick."

"Yeah, He might try it just for a change."

"You mustn't joke. God tests those He truly loves and confronts us with great challenges."

"Seems to me, He's going to love us to death," Dick said. "See you in a week."

He walked back into the cold and across the now dark corral to the stable, disturbing the deserved rest of his tired horse. Saddling it, he rode into the wind, past Tunstall's store and down the empty, silent street of Lincoln, to the trail to Eagle Creek and the valley on the other side where San Patricio lay, sheltering his men.

Nestled on the bank of a small tributary emptying into the Pecos was an old adobe home John Chisum had acquired with the land, a house built to accommodate a large family as well as protect them from Indians. The walls were three feet thick and the flat roof was ringed with what the natives called a *pretil*, a parapet interspersed with gunports. The roof was accessible from inside the house by a ladder set at such a low angle it was almost like climbing runged stairs.

Sue McSween ascended easily, holding her skirts immodestly aside because there was no one to see her. She had arrived the day before in a buggy Chisum had sent to meet her in Las Vegas. Having come home to join the fight, to avenge Tunstall's death and save her property in Lincoln, she considered Chisum her only ally. Her husband had apparently handled tactics so ineptly he was reduced to hiding in the mountains, his men branded as outlaws and banished from their homes. Since the deaths of Baker and Morton, the Regulators' only actions had been sporadic and indecisive battles, accidental skirmishes guided by no overall vision and with no gain achieved. Sue couldn't imagine a more dismal failure of strategy.

When far across the prairie she saw riders approaching, she raised the field glasses and studied the travelers. Two men on horseback, trotting quickly as if in a hurry yet riding tired mounts. She recognized the first horse because it was her mare, Pet. As her husband came into definition, she thought he looked like an old man with his stooped shoulders and dark planter's hat. Alone on the roof she said, "I won't let you quit, Mac. Nor lose, if I can help it."

Swirling her skirts with the impetus of decision, she left the roof and went to her room to repair her toilette before greeting her husband after a separation of three months.

When he came in and saw her there, her cheeks still pink from the chill of the roof, he thought her beautiful. "My dear," he said, coming forward to take her hands. His clothes were dusty and he smelled as though he hadn't bathed in days, his hair long and unkempt, his face haggard with fatigue.

"Oh, Mac," she whispered, shocked at the devastation she saw. Turning away, she wiped her tears before facing him again. "Dear Mac," she said.

"You look lovely, as always," he said. "I feel ashamed even touching you, as travel worn as I am. Did you miss me, darling?"

"I shouldn't have gone," she replied, walking to the window and looking out at the orchard. "I could have been a help to you."

"What could you have done?" he asked with a smile.

"Sometimes I think I would have killed Dolan myself."

He noticed she was wearing the locket Tunstall had given her. Mac remembered how happy she had been when she first showed it to him, how she had come running into the house like a child, so excited and pleased. And the next day, John had been embarrassed until Mac let him know he didn't disapprove of the gift, was in fact delighted with Sue's happiness. John had smiled his smile of warm sunlight, making Mac feel all was right with the world because they were friends. He sighed deeply and began unbuttoning his vest, watching her fondle the locket at the end of its long chain. "I remember when John gave that to you. It seems long ago."

She faced him with anger clouding her face. "I shan't take it off until his death is avenged."

Mac turned away, tugging at the knot in his tie and pulling it loose, then pouring water into the basin to wash.

Sue left him alone, staring out the window at the maze of pink apple blossoms alive with hornets. Determined not to indulge herself in a destructive onslaught of anger, she tried to quiet herself enough to avoid inflicting her wrath on the man she was tied to for life.

Mac felt miserable, washing in the basin. He had yearned for her presence since the moment she left, yet within minutes of their reunion, they were estranged. Feeling stronger now that he could face her with some semblance of order, he turned back and explained his plans.

She listened, straining for patience, seeing in his face reminders of happier times and wanting to retrieve them, to live as they had before ever hearing of an isolated county where a young lawyer would supposedly do well. When he finished speaking, she chose her words carefully and modulated her voice to express encouragement rather than the disdain she felt. "So you intend to show up in court and vindicate your name?"

"Yes," he answered, perceiving her true reaction yet admiring her effort to be supportive.

"Why do you expect more success than before?"

"Because last time was in Mesilla with the judge alone. This will be in Lincoln. Our neighbors will sit on the grand jury and they'll not indict me. I am innocent."

"And the only charge against you is the one for embezzlement?"

"Yes," he scoffed. "Which should have been settled in a civil court all along."

"And what of Brewer and the others? Will they be indicted for killing Morton and Baker?"

"So you've heard about that?"

"I've had the benefit of Chisum's knowledge. Ash Upson is saying the Regulators went through Agua Negra with the intention of killing their prisoners. Chisum doesn't disagree."

"I think public opinion is with us," Mac answered. "Morton and Baker were principals among the posse who killed Tunstall. Our warrant was legally issued. That it was revoked the day before it happened was unknown to Brewer's men. They acted in good faith of serving the law, and I think the jury will applaud their intent. After all, Brady did nothing to arrest the killers."

"How did he justify that?"

"He said the outlaws attached themselves to the posse and were outside his control. And also that Tunstall resisted arrest, which no one believes."

"No! But if he were here now, he'd act differently."

Mac sighed. "Perhaps. But I am not he. Don't expect it, Sue. I shall never retaliate with violence."

"Not even in defense?"

"I cannot."

"Will not," she argued. "Choose not to."

"However you wish to say it. I shall never carry a weapon nor use one against another man. Peace is not sown with violence."

Caring more for his survival than peace, she wanted to cry out that he was a fool. But she held her tongue. And when they left their room to join the Chisums for dinner, she walked at Mac's side as if she were proud to be there.

Sue wore her most demure gray silk for the meeting with the Regulators. Eager to assess the men Brewer had gathered, she went early into Chisum's cavernous parlor and chose a chair in a corner behind the hearth so the light would illuminate their faces.

They all saw her as they came through the door, but Brewer was the only one to approach. Watching him arrange his expression to one of polite welcome, she wondered what he really thought. She rose to accept his quick embrace, then smoothed her skirts as she settled back in the chair, nodding at an ottoman nearby. "Please join me a moment, Dick."

Reluctantly he complied. "It's good to see you home, Mrs. Mac."

"Thank you. Yet I hardly am, am I? At the moment we're guests of Mr. Chisum, but I look forward to returning to Lincoln. Tell me, are there flowers on John's grave?"

"No," he answered with surprise. "We're just coming out of winter."

"Are we coming out of winter, Dick? Will we win?"

He had enough respect for her to be honest. "Eventually. But we'll pay a high price. The lives of some of the men in this room."

She looked at them then, nine Americans and three natives, all young except Middleton, who was reputed to be the best. When she had come in, their rifles stacked in the hall evoked a smile of power from her lips. Now, looking at the pistols each man wore, at their rough clothing and scuffed boots, their brown faces and hungry eyes, she smiled again. "You've chosen well," she murmured, looking back at Brewer.

"They were John's friends," he answered, not liking the chill of her smile.

"He had a way with men, didn't he," she said, touching the locket on her breast.

He looked away to watch Mac and Chisum enter the room. Sue, or someone, had cut Mac's hair and pressed his suit, so he looked almost as fresh as Chisum. The old rancher was casually dressed but his clothes were clean and ironed, while the Regulators had been living in what they wore for three days now. Sitting beside the perfumed Mrs. McSween, Brewer was keenly aware that he must smell strongly to her delicate nose. Indeed the roomful of men probably smelled like animals to her, and he wondered if that's how she saw them. Wishing he'd moved back with his friends before Mac's arrival, he felt too uncomfortable to do so as the lawyer took the floor and began to speak.

"Thank you for coming," he said in a courtroom voice, his face composed with dignity. "I shall be brief. As you can see, Mrs. McSween has rejoined me. We intend to return to Lincoln and reside in our home. I am confident the grand jury will exonerate me of this charge Dolan has wholly fabricated, and it will be over." He paused, his gaze running across all the faces watching him. "I have good news, though it is unfortunate our circumstances are so melancholy that news of a man's death can be called good." Again he paused, and the fire crackled behind him. "Tom Hill has been killed while attempting to rob a sheepherder."

Murmurs of pleasure moved like a wave from the mouths of the men. Sue watched their bloodlust with approval.

"Jesse Evans was with him," Mac continued. "He was wounded and has sought medical care at Stanton. Apparently he was shot in the lungs and is confined to bed."

"Is he under arrest, then?" McNab asked.

"That, I don't know," Mac answered. "But with the deaths of three of the men who murdered John Tunstall, and a fourth confined at least for the moment, I think we can claim justice and be done with killing."

"Tell that to Dolan and Brady!" Brewer said. "You're dreaming, Mac, if you think anything's over."

To Sue's horror, Mac took a step back and sat heavily in a chair, leaning forward to hide his face in his hands. She burned with humiliation and impotence to rise and tell these men what should be done.

For long moments the quiet was broken only by the soft whisper of flames in the hearth. Finally Mac looked at the men. "The day after tomorrow I return to Lincoln," he said, his voice a hoarse whisper. "As soon as I arrive, Brady will try to arrest me. You must not let him. If I am arrested, I shall surely be killed." He stood up, struggling for dignity. "That's all I have to say, gentlemen. Goodnight."

The men were silent, watching him walk into the dark hall. No one moved or uttered a sound until Brewer, overcome with compassion, strode after him.

Still the men were silent. The rustle of Sue McSween's silk gown was like the sound of a distant cataract falling over a precipice as she moved to the chair her husband had just left. Standing with one hand draped on the back as if she were honoring the absent occupant, she was silhouetted against the fire, a rigid outline of bustle and breasts, a fluff of crimped curls and the yellow eyes of a tigress.

"Gentlemen," she said calmly, "Sheriff Brady is the only man standing between us and justice, the only power that can prevent my husband from appearing in court and proving all of the charges that led to the murder of John Tunstall spurious, so the condemnation will fall where it belongs: on the head of Jimmie Dolan."

She paused, but the men gave no response, so she made her point quickly. "Sheriff Brady carries the only warrant for my husband's arrest. Destroy that warrant, and it will be impossible to replace before the opening of court."

The men assessed her words in each other's eyes. Knowing it was only because she was a woman that they didn't clamor assent, she felt she would scream, trying to hold herself poised while she waited.

Finally Chisum stepped from the shadows. "I'll back that up. Five hundred dollars to the men who get Brady out of the way before Mac arrives in Lincoln." He let his words settle a moment, then smiled. "You boys work it out among yourselves," he said, offering his arm to Sue. "Mrs. McSween?"

She walked proudly beside him, thinking she deserved a husband who would stand with her as John Chisum did.

25

The Kid's little señorita in San Patricio was named Angelita Sedillos. At sixteen she was plump and pleasing, with long black braids falling over her full breasts. She lived with her grandfather in a three-room adobe on Eagle Creek. The grandfather amiably slept with the horses when Billy came visiting, so Angelita had the whole feather bed to share with the Kid, while Fred Waite and Hendry Brown spread their blankets on the parlor floor.

Hendry thought Angelita was a prize, but he knew, the "sisters" were whores who serviced Fort Stanton. As on other nights, he lay awake long after the working girls had left, listening to Billy and Angelita in the adjoining room. Only a blanket hung across the door to muffle the gentle murmur of Billy's voice and Angelita's husky laughter, the rustle of covers, and an occasional creak of the bed. Hendry listened to her soft little mewing, then heard the beginning of a cry quickly stifled.

He knew the feeling of clapping his hand over a woman's mouth to keep her from crying out as she came, and it made him hot to hear it. He twisted in his blankets and tried to sleep. It was quiet now, and gradually the tension in his body eased. He had just begun to drift off when they started up again, their lovemaking heralded by a murmur from the Kid followed by Angelita's silky giggle. When a moan escaped her, Hendry grabbed his coat and stomped outside.

It was cold in the middle of the night in the high mountain canyon. He sat cross-legged on the wooden portal, tucking his stocking feet beneath himself and bracing his back against the wall to keep from shivering. After a moment, the door opened and Fred came out.

Hunkering down beside him, Fred offered a cigarette already rolled. In the light of the match, Fred said, "Kinda hard to listen to, ain't it?" He smiled beneath his long dark moustache.

Hendry exhaled a strong jet of smoke. "Don't he ever sleep?"

"Not much," Fred admitted, flicking the match into the yard where its flame trembled in the dust, then went out.

"With her I don't blame him," Hendry said. *"My* sister asked for money."

Fred shrugged. "She's gotta eat."

"Does Billy pay Angelita?"

Fred puffed on his cigarette. "She's in love with him. He's the first man she's been with."

Hendry snorted with envy.

"He's good with women," Fred said.

"And with horses and guns and rich Englishmen. Isn't there anything he ain't good with?"

"The law," Fred answered softly. "He told me the law's had it in for him since he was a little tyke."

Hendry took a long drag on his butt, then flicked it into the yard. "You know what we're doing tomorrow, Fred?"

"Yeah."

"Shooting the sheriff," Hendry whispered. "That's really riding loose."

"I know it."

"But you're going?"

"I go with Billy."

"Is Brewer coming?"

"I don't think he even knows about it."

"Oh, he knows. He's just too smart."

"What about you?"

"Yeah, I ain't smart," Hendry said, standing up and shaking the cramps out of his legs. "You think they're finished yet?"

"Prob'ly. Billy only usually goes twice," Fred answered, following him back into the warmth of the house.

They met an hour before dawn in Francisco Trujillo's *choza,* crowding together in the small room as they decided who would go. Asserting leadership in Brewer's absence, McNab made the final selection, saying the natives were out because Brady had a Mexican wife. Doc Scurlock had stayed with Mac at Chisum's, and Charlie Bowdre had left to find Brewer. Their absence was accepted as a decision.

They were six when they rode out: McNab, Middleton, Bonney, Waite, Brown, and Big Jim Finlay. Finlay was a heavyset cowboy who had ridden for Tunstall. He was quiet when he wasn't drunk, nondescript except for his size, and he followed the Regulators simply to be in the company of friends.

Hendry Brown, as always, rode at the rear. Ahead of him, Billy rode behind Fred Waite, whose big bay blocked Billy's view of the others on the narrow trail climbing alongside Eagle Creek. Billy was thinking about his Winchester, hoping the sheriff had it with him when he took the fall.

Quietly, the six Regulators rode through the sleeping town of Lincoln. McNab leaned from his saddle to unlatch the corral gate and hold it as they filed past him and on into the stable behind Tunstall's store. They tied their horses ready to run, then left the door open to the morning chill and walked back across the corral to take up positions behind the gate, crouching low to keep out of sight. Billy was in the middle; Fred and Hendry on his right; McNab, Middleton, and Finlay on his left.

The morning sun flooded the narrow valley with light. On the other side of the street, across the meadow sprinkled with early wildflowers, Squire Wilson came out of his house and began hoeing a bed for onions. A neighbor boy stopped his play to watch the old man, who grumbled as he worked.

Out of sight behind the gate, Billy said, "We should've got a *muchacho* to let us know when he's coming."

"We'll hear him," McNab grunted.

"Yeah," Billy agreed, "but we could be playing monte in the stable while we wait."

McNab looked at him over his shoulder. "This ain't a church social."

Billy laughed. "I ain't never been to a church social where they play monte. How about it, Fred?"

"I ain't ever been to a church social," Fred answered, his voice tense. "Lincoln ain't even got a church."

"Fine by me," Billy said. "Everything that happens inside 'em is a lie."

"Tell me something that ain't," Middleton growled.

"What we're about to do ain't," Billy said. "It'll be easy pickings after this."

"You're *loco* if you believe that," Middleton retorted. "What we're about to do is shoot the hornets' nest outta the tree."

"What're you so touchy about, John?" Billy asked. "Ain't you ever laid an ambush before?"

"Plenty," he answered. "But I ain't never shot the law."

"Why, your feet've got goosebumps," Billy teased. "I can see 'em poking through your boots."

"Quit yapping," McNab snapped. "I think they're coming."

Billy stood up, his belly flat against the gate as he peered over the top. He drew his six-gun and cocked it with his thumb, listening to the crunch of gravel from the approaching men. To his friends, Billy whispered, "He ain't alone."

McNab pulled the Kid down out of sight.

Brady wasn't going to open court but to tack up a notice that the session had been postponed. Judge Bristol had written that he felt threatened and feared he couldn't travel from Mesilla in safety. Brady suspected it was Rynerson's doing. The district attorney wanted him to arrest McSween when he came into town, not knowing court had been postponed, then turn him over to Jesse Evans. Brady didn't like it but felt he had no choice. To balk now would be suicide.

He had taken four men with him to walk the half mile through town. They kept their coats tucked behind their pistols and carried rifles, Brady the Winchester confiscated from that whippersnapper Billy Bonney, which was almost new and too good for a punk like him. They passed in front of the Tunstall store, George Hindman and Jake Mathews walking on either side of the sheriff, Jim Longwell and Dad Peppin slightly behind.

Brady said, "I hope the Kid comes in with McSween. He rides too high and I aim to shorten his rope before I'm done."

Simultaneously, the Regulators stood up behind the gate and emptied their guns at the passing men. Brady went down with twelve bullets in his back. Hindman fell but crawled a short distance, then blacked out. Peppin, Mathews, and Longwell dived for shelter. Across the street, a bullet shattered both thighs of Squire Wilson. The neighbor boy, watching him fall, began to scream.

Billy leapt the gate through the thick cloud of smoke. He'd seen his rifle and meant to get it. Turning the sheriff over, Billy had the Winchester in his hand when someone jumped the gate behind him. As McNab knelt in the dust to search Brady's pockets for the warrant, Billy looked at the sheriff's face and smiled, seeing the dirt crusted on his open mouth. They were all the same now, equal men squaring off without a badge between them.

A shot rang out and McNab fell. A split second later Billy felt his own leg wet with heat. He looked down and saw blood on his thigh, then grinned at McNab. "Reckon we're kin now," Billy said. "Shot with the same bullet."

"Help me, Kid," McNab moaned.

Bullets whined past his ears, kicking up spurts of dust as Billy grabbed McNab and hauled him toward safety. The gate swung open and they escaped behind its protection.

Middleton, Brown, and Finlay were already mounted. Fred stood holding the reins of his horse and Billy's too. Billy smiled at his friend, wanting to make tracks but feeling McNab heavy on his shoulder. The first thing he did was slide his Winchester into the empty saddle scabbard on his fine gray mare.

Sam Corbet hurried from the store and lifted McNab off. "Can you ride, Kid?"

He looked down at the blood soaking his leg. "I'll be all right," he mumbled, tying his handkerchief in a quick tourniquet.

"Then go," Corbet urged. "I'll hide Frank."

Billy swung onto his mare, feeling his leg a lance of pain. He pulled his hat low over his eyes and dug in his spurs to follow the others. When his nimble mare leapt Brady's body, Billy looked down, past the blood dripping off his boot into the sheriff's face, and he laughed.

As they galloped down the empty street, Middleton yelled across at him, "You get the warrant?"

"Missed it," Billy said. "But I got my rifle."

For a long moment, the dust of their departure settled in silence over the street of Lincoln, where nothing moved. When George Hindman moaned and begged for water, Longwell filled his hat at the trough and carried it over, but by then, the deputy was dead. Longwell dumped the water in the dirt and stood staring down at Brady sprawled as the outlaws had left him, his face covered with a fine layer of sand.

Slowly the people came onto the street. In silent, mournful groups they gathered to stare at the corpses of their sheriff and his deputy. No one moved to gather the dead, no one sent for aid from the fort, no one did anything but stand in silence and stare at the blood in the pale morning sun.

Frank McNab was bleeding heavily. The hole in his hip felt like a nest of scorpions against his bone, and his leg kept wobbling out from under his weight. Dragging it behind him, he leaned on Corbet as they climbed the three steps into the store, then crossed to what had once been the Englishman's rooms.

Corbet opened the door without knocking. Mrs. Ealy and Miss Gates had been sewing, and their baskets had tumbled onto the floor, spilling gaily colored skeins of thread as the women dived for cover when the fusillade erupted outside their window. They sat now with their skirts disarrayed to reveal not only ankles but knees covered with black stockings. Dr. Ealy clutched his open Bible to his breast. He was on the floor, too, his chair overturned by his sudden lurch. All three stared at Sam Corbet half-dragging a bleeding McNab into their parlor.

"Remove the rug," Corbet barked at Mrs. Ealy. When she sat immobile, he shouted, "Move, woman! There's a cellar beneath where we can hide him."

Miss Gates yanked the rug aside, revealing the hatch, and Mrs. Ealy leaned from her knees to pull it open. As Corbet dragged the nearly unconscious McNab toward the cellar, he said to Miss Gates, "Clean all the blood from inside the store. Quick! They'll be here any second."

She didn't ask who *they* were but hurried to the kitchen for a bucket and towels. As she looked back into the parlor, she saw the hatch going down over Dr. Ealy, holding a lantern in one hand and his medical bag in the other. Outside she heard men in the street, and she hastened to her task of erasing the trail of blood that led to the parlor from the back door.

There was a great deal of blood, as if someone had walked along pouring slowly from a milkpail. Except it wasn't the wholesome white froth of milk, it was thickly coagulating blood that dispersed in her bucket until she was slopping thin red water to gather almost solid gobs of gore. Corbet brought her a fresh pail and another rag, and she bent to her work as he followed behind with a dry cloth. Just as they were cleaning the back threshold, a fist pounded on the front door.

Susan Gates took the pail and cloths to the kitchen and set them in a corner, wanting to throw them out but knowing it was foolhardy now that *they* were here. Returning to the parlor, she saw the rug had been replaced. A chair had been set in the middle of it, occupied by Mrs. Ealy holding her retrieved sewing basket in idle hands. Susan settled a chair beside her and picked up the stocking she had been darning, nodding at the minister's wife to resume work. She did, blindly flashing a needle in and out of a seam she had been removing.

Sam Corbet wiped his hands on his handkerchief as he walked across the store to open the door.

Dad Peppin barged in. "You're under arrest, all of you," he bawled, looking around and seeing only Corbet. "Search the whole damn place!" he yelled at his men. A dozen deputies tromped in and began opening doors and closets and crates, any space large enough to hide a man.

"We know they're here," Peppin said, crossing to the parlor and staring in at the women.

"Who are you looking for?" Corbet asked from behind him.

"You know damn well! McNab and the Kid were wounded and seen plain as day. Where are they?"

"We've seen no one," Corbet replied. "When the shooting started, we all dived for the floor. What happened?"

"They killed Brady and Hindman!" Peppin shouted.

The back door opened and Longwell dragged Widenmann inside. "Here's one of 'em. He was out in the stable, had a horse all saddled ready to go."

"You're under arrest!" Peppin bellowed.

"By whose authority?" Widenmann snapped.

"I was Brady's chief deputy. His job falls on me by rote."

"And I'm a deputy U.S. marshal! You're out of line, Peppin."

Charles Crawford poked his head through the front door. "The McSweens are coming!"

From the east came a smart black buggy drawn by a chestnut mare. The people recognized the lawyer and his wife, returning as if in triumph. She was beautiful in her deep purple traveling suit, a matching bonnet with a white plume set at a low angle over one eye, her husband dignified in his dark frock coat and broad felt hat. Behind them rode Barrier and Scurlock, holding rifles and watching the street with sharp eyes.

McSween trotted his horse past the corpses without hesitation. Neither he nor his wife even looked to see who lay dead beneath the swarm of flies. The people watched Mr. and Mrs. McSween stop in front of their home, watched the lawyer hand his wife down as if they had just returned from church and their piety were visible for all to see, and the people exchanged knowing looks with their neighbors, sharing without words the observation that the McSweens had expected to find the sheriff dead when they arrived.

Dad Peppin came tearing out of Tunstall's store, followed by a dozen men, to confront McSween before he was inside his home.

"You're under arrest!" Peppin shouted.

Mac gave him a small tight smile. "I don't recognize your authority, Mr. Peppin. Show me your commission as sheriff of Lincoln County."

"I ain't got one and you know it! Brady's body ain't even cold. But you killed him, your men did, and you'll hang for this, McSween!"

"Come back with a warrant," Mac said impatiently, turning away and closing the door in Peppin's face.

"I'll be back with a warrant," Peppin yelled from outside, "even if it's covered with Bill Brady's blood!"

Mac walked into the parlor to see Sue standing before the cold hearth. All those months of her absence, he had longed to have her home again, but everything was wrong now.

Sebrian came in from the kitchen and managed to smile. "It's good to see you again, Mrs. Mac."

"Thank you, Sebrian," she answered. "I had expected a quieter welcome than this."

"Yes'm," he said softly. As he crouched before the hearth to build a fire, Sebrian could feel the estrangement between the couple behind him. He felt it was tragic that her homecoming had been marked with murder. Standing up, he said, "I'll make some tea."

"Yes, please," she murmured, sitting in her chair before the crackling blaze.

Mac waited until Sebrian had left. Watching the firelight flicker on the beautiful face of his wife, Mac moaned, "You have doomed me."

The white plume of her bonnet glistened red in the firelight as she turned to meet his eyes. "Trust me, Mac. It was necessary."

"I shall never be clean again."

Her nostrils flared in repugnance. "You'll be alive."

"Forgive me," he said, burdened with the ferocity of her love. "You acted your conscience out of regard for my safety, I accept that. But I believe we have committed a grievous error."

David Shield came into the room and stopped, watching them with apprehension.

Wondering how much he had heard, Mac said heartily, "Come in, David, and say hello to Sue."

Shield whispered, "Did you do it?"

"Do what, David?" Mac asked pleasantly. "Will you have a cup of tea with us? Sebrian is just now making it."

Shield shook his head. "I must know, Mac. Did you order the Regulators to kill Sheriff Brady?"

"I did not. I abhor violence and have striven these past months to avoid it. You know that, David. I'm surprised at your doubt."

Shield nodded, glancing at Sue. "Eliza will be reassured to know we are innocent of implication," he said to Mac, as if attributing his worry to his wife. "I'll go tell her. Will you be coming to the office later?"

"Yes, I'm eager to resume work. How's your new clerk doing? Harvey Morris, isn't that his name?"

"Yes," Shield answered. "He's doing well enough. If you'll excuse me, until later, then?"

Mac watched him leave, then turned back to Sue. "He didn't believe me."

She shrugged. "You told the truth."

"Not entirely," he said, sinking heavily into the chair across from her.

Sebrian returned with the tea and they said no more. Sitting across the fire from each other as they sipped the beverage they had learned to appreciate from their friend John Tunstall, both of them remembered happier days.

They heard the horses first, the cadence of many animals walking slowly closer until it stopped in obedience to a curt, military command. Mac and Sue watched each other with trepidation as they waited for the summons.

It came with a pounding on the door. Sebrian opened it as courteously as if guests were expected for tea. Dad Peppin stormed in accompanied by Captain Purington, the commander at Fort Stanton. Outside, a troop of the Ninth Cavalry sat their horses with rifles held against their thighs, the barrels aimed at heaven.

"We know you're hiding them somewhere," Peppin said, motioning his deputies inside. "Search the house," he told them.

"I protest!" Mac cried. "Where is your warrant?"

"I have a warrant for your arrest right here," Peppin said, flapping the bloodstained paper in Mac's face. "We'll get one for murder later."

"I regret Brady's death as much as you," Mac replied coldly. "You still must have a search warrant to enter my home."

"I'm doing it on Purington's authority," Peppin answered. "Martial law supersedes even lawyers."

"Is that true, Captain?" Mac asked. "Have you authorized martial law in Lincoln?"

"I haven't authorized anything," Purington replied gruffly. "I'm here to protect lives and property. That's the extent of my duty."

"How convenient," Mac retorted. "Heavily supportive of one side yet innocent of action. Your very presence is an act, Captain. This man is committing a crime, entering my home without legal sanction. Protection from unlawful search is a right guaranteed in the Constitution you have sworn to uphold."

"Damn the Constitution and you for a fool, McSween!" Purington shouted. "I'm going back to the fort. Anyone who wants the protection of the U.S. Army can come along." He stomped out and mounted his horse, yanked its head around and started west, his troop following at a slow but inexorable exit from town.

Peppin waved the warrant in Mac's face. "You're still under arrest," he crowed.

"Then I place myself under the protection of Captain Purington," Mac replied quickly, taking Sue's arm and leading her out to the buggy still tied in front. "Come along, Sebrian," he called as he picked up the reins. "Lock the door, please."

Sebrian watched the last of Peppin's men leave, then pulled the door shut and turned the key. As he sprang up behind the luggage on the back of the buggy, he pretended not to notice that Mrs. Mac was crying.

26

When Charlie Bowdre told Dick Brewer of the plan to kill Brady, Brewer was against it. He knew the assassination could only hurt their cause, inspiring fear in the people and destroying any sympathy for McSween. He also knew that despite Brady's flaws he held some control over Dolan's men. With the sheriff dead, the county would be truly lawless, wide open and lethal. But since Chisum had offered recompense, Brewer didn't argue with the men who chose to accept it. He simply went back to his farm and waited to hear what happened.

When Middleton rode in on a lathered horse and told him the deed had been done, Brewer resumed his mantle of leadership. Deciding to act as if the ambush changed only the animosity of their enemies, he told Middleton to gather the Regulators after dark at George Coe's ranch, then watched him spur his tired horse toward San Patricio where the men had scattered in retreat.

Brewer didn't wait for dark. He saddled his horse and left, feeling the loneliness of an outcast as he rode through the mountains, avoiding the trails where he might be seen. When he reined up at the edge of the clearing around Coe's house, George came out of the barn with a rifle in his hands. The two men stared at each other, both remembering when a visitor had been welcomed with joy rather than grim faces over guns.

"Come on in, Dick," George said, offering a belated smile.

Brewer nudged his horse into the dim shelter of the stable. It smelled alive, not abandoned as his had become. He swung down and loosened his cinch, pulled the bridle off and then back on with the bit beneath the horse's chin, then tied the reins to a stall before turning around and looking at George, waiting in the rectangle of sunset falling through the open door. Brewer moved to its warmth and sat down on a stack of hay.

"They're coming," he said, closing his eyes and letting his head drop back against the wall of the tack room, savoring the comforting smell of horses and leather. "I asked the Regulators to meet me here after dark."

George pulled a shaft of hay from the stack and chewed on it awhile. "What's your plan?" he finally asked.

"You hear about Brady?"

"I imagine the whole county's heard by now."

"What do you think they'll say?"

"They'll be scared, Dick. Killing the law scares everybody. Personally, I ain't sorry 'cause I hated the man. I know it wasn't right, but some kind of justice has been delivered."

"I hope other folks feel the same," Brewer said. "Even so, I'm going to keep the men out of sight for a while."

"Where you gonna go?"

"Any ideas?"

"Well, I'll tell you," George said, warming to the subject. "There's a rascal name of Davis who's had an easy time stealing horses since most of us ain't been home. We could go over to his camp and see if we can't replevin some."

"I know him. He was with the posse that killed Tunstall. Where's his camp?"

"Clear the other side of Blazer's Mill, near Tularosa."

"Seems far enough. And replevining stolen horses sounds like a respectable mission for the Regulators."

"Useful, too. You can't be riding the same mounts all over kingdom come like you have been."

"I know it. What happened to Tunstall's riding stock?"

"We'll prob'ly find most of 'em in Davis' corral," George said with venom. Then, more softly, "Whyn't you come up to the house and eat something 'fore they get here? How long has it been since your last meal?"

"A while," he said, opening his eyes and staring at the rafters already lost in darkness. "George, they shot Brady in the back from ambush. You and I couldn't do that."

"No," his friend answered. "Let's be glad they're on our side."

Brewer managed a dry chuckle, then he followed the tall, lanky farmer to his house for a plate of biscuits and beans.

In twos and threes, the men arrived. George opened the door first to Middleton and Scurlock, then Bonney, Waite, and Brown. Trujillo and Salazar came with Chavez, followed by Bowdre, Frank Coe, and Big Jim Finlay. McNab was the only one missing. He was recuperating in the bed of the Kid's sweetheart, so well tended the men almost envied him.

Brewer didn't. He watched the faces of the five who had been there, searching for the quality that allowed them to shoot a man in the back. But they all looked the same: Middleton as sour as he'd been since Tunstall's death, Finlay as quiet, Hendry as sharp behind his severely manicured moustache, Fred as amiable beneath his huge floppy one, the Kid just as jovial walking with a limp as without. Noticing Billy's new trousers, Brewer recognized them from the stock in Tunstall's store. He wondered how they'd managed to get McNab out of Lincoln and remember the nicety of a pair of pants while dodging Dolan's men, and begrudgingly, he admired them.

When they rode out at dawn, he felt the same camaraderie as before.

The laughter that always came from the vicinity of the Kid, the sounds of their horses, the creak of leather and jingle of bridles as they rode together. The mountains were ablaze with wildflowers, the sky blue and the air crisp as they rode leisurely southwest toward the Tularosa Valley.

The first night they camped in an isolated glen. Brewer felt solitary and spread his blankets off by himself, watching his friends loll about the fire. New to the Regulators, the Coe cousins stared wide-eyed as the veterans regaled them with accounts of their adventures. Brewer listened to their bravado, laughing despite himself at their comic descriptions of facing death as if it were no more cantankerous than a bronc with a deceptive buck.

When they finally turned in, Brewer lay in his blankets and listened to the rhythm of their snoring join together like a chorus of toads beneath the silence of the forest. Wondering who was on guard, he squinted across the dying fire to see Billy walk over to check the horses, and like others before him, Brewer wondered if the Kid ever slept.

In the morning, they headed toward Blazer's Mill. A McSween partisan, Blazer was a tall, stooped man, frail and able to maintain his enterprise only because he had enough money to hire others to do the work. Inviting the Regulators to water their horses, Blazer noted sadly that George and Frank Coe rode with them now. He had hoped they could stay out of it. Looking at Brewer, he asked, "Did you know Buckshot Roberts is on your trail?"

"What for?" Brewer asked with annoyance.

"The bounty," Blazer said slowly. "Didn't you know there's a price on your lives for killing Brady and Hindman?"

Brewer shook his head.

"Dolan put up two hundred dollars for any of the Regulators, dead or alive," Blazer said, noting the shock in the eyes of Brewer and the Coes, the gleam of fight in the others. The Kid didn't even react to the news but simply watched his mare drinking from the trough.

"I don't like being the one to tell you," Blazer continued, "but it's best you know. That kinda money's gonna pull all kinds of scum into the county, as if we ain't got enough as 'tis."

"Yeah," Brewer mumbled, realizing he should have ridden with the others since he was equally condemned for the act.

"Buckshot was just here looking for his mail," Blazer said. "He told me he aims to collect some of them bounties, being as y'all got it in for him anyway."

The horses slurped noisily, blowing great sighs across the surface of water.

Dr. Blazer said kindly, "Why don't y'all come inside for some supper? Looks like you've ridden a ways."

Brewer accepted the invitation, wanting time to think before they moved out again. He knew it was the first of many meals they would beg or steal if forced to live off the land. Middleton and George Coe stood guard while the others sat down to a supper of beans and biscuits and buttermilk cool from the cellar. The men ate in hungry silence, waiting to hear Brewer tell them how it would be.

Coe and Middleton were sitting on the top step outside the back door, watching the road that followed the canyon down into the Tularosa Valley. The two-story building of the Indian Agency loomed to their left, deserted on this non-ration day. On the other side of the road was the sawmill, and between it and the road stood a stack of raw lumber. To their right was the stable and smith shop, empty because Blazer's workers had gone home for their midday meal.

The horses of the Regulators were hidden inside a high-plank corral, so there was no sign that the mill was different from any other early afternoon when Buckshot Roberts came ambling back.

Grizzled and filthy, he wasn't a popular man in Lincoln County, but he was known to be fearless. He'd ridden with the posse that killed Tunstall and was named on the warrant, so he'd holed up in Mesilla since the murder, only waiting for a check from the sale of his land before leaving the county permanently. The chance of being paid to kill men sworn to kill him, however, was too good to let pass. He planned on riding into San Patricio to flush a few of them out, then take their bodies back to Lincoln for the reward.

He was anxious to get his check, though. When he saw the dust rising over the mill, he went back hoping it was the freight wagon bringing the mail. If he hadn't expected to find any of the Regulators alone, neither had he expected to come across all of them together at Blazer's Mill. He knew that's what he'd done as soon as he saw Middleton and Coe guarding the kitchen door.

The sentries watched him amble his mule closer, then get off and tie it between the house and the empty Agency building. Wearing two six-shooters and a pair of *bandoleras* crisscrossing his chest, he set his rifle on the cracked toe of his boot and scowled at the sentries. Middleton and Coe stood up, their rifles ready.

Buckshot spat tobacco juice into the dust. "Yer cousin inside?" he asked George.

"What do you care?" Coe said, his cheek against the smooth stock of his rifle.

"Can I talk to 'im, think?" He spat again.

The men inside heard the voices. They all came out, eyeing the old man warily. George said, "He wants to talk to Frank."

"I know him," his cousin said. "I'll listen to what he has to say." He walked toward Roberts. "Come on, we'll talk over here."

Buckshot wouldn't turn around. He walked backward to the steps of the Agency. They sat down and stared at the Regulators watching them, George and Middleton still holding their rifles ready at their shoulders.

"Go on," Frank yelled, "leave us be awhile!" He watched them move out of sight behind the house, then looked at Roberts. "You sure walked into it, Buckshot. What do you want here anyway?"

"T'get out alive," the old man grumbled.

"If you surrender you've got a chance," Frank said. "Brewer won't let 'em hurt a man who surrenders."

Roberts snorted. "Like Morton and Baker? No sir, I'd as soon die fighting if it comes to that."

"Then there's nothing I can do for you," Frank said, standing up.

"Did the mail wagon come?" Buckshot asked, glancing around the yard.

Frank shook his head.

"Thanks fer the parley," the old man muttered, squinting up at him. "You go tell your friends I've come for their scalps. Go on, now. I'll not shoot you in the back."

Frank nodded and left. "It's no go," he told Brewer. "I tried to talk him into surrendering, but he's determined to take scalps."

Brewer looked past the corner of the house, remembering the weapons the old man wore. Because of the bounties, Buckshot had come to commit legal murder, while if the Regulators defended themselves they risked being hung. The injustice made Brewer angry, and part of his wrath was aimed at himself for not being in on ambushing Brady and guiding it to a more effective result. If he'd made up his mind to go that far, he would have killed Dolan too. Now he was left with a snake who'd had its rattle cut off, making it more dangerous. Believing he'd failed them, Brewer looked at his men.

"There's only one way to discourage bounty hunters," he said low and mean, "and that's to kill every one of 'em that comes along. I'm asking for volunteers."

Charlie Bowdre stepped forward. "I hate that ol' sonofabitch. I'll go."

"Deal me in," the Kid said.

"Me, too," George said.

"That's enough," Dick said. "You boys be ready to back us up. Let's go."

Bowdre was the first around the corner. He drew his gun and yelled, "We got a warrant for your arrest. Throw up your hands!"

"Fat chance," Buckshot snickered, firing his rifle.

Their guns went off simultaneously. Bowdre's bullet dug deep into Buckshot's groin. Buckshot's bullet struck Bowdre's gunbelt, slicing it in half and gouging his side as it glanced off to explode George's pistol and sever his trigger finger, continuing on to rip a tunnel through the edge of Middleton's gut.

Billy looked at three men down from a single bullet and whistled in admiration. He gave the old man a smile just as Buckshot fired again. Billy ducked back behind the corner of the house. George was wrapping his hand in a handkerchief already dripping blood. Middleton had torn his shirt open and was gawking at the flesh wound in his belly. Bowdre was looking at his gunbelt in the dust and fingering the sore spot against his hip.

"Goddamn, what a shot," Billy whispered.

He saw Brewer had made it behind the pile of lumber on the other side of the road, so they had Buckshot cornered. He had stumbled into a room of the Agency and pulled a feather mattress across the open door in front of him. Billy stepped out from behind the house and emptied his pistol at the old man anyway, watching his bullets hit the bed with puffs of dust. When his gun was empty, Buckshot's rifle gleamed in the sun and Billy dodged back behind the house just before a bullet knocked the edge of adobe off the wall beside him.

As he reloaded, he saw Brewer stand up behind the lumber and take a carefully chosen shot. Billy snapped his gun closed and was about to step out and fire when Brewer rose above the woodpile again. As Billy watched, the top of Brewer's head was blown off. He lurched backward to fall dead in the dirt.

Billy swallowed hard. "He got Dick," he said softly.

Coe, Middleton, and Bowdre came up closer, looking away from their wounds to see Brewer sprawled in a growing pool of blood.

As the knowledge spread among the men, a silence of impending fury fell over the mill. Dr. Blazer came out, drawn by the quiet, then froze as he saw Brewer dead. To no one in particular, he said, "Let me go check Roberts' condition. If he's gutshot, he can't live long."

The Kid smiled. Blazer hurried away from him, out into the yard in front of the Agency. "It's Dr. Blazer, Buckshot," he called. "Can I help you?"

"Don't bother," the old man growled. "I'm kilt."

"I'm coming in," Blazer answered, stepping over the bloody mattress. Roberts lay on his back, his belly a mass of gore. A *bandolera* was twisted around his arm, both his pistols lay loaded and ready within reach, and he held his rifle in hands slippery with blood. Blazer looked at him with pity and returned to report.

All the Regulators were gathered behind the house again, staring at Brewer in the sun across the road. For lack of any other apparent leader, Blazer said to the Kid, "Roberts is gutshot bad. He'll die within hours."

The Kid seemed lost in thought as he looked up at the new telegraph wire running from the Indian Agency to Fort Stanton. Suddenly he snapped back. "Soldiers coming," he said. "Let's ride." Firing his gun at Roberts, he ran for the corral. The others followed, emptying their rage into the feather bed protecting the dying man. They leapt on their horses and tore out of the yard, heading up Tularosa Creek.

Brewer's horse trotted out from the corral and whinnied its confusion at being left behind. Blazer walked over slowly, talking quietly to the animal until he could catch the reins dragging in the dust. He led the horse back inside and closed the gate.

He was halfway across to Roberts when the cavalry arrived. The young Negro sergeant reined up tight in front of him and barked, "We came at the request of Agent Bernstein. He said the Regulators are here."

"They were," Blazer answered, raising his eyes to the silhouette of Bernstein in an upstairs window. "They've gone," he told the sergeant. "Except for Dick Brewer. He'll be staying."

The sergeant followed Blazer's gaze to the body behind the woodpile.

Blazer cleared his throat. "There's a wounded man inside. Will you fetch Dr. Appel to tend him? I'm just a dentist, you know."

"I'll send a man, but we're going after the Regulators. Which direction did they take?"

"North!" Blazer exclaimed. "Back to Lincoln."

"They're crazy," the sergeant muttered, then yanked his horse around and divided his men.

Dr. Blazer sat on the stoop and waited for his workers to return so he could tell them where to dig the graves. Then he went inside and sat through the fading afternoon, watching Buckshot Roberts bleed to death.

The Kid rode hard at the head of the Regulators, trying to outdistance Brewer's death. Since the previous autumn when he'd first come to stay with George Coe, Billy had crisscrossed the Capitan and Sacramento mountains so often he knew every arroyo and canyon, every spring and meadow. What he didn't know was where to hide the pain he felt that a reprobate like Buckshot Roberts could destroy as fine a man as Richard Brewer.

But now the Kid concentrated on leading the Regulators the shortest route back to Coe's ranch on the Hondo. They left their horses saddled in the barn and congregated in the house, crowding the single room.

George opened his jug, took a long swallow, then passed it to Scurlock. As the whiskey traveled from man to man, George bent over the hearth and started a fire. He stayed hunkered down, watching the flames lick delicately at the tinder, then catch and snap on the seasoned pine he'd cut from the forest last summer.

He and his friend Dick Brewer had gone out with a wagon and spent a week toting wood back to their homes to be ready for winter. Here it was spring again, time to be planting crops, foaling mares, and riding into town with Dick to attend a *baile* and flirt with the señoritas. Except his fields weren't plowed yet, and his horses were all run off.

George stood up and looked for the jug. He saw Billy pass it without drinking, and George thought the Kid was smart for not getting drunk. But as for himself, George needed something to kill the pain.

The whiskey traveled around the room until every man had his turn. As Scurlock passed it to begin its second round, he said, "At least we got the bastard. He died slow and hard for killing Dick."

A general grumble of assent rose from the men, then the whiskey made its round again in a silence broken only the sounds of the men drinking and the slap of their hands as they passed the jug. When it came back to George, he felt it was getting light and he drug out another. Yanking the cork, he took a deep swig, then passed it on. "What're we gonna do now, boys?"

For the first time, the Kid spoke. "I'll ride over and tell McNab. Why don't we wait for him before making any decisions?"

"Good idea," Scurlock said. "We'll stay here. That all right with you, George?"

"I got another jug after this one," he answered glumly.

"I'll take Fred and Hendry," the Kid said. "Charlie, you want to come?"

Bowdre looked up with surprise. Truth be told he'd rather stay with the jug, but an invitation from the Kid wasn't something to turn down. "Sure, I reckon," he said.

As they walked across the moonlit yard, Billy stuck his hand out and said, "I want to congratulate you, Charlie. We was all shooting at the old buzzard, but you're the only one who hit him."

"Thanks," Bowdre answered, pleased someone had finally said it.

Billy threw his arm across Charlie's shoulder and asked confidentially, "You like green chile enchiladas?"

"I reckon," Charlie said, confused.

Walking behind them, Waite and Brown laughed. Hendry said, "Don't believe what he tells you about the sister."

27

Billy's friend Macky Nab was sitting at the table watching Angelita stir a pot of chile. She was a shy girl who had lived with her grandfather since her parents died of smallpox when she was nine. The small home they shared had a garden, a milk cow and chickens, and two fields of corn that usually brought sixty dollars from the Big Store in Lincoln. It wasn't enough to cover their debt for the supplies they needed over the year, but Dolan had always just marked their credit and let them keep charging against the promise of their crop.

This year, however, they had promised it not to Dolan but to the Englishman, who was partners with Macky Swain. When Dolan found out, he'd cut off their credit. They didn't have anything now other than what they grew themselves, and the gifts Billy brought.

Angelita had met Billy walking home from Lincoln early one evening. She had gone to town for coffee and sugar, intending to shop at Tunstall's store because of their new arrangement, but she had gotten a late start. After walking five hours, she found the Englishman's store closed, so she went to Dolan's. That's when she learned he'd cut off her credit. He leered and offered to make a private arrangement, and she ran all the way back to the trail toward Eagle Creek before stopping to catch her breath. Then she started the long walk home empty-handed.

Halfway up the mountain, Billy Bonney had come along the trail alone. He was so cheerful and friendly, she let him coax her onto his horse as he slid behind the saddle and put his arms around her to hold the reins. When he heard her story about the Englishman's store being closed, he laughed and said she should have just knocked on the door, that Sam Corbet lived in back and would've been glad to sell her anything. She admitted she hadn't thought to do that, then told him about going to Dolan.

Billy smiled and said he couldn't blame the man none for appreciating her beauty. She felt pleased, thinking Billy had a way of making the ugliness of the world seem harmless. When he dropped her off at home, she was disappointed he didn't accept her invitation to stay for supper. She watched him ride away thinking she would never see him again. But the next day he was back, with coffee and sugar and a shiny green ribbon for her hair.

On his next visit, her grandfather killed a rooster and she made chicken enchiladas smothered in green chile. Billy brought her two cans of peaches and her grandfather a box of bullets for his old hunting rifle. The three of them sat late at the table talking softly in Spanish, and Angelita thought she had never seen her grandfather enjoy himself so much with an American. Billy's Spanish was fluid and graceful, and the old man's eyes gleamed with appreciation, watching him speak.

That night her grandfather had walked Billy out and they stood talking by his horse for a long time. Angelita kept peeking at them through the window as she washed the dishes. When her grandfather came back inside, he wouldn't tell her what they'd been discussing. When she persisted, he became angry and told her not to meddle in the conversations of men.

Only later did she figure out they had decided her fate, agreeing like traders on how much she was worth. Certainly she hadn't put it together by the time of Billy's next visit. When her grandfather left the table saying he'd sleep in the barn, she watched him go with confusion. Then she looked at Billy's smile and felt glad, foolish girl that she'd been.

It was after Billy started sending her to find sisters for his friends that she realized what she'd done. At first she felt indignant, but she was obedient and did as he asked. Before long she knew the only difference between her and the sisters was they were paid in cash and she in gifts of food. And that she loved Billy. She came to see her love as a blessing to make up for having forfeited her right to be married in a church.

Superstitious and submissive, Angelita strove to bear her fate with dignity. But she didn't like Macky Nab, and that made her realize another way she was different from the sisters. She knew she would starve before bedding the man who stared at her so greedily without even pretending to be nice.

Frank McNab was feeling strong enough to walk with a stick used as a crutch. He'd been lucky the bullet missed the bone, that's what Dr. Ealy said as he cleaned the wound by pulling a silk scarf through the hole. If it had hit the bone, McNab would never have walked again. Yet here he was, feeling so horny he could hardly keep his hands off the Kid's girl. He didn't want to abuse these people's hospitality, and he certainly didn't want to antagonize the Kid, but he knew if he didn't leave soon he was apt to do both. When he heard four riders come into the yard, he stood up eagerly, hoping they were the Regulators.

Also knowing it could be Dolan's men, McNab kept himself hidden as he peered out a window. The sight of his friends sent him hobbling for the door, but Angelita flew past him in a swirl of calico he remembered seeing on a bolt in Tunstall's store.

McNab stood in the door and watched her wait while the Kid swung down. Then Angelita leapt to hold him, kicking her feet up as she hung on, laughing and kissing his cheek. "Billy, Billy," she said. "I'm so glad you're back."

The Kid disentangled her, eyeing McNab. "Has this crowbait been giving you trouble?" He smiled at Frank when he said it.

"No, no," Angelita was quick to say. "He's much better, see. I'm a good nurse, no?"

"Looks like it to me," the Kid said. "I brought another man hungry to taste some of your chile. You got enough?"

She nodded happily. "Come into the house," she pleaded, tugging at his hand. "Talk in the kitchen while I cook tortillas?"

"In a minute," he said. "Go along now."

Stepping out of the door to let her pass, McNab saw her look back at the Kid with longing just before she disappeared. McNab looked at the Kid, too, and saw from the change in his face that he brought bad news.

"We ran into Buckshot Roberts over at Blazer's Mill," the Kid said. "We killed Roberts, but he got Dick first."

McNab hung on to his crutch hard, knowing Brewer had given them a badge of legitimacy, usurped by the Santa Fe Ring's proclamation or not. With Brady dead, this was no time for the Regulators to lose their legitimacy. He asked the Kid, "Ain't there a justice of the peace in San Patricio?"

"Gregorio Trujillo," he answered, waiting for his point.

"I think I'll have myself appointed a deputy," McNab said. "The governor's proclamation only outlawed Wilson's court, not this one in Precinct Two. We'll be legal again with a constable's commission."

"Makes no difference to me," the Kid said. "But if you want to go, let's do it."

"I'll get my horse," McNab said.

"Why don't you lend him yours, Fred?" Billy suggested, then smiled at McNab. "You may be able to sit a horse, but I don't think you could saddle one." He looked at the three men who'd followed him. "We'll be back in a coupla hours."

McNab climbed up on Fred's big bay, feeling his hip complain as he swung his leg across. He looked down to see Angelita standing in the door near tears.

"We'll be right back," Billy told her.

With dismay, she watched him rein his horse down the trail with Macky Nab.

Now she had three men sitting at her table watching as she cooked. Fred she knew and didn't mind; he was gentle and Billy's friend, so hers too. Hendry Brown she didn't trust. She didn't like seeing his smile curl under his thin moustache lying like a whip above his mouth. The new one, Charlie Bowdre, was restless. The way he kept moving around the room made her nervous, but she didn't say anything. She had been brought up to accommodate the behavior of men. Even so, she was finding it difficult, because it wasn't Billy she was required to accommodate but an increasing parade of unpleasant strangers.

She served the men supper and washed their dishes, then scrubbed the stove, listening for the sound of horses to tell her the waiting was over. When Billy and Macky Nab finally returned, they sat with the others at the table, talking softly while they ate. She tried not to listen because the men spoke of killing and being killed, and she couldn't bear to think of losing Billy that way. She would rather he grow tired of her and find another girl. At least then she could think of him in her lonely times, and how he might be smiling remembering her.

The horses nickered as Billy and Angelita climbed into the loft to spread his blankets by the window. She saw Fred standing guard in the shadow of the house, and she turned to ask Billy why everything was suddenly so dangerous. He shushed her with a kiss, took her fast and hard, then threw himself off just as tense as before.

She waited, attuned to his moods. Finally he kissed her again, and she knew from his gentleness that he had conquered something within himself. On other nights she became an animal to please him, but this time their union was tender. And this time when Billy withdrew, he nestled her on his shoulder as they lay naked between his blankets, staring at the darkness in the rafters above.

Now she could speak; after satisfying her man, a woman had earned the right to say her mind. Angelita asked, "Was it a good friend of yours who died today?"

"Yeah," he answered, and she felt the tension sweep down his body again.

"I am sorry," she said. "Also I am glad it wasn't you."

"One day it might be," he said.

"I have been thinking," she said, gathering her courage. "My grandfather tells me stories of how it was in México with war in the countryside. It is becoming the same here. We can do as he did. We can go away." She took a deep breath. "Even if you don't wish to go with me, you should do it to save your life."

He laughed. "This is my life. Sharing love with a pretty girl, having a friend outside watching for coyotes that sneak around in the night. I can't think of nothing better."

"You make a joke of everything," she scoffed.

"That's no joke." He sat up to look at her in the dark. "I ain't coming back, Angie, not till this is over. I don't like seeing you with all those hardcases down there. You deserve better."

"Why are they good enough for you and not for me?"

" 'Cause I'm like 'em. I got a price on my head, dead or alive. I ain't gonna let it be known I spend time at your house."

"Why do you have a price on your head?" she whispered.

"For killing Brady."

"Why did you do that, Billy? Don't you see it will never go away? They will chase you until they catch you, then only bad will come."

"They'll never catch me," he said.

"You have caught yourself. Nothing good will come of this. Already what you have done is taking you away from me."

"God, Angie, if things were dif'rent, I could maybe offer you something worth having. If they hadn't killed Tunstall, I'd be running a horse ranch on the Peñasco with Fred, you know that? Tunstall was gonna set us up and then everything would've tumbled right. But that ain't what happened. I made a vow to get the men who killed him, and we've done it with five of 'em. Ol' Jesse's slick as butter but he'll dance to my tune sooner or later. Then maybe I can think about some kinda future."

She was crying and he lay down and cradled her against his shoulder again. "That's right," he murmured. "I'm telling you now so you won't let the men see you crying in the morning."

And she didn't. She cooked them all tortillas and eggs, watched them eat and then leave. Billy didn't look at her once the whole time. Not until they were riding out did he turn and tip his hat. She smiled bravely until he was gone.

Mac was staying in the same room at Fort Stanton he had occupied before. Sue was with him now, though the atmosphere between them was tense. She spoke more words to Barrier in the adjoining room than to her husband, who was preparing his defense for court.

The criminal charge was of no consequence to Mac. He could easily prove he had instructed his law partner to follow the court's stipulations. That would exonerate him of the embezzlement charge. After the civil case was resolved, he would be given a specified time to comply with the order of the court. Time that would allow him to gather the funds.

The truth was, Mac had loaned the Fritz money to Tunstall. Since he'd been forced to wait until the court named the heirs, the money had just been sitting in Mac's account and he hadn't seen any harm in making the loan, confident the Englishman would repay him before the case was settled. But that hadn't happened. Tunstall had been murdered. And because they'd never drawn up partnership papers, his accounts in St. Louis and Santa Fe were inaccessible to Mac. Wryly, he realized he didn't even possess a note on the loan to present a claim against Tunstall's estate.

So it was the civil case of Scholand and Fritz that worried him. They were suing for the entire amount of ten thousand dollars, disregarding his nearly six thousand deduction for collection expenses. Not all of that was profit, though he used the word with irony. The insurance company had declared bankruptcy and McSween was able to realize only eighty percent of the policy's value. To collect that amount, he had to pay nearly three thousand in bank and attorney fees in New York. His fee and travel expenses amounted to little more than a thousand dollars, which he considered just. However, whether the plaintiffs won the four thousand he offered or the entire ten, Mac didn't have the money.

His strategy lay in petitioning for a continuance due to the disruption of his life over the past months. If given merely ninety days, he felt confident he could raise the money. Once he was acquitted of the embezzlement charge, his business was sure to prosper. He was famous now as the lawyer fighting the Santa Fe Ring, and victory could only enhance his reputation.

In the sanctuary of the fort, Mac felt safe for the first time since Tunstall's death. Once exonerated, he could reside peacefully at home again. He and Sue could begin the process of reweaving their marriage, and the past would be left behind. He was just beginning to feel optimistic when he learned of Brewer's death.

Sue picked up the gossip around the fort first. Mac held the horror at bay until Doc Scurlock came to their door with a face of grief. Numbly Mac thanked the man for telling him, closed the door, then fell to his knees sobbing in anguish.

Sue tried to comfort him, crying herself, but Mac rebuffed her caresses. Brady's murder had doomed him. God no longer favored his endeavors. The things his soul had refused to touch were now his sorrowful meat.

28

Court finally convened on April 8. Assuming the presence of the judiciary would ensure their safety, Mac and Sue returned home. Sue stayed sequestered with Sebrian while Mac ventured into the street accompanied by Deputy Barrier, Doc Scurlock, and Frank McNab.

The village was crowded with fighters: rambunctious Regulators, rowdy Seven Rivers warriors, swaggering Dolanites, and the arrogant riffraff off the Rio Grande riding behind the outlaw John Kinney. Except for the Rio Grande outlaws, they were all citizens of Lincoln County and had all come to see justice done. Even the men who had taken no part in the fighting knew which side they were on, and they all wore guns. The street was an arena of ribald insults and threatening jeers, and Mac didn't feel safe walking it alone.

Daily, Prosecutor Rynerson and Judge Bristol were escorted from Fort Stanton by a bodyguard of soldiers. The courtroom audience was vocal with its sentiments, and Judge Bristol pounded the gavel often. Surrounded by Barrier, McNab, and Scurlock, Mac stood against the wall on one side of the room, facing Dolan with his bodyguards on the other, as the grand jury returned with their findings.

Dr. Blazer was their foreman. As the room fell silent, he remained standing while the other jurors sat down. Then he cleared his throat and read: "We, the grand jury for the April, 1878, term of the District Court for the County of Lincoln, deeply deplore the present insecurity of life and property, though it is but the revival and continuance of the troubles of past years.

"Your Honor charged us to investigate the case of Alexander A. McSween, Esquire, charged with the embezzlement of ten thousand dollars belonging to the estate of Emil Fritz, deceased. This we did, but were unable to find any evidence that would justify that accusation. We fully exonerate him of the charge and regret that a spirit of persecution has been shown in this matter."

The Regulators broke into cheers and hurrahs. Except for Scurlock and McNab, they were all standing by the rear door, and their noisy jubilation infected the audience with vociferous accord. Judge Bristol pounded his gavel, shouting that he would clear the court if silence wasn't restored. Everyone quieted down and turned expectantly to the jury.

Blazer sniffed, then read: "The murder of John H. Tunstall is without parallel for brutality and malice, and without a shadow of justification. By this inhuman act we lost one of our best and most useful men, one who brought intelligence, industry, and capital to the development of Lincoln County. We equally condemn the murder of our late sheriff, William Brady, and his deputy George Hindman. In each of the cases where the evidence warrants it, we have made presentment."

The audience was silent, waiting to hear who would be named.

"For the murder of John Tunstall," Blazer read, "we order indictments be issued against Jesse Evans as principal, and James J. Dolan and Jacob B. Mathews as accessories."

A murmur of approval swept through the crowd.

Blazer continued, "For the murders of William Brady and George Hindman, we order indictments be issued against John Middleton, Hendry Brown, Frederick Waite, and William H. Bonney, alias Kid. For the murder of Andrew L. 'Buckshot' Roberts, we order an indictment be issued against Charles Bowdre."

Now Dolan's men were laughing, though no indictment had been issued for the killing of Morton and Baker. Mac turned to watch the Regulators quickly slip from the courtroom, then met McNab's eyes, wondering why he had escaped indictment. It was evident, however, that any pleasure McNab felt at his own fate was marred by the condemnation of his friends. When he followed them out, Mac too left the courtroom, accompanied by Barrier and Scurlock.

Outside, Barrier bid him good-bye. Watching the deputy disappear in the crowd, Mac felt unable to fully accept that he was a free man. He turned to see Scurlock smiling at him.

"It's a good day, ain't it, Mr. Mac?"

"Yes," he answered. "A good day for new beginnings."

With resolution he walked through the boisterous crowd to the expected peace and quiet of his home. When he opened the door, however, his parlor was crowded with Regulators and partisans. Sue sat by the fire, laughing in celebration, as Mac scanned the faces for the men who had been indicted. None of them was there.

"Mac, darling," Sue said, crossing the room to kiss his cheek. "Congratulations," she murmured, her eyes flashing with happiness.

He patted her hand, then said softly, "I'll think I'll just go into the kitchen and have Sebrian fix me something to eat. Go on with your fun, Sue. I'm tired and won't be good company."

He turned away to avoid her protest, but before he was out of the room he heard her laugh anew at someone's joke. In the kitchen, he found Sebrian cooking alone.

"Congratulations, Mr. Mac," Sebrian said. "I surely am glad you've been 'xonerated."

"Thank you," Mac said, sitting heavily at the table. "Have you seen Fred or Billy?"

Sebrian's smile fell from his face as he shook his head.

"Middleton or Brown or Bowdre?"

"No, sir," he said. "Would you like me to find 'em?"

Mac sighed. "It can wait, I suppose. Is there anything to eat? I feel weak from hunger."

"I'll get right on it, Mr. Mac." He set the coffeepot on the fire and was taking a kidney pie from the pantry when Sue came in.

"There you are, darling!" She laughed. "I've just had the most wonderful idea. Let's have a party to celebrate our victory! We can invite John Chisum and all the Regulators and partisans, everyone who stood by us. Don't you think that's a wonderful idea?"

Mac searched her face for regret that five of their men had been indicted for murder. Seeing none, he answered distractedly, "Whatever you wish, Sue."

In the first halcyon weeks after court, peace was restored in Lincoln. John Copeland had been appointed sheriff, and even those Regulators under indictment felt free to walk the street without fear of arrest. They availed themselves of Mrs. Mac's open hospitality, and Sheriff Copeland was often seen laughing with the men who filled her parlor, watching them come and go even as he held warrants for their arrest.

A few days before Mrs. Mac's victory celebration, Dad Peppin and Jake Mathews rode to the Pecos to recruit a posse. Claiming to be deputies under the authority of their appointments by Brady, they were hoping to circumvent the lethargy of the present sheriff. In Seven Rivers, Peppin and Mathews enlisted twenty men to arrest the indicted Regulators who would openly flaunt their freedom at the celebration.

On the day of the party, the posse reached the Fritz ranch east of Lincoln shortly before noon. The house was built on a small plateau that crumbled as it approached the banks of the Rio Bonito. Hoping to ambush some of the Regulators riding to town, fifteen of the posse hid themselves behind the descending cliff. Half a mile down the road was an unoccupied tenant house. Another seven of the posse hid within its adobe walls.

Frank Coe and his farming partner Ab Saunders, accompanied by Frank McNab, fell into the trap. Riding a faster horse than the others, Coe was far in the lead when they passed the Fritz ranch, and for that reason alone he nearly escaped.

One moment there was only the cadence of hoofbeats beneath the birds singing in the trees. In the next, twenty rifles exploded the quiet. McNab's horse bucked in fright. He flip-flopped up and down, avoiding the bullets flying around him only because of the erratic action of his horse. When Saunders horse went down with a bullet through its heart, Ab ran into an arroyo.

The Olinger brothers pursued him on horseback, easily overtaking the running man and cornering him against a cliff of crusted sand. Bob Olinger shot Saunders in the hip. Yanking his horse around, Bob yelled to his brother, "He won't go anywhere!" Then he spurred back to battle, his long red hair flying beneath his roundtop sombrero.

Wallace Olinger looked regretfully at Saunders, moaning crumpled on the ground, then followed his brother. McNab's horse was still bucking but riderless now, and the Olingers saw the other men hightailing up a canyon into the mountains. They galloped after them and reined up just in time to see McNab shot through the head by the man known only as Indian. With a curdling cry for more blood, the half-breed Apache led the posse in pursuit of the last man.

Frank Coe had watched everything happen behind him, momentarily paralyzed with shock. When he saw he couldn't help his friends, he turned his mare to run just as a rifle shot shattered her head and she fell, pinning Frank's rifle beneath her. He propelled himself forward and hit the ground running.

Horsemen were coming up fast, already shooting though still out of range. A hundred yards ahead of Coe, an arroyo opened up and Frank scurried into its cover. He scrambled up the cliff, knowing he'd be in plain view when the riders rounded the bend but taking the risk because their horses couldn't follow. The dirt crumbled beneath his weight as he clambered up the wall. Bullets whizzed past his ears as he rolled over the edge, then sprang to his feet and kept running.

His lungs felt ready to explode. Blood pounded in his ears so loudly he could barely hear the gunfire behind him. He darted into another arroyo and fell on his knees to build a breastwork of rocks, but the ones big enough were too deeply embedded and he couldn't dig them out. He ran on, turning up a small fork off the arroyo and then another, hearing the men close behind. Panting hard, one of them said, "Leave him to hell." Bob Olinger answered, "Not yet."

Frank climbed out of the arroyo into a meadow stretching a mile to the timberline with no cover between him and the trees. Knowing he had to make a stand or be shot in the back, he bellied into a shallow depression and flattened himself close to the earth, waiting for the faces to come over the ridge.

The first was the half-Apache. Frank shot and missed and the Indian dove for cover. Then came Bob Olinger, buckskin fringe flapping as he hoisted his bulk over the edge. Frank shot straight at him but missed. Bob shot back. The bullet ran through Frank's hair like a gentle finger lightly rearranging his part. He was down to his last two cartridges when he heard Wallace Olinger shout, "Hold on. That's Frank Coe."

"Who'd you think?" Frank hollered back.

"We thought you was the Kid!" Bob Olinger jeered in angry disappointment.

Frank had no use for Bob, but he and Wallace were friends, so he called, "Wallace, if I surrender, do you give your word I won't be harmed?"

"Yeah, come on out," Wallace answered. "We weren't after you but the Kid."

His knees trembling, Frank Coe stood up and surrendered his weapon. They all returned along the route he had run in desperation only moments before, then they tied his hands and took him on a horse back to the Fritz ranch, where he was told to sit under a tree while the posse regrouped around him. He heard someone say McNab was dead and Saunders had been left bleeding in an arroyo, shot in the hip.

"Ain't you gonna help him?" Frank asked.

The men just laughed. Frank argued that Saunders was a nonpartisan, nothing more than a farmer. But he couldn't find a sympathetic ear until he saw John Jones at the edge of the crowd.

John had agreed to come on this foray, figuring he'd given Billy an open range this far. If his friend was always going to be in the center of action, there was nothing John could do but go against him. He hadn't planned on accosting the Kid directly, however, and when the posse chased Coe up the canyon thinking he was Billy, John returned to the ranch, stopping a moment to stare down at the corpse of McNab. John considered McNab a bounty hunter serving Chisum's greed, so felt no regret at his death. Ab Saunders was a different matter.

Merely nodding his intention to Coe, John took a wagon from the stable and found Saunders, unconscious from loss of blood. As gently as he could, he loaded the farmer into the wagon and drove him to Stanton.

On the road, John felt disgusted with the whole operation because Bob Olinger was riding so high. Crippling a cornered man wasn't anything glorious, and John was almost sorry Coe *hadn't* been the Kid because then Pecos Bob would be dead. When they rendezvoused later in Lincoln, John meant to steer clear of Bob Olinger and make his own stand. He would shoot to kill, as when he hunted deer. A clean kill was honorable, anything less was sadistic or inept, and John Jones laid claim to neither of those attributes.

Juan Trujillo, Francisco's ten-year-old brother, had been hunting deer in the mountains above the road when he heard the shooting. Cautiously he approached the edge of the plateau and looked down to see McNab killed, then watch Frank Coe's desperate flight and surrender. Juan returned to his horse and hurried back to San Patricio to tell Francisco.

His brother was just leaving for the fancy party at Macky Swain's with *el Chivato* and three other men. Francisco had told Juan all of them were *hombres malos* and he wasn't to mess with them ever. Breathlessly Juan told his tale in Spanish. Among the Americans only *el Chivato* understood, and he and Francisco exchanged looks that frightened Juan so badly he wished he hadn't told. "Now you will fight," he said in English.

"Now we will have a chance," Francisco replied, hugging the boy brusquely.

Smiling down from his horse, *el Chivato* said, "Thanks, pardie. We'll be ready for 'em."

Francisco rode out with the others, protected by a prayer from the lips of his brother.

Doc Scurlock, George Coe, and Hijenio Salazar were waiting with Charlie at Bowdre's farm. They rode into town with the Kid, Fred Waite, Hendry Brown, John Middleton, and Francisco Trujillo. All of them had worn their best clothes for the party, but now their faces were grim. Riding straight to McSween's, they stayed on their horses as Scurlock called for the lawyer to come out.

Mac opened the door and studied the men a moment, then closed it and walked toward them. Stopping just inside the picket gate, he asked, "Gentlemen?"

Scurlock laid it out baldly. "Some Seven Rivers men ambushed ours by the Fritz ranch. They killed McNab and captured Frank Coe. Saunders was with 'em but we don't know what happened to him."

"Why?" Mac cried. "What did they hope to gain?"

"Whatever it was they ain't got enough," Middleton said. "They're coming our way, not expecting us to be ready."

"They'll be wrong," George Coe said. "They hurt my cousin and I'll kill every one of 'em."

"You'll have help," Billy said, looking straight at Mac.

Mac looked away from the challenge in the Kid's eyes to see Francisco Trujillo watching him sadly. "Francisco, will you help me?" Mac asked.

"If I can," he answered, unhappy to be singled out.

"Will you intercept Mr. Chisum? Tell him the party has been canceled. Apparently our joy in victory was premature."

Francisco didn't feel he could deny the pious lawyer's request any more than he could a petition from a priest. So he answered that he would do it and rode east alone while his friends took defensive positions in town to wait for the enemy.

Mac went back inside where Sue waited by the table laid for her party. He closed the door and latched it, then turned to face her and said gently, "They killed McNab."

She had been regal, impervious, impatient. Now her posture fell, her mouth hardened in fear, and she hid her eyes. When she looked up again, tears spilled down her cheeks as she shook her head in bewilderment. "It isn't over, Mac?" she whispered.

"Among the men attacked," he said, "they killed only the one involved in Brady's murder."

"Who were they?" she wailed.

"Men from Seven Rivers."

"What do they want here?"

"Vengeance."

Anger conquered her fear. "You think killing Brady brought this on!"

He nodded. "We boast of innocence while our men are indicted for murder. Didn't you expect retribution to be laid at our door?"

"Why isn't it laid at Dolan's door?" she cried. "Or Murphy's, that drunken sodomite!"

"Mrs. McSween!"

"Answer me!" she screamed. "Quote me scripture on why the wicked win."

"And Moses said unto them, look to it; for evil is before you."

On the table was an empty plate. She picked it up and threw it at him. He ducked, showered with slivers of crystal when the plate shattered against the door. They stared at each other as Mac slowly stood up straight again.

"This will not do," he said softly. "We are married and our fates intertwined."

She felt frightened to have attacked her husband. "I'm sorry," she whispered. "It's just that I feel so helpless, Mac, and you are so obstinate."

"What would you have me do?"

She was silent.

"Pick up a gun and join the others on the rooftops? I hardly think I'd be an asset. You see, I feel helpless, too. There will be a battle today and I am powerless to stop it, even though one side fights in my name. Brewer could control them, and I had hope for McNab. But now they have no leader, Sue, and that makes them a mob. Dolan isn't leading the other side either. It's a plague of violence let loose."

"Let's leave," she said.

"What?"

"Pack a few things and disappear."

"Would you tell your sister?" he mocked. "Or simply abandon her, as you would the men fighting in our name?"

"But not for our purpose," she argued. "They're fighting for the love of it now."

"We set it off!" he shouted. "We started it and we'll stay until it's finished. If you had remained in the East you could still claim innocence, but both of us have blood on our hands, Mrs. McSween, and I'll hear no more talk of leaving. Now clear this table and bring me supper by the fire."

29

On the roof of the Ellis home at the other end of town, George Coe was looking at a Dolan man through field glasses. The man was sitting on a cow skull high on a hill studying the town below through his own field glasses. George said to Hendry Brown, "I'm gonna pick that feller off."

"No way," Hendry scoffed. "That must be eight hundred yards if it's a foot."

George raised his rifle, used the glasses to calculate his aim, and pulled the trigger.

Dutch Kruling fell off the cow skull, shot through his ankles.

"I hit him!" George crowed.

Hendry yanked the glasses out of George's hand and looked for himself. "I'll be damned," he said.

Inside the Big Store, the shot was heard as a call to battle. The Seven Rivers men ran from the building to join the fight, leaving their prisoner alone. Frank Coe crept down the stairs and out the side door, along the west end of the building and across the street to the river behind Wortley's, then followed the water to the other end of town and the home of Ike Ellis. When he climbed onto the roof, George greeted him with a wild tale of making an eight-hundred-yard shot.

Frank snorted his disbelief. "Where's the Kid?"

"You smell anything?" his cousin teased.

Frank sniffed the air, then shook his head.

"Neither could Kid." George laughed. "He claimed he can always smell a fight and this ain't what it smells like, so he's down by the river with Tulles."

Frank laughed, too, then remembered his partner, Ab Saunders.

"Prob'ly Kid's right," Frank said. "Think I'll ride over to Stanton and check on Ab."

"I'll go with you," George said.

When Sheriff Copeland realized Lincoln was in the possession of two opposing bands of warriors, he felt it incumbent on his office to do something. Yet he had no control over the Regulators, and the Seven Rivers men considered him fair game as a McSween partisan. So he did what Brady and Peppin had done before him: he requested troops from Fort Stanton to quell the violence.

Colonel N. A. M. Dudley was the new commander at Stanton. The soldiers called him "North American" because of his initials, but there was a hint of a slur in their jest. The Ninth Cavalry was composed entirely of Negroes, and perhaps they saw something inherently bureaucratic in the colonel's reputation for shifting responsibility onto others. Dudley sent Lieutenant Smith with a cavalry troop in response to the sheriff's summons.

Lieutenant Smith was up to the task. He strung his mounted soldiers along the snaking road through town, then rode up and down the single street calling for all men to lay down their arms or risk firing at the United States Army. When he returned to the sheriff, Smith asked, "Which side do you want arrested?"

Thoroughly disgusted, Copeland answered, "The whole damn business!"

Since the Regulators had been warned in time to take the best strategic positions, the Seven Rivers men offered to surrender on condition the lieutenant take them back to the fort. Lieutenant Smith agreed and Copeland watched them ride out, feeling he hadn't totally failed his office. Shortly afterward, Colonel Dudley wired the sheriff asking what he wanted done with the prisoners. Knowing he couldn't hold so many men in Lincoln's jail, Copeland suggested they be sent home. Dudley complied, and wrote in his journal that they'd all had a good scare.

Dolan put pen to paper, too, writing a letter to the editor of the Santa Fe *New Mexican,* a newspaper controlled by the Ring. He wrote in response to an editorial in the Mesilla *Independent* in which A. J. Fountain, owner and editor, had reported on the recent session of court.

Fountain explicitly laid blame for the continuing violence on the gangs of outlaws led by Jesse Evans and John Kinney. "It is alleged," Fountain wrote, "that the outlaws are employed by certain persons owning contracts to supply the government with beef, and that cattle stolen from the citizens by these outlaws are turned over to the government on these contracts."

No doubt existed in any reader's mind that the owners of the contracts were none other than the principals of The House. Dolan penned a virulent reply:

May 16, 1878

Gentlemen:

I see by the last issue of the *Independent* that its editors still continue to publish their malicious lies in regard to the Lincoln County troubles. The *Independent* says "outraged prominent citizens" have formed themselves into the "Regulators" to pursue justice.

Who are these prominent citizens and Regulators? One is William H. Bonney, alias Antrim, alias Kid, a renegade from Arizona where he killed a man in cold blood; Fred Waite of the Indian Territory, one of the murderers of Mr. Morton, Mr. Baker, Sheriff Brady, Deputy Hindman, Mr. Roberts, and probably others; Bowdre and Scurlock, who we helped purchase land when they first came to the county and who are now in arrears on their debts; the Coes, constant complainers who whine that we offer contracts too cheap to suit their taste. The balance of the so-called Regulators are tramps without name or character.

My character is so well known in New Mexico that I neither require nor seek endorsement for my veracity.

James J. Dolan

The maligned Regulators met at Clenny's monte house on the Hondo and elected Doc Scurlock their new captain. Their only legitimacy was possession of the tattered warrant issued by Squire Wilson in February. Under its guise, they rode to Dolan's cow camp on the Pecos to flush out more of the men who had ridden in the posse that killed Tunstall. Since the hut was unoccupied, they scattered the stock found in the corral. When a horseman bolted from a nearby arroyo, the Regulators took off in pursuit.

The foray was Francisco Trujillo's first taste of battle. He felt proud that he managed to shoot his gun at the fleeing man, though he found it difficult to aim from astride a galloping horse. The man was shooting back, and one of his bullets killed Francisco's mount. Francisco managed to jump clear, then leapt up behind Hijenio Salazar and they galloped after the others. Francisco saw the fleeing man's horse stumble, and watched him somersault through space, then land on his feet with his hands in the air as if it were an acrobatic act.

The Regulators milled their horses around him, grinning down at the man who'd killed McNab, the half-breed Apache known simply as Indian. Their smiles chilled Francisco's heart. "He has surrendered," Francisco said. "We should take him alive."

Francisco knew he looked ridiculous, sitting on the back of Hijenio's horse as he told the Americans what to do. Scurlock jerked his head at Hijenio, and he reined his horse away and kicked it into a trot to cut distance between them and the others. Francisco said, "Wait." Hijenio did but complained, "You don't want to know, *amigo.*"

Francisco twisted on the rump of the horse and watched Indian riding the other direction between *el Chivato* and Martín Chavez. Indian's hands were loose but he was unarmed. Suddenly his horse bolted and *el Chivato* and Martín pulled their pistols and shot the fleeing man in the back. Francisco watched him slump forward, then slide to the ground. *El Chivato* spurred his horse after the one running riderless away. He caught the reins and led it back to Francisco. "Here's the saddle I promised you," *el Chivato* said with a smile.

Francisco slid off the back of his friend's horse and took the reins of the new one. But when he turned to mount, he saw the saddle was drenched with blood. As he watched the blood slide down the skirt and drip off the stirrup, vomit gagged in his throat. He turned away, swallowing hard.

Softly Hijenio said, "I will clean it for you." He dismounted and led the new horse into the weeds, where he poured water from his canteen to wash away the blood, then wiped the saddle dry with bunches of buffalo grass.

When the Regulators scattered the cattle from Dolan's camp, they were dispersing the property of Thomas B. Catron, who now owned The House since Dolan had declared bankruptcy. Dolan traveled to Santa Fe to tell Catron. Catron went to Governor Axtell, and the governor went to Colonel Hatch, commander of all the militia in the territory. Hatch ordered Dudley to stop the Regulators at any cost.

In late May, the trial of Tunstall's killers was held in Mesilla. Of the men who had ridden with the Englishman that day, Brewer was dead and the other three under indictment, so only Widenmann appeared for the prosecution. Judge Bristol ridiculed his testimony.

"Mr. Widenmann," Bristol mocked, "you say you were running horseback, dust flying, balls whistling around, yet you could casually look back and recognize members of a large party coming full-speed three hundred yards behind. Your testimony in this matter will not be given much credence."

Jesse Evans testified that on the morning of February 18 he had been down on the Pecos, a day's ride from the scene. He denied any knowledge of what the other indicted men were doing, but Buck Morton and Frank Baker had been with him. The friends they were visiting took the stand and corroborated his story, so Jesse Evans was cleared of the charge. District Attorney Rynerson decided against prosecuting Dolan and Mathews for lack of evidence.

The butt of jokes around Mesilla, Widenmann left New Mexico. With the melancholy thought that his friend John Tunstall would be remembered only for having been murdered, Rob traveled east to his family's home in Ann Arbor, Michigan, carrying all of his belongings in the leather satchel embossed with Tunstall's name.

The threat of prosecution behind him, Jimmie Dolan again rode to Santa Fe, this time to call on the governor. When Axtell was led to inquire what could be done to restore order in Lincoln County, Dolan suggested he appoint a sheriff not inclined to protect outlaws. So the governor wrote the district attorney requesting candidates. Rynerson suggested Dad Peppin, Brady's former chief deputy. The end result was another of the governor's proclamations, this one a scorpion with three stingers: Sheriff Copeland was dismissed and Peppin officially appointed, all men were ordered to lay down their arms and return to their homes, and all legal posses were to be composed of federal troops under the leadership of the county sheriff.

McSween greeted the proclamation with alarm. It effectively put his men outside the law anywhere but their individual homes, where they could be shot down one by one. The only remedy he could advise was to flee. When he received advance news of Peppin's arrival, Mac was convinced of the wisdom of his advice.

Traveling with such a horde of riders that the approaching dust could be seen for miles, Sheriff Peppin led a troop of cavalry and thirty of the worst cutthroats John Kinney could scrape from the gutters of the Rio Grande. Fifty fighting men rode behind Peppin, and beside him rode Jimmie Dolan, recently returned from Santa Fe. People whose homes they passed ran ahead to tell neighbors, who ran ahead to tell their neighbors. The news traveled faster than the posse, reaching Mac an hour before Peppin rode into Lincoln.

Among Mac's friends, only three men were left in town: his law partner David Shield, the young law clerk Harvey Morris, and the Reverend Dr. Ealy. Mac asked the schoolteacher, Miss Gates, to stay with his wife, then took his leave at the front door of his home as if he were going to work.

"I'll be in the hills around San Patricio," he told Sue. "If you need to do so, Sebrian can always find me."

"Take me with you," she pleaded.

Mac shook his head. "You wouldn't like living in a peasant's hut."

"And if I never see you again?" she whispered.

"I shall return," he said, looking up the empty street of the deserted village. "When I do, you may shower me with the attention due a prodigal son, come home to work with the common man, as he should have done all along." He turned away and clumsily mounted Sue's mare, Pet.

Sue was frightened by his words. Holding to his leg in the saddle, she pleaded, "Promise me you won't fight, Mac. You'll be killed, you haven't any skill compared with them."

He smiled sadly. "I shan't fight, but I shall return and reside in my home, and it will be the Regulators who allow me that privilege. My moral stance is no more than a squeamish excuse. It tarnishes my soul." He turned his horse and slowly ambled down the street of Lincoln, heading east toward the trail to Eagle Creek and San Patricio.

A few days later, Peppin's posse returned to Lincoln after their first pursuit of the Regulators. Sue watched the posse move leisurely up the street and let its horses loose in Wortley's corral, her Pet among them. Trembling, she watched Dolan, Sheriff Peppin, and the outlaw John Kinney enter the Big Store, which was supposedly closed while Catron's brother-in-law took inventory for the bankruptcy sale. Yet Dolan seemed to have access to it as easily as before. Sue hated him, but she hated more not knowing the fate of her husband.

Running through her house to the kitchen where Sebrian kept a shotgun, she took it with her as she strode up the street. Then she stood in front of the store, brandishing the gun as she shouted, "I want to see Jimmie Dolan, right now, or someone will die!"

The men lounging on the porch laughed at her. From the corral behind her came more harsh laughter which curdled in her heart. "Jimmie!" she screamed. "Come out here and talk to me this minute!"

Grinning derisively, Dolan stepped through the door. "Always happy to oblige a lady," he said with a smirk, "especially when she carries a shotgun. Do you know how to use that, Sue?"

"Well enough," she retorted. "That's my mare you have in your corral. My husband rode that horse out of town, and I want to know where you got her."

"Which mare?" he asked, as if bored.

"The chestnut with Chisum's brand! Or are you in the habit of corralling horses wearing Chisum's brand?"

"Give her the mare," he muttered to his men, turning away.

"Wait!" she cried. "Where did you get her? Please, I must know."

Dolan turned back, thinking he would enjoy taming Sue McSween, who was obviously too feisty a wife for the pious lawyer. With a flicker of compassion, he said, "We didn't see your husband." Then he went inside, closing the door.

But his men weren't through. They spooked the horse so it was prancing nervously when they gave her its rope. Sue quieted the mare and led it down the street, seething at the catcalls the men hooted after her. Shaking with rage, she tied the horse to her picket fence, then spied Saturnino Baca watching from in front of his house up the road.

It wasn't his house. It belonged to her husband, but the Bacas had steadfastly refused to move for months. First they'd said they needed time to find another place, then that Mrs. Baca was pregnant and they would stay for the duration. Now she was confined after childbirth and couldn't be moved. Still carrying the shotgun, Sue strode angrily toward Saturnino.

"I suppose you're to blame for this!" she accused.

"Señora, I don't know what you mean," Baca answered, eyeing the shotgun.

"You sent the posse to San Patricio because you knew my husband's men would be there!"

"Everyone knows the Regulators hide in San Patricio," he replied haughtily. "As for my sending the posse, I am not a law officer, that is not my job."

Sue felt she must scream or go mad. "Very well! I have enough money and guns to kill you and all your family!" She wheeled around and ran for home, bolting the door and collapsing.

At the sound of the slamming door, Miss Gates hurried through the house and found Mrs. McSween prone on the floor, pounding the carpet with her fists. The teacher pulled the sobbing woman into her lap, saying nothing because no words of encouragement could truthfully pass her lips.

30

Mac awoke to the maddening squawks of a bluejay in the tree above him. He couldn't see the bird though it was directly overhead, its cry shattering the early morning peace of the mountain glen. Angrily he rolled over in his blankets and tried to lose the sound in regained sleep, but the jay refused to be ignored. Mac looked across at Scurlock bundled in his bedroll beyond the cold ashes of the fire.

"You want me to get rid of that devil, Mr. Mac?"

"Please."

Scurlock's gun fired and the bird fell in front of Mac, its headless neck a bloody pulp surrounded by delicate blue feathers. When he closed his eyes he could still see the vision of gore, so he looked again and saw the reality was much less hideous than his fantasy. He picked up a wing and sailed the tiny carcass far into the forest. Snuggling deeper into his blankets, he fell back asleep.

When he awoke, he thought it had been a dream. Then he saw three blue feathers on the grass in front of him. Staring at them, Mac remembered how easily his desire had been accomplished: the request for permission, the wish affirmed, the deed done and the remains discarded, leaving only peace.

Mac looked around the pristine forest of a beautiful July morning, thinking he might as well be in prison. It was simply that the boundaries of his jail served to keep him not in but out, leaving him free to go anywhere but home. He was tired of skulking through the forest like a fugitive, weary of camping in the mountains or begging the shelter of a peasant's hut. As with the maddening bluejay, he need not endure its squawk or run from its annoyance. There was another method.

When Scurlock roused himself to revive the coals of the fire, Mac stopped him. "I'm going home today, Doc," he announced. "Will you take me to the men so I may tell them?"

Scurlock smiled, as eager as Mac for an end to exile.

They rode northeast, skirting San Patricio and coming out on the Hondo behind Clenny's monte house. Clenny was a partisan who often gave food and lodging to the Regulators. He also kept women upstairs from his gaming room as another charm of his hospitality, though Mac was ignorant of that.

Leaving their horses hidden in the thicket along the river, Scurlock led Mac to the back of the saloon and into the kitchen. It was still early enough that no one was awake, and the house was silent as they passed down the hall and climbed the stairs. Just as they reached the second floor and were about to turn toward the door of the brothel, the ominous click of a cocking weapon stopped them.

"Where do you think you're going?" asked a soft Texas drawl.

Scurlock turned around and faced a tall, freckled stranger holding a forty-five aimed at his heart. "Who're you?"

"Tom O'Folliard," the youth answered.

Scurlock didn't know him. With a growing dread, he considered the possibility that the Regulators had left and he had led Mac into an ambush. Glancing at the closed door, he asked, "Who's in there?"

"You sure ask a lot of questions," the Texan said.

The door opened a crack, revealing John Middleton wearing long johns and holding a pistol. "Hey, Doc, Mac," he mumbled, his tongue thick. "S'alright, Tom." He opened the door wider, then looked at the lawyer. "Come on in, I guess."

Mac stepped into the room. Half a dozen wooden beds were built along the wall, and the men waking up in the beds hadn't slept alone. The others apparently had, those in blankets on the floor. They were all awake now, sitting up and shaking off a night of hard drinking.

In the blur of confused faces and bleary eyes, Mac saw Billy Bonney watching him from the far end of the room. The Kid's eyes were sharp, his smile curious. Then he looked down and spoke softly to a head of black tousled hair nestled in his bed. The girl murmured a protest. He insisted. *"Ay, Chivato,"* she complained, throwing off the covers and rising to stretch lazily, completely nude.

Though a married man, Mac had never seen a naked woman before. Her breasts rose firm and plump as she stretched her arms toward the ceiling, her waist tiny and her hips as round as halved peaches with a furry black pit.

She came down from her stretch and clapped her hands. Quickly gathering a flounce of a yellow skirt and a snip of a white blouse, she walked along the aisle shouting, *"¡Despiértense, muchachas!"* She poked and pulled at female appendages showing through the blankets as she came toward Mac and called, *"Andale, muchachas. Dejen los hombres."*

Mac watched five young Mexican women rise from the blankets. With playful squeals they snatched clothes from different beds, then scampered straight toward him. They were all nude, and not one of them even saw him standing by the door watching them pass. He looked at the Kid, maybe just because he was the only other sober man in the room.

Billy laughed. "You look like you died and went to heaven, Mac." The men struggling to get dressed joined in his laughter.

"I doubt I'll see such sights in heaven," Mac replied.

"If there ain't women in heaven," the Kid said, "I'd jus' as soon not go."

Several men mumbled assent, then Middleton and Scurlock came in and closed the door. "Who is that out there?" Scurlock asked the Kid. "Middleton says he came with you."

"That's right," Billy said, buttoning his pants as he smiled down the room at Doc.

"What's he want with us?"

"Says he wants to be a Regulator," the Kid answered, stepping into a boot and pounding it on the floor as he worked his foot in, the spur singing prettily. He picked up his other boot. "Says he wants to fight for justice, and he rode all the way from Texas to do it."

Snickers of amusement fluttered through the room. Scurlock watched the Kid work his foot into his second boot, then asked, "Is he a fighter?"

"I can teach him," Billy said, buckling on his gunbelt. "He's got promise."

"Let's hope he lives long enough to prove it," Hendry Brown said with a chuckle, buckling on his own gunbelt.

Mac watched the men reassemble themselves as a fighting force. In a remarkably short time they were seated on the wooden pallets, their blankets rolled to go, their eyes focused, their guns ready to do his bidding.

"Gentlemen," he said in the sudden quiet, "today I shall return to Lincoln and I shan't be driven from my home again." The men received this news with a quiet expectancy as Mac pulled a letter from his pocket. "I have composed a statement of our intentions, and have taken the liberty of signing it, simply, 'Regulator.' I hope I don't assume too much in calling myself one of you."

"Welcome to the fight, Mac," the Kid said.

"Hell, no! You *are* one of us!" George Coe called.

"You're our leader, course you can use our name," Big Jim agreed.

"Thank you," the lawyer answered, touched by their generosity. "Allow me to read the letter. It is addressed to the present occupant of Dolan's store: In camp, July thirteenth, 1878. Mr. Walz—sir: We are all aware that your brother-in-law, T. B. Catron, sustains the Dolan-Kinney party, and take this method of informing you that if any property belonging to the residents of this county is stolen or destroyed, Mr. Catron's property will be dealt with in the same manner. . . ."

Mac was interrupted by the men hooting their approval. He held up a hand for quiet, then continued reading: "We know the Tunstall estate cattle are pledged to Kinney. If they are taken from this county, a similar number will be taken from Catron. It is our object to protect property, but the man who deals destruction shall have destruction dealt him. Steal from the poorest or richest among us, and the full measure of injury you do shall be returned.

"As I said," Mac finished, "I have signed the letter, simply, 'Regulator.' "

"All right, Mac," the Kid congratulated him. "Now you're telling 'em." And the men clamored approval.

Mac waited until they were quiet again, then said, "Yesterday I learned the military can no longer form a *posse comitatus* and ride in the service of the sheriff. Congress passed the law to curtail the abuse of voters at southern polls, but it aids our cause. We should make our stand now, while Dolan cannot summon troops to assist him. Are you with me?"

The room rumbled with their assent.

Mac felt humbly pleased at their loyalty. These men dedicated to his purpose were young and uneducated, most of them without property other than their horses and guns, certainly a far cry from the audience he had expected to address in the prime of his life. He had expected acclaim from senators and the moral leaders of the nation. Instead he found himself loved by a small band of guerrilla fighters, and the irony was not lost on Alexander McSween.

As they rode up the Hondo Valley and climbed the trail along Eagle Creek, the news of their advance spread through the mountains. They entered town shortly after sunset on the evening of July 14, a Sunday on which Lincoln had seen morning church services held in the McSween parlor. By nightfall, sixty men had come to fight with the Regulators, half of them Mexicans who fought against the oppression of The House, the others Americans who fought to avenge the deaths of Tunstall, Brewer, and McNab.

Twenty Mexican sharpshooters under Martín Chavez occupied the Montaño home, availing themselves of its flat roof. Taking advantage of the territorial representative's absence, five Mexicans broke into the Patrón house, knocking extra gunports in the *pretil* around the roof. Doc Scurlock, John Middleton, Frank Coe, and Charlie Bowdre fortified themselves in the Ellis home to defend the east end of town. Others camped in the thickets along the river and on the northern hills, giving them a vantage over both ends of the street. George Coe, Hendry Brown, and Fred Waite secreted themselves inside the Tunstall store, unbeknown to Dr. and Mrs. Ealy, who were spending a quiet evening with their daughters in their parlor.

Into his home Mac led a combination of fighters and noncombatants. The Kid eagerly volunteered to be in the hot spot. He brought Tom O'Folliard, the tall young Texan who had come to fight for justice. Big Jim Finlay was an asset, but Tom Cullins and Joe Smith came with more enthusiasm than experience. They were complemented by Hijenio Salazar, José Chavirra, Francisco Zamora, and Vicente Romero, all capable fighters, and the youthful Ignacio Gonzales and Harvey Morris, the bespectacled young law clerk. Also in the house were Sebrian Bates, Mrs. McSween, the schoolteacher Miss Gates, and Mrs. Shield and her five daughters. David Shield was interviewing with a law firm in Las Vegas, not suspecting he had left his family at the crucial moment.

McSween's sudden decision to reoccupy his home took Sheriff Peppin by surprise. Most of his men were in the mountains hunting the Regulators with Kinney. Peppin dispatched a rider to bring them back, then sent five men to fortify the *torreón*.

From the roof of the Montaño house, Martín Chavez watched Saturnino Baca carrying food and water to the *torreón* from his home next door. Martín sent a messenger relaying this information to McSween. Mac responded with a written order of eviction.

Vividly remembering Sue's threat, Baca wrote a petition to Colonel Dudley asking him to intervene. Baca explained his wife had recently been delivered of a son and was accustomed to a confinement of forty days. To ask him to move now was out of the question, and he begged for protection from the fort. Because of the restrictions placed on the army, Dudley could do no more than send Dr. Appel to investigate.

Early Monday morning, the post surgeon drove his buggy into Lincoln, hurrying through the hot wind raising dust along the road. He called first on the McSweens and found the house as silent as if they were alone, which was not what he had been told to expect.

Mrs. McSween didn't participate in the discussion, but her eyes flashed so violently that Appel often found himself looking at her as he listened to her husband. The lawyer was outwardly calm, yet he was so pale and his voice so soft, even while his words were strident, that Appel privately diagnosed him as suffering from psychic fatigue. Still, the lawyer's solution to the problem was reasonable: evacuate the *torreón* and he would have no objection to the Bacas remaining in the house.

Appel carried this message to the men in the *torreón*. They argued that the Regulators would claim it as soon as they left. Baca complained that in such case he would be no safer than before, and suggested Dudley send soldiers to occupy the *torreón*.

When Appel returned to the lawyer and asked if he would agree to this plan, Mac replied, "That would be acceptable, if the soldiers do not assist my enemies in using either the *torreón* or Baca's house to attack me or my men. But if Colonel Dudley steps one inch across the line of neutrality, you may assure him he will be called to account for it in future."

Appel took a step away. "Threats will not aid your cause, sir."

"If they were all I had, I would agree," Mac answered. "But they are neither idle nor without strength. I shall not be driven from my home again."

Appel turned and left. He reported his findings to the sheriff, then climbed into his buggy and started back to the fort. As he drove along the road, the trees were nearly doubled over by the howling wind, the sky obscured beyond a mass of swirling dust. He kept remembering McSween's haunted eyes as he vowed not to be driven from his home, and the mocking smile of his wife, as if she were Lady Macbeth speaking to an emissary of the king. Appel hadn't liked either one of them, yet he admired the ferocity of their union.

A few miles toward the fort, he met Kinney riding at the head of fifty men. They reined up and milled their horses around his carriage.

"What's it like in Lincoln?" Kinney shouted.

"Terrible," the doctor said. "The village is almost deserted, there's less than a dozen families left in their homes."

"And McSween?"

"The Regulators have taken the whole town, all except the tower, Dolan's store, and the Wortley."

"Yeah!" Kinney yelled, yanking his horse around and leading his men into battle.

Dr. Appel watched them disappear in the dust storm, then clucked his horse forward and continued his melancholy journey.

Sheriff Dad Peppin was a butcher by trade with no training in strategy. When Kinney and the others tore into the west end of town shooting off their guns to announce their arrival, the sheriff relied heavily on Dolan's advice. Gathering his men in the yard behind Wortley's, Peppin asked for a single volunteer to serve the warrants on the outlaws in the McSween home. Jack Long agreed to do it.

Holding his hands well away from his weapon, Long walked up the road through the nearly blinding dust and stopped in front of the lawyer's house. "I have warrants for the following men," he shouted. "Alexander McSween, William H. Bonney, George Coe, Frank Coe, Josiah Scurlock, Charles Bowdre, and Hendry Brown. Send 'em out and we won't bother you no more."

Behind windows fortified with feather beds and furniture, the Regulators stood watching with drawn guns. Tom O'Folliard grinned across at Billy. "What do you say, Kid, should I shoot the bastard?"

"He had the nerve to come alone," Billy said. "Let's jus' make sure he don't doubt his welcome." He aimed his pistol a good yard away from Long and pulled the trigger.

Long flinched as the bullet dug into the road a few feet from where he stood. When his hat flew off accompanied by the high-pitched whine of another bullet, he ran back toward Wortley's.

Inside the house, the Regulators laughed; but the Kid wasn't amused. He turned on O'Folliard and warned, "Don't get fancy on me, Tom. This ain't the time to show off."

The men quieted and looked away. When Tom apologized, Billy nodded, then left for the kitchen.

Sebrian and the schoolteacher were cooking at the stove. Big Jim was sitting at the table sharing a bottle of whiskey with Tom Cullins and Joe Smith. Billy walked in with a friendly smile for the cooks and a frown for the drinkers.

"You got something to eat?" he asked Sebrian.

"Sure thing, Mr. Bonney. Sit yourself down."

"Don't call me that," Billy answered, moving to the table and picking up the whiskey. He took a couple of steps backward, smiling at the men at the table as he said, "Most folks jus' call me Kid."

"I'll call you a thief if you don't bring my bottle back," Finlay complained.

Billy set the whiskey inside a cupboard and shut the door. "We're gonna be here a long while, Big Jim. You don't want to be napping at the wrong time."

"I can handle liquor," he muttered.

Billy pulled a chair out and sat down just as Sebrian placed a bowl of posole and a plate of tortillas in front of him. "Thank you, Sebrian," he said, digging into the food.

The seated men sullenly watched him. In search of a more pleasant countenance, he looked up at Miss Gates. She gave him such a radiant smile, he nearly blushed. Goddamn, he thought, concentrating on his posole, the schoolmarm approves of me! When he finished eating, he went back to the parlor and resumed his post by the window.

Sporadic gunfire was heard all afternoon, but no messenger brought news to the house. The McSweens were sequestered in their bedroom, and Mrs. Shield kept her daughters in their wing, so the Regulators had free roam of the front rooms. They spoke softly among themselves, speculating on what was happening beneath the dust storm that swirled over Lincoln.

Tuesday dawned clear and still. Peppin sent his best marksmen to the southern hills to drive the men from Montaño's roof. By late afternoon they finally succeeded, although Martín's men managed to escape without being hit. Only Charlie Crawford was shot in the process. He was left on the hot hillside, crippled and bleeding, because none of his friends dared rescue him.

Sheriff Peppin wired Dudley, pleading for the army's intervention on behalf of the women and children still in town. But the commander's hands were tied by orders. He sent a courier with his message of regret, a young cavalryman named Berry Robinson.

As he rode into the west end of town, the soldier was fired upon. His horse reared so abruptly, he was thrown. As he picked himself up, he decided the gunfire had come from the far side of Wortley's corral, but he could see no one through the frightened horses milling inside the enclosure.

At the hotel, Dolan welcomed him with a grin of glee. "Now we got 'em," he crowed. "Sit down, Private, while we write our reply to the colonel's letter."

When Dudley read, and then heard from the man himself, that a soldier of the U.S. Army had been fired upon by civilian combatants, he chafed beneath orders. But again he could do nothing more than send Dr. Appel to investigate.

On Wednesday morning, the McSweens made no pretense of being alone. They met the post surgeon at their door with ten gunmen visible in the room behind them.

Upon questioning, Mac stated they had seen the soldier approaching the Wortley but that no one inside his home had fired a gun all day. In fact, no firing had been heard in the village except the one shot that came from the vicinity of the hotel's corral. When Dolan and Peppin contradicted the lawyer, Dr. Appel returned to the colonel with a report stating that the shot had been fired by parties concealed within McSween's home.

Colonel Dudley saw the attack as an intolerable affront to his personal dignity, a view reinforced by Jimmie Dolan when he visited the colonel that afternoon, bringing a bottle of his finest whiskey. Halfway through the bottle, Dolan began to drop innuendoes about the duties of a soldier to defend the peace and prosperity of his country, expounding on the sentiment that an army officer was a man who loved law and order, and by the nature of his makeup felt honor-bound to protect women and children.

"Unlike Tunstall," Dolan continued, "who started these troubles by arming ruffians like the Kid. Half of Tunstall's land holdings were fraudulent because he paid men to file in his name to get around the citizenship requirement. That's the sort of character he had. And this lawyer is worse. McSween's never seen military service and never will. He's from Canada someplace, wasn't even born an American. You should see the men who follow him. Dirt farmers, most of them, the Mexicans anyway. Half of the Americans, too, and the other half paid killers. They keep the people terrorized."

"I know," Dudley agreed, pouring himself another drink. "When

Widenmann was here, he and Bowdre would strut around the fort like two walking Gatling guns."

Jimmie laughed. "Don't you have a Gatling gun in your arsenal, Colonel?"

"Yes. And a mountain howitzer, too. That would command Lincoln, wouldn't it? I could level a house and everyone in it with one volley."

Dolan smiled. "Your mere presence would restore peace, and allow the women and children to feel safe in their homes."

Dudley tugged at one end of his walrus moustache. "I suppose I could ride in and bivouac on neutral ground, taking no action, you understand. What do you think?"

"I think it's a brilliant idea," Dolan replied, standing up. "I'll leave you to your duties."

"Your whiskey, sir," Dudley said, nodding toward the bottle on the table.

"A gift. I've several crates of it in Lincoln."

Left alone, Colonel Dudley called for his adjunct and gave orders for all the artillery on the fort to be readied for action. Then he requested that his five junior officers report to his quarters.

Joining him, the officers avoided each other's eyes in the presence of their inebriated commander. When he presented his statement of agreement for each of them to sign, sharing the responsibility for occupying the town, the officers saw the wiliness of his act but never guessed the deception behind it. They signed the statement vowing a humanitarian purpose of protecting women and children with the army's presence in the embattled village, and all but one followed Dudley to Lincoln. The officer who stayed behind would have gone too, except someone had to mind the fort in case the Apaches should feel ignored.

On the dawn of July 19, Colonel Dudley left Stanton with four junior officers, eleven mounted cavalry, twenty-four infantry, a Gatling gun, and a mountain howitzer. The troops moved slowly and stopped outside the village at nine-thirty.

Dudley sat his horse in contemplation. Just as he had needed a document proving his officers concurred with his plan, he now needed another justifying his support of Sheriff Peppin. He called his adjunct. "Purington!"

"Yes, sir," the captain answered, nudging his horse closer.

"Where's that justice of the peace the Regulators shot when they killed Brady?"

Purington thrust his chin behind them. "He's staying with relatives in a hut yonder, sir."

"Fetch him," Dudley said.

The captain turned his horse away and returned quickly with the rotund little man.

Squire Wilson rode a burro with two crutches tied to its saddle, his pink face moist with worry as he waited to learn what the army wanted. On his tall dun gelding, Dudley towered above Wilson in a dark dress uniform bespangled with ribbons and a monocle catching the sun.

"I want you to issue a warrant against McSween and the men with him," the colonel commanded.

Wilson shifted to ease the aching of his thighbones. "Mr. Mac is in his home," he answered with the puny force of his resistance. "I guess he has a right to company if he wants."

"They fired on one of my soldiers! I want warrants against all of them for attempted murder."

"But Colonel," Wilson argued timidly, "surely that's a military affair outside civil jurisdiction."

"Soldiers are entitled to equal protection under the law, the same as anyone."

"But my commission was revoked by the governor!" Wilson crowed.

"That was an error. You've been reinstated with full powers."

"I've received no notice of that."

"You will. Now do as you're told. Issue a warrant."

In the cool of the morning, Wilson could smell his own sweat. Summoning all of his courage, he said, "McSween's done nothing wrong, sir. Why is he being hounded?"

"So you're with them, are you?" the colonel retorted. "If so, I'll lock you in irons in the stockade. Is that what you want?"

"No, sir," Wilson answered in defeat.

"Then write me a warrant!"

"I'll need affidavits," he replied petulantly. "I can't issue a warrant out of pure air, even for a colonel."

Dudley glowered at the pesky little man. "Come with us."

Squire Juan Bautista Wilson was a shy, reclusive man who liked nothing better than sipping hot chocolate in front of the fire, listening to a woman work in the kitchen over the quiet sounds of children doing lessons at the table. He did not like war, had never sought confrontation of any kind. He didn't even bear a grudge for his wounds in the hope that would serve him well with the Regulators. Now, riding his burro at the head of the soldiers marching into town, he knew he would be seen by everyone as a traitor.

Dudley stopped his troops at parade rest in front of the Wortley, yanked his horse to attention and sat up straight. Addressing the men who watched from the portal, he asked for Peppin, who was finally located in the privy. He came out red-faced, stuffing his shirttails into his trousers as he crossed the yard to greet the colonel.

Dudley twitched his walrus moustache in an effort not to laugh at the bumbling butcher of a sheriff. Beginning with a guttural harrumph, the colonel announced, "Under General Order Number Forty-nine, issued Seven July this year, the U.S. Army is forbidden to interfere in civil matters, compelling us to remain neutral in this dispute. We are not here to assist either side, but to offer protection to noncombatants. Anyone seeking the sanctuary of the army may come to my camp and receive it." He waited to let his words sink in, then smiled at Peppin. "If you'd be good enough, Sheriff, to escort me to a suitable bivouac?"

When Peppin led the colonel and his troops down the street, Dolan's men fell in with the ranks.

Inside the McSween home, everyone stood behind the front windows watching the army arrive. Sue McSween put her hand to her throat as Mac frowned. The Kid cursed beneath his breath, and Tom O'Folliard felt his first intimation of fear. Susan Gates whispered a prayer of petition, to which Sebrian uttered a solemn amen. Big Jim Finlay cocked his Winchester with threat. Hijenio Salazar made the sign of the cross over the *bandolera* on his chest. Joe Smith and Tom Cullins paled. Harvey Morris swallowed hard. Zamora, Chavirra, and Romero exchanged wary warnings with their eyes, and Ignacio Gonzales wiped his sweaty hands on his trousers.

Inside the Tunstall store, Fred Waite, Hendry Brown, and George Coe tasted the bitterness of anarchy as they watched Dolan's men drop out of the ranks to take up defensive positions they could never have reached on their own. In their private rooms at the other end of the building, the Ealys watched with relief, thinking the army would ensure their safety.

Martín Chavez had no such illusion. As the troops passed the Montaño house, he held his men back, even though their trigger fingers itched to fell the colonel with a sniper's bullet.

The troops camped on the north side of the road near the jail. As Sheriff Peppin quickly explained the position of the enemy, Colonel Dudley smiled at Dolan's wiliness. The merchant had placed him between the group of insurrectionists within the Montaño house and those fortified in the Ellis home on the eastern edge of town. In mere choice of site, the army had effectively sliced McSween's forces apart.

When his soldiers were bivouacked, Colonel Dudley remounted his horse and led a detachment of infantry and the mountain howitzer into position directly in front of the Montaño home. Holding his baton high as if prepared to give the order to fire, he shouted, "Everyone inside this building is ordered to evacuate. If any person fires one shot at or toward my soldiers, I will level the house. Anyone choosing to vacate now may do so under my protection."

"*Chingada su madre,*" Martín Chavez muttered. He had been beaten; the truth was as ugly as a pimple on a whore's butt. "*Vámonos, muchachos,*" he said. "*Corran por sus caballos.*"

In a frenzy of banging doors, the twenty fighters abandoned the house and tore down the street toward the Ellis corral. The five men inside Patrón's home ran too. The men in the *torreón* saw them and yelled to Sheriff Peppin, who sent men running between the soldiers and the houses, firing after the fleeing fighters. The Mexicans managed to mount and spur their horses out of range without being hit.

When Middleton, Scurlock, Frank Coe, and Charlie Bowdre saw Martín's men take flight, they were infected with the high emotion of retreat. In near panic, they galloped after the Mexicans to reconnoiter in the hills north of town.

Colonel Dudley returned to his tent feeling he had earned himself a drink. In the first hour of the army's presence in the village, McSween's forces had been depleted to the fighters in his home.

31

As head of the committee that investigated the Berry Robinson incident, Dr. Appel signed the affidavit against McSween. Squire Wilson issued a warrant, and Colonel Dudley sent three soldiers to deliver it to Sheriff Peppin in the Wortley. Peppin gave the warrant to Marion Turner, who took Milo Pierce and Bob Olinger to approach the besieged house. John Jones watched them walk up the street, not yet ready to confront his friend inside.

Big Jim Finlay had been nipping at his whiskey again. He kept the bottle in a hutch he'd shoved up against the window he guarded. There was a crack between the cupboard and the wall just wide enough for his gunbarrel to poke past the jagged edges of broken glass. When he saw the Seven Rivers men approaching, he wanted to shoot them down. "Let's get 'em," he said thickly.

"Wait," Billy said. "They've come to parley."

Finlay glared at him, wondering when the Kid had become leader of the Regulators. But Big Jim's vision was blurred and he didn't care to argue, so he let the hammer fall back on his gun with a solemn click of concession.

Turner yelled, "We've got a warrant for the arrest of everyone in the house."

"We've got a warrant for you, too!" Big Jim shouted back.

"Why don't you come out and serve it, then?" Turner mocked.

"Our guns don't need to come out to be heard," Finlay jibed.

"You cussed fools!" Turner yelled. "All your friends lit out and we've got you surrounded. Why don't you surrender and be done with it?"

The Kid answered him. "Maybe we like breathing too much," he said.

Turner and his men walked back toward the Wortley.

"We should've shot 'em down," Big Jim snarled.

Billy looked at him hard, then shifted his gaze to McSween in the corner.

The lawyer was reading his Bible, his wife sitting on the floor by his chair. Mac felt Billy's eyes and looked up. "You did right," Mac said, his voice barely a whisper. "They came to offer us surrender and should not have been harmed. You were also right not to accept their offer, though I'm afraid we're doomed either way."

"I ain't doomed," the Kid said. "You're gonna have to pick up a gun and use it before this is over."

"I shan't do it, Billy," Mac replied. "Don't count on me in your plans."

Billy looked at the lawyer's wife, staring at her hands folded in her lap, pale and graceful against her dark skirt. "You're gonna have to leave, Mrs. Mac."

Her eyes were ferocious. "I won't stay so long as to impede you," she said firmly, "but I shan't leave just yet."

"Suit yourself," he said, looking out the window to see three soldiers duck around the corner of Tunstall's store. Calling to the Mexicans in the kitchen, he asked, "Hijenio, you see any soldiers back there?"

"*Sí, Chivato,*" came the reply. "On the hill behind us."

"Holy shit," Billy said.

Mac smiled at the profanity, grimly amused by its aptness. But when he looked at his wife, his smile faded. Unable to bear the accusation in her eyes, he returned to his Bible.

He wasn't really reading. His eye would grasp at phrases—*I was not in safety*—that clamored in his mind—*neither had I rest*—with the condemnation in his wife's eyes—*neither was I quiet*—and his conviction of doom—*yet trouble came.* My God, he prayed in silence, is my sin so great that I must lose my life?

Billy saw the soldiers bustling around the howitzer up the street. As he watched, they lifted the trunnions, swiveled the artillery on its wheels, and rolled it into position directly in front of him. "They got a cannon out front now," he said.

"We've children in the house!" Sue cried. "Have they no mercy?"

No one answered, and she turned with vigor to her husband. "You must do something, Mac! For God's sake, don't let them blow us all up!"

Slowly he fumbled in his mind for an action that might prove effective. "I shall write Dudley a letter," he finally said. "Bring me my satchel, Sue."

She rose to comply, thinking Mac had fought the whole war with letters and gained nothing, yet he would pen another missive and send it to oblivion with their lives.

When Mac saw that the stationery was letterhead from the Lincoln County Bank, a sob mangled his throat. He forced himself to concentrate on the present, but his usual adept turn of phrase failed him. He wrote:

> Lincoln County Bank Building
> Lincoln, N.M., 7/19/1878

Colonel Dudley, U.S.A.

Would you have the kindness to let me know why soldiers surround my house. Before blowing up my property, I would like to know the reason.

> Respectfully,
>
> A. A. McSween

When he finished he looked at the three women: his wife, her sister, and the schoolteacher. "I must ask for a volunteer to deliver my message," he said, his voice heavy with regret.

Minnie Shield stood up from the huddle of children. She was twelve years old and considered herself fearless. "I'll go," she said.

"Minnie!" Eliza cried. "You'll do no such thing."

"Let me go, Mama. I'm not afraid."

"Let her do it," Sue said, admiring the girl's pluck. "She'll not be harmed and can keep her head."

Mac handed her the envelope. "Don't run," he instructed. "Walk with dignity."

"Yes, sir," she said. Solemnly carrying the letter, she walked past the eyes of everyone in the room. Without a word she walked past Sebrian in the kitchen, out the back door, and along the east side of the house to the front gate. She hoped the Ealy girls would see how brave she was when she passed in front of Tunstall's store.

Inside the store, Fred Waite watched her come through the front gate wishing he could go in as easily. He felt he'd betrayed the Kid by not being with him, and he wanted to make amends for his mistake. When the little girl was a hundred yards down the street, he said to George and Hendry, "I'm going."

All three slipped out the back door and through the corral to the side gate facing the house. They hesitated behind the adobe wall, then started to bolt. Men on Wortley's roof opened fire, forcing the three to retreat back to the warehouse behind the store. They dug their way to the top of the loose mountain of oats piled against one wall and lay on their bellies poking their guns through the small windows open at the ceiling.

George squinted across the forty yards to the back of the house and said, "Guess this is as close as we get."

"Not a bad spot," Hendry said. "We can pick off anybody coming at 'em from behind."

Fred sucked on his moustache. "If Billy wasn't in there, I'd jus' ride away."

Hendry grunted his agreement.

"Not me," George said. "Miss Gates is in that house, and Mrs. Mac and Mrs. Shield and all them little girls. 'Sides, if we run now, what was it all for? I feel so full of piss all I can do is hate. There's nothing I want more'n Dolan men in the sight of my gun."

"You're gonna get 'em," Hendry said.

"Here comes the girl," Fred whispered.

They watched her round the corner of the house and go in through the back. She carried the letter through the kitchen and on into the parlor where she gave it to Mr. McSween.

He sat staring at the colonel's reply so long, Billy finally asked what it said. Mac handed him the note, then everyone watched him read it.

Billy looked at the little girl. "You get this from the colonel?"

She nodded, intimidated into silence.

"You sure?" Billy asked softly, encouraging her.

"I saw him write it," she managed to say.

Billy gave the letter back to Mac. "The coward wouldn't even sign his name."

Sue took the paper and read quickly:

I am directed by the commanding officer to inform you that no soldiers have surrounded your house and that he desires to hold no correspondence with you; if you desire to blow up your house, the commanding officer does not object, provided it does not injure any United States soldiers.

"Blow up our own home?" she exclaimed. "The man's mad!"

Sheriff Peppin stood beside the Wortley with his ear tuned to the whispering voice of Jimmie Dolan. Peppin nodded agreement to the plan, then walked around back to fetch Jack Long. Crouching in the dirt, Peppin drew a map of the McSween house, the yard, and the gates in the fence. He pointed out the woodpile, then gave Long a can of coal oil and sent him to work.

Long took "Dummy" because he was mute and deaf and placid as an old mule. He mimicked whatever anyone showed him to do, asked no questions and offered no complaints. Stealing through the tules along the river, they crept up behind the house and managed to get inside the stable unobserved. From there they ran across the yard and behind the small projecting ell of the kitchen, safe from the men suddenly shooting at them from the warehouse behind the store.

Incredibly, the door was unlocked. They stepped inside with drawn guns. Sebrian looked up from the stove thinking he'd met his death. "Out," Long whispered, waving his pistol.

Sebrian ran across the bright strip of sunshine to the stable. As a last act of defiance, he latched the door from the inside, then went out the back and kept running until he reached a friend's house and was taken in.

Working fast, Long and Dummy poured coal oil on the wooden floor of the kitchen, scattered shavings from the kindling box, then dropped a burning match and slipped out the back door.

As the Regulators in the warehouse peppered their path with bullets, Long and Dummy made for the shelter of the stable. Discovering the locked door, they ran for the next nearest haven, past the chicken house with its useless slatted walls to the privy on the edge of the river. Its thin planks were no protection. For a brief second they danced between deadly slugs, then abandoned dignity and jumped feet-first into the vault. Crawling through the muck only to be greeted at the other end by a rain of bullets, they remained trapped in the cesspool, much to the glee of Waite, Brown, and Coe, who kept them there.

Wanting to tell Sebrian how brave she had been walking to the colonel's camp, Minnie Shield snuck away from her sisters and crossed the rooms to the kitchen. "Fire, Mama!" she screamed. "There's a fire in the kitchen!"

Eliza ran, grabbed the two buckets of water standing by the wall, and doused the flames. She looked up to see the Kid watching from the door. He smiled at her, then was gone so quickly he seemed an apparition in the smoke.

Minnie ran out to tell everyone: "They set fire to the kitchen! But I saw it and Mama doused the buckets on it." She looked at the Kid for confirmation.

"It was good work," he said, "but there's no more water in the house."

Jumping to her feet, Sue cried, "Will they burn us out? Destroy everything we own?"

No one answered. She raised her hands to cover her ears, trying to think over the racket of gunfire from behind the house. Suddenly a fusillade erupted from across the street. Bullets flew through windows, piercing the barricades of furniture. Wood splintered and glass shattered as everyone fell to the floor.

The Regulators began shooting back, careless of the soldiers who stood with the enemy. It was earsplitting, so loud each shot nearly drove Sue mad. Bullets whistled into the room with high-pitched whines ending in dull thuds as they crumbled the adobe walls, shattering anything in the way.

The littlest girls were crying, the others huddled silenced by fear. Eliza hid her face in her oldest daughter's lap, praying fervently for rescue. Miss Gates was also praying, but her petition included everyone in the house as well as the other men, wherever they were.

Ignacio Gonzales cried out, dropped his gun and spun holding his arm, spurting blood on the carpet as he twirled.

"Come here!" the schoolteacher commanded. He whimpered as she tore strips from a tablecloth to bandage his wound. With each explosion of gunfire he winced in fright, and she realized he was a child, not more than fifteen.

Finally it was quiet again. There was only the heavy breathing of the men, the metallic revolution of their weapons as they reloaded, the crying of the little girls, and their mother's softly whispered hushing sounds.

Sue McSween searched her mind for a solution. In the patriarchy of her world, she could only petition power. She sat up and announced, "I believe I will go see Dudley."

Mac looked at her, his eyes full of terror. "Will you return?"

"I won't abandon my sister and nieces," she retorted, then repented. "I'll come back. I shan't leave you without saying good-bye."

On her hands and knees, Sue McSween crept across her Belgian carpet littered with broken glass and crumbled adobe. When the Kid opened her front door, she stood up and stepped out, hearing him close it behind her as she brushed dust from her skirt. Then she looked down the long empty street to Dudley's camp.

She wished she'd fixed her hair before coming out. There was nothing for it now but to walk as proudly as she could through her enemies. A bullet plopped near her feet, spraying sand across her dark skirt like an apron of quickly falling lace. She told herself she didn't care if they shot her. She would rather die than watch her husband die. As she resolutely marched on, Dolan's men played with her courage.

Though they wouldn't shoot any woman, they teased her with shots landing close enough that she moved through a cloud of dust. Even in their derision, they admired the cut of her spine.

She was quivering with rage when she reached Dudley's tent. Watching the colonel rise from a table holding a bottle of whiskey, her lip curled in disgust. "Why are soldiers surrounding my husband's house?"

"I assure you, madam," he answered stiffly, "I have come to Lincoln solely for the purpose of protecting women and children. I do not intend to take sides in the fight, nor shall I permit any of my men to do so."

"That's too thin, Colonel."

He raised his head with a sneer. "I'm not accustomed to conversing with women who use such vulgarisms as 'too thin.' "

It required all her constraint not to strike him. Keeping her voice low, she pointed out, "You have a cannon aimed at my home."

"If you'll take a closer look"—he smirked—"you'll see the howitzer is aimed in the opposite direction."

"There are three women and five children inside!" she shouted. "Will you not protect us?"

"Any noncombatants may avail themselves of the army's protection."

"Will you allow my husband and his men to surrender to you, under your guarantee of safe passage to Stanton?"

"I'm sorry," he answered. "I cannot interfere with the sheriff."

"They're setting fire to our house!" she cried.

Incredibly, he laughed. "I can't see that to be of any consequence since your husband himself threatened to blow it up."

"He did no such thing!"

"I have it in writing."

"Let me see it."

"No, you would tear it up."

"I demand that you let me see it!" she screamed.

Wincing at her shriek, he capitulated. "Very well. But if you make one false move, I'll have my sentry shoot you."

She snatched the paper from his hands and read in Mac's handwriting: *Before blowing up my property, I would like to know the reason.* "He was distraught," she whispered. "He didn't mean what it implies." Her voice gaining strength, she accused, "You've chosen to misconstrue his meaning."

Dudley whipped the paper from her hands. "McSween is a man of little principle. Any woman married to him must be of low character."

She recoiled. "And you, sir, are cruel! To sit here drinking whiskey while Dolan and Peppin destroy us! If I live, I'll do everything in my power to bring justice on your head."

She spun away and ran for home, oblivious to the enemies watching her flight. She wanted only to cry in her husband's arms and have it all disappear. It was a nightmare. They were doomed. When she looked ahead, she saw flames licking up over the roof of her house. She ran for the door, slipping in and crying at the room full of expectant faces, "The house is on fire!"

"We know," Mac answered in a husky voice. "We've tried our best to put it out, but with no water . . ."

"Oh Mac," she moaned, "Dudley will do nothing to help us."

Silently the fighters gathered in a huddle around the lawyer. Sue sat with the women and children as they listened to the men deciding the short future before them.

"Adobe burns slow," the Kid said. "I figure the fire won't get clear around till after sunset. We can stick it that long."

"What's your plan?" Big Jim asked, eager for hope.

"Soon as it's dark we'll make a break. We only gotta cross about a hundred yards to the river. If we run fast and shoot fast, most of us'll get through." He looked at the women. "You best leave before then. Skirts ain't much good to run in."

"I'd leave right now if I had somewhere to go," Eliza whimpered.

"You can go to the Ealys," Sue said calmly. "I think you should. Now, while it's quiet."

As Eliza and the children gathered the few belongings they would take, Miss Gates picked up the small valise she had prepared for her own departure. "And you, Mrs. McSween?" she asked softly.

Sue shook her head, then looked at the Kid. "I'll leave before I become a problem."

"I'll stay with Mrs. McSween," Miss Gates announced, sitting back down.

Billy shrugged. "Let's go, girls," he said lightly to the children.

Ignacio Gonzales stood up holding his bloody arm. "I want to go, too. I'm wounded and can't shoot anymore."

The Kid spun on him with venom. "You damned coward! We're all sticking till dark. Take it like a man or I'll kill you right now."

He watched Gonzales slink into a corner. Looking back at the little girls, frozen in terror, Billy smiled. "You be good and do like your mama tells you. Promise?" The honey of his voice was so sweet they all nodded, not afraid of him anymore.

Eliza led her daughters to sanctuary with the Reverend Dr. Ealy. Shortly after their arrival, the recommenced firing exploded a keg of gunpowder in the store and Dr. Ealy decided to find safer quarters for the women and children in his care. He sent his wife alone to petition Colonel Dudley for help. A wagon was dispatched to move the noncombatants to the empty Patrón home.

As the sun crept through the afternoon, the fire begun in Sue McSween's kitchen smoldered into the room which should have been the nursery and poked its red hot nose into the dining room. The air was thick with smoke, the remaining rooms along the front a jumble of furniture they had tried to save then given up on, all the pleasures of her fondly decorated home being burned to ashes.

Sue sat and watched. When the fire claimed her chiffonier she thought of the locket from Tunstall nestled in her silk and lace. If she braved the flames to retrieve it now, it would sear her flesh. Better to let it go, to concentrate on holding her mind together, to feel the presence of her husband for a few moments more.

Mac sat despondently in the corner, staring in front of himself but obviously seeing nothing. Beyond him on the floor was the wounded Ignacio, crouched behind the chair in fear of the Kid. The men sweated in the heat, their eyes burning with smoke. No one fired from either side, everyone waiting for the remnant of the Regulators to make their move.

Only the Kid was cheerful, teasing the men about the next little señorita they'd have in their blankets. The Mexicans laughed at his jokes, appreciating the diversion, but the Americans were sour, silent and tense.

At one point, Billy walked over and shook McSween by the shoulders. "Snap out of it, Mac. It ain't over yet, we're gonna make a break."

Mac stared at the Kid as if uncomprehending. "I am doomed," he finally said, shifting his eyes to his wife.

She cried out to hear it, letting herself fall against the bony hardness of his knees. The men withdrew, leaving them as much privacy as could be had in the last three rooms free from the smoldering advance of the fire.

When the sun dropped below the peaks, diffusing the light to a somber haze through the smoke, Billy decided the women should leave before they were mistaken in the gloom for men. Gently, he told the lawyer's wife it was time.

She looked up into her husband's face, his eyes catching the red light of the fire. "If you run with the Kid," she whispered, "you might make it through."

With a melancholy smile he said, "I am weary of being a refugee."

"Oh Mac," she moaned. "How can I bear to just walk away and leave you?"

"You must," he answered simply.

"And tomorrow?"

Reaching out to touch her cheek, he said, "Thou shalt seek me in the morning, but I shall not be."

"But what shall I do, Mac?"

"Find yourself a husband without ambition," he suggested wryly.

She sobbed. "Our life could have been so wonderful."

"Now is not the time for reminiscence," he said gently. "You must leave while there's yet light."

"Oh!" she cried at the difficulty of parting.

"Miss Gates," he called. And when she came, he smiled at her fortitude. "Thank you for staying with my wife. Take her to her sister, will you be so kind?"

Sue let her husband lift her to her feet and hold her in his arms. She clung to him, inhaling his scent. Then she sobbed again, hearing his prayer for her protection. But she could not utter a prayer in return.

As Miss Gates led her from the room, Sue didn't look at the ruins of her home. In her sister's kitchen she stopped, remembering for one brief moment a night she had stood there with Mac and talked of Eliza's coming and John Tunstall's return from St. Louis. All her happiness then, all her prospects for a full and rich life, had been stolen. Not by God, but by men named Dolan and Dudley and Dad Peppin. She looked at Miss Gates and vowed, "I shall have my revenge."

"Oh, Mrs. McSween," the schoolteacher said. "I feel so destitute for you."

Her sympathy was the first Sue had received. She embraced the bearer with fresh tears, the two of them clinging together for a moment of grief. Holding to each other's waist, they opened the door and walked out under the mauve sky of sunset.

As the dark day dimmed into night, the walls of the smoldering house shone through the dusk. The roof was burning with long tendrils of flames snapping in the wind, the adobe glowing like a lantern around the eye of the fire.

Dolan's men crept closer. They surrounded the last unburnt room, knowing the Regulators were breathing scorched air and about to make their break. The remaining walls sheltered the yard from the light of the flames, so there was a blotch of darkness behind the house. Between the chicken coop and the privy was a gate through which the enemy stalked.

The three Regulators in the warehouse shot at the intruders, inspiring a fusillade in return so they had to keep away from the windows. The flames sent slivers of light dancing into their perch. Well aware of the combustible nature of their haven, they agreed that as soon as they saw the Kid get out, they would make a run for it, too.

Inside the house, Billy crouched in the center of the room, staying low to avoid the worst of the smoke as he studied the men around him. They didn't look like fighters. They looked whipped and it hadn't even started yet. McSween sat crosslegged on the floor clutching his Bible to his chest, his lips moving in mumbled prayer.

Billy rose and stretched. Kicking his feet to limber his muscles after five days of sitting around, he crossed to stand before Mac. "It's time to trade your Bible for a gun," the Kid said softly.

Mac looked up as if he hadn't understood.

The Kid winked. "A gun'll do you better than your religion right now."

"Perhaps that's true for you," Mac conceded. "For myself, I shall die believing otherwise."

"Why die without a fight?"

McSween gathered himself to his feet. "It is who I am," he said.

Billy grinned. "I didn't think you'd stick it. I've been waiting for you to pick up a gun ever since they killed Tunstall." He pulled his pistol from his holster, spun the cylinder to make sure it carried a full load, then took another from his belt.

"We're dif'rent, Mac," he said. "But I ain't ashamed I fought your cause. When you get to heaven say hello to my mother, will you? Her name's Katherine McCarty." He laughed at himself but wouldn't take it back. "Good luck to you, Mac."

The Kid turned to his men and whispered, "This is the plan: I'll take four of you and run out shooting. While they're concentrating on us running through the side gate, the rest of you make a break for the back. Run fast and shoot straight. Who's going with me?"

"I'm going," O'Folliard said, stepping forward with a pistol in each hand.

"Me, too," Big Jim said.

"I've had enough of breathing smoke," Chavirra said.

In a voice tight with tension, Harvey Morris said, "Let me go first."

They bunched near the door, waiting for the Kid's signal. He looked at McSween. "As soon as you hear the shooting start, hightail it for the back gate. Don't wait or you'll miss your chance."

Mac nodded and smiled encouragingly. "God be with you," he said.

The Kid laughed. "God and Lady Luck. Let's go."

He flung the door open and Harvey Morris dashed out, blindly firing a gun in both hands as he ran for the gate. Billy jumped after him, O'Folliard on his heels, Chavirra and Finlay right behind. Guns spoke through the shadows, sending flares of light flashing from the dark.

Billy sucked the cool air into his lungs as he ran and fired. He saw Harvey go down in front of the gate, half his head blown away. Billy kept running and shooting, hearing the guns of his friends and a hundred retorts exploding the night into shrapnel of sound.

From the shadows John Jones yelled, "Let 'em go. It's McSween we want!"

Billy leapt over Harvey and went down, tumbling through the gate. Bullets screamed from the corner of Tunstall's store. He looked up and saw soldiers, their rifles belching lead. Scrambling to his feet, he ran into the tules and on to the river. The cool water tasted like salvation, the far bank beckoning with a reward sweeter than anything St. Peter had to offer. Crawling into the dark reeds, Billy grinned at Tom O'Folliard, who grinned back.

In a last-moment impulse for survival, Mac jumped to his feet to rush for the door. At exactly the same instant, Ignacio Gonzales leapt up to do the same. The two men collided, smacking their faces together, then staggered back, both stunned from the blow. Mac's nose had been broken. Blood gushed over his mouth. Ignacio looked at him briefly, then ran out screaming, "I want to surrender. Will someone accept my surrender?"

"I will," Bob Beckwith answered, stepping out of the shadows.

Vicente Romero pushed Ignacio aside. "We will never surrender," Romero said, shooting Beckwith in the eye.

Romero, Salazar, and Zamora plunged into the yard, shooting point-blank into the crowd of men pressing forward. They shot back and all three went down, Romero and Zamora dying instantly. Hijenio Salazar was knocked unconscious from the impact of two bullets. Only Ignacio escaped into the darkness and disappeared along the river.

Mac stepped to the door. Blood filled his mouth as he said, "I am

McSween." Five bullets pierced his body and he fell to his knees. "My God, save me!" he sobbed. His prayer was answered with the silence of eternity.

A jubilant cry erupted from the killers' throats, filling the village of Lincoln with the howl of their victory.

Billy and Tom heard it, running over the mountains toward San Patricio. Fred, Hendry, and George heard it, pulling themselves out of the river onto the safety of the far shore. Sue McSween heard it, and fell with a moan into the lap of Miss Gates. Colonel Dudley heard it and poured himself another glass of whiskey. Jimmie Dolan heard it and smiled. Ordering a henchman to gather a crate of reward, he walked down the street to join the celebration.

Even from far away he could hear fiddling over inane yells and random shots. On the edge of the yard, Dolan paused to admire the scene. The collapsing roof was ablaze, lighting the ground between long batwings of shadow flashing across men dancing in grotesque postures of triumph. Under gunpoint, Sebrian Bates sat on the adobe wall fiddling jigs while tears ran down his face, shining red in the light of the fire. Dolan smiled wryly at the frenetic, clumsy music, then admitted it was no worse than the dancing of the men, their arms akimbo as they leapt over the corpses of the fallen enemy.

Nodding at his henchman to distribute bottles of The House's finest whiskey, Dolan walked through the yard grinning. The men greeted his gifts with joy, each man taking a bottle for himself. They swigged as they danced, shooting off their guns and laughing at the fiddler who cried while he played.

"Who's this?" Dolan jeered, stumbling on a corpse, then kicking it over with his boot. "McSween! I'll be damned if he's not still holding on to that Bible of his!"

"Where's his gun?" John Kinney asked.

"The damned fool didn't own one!"

Hijenio Salazar opened his eyes. He saw the flicker of flames first, then heard the laughter, then, incredibly, a fiddle. Boots were stomping all around and he realized he was in the middle of the yard, in plain view of everyone. Macky Swain lay dead before the door, next to Beckwith from Seven Rivers, and Vicente Romero who had refused to surrender, and Francisco Zamora, never to hunt deer or flirt with señoritas again, and Harvey Morris, the innocent law clerk from Kansas.

Hijenio thought he must be dead, too. Then the pain came to tell him he was still alive. He saw boots approaching and closed his eyes, praying silently, *Santa María, Madre de Dios, ayúdame.*

Two men stood over him, one of them cocking his pistol.

"Don't waste a bullet on that greaser," the other man said. "He's dead as a herring."

"One way to find out," the first said, kicking Hijenio hard in the side.

Hijenio felt he would faint. He couldn't let himself, afraid he would moan. The Mother of his God answered his prayer and allowed him the grace of suffering in silence. As his laughing tormentors went away, he sang praises to his Lady that she might not desert him.

Far into the night, the killers danced a macabre ballet with the shadows from the burning house. They carried away only Beckwith's body out of respect. On McSween they piled planks from the chicken coop and set them on fire, then threw empty bottles into the flames consuming the corpse.

Hijenio waited for the revelers to drink themselves into a stupor, dance themselves to exhaustion. The fiddler played slower and slower, but still he played on. The house burned out, leaving only smoldering ruins lighting the yard as if with the red haze of hell.

Hijenio held to consciousness. He counted the men who stumbled away, and he counted the men who stayed to finish the whiskey and shout drunken curses at the sky. Finally the last two staggered from the yard. The fiddler dropped down the far side of the wall and disappeared, and Hijenio Salazar began to drag himself toward the river.

In the morning, Colonel Dudley took Dr. Appel to survey the deserted, smoky town. As they neared Tunstall's store, they saw the doors standing open and debris scattered in front: spilled flour, shreds of cloth, empty food tins, broken bottles. Inside, shadowy figures helped themselves to the merchandise that remained. Dudley walked on, telling himself looting was a civil affair.

The adobe house that had once been home to the McSweens still smoldered, everything inside its collapsed walls charred into ashes. Twitching his moustache against the stench of burnt flesh, Dudley turned the corner of the ruins and surveyed the carnage in the backyard.

Four corpses lay amid the clutter of empty bottles and broken glass. Chickens scratched around the bodies, picking at the dead eyes. Dudley and Appel had to step over Harvey Morris, sprawled just inside the gate.

Two of the dead were Mexican, of no consequence to Dudley. When he looked at the burned-out pyre over McSween, he snorted with disdain to see the lawyer had barely made it beyond his own door. Appel shooed the chickens off their morbid feast, spied a quilt left crumpled in the yard, and spread it over the lawyer's body. When he looked up, the colonel saw censure in the doctor's eyes, and Dudley retreated toward the whiskey in his tent.

This time when they passed in front of Tunstall's store, they heard laughter from inside and stopped to investigate. Jesse Evans stood before a mirror in his underwear, holding a pilfered new suit. John Kinney sat on the counter fishing peaches from a can. They both grinned at the colonel. He let his gaze take in the ransacked store, the gaping safe against the wall, the gun case smashed and emptied, its supply of ammunition gone. All the merchandise had been destroyed or carried off. Dudley's throat felt dry and he turned away.

Men were coming onto the street, hungover and drinking again. Occasionally gunfire erupted as a fighter relived his moment of glory. Dudley and Appel walked past the deserted *torreón* and the gutted Montaño home, stripped by looters. Patrón's house was shuttered as if empty, but one sign spoke for the people inside: lifting gently in the morning breeze, a woman's long black veil of mourning nailed to the door.

Dudley stopped stock still, seeing it.

Unable to resist taunting his commander, Appel mocked, "Hell hath no fury?"

"What can she do, now that she's alone?"

"Is she? I don't believe I saw the Kid's corpse in the wreckage of her home."

32

He remembered crossing the Guadalupes after he lost his horse to the Apache, walking in boots too small until his feet felt like stumps sloshing blood. Now, accompanied by Tom O'Folliard, he walked in boots John Jones had outgrown, over the crest of the forest to Eagle Creek and down into the Hondo Valley, free by the grace of the man whose boots he wore.

After so many hours of breathing smoke, Billy breathed deep of the fresh night air. The guns on his belt were all he had to his name. His horse and rifle had been left behind. Even so, he felt happy just to be alive; melancholy too, sorrow a companion to his pleasure in the starlit forest.

Billy was eighteen and had killed one man and had a part in killing six others. He'd seen men he admired murdered by the law, and he'd shot into the darkness hiding a good friend who had shot back. He was alive by the grace of that friend. Even now he could go to John's home and feel welcome. Lots of people in the county would take him in. He wouldn't

go hungry or cold in the rain. He would even get another horse and outfit and maybe a rifle as good as the Winchester he'd lost. But what would
he do?

In the soft light of dusk, he and Tom finally reached George Coe's
farm. They were hailed by Fred Waite, watching from a window. He
came out to greet them, hugging Billy with the joy of reunion, then
shaking hands with Tom and welcoming them back to what was left of
the Regulators. Sitting around Coe's kitchen were George and his cousin
Frank, Charlie Bowdre, John Middleton, Doc Scurlock, and Hendry
Brown, all with grim faces.

Billy looked at Fred, who shrugged. "Ain't much to be happy
about," he said.

A jug of whiskey sat on the table, and Middleton and Bowdre were
well on their way to getting drunk. George seemed more relaxed than he
had in months, as if something had broken loose inside and he was better
off for it. A pot of beans simmered on the stove, the coffeepot sizzling
beside it, and a ball of biscuit dough waited on the counter to be rolled
out, as if George had set up housekeeping again. His quiet whistling was
a peaceful sound amid the gloomy faces.

They knew anyone riding by would see the smoke from the chimney
and guess who was likely to be inside. Their desperation was their defense. So they sat and waited for supper, a lethargy palpable among them,
a lack of ambition that came from the extreme expense of energy in the
days of battle. They talked it out, what each had done and seen and
known of the others. They cursed the soldiers as their downfall, pitied
McSween's widow, and grumbled about the injustice of Dolan having
the army on his side.

When Middleton's and Bowdre's drunken complaints became too
maudlin for Billy to take, he walked out to the barn to look over the
horses. Like shadows, Tom O'Folliard and Fred Waite followed him.
After a moment the Coes, Hendry Brown, and Doc Scurlock came, too.
They all stood looking at the string of animals tied to the stalls. Hendry
asked Billy, "Did you lose that gray mare Tunstall gave you?"

"Guess Dolan's got her by now," he answered.

"Everybody's the same," Fred said. "We all hightailed it on foot."

"Except for us in the Ellis house," Scurlock said. "If we'd known how
it was gonna turn out, we'd have brung your horses with us."

"Would've been a hell of a note to run clear down there and find 'em
gone," Billy conceded without rancor.

"Dudley aimed his howitzer at the Montaño house and Chavez had to
run or be blown up," Frank Coe said, though no one had asked. "When
we saw them coming, we thought it best to leave, too, thinking we could

help you from the hills. But the army kept us pinned so we couldn't get close from any direction. When they turned that Gatling gun on us, our rifles were suddenly real puny."

"Soldiers shot at me, too," Billy said. "From Tunstall's store when I was making my break."

"We oughta get Dudley for what he done," Hendry Brown said.

"Not me," George said. He hesitated, then looked at the Kid. "Something come over me this morning. Hendry and Fred and me were so tuckered when we finally made it out of there, we lay down on the hill south of town and fell asleep, wide open for attack. Course we was hidden in the trees and it would've taken a lucky accident for anyone to find us. I slept like a babe. When I woke up, the sun was jus' cresting the peaks and the whole valley was misty with smoke, all golden and pink. I heard the birds singing and smelled the pines so fresh and clean, and all my hard feelings died. I didn't want to hate anyone anymore, nor kill anyone neither. I jus' wanted to come home, so that's what I did."

Billy thought a minute, then said, "I might feel the same if this was mine. You got the prettiest spread in the county, and that's a fact. Did I ever tell you how much I admire this barn?"

"No, I don't reckon," George answered, pleased because he'd built it himself. "It's solid, all right. This here barn'll stand a hundred years, and when it finally gets too rickety and a danger in high wind, I want it to be a Coe that brings her down. I aim to stick to this land."

"I would too, if it was mine," Billy said. "I sure am hungry. You reckon them beans are ready yet?"

After supper, the Regulators sat around George's table and discussed their future. It was generally agreed that what they needed first was horses. Billy suggested they make a raid on the Fritz ranch. Everyone admitted Fritz was holding the best of Dolan's stock and it would be a rich cache, but they doubted the horses they had were up to the exertion and opted for easier prey.

Across the mountains near Blazer's Mill, the Mescaleros kept a herd. If the Regulators timed it right, they could get away with a dozen fast ponies. George said that while they were over there, he'd like to see Brewer's grave. A silence followed his words as each man remembered their fallen friend and leader.

Mentally they counted their dead: Tunstall, Brewer, McNab, McSween, Morris, Zamora, Romero, and Hijenio Salazar, who was not dead but they hadn't yet learned of his survival. They thought they had lost eight men, and even when they eventually adjusted the number to seven, it didn't diminish the injustice they felt knowing their friends had died fighting for the right to a peaceable life.

Several days later, Billy, George, and Hendry set off to replenish their remuda with Indian stock. They rode down Tularosa Canyon, approaching from the north so they could pay their respects at Brewer's grave, which lay between them and the meadow where the herd was pastured. A clear icy spring gurgled out of the mountain north of Blazer's Mill. The Kid dismounted and was watching his horse drink from the stream when a posse rode up.

Atanacio Martínez was leading twenty Mexicans to attach a herd of cattle. When he laboriously explained that he had legal sanction to replevin the herd and was acting within the undisputed bounds of the law, Billy asked if he wanted any help.

"I don't think that would be wise, *Chivato,*" Atanacio answered as politely as he could. "You should stay out of sight until what happened in Lincoln dies down. Just lay low and people will forget."

Billy laughed. "I won't forget, and I doubt anyone else will either. But you go on with your business. We was jus' watering our horses and won't get in your way."

He watched Atanacio lead his posse down the mountain, then said to George and Hendry, "They'll be our cover. While everyone's watching 'em ride by, we'll slip in and catch what we want."

He stood there a moment more, calculating how long it would take the posse to get past the Agency. "We got a few minutes," he said, dropping to his belly and drinking from the spring. He smiled at the reflection of his horse in the pool, its whiskers and huge slurping lips taking in water.

Without warning, gunfire exploded. His horse spurted blood from its nostrils and fell over dead. Billy leapt up behind George and they galloped for cover, then wheeled around to reconnoiter. The shooting was coming from the Agency. Curious as to who Martínez had intercepted, they edged their horses nearer until, from a crag projecting over the canyon, they looked down on the yard of the mill.

Atanacio was afoot. They watched the Agency clerk, a man named Bernstein, spur his horse closer, still shooting, and corner Martínez behind a tree. There was nothing Atanacio could do but defend himself, and they saw the clerk fall to the ground.

"Stupid Jew," Hendry growled. "What the fuck was he doing attacking a constable like that?"

"Maybe he thought they'd come to steal the Indians' ponies," George guessed wryly.

"Don't guess he'll do it again," Billy said. Then, more urgently, "Look down there."

A troop of cavalry was riding pell-mell up the road. The Regulators spun around and cut distance fast, still not understanding what had happened.

They had gone only a few miles when Billy noticed blood dripping from the chest of Hendry's horse. He called to Brown and they all stopped and looked at the wound. Hendry cursed when he saw it. As if only waiting to hear the pronouncement of its doom, the horse fell on its knees and stayed there, wheezing hard. Without another word, Hendry pulled his saddle and bridle off, then shot the horse in the head. That left them one mount between them and they had to admit their raid had been an unmitigated disaster.

Billy knew an old man, Onofre Ochoa, who lived with his wife a few miles east. He offered to walk over and stay with them until someone made it back with a horse. Hefting Hendry's saddle, Billy parted from his friends.

The saddle added extra weight to his boots pushing into the soil, but he didn't think anyone would track him. What happened at the Agency had nothing to do with him. He'd just been in the way and lost his horse because of it. Certainly he didn't think he was placing the Ochoas in danger.

Billy and the Ochoas sat openly by the lamp at their table that night, sharing their simple food, then talking and laughing around the hearth of the one-room home. Billy felt honored when they pulled the top mattress off their bed and laid it in the corner for him. He slept soundly for three or four hours, the way he always did; a deep, dreamless sleep that came quickly and left as abruptly.

A few hours after midnight, horses approached through the darkness outside. Billy heard whispering and the jingle of bridles. Taking his gunbelt, he quietly crawled across to his friends. "*Amigos,*" he whispered. "Be silent, wake up." To them, he formulated his plan: "Hide me in your bed, *por favor.* Put the other mattress on top and fix the blankets and pretend to be sleeping."

"*Andale,*" Señora Ochoa said.

Billy held his pistol ready as he lay facedown and felt the other mattress cover him. He heard the blankets rustle on top. Then, feeling the weight of the Ochoas, he squirmed to find a pocket of air.

Heavy pounding broke the silence, a fist on the door. "Open up. It's the United States Army out here. We've got you surrounded."

As if they had been asleep, the Ochoas waited until the pounding came again. Then the señora got up and unlatched the door. She sped back before they could see her nightgown, and her leap crushed the air out of Billy's lungs. He had to gasp for more even while he heard the boots of many men on the earthen floor.

"We're looking for the Kid," a surly voice barked. "We tracked him here."

"You are mistaken," Señor Ochoa answered, a quaver of fear in his voice. "We are alone. See for yourself."

Billy heard the hiss of a match being struck. After a moment, the officer growled, "The Kid killed the clerk over at the Indian Agency. Anyone who hides him is an accessory to murder. *¿Entienden?*"

"*Sí,*" Ochoa answered. "We have seen no one."

A terse command for his soldiers to mount up was the only farewell the officer gave, but it was welcome. The three people in the house listened until the sounds of hoofbeats faded in the distance. Only then did Billy come out. He sat on the floor with his pistol limp in his hand as he leaned between his knees. When he could breathe easily again, he grinned up at his friends. "Outsmarted 'em that time, didn't we?"

"*Sí, Chivato,*" the old man said with admiration. "You're quick like a fox. They will never catch you."

Billy laughed. "You were pretty foxy yourself, Grandpa. Many thanks." He stood up and holstered his gun. "I didn't do what they said. I wouldn't have come here if I'd known they was tracking me."

"We know that," the señora answered. "We would have hidden you even so."

He marveled at their loyalty. "Go back to sleep. I'll keep a lookout for the rest of the night."

He went outside to sit in the shadow of a pine and watch the starlit yard. Yet even while he enjoyed the beauty of the scene, his mood was shrouded with knowing he'd been blamed for Bernstein's death. When the moon broke from behind clouds and illuminated his friends' humble home, he marveled again that they would risk their lives to help him. They were simple, peaceable folk, their only weapon a hunting rifle. Yet they had defied the United States Army and hidden him without fear. Well, maybe with fear. He'd heard their voices tremble when speaking to the officer, but that they felt afraid only magnified the worth of their loyalty.

Billy thought it was people such as the Ochoas who should reap the bounty of the earth. That the army defended Dolan instead of them festered in Billy's long-standing antipathy for the law to ordain his fate with a simple declaration of revolt. If the powers that be were going to blame him for crimes he didn't commit, he'd make sure they paid for the crimes they did. He was free now, following nobody's instincts but his own, and he was keenly adept at making trouble. He vowed to pester the authorities until they wished they'd never heard of the man the *pobres* called *el Chivato.*

33

In Fort Sumner, Sallie Chisum was sitting on the roof of an old, dilapidated carriage talking with her friend Paulita Maxwell. The faded grandeur of the carriage was a remnant of the wealth of Paulita's father, Lucien, who had once owned the fabled Maxwell Land Grant in the northeast corner of the territory. In 1869, he had sold the nearly two million acres for six hundred and fifty thousand dollars.

Lucien had been a rancher, however, more than a businessman, and his founding of the First National Bank in Santa Fe ended in financial loss when he sold out to Thomas Catron. Maxwell had moved his family into the abandoned fort at Sumner, purchasing the buildings and adjacent land from the government. Sorely missing the high plains of his Cimarron country, Lucien had been unhappy in the low prairie along the Pecos. He died in 1875, leaving his son to manage the remnant of his estate.

Peter Menard Maxwell was landlord to the people who rented rooms in the long buildings that had once housed soldiers. He lived with his sister and mother and their Navajo servant, Deluvina, in the large house that had formerly been officers' quarters. The imposing frame edifice, a commodious Victorian structure consisting of twenty rooms on two floors, faced the old parade ground and backed on the river.

Fort Sumner was a mecca for travelers. Anyone coming north from the lower Pecos, northwest out of Texas, west off the Staked Plain, south from Las Vegas or Santa Fe, or east from Lincoln or Mesilla, came through the town of the Maxwells. The sheriff of San Miguel County resided in Las Vegas, one hundred miles to the north, so there was no law in Sumner except for the gentle will of Paulita's brother and the general desire among the people for peace.

Maybe it was the river's influence. The sultry summer nights followed by oven-hot dawns swamping the plaza with sun, the bees droning in the peach orchards, the mutts sleeping in the shade of cottonwoods lining the road created a thirst for a happy antidote to boredom: a *baile,* a contest, or simply talking with a friend. Fort Sumner was a somnolent town because the people who visited were often in retreat from somewhere else.

Sallie Chisum was one of those who arrived seeking sanctuary. Three years older than Paulita, but nowhere near the beauty, Sallie struggled to compensate with the fact that she had been hostess for her Uncle John, the lady of a house where dinner was often served to a dozen strangers from a dozen different places. She wanted to impress her friend but wouldn't lie to do it, just brag a little, flaunting her worldly knowledge before the other's fifteen-year-old innocence.

Alternately watching her friend's face and the horses in the corral, slapping flies away with their long black tails, Sallie said, "There was a battle in Lincoln and the lawyer was killed. Now outlaws roam pretty much at will and no place in the county is safe."

"Wasn't the lawyer a friend of your Uncle John's?" Paulita asked.

"Mr. McSween used to visit us quite often," Sallie answered thoughtfully. "His wife, too, though I can't say I cared for her, poor thing. She's a widow now and left penniless, we hear."

"Why didn't you like her?" Paulita asked.

Sallie thought a moment, drawing her knees up beneath her skirts and hugging them on the cracked roof of the carriage. "She was too friendly with men, like she was easy," she finally said. "Actually I think men are afraid of her." Sallie smiled sadly, suddenly remembering Dick Brewer apologizing for inadvertently swearing. He had stood awkwardly in the hall as if poised for flight, his eyes burning with humiliation as he expressed his regret for offending her, looking so handsome she felt tempted to kiss him. He was dead now, like so many others. She looked at Paulita. "Most of the men down there are afraid of women. They treat us like fine china to be left on the shelf."

"How dull," Paulita said.

"Not always," Sallie was quick to counter. "Some of them are downright bold. We're here because Billy Bonney came calling at Bosque Grande and Father decided it was time to move."

"Is he a beau of yours?" the girl asked with a sparkle in her dark eyes.

"No, we're just friends," Sallie answered. "He came to see Uncle John, not me. But he made me promise not to tell anyone and I haven't till now. Do you think I should tell my father?"

"That Billy Bonney wants to see your uncle? Is it so important?"

"He's killed a lot of men."

"So has Billy Bonney," Paulita answered innocently.

Sallie looked at her angrily a moment, then realized the girl was only repeating what she'd heard. And, truth be told, Uncle John probably had been forced into situations when he'd ordered a man's death. She was sure it had always been justified, that they were men who needed killing. She realized she'd heard that phrase from Billy and she repeated it now in a puzzled tone. "He said he only killed men who needed it."

"Billy Bonney said that?" Paulita laughed. "Does he think he's Don Quixote fighting for justice?"

"Who?"

"A book I read in school," Paulita said. When her friend still looked puzzled, Paulita added, "It's only a funny story. Your Billy Bonney made me think of it: the same kind of glorious purpose that in the end is just silly."

"Death isn't silly," Sallie replied earnestly. "I once talked with a man who was killed the next day. He knew it was going to happen and I begged Uncle John to intervene, but he wouldn't. Billy was with the men who killed him. I knew Sheriff Brady, and Billy killed him. I knew Dick Brewer and Alex McSween and John Tunstall and Frank McNab. I can't say any of them deserved to die. They seemed like decent men to me." She sighed. "It's hard to understand."

"It's war," Paulita said. "Mother says it's always hard for women to understand."

Sallie nodded, feeling worried. "I told Billy we were coming to Sumner," she whispered. "I told him Uncle John was meeting us here and Billy made me promise not to tell that he knows."

"How did he make you?" Paulita whispered back.

"We made a deal," Sallie said, watching her friend's face. "I made him promise not to hurt Uncle John."

"Good for you! Then you have nothing to worry about."

"Do you think so? My father is afraid of Billy."

"My brother says Heiskell Jones thinks well of Billy Bonney and that's good enough for him. So maybe, if he follows you here, I'll get to meet this famous Billy the Kid. Anyway, I think your father is only trying to protect you."

"That's silly."

"Of course," Paulita agreed. "All of life is silly, don't you think?"

"Maybe when you're fifteen," Sallie teased. "When you're eighteen, you'll see how serious it is."

"You've learned about death, is all," Paulita answered, her beauty illuminated by the sadness washing across her face. "See that cemetery down there? My father is buried in that *camposanto* and I will be, too, someday. Death is the silliest thing of all."

"I've bet my life on this man," Billy said to the small crowd Fred had collected from the saloon. "Today I'm betting that he can outshoot any man here. What do you say? Any takers?"

"He ain't got no trigger finger!" Beaver Smith yelled.

Billy grinned. "I'm still betting he can outshoot any one of you."

George Coe wanted to hide his mangled hand in his pocket but knew it was the hook to bring in bets.

"Why don't *you* shoot, Kid?" Barney Mason hollered. "Around here
we heard you was the best shooter in the war."

"Hell, boys," Billy said, "I want it to be a fair contest. Ain't there
one of you thinks he can outshoot a three-fingered man? Why, George
ain't got but half a thumb!"

"I'll shoot agin 'im," a sour-smelling buffalo hunter growled, stepping into the clearing around Billy and George. "I kin outshoot anybody, even the Kid, whoever he is."

Billy smiled. "All you gotta do is outshoot George. Set up the
bottles, Fred. All right! The bank's open. Who wants to place a bet?"

Two dozen men were standing in front of the only saloon in Fort
Sumner. They were rowdy, loud, and boisterous, quick to part with their
money. Despite the heat of August, most wore vests and rumpled jack-
ets. They all wore high leather boots adorned with spurs, and six-shooters heavy on their cartridge belts. All were dirty, hot and sweaty,
shouting and laughing and grumbling and cursing as they paid their
bets into the small, almost feminine hands of Billy Bonney. They eyed
the Kid as much as the shooter he promoted, seeing the famous fighter
for the first time.

He seemed benign, showing his crooked teeth in a constant grin,
making the men laugh at his jokes, putting them at ease. They almost
couldn't believe he was the Kid they'd heard so much about, except he
wouldn't shoot, letting his reputation speak for him. Besides, who would
be foolhardy enough to say he was the Kid if he wasn't? Crazy enough to
take on the Kid's enemies—Dolan and Catron and the Santa Fe Ring?

So they bet as much to get close to him as because they cared about
the contest. To see his gray-blue eyes dance in his long peach-fuzz face,
feel his crooked grin aimed at them, maybe brush his hand lightly as
they exchanged the sweaty coins and wadded scrip of their bets. They
eyed his gun, noted it was a Colt's Lightning Action, and they thought
to themselves it was the Kid all right.

The targets were bottles set on a makeshift platform eighty yards
down the road. Each contestant got the chance to shoot five and Coe
went first. A hush fell as George raised his Winchester and took his time
aiming.

He felt confident, yet the edge of need was there to make him extra
careful. The Regulators were busted and Billy had thought up this contest to raise money. They'd all pooled their cartridges to have enough to
compete, and they would all be broke and without ammo if George lost.
But it was even harder than that because between them they'd only had
twenty shells.

George planted his feet firmly a little farther apart, squinted down the barrel and fired, swiveling his shoulder to sight the next bottle, hearing it break as he swiveled to the next. But he forgot to count and wasted a sixth shot. He grimaced at Billy as he stepped back, lowering his rifle.

A cheer went up from the spectators backing the Kid's man, and a grumble from those backing the buffalo hunter. He had a Sharp's .50-50, a cannon to use on bottles, with a trajectory that would continue for eight hundred yards compared to the Winchester's three hundred and fifty.

"I hope no one's coming up the road," Billy whispered to George.

"For the next hundred miles," George answered with a laugh.

The buffalo hunter turned to glare over his shoulder.

"Sorry," the Kid apologized with a grin.

The Sharp's' boom was so loud it obliterated the sound of breaking glass as the bottles shattered. The buffalo hunter stepped back to applause from his supporters.

George wiped the sweat off his face with the sleeve of his shirt and stepped into position as Fred placed a fresh row of bottles on the platform. The other Regulators were standing beneath a tree in front of the saloon, a huge cottonwood that threw its shade across to where George stood holding his rifle. The men gave him thumbs up.

Bam, bam, bam, bam, bam! All five bottles exploded in the sunlight. He could hear Billy laughing and felt smug with pride as he stepped back beside him, unable to look at anyone, afraid he would blush with embarrassment at feeling so proud.

While Fred set up the bottles, Billy let his gaze rove across the crowd. They were mostly Mexican, slight and dark, their faces honed with intensity, body and soul into the contest. The buffalo hunter's partner was dressed in buckskin reeking of blood and the sweat of months without a bath. His face was noncommittal, as if it weren't his partner competing. Yet he had bet on him, so he cared. He just wore a habitual poker face that made him look mean.

So did the Regulators, Billy noted. He decided he liked the Mexicans better. They lived with their hearts, alive in each moment, and he preferred their company to the devious treachery of Americans. He trusted Mexican people more than he did most of his friends. It seemed a Mexican's life was simple, his decisions clean-cut. With Americans, so many elements came into play that Billy was never sure how someone would fall until he was down.

A tall man crouched in the door of the saloon, his apron marking him as the barkeep. He was so tall he had to bend his knees to keep his head from hitting the lintel, and these buildings were left over from the fort. They hadn't been built by Mexicans, who often made their doors so low even Billy had to stoop to step inside.

Billy was five nine and the bartender had to be four, maybe even five inches over six feet. He had a flop of dark hair and a black killer moustache drooping over his pale bony face. His blue eyes caught the Kid's and the two men nodded at each other, then Boom! went the buffalo hunter's Sharp's and Billy looked back and watched the five bottles disappear from the plank.

"Damn!" George swore beneath his breath.

"He can't keep it up," Billy whispered. "That cannon gets heavy."

"So do buffalo hides," George muttered as he moved into position. He had already slipped once and couldn't do it again. Raising his rifle, he squeezed the trigger with his middle finger five times, but only four bottles fell.

He stepped back, too ashamed to look at Billy, but the Kid said, "That's all right. Ol' Buffalo ain't shot yet."

The hunter was arrogant. He took his stance and hefted the heavy rifle to his shoulder without hesitation, fired once and missed. A cry of victory went up from the men backing Coe. Thinking no matter how well the hunter did now there would be another round, the bettors didn't know George was short of enough cartridges to finish.

The hunter grumbled and stepped back into position, raised his rifle and took his time aiming. Boom! The second bottle disappeared. Boom! the third was gone and Boom! the fourth. Boom! the fifth still sparkled in the sun, a glittering pair with the first. Fred let loose a war whoop of victory and Billy danced a jig around George, who was laughing again now that he'd won.

The Regulators divvied the money there under the cottonwood. Billy returned a dime for every cartridge thrown into the pot and split what was left among the men, each getting three dollars as their cut, Fred an extra two for working the bottles, Billy an extra five for taking the bets, George an even ten. That left Billy eight dollars, plenty to get into a monte game and win enough to tide him over until Chisum hit town.

Everyone headed into the saloon to celebrate, except Billy, Tom, and the Coes. As they ambled back to their camp by the river, George and Frank explained they had been asked to help their cousin drive a herd from the Sugareet to the San Juan, and they figured this was a good time to make themselves scarce around Lincoln.

"You ain't leaving your land?" Billy asked, incredulous.

"We'll be back," George said.

"I guess what we're saying," Frank explained, "is we're leaving the Regulators."

Billy laughed. "There ain't no more Regulators. We're nothing but outlaws now."

Sauntering into the shade of camp, the Coes waited until the Kid was seated on a boulder, then George said, "That's jus' it, Billy. We don't want to be outlaws. We figure the war is over and we want to be farmers again."

Billy looked up the dusty bed of the Pecos, a thread of dirty water barely moving between sandbars. The war had stripped him of his only possessions and he meant to collect value with interest. Chisum still owed him wages, and Jesse Evans was still running loose. Dolan had still gotten away with murder: Mac, Tunstall, Brewer, McNab, Morris, Romero, and Zamora were still dead. Billy couldn't bring himself to just walk away from all that. He was a fighter. Neither a farmer like George, whose fine red barn would stand a hundred years, nor like Frank, who had been Tunstall's neighbor and would have been Billy's if Tunstall had lived.

If Tunstall had lived . . . That speculative future was becoming a mythical reality in Billy's mind, a lost opportunity to be like everyone else. Not really like everyone else. Most folks just sat back and let whatever was happening roll right over them, but Billy was a performer. His mere presence stirred things up somehow, made people laugh, kept their conversation lively, and he never expected to be a follower again.

But for the Coes life was different, and Billy accepted that for them the war was over. He'd known it since George's near-religious awakening on the mountain overlooking Lincoln. All his hard feelings had died, he'd said. That wasn't true for Billy. He hadn't experienced any revelation on the mountaintop, but he wasn't one to bear a grudge out of envy. He smiled at the two lanky farmers, saying he'd be glad to receive an invitation to supper when they came back.

They all laughed and joked about the homecoming for a few minutes, then George asked, "What'll you do now, Billy?"

"I got an appointment with Chisum," the Kid said, looking up the river again, watching the heavy water move through the mud. "He promised us five hundred dollars to kill Brady. I aim to collect."

There was silence in the camp, only the whine of cicada in the trees overhead. "We wasn't there," George finally said.

Billy shrugged, his smile wry but his eyes veiled.

"Why don't you come with us?" Frank suggested. "I'm sure my brother can use another drover."

The Kid laughed. "I herded cows once. All I got was an eyeful of shit and shortchanged at the end. No thanks." He stood up and clinked the coins in his pocket. "Let's get some supper and check out the monte tables."

Tom O'Folliard pulled himself to his feet, but the Coes remained on their blankets.

"Reckon we oughta save our money for the trip," George said.

"Supper's on me," Billy answered, then grinned. "Maybe later I can talk you into staking me in a game."

Frank laughed, and he and his cousin followed the Kid and Tom into the lengthening shadows of evening.

34

Beaver Smith's saloon was long, narrow, and dark, with a few scarred tables scattered between the bar and the batwing door. There were two lamps behind the bar and a lantern suspended from the ceiling, but no windows to let in light. Even the door was shaded by a huge cottonwood, like those lining the avenue leading into town. Planted by the soldiers twenty years before, the trees were stately now, providing a graceful entrance to anyone coming from Vegas or Lincoln.

The avenue ran north and south along the river. Two of the three smaller roads, turning east with military precision, were lined by flat-roofed adobe barracks. The most southerly road traveled through untouched prairie past the *camposanto* southeast of town. The Regulators had camped nearly parallel to the cemetery, though they didn't even know it existed. About a mile west of it, along the bank of the river, their camp swarmed with mosquitoes, so the Regulators were not eager to return to their blankets from the convivial comfort of Beaver Smith's saloon.

Cagily ready for trouble, the barkeep had watched the men all evening. The Lincoln County War had not passed unobserved by the outside world. All the territorial newspapers carried accounts from citizens who sounded off in letters to the editor, usually under a nom de plume, so the reports were blatantly biased. But through the hyperbolic prose and partisan distortions, the story emerged into the world at large. Even the big eastern papers carried items about the war in the remote territory of New Mexico, and even they regaled their readers with the exploits of Billy the Kid.

No doubt unwittingly, Dolan himself had initiated the Kid's fame by listing Billy first when he debunked the "outraged prominent citizens" fighting for McSween. "A renegade," Dolan called the Kid, "a cold-blooded killer." After that, editors always wanted Billy's name in the stories. If they didn't have news of the young fighter, they invented it.

In Beaver Smith's saloon that hot night toward the end of August, 1878, the barkeep watched Billy Bonney playing monte for several hours, watched the ebullience that surrounded him like an aura of high energy, always this chatter and laughter coming from the men playing with the Kid, while those at the other tables stared sullenly at their cards in silence. Yet the barkeep saw that all eyes in the room watched the Kid unobtrusively.

When the last game had ended, Billy felt restless. He'd won back the money spent on supper and then some, but now only the Regulators were left in the saloon and they guarded their funds from his skill with cards. When he asked the barkeep to play a hand, the man answered with a southern accent that he wasn't allowed to gamble while working but would enjoy a game later.

"Yeah, well, who knows if I'll be around later," Billy said, returning to the table where O'Folliard and the Coes waited. "Think I'll go for a walk," he said as he passed, headed for the door.

Tom stood up and followed him. The other men all watched in silence, each man's thoughts like a secret cocoon inside his mind. Anyone would be a fool not to like the Kid, and a fool not to fear him, too. This ambivalence kept his companions on the edge of expectation, ruffling their lethargy with the acute awareness that momentarily everything could change.

The barkeep found the Kid's acuity challenging and looked forward to meeting his pale eyes over a deck of cards. The other men in the room awaited trouble with Billy. In war he had been a great companion. Now that peace had come, they watched the Kid warily to see how he'd fall. They all liked him and hoped he'd fall in a way that wouldn't put them in jeopardy.

To Scurlock and Bowdre, Billy was a friend they hoped to use for their own purposes. Middleton was tired and content to follow the Kid's lead for a while. The Coes truly loved the Kid, Hendry Brown admired him, and Fred Waite felt both those emotions mixed with a nostalgia for days past.

Tom O'Folliard, following the Kid onto the dark street in front of the saloon, revered him as a hero. Tom was several inches taller, pudgy, and with feet so large he was nicknamed Big Foot. He had a baby face and elephantine ears beneath fine, tawny hair. Though his gunhand was decent, his prime asset was his devotion to Billy, and the Kid had been quick to see the advantages.

They walked south along the avenue, then turned east. Rented to families, the former barracks were now a series of one-room apartments, their open doors showing interiors brightly painted the vivid colors of the tropics and crowded with furniture. The families were seated along the portal on blankets and chairs. Men smoked dark cigarillos and women cradled toddlers asleep in their rebozos, watching the older children play marbles and tag in the dusty road.

The aromas of late suppers—beef and chile, frijoles and tortillas—mingled with the humidity of the river into a heavy, sensual atmosphere. Light fell from the open doors across the wide dark street, sporadically illuminating the two men walking through, the jingle of their spurs singing in the lull of conversation and play caused by their passing. The curiosity of the people was friendly, and the two strangers suffered it with grace.

Billy liked the town already, feeling at ease with these simple people who lived in one room and spent their evenings watching children play. He smiled comfortably at Tom as they turned in front of the plaza and found themselves enveloped in the sultry sweetness of a flower garden stretching away from the path.

The perfume of hundreds of blossoms ripening in the heat was heady on the humid air. Billy pulled his knife from his belt, leaned across the fence to choose the biggest white rose, and cut it off. "My ma loved roses," he said, stepping back beside Tom with a crooked grin.

"Where is she?" Tom asked, thinking of his own mother, who had begged him not to go to Lincoln.

Billy lifted the flower to his nose and held it there a long moment. Then he looked at his friend and laughed as he tossed the rose away. "She died puking her blood in my arms," he said, moving on down the path.

"Gosh, I'm sorry," Tom mumbled.

"So am I," Billy said.

They passed in front of another flower garden. This time they didn't stop but continued to the looming house beside it, through the picket gate and up the steps to the front porch. Standing in a dapple of colored light falling through the stained glass window in the massive door, Billy knocked, then took his hat off while he waited.

A plump Navajo woman opened the door and surveyed him critically.

"My name's Billy Bonney," the Kid said. "Is Miss Chisum at home?"

The woman flicked her gaze to the tall boy behind him, then said in a husky voice, "Miss Sallie's taking a bath, getting ready to see her Uncle John, who's coming in the morning."

Billy laughed and thanked her, then said, "Tell her I called, will you?"

She nodded and closed the door. Billy turned to Tom and laughed again with delight that it had been so easy.

From the shadows on the far end of the veranda, a soft feminine voice said, "You could have asked me. I would have told you what you came to find out."

Billy stood in the light falling through the stained glass, a pattern of blue and green on the wooden floor. He stepped into the shadows and tried to focus on the girl in the swing. "What was it I came to find out?" he asked, seeing only a slender silhouette against the pale slats.

"When John Chisum's coming," she said.

She stood up and walked toward the men, the rustle of her skirts sounding like the flow of high mountain water. As she passed between them, she was a breeze of lilies, a cool refreshing scent.

"How'd you know?" Billy asked.

"Sallie told me," she answered. In the flowery pattern of light from the door, she turned and smiled. "My name's Paulita Maxwell. I'm pleased to meet you, Billy Bonney."

"The pleasure's mine," he said politely. "This here's Tom O'Folliard."

She gave Tom a small smile, then said, "Good evening, gentlemen," and disappeared behind the stained glass panel of the door.

"Whew," Tom whispered. "Pretty classy."

Billy made no reply, skipping down the steps and starting briskly back toward Beaver Smith's, his mind already on business. Chisum was expected tomorrow and Billy didn't intend to let the old man get comfy before hitting him up. For now he had an evening to get through when he felt so wired he knew sleep was half the night away. He went back to the saloon and waited for the barkeep's shift to end.

When it did, the tall, lanky Southerner carried a bottle of whiskey to the Kid's table. "Name's Pat Garrett," he drawled, extending his hand.

"Billy Bonney," he said, standing as they shook. He introduced Tom, Fred, and Hendry, who nodded from their seats.

Garrett set the bottle down and folded himself into a chair. "What'll it be, boys? Monte?"

"That's my game," Billy answered.

"Ever play casino?" Garrett asked, a twinkle in his blue eyes.

Billy shook his head.

"Want to learn?"

He shrugged. "Sure."

"Fine," Garrett said, flashing strong white teeth between the wings of his black moustache as he smiled. "This is it: Face cards are worthless, aces count one, and the rest pip. The ten of diamonds is big casino, the two of spades little casino. Either one of 'em takes the pot. You get four cards." He dealt them out facedown. "I get four, and the table gets four faceup. Go ahead, look at your cards. Normally we'd place our bets now, but this is a dry run. If you have the ten of diamonds or two of spades, you've won. Do you?"

Billy shook his head.

"Good. Okay, now see, I've got a six here, the suit doesn't matter. So I can take this four and this two. I could also take a five and ace if they were there. Get it?"

"Yeah," Billy said.

"You play."

Billy laid his seven of spades down and took the five and two from the table.

"So we bet again, get a new deal. Right now you have seven points and I have six. Twenty-one beats anything short of a casino. Understand?"

"I'm ready," the Kid said.

Fred laughed, standing up. "I'm turning in."

"Me, too," Hendry said. "I couldn't play that game sober, I don't believe."

Garrett looked at Tom.

"I'll just watch," he said, leaning back in his chair and hooking his thumbs in his gunbelt.

Garrett poured himself a drink as Fred and Hendry clumped across the room and out the door. "You want a drink, Kid?"

Billy shook his head with a friendly smile.

"Not even now that all your tin soldiers are safely tucked in their blankets?"

The Kid's eyes flashed cold and Garrett felt pleased to have raised his ire so quickly. No doubt the Kid was good but he operated from emotion, and Garrett thought his own intellect was superior. He dealt the cards.

Through the hours, Garrett continually nipped at the bottle as he and the Kid played without stopping, without even talking much. There was just the slap of the deals, the slide of the coins, the riffle of the cards. Tom dozed in his chair, his hat over his eyes.

Beaver Smith closed the bar and yelled for Garrett to lock up when he left. They played for hours after that. Gradually the Kid started edging into Garrett's winnings, until when they finally quit they were about even. They scraped their money off the table and smiled at each other with appreciation. Few men were gambling fools as they were, and the future promised a rewarding friendship between them.

That night, though, Garrett was tired. He had worked all day and was just about to say goodnight when Billy asked if there were any whores still awake in Sumner.

"I know some cost two dollars," Garrett answered. "Let you stay the night."

"What do they look like?"

"It's dark when I get there and they're gone in the morning, so I can't really say."

Billy laughed and tapped his boot against Tom's chair. "Hey Big Foot, want to go find a whore?"

"Sure," O'Folliard answered, though he hadn't really heard the question.

"Well, come on, boys," Garrett said. "I think I can stay awake just long enough to get my money's worth."

The gray light of dawn found Billy sitting in the window seat of the whore's room, watching her face emerge from the shadows. He'd found it was interesting to make love to a woman he'd never seen, allowing his hands to make judgments as they explored her body.

She was small and slender, that much he'd learned, passive and acquiescent, her only words a softly mumbled greeting in Spanish followed through the night with quiet moans. He took them for sounds of pleasure but obviously preferred thinking that. In truth, he had no idea what her response had been. He waited now for the light to reveal it in her eyes.

Not a beauty, she was young and unmarred by pox, her skin the cocoa color of the Pecos at flood. Her broad nose marked her for mestizo, and her hair was long and straight and black as an Apache's. She opened her eyes, lazily closed them again, then opened them wide as she realized he was watching her.

She had overslept, sinking into a dreamless oblivion after his gentle possession that came like a wave again and again until she fell asleep in his arms. She was not oblivious now as she realized she was jeopardizing the secrecy of her activities. That was why she and the others slipped in and out of the whorehouse under cover of darkness: to protect their reputations as well as those of their families. She hurried now to dress and get away.

He watched her in silence, thinking her beauty was enhanced by the light in her eyes, and that her shyness proved she was new to the profession. "What's your name?" he asked.

"I'm not supposed to say," she whispered, pulling her blouse over her breasts, tucking it into her skirt then tying a sash around her waist.

"Can I see you again?"

She shrugged. "If you come again, perhaps."

"How can I ask for you if I don't know your name?"

She turned to the mirror above the washstand, combing her fingers through the length of her hair until every strand lay smoothly in place. He was watching her in the mirror, his smile so full of appreciation that she thought she saw more in his eyes than fondness for a whore, and she gambled with her fate. "You could come to my sister's," she answered, turning to face him.

"Where's that?"

"Across the plaza," she said quickly. "The third house from the far end. I must go now." She waited to be dismissed.

"My money's on the bureau," he said with a playful smile. "Take what you need."

She walked closer to look at the coins spread on the dresser. Among the small change were a dozen silver dollars and a Gold Eagle. She would get half of the two dollars he'd paid to come upstairs, so she picked five dollars from the coins, though she eyed the Eagle. She saw he was amused by her choice.

He said, "Why don'cha stay at your sister's tonight and I'll come calling?"

"I would like that very much," she said. "I must go now."

"Won't you tell me your name?" he coaxed. "I'll tell you mine. It's Billy Bonney, but most folks call me Kid."

Her eyes widened and she fell back on her native tongue. "Me llamo Abrana García," she whispered, then disappeared out the door.

He listened to her bare feet on the stairs and watched from the window as she emerged on the street, running without looking back as she hurried to escape the prying eyes of her neighbors. At the corner near the orchard, he saw her look up fearfully and guessed she'd been spotted. Energy tingled in his veins as he recognized the ambling form of John Chisum.

The whole town was asleep and Billy thought he couldn't have asked for a better time to make his play. He walked downstairs and into the bright sunshine of early morning.

John Chisum stood at the corner of the orchard planted to feed the thousands of Apaches and Navajos confined nearby when Sumner had been a fort. Peaches were scattered festering in the grass, and those still on the trees had split open, their sugar nectar for swarming bees. There was an overabundance of peaches in Sumner; what should have been a delicacy made children complain of eating them again. Staring at the acres of rotting fruit, Chisum felt melancholy, reflecting on the waste.

The war was over. The Santa Fe Ring had won, and Chisum was pulling out. He was going back to Texas, to the Panhandle this time, to breed a select herd of cattle and indulge his passion for horticulture. He hoped Sallie would stay with him, marry and raise children in his home. He missed being a grandfather more than he had ever longed for fatherhood.

When he looked up and saw the Kid walking toward him, Chisum felt eager to get one more severance out of the way. Assessing the Kid's approach—the stealth of his gait, the tension of his hand near his gun— Chisum knew he was coming for revenge or money, nothing else motivated men to kill. "Morning, Billy," he said pleasantly, turning to face him.

"You owe us five hundred dollars," the Kid said with a smile.

Chisum smiled back. "Do I?"

The Kid pulled his gun and nudged it into Chisum's gut.

Chisum chuckled. "You know I'm always unarmed." Then, hesitating for permission, "Let me get a smoke, will you? I talk better that way."

The Kid stepped back, still holding his gun as he watched Chisum reach into the pocket of his shirt and take out a pipe, fill it with tobacco, tamp it down and strike a match on the dilapidated fence around the orchard.

"Now, Billy," he began, emitting a cloud of fragrant smoke. "You could talk to me about that five hundred dollars till your hair's as white as mine and never convince me to pay it."

"You promised it."

Chisum took his pipe from his mouth. "I know you won't shoot an unarmed man, so you may as well put your gun away."

"The last men who cheated me were Morton and Baker," the Kid said.

Chisum puffed on his pipe, thinking of the day he'd watched those men ride out of his yard surrounded by Regulators. He'd kept himself clean until Mac had collapsed and Sue stood up so fierce and proud she'd deserved backing, dammit. But Chisum knew it had been a mistake. Killing the law proved too unsavory for even McSween's reputation, and Chisum wanted no vestige of his complicity left.

"Just between you and me," he finally said, "it's true I promised that money, but I'll deny it in front of anyone else. I gave you boys credit at my store, never asked for payment and never received any. You ran up way over five hundred dollars in cartridges alone. You boys used a lot of bullets those last few months. I think that counts, and the way I see it, we're square."

The Kid laughed. "You motherfucking sonofabitch. Tunstall and Mac never would've pushed Dolan so hard without trusting that you were behind 'em. But every time a showdown came, you were out of the territory. Now you're pulling out for good and think you can jus' walk away clean." He shook his head in mock disbelief, then holstered his gun. "I won't kill you, Chisum, but not for any reason that has anything to do with you. I'll take the five hundred from your herd with int'rest, till you wish you'd been honest with me when you had the chance."

When Billy sauntered into the camp of defunct Regulators sitting lazily around second cups of coffee, George was just saying that anyone who wanted to ride to the Sugareet with him and Frank was welcome. Billy felt all the men look at him, waiting for his reaction to the Coes' invitation.

He poured himself a cup of coffee, winked at Tom sitting on a log, then settled himself on his favorite boulder near the river. "You all can do exactly as you please," Billy said. "There's nothing holding us together now. I jus' seen Chisum and he refused to pay, says we run up more'n that buying bullets at his store, so we're square."

"Sonofabitch," Hendry grumbled. "We used those bullets defending his interest."

"Aw, I never thought he'd pay," Middleton said.

Billy laughed. "Me neither. But I let him know he won't get away with it."

There was a long silence, the sludge of the river suddenly loud beneath the whine of cicadas in the cottonwoods. His voice heavy with dread, Fred asked, "What're you thinking of, Billy?"

"I told Chisum I'd steal the five hundred from his herd, and I aim to do it."

"You're heading for disaster," Frank warned. "Any strike against Chisum will bring a posse after you."

"That's nothing new," Billy said.

"But it's dif'rent now," George argued. "Find yourself a way to make an honest living and what happened will blow over. If you go on like this, they'll get you for sure."

Billy shrugged. "I'll give 'em hell in the meantime."

"They'll give you hell," Middleton said. "You won't be able to fuck a whore without a gun in your hand."

"Does that mean you're leaving for the Sugareet, John?" Billy asked, his voice noncommittal.

"Nah, I'm not a drover," Middleton answered. "Anyway, I ain't got traveling money right now."

"That's exactly it," Billy crowed. "We're all broke. I say we raid the Fritz ranch and make off with Dolan's prime horses. Drive 'em over to Tascosa and live high for a spell. I hear they're hungry for good horses in the Panhandle."

"Lincoln's wide open," George said. "John Kinney's gang has been joined by a bunch from Texas calling themselves Selman's Scouts. I hear they're tearing things up pretty bad."

Billy laughed. "I ain't afraid of Kinney or Selman, and none of us are new to their game. We'll be in and out before they ever catch our wind."

"I'll go," Fred said, so solemnly they all turned to look at him. "I need money to move on, but this is it for me, Billy. I've nothing in Lincoln to go back for."

"I feel the same," Hendry said. "All I ever got from that country was shot at and shortchanged on my wages. Don't seem like a healthy place."

"Guess that goes for me," Middleton muttered.

Charlie and Doc said they'd go, so with Tom and Billy they were seven. "No use sitting here," the Kid said. "Let's ride."

George and Frank Coe had hoped Billy would come with them. Certain he was embarking on a path to tragedy, they felt no inclination to follow. Yet, watching the men joking and laughing as they saddled their horses, the Coes envied Billy's enjoyment of life. They faced months of hard work herding cattle across the rugged northern mountains, then coming home to the shambles of their farms and beginning again to build an enterprise. Billy faced lazy days of freedom, long hot nights in the company of whores, and a living pilfered from other men's herds. The Coes felt a twinge of jealousy when they were honest with themselves.

They were generally honest men, wanting nothing more than to be left in peace to farm their land. They knew, however, that Billy's path promised every pleasure but peace. When the time came to part, George and Frank felt melancholy as they watched the Kid ride into the vast prairie on the dark side of the law.

35

Henry Hoyt was carrying the mail from Fort Bascome to Tascosa, riding his poor horse slowly through the night as he journeyed alone across the high plains. Twenty-four years old and a medical doctor by trade, he had come West to indulge himself in an itinerant apprenticeship before forging his career in the higher echelons of eastern opportunities.

Tascosa was a minuscule village constructed of mud. The plaza was no more than a hundred yards square, with McMasters' store on the north side, Rinehart's on the west, a blacksmith shop on the south, and on the east the home of Pedro Romero and his family. Hoyt's services as a doctor were needed only sporadically. He treated mainly gunshot wounds, occasionally a knifing. Wryly dissatisfied with his grand experiment of being a frontier doctor, he would have relocated to Las Vegas or the growing town of Albuquerque except that few of his patients had money to pay him, so he was stuck.

When the mail carrier took ill, Hoyt volunteered to make the trip, thinking he would pass a few days seeing the country and get paid at the end of his ride. The Comanches were said to be gathering again, forcing him to travel at night, and he had to rest his old nag so often his progress was slow. When the first tinge of sunrise showed on the horizon, he was still an hour from home.

The trail led through a dry arroyo slicing down toward the river. As he came out on the floodplain, he saw five men traveling north with a herd of horses. Hoyt stopped to admire the quality of the herd. After a moment, one of the men left his companions to canter over.

He was riding a magnificent sorrel stallion, its flashy red coat shimmering under a flaxen mane and tail. The horse was the best Hoyt had seen on the frontier, and he whistled in appreciation. As the man approached, Hoyt saw he was young and heavily armed.

Barely holding the feisty sorrel in place, he gave Hoyt a grin and said, "Howdy, *amigo,* can you tell me where there's a ranch around here? We heard the Panhandle's short of horses and brought a herd to sell."

"Excellent stock," Hoyt answered, thinking the young man's crooked teeth marred an otherwise pleasant face.

"Looks like you could use a better mount yourself," he said. "I'll give you a fair price."

"Ummm," Hoyt murmured, knowing he hadn't enough money for such a fine horse. "Maybe, we'll see. But as for your question, the ranchers come into Tascosa to buy supplies now and then. If you corral your herd there, they'll all see them eventually."

"Which way to Tascosa?" the stranger asked.

"Straight across the Canadian. There's good grazing between the creek and the river, if you can stand the mosquitoes."

"Thanks. You oughta come on down and see if there's one you want. We should be all settled in by the time you mosey into town." He laughed, whirling the powerful horse so it reared as it spun around, then he galloped back to his friends.

Hoyt kicked his beast into its ambling gait and soon lost the dust of the herd ahead of him. He would have sworn he could have walked the last mile faster than his horse managed to cover it, and he felt cranky when he finally reached the plaza. Carrying the mail sack into the McMasters store, he traded it for four silver dollars.

"Did you hear Billy the Kid's gang is in town?" McMasters asked.

"No," Hoyt answered. "And I'm too tired to care. All I want is supper and bed."

"They brought a remuda of horses for sale," McMasters said. "You should buy yourself one if you intend to make the mail trip again. Course, they'll all be stolen, but if you get a bill of sale you're clear with the law."

"A herd of horses?" Hoyt asked with an amazing suspicion. "What does Billy the Kid look like?"

"Kind of a small fellow. Laughs a lot and has crooked teeth."

"I met him! I spoke with him on the road just now coming into town." He decided not to mention that he had given the outlaw directions. "You're right about my horse. I think I'll wander down and see what price the Kid's asking."

"You best watch your step, Doc," McMasters warned. "Those men aren't just horsethieves, they're killers, every one of 'em."

"I've heard those stories about the Lincoln County War and I believe they're mostly exaggerated."

"Uh-huh. You best take a gun."

Hoyt laughed. "If they're even half as good as their reputation, I'd be as helpless with a weapon as without. Besides, I've discovered that men who live by their guns generally value having a doctor around. I'll come back with the best horse in their remuda, you wait and see."

Henry Hoyt looked at the Kid differently now that he knew who he was. Billy sensed it and figured he could use his new-found reputation to advantage. People with expectations didn't always watch what was really going on, making them putty in the hands of a good horse trader.

From where they walked through the tall grass toward the herd, the edges of the river's shallow bed were just high enough to obscure the water. The sky was bright blue, the sun warm on their backs as they approached the horses grazing inside a circle of rope laced through the cottonwoods.

"How good a rider are you?" Billy asked. "You want a horse with spirit or one you never have to fight?"

Grasping for a flippant remark, Hoyt said, "A good horse is like a good woman: they both try hard to please."

Billy laughed. "I like a little spit in 'em, myself." He beckoned Hoyt to the edge of the corral where they crouched in the grass. "This is the way to look at horses," Billy said. "Watch how their chest muscles ripple, the power in their haunches, look for that drive to be there when you need it."

Hoyt imagined there had been times when the Kid relied on a horse to save his life, and his own journeys paled in comparison. "I met John Chisum on the way here," he said, studying his companion's face. "Around the fire at night he told some hair-raising stories about the Lincoln County War."

"Chisum wasn't there," Billy replied, squinting across at Hoyt to see if he could take a hint.

Hoyt could. "I admired that sorrel you were riding. Are you selling him, too?"

"Might. If I get a good price. He's a damn good horse."

They both watched the copper-colored stallion, his blond mane dragging in the grass as he grazed.

"I'll sell that black mare there for fifty."

Hoyt looked at the mare. "Could I ride her first?"

"Take her out now. I'll saddle her if you like."

Hoyt shook his head. "I'm going to bed. Perhaps we could have our ride tomorrow?"

"All right." They shook hands and Billy watched the doctor walk away, thinking he would sell the sorrel to Henry Hoyt for a hundred dollars before he was done.

The next morning, the other outlaws looked Hoyt over like a new breed of pigeon. He ignored them, following Billy to where the stallion and black mare were saddled and waiting. Billy swung onto the mare and grinned down at Hoyt. "I'll give you one piece of advice. Soon as your foot's in the stirrup, far as Dandy Dick's concerned, you're on and you best be there quick as you can."

When Hoyt untied the reins and threw the far one over the horse's neck, Dandy Dick stood quivering in place. But as Hoyt grabbed the horn and put his foot in the stirrup, the sorrel danced out from under him. He lunged fast for what felt like empty air and caught his seat in the saddle. The sorrel half-reared, then stomped in place, chewing noisily on the bit.

With a grin of congratulation, the Kid turned the mare and kicked her into a run.

Hoyt merely relaxed his rein and the sorrel surged ahead. As they galloped across the plains, the cadence of hooves beating a drumbeat of freedom made him laugh with sheer pleasure. Far in the lead, he turned Dandy Dick to climb a steep bluff, then reined around to look over the valley as his companion caught up. In a sudden burst of joy, Hoyt said, "My God, this is beautiful country!"

The Kid tugged his hat lower over his eyes as he looked more intently at the green plains cut by the muddy Canadian. Far to the west, a plateau stretched across the horizon, one giant slab of red rock reaching north. "Kinda flat," he said.

"Have you been East?" Hoyt asked, forgetting the frontier code of not prying into another man's past. "Ever seen a really big city?"

The Kid shook his head, an ambiguous smile on his mouth.

"Parts of them aren't so pretty, the tenements and such, but the gardens are magnificent, and the theaters and museums are astounding."

The Kid laughed. "A lotta stuff astounds me right here."

"Like what?" Hoyt asked.

The Kid looked across to the red plateau where New Mexico began. "Oh, why some men kill wearing badges and that's all right by the law, while others kill defending themselves from the badges and it ain't." He squinted at Hoyt. "Don't s'pose you think much about things like that."

"No," he admitted. "But there are other ways to settle disputes. I've heard John Chisum never wears a gun."

"I don't have any respect for men like Chisum. They took all they got by being meaner'n the rest of us, and that's a fact."

"Surely you'll admit there's greatness in the man to have come to an untamed wilderness and made it productive."

The Kid looked away, whistling softly between his teeth.

Carefully, Hoyt asked, "Don't you see *any* virtue in men like Chisum?"

"No, I don't," the outlaw answered, stopping his tune in midphrase. "I know an old Mexican couple who lied to some soldiers to save me from arrest. I see virtue in their courage, but the likes of John Chisum is rot in the porridge."

"You must have cause to feel as strongly as you do," Hoyt said thoughtfully. "Most people would disagree with you, though."

"Does that make 'em right?"

"Not necessarily, but it behooves a man to value the opinions generally held, if only because we live in a democracy."

The Kid grinned. "I heard that before: the world's built on the Ten Commandments and it would behoove you to follow along. A nice church-going lady told me that once."

"What answer did you give her?"

"Chisum don't follow the Ten Commandments. Jimmie Dolan neither. Nobody pays any attention to 'em, near as I can see, 'cept when they want to keep somebody else down."

"Dolan is the man you fought in the war?"

"Yeah, and he beat us 'cause he had the law on his side, making his killings legal while ours were hanging offenses."

Boldly, Hoyt asked, "Don't you have any qualms about killing a man?"

The Kid shrugged. "A dead man won't bother me anymore. That's all I'm thinking when I pull the trigger."

"And you never feel regret?"

"No, 'cause I'm alive and they ain't. It makes me feel good."

"Isn't that just as selfish as what you accuse Chisum of?"

"Maybe," the Kid said. "But the only profit I get from my gun is staying alive. I don't live rich and stomp on the men who put me there. 'Sides, I can't see why a man needs eighty thousand cattle or thousands of dollars in some bank somewhere. Long as I have a good horse, a gun I can depend on and plenty of bullets, I can find what I need. I don't want any more'n that." He reined his horse around to face down the hill. "What do you say we race back to camp?"

Without waiting for an answer, he spurred the mare and sent her skittering down the bluff and into a dead run across the prairie.

He had stolen a head start and Hoyt was behind for the first hundred yards, but the sorrel was faster and he knew they'd win without trying. As they galloped far into the lead, he suddenly wondered if he'd be able to stop the powerful horse. He pictured himself bursting into the outlaws' camp, kicking the fire all over their blankets and upsetting the coffeepot, exciting the herd so they broke through the rope corral and scattered loose on the prairie.

The only consolation he could imagine from such an event was that he and the sorrel would be halfway to Dodge City before the outlaws could pick themselves up. The fantasy of absconding with the prize of a herd belonging to notorious horsethieves made Hoyt laugh. Without thinking, he reined the sorrel and turned him to stand dancing while they waited for the Kid to catch up.

As they ambled back to camp, the Kid kept extolling the sorrel's virtues and Hoyt kept nodding agreement but remained silent in the pauses meant to be filled with his decision.

When they reined up beneath the cottonwoods, Hoyt saw the Mexican boy who worked for McMasters hunkered over the fire drinking coffee. The Kid swung off the mare, unsaddled and let her loose in the corral, then did the same for Dandy Dick, taking over for Hoyt, who had barely unknotted his cinch.

Watching how quick he was, Hoyt thought the Kid was unusually good with horses. "I like that Dandy Dick," Hoyt said.

The Kid grinned as he let the sorrel loose with the others. "I'll save him for you, Henry. Do you know this little *muchacho* in our camp?"

"Yes, he lives in town."

"Good," he said, walking toward the fire. "Howdy, pardie. Name's Billy Bonney. What's yours?"

"Carlos Hernandez," the boy said, standing up respectfully. He had been told these men were *hombres malos* and he was to mind his manners carefully.

"You come to buy a horse?" the Kid teased, picking up his canteen and yanking the cork.

Carlos shook his head. "I come to say that Señor William Bonney is asked to a meeting."

"Meeting with who?" Mr. Bonney asked. He lifted the canteen and took a long drink of water.

Carlos waited until he was through, then said, "All the big *rancheros,* señor. They ask respectfully. They told me to tell you so."

"You know anything about this?" Billy asked, handing the canteen to Hoyt.

He shook his head.

The Kid looked back at the boy. "When is this meeting?"

"Right now, señor. They are waiting."

Billy pulled his pistol and checked the rounds, snapped the chamber closed and dropped the gun back in his holster, then looked at Hoyt. "Want to come?"

"You bet!"

"Stay put till I get back," the Kid told his men.

As they sauntered up the road toward the plaza, the Kid talked to the boy. They spoke in Spanish, a language Hoyt didn't know, but he saw Carlos preen beneath the outlaw's attention. When they crossed beneath the portal of McMasters' store, they were laughing softly.

The room was low and dark, the three ranchers seated around the cold stove. Tom Bugbee of the Quarter Circle T was there, and Bill McCarty of the LIT, and Charles Goodnight himself from the JA. The merchants of Tascosa, George Howard, Jim McMasters, and Elmer Rinehart, were there, as well as Don Casimiro Romero, patriarch of the largest Mexican family on the Panhandle.

Walking in behind the Kid, Hoyt felt the men's reception as a fierce field of resentment. He knew the ranchers had carved their survival out of land once owned by Comanches, and they didn't spook easily. That the Kid's presence made them wary impressed Hoyt. He moved to the side to watch from a neutral position.

Bill McCarty of the LIT took the floor. He introduced everyone, then said gruffly, "You understand how we feel, Kid, I'm sure. A man with your reputation, the news you're here spreads like wildfire. All sorts of riffraff start drifting in. Changes the complexion of our community and causes us concern. You understand that, don't you?"

The Kid laughed. "Can't say I do. But I'm jus' one of those drifting by. I don't aim to stay."

McCarty nodded. "What exactly are your intentions?"

"I heard you were short of horses, so I gathered a bunch to help you out."

Charles Goodnight spoke, his soft voice testifying to his power. "We're doing our best to make this a law-abiding country, Kid, and much prefer not to have trouble with anyone. So let's come to an understanding: as long as you don't depredate in the Panhandle, we'll leave you alone."

The Kid smiled. "All we want is to be left alone. Unless any of you want to buy some good horses. Then we'd be glad to let you look over our herd. You're welcome at our camp anytime, gentlemen." Tipping his hat, he walked out.

Hoyt laughed, impressed with the Kid's aplomb. The ranchers looked at him hard.

"You find the likes of him amusing?" Bugbee grumbled.

"I think he handled himself amazingly well in a situation you did your best to make uncomfortable for him."

"We intended to make him uncomfortable," McCarty said. "We don't want Tascosa getting a reputation for harboring outlaws."

"As I understand it," Hoyt replied, "he hasn't broken any laws in Texas."

"Give him time," Goodnight said. "Fellows like him breed trouble like horseshit breeds flies."

* * *

Several days later, Hoyt returned to McMasters' store from setting a broken arm for a boy who had fallen off the roof of his home. Hoyt felt pleased with his work, thinking the arm would heal so well the boy would never feel it had been broken. As he ambled into the saloon, however, his good mood was punctured by the sight of the Kid's men, rowdy and drunk over a game of poker.

They were playing for bullets, and Hoyt suddenly realized they needed to sell their remuda before moving on. He made a mental note to pass this insight along to the ranchers, then walked to the bar. With studied nonchalance, he asked McMasters for a lemonade.

The merchant pulled a pitcher from beneath the counter and poured him a glass, saying softly, "They've been in here for hours. I expect trouble."

Hoyt sipped his sweet, tepid drink, noting a half-empty whiskey bottle at Middleton's elbow. As the outlaw dealt a new hand, he clumsily knocked the bottle off the table and it broke on the floor.

"You sonofabitch," Middleton growled at Fred Waite, who was sitting beside him.

"Fuck you!" the half-breed retorted, pushing his chair back and stalking out. Hendry Brown and Tom O'Folliard slumped deeper in their seats.

"Barkeep!" Middleton yelled. "Bring me another."

"Should I do it?" McMasters whispered to Hoyt.

"He might drink himself into a stupor," he reasoned.

"Yeah, and he might raise hell before he gets there," the merchant answered, his face pinched.

"Goddammit!" Middleton shouted, staggering to his feet. "I don't think you understand who I am. I killed more men in the Lincoln County War than everybody else put together. When I want something, I want it now!"

The Kid stepped through the door. Not seeing him, Middleton came out from behind the table with his hand on the butt of his pistol as he snarled at the merchant, "Guess I'll have to teach you what I mean."

"Middleton, you idiot!" the Kid exploded. "Light out for camp and stay there."

Middleton wheeled, squinting at the Kid suddenly in front of him. "Aw, you're jus' showing off," Middleton finally said. "You wouldn't talk that way if we was alone."

"If that's how you feel," the Kid answered softly, "let's step outside and we will be alone."

Hoyt watched Middleton's face slither into a puddle of obeisance.

"Aw, you know I was only joshing," he whined.

"It ain't no joke," the Kid snapped. "Now git." He watched him go, then sauntered toward the bar as if nothing had happened.

"Howdy, Kid," Brown said, his voice thick with camaraderie.

"Hey, Billy," Tom called with a grin.

"Howdy, boys," he answered, walking straight to Hoyt and shaking his hand. "Good to see you, Henry. You made up your mind about that sorrel yet?"

"I'm still thinking about it," he answered, then couldn't resist adding, "That was an impressive performance."

"What was?" the Kid asked, his eyes dancing in fun.

"The way you controlled Middleton. You had him cringing like a dog."

"He's going sour on me," was all the Kid said. "What'cha drinking?"

"Lemonade. Can I buy you one?"

"Yeah, a bucket. The water 'round here tastes like puke."

"That's why we're drinking so early," Hendry called from the table. "The water tastes like shit."

The Kid shifted around to face him. "Whiskey makes you careless, *amigo,* and that ain't something we can afford."

"Yeah, you're right," he conceded. "Guess I'll go sleep it off." He pulled himself to his feet and walked out.

Tom grinned and said, "I ain't drinking."

When the Kid turned back around, Hoyt asked eagerly, "Don't you drink spirits, Billy?"

He shook his head.

Hoyt laughed. "Hail fellow, well met! I'm a teetotaler, too."

McMasters set another glass of lemonade on the counter. "Glad you happened along just then," he said with a smile. "I was afraid I'd have to use my scattergun on your friend."

The outlaw neither smiled nor made a reply. McMasters, sensing he was unwelcome, left the room.

The Kid sipped thoughtfully a moment, then asked, "What's a teetotaler?"

"Someone who practices abstinence from alcohol," Hoyt explained. "There's a whole movement of us in the East. We're working to have liquor made illegal."

The Kid laughed. "I wouldn't want to go that far. The way it is now, I've got an edge jus' 'cause I'm sober."

"You'd have an edge in any crowd," Hoyt said sincerely. "The other night, you walked into that meeting with the wealthiest men in the Panhandle and conducted yourself with as much poise and sangfroid as any man there."

The Kid sipped his lemonade, then admitted with a crooked smile, "I don't know what those words mean."

"They mean you can hold your own," Hoyt said, "among any men you care to tangle with."

He shrugged. "Yeah, I suppose."

"Why, you have amazing leadership abilities!" Hoyt exclaimed. "There are a hundred jobs you could succeed at and be respected for, other than the path you're on now."

"Like what?" he asked playfully.

"Well, foreman on a ranch. Most of their job involves seeing that other men get the work done."

The Kid nodded as if considering the suggestion. "You mean, work for some bastard like Chisum?"

Hoyt was taken aback by the sudden profanity. "When I met the man, he spoke highly of you."

"I bet he said I was a good fighter, wasn't that it?"

"Well, specifically, yes. But it was evident he likes you."

"Fighters are dirt to Chisum," the Kid answered. "Handfuls of dust he throws in his enemy's face then lets blow away on the wind. That'll be the fate of everybody if the Chisums and Dolans of this world hold sway."

Hoyt decided to change the subject. "The Romeros are having a *baile* next week. I've been given permission to invite you."

The Kid laughed. "You mean they'll let us near their daughters?"

"If you promise to be on your best behavior. But there is one condition."

"If you're gonna say I can't coax a señorita to go walking in the woods, I ain't coming," he warned.

"There aren't any woods around." Hoyt laughed. "Anyway, it isn't anything that serious. All the men leave their guns here in McMasters' store during the dance. We find things work out better that way."

The Kid shrugged. "Fine by me. It'll be a pleasure to kick up my heels at some fiddle music again."

"I wasn't sure you'd still be around," Hoyt said, pleased. "How's your horsetrading working out?"

"Pretty good. Got an offer of a hundred dollars for Dandy Dick the other day, but I couldn't bring myself to part with him yet."

"I don't know who could afford more than a hundred," Hoyt murmured.

"Guess I'm sentimental about Dandy Dick," the Kid mused. "He's worth more than money. But I won't be taking him back to Lincoln, so somebody's gonna get him."

The band consisted of three fiddles, a piano, and five guitars. They played boot-stomping jigs, frenetic waltzes, and slower, more romantic Virginia reels. The hall was brightly lit with lanterns strung along the walls, and despite the open door, the energy of so many people filled the room with heat. Most of them came from long, lonely months on the prairie. They met to gossip and share the light of life in each other's eyes, to feel they were more than just pillars of endurance against the fierce winds sweeping across the plains.

To them, Billy the Kid was a subject of gossip. They enjoyed conjecturing on the truth of the tales told about him, and often spent time dissecting what they could understand of the causes of the Lincoln County War. But the news that touched their hearts with fear was of Victorio, the Apache chief who had gathered a war party and left the reservation, intent on revenge. Indians frightened the settlers more than the men who had fought for either side in the Lincoln County War. All fears were forgotten, however, that boisterous October night at the Romeros' *baile.*

Laughter floated above the music. The thud of boots on the hard-packed dirt floor kept time with the clap of hands, and the chatter of conversations filled every last cranny of quiet. There were fifteen women and twice as many men. Even the old ladies were pressed into service, coaxed with overblown compliments that made them blush. Beneath the stern chaperonage of Don Casimiro, not one girl went walking with a man in the moonlight.

Hoyt watched the Kid dancing through a reel with Señorita Piedad, a niece of Don Casimiro's. The young beauty flirted coquettishly, protected by the understanding that the recipient of her attentions could do no more than hold her waist and lift her hand for the sashay down the aisle.

Hoyt chuckled as he watched the charade, thinking the old Spanish customs had their charms. When the Kid had escorted the señorita back to her mother, Hoyt caught his eye. Together they stepped into the cool, crisp air of midnight and walked away from the noise of the crowd, ambling into the darkness toward the plaza.

"Señorita Piedad's a beautiful girl, isn't she?" Hoyt asked, looking with appreciation at the depth of stars in the black sky.

"Yeah, she is," the Kid answered, giving him a quizzical look.

"If a man married into her family, he'd find himself a man of property."

"Is this your way of telling me hands off?" the Kid teased.

"Exactly the opposite! I was thinking of you."

"I can get my own women, thanks," he replied.

Boldly sailing on under a flag of noblesse oblige, Hoyt said, "You wouldn't be the first to marry a wealthy girl to get a start in some enterprise or other. With capital, there are many things a man with your abilities could accomplish."

"Maybe," the Kid admitted, "but I can't see myself a married man."

"There are other ways, then. I'd write you a letter of recommendation. Even Mr. Chisum, I'm sure, would recommend you if asked. You have opportunities if you'd avail yourself of them."

The Kid primed the pump in front of McMasters' store and took a long drink, then spit a stream of silver on the ground. "I like my life," he said.

"You're not really going back to Lincoln?"

"Yeah, I am."

"Why?"

"I have friends there."

"And enemies!"

He grinned. "Like you said the other day, I can hold my own."

Hoyt snorted with defeat. "I don't understand you."

"No reason why you should. We grew up in dif'rent worlds. Come on, I'll race you back to the *baile.*"

As with the sorrel and the mare, the Kid stole a head start, but Hoyt was taller and soon passed him. When he neared the door, Hoyt started to slow down, but the Kid sailed on by just as the music stopped. He was still running full speed, and he tripped on the threshold and slid on his belly into the quickly parting crowd. Hoyt ran after him, straight into the barrel of Middleton's gun.

Instantly, the Kid's men surrounded his prostrate form, their pistols drawn from concealment. Hoyt stepped back, so surprised he felt as if the wind had been knocked out of him.

Billy sat up, rubbing his elbow. "It's okay, *amigos,*" he said. "I jus' tripped, is all."

Don Casimiro strode through the people, who parted like the Red Sea. "What is the meaning of this? You were told our rule about weapons, yet you disobey and bring them anyway?"

Billy stood up and shrugged. "I got one, too, Don Casimiro. We jus' didn't think it wise to come without 'em." He shrugged again, throwing an apologetic look to Hoyt.

"You will understand, then," Don Casimiro pronounced, "that I think it wise to bar you from all future *bailes*. Please leave my home."

The five outlaws strode from the hall and walked in silence down the dirt road. It wasn't until they were back in camp, slapping mosquitoes, that anyone spoke.

"I felt like a fucking nigger," Fred muttered, looking at Billy. "I've never been thrown out like that before, like I wasn't good enough to dance with their women."

"It was my fault," Billy said. "Hoyt and I were having a race and I couldn't stand it that he was beating me again, like he did on the horses."

"You can't be best at everything," Middleton grumbled. "What were we s'posed to think when you come sliding in on your belly like that?"

"I didn't have time to consider it. I jus' tripped."

"If you hadn't tripped," Middleton continued, "you would've come running pell-mell into the middle of everybody and it wouldn't've been any better. You're crazy, Kid, and it's gonna get us all killed. I'm pulling out."

"That don't surprise me none," Billy said with an easy smile. "For myself, I'm heading back to Lincoln. Anyone wants to come is welcome. Anyone who don't, that's fine, too."

"What're you going back for?" Fred asked in disbelief.

"You're walking straight into a noose," Middleton warned.

"You're a *loco* sonofabitch," Hendry said with a grin. "You're going back just to give 'em hell, ain't you?"

"Can't think of nothing better to do," Billy answered.

"Well, I can," Hendry said. "I hear any man with balls can get a job as a lawman up in Kansas."

"I always figured," the Kid said, "that lawmen are killers who've lost their nerve."

Middleton slapped a mosquito on his face.

Quietly, Fred said, "I'm going north, too, Billy."

"All right," he said softly, shifting his gaze to Tom. "How about it, Big Foot? You going home to your mama?"

"I'd rather ride with you," Tom answered.

"You're crazy or stupid, I don't know which," Hendry mocked. He felt the Kid's gaze, sharp as a knife. "Just voicing my opinion," Hendry said, sliding into his blankets and turning his back.

Middleton and Fred disappeared beneath their blankets too, and after a few minutes Tom was driven by the mosquitoes to cover himself for protection. Billy felt wired with tension, hours from sleep. He stood up and walked over to the rope corral. The night was silent except for an occasional hoot from an owl or the yelp of coyotes off the far ridge.

Billy knew it was foolhardy to go back to Lincoln, yet if he let himself be exiled from where he wanted to be, then Dolan had beaten him, too, not just Tunstall and Mac. Unlike them, Billy was still alive. He would go where he chose and do as he pleased, and it would be up to his enemies to stop him if they could.

In the morning, the men broke camp in sullen silence. They divided the remainder of the herd, letting Billy keep Dandy Dick without argument. He also kept a tall bay mare that was quick and smart, then shook hands with his friends and watched them ride out, leaving him with only O'Folliard.

George Howard, Jim McMasters, and Henry Hoyt stood leaning on the counter in McMasters' store as they chuckled about the high point of the *baile* the night before. They broke off talking as the Kid came in.

"I jus' come to say *adiós*," he said. "Me and my friends are moving out."

"I'm sorry to hear that," Hoyt said sincerely. "I hope it's not because of what happened at the dance."

The Kid laughed. "No, I've jus' done what I come for and it's time to vamoose. Before I leave, though, I want to give you a present." He looked at McMasters. "You got paper and pen I can borrow?"

The merchant shrugged, pulled them from a drawer beneath the counter and handed them over.

The Kid stared down at the paper a moment, then wrote a short paragraph. When he'd finished, he pushed the paper toward McMasters. "Will you witness that? You, too, Mr. Howard?" He smiled at Hoyt. "I don't want anyone saying you stole that horse."

"Which horse?" Hoyt asked, barely daring to hope.

With a grin, George Howard slid the paper toward Hoyt.

Without picking it up, he read:

> Tascosa, Texas
> Thursday, Oct. 24th 1878
>
> Know all persons by these presents that I do hereby sell and deliver to Henry F. Hoyt one sorrel horse for a sum in hand received.
>
> W. H. Bonney

"The sorrel?" Hoyt cried. "I'm speechless, Billy. Where is he?"

The Kid laughed. "Tied outside."

Hoyt started for the door but Billy caught his arm, picked up the bill of sale and handed it to him. "You best not lose this."

"Thanks," Hoyt said, stuffing it into his pocket, then hurrying out to admire his horse.

McMasters and Howard followed. They stood on the portal as the outlaw swung onto a bay mare.

Hoyt reached up to shake his hand. "I feel terrible just taking him. You must let me pay you something."

The Kid shook his head, gathering his reins.

"Wait," Hoyt cried. Reaching into his vest pocket, he pulled out a lady's gold watch on a long chain. "I bought this off a Comanchero a few months ago," he said, pressing it into the Kid's hand. "Maybe you know a señorita who'll be looking for a present when you get back."

The Kid laughed. "There is a girl in Sumner who'll be mad at me when I see her again. Thanks, *amigo.* See you around."

"I hope so," Hoyt called, watching the two outlaws ride up the road until they disappeared from sight. He turned back to survey his horse, then grinned at the merchants.

"You know the story on that horse?" McMasters asked.

"No," Hoyt said.

"Middleton told me one afternoon when we were alone. This here fine sorrel stud was ridden into Lincoln by Sheriff Brady the day Billy the Kid's gang shot him down. They didn't get away with him then, though. They stole him from the Fritz ranch where Jimmie Dolan had taken him, along with anyone else's horse that happened to be running loose after a battle. That there is Dandy Dick, and he was given to Brady by none other than Major Murphy himself. You got yourself a relic of the Lincoln County War, Doc." McMasters laughed. "Yes, sir, you got yourself a real prize!"

36

The Widow McSween fled Lincoln in fear of her life. Without once visiting her husband's grave, she rode out of town with her face hidden by the deep brim of a sunbonnet. She fled to her sister's new home in Las Vegas and begged the charity of David Shield. On the first evening of her arrival, Sue undammed the terror she felt, the horror and sorrow, in sobs of grief and blasphemous cries of injustice. Then Eliza helped her sister move into their tiny spare room.

Early in September, a one-armed man called at the Shield home and asked to see Mrs. McSween. Eliza left him in the parlor and went outside to call her sister, who was sitting in the sun in the backyard.

Sue was wearing the one dress she owned, a frock of midnight blue already washed many times since she'd left Lincoln. Lightened by her idle hours in the sun, her auburn hair was streaked with gold and its woven braid resembled a crown. Her face was solemn with mourning, alive with a reawakening sense of survival, and the man in the parlor thought her beautiful as she stopped in the door and said with dignity, "I am Mrs. McSween."

"Houston Chapman, madam," he said. "I'm an attorney representing the Territorial Life Insurance Company and I've come about your husband's policy."

A flash of energy ignited within her, but she was cautious, wary of deception. "I know of no policy."

He shrugged with compassion, the folded empty sleeve of his jacket swinging in the air. "That's often the case. May we sit down?"

"Forgive me," she said, crossing the room and choosing a chair.

The lawyer sat on the edge of the settee. "Allow me to express my sincere sorrow at your plight."

"Thank you," she answered politely.

He withdrew a check from his pocket and handed it to her. "I know it's small compensation, but your husband wished you to have it."

When she saw it was for ten thousand dollars, a glacier of fear thawed within her. Laying the check aside, she asked, "Do you have a copy of the policy?"

"I'm sorry, I don't," Chapman replied with regret. "I'm sure you'll find your husband's copy in his papers, when you feel strong enough to go through them."

"My home was burned."

"Yes, a terrible thing."

"I left his papers in his office. Corbet's there but the store is closed. It was looted, even the account books torn apart and strewn on the floor. What they didn't want, they destroyed like animals."

"Yes," Chapman murmured.

Her words tumbled in a rush, unleashed by his sympathy. "I hadn't intended to let them push me out as they do everyone they don't like, push them out or kill them. They're the criminals, you know. Dolan and Dudley and that ridiculous excuse for a sheriff. No one can control the scum they imported—Kinney and Selman. Dolan won't poke his nose out of the fort! Now that he's killed my husband and Tunstall, he hides from the men he hired to do it! They've done terrible things, Mr. Chapman. The worst happened just before I left. Kinney's gang down at Dowlin's Mill defiled two young women, wives of some workers there. Dragged them from their homes and stripped them naked and violated them. All of the men taking turns. There were five of them, I heard."

"Good heavens!" Chapman exclaimed. "Wasn't anything done?"

"Oh yes," she bit off with sarcasm. "Kinney's appointment as deputy sheriff was revoked." Taking a deep breath to calm herself, she said, "Many atrocities were committed in the Lincoln County War, Mr. Chapman, but none of our men ever committed so abominable a crime."

"It's well you removed yourself to safety."

"Yes," she said, looking at the check and thinking now she could fulfill her vow of revenge.

Chapman broke into her thoughts. "A moment ago, Mrs. McSween, you said Dudley and Dolan are the criminals. Were you referring to Colonel Dudley, commander at Fort Stanton?"

"A despicable excuse for a man! He's a drunkard, a liar, and a pig!"

"Unfortunately, not criminal attributes," Chapman answered with a smile.

"Colonel Dudley is responsible for my husband's death," she declared, her voice cold with control. "He could have saved my husband and he refused, though I begged him. I begged him, Mr. Chapman, though I despise the man. He aimed a cannon at our home and threatened to blow us up, his soldiers fired at us while he sat in his tent drinking whiskey and giving pompous speeches about the army's neutrality. The army was not neutral. Colonel Dudley is directly responsible for the destruction of my home and the murder of my husband and four other men."

"Can you prove these allegations, Mrs. McSween?"

"There were witnesses to everything that happened. Go to Lincoln, ask anyone who's not in Dolan's employ!"

"Do you think these witnesses would testify in court?"

She studied his face, his long aquiline nose above a small, thin-lipped smile, the sandy hair falling into his hazel eyes. He was slight of build and lacking an arm, but there was an intensity behind his placid demeanor that attested to an inordinate drive to compete and win.

Sue McSween smiled at Houston Chapman, and a partnership was born. "Some of the men would," she answered, "although many of them are under indictment and might be hesitant to return to Lincoln."

"Perhaps we could work out an offer of immunity to secure their testimony. Is there any other evidence you can think of?"

"Dudley wrote my husband a note."

"Do you still have it?"

"I left it on the dining room table. It burned with everything else."

"Who read it?"

"My husband and myself." Then, remembering, "Billy Bonney. Mac handed it to him, I don't know why. The Kid had assumed leadership by then, I guess that was reason enough. He was the only one who retained any presence of mind."

"Do you think Billy Bonney would testify against Colonel Dudley?"

"Yes, I do," she said.

Accompanied by her lawyer, Sue McSween returned to Lincoln and established residence in the house she had finally wrenched from Saturnino Baca. Chapman stayed in Tunstall's old rooms, and they spent their days organizing the shreds of documents relating to Mac's and Tunstall's accounts.

She hired a detective to find Tunstall's cattle and replevined what was left of the herd. By the time she paid the detective and the drovers, then pasturage until the cattle were sold, she realized a loss of two hundred twenty-three dollars. The ranch on the Feliz and two others on the Peñasco had been purchased under the Desert Land Act, not in Tunstall's name but in the name of American citizens. The improvements necessary to secure title hadn't been made and the land was forfeited. The store had been looted, everything of value stolen or destroyed. The building itself was worth five hundred dollars, but it cost four hundred to repair the damage the looters had done. Mac's estate consisted of a charred, empty lot, the house Sue was living in, and a bank account in Santa Fe with the paltry balance of forty-six dollars and eighty-seven cents. Such were the remains of their ambition.

Refusing to accept defeat, Sue and her lawyer pored over the books for weeks, but struggle though they did, she was unable to recoup anything.

Christmas was only four days off. She had no desire to celebrate the holidays but had told Sebrian to go ahead with the turkey dinner he'd planned. He backed away from her in silence, something she noticed a lot of people did lately. She cared only that they left her in peace to settle her affairs.

There were three rooms to her home: a box of a parlor, a closet of a bedroom, and the long commodious kitchen. She took satisfaction coming in from the office to the comforting aromas of dinner cooking and coffee hot on the stove. Feeling strong in her bitterness, justified in her revenge, she alleviated her loneliness only with Sebrian's loyal companionship.

One night she had a visitor. He wasn't a person she especially liked.

In the days he'd lived in her home protecting her husband, she had often felt afraid of him because he seemed impervious to command. Yet the damp December dusk she came home to find Billy Bonney at her kitchen table, she felt a rush of joy.

She greeted him effusively as she removed her shoes and left them by the back door, begging him to excuse her but the ground was muddy and she cared so much about the floor. Then she noticed his tracks dried into a lacy coverlet of mud, as if it had taken him a while to settle into the chair, and she laughed. Sebrian beamed at Billy, the first person to elicit that old laughter from Mrs. Mac.

"Coffee, please, Sebrian," she said, taking the chair closest to the Kid and meeting his eyes. "I've always wished to thank you for everything you did for my husband. Hijenio Salazar told me of how you tried to get Mac to defend himself, and I want to thank you for that."

The Kid smiled. "We needed all the shooters we could get."

"Where are they now?" she asked. "The others who were with us?"

"They've mostly left the county, except Tom O'Folliard, Doc, Charlie and me."

"John Middleton? Hendry and Fred?"

"Fred's in the Nations, the other two in Kansas, last I heard."

"And the Coes?"

"They're up north in the Cimarron country."

Sebrian set two cups of coffee on the table, then went outside to fetch more wood, leaving the door open for the moment he was gone. Feeling the cold air blow in off the snow, Sue tucked her stocking feet beneath her skirts as she huddled over her coffee, breathing the steam into her face for warmth.

Billy watched her. He knew she was leading up to asking him for help; he'd seen people do that a hundred times already. On the basis of old friendships, he'd been asked to replevin herds, encourage men to settle debts, or curtail their fun at someone's expense, that someone being a friend of the Kid's and coming to him for protection.

He usually obliged. He wasn't doing much anyway, just staying around Sumner beating Garrett at casino and sleeping with Abrana every night. He was always happy to ride into the country as a favor for a friend, and pick up a few steers or horses for himself along the way. It was a comfortable life, but he wasn't opposed to helping Mrs. Mac with her vendetta. He'd heard the gossip and knew that's what she was aiming for. He just didn't know what exactly she wanted him to do.

When Sebrian came back and closed the door, she still seemed at a loss, so Billy prodded her. "I heard you wanted to see me," he said.

She sat up straight and smiled her gratitude. "I'm taking Dudley to court," she answered. "Charging him with murder and arson. Will you testify as an eyewitness?"

Billy laughed. "I have a hunch if I go into a courtroom, I'll come out feeling a lot worse than when I went in."

She was ready for his objection. "What if my attorney worked out an immunity and brought you in under Governor Wallace's amnesty?"

"I don't qualify for the amnesty. I've already been indicted."

"I'm saying we could have an exception made. Would you testify if my attorney could arrange things to your advantage?"

"The gov'nor ain't gonna make any exception for me. But sure, if you can guarantee I won't be arrested, I'll testify against Dudley or Dolan or any of 'em." He smiled. "As long as I get to keep my gun."

She looked down, fighting tears of disappointment.

"Mrs. Mac," he explained gently. "It would give me pleasure to see Dudley held accountable for what he done, but I don't have faith in courtrooms or anything that happens inside of 'em. And I don't have any faith in any promise of immunity, either. So I guess my answer's no. That's the only way I can see to call it."

She managed to smile. "Where are you staying? Did you come to town alone?"

He shook his head. "Tom, Charlie, and Doc are over at Stockton's saloon."

"You can sleep in the store, if you like. My lawyer is staying in Tunstall's rooms now, but he's gone to Vegas this week. You're welcome to sleep in the big room. The stove's still there. Sam'll let you in."

"Thanks," he said, standing up. "It was good to see you, Mrs. Mac, and I wish you luck against Dudley."

She nodded and watched him leaving. When he had opened the door, she called, "Kid, if we can arrange the immunity, where would I reach you?"

He seemed amused at the prospect. "I'm generally around Sumner these days. If you get word to Pat Garrett at Beaver Smith's saloon, he'll see I get the message." He nodded at Sebrian and left.

In the morning, Sue found the men bundled in their blankets around the stove. They all opened their eyes to see who had come in, then went back to sleep. Walking softly, she continued across the room to Mac's office.

The Kid was building a fire in the stove. He looked up and smiled at her when she came in. As she stood in the doorway removing her cloak and gloves, she watched him add wood until the blaze glowed on his face. "Thanks for the fire," she said. "Sam usually does that."

"Yeah, well, he was out drinking last night so I told him I'd do it."

He stood up and admired her figure as she reached on tiptoe to hang her cloak.

When she turned, she saw his appraisal and gave him a flippant, inquiring look.

"That's the dress you wore the last day of the battle," he said, thinking she was angry because of the way he'd looked her over, as if she wasn't a woman.

"I'm surprised you remember," she said, feeling pleased despite herself as she sat down behind the protection of Mac's desk.

The Kid smiled. "I generally have an appreciative eye for pretty ladies."

"So I've heard. Though the appeal of your charm has always been a mystery to me."

"Yeah, we don't like each other much, do we?" he teased.

She laughed. "Oh, I don't know. I love to see Dolan run to Stanton whenever you come to town."

"Has he done that?" Billy asked with surprise.

"Yes," she gloated. "Colonel Dudley's also sent soldiers to protect Catron's store. You certainly strike fear in their hearts, Kid."

He had seen the same bloodlust in her eyes when she'd stood in Chisum's parlor and asked the Regulators to kill for her. He didn't like seeing it there, though if he'd seen the same in a man he would have respected the drive, if not the motive.

She saw the change in his attitude, knowing it was because she didn't fulfill his expectations of feminine virtue and he blamed her for that. She scorned men now. It was the only way she could deal with them: let them know she didn't care one whit what they thought of her, she wanted the job done. So she laughed at the young gunfighter, thinking he probably preferred his women submissive and cringing. But it was a friendly laugh, because she needed him in her case against Dudley.

"Sebrian's making breakfast for you all," she said. "He'll be disappointed if you don't show up."

"Thanks, Mrs. Mac," he said, then was gone. Outside her office anyway.

She could hear him moving around the store, his light step and the jingle of his spurs. She looked at the fire in the stove the Kid had left open. The flames were crimson and blue, consuming the wood, as they had been on the adobe of her home, creeping inexorably closer. She had listened to those same footsteps—the Kid never would be still—the light tap of his boots accompanied by the silver song from his spurs.

Sebrian had told her spurs were always made of high-quality steel, and it was the music accompanying their every step that induced a man to buy one set over another. She thought about that as she listened to the Kid moving around the emptiness of Tunstall's store, and about music and her piano, which was now charred ashes beneath the snow of winter.

Someone else was up, clumping heavily, dropping things as he fumbled to dress. The Kid paced, pausing before the windows, retreating back behind the counter, then out again. Sue in her office listened. His footsteps brought back memories of days of terror punctuated by the Kid's soft chatter and easy laughter. The laughter came again, then she heard the outside door close. She moved to the door of her office and watched the Kid and Tom O'Folliard walking down the street toward Sebrian's breakfast. Seeing that Scurlock and Bowdre still slept in their blankets, she went back to work.

The snow melting off the roof of Mrs. Mac's house fell in such a noisy downpour it sounded like rain, though the sky outside the windows was blue. Billy was enjoying listening to Sebrian's gossip as he finished a second plate of pancakes. He pushed his empty plate away and leaned back in his chair, completely at ease as he watched the door slowly swing open. At first he thought it was caught by the wind, then he saw Sheriff Kimball, Jack Long, and Jake Mathews holding guns aimed straight at him.

"Sonofabitch," Billy said.

"Hands up real slow," Kimball said, stepping into the room followed by the others. "Stand up. Keep your hands away from your guns."

Billy complied with a grin. "You got me, boys. What're you gonna do, stare me to death?"

Tom was still chewing a mouthful of pancakes as he stood up and raised his hands. He looked worriedly at Billy, seeing his easy smile and his eyes dancing as if in fun; but Tom knew the Kid now, and he could see the anger coiling for its chance.

"Get their guns," Kimball said.

Jake Mathews had ridden with the posse that killed Tunstall and been indicted for the murder, but he was still a deputy. Lifting the Kid's pistol from its holster, Mathews grinned and said, "You're under arrest."

"What for?" Billy asked, looking at Kimball.

"We got a hundred warrants against you," Mathews said. "Take your pick."

Billy laughed, still looking only at Kimball. "You're s'posed to tell me the charge, Sheriff. Ain't you ever made an arrest?"

"Reckon you know what you're indicted for, Kid," Kimball answered. "Let's go."

"Sorry I won't be able to help with the dishes, Sebrian," Billy said as he walked out first.

Knowing what was waiting for him, Billy feasted his eyes on the blue sky. He walked along appreciating the warmth of the sun and enjoying watching the children play, excited with the coming of Christmas. Then he descended the ladder into the dungeon and listened to the hatch being locked from above.

He stood in the dark a moment before walking across the room, remembering how many steps it was because he'd paced it so many times on his last visit. Striking a match, he lit the tallow candle stuck into a niche in the damp earthen wall, turned around and met Tom's eyes.

Thinking he'd never seen the Kid so angry, O'Folliard hunkered on the floor and hugged his knees for warmth. Billy paced, each crunch of his boots on the moist gravel accompanied by the jangle of a spur, his rhythm never changing.

It felt like hours, they couldn't tell, but finally the hatch opened and Sam Corbet's long body climbed down the ladder.

The Kid laughed and shook Corbet's hand. "I'd offer you a chair, Sam, but they're all kinda dirty."

Corbet laughed too. "I'm sorry this happened, Kid. Our new sheriff is overzealous, in support of Dolan, of course. Scurlock and Bowdre will have you out as soon as it's dark. They wanted me to tell you that."

"Good. 'Cause I sure don't like being here. This is a terrible place to put a man."

Corbet looked around at the snow-soaked walls, the lone candle as the only source of heat, the damp dirt the only surface to sit or sleep on. "I don't suppose jails are ever real nice."

The Kid looked at him hard. "I'm tired of this shit, you know that? I'm tired of seeing someone with a warrant pop through a door every time I sit down."

"I can understand that you would be," Sam answered dryly.

"Yeah, well, I'm gonna stop it. I'm going to Dolan himself and ask for a truce."

"Wouldn't it be better to stand trial and clear your name? No jury in Lincoln will convict you."

"Why bother with Bristol's court? If Dolan agrees to let me alone, all his soldiers will follow suit."

"It's a good goal, however you go about it. I think we're all ready for peace."

"How long till dark?" he asked, starting to pace again.

"Five hours," Sam answered, his eyes following the Kid.

"Tell Doc and Charlie to get us some guns."

"There are no guns for sale in Lincoln. They're only available at Stanton and you have to go through Dudley to get one."

"Sonofabitch," the Kid said.

"They tried to confiscate your horses, claiming property belonging to a person under arrest was to be held by the sheriff. Mrs. Mac tore out there with a shotgun and said the horses were hers and if the men didn't get off her property she'd shoot somebody."

The Kid laughed.

"So you'll have your horses tonight," Sam said, "and we'll do our best about the guns."

"Thanks," the Kid said, stopping to shake Sam's hand.

Corbet knocked on the hatch and waited for it to be opened, then climbed into the bright light of sunshine.

After a moment, Tom asked, "You gonna go see Dolan fresh from breaking outta here?"

Billy chuckled. "That'd be sticking it up his nose, wouldn't it?" He started to pace again. "Reckon I'll write him a letter."

"And say what?" Tom asked.

Billy shrugged in mid-stride. "Jus' that we got no more reason to bother each other."

"What about Jesse Evans?" Tom asked. "You gonna let him slide?"

Billy stopped and stared into the flame of the lone candle illuminating the dungeon, seeing Jesse's blue eyes laughing as he pulled a trigger, knowing he'd laughed watching Tunstall fall. But to make a truce, both sides needed something of value to place on the table. "Yeah," he said to Tom, starting to pace again.

With relief, Tom asked, "Where will we go in the meantime?"

The Kid laughed. "Back to Sumner!"

37

Under the clear sky of a February day, Deluvina Maxwell decided to celebrate her birthday. A full-blooded Navajo, she had been captured by Apaches when she was nine. The Apaches sold her to Comancheros, who in turn sold her to Lucien Maxwell, who kept her as a slave. When the Emancipation Proclamation freed the slaves it didn't change her life. As a member of the Maxwell household, Deluvina was held in high esteem by the villagers, and she truly loved the women she served, the beautiful Luz and her vivacious daughter Paulita.

Yet Deluvina was Navajo. She believed in visions and occasional extreme expressions of emotion, and she wanted this birthday to be memorable. So just before dusk, she slipped out of the Maxwell house and headed toward Beaver Smith's saloon.

She stepped carefully along the muddy road, fearful of soiling the dress she had been given as a birthday present. She also walked quickly, wanting to reach her destination before she was missed at home.

The men in the saloon all looked up, seeing a short, plump Indian woman with long black braids hanging over her ample breasts. She walked solemnly across to the bar, met Beaver Smith's eyes, and ordered a whiskey.

"Now, Deluvina," he wheedled, wanting to avoid trouble with the Maxwells, "you know it's against the law for a woman to be in here a'tall. And you're an Indian, to boot!"

"Give her a drink if she wants one," the Kid said from the far end of the bar.

Remembering he'd come calling for Sallie Chisum one night, Deluvina smiled. "There's a brave boy. He's not afraid of the law."

Billy came up closer, glad for the diversion. "Come on, Beaver, give her a drink. We'll liven up this pit of gloom."

Reluctantly the bartender poured out a shot of whiskey. Deluvina downed it in one gulp, then held on to keep her balance as the ninety-proof liquor hit her brain. Billy reached out to catch her if she fell, but she gestured triumphantly that she was fine. "Another one," she said.

Billy nodded at Beaver Smith, then slid a silver dollar on the bar. "Reckon that'll buy her enough."

"Thank you, señor," she said. "Today is my birthday." She watched the shotglass being filled.

"How old are you?" Billy asked, wondering if she would drink this one as fast as the first. She was a pretty woman, with flashing black eyes and smooth, moist skin. If she didn't drink herself sick, he figured it might be fun to take her to bed, the mood she was in.

"I'm thirty-one and I'm Navajo," she replied, giving him a scrutiny. "Did you know that?"

He shook his head. "I guessed some kinda Injun."

"Only on my birthday," she said. "The rest of the time I'm American like anyone else. But on this day, I remember who I really am." She lifted the glass and drank it down.

Billy watched her sway as the whiskey hit. Again she kept her feet and came back grinning. Then she dropped her chin, rolled her eyes, and let out a bloodcurdling scream that would have brought any Indian within a hundred miles running to the rescue.

But there were only drifters whiling away time on a cold afternoon, and they all yelled back. Some yipped like coyotes, some howled like

Comanches, some gave rebel yells from battles they'd lost but couldn't forget. Billy leaned close and harmonized with Deluvina, their voices mimicking the mournful call of wolves after a kill. The eerie duet sent shivers down every spine in the room until Deluvina collapsed against him in giggles.

After a moment she stood up straight, struggling to show only calm before these white eyes she was playing with. "Another!" she announced, slapping the bar.

"You sure?" Billy asked.

She nodded, and he gestured for Beaver Smith to pour.

The barkeep balked. "This ain't a good idea, Kid."

"Relax, no one's gonna hurt her."

"It's against the law for her to even be in here."

"It's against the law for me to be out of jail," Billy retorted. "So the fuck what?"

"Yeah! So the fuck what!" Deluvina echoed. Then she laughed, watching her glass being filled again. She downed it, squeezing her eyes closed as she waited for the impact to pass. "Listen, Kid," she said, leaning on him heavily. "Is it okay if I call you that?" she asked, looking straight into his blue eyes, so clear and sharp, like none she'd ever seen before, the way they followed her every move.

"Sure, Deluvina," he said softly. "We're friends, right? You can call me anything you want."

"Thanks," she said. "You're a true heart. I say so and I'm Navajo. Indians know about true hearts, don't they?"

"I've always heard that," he answered.

She studied him solemnly a moment, then grinned. With a wild whoop, she vaulted onto the bar and began dancing, howling with joyous liberation as she pranced up and down. Twirling her skirts high, she unbraided her hair and combed it loose until it flew around her like a giant sweeping wing of ebony.

The men clapped and stomped. When she stopped, their drumming rolled on. They shouted for her to dance some more, to have another drink, to howl like a wolf again. She held up her hands for silence.

"There is something else Navajos are best at," she declared. "We not only dance in the path of beauty, we ride with the wind. I challenge any man here to a horse race. I bet my virtue on it." She leapt to the floor and ran outside.

The men stared after her, then followed her out. She swayed drunkenly in the road until Billy came up and put his arms around her, afraid she would fall in the mud. She leaned close against him, looking up to meet his eyes. "Will you do it?" she cooed. "Will you race me?"

"I would, Deluvina. But you ain't got a horse."

"Someone'll lend me a horse." She spun away from him. "Won't someone?" she asked of the crowd. "I can ride any horse any man can."

Billy laughed. "I don't know about that. You got a skirt on, for one thing."

"No problem," she answered, taking a few staggering steps. The sunset was red in the sky, the wet road already icing over. In the cold air, she felt clear and calm. Seeing the horse she wanted, she screamed her war whoop leaping toward it.

Billy shouted, "No, Deluvina, not that one!"

Quickly she untied the rangy bay, but the mare was already alarmed by her bloodcurdling scream and shied away from her. Deluvina pulled hard on the reins to get the animal close, then lunged for the saddle, caught one stirrup and held on to the horn, standing on the horse's side as she yanked it out of the Kid's reach.

Kicking her leg across, she managed to gain a seat, her skirts bunched high around her hips. The stirrups were too long, though, and the horse didn't like her. She was holding on with the reins and it didn't understand the fierce sawing on the bit. It began to buck. Deluvina dropped the reins and grabbed for the horn with both hands. An empty stirrup socked her in the knee, then she lost her seat and was sailing through the air, coming down, and wham! she was on the ground, out cold.

Billy caught his horse, quieting the mare as he led it back to the fallen woman. Deluvina sat up dizzily. Her skirt and petticoats were twisted high on one hip, revealing her black stocking and a strip of smooth, brown flesh, and the bodice of her dress had ripped into a risqué décolletage. Billy grinned as he pulled his blanket off from behind his saddle and handed it to her. "I think we best take you home, Deluvina."

She put a hand to her temple and moaned, "I hit my head."

"Maybe I should carry her," O'Folliard suggested, looking to Billy for permission.

"Good idea," he answered. He returned to the hitching rail for Tom's horse, telling the crowd, "Go back inside and have another drink. Show's over." Then leading the two horses, he followed Tom carrying Deluvina home.

At the Maxwell house, Billy knocked as Tom stood in the dapple of blue light falling through the stained glass. Pete opened the door, looked them over and said, "She went drinking again."

Billy laughed. "I didn't know it was again, but that's what she did. Then she tried to mount a horse she didn't have no business on and got herself thrown. Her dress is kinda muddy, and torn some, too. That's why we wrapped her in the blanket."

"Bring her in," Pete said with overblown patience. "I've carried her often enough to know how heavy she is." He beckoned for Tom to follow him down the hall.

Billy waited in the parlor, looking around. The Maxwells represented old money in the territory and their possessions reflected a kingly grandeur. There was also an air of a dead past that dragged at the lives of the people who lived in this room. He didn't like it and had just made up his mind to wait outside when Paulita came in from the hall.

"You're not leaving, Mr. Bonney," she asked, "before we've had a chance to thank you?"

He had forgotten how pretty she was, how lively the light in her dark eyes. "You oughta thank Tom," he said. "He's the one carried her here. All I did was follow along with the horses."

"I shall thank him. Could you both stay for dinner, have you eaten yet? It would make us happy to repay your kindness."

"I guess we could do that," Billy said. "Is there a place we can wash up?"

She smiled as if he had made the perfect reply.

He followed her down the hall to a room with clean towels and fresh water in the pitcher. After a moment, Tom joined him and they made themselves as presentable as possible.

When they entered the dining room, Billy saw Pete frown at their guns. Mrs. Maxwell sat at one end of the table, Paulita across from the guests. At the other end, Pete served each plate and passed it down while explaining that Deluvina was a devoted servant and only occasionally got it into her head to become an Indian again. "She's a wild critter when she's liquored up," he finished, "but she's part of our family and we endure her lapses."

"Oh, we love her to death," Paulita said. She smiled at Billy. "I wish I could see her cutting loose sometime."

Billy laughed. "It was a sight. She let her hair down and was stomping and hollering on the bar."

Paulita laughed, too, but her mother was less amused. "I don't understand," Luz Maxwell said, "why she insists on going to the saloon. If she must drink, why can't she do it at home?"

"Under your censoring eye, Mama?" Pete asked with affection. He passed the last plate to Billy and settled into his chair. "Besides, her rampages always end with a contest. Who could she challenge here to anything rowdier than a sewing bee? What was it this time, gentlemen? A shooting match with bow and arrows? She did that once in Cimarron."

"A horse race," Billy said. "But she chose the wrong horse."

"Yours?" Paulita asked.

"Yes, ma'am. She spooked her so bad, running at her screaming bloody murder, there was no way my mare wanted to be anywhere near her. I encourage my horses to rely on their own judgment, it's helped me out now and then."

Paulita smiled, wondering if he encouraged his women to rely on their own judgment, too.

There was a silence broken only by the sounds of cutlery. Then Luz Maxwell asked, "Mr. Bonney, have you seen Mrs. McSween since the death of her husband?"

"I seen her shortly 'fore Christmas," he said. "She seemed to be doing okay, near as I could tell. I was never a close friend of hers."

Pete snorted. "Nobody is, from what I hear. Everyone else is willing to let the past die, but she and that fancy lawyer she's hired keep stirring the troubles up all over again. She's gathering affidavits against Dudley and he's gathering affidavits against her. It makes people remember they have cause to hate their neighbors when they'd come close to forgetting. She should let it go."

"She lost her husband, Peter," Mrs. Maxwell said. "I admire her for fighting back."

"So do I," Paulita said, giving Billy a brilliant smile.

"It's just going to get more men killed," Pete argued. "Don't you agree with me, Kid?"

Billy had been watching Paulita over the rim of his cup, aware that she was flirting with him. He set the cup down and smiled at Pete. "I think most men are hoping to fall under the amnesty."

"How about you?" Maxwell asked. "Are you going to settle down and live peaceably now?"

"I figure I'm already doing that," Billy said.

"You know, Pat Garrett worked for me awhile back," Pete continued, as if changing the subject. "I hear he's a friend of yours."

"Yeah, I know Pat. He's a mighty poor poker player, I'll say that. The Mexicans call him *Juan Largo* 'cause he's so tall."

"I've heard they call him Big Casino and you Little Casino," Paulita said.

Billy laughed. "I hadn't heard that."

Maxwell frowned at his sister, then turned to the Kid again. "I caught Garrett stealing some of my cattle with Barney Mason and I fired him because of it. Did you know that?"

"No, I didn't," Billy answered, catching his drift.

"The old way of doing business doesn't cut it anymore. A lot of people are having to change their habits."

"Oh, Pete, that's always true," Paulita scolded. "How serious you are sometimes. Life is always changing. The world looks different every day."

Her mother laughed with affection. "You're such a philosopher, little one. Where is Deluvina? Oh yes, sleeping it off." She gave an embarrassed laugh. "I guess we clear up ourselves, dear."

Paulita rose and helped her mother remove the dishes from the table, making a special point to lean close to Billy as often as she could, letting him inhale her scent and hear the rustle of her skirts as she moved around him. Her brother saw that she was flirting with the Kid and thought it funny, knowing he was living with Abrana García in the quarters.

It was nearly ten o'clock when Billy and Tom led their horses into the stable and walked over to Abrana's room in the long row of barracks. She was waiting for him, sitting on a rawhide settee in the shadow of the portal. He saw the chain of her watch first, the one he'd given her when he came back from Tascosa, catching light as it dangled outside her shawl.

Tom went inside to spread his blankets on the floor as Billy sat down. He looked the length of the frost-encrusted plaza to the Maxwell home, wondering how far Paulita would carry her flirtation before drawing her skirts back out of the mud.

Abrana had been to the Maxwell house just that afternoon, showing some lace she hoped to sell. Mrs. Maxwell had called her daughter to look at the lace. When Paulita leaned close, Abrana had been taken by the delicate scent of the rich girl's perfume, and she knew she wasn't mistaking the fragrance she was now picking up off Billy's clothes. She waited for him to touch her.

Finally he came back from his thoughts. He lifted a strand of her hair from where it fell over her breast and held it to his nose a moment, inhaling her scent. But it wasn't enough. Trying to control the anger in her voice, she said, "You've been at the Maxwells'."

He laughed. "Deluvina got drunk. It was the damnedest thing. She was whooping and stomping on the bar. I've never seen anything like it."

"So you took her home."

"Tom carried her. Said she was heavy, too."

"And stayed for dinner."

"Yeah," he said, catching on.

"And until ten o'clock, knowing I'd be here waiting when you got around to dropping by."

"You're here, ain't you?" he asked in a coaxing tone, pulling her close. "Don't fight me tonight, Abrana. I'm leaving in the morning."

"Where are you going?" she pouted.

"I have an appointment in Lincoln."

"Don't go," she pleaded, raising her face to his. "There's nothing but trouble for you there, Billy."

"You shouldn't worry," he said, kissing her mouth. "Jus' give me some loving before I go."

Obediently she followed him into the one room of her home, stepping over his friend already snoring on the floor. But when they were in bed, she could still smell the delicate perfume. As she lay beneath Billy's love, Abrana became convinced he was thinking of the rich girl as he moved inside her. In frustration she cried out, "You're fucking Paulita, not me!"

He pulled back fast and slapped her hard. "Don't ever use that word with her name," he said.

She stared at him through the tears caused by his blow.

Softly he said, "We're the only two people in this bed, Abrana. You're the only woman I'm fucking."

"So you fuck Abrana and make love to Paulita!" she retorted.

"I don't do anything to Paulita," he answered impatiently. "She's a lady and I'd kill the man who tried. You're a whore who hasn't complained about my fucking before tonight."

"I'm not complaining, Billy!" she cried. "I'm afraid of losing you."

"Jus' 'cause I had dinner at the Maxwells'?"

She was contrite. "I'm sorry," she whispered. "Please come back." She reached for him. "Come back to me now and after Lincoln," she pleaded.

But he'd lost the inclination and was already leaving. When he reached to take his gunbelt from her headboard, she touched his hand, sniffling. He said nothing. As soon as he was out the door, Tom O'Folliard picked up his blankets and followed him.

They slept in the hayloft of the stable that night. Tom had never known Billy to hit a woman before, but he thought Abrana deserved it the way she'd carried on. It made him wonder about Paulita, though; if maybe Abrana wasn't right and something was happening between them. In the morning he didn't wonder anymore. He saw it with his own eyes.

As they saddled their horses, Billy remarked that he'd left his blanket with Deluvina. On their way out of town they stopped at the Maxwell house to retrieve it. Paulita was in the yard, looking lovely in a blue dress that set off her fair complexion and dark hair blowing loose in the wind.

Billy stayed on his horse, smiling down at her as he asked for the blanket. He watched her walk away, then stared at the door as if he could see her inside the house.

When she came back, the red blanket was draped over her head, enveloping her body as she walked toward them. Her eyes laughing over a radiant smile, she stood before Billy and said, "I thought if I made myself into a squaw, you might take me with you."

Billy gently pulled the blanket off. She let it go, standing proud beneath his scrutiny.

"I'll be back," he said, laying the blanket across the saddle in front of him.

"I'll be waiting," she answered boldly.

38

It was nearly dark on the afternoon of February 18, 1879, exactly one year after the death of John Tunstall, almost to the hour. Sue McSween wasn't aware of the anniversary, however, as she stood watching from the windows of Tunstall's store for her attorney to return from Santa Fe. When she noticed Doc Scurlock and Charlie Bowdre tying their horses in front of Stockton's saloon, she murmured, "I wish Mr. Chapman would come."

"The roads are icy, Mrs. Mac," Sam Corbet said, crouching before the potbelly stove to bank the coals.

She pulled her shawl tighter against the chill, watching Hijenio Salazar go into Montaño's store. "Is the stable ready for Houston's horse?"

"Yes, ma'am. Why don't you go on home before it gets dark? Mr. Chapman'll be along shortly, I'm sure."

"I think I shall," she said, seeing Jesse Evans and Jake Mathews ride up the street. She turned away in disgust and walked back to her office. As she buttoned her cloak, then tied her wool bonnet beneath her chin, she thought about all those men she had seen while watching from the window, men she hadn't seen in Lincoln in months, not all at the same time.

She crossed the front room again, bid Sam goodnight then stepped outside, pausing to study the snowy dusk. Up the street she saw Jimmie Dolan getting off his horse in front of Wortley's. Impulsively she went back inside and closed the door. Corbet was piling more wood beside the stove. He looked up, his long, mournful face apprehensive.

"What's going on, Sam?" she asked.

He crossed the room to stand above her, his hand on the knob, ready to open the door. "It's best you go home and stay there, Mrs. Mac."

"Not until you tell me why all these men are in town. All the fighters, what's left of them anyway. The Kid's the only one I haven't seen."

"He'll be along," Corbet said. "They've called a truce and are meeting tonight to work out a peace."

"Why wasn't I told?"

"It's between the fighters, Mrs. Mac. They're doing it on their own."

"Did they think I'd stand in their way?"

"No, ma'am. Leastways, I'm sure none of our men thought that."

"Then why wasn't I told? Tell me, Sam!"

"On account of Mr. Chapman," he answered. "Nobody wanted to include him."

She laughed in relief. "He'd certainly try to run the meeting, wouldn't he?"

"Yes, ma'am, I reckon he would," Corbet said, pleased to see her laugh. "But there's likely to be some heavy drinking in town tonight and it's best you get home before dark. These men get drunk, they might shoot off their guns for no reason at all. So it isn't a good night for a lady to be out." He opened the door.

"Thank you, Sam," she said, turning away and hurrying toward home. When she arrived, she told Sebrian to lock the door and not open it again for anyone but Mr. Chapman.

Sebrian was to disobey her. The man he would let in was at that moment riding the old Indian trail north of the river toward Tunstall's store. Sam Corbet stepped out the back door into the biting cold, then walked across the corral to watch by the gate.

Hijenio Salazar was the first to arrive. He led his horse into the stable, left it saddled ready to go, then walked back to wait with Sam. There was no wind and the sky was black now, the stars sharp.

Hijenio raised his head. "Riders in the river," he whispered.

Then Corbet, too, heard them splashing through the icy water. As the Kid and O'Folliard came around the adobe wall, Sam pulled the gate open just wide enough to let them pass, then closed and latched it securely again.

Billy grinned. "*¿Qué tal, amigo?* Howdy, Sam." He swung down and handed his reins to Corbet. "You got some grain for my mare? She's come a long way."

"I'll take care of her," he said, nodding at O'Folliard and accepting his reins, too. "Go on," Sam said to Billy. "It's past time."

He laughed. "They'll wait." He drew his gun and loaded the sixth chamber, then eased the cylinder closed and slid the pistol back in its holster. "Never know about these peace parleys," he said. "You ready, Tom?"

"Whenever," the Texan drawled.

"¿Listo, Hijenio?"

"Sí, Chivato."

"Andale," he said.

Corbet stood holding their horses, watching them go. "Good luck," he called.

As the remnant of the Regulators walked through the darkness along the river, skirting backyards in the ribbon of ink beneath the trees, Billy was worried about Hijenio. He had been wounded and kicked by the very men they were on their way to meet. Billy knew, if they'd kicked and held a gun to his head, he couldn't meet them afterward without giving it back. But Hijenio still lived in the county and had vowed to keep the peace if it was made. He would be the only Mexican at the parley, and Billy felt it right that one was included. They walked past the torreón and Mrs. Mac's house, the empty lot where Dudley had camped, and the dark hut of the jail.

"You okay, amigo?" Billy asked.

"Sí," Hijenio answered. "I won't shoot unless they give me reason."

"They give us a reason," Billy said, "we'll all be shooting."

They approached the small adobe house abandoned by a farmer during the war. The Kid and his men were the last to arrive. He stood in the open door a moment, surveying the scene lit only by a fire blazing in the hearth.

Jimmie Dolan was leaning against the table, Jesse Evans standing beside him with a mocking smile, Jake Mathews and Will Campbell behind them, so Billy and his friends were outnumbered.

"Close the door, Kid," Dolan said. "Or aren't you staying?"

Billy took a step farther in, Tom at his side, Hijenio closing the door behind them.

Jesse said, "We oughta kill the Kid now. You can't deal with a renegade."

"Back off, Jesse," Dolan said, smiling at Billy. "We've come to discuss a truce, if I understood your letter, Kid. The punctuation was rather unorthodox."

"You understood it. There ain't no more profit in us fighting."

"Never was," Dolan replied. "The war wiped me out."

"You're alive," Billy said.

"And we both want to stay that way, is that the main thrust of our agreement?"

"Pretty much."

"Let's write our treaty out to make it official," Dolan said, taking a pencil and folded sheet of paper from his pocket. "Any objections to my being secretary?"

"A man's word is good enough for me," Billy said.

"I have a legal bent of mind," Dolan answered, flattening the paper on the table. "I should think you would've learned something about law from McSween."

"I learned what it got him."

"Yes," Dolan said, smiling as he wrote. "How does this sound: No party to this agreement will kill any other party to this agreement."

"What if we change our minds?" Jesse asked, his eyes pinned on the Kid.

"All right," Dolan said. "We'll add a clause at the end: without first withdrawing from the agreement. How does that suit you?"

"I'll accept it," Jesse said, "against my better judgment."

"Kid?"

"Yeah," he answered, watching Jesse's silhouette against the fire.

"Anyone opposed?" Dolan waited a moment, then wrote the addendum. "Next point: We'll kill no officer of the army for anything done in the past."

Billy laughed. "Why're you protecting Dudley?"

"A favor to a friend," Dolan replied, meeting his eyes.

Billy shrugged. "No sweat to me. How do you feel about it, Tom?"

"I ain't aiming to kill any soldiers," he drawled, the laziness in his voice belying the tension of his posture.

"Hijenio?" Billy asked, throwing him a quick glance.

The Mexican's eyes glittered like obsidian in the firelight. "I agree."

"Good," Dolan said, bending over the paper to write it down.

"As long as we're taking care of other people," Billy said, "I think we should agree that anyone who acted as a friend to either side won't be killed."

Dolan sniffed, then wrote it down. "One more clause," he said. "No one here will give evidence in a court of law against anyone else here. Is that agreeable?"

Billy thought about Mrs. Mac's vendetta against Dudley. "You talking about the men actually in this room?"

Dolan knew the Kid was thinking of Dudley, but his friendship for the colonel didn't extend far enough to include the military on this point. "Yes," he answered.

"I got a clause to add," Mathews said, making Dolan wince so Billy knew it hadn't been part of his plan. "If any of us gets arrested, we should agree to set each other loose."

"Ain't you got friends to do that?" Billy jibed.

"Seems to me, that's the point of our agreement," Mathews said. "There's not a lot of us left from the war. If the law comes down, I think we should stick together."

"I don't see that as necessary," Dolan protested.

Billy laughed. "Easy to say when you own the judge. Put it in."

"You're agreeing to something illegal," Dolan argued. "Believe me, gentlemen, it's better done with a handshake."

"I like it, too," Jesse said.

Dolan sighed and bent over the page, asking warily, "Anything else?"

"Yeah," Jesse said. "Anyone breaking this agreement will be killed."

"I don't think that's necessary," Dolan said again. "Certainly that's implied, gentlemen?"

"Write it down," Billy said, matching Jesse's smile.

Dolan wrote it down. When he finished, he signed the agreement with a flourish, then handed the pencil to the Kid.

Billy took his time, writing *William H. Bonney* in a neat script. He handed the pencil to Jesse, whose eyes mocked him as if with a trick. Jesse pulled the paper over and scrawled his name, then handed the pencil to Mathews. It traveled to Campbell, O'Folliard, and Salazar, who asked Billy to write out his name, then solemnly marked an X beneath it.

Dolan pocketed the paper. "I'll have copies written out. Tomorrow you can stop by and pick one up." He smiled fondly at the Kid, having wanted his gun for a long time. "Why don't we go someplace and celebrate our friendship? Drinks are on me."

"If we're really friends, Kid," Jesse taunted, "you'll come drinking with us."

"All right," Billy answered. "I guess we can do that."

They walked to Stockton's saloon. Scurlock and Bowdre were already there. They and the Kid exchanged nods, communicating that the peace had been made, then Doc and Charlie slipped out the back door. With Tom at his side, Billy let his drink sit in front of him, watching the others throw down shots like water. The celebration had been joined by half a dozen more Dolan men and the room was rowdy. Jesse came over and leaned on the bar.

"So we're finally on the same side again," he teased, draining his glass. When he turned to look at the others, Billy switched drinks.

"Looks that way," he agreed. "Being as there ain't no sides anymore."

Hijenio came over. "I'm saying *buenas noches, Chivato.*"

Billy shook hands and watched him leave, then looked at Jesse, who laughed and said, "You sure warm up to the greasers."

"I like their women," Billy answered, and Jesse guffawed out of all proportion to the joke.

After a while, they walked down the street to the Ellis saloon. Billy stood at the bar with another full drink, talking with Ike Ellis as they watched the revelers.

"You're sure moving in strange company tonight, Kid," Ike said.

Billy grinned. "We're celebrating peace."

"Glad to hear it," the old man said. "We all knew of your meeting and were sure glad you called it. Had a hell of a time convincing Sebrian not to tell Mrs. Mac, though. We were afraid if her lawyer heard of it, well, Lord knows what he would have done but it wouldn't have been peaceful."

"Never met the man," Billy said. "Folks don't seem to like him much."

"Nobody likes him except Mrs. Mac. He's only got one arm and feels he has to be twice as ornery because of it."

Seeing Dolan walk toward them, Billy asked quietly, "What's your excuse for Jimmie?" He and Ike laughed.

Dolan leaned against the bar. "What do you say we have another drink, Kid?"

"Here, have mine," Billy said, pushing the full glass toward him.

"Aren't you drinking?" he asked suspiciously.

Billy shrugged. "I jus' ain't built up your tolerance, Jimmie."

"It was Murphy got me started," he said thoughtfully, sipping from the glass. "You try to keep up with him, you better have your wits about you."

"I've always heard so."

"Wasn't easy, getting in with Murphy. I don't think you ever appreciated that. You were always against me and I couldn't figure it out. You should've been with us from the start."

Wanting to say he'd never developed a taste for sodomy, Billy held his tongue.

"McSween was a self-righteous bastard," Dolan said, "and Tunstall an arrogant sonofabitch, 'cause he was English, I guess. I couldn't see any other reason. But you're one of us—an American boy. I never could figure you siding with those foreigners."

"I liked 'em," he said.

"It wasn't anything personal, Kid. It was just business, all along."

"That's the dif'rence between us, Jimmie. With me, everything's personal."

"A dangerous way to live," Dolan pronounced. "Doesn't leave any room to roll with the punches."

Billy laughed. "Ain't gonna be no punches coming from you. Who else do I have to worry about?"

"Nobody," Dolan said. "I say you're free to come and go and I own Lincoln now." He surveyed the low, dark room filled with his men. They were boisterous with drink as they played billiards and told lewd jokes, smoking and spitting on the floor; a rough collection of men who lived by their guns. "No matter what anyone thinks of what happened," he said, looking back at the Kid, "I won. From here on out, you're welcome in Lincoln."

"I know a lot of other folks feel that way," Billy answered, winking at Ike.

"I'm hungry," Dolan said. "Want to go get some oysters?"

"All right. I didn't have any supper." Billy reached across the bar to shake hands with Ike.

"Be careful," Ike whispered. "Liquor doesn't bring out the best in that man."

"Thanks," Billy said, but he didn't think Dolan would pull a doublecross. He'd been as eager as any of them to agree to the truce.

Billy caught Tom's eye and the two of them walked into the cold night with Dolan and his bodyguards. They were all drunk except Billy. Tom wasn't as far gone as the others, but he was feeling loose, relying on the Kid's judgment.

Dolan and Will Campbell were leading the way, Billy and Tom between them and Jesse Evans and Jake Mathews taking up the rear. Noticing he and Tom were blocked in, Billy gradually dropped back to walk even with Jesse.

They came to a long stretch of darkness, their boots crunching on the snow. When Jesse and Mathews laughed about a whore they'd once shared, Dolan called back that he could send for some women if they wanted. Crossing the swatch of light falling between Stockton's saloon and Mrs. Mac's house, they walked into the pitch dark in front of the *torreón,* laughing curses as they slid on the ice. At the other end, they were in front of Tunstall's store.

A man stood at the door holding a white cloth to his face as he fumbled with keys in the lock.

Campbell lurched to a stop in the road. "Who the hell are you?"

The man turned and stepped from under the portal, revealing in the starlight that he was missing an arm. "My name is Chapman," he answered haughtily.

"It's the bitch's lawyer!" Campbell crowed.

Mathews stepped up next to him. "What'cha got that cloth on your face for?"

"I have a toothache," Chapman said curtly. "If you gentlemen have no business with me, I'll say goodnight."

"Oh, we got business," Campbell said, drawing his gun and jabbing it into the lawyer's chest.

"Am I talking to Mr. Dolan?" Chapman sneered.

"No," Jesse shouted from beside Billy, "but you're talking to damn good friends of his!"

Billy started to edge away, brushing past Tom to let him know. Jesse drew his gun and poked it into the Kid's back. "Don't make another move," Jesse said.

Dolan laughed, drawing his own gun and shooting into the air. Campbell pulled the trigger.

"My God!" Chapman cried. He staggered a few steps into the road then fell on his back, flames flickering on his coat from the powder burns.

The silence was broken only by the hissing of wet blood on burning wool. The lawyer was already dead.

"Let's get something to eat," Dolan said, walking up the road toward McCullum's Oyster Bar. Mathews and Campbell followed him, guffawing at the corpse.

Jesse wagged his pistol at the Kid and Tom. "After y'all," he said.

Billy stole a glance at Tom. He seemed sober now, but Billy guessed they all were after what happened. In his opinion, the peace treaty had just been broken, and he and Tom were close to being prisoners. He figured his best chance lay in pretending he hadn't noticed it yet, which wasn't easy with a gun in his back.

Ahead of them Campbell fired a couple of rounds in the air, hollering with jubilation. He walked backward a few steps, calling to Jesse, "I promised God and Colonel Dudley I'd kill Chapman tonight, and damn if I didn't!"

"Yeah, you did." Jesse laughed. "Didn't he, Kid?"

"No argument," Billy said. He'd begun to think it was a setup from the beginning: Dolan hadn't wanted a truce, he'd just wanted all the guns on his side, and killing Chapman was meant to make them guilty together. But Billy didn't see it that way.

As they came near the restaurant, he watched Jesse holster his gun. Billy laughed, as if pulling the gun had been a joke. He caught Tom's eye to let him know they were taking their first chance out, then they all strolled into the oyster bar.

Edgar Walz, Catron's brother-in-law and the man running the Big Store, was sitting at a table alone. Dolan greeted him effusively. Watching the heavily armed men joining him at the long table, Walz didn't look happy. When the barkeep came, Walz told him to wrap his order as a carry-out. Dolan laughed and asked if he didn't like their company.

"I have a toothache," Walz explained with a quick lie.

"Then oysters are just the thing!" Dolan congratulated him. "You don't have to chew 'em, they slide down!"

"Don't go near Tunstall's store, though," Campbell advised. "It's unhealthy for people with toothaches tonight."

"What do you mean?" Walz asked nervously.

Dolan looked up at the barkeep. "Bring us six dozen of them New Jersey oysters and a coupla pitchers of beer." He waited until the man left the room, then leaned close to Walz. "We killed Chapman," he whispered in triumph.

Walz's eyes flew from face to face, then he looked back at Dolan. "My God, man," he moaned.

"Don't worry about it," Dolan said. "It'll make Dudley happy, and that'll make Catron happy up in Santa Fe."

"Listen," Campbell said suddenly, "we should've left a gun in his hand so it'd look like self-defense."

Dolan shifted his eyes back to Walz. "You're going that way, aren't you, Edgar?"

"I won't do it," he whispered. "I'll not be involved."

"I'll do it," Billy offered.

Campbell grinned. "I always heard you had balls, Kid," he said, handing him an extra gun he'd carried in his pocket.

Billy stood up and met Tom's eyes, then sauntered out the door. As soon as he was in the street, he ran through the dark to Tunstall's store. From Chapman's body came the nauseating smell of burning flesh, strong in the air. Billy didn't stop. He vaulted the gate into the corral and kept running to the stable. His mare was still saddled.

"Sorry we have to do this, girl," he said, swinging on. "I know you deserve a rest, but this ain't the time." He dug in his spurs, leapt the gate, and galloped east down the street. Immediately he reined in behind Mrs. Mac's house to hold his prancing mare as he called for Sebrian.

The tall, dark man came out from the kitchen.

Mrs. Mac appeared in the door. "What is it? What's happened?"

"Come hold my mare, will you, Sebrian?" Billy asked, stepping down. He gave him the reins and walked into the house, closing the door so his horse wouldn't be illuminated in the yard. To the widow, he said, "They killed Chapman."

Her hand flew to her throat. "But he was just here! Who did it?"

"Dolan, Mathews, fellow named Campbell. Jesse Evans was with 'em but Campbell pulled the trigger."

Seeing her swoon, he caught her as she fell, then carried her into the parlor and lay her on the settee. Quickly he unbuttoned her dress, yanked open the bow of her corset and loosened its laces, his fingers brushing her skin. Her breasts were flushed, scattered with freckles. When he saw them rise as she took in air, he stood up and moved away from her.

She awoke to the sound of his spurs as he paced, his steps measured and metallic, and she thought she would never be done with hearing his footsteps walk through her life. Presaging violence or echoing grief, death always came with the silver song of Billy Bonney's spurs. She sat up, pulling her dress closed as she met his eyes, seeing them soften with compassion.

"You fainted," he said. "I opened your laces so you could breathe."

She nodded, feeling their intimacy had gone far beyond sex. "Is it true?" she whispered. "They've killed Houston?"

"If he's Chapman."

She bent low over her knees.

He watched her a moment, then said, "I gotta go, Mrs. Mac."

Her face was ravaged with hurt. "Help me," she pleaded. "You've always been so good at keeping your spirits up, Kid. Can't you say something to help me before you go?"

He searched his mind for something to tell her, she who had lost her husband and her home, most of her friends, and now her lawyer to the venom of her enemies, yet asked only for help to keep going. "You're a strong woman, Mrs. Mac," he said. "You gotta help yourself."

She listened to his spurs crossing the kitchen, the sound of the door, then his horse galloping away. Standing up with resolution, she called Sebrian and told him to find Chapman's body and bury it with the others.

That cold night marking the first anniversary of Tunstall's death, the Kid met Tom at the mouth of Salazar Canyon, then they headed for Hijenio's house to tell him the outcome of the peace.

*   *   *

The murder of Chapman brought Governor Wallace to Lincoln. After writing his wife before Christmas that he saw the necessity of making the journey, he procrastinated two months and would have dawdled yet another if left to his own inclination.

He was close to finishing Book Two of his novel, a biblical epic he was calling *Ben Hur.* Judah had just been arrested for his accidental attack on the Roman procurator and condemned to the galleys. Wallace felt if he could continue the flow through the first appearance of the Nazarene, he could then comfortably lay his novel aside and take up the much more cantankerous problems of Lincoln County.

He had listened to partisans from both sides and thought them all contentious and petty. But then, what was a range war instigated by two opposing mercantile firms compared to the King of Kings?

Wallace was disturbed by a visitor just when he'd reached the scene where Jesus gives Judah water at the well. Knowing only bad tidings interrupted the sanctuary of midnight, the governor was not pleased to see Juan Patrón. Stifling his displeasure, Wallace smiled and said, "Mr. Patrón, please come in." He gestured toward the chair in front of his desk, reseating himself and trying to keep his eyes off the manuscript spread before him. "May I offer you coffee or other refreshment?"

Patrón shook his head. His eyes were black in his broad face, his complexion too swarthy for the governor's taste. Among the darker races, Wallace preferred the Arabs' aquiline noses and thin lips. Mexicans were short and squat, nothing more than mestizos with only the Inquisition as their intellectual heritage. Yet Wallace wanted to be fair to the people he governed. With a silent sigh, he pushed his personal aversions from his mind.

Aware of the governor's prejudice, Patrón said bluntly, "Dolan killed Mrs. McSween's attorney."

"Chapman?" Wallace asked rhetorically. "How did it happen?"

"Dolan and his party ambushed their victim in the dark," Patrón said bitterly. "Chapman was unarmed. They burned his body." Wallace winced and Patrón drove hard. "One of them was heard to shout, 'I promised God and Colonel Dudley I'd kill Chapman tonight and I've done it!' "

Lew Wallace was a military man, having served the Union in the War of Rebellion, and he received the slur against a fellow officer as a personal affront.

In his silence, Patrón said, "Chapman was gathering affidavits against Dudley, I'm sure he told you himself. He had evidence that Dudley is guilty of arson and murder in the death of McSween."

"Evidence, not proof," Wallace said.

"Chapman is dead!" Patrón shouted. "Everyone who opposes Dolan is murdered! Anarchy rules in Lincoln. It is your domain. Govern it!"

Wallace chose not to take offense at Patrón's vehement command. Rising, he said, "I shall go to Lincoln immediately and investigate matters for myself." He paused. "How was the town when you left?"

"Quiet as a tomb. Lincoln is occupied by Dudley's troops at the moment."

"Martial law hasn't been declared! The man's overstepped his authority."

"Many times, Governor. Do I have your word? I left my family in Lincoln and would like to return, if I can be assured that you will come yourself."

"I'll begin arrangements immediately," Wallace said. "You can tell the people to expect me in . . . how far a journey is it?"

"Three days with a good horse," Patrón replied dryly.

"Four with an entourage, then. I shall leave, let's see, two days from now. It will take that long to tie up loose ends, you understand." With longing, he scanned the pages of his manuscript, then forced himself to look back at Patrón. "I'll leave on the second and arrive on the sixth. Call a town meeting for the night of my arrival. I'll want to hear all opinions on the issues."

"It shall be done," Patrón answered. "Goodnight, sir."

He turned and walked through the musty hall of the Palace to the plaza, blanketed with snow. As Juan Patrón headed down San Francisco Street toward Herlow's Hotel, he was thinking that if law didn't come to Lincoln now, only he and the Kid were left for Dolan to kill.

39

The village of Las Tablas lay twenty miles northwest of Lincoln in the Capitan Mountains, a cluster of adobe huts that were home to a dozen Mexican families. Billy was staying with a young couple who had a new baby, Tom with some old folks whose children had long ago left home. Hijenio had found the quarters, asking as a personal favor that the villagers shelter his friends.

The hosts accommodated them graciously. The strangers were polite, helped with chores, spoke Spanish, and were pleasant companions. The people knew, of course, that two Americans would not seek sanctuary in their village unless they were hiding, most likely from the law. But the law in Lincoln County was capricious, and the farmers of Las Tablas felt more protected by gaining the gratitude of *el Chivato* than by cooperating with the law.

The peace of their village was disrupted by his presence in only one way. The silence normally broken merely by the laughter of children, wood being split into kindling, burros braying, and cows lowing to be milked was now shattered with the noise of gunfire.

For hours each afternoon, *el Chivato* walked in a nearby meadow and shot at anything attracting his eye. The echoes reverberating off the mountains filled the people's thoughts with war. Isolated and illiterate though they were, gossip carried news of the governor's impending arrival, and they came to understand it was this event that kept *el Chivato* and his friend in their village.

Hijenio Salazar visited often, bringing a fresh supply of ammunition that the people noticed the outlaw no longer paid for. Having hoped for a few dollars for themselves, they came to the realization that he was broke, but it only endeared him more. They saw him as a special citizen who earned his keep with his good company and excellent gun.

Toward the middle of March, Hijenio found Billy practicing in the meadow with Tom. Loping his horse across the mush of melted snow, Hijenio tied his reins so his horse could graze, then walked with his friends to sit on an outcrop of rocks, warm and dry in the afternoon sun.

"The governor is in Lincoln," Hijenio said. "He sees people in the courthouse and is listening to everyone."

Billy spotted a sparrow on a chamisa bush, knowing he could pick the bird off but feeling lazy. "Did you get me more ammo?"

"*Sí, amigo.* Montaño gave it to me last night. Listen to what he told me: The governor took away command from Dudley. He is still at Stanton but will leave any day. Captain Purington is top *jefe* now. The governor gave out a list of men he wants arrested, and the army can do it without warrants because he says so."

"Who's on the list?"

"Everybody, *hombre.* I brought one, *mira.*"

It had been printed at Stanton and could have been a roll call for men on both sides of the war. Billy handed it back and said, "The gov'nor's getting good information. Is everybody talking to him?"

"*Sí,* mostly Juan Patrón and Ike Ellis. Also Montaño, because the governor's staying in his house. Mrs. Mac spent a long time with him. Montaño said it was the first time he had seen her dressed as a widow."

Billy laughed. "So she's in with the gov, huh?"

"She has a new lawyer." Hijenio shrugged. "The *bruja* never quits."

Pulling his pistol, Billy opened the cylinder and flicked the empty shells onto the ground. "What's the name of her lawyer?"

"I forget his name, *hombre,* but there is more to tell you. Someone wrote a letter to the newspaper in Cruces saying how Chapman was killed. The letter said you and Tom tried to get away, but Jesse Evans made you stay at gunpoint."

"Who wrote it?"

"He signed only 'Max.' I suspect it was Sam Corbet but it is dangerous to even *think* you know who did it. Dolan is in jail because of it. The governor is holding him, Jesse Evans, Jake Mathews, and Will Campbell at Stanton."

Billy laughed, loading his gun.

"The governor has put up a reward for you," Hijenio said. "One thousand dollars for you alive as a witness."

"I'm glad it's alive," Billy said, shooting the sparrow off a twig forty yards away.

"He wants you to testify against Dolan and the others. Montaño thinks you should do it. Mrs. Mac said the same. Patrón, also. It is murder, they say, and Dolan will hang. You were there and saw it."

Billy flipped open his gun and replaced the spent cartridge. "How long do you think I'd stay alive if I testified against Dolan?"

Hijenio shrugged. "Is a risky business."

Billy looked at Tom.

"I think you should do it, Kid," he said.

"You were a witness, too," Billy said.

"Ain't no reward for my testimony."

"That true?" Billy asked Hijenio. "Tom ain't included in the reward?"

"That's the way it is," he answered unhappily.

"Sonofabitch," Billy said, standing up. He took a few steps away, then turned back. "I got to think this over. Can you stick around?"

"*Sí, amigo.* I will stay till morning."

Billy walked far into the meadow, a cool breeze moving across the valley as the sun fell below the peaks. Before him yawned a dark canyon rising into the mountains; behind him was the village, its lamp-lit windows warm with welcome. He stopped and stood suspended between them.

He was a man nineteen years old whose reputation was bigger than he was. Everywhere he went, people knew his name. Most of them welcomed him, but in too many places someone asked him to leave, saying he attracted the wrong element. In Tascosa, he'd laughed it off, but fondness for the experience hadn't grown with repetition. The easiest solution was to leave the territory and go someplace where nobody knew who he was. But Billy couldn't bring himself to do it. His reputation was all he owned.

On the other hand, he knew his freedom would diminish as long as he was outlawed. Billy liked to move around the country and feel welcome wherever he went. That was why he'd quit the Banditti in the first place, and since returning from Tascosa, he'd kept himself clean, though he was as outlawed as Jesse Evans anyway. Now Jesse, Jake Mathews, and Jimmie Dolan were in jail, and it fell on Billy to testify and hang them. Mac had always insisted the law would win, but Billy had never believed it.

He didn't trust judges or anything happening inside a courtroom, but it was a long shot he'd make it that far. Even if he did, he was gambling the governor could assure a fair trial, and that once Dolan was hung, the Ring wouldn't retaliate. Billy stood to lose his life to gain his freedom. He was a gambler, and he decided to do it.

Walking back to the home of his friends, he asked for paper and pen. As the wife went out to search the village, Billy stood before the fire, smiling at Hijenio and Tom.

"I'm gonna write the gov'nor," he told them. "If he agrees to my terms, I'll do it."

"*Andale, amigo,*" Hijenio said.

"I'll stick with you," Tom promised.

"You go into this," Billy warned, "you'll be in deep. You best think of your own int'rests."

"I am," he answered.

The woman came back with a blank sheet of paper, a quill, a bottle of ink, and one tattered envelope. "Hey, this is great!" Billy said, making her blush. He sat at the table, spread the paper flat, and opened the ink. "What's the date, Hijenio?"

"I don't know."

"Never mind. Let's see: To His Excellency the Gov'nor, General Lew Wallace," he enunciated as he wrote. "Dear Sir. You put one of them double dots after 'sir,' don'cha, Tom?"

"You got me."

Billy looked at them and laughed. "Guess I'm on my own." He bent over the paper, stating his position as clearly as he could. When he was finished, he read it aloud to his friends.

Dear Sir:

I have heard that you will give one thousand $dollars for my body which as I can understand it means alive as a Witness. I

know it is as a witness against those that Murdered Mr. Chapman. if it was so as that I could appear at Court I could give the
desired information, but I have indictments against me for
things that happened in the late Lincoln County War and am
afraid to give up because my enemies would kill me. the day Mr.
Chapman was murdered I was in Lincoln at the request of good
Citizens to meet Mr. J. J. Dolan to meet as Friends. so as to be
able to lay aside our arms and go to Work. I was present When
Mr. Chapman was Murdered and know who did it and if it were
not for those indictments I would have made it clear before now.
if it is in your power to Anully those indictments I hope you will
do so as to give me a chance to explain. please send me an answer
telling me what you can do You can send answer by bearer I have
no Wish to fight any more indeed I have not raised an arm since
Your amnesty proclamation. a's to my Character I refer to any of
the Citizens. for the majority of them are my Friends and have
been helping me all they could.

Waiting an answer I remain
Your Obedeint Servant

W. H. Bonney

"What do you think?" he asked, watching their faces.

"It's a good letter," Tom said, amazed the Kid could turn it out so
fast.

Hijenio was impressed, too. "I will take it now," he said, standing
up.

"Whoa!" Billy laughed. "I thought you were staying till morning."

"My horse has rested and we both know the way down the mountain
in the dark. I will be in Lincoln by dawn." Sensing the Kid's hesitation,
Hijenio said, "You have many friends in Lincoln. We will protect you."

Folding the letter and sealing it in the envelope, Billy handed it over.

The governor was at breakfast when Montaño brought him the envelope.
Thinking it was another petition from a peasant having cow trouble with
his neighbor, Wallace asked, "Who brought it?"

"A boy," Montaño said. "He's waiting for your answer."

"Indeed?" Wallace laughed. "Do you know who it's from?"

"Yes, Your Excellency. It's from the Kid."

"Ah," Wallace said. "Allow me a moment?"

Left alone, the governor scanned the letter for content, smiled at the
offer, then perused the script more leisurely.

A novelist who prided himself on his eloquent style, Lew Wallace was amused by the Kid's letter. He had capitalized Friends, Murder, Work, Witness, Citizens, Court, and Character, and the governor thought those errors revealing of the man who had written them. Noting he'd misspelled *obedient,* Wallace suspected the Kid would have a similar problem with the action. "Anully" was a prize. Wallace chuckled as he rang the bell for his secretary. Requesting stationery, he then asked for Señor Montaño, and was writing when his host returned. "The Kid has asked for a meeting," Wallace said. "Can you recommend a place?"

Montaño smiled. "Squire Wilson's *casita* is isolated, and no one would suspect him of such courage."

Wallace laughed. "Yes, I know the house." He finished his letter, sealed it in his official envelope, and handed it over. "Let's hope he comes."

The little boy put the governor's letter inside his shirt and ran west through town, then into the brush where Hijenio waited. He rewarded the boy with a nickel, tightened his cinch and swung on. "Remember, *muchacho,* tell no one," he said from the height of his horse. The boy nodded solemnly, and Hijenio reined away to take the letter into the mountains.

He found Billy currying his mare in the lean-to stable. Walking into the small space, Hijenio reached across the horse's back to hand Billy the letter.

Billy looked at it a minute, then turned it over to study the official seal. It impressed him, holding a letter from the governor. It made the scheme seem plausible.

"Open it, *hombre,*" Hijenio urged.

Billy pulled his knife and cut the seal, slid the letter out and read it:

15 March 1879

W. H. Bonney,

Come to the house of Squire Wilson at nine o'clock next Monday night. I have authority to exempt you from prosecution if you will testify to what you say you know. The object of our meeting is to arrange the matter in a way to make your life safe. To do that the utmost secrecy is to be used. So come alone. Don't tell anybody—not a living soul—where you are coming or the object. If you could trust Jesse Evans, you can trust me.

Lew. Wallace

Billy laughed at the remark about Jesse Evans, then read the letter aloud
to Hijenio.

"*Pinche,*" he whispered. "Will you go?"

"What day is this?"

"Saturday, I think."

"Good. I've got time to see Tulles on the way."

"You go to a woman now? And her, of all of them?"

"Nobody's gonna mess with Juan Patrón's sister."

"Except Juan Patrón," Hijenio said.

At eight-thirty on Monday night, Lew Wallace was sitting before the
fire in Squire Wilson's home. Since coming to Lincoln the governor had
heard a great deal about Billy Bonney, and he was convinced the outlaw
had committed the crimes he was indicted for, as well as many rumored
ones. Yet there was another quality to the Kid's reputation that intrigued Wallace.

Mrs. McSween's eyes glinted with cunning when she spoke of him.
Her servant, Sebrian Bates, gushed with praise. Juan Patrón dropped his
voice in respect. Captain Purington beamed with admiration describing
the outlaw's elusiveness. Sam Corbet thought him a fine citizen, and José
Montaño said he was an asset to the community and they wished for his
pardon. So Lew Wallace waited for the Kid with curiosity, yet also his
mind wandered to his novel, which waited on his return to Santa Fe.

He would have to describe Jesus of Nazareth. The physical attributes
given the Lord had to be perfect, making his readers marvel at his powers
of description. The Lord's hair would be golden, his features symmetri-
cal, his eyes pale blue, aglow with loving wisdom. The governor found
pleasing a multitude while describing their God a puzzle far more in-
triguing than government.

A knock came on the door. Wallace nodded at Squire Wilson, then
watched the pudgy man trudge across the room and whisper, "Who is
it?"

"Me," came a young voice.

Wilson opened the door and the Kid's silhouette loomed on the
threshold, a pistol in one hand and a rifle in the other. "I was sent for to
meet the gov'nor. Is he here?"

"I am Governor Wallace," he said, rising.

The Kid's eyes searched the room as he stepped inside. When Wilson
closed the door, the Kid glanced behind himself, then looked at Wallace
and said softly, "I was promised protection."

"I have been true to my promise," he answered. "This man, whom
you know, and I are the only persons in the house."

The outlaw assessed him a moment, with eyes so pale they made Wallace feel cold. Finally the Kid holstered his pistol, leaned his carbine against the wall, and held out his hand.

The governor smiled down on him, thinking he was a slight man to cast such a long shadow. As Wallace settled himself in front of the fire and invited his guest to do the same, he felt the outlaw's scrutiny.

"Well, now," Wallace said, collecting his thoughts. "This is my plan: You will surrender to arrest and testify against the killers of Chapman. In return, I will pardon you of all crimes committed heretofore."

"Pardon? That means I go free?"

"Yes. You are forgiven."

"You can do that? Stop the law from acting against me?"

"It's within my powers as governor of the territory."

"Damn!" The Kid grinned. "You think Dolan will be convicted if I testify?"

"You were an eyewitness. Do you think the jury will believe you?"

"Yeah, I do." He stood up and began pacing the floor.

Wallace watched with amusement. "I wouldn't keep you in jail. We could confine you in Patrón's home."

The Kid looked at him hard. "I'd have to be arrested?"

"Yes, but it would be a matter of appearances only, going through the motions to appease the courts. I've promised you a pardon."

"But they'd take my guns. I'd have to ride into Lincoln unarmed."

"If our plan is to work, absolute secrecy must be maintained by both of us. You'll be inside the house under twenty-four-hour guard before anyone knows you're in town."

The Kid stopped in front of the fireplace and stared at the flames. He moved again abruptly to resume pacing the floor. "I don't know," he said. "I let myself get arrested once and swore I'd never be that stupid again."

"This isn't stupid, it's wise. Convict Dolan of murder and he'll hang. You'll be pardoned. The war will be over and everyone can go back to work." He restrained a smile, remembering the Kid had capitalized that word in his letter. "With your help, we can make it happen."

"S'pose you'll have me handcuffed." The Kid laughed. "That don't matter. I can get out of bracelets easy 'cause my hands are so small. I can get out of any jail ever built, too. Don't think I'll be at your mercy 'cause I'm under arrest."

"I would never think that," Wallace answered, stifling his resentment at the threat.

"I'll write you a letter and let you know," the Kid said, holding out his hand.

Wallace stood up and shook with him. "I'll hope for cooperation."

"But you'll take what you get, huh, Gov?"

Wallace thought of the reward for the Kid's capture and suspected the Kid was thinking of it too. "I'll do everything in my power to find peace for Lincoln County. Oppose me and you'll be an outlaw forever. Work with me and you'll be exonerated of all misdeeds."

The Kid laughed, picking up his rifle. "I heard that word before. McSween used it after he was cleared in court. Three months later he was dead. I'd rather be alive than exonerated, Gov'nor, and that might be the choice I'm making. I'll let you know." He slipped out the door and was gone.

Wallace sat back down and stared into the fire. The Kid's eyes had been so animated. They were alive with intelligence, even a kind of goodness in the sense of meeting a man square, but they held another quality: an ability to call judgment without mercy. Wallace thought the Kid would have made a good governor. He was of the earth, wily in the ways of men, and lethal as a guillotine.

As he walked back to Montaño's house, Lew Wallace decided he must change his description of Jesus. His eyes couldn't be pale; they must be as dark as the sky at dusk.

Two nights later, Hijenio brought bad news to Billy and Tom staying upstairs at Clenny's monte house. "Jesse Evans and Will Campbell escaped from Stanton last night. Some say their guard let them out. ¿Quién sabe? They are gone."

"Sonofabitch," Billy said. "Does that mean the deal's off?"

"Only if you say so."

"It's a lot more dangerous with Jesse loose," Tom said.

Billy turned around and peered through the shutters at the frozen wagon ruts in the empty road, rosy in the sunset. Jesse's escape had upped the ante, but by taking the gamble, Billy stood to gain what Jesse never would: Freedom. Pardon. Amnesty. Billy sent Hijenio to fetch writing implements, then penned his plan to Wallace:

Sir:

> I accept the promise you made but be sure and have men come that you can depend on. I am not afraid to die like a man fighting but I would not like to be killed like a dog unarmed.
>
> You will never catch Jesse Evans on the road. Watch Fritzes, Captain Bacas ranch and the Brewery. They will either go to Seven Rivers or to Jicarilla mountains. They will stay close untill

the scouting parties come in Give a spy a pair of glasses and let him get on the mountain back of Fritzes and watch

It is not my place to advise you, but I am anxious to have them caught, and perhaps know how men hide from soldiers better than you. Please excuse me for having so much to say and I still remain.

Yours truly

W. H. Bonney

P.S. Tell the sheriff to come to Junction tomorrow, but not before 3 oclock for I may not be there before. Do not send soldiers.

At the appointed hour, Billy and Tom rode their horses into the middle of Sheriff Kimball's posse and surrendered their guns. Their hands were cuffed behind their backs and their horses led along the road into Lincoln. A cold wind blew through the valley, dipping down off the snow and chilling the outlaws who rode with their coats open. Wallace had promised secrecy but the street of Lincoln was lined with citizens braving the cold to see the Kid brought in. When they came abreast of the jail, Kimball kept riding without looking back. The deputies all dismounted and told their prisoners to get down.

Billy looked at the jail, then at Longwell, the man he knew best among the posse. "I promised myself I'd never go in that hole again," he said. He wanted to add that the governor had also promised he wasn't to be kept there, but their arrangement was secret.

"I'm sorry," Longwell said. "I wish it could be another way."

Billy sat his horse, his hands still cuffed behind his back.

"Come on, Kid," Longwell wheedled. "Don't make trouble for me."

Billy kicked his leg over his horse's head and slid down. "I won't do that. But I wish the sonofabitch who gave the order was in your boots."

Longwell grimaced as he lifted the hatch and a draft of cold damp hit his face.

"I can't climb a ladder like this," Billy said, slipping off his handcuffs and tossing them to an astonished deputy. Untying his blanket from behind his saddle, Billy asked Longwell, "Take good care of my mare, will you?"

"Sure, Kid," he answered, unlocking O'Folliard's cuffs.

Billy took a long look at the gray skies, then at the people, most of whom he knew, watching from a distance. "Come on, Tom," he said, descending into the hole.

The hours of cold were a trial of faith for Billy. His thoughts were turning to escape when, late the following afternoon, Longwell opened the hatch and announced they were being transferred to the home of Juan Patrón.

Billy and Tom stood blinking in the bright sun while their wrists were cuffed behind their backs. Surrounded by men carrying rifles, the prisoners were walked across the street to where Juan Patrón stood in his open door, beaming a welcome. He asked the deputies for the keys to the manacles, then closed the door in their faces. Billy slipped his hands free and dropped the cuffs on the carpet, admiring his accommodations.

Two beds were pushed against the walls, and a square table with four chairs sat in the center of the room. "You done real good for us, Juan," Billy said.

"Thank the governor," Patrón answered, walking toward a door. "We're being paid well to keep you. Just a minute." He stepped into another room.

Tom was rubbing his wrists. "This looks comfy, don't it, Billy?"

"Yeah," he said, checking the view from the windows. In front stood Longwell; on the side, Pantaleón Gallegos.

"The governor sent you a gift," Patrón said, coming back, "as an apology for having to keep you in the jail overnight." He set a box of cigars and a bottle of Kentucky bourbon on the table.

Billy opened the box, releasing a strong fragrance of tobacco.

"They're excellent cigars," Patrón murmured.

"Have one," Billy said, taking one for himself. "You got a match, Tom?"

"Oh, you must trim it first," Patrón said, removing the tiny knife from its loop in the top of the wooden box. Deftly he demonstrated how it was done, then handed the knife to Billy.

Billy admired the knife as he cut the fat roll of leaves with a clean slice. He handed it to Tom, who trimmed his own cigar, then struck a match and held it for each of them.

Billy walked around the room, puffing on the cigar.

"Can I open the whiskey?" Tom asked.

"It's yours," Billy said.

"Gosh, thanks." He and Patrón tasted tiny sips. "You should try some, Kid," Tom called to where Billy looked out a window. "It's the best I've ever had."

"No thanks," he said, seeing Mrs. Mac coming down the street with an old man. Her new lawyer, Billy guessed.

"I must be about my duties," Patrón said. "My mother and sisters are just beyond that door. If you want anything, please knock and they'll supply your needs."

"Thanks, Juan," Billy said, turning to face him. "I seen Tulles the other night."

Patrón frowned. "I consider my sister a family concern, Kid. Please don't take offense if I'd rather not discuss her." He started to leave, then turned back at the door. "Was she well?"

"Yeah. A bit lonely, is all."

Patrón winced, then went out, closing the door.

"This is great!" Tom said. "It's like they put us in a fucking hotel!" He walked over and flopped down on one of the beds.

"Don't go to sleep yet," Billy said. "We're getting comp'ny."

A knock came on the door and Tom sat up with surprise.

Longwell came in. "Mrs. McSween is here. You want to see her?"

"Sure," Billy said, laying his cigar in a bowl on the table.

"I hate to tell you this, Kid," Longwell said. "But you gotta wear your cuffs for visitors. We'll leave the key and you can take 'em off when you're alone, but I got orders to keep you cuffed and I gotta make it look like I'm doing that."

"No problem," Billy said, picking his pair off the floor and slipping them on.

Tom felt more unhappy snapping the manacles around his wrists.

Longwell opened the door. "Come on in," he said, going back out and closing the visitors inside.

Mrs. Mac looked thinner, her eyes more conniving. She grimaced at Billy's shackles, then smiled radiantly. "This is only temporary, Kid. It's the best way, believe me."

"That's what I'm trying to do, Mrs. Mac," he answered. "But I'm not believing a hundred percent yet. I'm still watching to see what comes down at the end."

"No less than amnesty for you," she said, turning to her companion. "This is Ira Leonard. Judge Leonard, Billy Bonney and Tom O'Folliard. He's my new attorney, Kid, and I brought him along thinking you might want him to represent you."

Billy walked a few steps away, then turned back. "Wallace promised me a pardon. What do I need a lawyer for?"

Judge Leonard cleared his throat. "It's always best to go before the court represented by counsel, Mr. Bonney."

"You think the gov'nor will go back on his word?"

"No," Leonard was quick to reply. "But he hasn't decreed the pardon yet and, forgive an old adage, there's many a slip 'twixt the cup and the lip.''

Billy laughed. "If I decide I need a lawyer, I'll let you know."

There was a silence before Mrs. Mac said, "We all think you're brave, Kid, to testify against Dolan. Everyone is raving about your courage."

He knew her well enough to understand her praise always preceded a request. "I bet Dudley ain't," he said.

She laughed. "I'm sure not. Have you thought about what I asked? I'm not a governor and can't promise a pardon, only my undying gratitude."

He didn't consider that a paltry prize, suspecting Mrs. Mac would always be able to offer sanctuary of some sort. Nodding, he said, "I can't see it's much dif'rent from testifying against Dolan."

"Wonderful!" she exclaimed. Turning to her lawyer, she held to his arm. "We've got him, Ira!"

Judge Leonard met the Kid's eyes and they both laughed. Having accomplished her mission, Sue McSween swept her attorney out of the house.

Tom watched Billy shuck his cuffs, relight his cigar, and start pacing the room. "What do you think, Kid?"

"Play the cards as they fall," he said, looking out the window toward the trail to Eagle Creek.

Tom found the key and unlocked his cuffs, then sat on the bed again. "You like them cigars?"

"Yeah," he said, still looking out the window. "They make me feel like a gov'nor, with a prick big enough to fuck the whole territory."

Tom shifted uncomfortably. "Don'cha trust him?"

"As much as I trust Jesse Evans," he answered. Abruptly he walked to the front door and yanked it open. Longwell jerked back, drawing his gun. Billy laughed. "I jus' wanted to ask when court's s'posed to open."

"Fourteenth," Longwell said. "Don't come busting out like that, Kid. I'd hate to shoot you by accident."

"That'd be a poor way to die. How long away is the fourteenth?"

"Three weeks."

Billy nodded and closed the door. Sitting down at the table, he said, "Let's play some monte."

"All right," Tom said, moving to join him. "We ain't got any bullets. What're we gonna play for?"

"Cigars," Billy said.

40

Governor Wallace was facing the first session of court held in Lincoln for over a year, along with the almost concurrent court of inquiry against Colonel Dudley. Having determined Judge Bristol was biased, Wallace tried to replace him with Ira Leonard, but his petition was so slowly winding its way through channels that he had little hope of timely success. So he appointed Leonard a special prosecutor to protect the territory's interests. District Attorney Rynerson balked, claiming bias on Leonard's part because he represented Mrs. McSween at the court of inquiry. Wallace declared the district court independent from the inquiry and commanded Rynerson to work with Leonard.

The district attorney didn't argue with Wallace again, he simply ignored him. The Santa Fe Ring had decided the new governor was naive about territorial politics and instructed Rynerson to circumvent him. Commerce would rule as it always had, the banks and large landowners calling the shots. Government was merely a ritual of protocol.

Well aware of the Ring's opinion, Wallace trusted in the powers vested in his office to achieve his ends. As both sides sharpened their scythes for the harvest of court, he strove to care about the issues involved, but in his heart he longed to return to his novel in Santa Fe.

One afternoon, after listening to an especially virulent accusation of theft between neighbors, Wallace told his secretary he would be out for a while. Ignoring the room full of waiting petitioners, he walked down the dusty street of Lincoln to the house of Patrón. Wallace couldn't have explained his desire to see the young outlaw again, but that the Kid's charm was shrouded with death added piquancy to his appeal. Wallace could well understand the satisfaction of executing a particularly tiresome problem.

He walked in on the Kid, Tom O'Folliard, and Sam Corbet playing poker for cigars. Corbet was the only one embarrassed. The Kid laughed as he stood up and offered the governor his hand. Wallace accepted the handshake, not failing to notice the prisoners weren't wearing the shackles he'd ordered. He turned away to greet Corbet with a condescension easily read as a dismissal, and the store clerk left meekly. Watching O'Folliard gather the cards, Wallace recognized the attitude of an underling practiced at the deception of minding his own business. "Let's go for a walk, shall we?" Wallace asked the Kid.

The outlaw was obviously pleased. When they stepped outside,

Longwell asked, "What's going on, Gov'nor? I ain't got orders about this."

"We're just going for a walk. You may come along if you wish."

Longwell's face was screwed with worry as he asked the Kid, "Will you give your word you won't try to escape?"

The Kid looked at Wallace a moment, then said, "Yeah, I give my word."

"All right," Longwell said. "But I'll be right behind you."

"Don't get lost," the Kid teased.

They crossed the broad meadow scattered with adobe homes and newly planted gardens, the evening breeze cool on their faces.

"They been keeping you busy?" the Kid asked in a conversational tone.

Wallace snorted. "Are you managing to stay occupied?"

"I get a lot of comp'ny. Thanks for the cigars. I like 'em."

Wallace smiled. "And the bourbon?"

"I gave that to Tom. He's got more of a thirst than I do."

At the end of the meadow, Wallace turned east, following a trail along the edge of the hills. After a moment, he stopped and studied the Kid thoughtfully. "The other day, two urchins were discussing shooting skills outside my window. One of the boys said Middleton was the best in the county. The other said John Jones was better than Middleton, but you were better than John Jones."

The Kid laughed. "I'd hate to face it out with either one of 'em when they were sober."

"Do you think you would win?"

"I'd stand a good chance."

"I'm a fair show at weapons myself. Would you demonstrate your skill for me?"

Amazement flashed on the Kid's face. "I ain't got no gun."

Wallace turned to the deputy standing a short distance away. "Give Mr. Bonney your pistol, will you? He's going to demonstrate his skill."

Longwell's mouth fell open. Finally he said, "Aw, Gov'nor, you can't mean I should jus' give him my gun? What'll I tell the sheriff if he escapes?"

"He's given you his word," Wallace replied dryly.

Longwell glared at the Kid, who was grinning. "Aw, hell," the deputy said, handing the pistol over.

The Kid checked the chambers, then hefted the gun. "What do you want me to shoot, Gov?"

Wallace looked around. "The juniper sprig growing out of that rock?"

The Kid fired and the top of the tree was gone. "That was too easy. How about the bluejay on that cottonwood down there?"

"If you think you can do it," Wallace agreed. He watched the Kid raise the gun and pull the trigger, then looked at Longwell. "Did he hit it? I was watching his form."

"Yeah, he hit it," Longwell said with disgust.

Wallace looked back at the Kid. "Do you have an explanation for your unusual skill?"

"I jus' point like with my finger." He smiled, aiming the gun at the governor's chest. "If a man points his finger, it jus' naturally hits what he wants."

Wallace looked down at the weapon a few inches from his heart, then met the Kid's eyes dancing in fun. Wallace smiled. "I can see you would be a formidable enemy."

The Kid laughed, tossing the gun to the deputy. "You ain't got nothing to worry about, Gov, long as we're friends."

For the second time, Wallace stifled resentment at the Kid's threat. He turned and began walking back, the deputy falling in behind them again. "Everything's progressing well on our case," the governor said, suddenly eager to be away from the Kid. "It's unfortunate we lost Campbell and Evans, of course, but we should be able to convict Dolan of being an accessory to Chapman's murder. The trial probably won't be held until the next term of court, so I'll need you to promise that you'll return to testify."

"You mean you're letting me go?" the Kid asked.

Wallace glanced at him, marveling again at his youth. "After you've testified before the grand jury and we indict Dolan, I'll issue the pardon and you'll be free on your own recognizance until the trial. I'm pushing for it to be held this term, but Dolan's attorneys will no doubt win a continuance from Bristol. Does all this make sense to you?"

"I'm following it," he said. "When's the inquiry against Dudley? I told Mrs. Mac I'd testify for her, too."

"You're not to testify *for* anyone but to tell the truth."

The Kid shrugged. "It's the same thing."

Wallace stopped and held out his hand. "I'll leave you here. We've struck a good bargain that will benefit both of us. Don't you agree?"

"It seems that way now," he answered.

Wallace watched him walk away, wondering if the pardon was wise. That the Kid was capable of murder without remorse was obvious in the charm of his arrogance, as if death were no more than a turn of the cards and survival a matter of luck. Such an attitude didn't bode well for the Kid's rehabilitation.

Avoiding the courthouse filled with waiting petitioners, Wallace went to his quarters and wrote a letter to his friend Carl Schurz, secretary of the interior. Becoming discouraged with even that normally pleasant task, he requested that dinner he brought to his room and he ate in solitude, then stared at blank sheets of paper, trying to recollect the next step in his novel.

The lamps had been lit and his supper tray removed by the daughter of his host, yet still Wallace sat at his desk, writing sentences on pages he would burn in Santa Fe as useless. When he heard music, he stopped writing and walked outside to investigate.

His guard followed as he took a few steps closer to the sound of guitars and a violin accompanying voices singing in Spanish. "Is it a *baile* or a *fiesta*?" Wallace asked, proud of his Spanish.

"Neither one, sir," his guard answered. "They're serenading the Kid."

"Indeed!" He laughed, eagerly moving closer.

"This is a good way to get killed," his guard warned.

"Don't be silly. No one will shoot the governor."

"We're just men lurking in the dark to them guarding the Kid," the man answered unhappily.

Wallace stopped in the shadows behind Patrón's house. Illuminated by the lamplight falling through an open window, a dozen men dressed in homespun *campesino* garments were singing with women who sat in the swirls of their colorful skirts. Three peasants strummed guitars in flamenco rhythms, while the fiddle of Sebrian Bates blended the melancholy of the Confederacy with the lost rhapsodies of the gypsies. The Kid was leaning out the window and singing too, all their faces earnestly expressing the Spanish lyrics of a heroic ballad as they harmonized around a humble melody, hungry with the yearning of the dispossessed.

Wallace turned away, feeling he was intruding on an intimate ceremony. As he walked back to his room, he felt saddened by the scene, though he couldn't say why. It had been lovely, expressive of joy and courage, a passionate, heartfelt sharing of hope, and it should have left him more keenly aware of the human spirit's will to triumph over tragedy. Instead, he felt suffering was a force beyond anyone's power to amend.

Back at his desk, he resumed the letter to Schurz he had earlier abandoned. After sitting several moments sipping his fine Kentucky bourbon, he wrote that in a few days he would return to Santa Fe and his beloved *Ben Hur*, and of how much he looked forward to walking with the ancients again after conversing solely with illiterate peasants. "Although they are not without charm," he wrote. "A precious specimen nicknamed 'The Kid,' whom the sheriff is holding here in the plaza, is an object of tender regard. I heard singing, and going to the door, I found the minstrels of the village actually serenading the fellow in his prison."

When court convened on April 14, 1879, the murder of Chapman was first on the docket. Shackled hand and foot, the territory's star witness was led into the crowded room to take the stand. Mrs. Mac was in the audience, smiling encouragement. District Attorney Rynerson glowered from the prosecution table, and beside him sat Ira Leonard, Mrs. Mac's attorney. At the defendant's table were two attorneys from the Santa Fe law firm of Catron and Thornton. Jimmie Dolan smirked from behind them, unshackled but apparently in the custody of the army officer beside him.

When the recorder asked the witness to place his right hand on the Bible, a sudden hush fell over the courtroom as everyone listened to the Kid swear to tell the truth.

Rynerson stood up. "What is your name and place of residence, please?"

"My name is William Bonney. I reside in Lincoln."

"Are you not also known as Kid, Billy Kid, and Billy the Kid?" Rynerson sneered.

"Folks call me a lot of things," he answered.

"I'm sure. Have you not also been known as Kid Antrim?"

"I was once, but Antrim is my stepfather's name."

"Were you not called Kid Antrim when you murdered Francis Cahill in Camp Grant, Arizona?"

"Objection!" Ira Leonard shouted, standing abruptly.

Judge Bristol looked amused. "It's not appropriate, Mr. Leonard, to object against your own cocounsel."

"I'm here at the stipulation of Governor Wallace," Leonard said. "I represent the territory's interest in justice, Your Honor."

The judge chuckled. "We're all here to do that. On what grounds are you basing your objection?"

"Any act occurring in Arizona is irrelevant to our proceedings."

"I fail to see," Rynerson mocked, "how the character of the witness is irrelevant." He turned to the judge. "I wish to establish that this man has several indictments for murder against him, so the court can weigh his testimony accordingly."

"That is inadmissible!" Leonard shouted. "I demand it be stricken from the record!"

Bristol shrugged, knowing the record would be destroyed at close of court. "So ordered. Proceed, Mr. Prosecutor."

Rynerson turned to the witness. "Mr. Bonney, where were you on the morning of April first 1878?"

"Objection!" Leonard said, again rising and glaring at Rynerson.

"On what grounds this time, Mr. Leonard?" Judge Bristol asked. "We're talking of a crime that occurred right here in Lincoln. Surely that's relevant."

"It is not," Leonard argued. "It has no bearing on the crime before the court."

"I'm attempting to establish the character of the witness," Rynerson said as if to a child.

"He is the prosecution's witness."

"Yes, but this court is after justice and I believe the witness himself committed the crime."

"Your duty is to question him as to what he knows!" Leonard retorted. "If in the course of his testimony you can prove your allegation, you will be correct to do so. But to suggest it now invalidates anything that comes hereafter."

"I doubt that," Rynerson replied, turning away. "Where were you, Mr. Bonney, on the morning of April first, 1878, when the sheriff of this county was assassinated?"

The Kid only smiled.

"Let the record show," Rynerson said, "that the witness remains silent. Where were you then, Mr. Bonney, on the night of February eighteenth, 1879?"

"I was in Lincoln."

"Both times, no doubt," Rynerson said. "What were you doing in Lincoln on February eighteenth of this year?"

"Watching Dolan's gunman kill Houston Chapman."

Without bothering to stand the defense attorney drawled, "Objection. No connection between my client and the witness has been established."

"Sustained," Bristol said. "Strike the defendant's answer from the record."

Rynerson smiled. "What brought you to Lincoln, Mr. Bonney, on the night under discussion?"

"I came to make a peace treaty."

"A peace treaty that ended with murder?"

"That's what happened."

"Were you with the party responsible for Chapman's death?"

"Yeah, and I saw Will Campbell pull the trigger. Ask Jake Mathews. He was there, along with Jesse Evans and Jimmie Dolan."

"Just answer the question, please. Were you in possession of a firearm at the time?"

"I always have a gun."

"Not now," Rynerson replied softly. "Not ever again, if I have my way." He turned to Bristol and raised his voice. "I dismiss the witness."

"The witness is dismissed," Bristol echoed, and four deputies came forward to escort the prisoner from the court.

Seeing that Mrs. Mac looked worried, and thinking Leonard seemed as useless as an empty gun, Billy felt the beginning nudge of betrayal. He hadn't failed to notice the absence of Governor Wallace or any mention of a pardon.

Sam Corbet was standing by the door. As Billy was led past, Corbet whispered, "You got it in, Kid, that's what counts."

Billy had his doubts, but he decided to stay in the game awhile, trusting his instincts to know when the last card had fallen against him.

Toward the end of the court session, the clerk called the case of the Territory of New Mexico versus John Middleton, Hendry Brown, Frederick Waite, and William Bonney, alias Kid, on the charge of murdering William Brady and George Hindman. Billy was the only defendant to appear. Unrepresented by counsel, he pleaded not guilty, then waited for the announcement of his pardon. Knowing the governor had returned to Santa Fe, Billy assumed the duty had been relegated to Leonard.

Finally the judge read a declaration of the governor's intention to pardon William H. Bonney for all crimes committed heretofore.

Rynerson jerked to his feet as if shocked with outrage. "I refuse to recognize such a pardon! It would be a travesty of our entire proceedings to allow this vicious and reprehensible killer to go free. I petition the court to change the venue of his trial to Mesilla for the next term of court."

"So ordered," Bristol pronounced. "Return the prisoner to confinement."

As he was led shackled from the courtroom, Billy looked at Ira Leonard. The attorney nodded, signaling he would arrange a visit. When Leonard came, he assured Billy that the district attorney had no power to override the governor's pardon, explaining that Billy was being held merely to testify in the court of inquiry against Dudley. Even if Billy's case proceeded to trial in Mesilla and he was convicted, still the governor's pardon would prevail. Leonard advised Billy to be patient, saying his enemies wanted him to bolt so they could hunt him as an outlaw again. Only in the pardon lay freedom. Billy listened, and he waited. But his hope was diminishing.

Tom O'Folliard was no longer allowed to stay at Patrón's. The only indictment against him had been for stealing horses from the Fritz ranch, for which he pleaded the amnesty. Sleeping in Tunstall's empty store, he still spent most of his days with Billy. They were rarely alone. A constant string of visitors came to call at the commodious jail, and the days passed pleasantly for Billy.

The long, lonely nights were more difficult. He spent hours watching the stars move across the patches of sky visible through the tree outside his window. Longing to be on a fast horse riding under those stars again, he craved to be away from courtrooms and badges and men telling him what to do.

Finally, toward the end of May, Billy was called to testify before the military court of inquiry. Under heavy guard and again shackled, he was escorted into the same courtroom. Mrs. Mac, sitting in the audience, looked ill. Behind the defense table sat Colonel Dudley, sneering at him with apparent hatred.

The prosecutor was named Humphries. He began by asking Billy to tell everything he knew of the actions of the troops on the 19th of July last. Billy said he'd seen the troops come into town accompanied by Peppin's posse, that the army had pointed a cannon at McSween's house, soldiers had fired at the house, and that three soldiers near Tunstall's store had fired at him while he was making his escape.

Dudley was given the floor to cross-examine. "What were you and the others with you," the colonel asked, "doing in McSween's house that day?"

"We came there with Mac."

"Weren't you engaged in resisting the sheriff at the time you were in the house?"

"Objection," Humphries said, half-standing behind his table. "You're asking the witness to incriminate himself."

"Sustained," Colonel Pennypacker, president of the court of inquiry, answered.

Dudley frowned. "Were you not, and were not the parties with you in the McSween house on the nineteenth day of July last, engaged in firing at the sheriff's posse?"

"Colonel Dudley," Pennypacker said with strained patience. "It's outside the bounds of proper cross-examination to ask the witness to incriminate himself. Please rephrase your question."

Dudley tugged at one end of his walrus moustache. "Who was killed first that day, Bob Beckwith or the McSween men?"

"Harvey Morris, McSween man, was killed first."

"How many shots did those soldiers fire, those you say fired from the Tunstall building?"

"I seen 'em fire one volley."

"What did they fire at?"

"Me."

"Were other McSween men with you at the time?"

"Jus' a short way behind."

"Were you looking back at them?"

"No, I wasn't."

"How then do you know they were within range of the volley?"

" 'Cause there was a high fence behind and a good many guns to keep 'em there. I could hear the guns speak."

"Did you know any of the soldiers that you say fired at you?"

"No, I'm not acquainted with 'em."

"How many soldiers were with Peppin when he passed the McSween house each time that day, according to you?"

"Three."

"How many soldiers fired at you?"

"Three."

"The soldiers appeared to go in companies of threes that day, did they not?" he mocked.

Billy smiled. "All I ever seen was three in a crowd."

Dudley stared at him a long moment, then turned away. "I'm finished with the witness."

"The witness is excused," Pennypacker said.

Billy shrugged at Mrs. Mac on his way out, not sure his testimony had accomplished much. Back in his room, however, he had more to ponder than Mrs. Mac's vendetta as he waited in confinement for the pardon to be real.

Late one night, Juan Patrón paid him a visit. A politician by trade, Patrón had decided the best approach was a pretense of friendship. He knocked softly, then opened the door, calling, "Kid, you awake?"

"Come on in, Juan," he answered, desperately, it seemed to Patrón. Only one candle burned in the center of the table, barely illuminating the outlaw sitting fully clothed on his bed, the window open to the warm June night.

Patrón moved a chair over to sit near the bed. "I've just intercepted Tulles," he said softly. "She won't be coming tonight, or any other night. I tried to explain things before, Kid. My mother is old and her heart is weak. She has suffered greatly since the death of my father, and becomes overwrought when she sees Tulles."

The Kid was listening without apparent resentment, so Patrón continued. "I know my sister sees many men and takes them into her bed. I don't blame the men, except perhaps the first. I lay the responsibility on my sister, knowing she could have married and lived respectably rather than flouting propriety. My mother has forbidden her in this house, and I abide by my mother's wish."

The Kid nodded, then said, "I don't understand, Juan, how you can jus' turn your back on her. You haven't stopped loving her, I can see that."

"Neither have I ceased supporting her financially. I have two other sisters. Shall I encourage them to follow in her footsteps?"

"She seems to enjoy herself most of the time."

"Would you marry her?"

He laughed. "I hadn't considered it."

"No man ever will. That's exactly my point."

The Kid nodded again. "How come you ain't married, Juan? What do you do with all your extra juice?"

"I give my heart and soul to helping my people. It takes much more than I'm able to give."

"I think I can understand what you mean since being in here. This working with the law is like going into a fistfight with your hands tied behind your back."

Patrón made his move. "Do you still have faith in the governor's pardon?"

"Not much."

"If they take you to Mesilla, they'll handpick the jury. There's no doubt you'll be convicted."

"And have only the pardon between me and hanging. I've thought it through."

"Anytime you're ready, I'll give you a horse and a Winchester. Then let's see if they catch you."

"I'm ready now."

Patrón smiled with victory. "*Andale.* I'll bring the horse around back and return for you in five minutes."

The Kid caught him at the door. "Get word to Tom," he whispered. "And make sure I get plenty of ammo."

"Don't worry," Patrón said.

"And Juan," the Kid said, "pick a horse that can run."

41

Late in August, Pat Garrett was ambling through the moonlit prairie on his way home from visiting Captain Joseph Lea on his ranch near Roswell. Filling the vacuum of leadership left by Chisum's departure, Lea had spent the evening expounding on his visions of the future, which included Garrett as a cornerstone of law and order.

Pat had never considered being a lawman, but he had contemplated being rich. He knew one way to do it was attach himself to the coattails of the wealthy and catch what they dropped. Having kept his nose clean since Pete Maxwell fired him for rustling, Garrett guessed he could wear a badge if it paid more than tending bar for Beaver Smith.

As his ride brought him closer to Fort Sumner, Garrett's thoughts turned to his wife. When he'd married Juanita Gutierrez two years before, his refusal to undergo the hypocrisy of a church ceremony had broken the heart of his Catholic wife. So said the old women of the village, who whispered that Juanita died of shame because she hadn't been married in the eyes of God.

Garrett knew why she died—he'd sat beside her through the hours of her miscarriage—but he didn't argue with the old women. He buried his wife according to the rites of the Catholic Church and she lay in peace, everyone agreed. After that, he contented himself with whores and didn't think of a family much. But since he'd passed thirty, he had to admit it was time if he was going to do it.

The country he rode through was peaceful, the moonlight illuminating the trail that cut across the prairie. When Garrett saw two horses under a cottonwood tree, he reined up, then edged closer, curious. The nearest house was Samaniego's, and Pat had seen Miguel in Roswell just before leaving. When he caught a flash of moonlight off gunmetal, he stopped his horse short.

"Evening, Pat," came a soft Texas drawl as a lanky youth emerged from the shadows.

Recognizing Tom O'Folliard, Garrett looked around. "Where's Billy?"

Tom jerked his head at the Samaniego house.

Garrett smiled. "You always hold his horse when he goes visiting?"

"Sometimes he likes to get away fast."

"I can understand that, if he makes a habit of visiting other men's wives." He studied the boy before him, then asked playfully, "What happens if he stays the night?"

"I'm used to sleeping on the ground," Tom replied. "Last time I had a bed was in jail."

Garrett laughed. "Tell Billy I'm looking forward to playing some poker," he said, reining his horse toward town.

Tom returned to his blanket in the dark shadow beneath the cottonwood. Despite Garrett's laughter, Tom felt content being whatever the Kid wanted him to be, and he didn't care how many people thought him a fool because of it. He didn't even want women. He felt uncomfortable in their company and only laid them when the Kid bought him one. Tom had felt the Kid's disdain, but he figured he knew Billy better than anyone, knew the sometimes mournful moods behind his always cheerful smile, his restlessness which kept them moving as if in search of a home. It was all balanced by those rare moments of recognition. Like when they had to go into that hole of a jail in Lincoln, and it was taking all of Billy's stamina to force his boots down that ladder. He'd turned and said, "Come on, Tom," and Tom would have followed him into the bowels of hell.

To be the Kid's partner meant a lot in the world they lived in. It meant Tom was adept with a gun, an excellent horseman, capable of living off the land, and afraid of no one. Tom had a reputation because he rode with the Kid. People moved around him with more respect than if he'd just been Tom O'Folliard from Texas. Yet that's who he was, a boy with a personality as lanky as his body, a babyface trying hard to please, an innocence that blinded him to the danger of his companion. Now he enjoyed the Kid's popularity; their enemies were in the distant mountains, and life was easy.

The beginning of change was heralded by a pig attack. After nipping at a bottle most of the afternoon, Pat Garrett was attempting to herd the Gutierrez pigs into their pen when he slipped on some shit and careened full height into the sows, who took offense. His legs and arms were badly bitten before he managed to achieve the safety of a fence pole.

The Gutierrezes had come running, corralled the disgruntled beasts, and helped Juan Largo into their home where they insisted he remain for his convalescence. He was given a cot on the summer porch, with a box at one end of the bed to accommodate his stretch, and showered with the attentions of the Gutierrez daughters. Once a part of their family, he had drifted away since the death of his wife, and he discovered he enjoyed being back among them. He had only one complaint about his period of recuperation: the absence of whiskey and cigars.

The Kid rescued him, arriving one afternoon with a paper-wrapped package tied with string. "Brought you a present, Pat," he said with a wink.

Garrett tore off the paper to get at the bottle of rye and box of cigars. Just then the screen door opened and a young woman came out. He slid the whiskey under his pillow and looked up with a grin. "Come see what the Kid brought me, Apolinaria," he said, displaying the cigars.

"Smelly things," she said. "Hello, Kid."

She was a pretty girl, with skin as smooth as whipped cocoa and shiny black hair piled high on her head. Even next to Billy she was tiny. Next to Garrett she looked like a fairy.

"Bet you got your hands full taking care of Pat," Billy said.

"He's not so bad once you learn his growl has no teeth." She smiled fondly at her patient. "I thought you might like a shave before dinner."

Garrett ran his hand over the thick stubble on his face. "Guess I should." He looked at her craftily. "Will you let us smoke our cigars?"

"I suppose I can stand it."

"Okay, you can shave me," he said, then watched her go back inside for the accoutrements. He grinned at Billy. "She takes such good care of me, I may have to marry her."

"No fooling?" Billy laughed. "Guess that does call for a cigar."

They were puffing contentedly when Apolinaria returned. She set everything down, then opened the porch door to let the smoke escape on the breeze. The wind lifted her skirt, revealing a petticoat as blinding as sunlight. She batted it down, and blushed as she walked back to the men. Waiting with mock impatience for Pat to sit up, she lifted a towel from the water and wrapped his face, then stropped the razor. When she unwound the towel, Pat winked at Billy and he laughed, making Apolinaria look at him. "Have you never been shaved by a woman, Kid?" she asked, lathering Pat's face.

"I ain't got much need to shave often," he said.

Garrett chuckled and Apolinaria jerked the razor away. "Ay! hold still," she warned.

"You keep smoking cigars, Kid," he said, "you'll be as bristly as me when you get as old."

"You ain't old, Pat. Tell him, Apolinaria. He's always saying he's old."

She shrugged, continuing with her work. Watching the pretty girl so earnest in her task, the man pretending to submit yet obviously loving her attentions, Billy felt melancholy all of a sudden. "See you later," he said, starting for the door.

"Come back tonight and we'll play some poker," Garrett called after him.

"Ay!" Apolinaria protested. "Do you want me to cut you?"

Billy walked up the road following the river. He'd resisted seeing

Paulita since returning from Lincoln, but Apolinaria made him yearn to spend time with a lady. Approaching the back door of the Maxwell house, he called to Deluvina working in the kitchen.

Her face lit with joy as she hurried to open the door. "Billy! It's been too long since I've seen you. Are you hungry? Would you like some pie and a glass of buttermilk?"

He laughed. "How you been, Deluvina?"

"I've been good. No more tantrums." She smiled mischievously. "For a while, anyway."

Paulita came into the room. She stopped, composing her face. "Billy, how nice to see you," she murmured.

"Evening, Paulita," he said with an easy smile. "I thought maybe you'd like to go for a walk, with me, I mean."

Deluvina looked back and forth between them. Recognizing that a romance was blooming between her mistress and the Kid, she turned away and busied herself at the counter.

"I'd like that very much," Paulita said. "Tell Mother I won't be late, will you, Deluvina?"

"*Sí, niña.*" As she watched Billy open the door for Paulita, Deluvina felt pleased.

Walking within earshot of the people under the portals, Billy and Paulita conversed in the light chatter of renewed acquaintance. Finally they came to the end of the plaza and were free of an audience. "So how have you been, Billy?" Paulita asked earnestly.

"I been doing okay. You're prettier'n ever, your life must be suiting you."

She laughed, pleased with the compliment. "Oh, we have our *bailes* and suppers, but really, nothing ever happens in Sumner."

He took hold of her elbow and continued her walking. "What do you want to happen?"

"I'm sixteen now," she said. "My sister married at sixteen. It was against my father's wishes but he forgave her before he died. As he should have, since my mother was only nine when he married her, though it wasn't consummated for seven years."

He was surprised she knew that word. "What was the holdup?"

"You mean besides the fact that she was only nine?" she teased. "My father went on Frémont's expedition to California in between."

"Your father was an important man, wasn't he."

"He was important to me. I still miss him."

"I think of my mother pretty often, too."

"Did she die?"

"Yeah."

"And your father?"

He hesitated, then said, "I never knew him. They weren't married, my parents."

"That must be hard," she murmured.

He shrugged. "Don't miss what you never knew."

They were walking along the edge of the corral now. Paulita stopped and looked in at the horses. "Is one of these yours?"

"I keep mine inside. That way I don't have to catch it when I'm ready to go."

She nodded. "What happened in Lincoln? Do you mind that I ask?"

"No, I don't mind." He lifted a strand of her hair to inhale her scent. "What happened was," he said, letting loose of the curl and watching it bounce against her breast, "I played a waiting game with myself and finally got tired of it and walked out."

"I heard you were pardoned by the governor," she said, wishing he'd touch her again.

"The gov'nor said so." He took her elbow and guided her on. "But the district attorney refused to recognize the pardon and bound me over for trial anyway."

"Seems to me, if the governor says you're pardoned then it's true."

"It seemed that way to me, too." He laughed. "But it didn't feel that way standing in court wearing shackles."

"Can the sheriff really arrest you?"

"He can try."

They turned west along a row of quarters lined with curious eyes. Too late Billy saw light reflect off the gold watch chain, then Abrana stepped from the shadows into their path.

Stopping in surprise, Paulita said, "Good evening, Abrana."

"*Buenas tardes,* Señorita Maxwell," she answered, dropping her gaze. Then she raised her eyes to Billy.

"Evening, Miss García," he said with a smile.

She retreated into the shadows, her dark eyes flashing with invitation.

Billy and Paulita walked on in silence, then she said, "Abrana makes beautiful lace."

"Oh yeah? I didn't know that."

As they neared the corner, Charlie Bowdre stepped out of a lighted doorway and laughed with pleasure. "Goddamn, Kid, it's good to see you!" Coming forward to shake hands, he recognized Paulita and said with chagrin, "Sorry, Miss Maxwell, I thought you were one of the companions this galoot usually wastes time with." He smiled at the Kid. "Can you come in for a minute? I'd like you to meet my wife."

"When did you get married, Charlie?" he asked in surprise.

"Awhile back. I've been keeping her on the sly. Come on in and meet her."

A small, well-curved woman, Manuelita was shy in front of the man she'd heard so much about as well as the sister of the big *patrón*. When she offered them coffee and Paulita rose to help, the men walked back onto the portal. Hunkering in the shadows, they stared across the dark road at the empty dance hall.

"Ain't that something about Dolan?" Charlie asked.

"What's that?"

"Bristol dismissed all charges against him."

"All of 'em? Killing Tunstall and Chapman and everything that happened when Mac died?"

"That's what I heard. Insufficient evidence or some bullshit."

Billy was quiet a moment, then laughed. "Ol' Jimmie's sure a weasel, ain't he?"

"That's one word," Charlie said. "The same thing happened with Dudley. Cleared of all charges and sent to another fort back East."

"No shit," Billy said.

"Only the indictments for the Regulators are left on the books."

"Yeah, we're outlawed for sure."

"It ain't fair jus' 'cause we got indicted before the amnesty."

Billy smiled. "Nobody's got the balls to arrest us."

"I hope you're right 'cause I sure ain't got money to pay any lawyer."

"I thought you was working for Yerby?"

"Yeah, but being a drover don't pay a man enough to live decent."

"If Chisum had anted up his due, we would've come out of the war with a stake."

"Guess that's right," Charlie said.

"Would you be int'rested in rustling some of his cows?"

"Might."

Manuelita called from inside the house, "Charlie, is ready."

"I'll let you know when," Billy said.

They walked back inside and tried to be sociable, minding their language in the presence of a lady. They were all relieved when Paulita announced she was sorry to leave so soon but had promised not to be late.

As they cut through the yard of the dance hall, Billy said he'd like to dance with her sometime. She replied she would anticipate the honor with pleasure, making him chuckle at the precision of her manners. He held her hand as they walked through the flower garden to the house, then followed the wraparound veranda to the front where she led him across to the swing. They sat at opposite ends, not touching in the darkness.

"I missed you, Billy," she said.

"Did you? That surprises me."

"Why?"

"Rich girl like you are, why waste time thinking about me?"

"I find it a very pleasant pastime." When he didn't reply, she said, "I've thought about you kissing me quite often."

"You want me to kiss you, Paulita?"

"Very much," she said, touching his arm.

He leaned close and gave her a gentle, chaste kiss.

"That isn't the way I imagined it," she teased.

Finding her invitation impossible to resist, he pulled her tight and kissed her properly. But he'd barely begun when a lamp in the room behind them suddenly flooded the swing with light. He broke away, springing to his feet and stepping into the shadows.

She sat up, watching him settle on the railing of the porch.

A door opened and Pete Maxwell stepped out in his shirtsleeves. He greeted Paulita, then saw Billy. "Oh hello, Kid, I thought I heard voices."

"You must be exhausted after your long ride from Seven Rivers," Paulita said, wanting to hurry her brother away.

"Yes, it was a bitter journey." He looked back at Billy. "I hate to be the one to tell you, Kid, but John Jones was killed the day before yesterday."

Billy jerked to his feet and took a step backward. "By who?"

"Bob Olinger. A dispute over cattle, what else? I'm sorry, I know you were friends. Don't stay out late, Paulita," he said, returning toward his room.

"I gotta go," Billy mumbled, descending the steps and disappearing in the darkness along the road.

Paulita started to follow him, but her brother called her back. "He's not a lapdog you can cuddle, Paulita. He lives wild and feels hurt. Leave him alone." Trusting her to obey him, he went inside and closed the door.

Paulita ran after Billy, catching up beside the orchard. He turned in surprise at the sound of her footsteps, then pulled her into the deeper darkness beneath the trees.

"Oh, Billy," she said, holding him close. "I'm so sorry about your friend."

He held her a moment, then broke away. "You shouldn't be here."

"Sit with me awhile," she said, dropping onto the grass.

He hesitated, then sat down beside her.

"I want to be here with you," she said. "Is that wrong?"

"Most folks would say so."

"Why?"

"You know why, Paulita. Damn, if you ain't a little tease. You act like this with other men, you won't be a lady long."

"You're the only man I act like this with."

"You shouldn't do it. I know a girl was loose with men and now can't go home 'cause of it. Her mother faints if she runs into her somewhere." He softened his voice. "I wouldn't want that to happen to you."

Paulita laughed. "I'll bet she's Mexican."

"So?"

"My mother's French. She would never disown me for falling in love."

He had a keen desire to be alone on the prairie where he could shoot the bejesus out of something for a while. "I better walk you home," he said.

"Kiss me first," she whispered, sliding closer.

"God, Paulita." He laid her down in the grass as he kissed her, having to work at keeping his hands still. Finally he sat up and looked at her in the patch of moonlight beneath him.

"Promise me something, Billy. Don't go to Seven Rivers looking for the man who killed your friend."

He was surprised to think she might really care for him. "John's mother will be wanting to see me," he said.

"Then go later, when the hurt isn't so fresh. Stay here with me for a while."

Thinking he'd never received such a tempting invitation, he stood up and held a hand down to help her. "I better walk you home," he said again.

When she pressed herself close, he kept her at a proper distance by holding her elbow as they returned to her house. He left her at the gate, feeling he'd managed her well.

Finding Tom in Beaver Smith's saloon, Billy met his eyes from the door and told him without words they were leaving. They rode southeast to the Portales and camped by a spring. Long after Tom was asleep, Billy sat up alone, listening to the coyotes howl in the wilderness.

The Kid stayed clear of Sumner so long his friends thought he'd left that part of the country, and more than a few suspected he'd ridden down to Seven Rivers to avenge the death of John Jones. But from what Billy was able to learn, the fight had been fair. John had just met with bad luck. Billy was willing to leave it at that unless he chanced to cause Olinger some bad luck of his own. When the Kid finally returned to Sumner, he heard news that inspired retribution of another sort.

The Chisums were driving a herd north just across the Texas line. After picking up the gossip in Beaver Smith's saloon, Billy got word to Charlie Bowdre. One night early in October, he and Tom walked over to Bowdre's house. Charlie wasn't home yet so Billy and Tom waited on the portal. After a few minutes, they saw Bowdre and Doc Scurlock and the new man, Pickett, coming across the plaza. Billy assessed Pickett and decided he looked all right. After all, they were just taking a few cows.

On the flat plains east of the Portales, they found Chisum's herd. They waited out of sight until the night crew rode in for replacements, then Billy crept up on the remuda. At the same moment that he ran off the horses, his friends stampeded the cattle. Left on foot, there was nothing the drovers could do but shoot after shadows in the dark.

It had been easy to sneak up on the remuda because Chisum never kept his horses between the chuckwagon and herd as wiser trail bosses did. The remuda had been held inside a rope corral off by itself, so it was child's play for Billy to mosey in among them, hanging off the side of his horse Comanche-style. He'd cut the rope and fired his pistol, laughing as he looked back at the startled drovers lurching from their blankets. Controlling the herd of cattle, however, was something else.

The night was so black Billy couldn't see his mare beneath him. Galloping within the stampeding herd, he remembered the many prairie dog towns and numerous arroyos snaking through the country, knowing he wouldn't suspect they were in one until he felt his mare fall beneath him. Hurtling through the dark, he rode with a wild flow of energy, powerless to affect his fate.

Billy lived with a taut sense of command. He knew how to bend the odds of any game to his advantage. But what was happening now made him realize life was always a stampede, driven by whim, untamed by any one man's desire. And the truth was, no matter what Billy thought of what was happening, he didn't know the first thing about calling it quits.

Tom O'Folliard did. He'd worked as a ranch hand and learned a thing or two about controlling cattle. Recognizing that this herd was trail broke, he spurred his horse to ride point and gradually shifted them to the right. No herd ever turned left, it was an unwritten law of nature, so Tom eased the lead steers around to the right until they were coming up against the herd's tail, and gradually they all swirled into a spiral of dissipating energy.

By the time the sun broke over the distant ridge of mountains, Tom was circling back to find Billy. They laughed at each other in the early light of dawn, sitting their horses and admiring the hundred head of prime beef they'd acquired.

They drove them across the New Mexico line to just north of Sumner, where they grazed them on open range. Leaving the others to watch the cattle, Billy rode into town. In Beaver Smith's Saloon, he announced he had a herd to sell, if anyone was interested.

Two buyers from Colorado asked if he represented Chisum's outfit. Tongue-in-cheek, Billy said he guessed he did. When they saw the herd wearing Chisum's brand, they paid Billy eighteen hundred dollars cash.

Billy and his friends rode back to their old camp alongside the Pecos, where Billy sat on his favorite boulder as he divided the money. They kept laughing, taking great delight in anticipating Chisum's wrath, until the money was split and Scurlock grew solemn.

"I'm pulling out, Kid," he said. "Moving my family to Kansas. Chisum ain't gonna take this laying down and, joke all you want, I don't aim to catch the hell he's gonna raise."

Billy fanned the money in his hand. "You got a family, Doc," he said after a moment. "I can understand you gotta take care of 'em."

"Glad you feel that way," Scurlock said, standing up and shaking Billy's hand. "If you see me again, I'll be using a dif'rent name, so I'd appreciate it, Kid, if you don't let on that you know me. The law's coming down hard, and I want to make it to be a grandfather before I die."

Billy watched him walk away, thinking of Scurlock's farm abandoned on the Hondo. Bowdre's was the same. The Coes were still up north, too afraid to return. The Regulators had lost more than the war, they'd lost their land and, being outlawed, any chance for a legal livelihood in Lincoln County. It rankled inside Billy when he let himself think about it.

A few mornings later, Billy was playing casino with Garrett in Beaver Smith's when Maxwell walked in. Garrett stood up and offered his services, but Pete frowned and said he'd come to see Mr. Bonney. Billy chuckled at the animosity between them as he followed Pete outside.

"Jim Chisum's in town," Maxwell explained. "He lost a herd to rustlers but found the cattle pastured north of here. The men who bought them have already gone back to Colorado, leaving only hired drovers to trail them to Trinidad. The foreman has a bill of sale but Chisum is insisting he has right of replevin. The Chisums do what they want, regardless. I don't much care, as long as they don't take any of mine along. What I'd like you to do is ride up there, make sure none of my cattle have wandered into their herd, and cut them out if they have. My brand is the XIX. Can you do that?"

Billy grinned. "I'll go right now."

"Thanks," Pete said. "Come to the house for supper when you get back."

Smiling at his chance to bedevil Chisum, Billy returned to the saloon and called Tom. Garrett asked what was up, but Billy shook his head with a grin. All the way out to the herd, he couldn't stop laughing at his luck. When they saw Chisum and his trail boss on a knoll overlooking the cattle, Billy rode right up and grinned a howdy-do.

Abiding by family tradition, Jim Chisum wore no handgun. He carried a carbine in his saddle scabbard but knew he didn't have a chance in hell of getting it out to use against the Kid. "You goddamned sonofabitch!" Chisum snarled. "You dare come riding up here?"

Billy smiled. "Maxwell sent me to check over your herd for any of his that maybe strayed in."

"Them's all Chisum cattle down there. You should know that well enough."

Billy shrugged. "I aim to check over your herd for Pete's strays. Any objections?"

"Go ahead and look," Chisum muttered.

Billy nodded at Tom, who turned his horse into the herd and started cutting out steers. The three men on the knoll watched for a while, then the foreman said, "If he ever wants a job as a cowboy, you have him look me up."

"I'll be sure and tell Tom you said that," Billy answered. Then he looked at Chisum. "I got a message for your brother John. Tell him I collected the debt he owed with int'erest, like I said I would."

Chisum stared in an angry silence until Tom had finished cutting out two dozen steers. "I want to look at those animals," Chisum said, wheeling his horse and galloping down the hill.

Billy gestured for the foreman to precede him, then followed and grinned at Tom, who sat on his horse wiping sweat from his face with a dirty handkerchief.

"These brands are all smudged," Chisum scoffed. "You can't tell me that's the XIX on their hides."

"Looks like it to me," Billy said. "Don't it to you, Tom?"

"I cut 'em out," he answered, stuffing his kerchief into his pocket, then resting his hand on his thigh near his gun.

"You won't get away with this, Kid!" Chisum threatened. "You're stealing these cattle after you already stole 'em once!"

"You can take 'em if you want," Billy said with a smile, "but you'll take some lead with 'em."

"Move the herd out. Now!" Chisum told his foreman. Then he glared back at Billy. "Your freewheeling days are growing short, Kid."

Billy laughed. "Jus' tell your brother we're even."

"Not by a whisper of a prayer," Chisum yelled, spurring his horse away.

When Jim Chisum returned to his brother's ranch, he found him having dinner with Captain Lea and Ash Upson, who had accompanied Lea on this trip to the Panhandle. The three men looked up when Jim came in, dirty and travel worn.

He told them what happened. "The Kid stole the whole damn herd. Stampeded our remuda first so we couldn't go after him. By the time I got to Sumner, he'd already sold 'em to the buyers from Colorado and pocketed the eighteen hundred dollars!"

"Are you sure it was Billy?" John Chisum asked.

"We saw him plain when he was running off the horses. He was laughing, the sonofabitch! Then when we'd replevined the herd and were just about to head home, he came riding up and said Pete Maxwell sent him to check for strays. He cut out two dozen prime steers. Said we could take 'em but we'd take some lead with us if we tried. The goddamned punk! He's riding too high to let him get away with this."

"Did he make off with the remuda, too?"

"Nah, we collected the horses running loose on the prairie. Took us a full day to do it!"

"Go get some rest," John Chisum said with sympathy. "We'll talk again in the morning." He watched him leave, then looked at Lea. "The Kid's getting pretty bold."

"If Jim saw him, I guess he did it," Lea said. "But he'd have to be a dozen men to do all the things people say he does."

"True. But having it bandied about gives other men the notion they can get away with it too. He's gotta be stopped."

"Won't be easy. You have someone in mind?"

"I think I do."

"Is he good enough?"

Chisum laughed. "No, but he's stupid enough to try and he might get lucky."

"Who is he?"

"Fellow here at the ranch, name of Joe Grant."

Never one to mind his tongue anyway, Ash Upson was feeling his whiskey. "The war won't be over," he predicted, "till Billy's dead."

42

The winter wind on the Great Plains sweeps off the ice on the Canadian Rockies and blows in gales all the way into the bowels of Texas, freezing everything in between. Along the Pecos, the winter of 1879 was bitterly cold. In Fort Sumner, the plaza was crisscrossed with frozen wagon ruts, a corrugated expanse of badlands treacherous for foot or hoof. Few people braved the cold. Those who did hurried about their business, escaping from the wind in the shortest possible time.

Beaver Smith's had become home for the wandering transients who habitually slept outdoors. The long, narrow saloon had been filled around the clock by the same half-dozen hardcases when the Kid and O'Folliard walked in on Christmas Day. They had come back from Vegas on some sentimental notion to be in Sumner for Christmas. At the time it had seemed like a grand idea. Now, in the middle of a blizzard, it looked like a dumb one.

Inside the saloon were five men Billy knew and one he'd never seen, all rowdy with cabin fever. He and Tom bellied up to the bar and ordered whiskey, then turned around to survey their company. The men were stupid after drinking for days, surly at being trapped inside by the weather. Billy turned back around and muttered to Tom, "Drink up, *amigo.* I don't care for the mood in here."

Tom sighed and sipped at his whiskey, knowing he was to drink Billy's, too, and not wanting to guzzle the ninety-proof liquor.

Billy turned around again and asked the room at large, "Anyone want to play some poker?"

"We're broke, Kid," Hank Wickham said. He was a drifter pushing thirty, a perennial ne'er-do-well. "We've been in here for three god-damned days and drunk up all our money. Don't even have enough to buy another drink."

"You want a drink, I'll buy you one," Billy said. "Any or all of you." He cast his gaze around the others, then looked at the stranger. "How about it, pard? Can I buy you a drink?"

The man was thick and dark, with a stringy beard nearly covering his face. He wore his pants tucked into a pair of fancy boots, and from his holster gleamed the ivory handle of a Colt's .45, a long pistol reaching halfway to his knee. A smile of feigned friendliness spread across his face as he came forward. Letting the Kid pour him a drink, the stranger downed it in one gulp.

Billy laughed and pushed the bottle toward him, then walked away.

At the end of the room he looked back at the barflies clustered around the fresh whiskey, and he wanted to leave. Like the others, however, he had nowhere to go. Eventually he would beg a bed for the night, but it wasn't yet dusk. He was too dirty to show up at the Maxwell house on Christmas Day, and Abrana had put her foot down about Tom sleeping on her floor, so Billy didn't go there when he needed a bed for the night.

Wondering why they hadn't stayed in the hotel in Vegas a few more days, Billy sat down in a corner and pulled his hat over his eyes, keeping one ear cocked to the carousers at the bar.

He woke up surprised that he'd managed to sleep. As he looked at Tom, his friend nodded, telling him he hadn't been defenseless. Billy stood up and stretched, then sauntered over to lean across the bar and holler for Beaver Smith.

"He's gone home," Tom said. "Got sick of the smell, is what he told me."

Billy laughed and walked into the kitchen. He found a pot of coffee boiled thick, poured half a cupful and filled it with cream, then carried it back to the bar where he stood next to Tom and surveyed the drunks.

They were all sodden except the stranger. He had an aggressive energy about him that made Billy think the stranger had a bone to pick with someone in the room. The man saw him watching and came over.

"Name's Joe Grant," he said, his words slurred. "I'm from Texas."

"Good for you, Joe." Billy smiled, looking down at the man's fancy pistol. "That's a fine gun you have. Would you let me take a look at it?"

Grant's face flushed with pride. He slid the forty-five out, twirled it on his finger a few times, then handed it over with a flourish.

Billy admired the engraving along the barrel and the antelope heads carved into the ivory grip. He opened the cylinder, saw half the chambers were empty, and spun it so the next three times the gun fired the hammer would fall on nothing. Then he handed the gun back, saying, "That's a beauty."

"Hey, you bought me a drink," Grant said. "Let me buy you one."

"I'm all right," Billy said.

Grant walked behind the bar. "What'cha want? We got our pick here."

"I'm okay with coffee for now."

"Aw, there must be something," Grant muttered, using his pistol to knock a bottle to the floor.

As the other men retreated to the far end of the room, Billy and Tom exchanged wry smiles of amusement.

Grant knocked more bottles over, smashing one where it stood on the shelf. He turned to Billy and growled, "I bet I kill a man today before you do."

Billy laughed. "What do you want to kill anybody for? Have another drink."

Grant faced the bottles, knocking them down until glass showered on the floor, liquor dripping like the sound of someone puking.

Not liking Grant so close to the scattergun under the counter, Billy walked behind the bar. "Let me help you break up housekeeping," he said, drawing his own gun and knocking a bottle off the shelf.

Wheeling on O'Folliard, Grant announced, "I'm gonna kill Billy the Kid."

"You got the wrong pig by the ear, Joe," Billy said.

Grant whirled pulling the trigger, but only a metallic click broke the silence. He uselessly pulled the trigger again, his face sick.

The explosion of Billy's gun reverberated in the bones of his hand as the barrel gasped a wisp of smoke. The bullet knocked Grant backward and splattered his brains all over Beaver Smith's clean glassware. Billy walked past the corpse with disgust. "I've been outta the gate too often to let a fool of his caliber overhaul my baggage."

Hank Wickham called, "You best be careful, Kid. He might not be dead."

"He's dead," Billy said, opening the door for Tom and following him into the bitter cold.

The stars were just coming out as they walked back to the stable and into the stall of Billy's mare. They both stood close, warming themselves with her heat.

Billy finally said, "Goddamned stupid bounty hunter. Did you see his boots? And that flashy gun? Somebody give 'em to him. Prob'ly promised him a pony when he finished the job."

"Dolan?" Tom asked.

Billy shook his head. "I ain't bothering him. Must be Chisum."

Tom shivered. "What're we gonna do now, Billy?"

"We'll go to Yerby's," he said, deciding as he spoke. "Charlie'll be there."

"It's twenty fucking miles," Tom complained, moving to his own horse. "I hope it don't snow 'fore we get there."

"You got a better idea?"

Tom tossed his saddle onto his horse's back. "No, 'cause you jus' killed a man."

"What would you've done?"

"The same," he admitted, reaching under his horse's belly for the cinch. "I'm jus' saying that's why we can't stay in Sumner tonight, that's all."

Billy set about saddling his mare, stewing with anger. He knew Joe Grant had been sent to kill him, and also that there was only one way to deal with that situation. Anyone who blamed him had never been stalked by death and wasn't qualified to judge. But still, he knew he would be judged. People would say death followed Billy Bonney and it was better not to share his company.

He and Tom led their horses into the cold night. Billy swung on and reached across to punch Tom in the arm. "What the hell, *amigo.* We're alive, ain't we?"

"Yeah," Tom answered with a smile, following him into the hard wind threatening a fresh blizzard. Tom's only consolation was that the new snow would cover their tracks, if anyone chose to pursue them.

No one did. In the month of December 1879, nine men met violent deaths in San Miguel County. Joe Grant was just one insignificant more. No indictment was ever issued for the killing, no coroner's jury ever convened. Joe Grant was buried without ceremony and would have passed from history, except for the fame of the man who had killed him.

A wedding brought the Kid back to Sumner. Pat Garrett married Apolinaria Gutierrez on January 14 in a church ceremony, and the entire town was invited to the fiesta afterward.

In the long single-story adobe home of the family, door after door led to another room of food and music. As mariachi bands clashed in the closed house, the guests shouted above the happy din and feasted on enchiladas, tamales, and buñuelos dripping with honey.

Champagne had been toasted to the bride and groom, but otherwise no liquor was served except in the dining room, reserved exclusively for the pleasures of men. There they were allowed to drink whiskey and smoke cigars, leaving the windows open on the cold, sunny day as a fire blazed in the hearth. When the Kid and Tom O'Folliard arrived late in the afternoon, Garrett was well on his way to an inebriated wedding night.

"What does this mean, Pat?" Billy asked after congratulating him. "No more all-night poker games?"

"Hell, no," the bridegroom answered. "My wife rules the house, but what I do outside of it is my business."

"Does she know that?" Billy teased.

"Yeah, I'm level with my friends," Garrett said, eyeing him carefully. "And I consider her my best friend. You boys should think about getting hitched."

Tom laughed. "You know any women want to live on a horse?"

Garrett laughed, too. "Heard you have a place near the Portales, Kid. I was up to see it the other day."

"Oh yeah?" he asked, surprised Garrett had been able to find it. "What'd you think?"

"Fine springs. You could run a lot of cattle off those streams."

"I run a few now and then," Billy said with a smile.

Again, Garrett scrutinized him carefully, then said, "Come outside with me a minute."

Billy smiled at Tom, already digging into the platters of food, as he followed Garrett into the patio enclosed by the house. The day was cold, the sun nearly gone, the sky bleeding into the trees. Garrett took a long time lighting his cigar. Billy kept his hands deep in his pockets while he waited.

"I'm moving to Roswell," Garrett finally said.

Billy smiled at him, waiting.

"I aim to establish residence in Lincoln County so I can run for sheriff next year."

Billy laughed to cover the hurt that slashed through his mind like the steel blade of a knife. "Never figured you for a lawman, Pat."

"You figured wrong."

Reading the answer in Garrett's eyes, Billy asked anyway, "Does this mean you're giving me fair warning or something?"

Garrett nodded. "The men backing me asked only one question in the interview: if I could rid them of you."

Billy studied the friend who had suddenly become an enemy. "Seems like we're always taking sides, like in the war."

"Still the same war. Just healing pains throwing off the last poisons."

"And I'm one of 'em?"

"Tell you the truth, Kid, I don't think so. But I'm not being elected to think, just to do what they want. I know of a dozen men who rustle more cattle than you, but nobody sees them. The ranchers think you're a bad example to the young folks growing up, and the church ladies get near hysterical at mention of your name."

"Church ladies," Billy scoffed. "Who cares about them?"

"I thought that way once. When I lost my first wife, the old ladies caught on to the idea that she'd died of shame because we weren't married in the Church. They twisted that knife until I felt so guilty I was begging for mercy, and I learned to let the church ladies have their say. Give them their ceremonies, take a bath when they tell you to, kill an outlaw if that's what they want. It's all part of growing old gracefully."

Billy laughed. "You always was worried about getting old, Pat. I hope you make it."

"Thanks, Kid. I just wanted to let you know what I'm doing, being as you're a major part of it."

"I appreciate your telling me, but you ain't been elected yet."

Garrett laughed. "That's true."

"Let's go back to the party," Billy said, shivering from the cold. "This sure has been a gloomy talk for a wedding. Hope it don't mean Apolinaria ends up a widow before her time."

Garrett put his hand on the doorknob. "You should think about leaving the territory, Billy. It's an old custom, isn't it, to give advice on your wedding day?"

"I appreciate the thought, but I'm freezing out here, Pat. If you don't let me inside, you can deliver my frozen corpse to the church ladies in jus' about another minute."

So they went back inside laughing. Apolinaria was relieved, watching fretfully for their return. She crossed the room to embrace the Kid. "Goodness, you're shivering. It's frightfully cold, isn't it? Who would ever think to get married in winter?"

"Makes it nice to snuggle in bed." Billy smiled, leaning to kiss her cheek. "I get to do that, don't I? Kiss the bride?"

She blushed and whispered, "Paulita's in the parlor. She's been asking about you."

"Oh yeah? Then I'll jus' go say hello." He caught Tom's eye, then looked back at Garrett. *"Buena suerte,"* Billy said.

The house was crowded, the air dense. He wanted to get away from the faces rejoicing at Garrett's good fortune, out of the house of the woman who would bear his children, the noise of relatives and friends celebrating while Billy felt betrayed. He found Paulita talking with another woman. "Can I walk you home?"

"I'll get my cloak," she said, with no more than a murmured apology to the woman she was leaving.

Billy followed her to the front door. As soon as she reached for her cloak, he beat her to it and settled it on her shoulders. They smiled at each other as they walked out into the cold, dark night with a crescent moon rising in the east.

She stretched on her tiptoes to kiss his cheek. "It's been so long since I've seen you, Billy. Where have you been?"

"I've been working," he boasted. "I've got some cattle up by the Portales and I've been branding 'em and turning 'em loose on the range."

"That's wonderful! How many do you have?"

He thought of her brother's herd numbering in the thousands, and he laughed. "Every time I need money I sell some, so I ain't got more'n twenty, thirty head right now."

"It's a beginning," she said. "Is there a house on your land?"

He opened the gate into her yard, then held it for Tom before letting it go, both of them laughing at her question. "There's a cave," Billy said, guiding her with his hand in the small of her back. "But it ain't much good when it's cold like this."

"Where do you stay?" she asked, pausing at the bottom of the kitchen steps.

"Around. I'm glad I got to see you even for such a short time."

"Why don't you come in? Everyone will still be at the wedding except Pete, who rode out to the north range. He doesn't like Pat Garrett, you know."

"I picked up on that. We'd love to come in, wouldn't we, Tom?"

Not knowing where else they'd go, Tom said, "Guess it'd be all right if we stay in the kitchen."

Paulita laughed as she opened the door, tingling with anticipation. Then she saw her brother taking a pie from the cupboard, and she quickly changed her smile. "Pete! How nice to see you!" She gave Billy a wry grin, then crossed the room to give her brother a hug. "You came home early."

"Yes," he said. "Hello, Kid, Tom. Come on in. How was the wedding?"

"Gloomy," Billy said.

"Wonderful!" Paulita said at the same time.

Pete looked back and forth between them with a smile. "I was just about to have some pie. If you boys don't have to run off, why don't you join me?"

"I ain't hungry," Billy said, taking a chair. "But I'll sit with you awhile."

"You sit, too, Pete," Paulita said. "I'll cut your pie. Tom, would you like some?"

"Yes, ma'am. We were hardly at the wedding long enough to eat."

"Couldn't stomach it, eh?" Pete chuckled. "I never cared for Garrett myself. He's a cold bastard when it comes down to it."

"I know what you mean," Billy said.

"Did you hear they're running him for sheriff of Lincoln County next year?"

"He told me he was gonna run," Billy answered, meeting Tom's eyes. The Texan didn't look happy with the news. "Don't mean he'll get elected," Billy said.

"Odds are he will," Pete said. "Both Dolan and Chisum are backing him."

"Chisum's working with Dolan? Sonofabitch!"

"Lea's in with them, too," Pete said. "Even Catron's putting the votes he owns behind Garrett. Who else have they got? Kimball?"

"He's all right with me," Billy said, in control of his anger again. As Paulita set the plates on the table, he gave her a seductive smile.

Pete didn't see the smile. "Well, this is San Miguel County, Kid," he said around his first mouthful of pie, "and you're welcome anytime you need a place to stay. I can put you up at a dozen different line camps and give you all the fresh horses you need."

"I appreciate that, Pete."

"You're getting railroaded by this combine of *ricos* and I'll help you all I can. But my best advice is to leave the territory, at least for a while. They got it in their minds you're responsible for every crime committed anywhere near the Pecos, and they won't rest till you're stopped. Let them get this stampede of law and order out of their pants and things'll settle back to business-as-usual damn quick."

"Such language," Paulita scolded. "And the idea isn't much better."

"I thought you went to bed," Pete said, looking at her fondly. "Young girls always get so excited at weddings. Look at her blush." He grinned at Billy. "Time I started picking over the Rio Grande ranchers for a husband," he teased.

"Our father tried that with Ginny," Paulita answered. "Look what she did."

"She chose wisely," Pete said, scraping the last crumbs off his plate. "I'm not sure you will."

"Oh, pooh," she replied, gathering the dishes. "Any more pie, gentlemen?"

"No, thanks," Pete said, standing up. "I'm off to bed. Leave the lamp lit for your mother."

"Of course," she said, smiling at Billy as her brother left the room. "Let's go into the parlor, shall we?"

Billy looked at Tom, who shrugged and said, "Guess I will have another piece of pie."

"Help yourself," Paulita said. "There's two more whole ones in the cupboard." She took Billy's hand and led him to sit on the horsehair settee.

"Will you take me out to see your land sometime?" she asked. "I'm pretty good on a horse."

"Sure," he said, trying to relax under the reproachful eyes of her ancestors staring down from their portraits on the walls.

In the silence that followed, she sorted through her mind for a topic. "I bought some lace yesterday from Manuelita Bowdre and Abrana García. They came here together and I overheard Abrana say something about you."

"Oh yeah? What'd she say?"

"She spoke in Spanish, and I'd left the room to get my purse, but I was just right there in the hall. I heard her say that you are *muy hombre* in bed."

Billy laughed. "You must've misunderstood her. Your Spanish ain't that good."

"But I know all the dirty words."

"Hush, Paulita. Look at all these old folks on the wall. Don't you think they can hear you?"

She laughed. "They're just cardboard. I'd burn them if they were mine."

"Ain't they?"

"They're my ancestors, but the portraits will go to Pete's children. He's the only son and will continue the family name."

"Is he really gonna marry you off to a rich rancher?"

"He speaks of it. What do you think? Could such a man make me happy?"

Billy smiled. "Seems he might overpower such a little thing as you."

"He would be rough? Treat me like his cows? Get along little dogie, into that chute, like that?"

"He might," Billy said, leaning to kiss her. She was warm, her arms encircling him eagerly. He moved away from her again.

"Why are you so shy?" she teased.

"I ain't ever been called that before," he said.

"But you are with me."

"I like you too much, maybe."

"Perhaps I would find it better if you liked me in the way you do Abrana."

"She's jus' a whore, Paulita. I use that word 'cause you said you know 'em all already."

"She makes beautiful lace. Maybe your love inspires her."

Paulita looked so pretty half-reclining on the settee, he couldn't resist stealing another kiss. Though he couldn't rightly call it stealing.

43

The Kid campaigned in all the outlying regions of Lincoln County, trying to get the people to vote the way they wanted, not the way the man who held their debts told them to. But the people saw the alliance between Chisum and Dolan as a step toward peace.

They were weary of war, and the main vestige was the outlaws running loose, doing as they pleased. The people wanted law and order. Pat Garrett, promising to deliver it, garnered three hundred twenty votes to Kimball's one hundred seventy-nine. The *ricos* were so anxious to be free of the Kid, they had Kimball swear Garrett in as a deputy until he took the oath as sheriff. With a few handpicked men, he set off on the task he would later call bringing the Kid to justice.

Billy kept moving, living on his gambling skills and supplementing his income by rustling. In the spring, he found twenty-eight head of cattle wandering his land near the Portales. He and Tom gathered them into a herd and drove them to Pat Coughlin's near Tularosa, selling them for ten dollars a head. A few months later, they stumbled across a couple of horses near Bosque Grande, took them to Padrino's in Puerto de Luna and sold them for a hundred dollars. In November, they found half a dozen cows wandering loose north of the Capitans, herded them to White Oaks and sold them to the Dedrick brothers.

As they were leaving the Oaks, Billy announced he wanted to visit his old friend Hijenio. Tom didn't like going so close to Lincoln, but he figured if they stayed in the mountains they could slip through without being seen. When they reached the mouth of Salazar Canyon, however, the Kid kept riding the road into town. Without a word, Tom followed along.

The Big Store was closed now, its windows shuttered and its front door padlocked with a chain. As they rounded the curve, they saw a new sign on the roof of Tunstall's store: J. J. DOLAN MERCANTILE COMPANY. Billy sat his horse in the middle of the road for a long time, staring at that sign.

He clucked his mare forward and rode over the place where Brady had fallen, past the corral without looking at the graves of Mac and Tunstall in the adjoining field, past the courthouse where he'd testified in shackles, the Baca house where Mrs. Mac still lived, the Patrón home where he'd stayed so long waiting on the governor's pardon. All down the street people called out, "Howdy, Kid." "Good to see you, Kid." "*Andale, Chivato,* you have returned!"

Billy smiled a greeting to each of them but didn't stop as he walked his horse through the middle of town. When he came out the other end, he caught the trail to Eagle Creek, climbed the mountain and skittered down the other side into San Patricio.

George Coe's farm was just up the Hondo, what had once been Dick Brewer's a little farther on. No one was there now and Billy turned his horse east again. They stopped at Clenny's monte house for the night, and in the morning rode down into the Pecos Valley and south to Rocky Arroyo.

It was sunset when they arrived, one of those long cobalt twilights of late autumn. Ma'am Jones was sitting on the porch swing watching two riders approach. Her husband Heiskell sat beside her, and their son Jim stood in the door with a rifle. The other children were inside washing the supper dishes. All of a sudden, Ma'am gave a cry and ran down the steps and across the yard.

Billy spurred his horse to meet her, reaching down to lift her into the saddle in front of him. She was laughing and crying both, kissing his face as they rode back to the house. Jim came from the porch to help her down, then Billy swung off and shook hands with him and Heiskell and introduced Tom.

The rest of the family came out on the porch. Billy smiled up at Minnie, appreciating her pristine beauty, as the children all called greetings to the friend of their brother who had been killed. Five-year-old Nib came down the steps. The last time they'd seen each other, Nib was a toddler teething on John's six-gun. Now he walked straight across to the Kid. Billy crouched and extended his hand. "Howdy, pardie," he said softly. "Do you remember me?"

Nib nodded, solemnly shaking his hand. "You were John's friend."

"That's right." Hearing Ma'am sniffle behind him, Billy said, "You remember your brother real good now. He loved you a lot."

"When I get grown, I'm gonna kill the man who killed him."

"Hush, Nib!" Ma'am cried. "You'll break my heart if you say that again."

Billy stood up to escape the demand for vengeance written in the boy's eyes.

"Walk with me, Billy," Ma'am said. Then to the others, "Let us be by ourselves awhile."

She took Billy's arm and guided him to the family cemetery on the crest of the arroyo. Marking John's grave, a brown stone caught the sunset to gleam red above the pale earth. Ma'am sank to her knees and reached a hand up for Billy. "Pray with me," she said.

The Kid let himself fall to his knees beside her, remembering the times he'd gone to church with his mother, the strangeness of kneeling to a power no one could prove. Sliding his arm around Ma'am's waist, he held her while she prayed aloud, asking for the redemption of all the men who had died in the war, and God's blessing on her firstborn son, whom she had sinned against by loving more than the others, so that he was taken from her in punishment of her pride. When she finished, she turned imploring eyes on Billy.

"Promise you won't take vengeance for John's death."

"It don't make me fond of Olinger," he said, starting to get up.

She held him beside her. "Promise me, Billy. I've seen men who are hunted. When they come to supper they sit with their backs to the wall, always watching the door, always afraid. I don't want that for you."

"I ain't afraid," he said to reassure her.

She clutched him more strongly. "There's been too many killings. I don't want any more mothers to suffer as I have. I saw Mrs. Beckwith after Bob was killed in Lincoln. If you could see what it does to us, Billy. If every man who kills would have to tell the bereaved mother, we'd be done with killing. It's more than we can bear."

She was crying. He pulled her close and murmured into the lemon scent of her hair, "If that's what you want, I promise I won't go out of my way to cross Olinger."

"Bless you," she whispered, her face against his shirt.

Looking down at the grave, Billy thought that the only thing left of John was his mother's tears. Billy knew he wouldn't even have that when his time came. "Come on, Ma'am," he said gently, lifting her to her feet. "Let's go back to the house before it gets so dark we lose our way."

She blew her nose on a tiny handkerchief, then smiled. "I'm glad you came to see me, Billy. I've been waiting."

"Yeah, I meant to come sooner," he said, tucking her hand in his arm as they walked. "This girl up in Sumner convinced me to let things cool down first."

"She sounds wise. Are you getting serious with her?"

He shook his head. "She's like Minnie, good and clean." He shrugged. "I ain't got much to offer a woman like that."

"You could. If you left the territory and started over someplace new, you could offer a woman what she really wants: a fine strong man to be her partner through life."

"Am I that?" He laughed. "I think you got me confused with John."

"He thought the world of you, Billy. So do I. Come on in and have some supper, we've plenty left."

Billy and Tom spent the night there before the hearth. In the morning, Heiskell was driving a team into Seven Rivers to pick up supplies.

Billy tied his horse to the back of the wagon and rode beside Heiskell the first few miles. Tom followed, reining his skittish horse to stay behind the mules. Eight-year-old Sammie rode in the bed of the wagon, standing behind the seat listening to his father and Billy talk.

"Ma'am's right," Heiskell said. "You oughta make a fresh start someplace else. The West's a big place."

"Thing of it is, I like it here." Billy smiled. "Me and John used to have us some times. It don't seem right, him not being here anymore."

"Do you know how it happened?"

"Not exactly."

"I got Charlie Slaughter to ask Jim Ramer for me. He said John killed Jack Beckwith in a fair draw. John tried to settle it some other way, but couldn't refuse when it was forced on him. A coupla days later, he rode over to Milo Pierce to explain things. Milo was lying on a cot on the porch. When John got down and shook hands with him, Milo held on to his hand. Right hand, of course. Bob Olinger come out of the barn and shot John in the back."

Billy groaned, stabbed with regret at the promise he'd made Ma'am.

"Jim Ramer was there and saw the whole thing. They told him if he ever told the truth about it, he could expect what John got."

"Motherfucking bastards," Billy muttered.

"Yes," Heiskell agreed. "I tried to keep it from Ma'am, but she insisted on bathing him herself."

"There's nobody like her," Billy said, smiling again.

"Do you know the new sheriff at Lincoln?"

"Yeah. Chisum and Dolan put him in to get me."

"He's sheriff, Billy, and whatever he does will have the protection of the law."

Billy laughed. "It ain't been long since I rode under a badge and Garrett was rustling cows. The law's a funny thing, ain't it?"

"Still the law," Heiskell said.

"Guess I better get off here," Billy said. "You don't want to ride into town with me."

He swung onto his mare and smiled down at Sammie in the wagon. Standing up in his stirrups, Billy dug into his pocket and pulled out some coins, then handed them to the wide-eyed boy, chuckling at his delight. "The game ain't over yet, Pa Jones," Billy said. "I still got a coupla cards up my sleeve."

He tipped his hat and turned his horse north, Tom falling in behind. When they reached the outskirts of Sumner, Billy sent Tom on to Yerby's and rode into town alone. He went first to the whorehouse to buy a bath. The women fawned over him, knowing he was generous and gentle, but he wasn't interested that night. Dressed in clean clothes, he walked over to the Maxwell house.

Paulita was sitting on the porch alone. When she saw him coming, she ran down to kiss him openly by the gate. He looked at the house, the windows dark. "Ain't nobody home?"

She shook her head. "Would you like to come in?"

"Yeah," he said, then followed her up the steps and into the parlor. Sitting on the settee as they had before, he looked at her ancestors staring down from the wall.

"Why do they bother you so?" she asked softly.

He didn't answer, merely stood up and began pacing the floor.

Admiring the agility of his step accompanied by the silver song of his spurs, she loved him passionately.

He stopped in front of her. Studying her face, he laughed at his hesitation, then asked, "Would you ever consider marrying someone like me?"

"What do you mean? How like you?"

His foot tapped on the carpet as he searched her face for ridicule. Seeing none, he answered honestly, "A man who's been indicted for murder, who did the killings and would do 'em again. Who would take you from your family and prob'ly shame the family, too, so all the old ladies would gossip about the Maxwell daughter who ran away with an outlaw."

"If I loved a man and he loved me," she said, "I would go with him proudly wherever he asked, no matter what he had done, or what the world might be pleased to think of us."

He lifted her up before him and kissed her. She was like a willow in his hands, supple and strong. In her he found a sense of kin he'd thought was gone forever when he lost his mother. He held Paulita close, accepting her love so deeply that he claimed her there in the parlor of the great Maxwell family, possessed her in spirit, heart and soul, without touching her other than to kiss her mouth and hold her in his arms.

She waited for him to say the words that would complete their union. Instead he brushed her dark curls away from her face and said, "I'll be gone for a while, but I'll be back."

"Don't leave me again," she murmured.

"There's a lawyer in the Oaks. A while ago he said he'd be willing to take my case, help clear my name. It's worth a try, don'cha think?"

"You won't go to Lincoln?"

"Prob'ly not. But I got a lot of friends there. I might stop by and say hello. Might even pay a call on Garrett if he's in town."

"Promise me you won't go to Lincoln," she pleaded.

"Don't do this, Paulita," he warned.

She looked into his eyes a long moment, seeing for the first time what it meant to be his woman: obedience, immediate and unquestioning. "I will be what you want, Billy," she said, "if you will come back to me alive."

He laughed. "I won't be back any other way."

When Billy rode up to Yerby's line camp to tell Tom what he'd decided, he found his friend in the grips of a cold. The Texan protested he was fine, but a hard wind was blowing, so Billy left him behind. Riding north first to Puerto de Luna, Billy felt the strangeness of traveling alone for the first time in three years.

In Puerto de Luna, he went into a small *tendejón* on the edge of the village. At the table were two men he knew slightly. One was bad company, the other a novice at running on the loose side of the law, but Billy was lonely so he ambled over to chat. Standing by their table, he loaded boxes of cartridges into his saddlebags.

"Looks like you aim to do a lot of shooting, Kid," Dave Rudabaugh said, a grin showing through his black beard.

"Always like to be ready. Which direction you riding from here?"

"Anywhere but Vegas," the fat man answered.

"I'm going down to the Oaks, thought you might want to ride along," Billy said, wondering if he was really that lonely.

The young blond novice, Billie Wilson, was pleased for a change of company and said so. Rudabaugh hoisted his bulk into the saddle and rode between the two Billies as they joked and chattered on the trail. When they camped in an arroyo that night, Rudabaugh pulled a bottle from his saddlebags and passed it around, but it came back so fast he quit bothering. After a while, his tongue was loose and he rambled. Wilson fell asleep in his blankets. The Kid was leaning against his saddle, staring up at the stars, when the older man mentioned a friend named Webb.

"He's down by Roswell," Rudabaugh said, "visiting the Dedrick brothers. You know 'em?"

"Yeah," Billy answered. "They run a stable in the Oaks. They're good friends of mine."

"They're into some funny business these days," Rudabaugh warned. "It's gonna bring the marshal down hard."

"Sherman's the marshal and I ain't seen him once."

"Knock on wood, Kid. You're riding into Garrett's county and I've heard he's a mean sonofabitch."

Billy laughed but said nothing.

Rudabaugh asked in a suspicious tone, "You got business coming down?"

"I'm gonna meet with a lawyer about clearing my name," Billy said, watching to see Rudabaugh's opinion of his chances.

"You must be joking! I've heard you're always pulling the other fella's leg." Rudabaugh guffawed loudly. "That's a good one, Kid."

As if it were a joke, Billy said, "The gov'nor gave me a pardon."

"I heard about that. But you've killed a man since and done a few other illegal acts, if I can believe half of what I hear. Webb told me San Miguel has a warrant against you for running a gaming table without a license."

"Aw, that don't count."

"They got a piece of paper on you, it all counts when you're standing in front of a judge. Hell, you've been outta the gate more'n once, you know that." He snorted grumpily. "I'm going to sleep."

Within minutes he was snoring and Billy was alone. The wind had whipped all trace of moisture from the air, leaving only a dry chill that permeated to the bone. Billy lay wrapped in his blankets, hours from sleep, trying to assess his odds. He'd stand trial anytime for the killing of Joe Grant, certain he'd be acquitted. As for the rustling, it was penny-ante and wouldn't amount to much of a sentence if he was convicted. It was the killing of Sheriff Brady that hounded him, and it was that crime the pardon had been meant to forgive.

In the morning, Rudabaugh and Wilson awoke to a camp without the Kid. They had rekindled the fire and guzzled their breakfast of boiled coffee when he came back herding six horses. Leaving them to graze, he rode up to the fire and asked, "You boys intend on traveling today or you gonna sleep another twelve hours?"

"Where you been, Kid?" Wilson asked, glad to see him. "We thought you'd left us."

"I gathered a few horses to sell." He smiled at Rudabaugh. "You gotta pay lawyers 'fore they'll let you in the door."

Rudabaugh laughed, emptying the coffeepot into the fire, then moved to his horse. As he tossed the saddle onto the big gelding's back, he grinned at Wilson. "You know what he jus' did?"

Wilson shook his head with a nervous smile.

Rudabaugh laughed loudly. "He jus' stole a herd of horses to pay a lawyer to clear his name!"

Wilson looked at the Kid to see how he was taking the joke, but he was already riding away, herding the horses southwest into the prairie. Rudabaugh and Wilson galloped to catch up, and together they ambled toward the Greathouse ranch, forty miles north of the Oaks.

Whiskey Jim Greathouse bought four of the Kid's horses but didn't want the other two, so Billy turned them loose to wander home again. The eighty dollars in his pocket seemed like enough, though he really had no idea what a lawyer cost.

As they rode toward the Oaks, Billy came to the realization that if he'd hired Ira Leonard in the first place, Mrs. Mac would have footed the bill. Not hiring him had been a mistake. When the district attorney asked for a change of venue, a lawyer could have fought it. All Billy could do was stand there and watch it happen. Even if he'd hired Leonard then, something might have been done. It was walking out of jail that broke the contract. And even though he knew he'd waited far too long for the governor to keep his promise, Billy suspected if he'd waited a little longer he might have had his pardon.

Remembering Juan Patrón's eagerness to have him gone, Billy also suspected he'd been manipulated to do what Patrón wanted against his own interests. He couldn't help wonder if the governor hadn't done that too, but always in his mind he came back to the idea that a long shot was worth the try.

The sheriff-elect of Lincoln County had been summoned to meet with an agent of the Treasury Department, Azariah Wild, sent from Washington to investigate the problem of counterfeit money. Sitting in the agent's room in the Wortley Hotel, Garrett listened to Wild say he was certain the contraband wasn't being manufactured in New Mexico, but a lot of it was changing hands in the territory. When he'd given his list of suspects to the U.S. marshal, however, John Sherman had refused to act.

"Who was on the list?" Garrett asked.

"Sam Dedrick, John Webb, Tom Cooper, and William Bonney."

"What did the marshal say when you presented this list of men you wanted arrested?" Garrett asked, tongue-in-cheek.

"He said he preferred not to."

Garrett laughed. "Well, you know, Sherman's an eastern boy. I think the appointment's a little rougher than he anticipated."

"I intend to accomplish my mission, Sheriff," Wild said. "I need an officer of the law to execute my plan."

"And what is your plan?"

"To form a posse, ride into White Oaks and arrest the felons," he answered, as if it were obvious.

"Such a posse would cost a lot of money to outfit," Garrett said, hiding his opinion that the plan was ludicrous.

"Money's no problem. I'm authorized to pay a salary of two dollars a day plus per diem for food, lodging, and stabling of mounts."

Garrett took a cigar from his vest and set about trimming it methodically. "I'd like to help you," he answered, lighting his cigar and blowing a smoke ring at the ceiling, "but I'm after the Kid right now."

"Our purposes are not crossed. I have information that links Bonney to the counterfeiting scheme."

Garrett had never known the Kid to be much interested in money and he didn't believe it. But not inclined to look a gift horse in the mouth, he said, "What we need is a spy to get us some inside dirt."

"I intend to outfit myself as a miner, ride into White Oaks, and do that myself," Wild answered.

Garrett smiled. "You best start calling it the Oaks or you'll be pinned for a stranger right off, and these men are real shy of strangers."

"Do you have a man who could better serve our purpose?"

"Barney Mason," Garrett answered. "Captain Lea will vouch for him if you don't trust my judgment." He was thinking how pleased Apolinaria would be that he'd found her no-account brother-in-law a job.

So Garrett rode to Sumner and enlisted Barney Mason, his old cattle rustling buddy, as a deputy in the service of the Treasury Department. Then he rode home to Roswell to tell Apolinaria he was starting in earnest on his manhunt for the Kid, because he'd finally found someone to finance it.

On the night of November 20, Barney Mason rode into the Oaks. A petty thief and coward, he was generally considered harmless and sometimes useful. That he was related to Garrett wasn't held against him. The Gutierrez family was abundant with daughters, so half the men in Sumner were related to Garrett. Besides, it hadn't been that long since the sheriff of Lincoln County had been a scoundrel with the rest of them, and if you discounted all the men he'd been friends with before going over to the law, you wouldn't be left with many.

Barney Mason rode his horse to the corral of Dedrick's Stables and saw four men standing in the slush of melted snow by the office door. He swung down and approached cautiously, nervous because he was hiding something. The Kid, Dave Rudabaugh, Billie Wilson, and Sam Dedrick stopped talking as Barney approached. He greeted them, then said something lame about being surprised to see the Kid so far from Sumner.

"What'cha doing here yourself?" he asked with a bedeviling grin.

Barney always felt the Kid was playing with him in a way he could never figure out. "I jus' come over to take a herd of horses I seen running loose."

"All by yourself?" the Kid mocked.

Trying to cover his lie, Barney said, "I was hoping someone here would ride along."

"I don't know anybody would ride with you, Barney, and that's a fact." The Kid walked into the stable, followed by Rudabaugh and Wilson.

"He don't seem to like me much," Barney said to Sam Dedrick.

"Don't worry about it. The Kid's mad 'cause some man he was s'posed to meet didn't show. You want to put your horse away?"

"Reckon," Barney said, unhappily leading it into the stable.

The Kid and his men were mounting up. As Dedrick held the door open for them, Barney watched the outlaws ride out, huddled against the wind. As soon as they were well on their way, he ran up the street to the sheriff's office and told them he'd just seen the Kid leaving town. Deputy Hudgens raised a posse and left White Oaks before midnight, easily following the outlaws' trail through the fresh snow into the Jicarilla Mountains.

Billy was warming his hands over the remnants of the breakfast fire as a strong wind rushed through the pines, carrying the sounds of the posse away from the camp. Having left his coat and gloves on his blanket spread in the snow, Billy hunkered close to the embers, thinking of nothing but thawing his hands so they'd be supple again, not frozen near stiff. He wasn't even thinking about Judge Leonard. The lawyer must have confused the date, and Billy had decided he would go back in a few days and try again. If the lawyer had chickened out and wouldn't take his case, there was time to think it through when he was sure that's how it was. Right now his thoughts didn't go beyond getting warm.

The first indication something was wrong was the high ping of a rifle. When his mare grunted and fell over dead, Billy didn't wait to reconnoiter. He ran for the trees. Wilson was right on his heels, abandoning his own horse. They passed Rudabaugh pulling his pants up in the bushes just as a fusillade erupted behind them. Grabbing his gunbelt, he ran after the two Billies.

The snow was deep, laced with crevices that bogged them to their waists. Following the Kid straight uphill, Rudabaugh was soon puffing hard, sweat dripping from his nose. He was falling behind, but drove himself on. They floundered over the crest to the other side, then slid half the time so they bounced down the mountain to plow through the drifts on the plains toward the Greathouse ranch, thirty miles away.

Their sweat-soaked clothes froze in the wind. Coats and gloves left behind, they kept their hands deep in the pockets of their trousers. Icicles collected on the ends of their noses, and only the heat of motion saved them from freezing.

When they arrived at the ranch, Steck, the German cook, took them into the kitchen beside the piping hot stove, gave them blankets and coffee, then left to tell Greathouse he had company. When Steck came back the outlaws were asleep on the floor, wrapped in the blankets around the stove. He quietly left them alone.

Whiskey Jim Greathouse knew the Kid and had met the others on their visit a few days before. He didn't know there was a posse on their trail so took no special precautions. When the household went to sleep that night, they locked the doors but never thought to post a guard.

In the morning, Steck walked out to the woodpile. With several logs in the crook of his arm, he looked up into the barrel of a forty-five an inch from his nose. The man behind it told him to be quiet and move into the forest. Steck complied.

Behind bulwarks of boulders, the posse lay in the snow. Steck shivered in his shirtsleeves as he was told to crawl across to the deputy sheriff. As soon as he got there, Hudgens asked, "Who's inside?"

"Greathouse," Steck answered through chattering teeth. "Three other men I don't know."

"Is the Kid one of 'em?"

"I don't know him," Steck lied.

"He's small, wiry, has crooked teeth. Riding with a fat, bearded man named Rudabaugh and one with yellow hair named Wilson. That sound like the men inside?"

Steck nodded, hugging himself against the cold.

Hudgens pulled a pad of notepaper and a pencil out of his pocket, then wrote a note asking the Kid to surrender. "Give this to the Kid, understand? Get going."

Steck clutched the note in his hand as he scurried back across the yard. The Kid was awake in his blanket by the stove. Greathouse, standing in the far door, looked worried. Steck advanced silently and handed over the note.

Waking up in a friend's warm kitchen, Billy had been feeling optimistic again. He'd decided the attack of the day before came from Dolan's men making sure his welcome in Lincoln County was understood. Reading the deputy's demand for surrender didn't dissuade him from that opinion. He crumpled the note and threw it into the open door of the stove. "Go tell Hudgens he can take me as a corpse."

Rudabaugh sat up. "What the fuck?" he grumbled.

"There's a posse outside." The Kid smiled. "Go tell 'em what I said, Steck."

Steck reached for his coat, but Greathouse stopped him. "I'll go," he said. "That all right with you, Kid?"

"I like it better. Steck can start breakfast while you're gone."

Greathouse buttoned his coat as he crossed the yard, following

Steck's tracks through the snow to the posse. When he relayed the Kid's message to Hudgens, the deputy swore under his breath, then growled, "I want the Kid and the men with him."

"Go get 'em," Greathouse mocked.

The deputy's fist sent him sprawling. "We know you're in with 'em, so don't pull no shit."

Hudgens stared at the house with smoke billowing from the chimney, knowing the outlaws were warm and well fed while his men were cold and without provisions. They couldn't wait them out and he didn't want to attack pointblank. That left negotiation. Deciding he'd approached the wrong man, he wrote a note to Billie Wilson, promising protection if he would surrender.

When Greathouse took the message back to the kitchen, the outlaws were eating. He handed the note to Wilson.

Wilson read the note, then looked at the Kid. "They're offering us protection if we surrender."

"What'cha gonna do, Billie?" the Kid asked, sopping his eggs up with a crust of bread.

Wilson looked at Rudabaugh. "What do you think, Dave?"

"Who's heading the posse?" he asked Greathouse.

"Hudgens."

"Who's with him?"

Greathouse named the men, watching the Kid clean his plate.

"Jim Carlyle?" Wilson asked. "You saw him for sure?"

"Yeah," Greathouse said.

"Tell them I'll surrender to Carlyle on his guarantee," Wilson said.

"What about you, Kid?" Greathouse asked. "You go along with that?"

The Kid smiled. "Why don'cha send him in and we'll talk about it?"

When Greathouse took that message to Hudgens, the deputy refused to allow it. But Carlyle volunteered. Arguing that the Kid wouldn't harm a man who came to parley, he took off his gun and walked across the yard.

Steck was alone in the kitchen. The cook nodded at the far door and Carlyle walked into the tavern, lit only by a blazing fire and the filtered sun through the deep windowboxes. The Kid stood at the far end of the room, watching him. Rudabaugh and Wilson were drinking whiskey at the bar. Wilson called, "Come on in, Jim, and have a drink."

"It's a little early for me," Carlyle answered, stuffing his gloves into the pocket of his coat. "You boys got yourself in a fix this time."

"Same one you're in," the Kid said.

"Wait a minute. I came in peace, trusting your word."

"I didn't give my word," the Kid said, walking toward him. "You came riding into our camp, killed my mare and made me run for my life. I don't call that peaceable."

"We were trying to make an arrest. You didn't expect us to announce ourselves, did you?"

"Well, you know, I kinda did," the Kid answered, stopping a few yards away. "To arrest a man, you're s'posed to have a warrant. You fellows have a warrant on you?"

"We didn't have time for that. We heard you were in town and came after you."

"For what?" he asked, his eyes glittering with ridicule.

Carlyle shrugged uncomfortably. "There's half a dozen warrants against you."

"For what?"

"Larceny, mostly. Rustling."

The Kid walked right up to him and yanked the gloves out of his pocket. "These are mine. You picked 'em off my blanket after shooting into my camp. Don't you think you got a lot of nerve to accuse me of theft?"

Carlyle swallowed hard. "Property belonging to outlaws is to be confiscated by the law."

Backing a few steps away, the Kid dropped his gloves on a table. "That's how they beat Tunstall, you know that? They declared him an outlaw and took his cattle and then his ranch. Now Dolan's got his name on the goddamned store."

"That was the war, Kid," Carlyle said.

"It's still Dolan, though, ain't it?"

"Reckon," he admitted, sorry he'd come.

The Kid turned around and walked to the other end of the room, close to the fire.

Wilson said, "Come on over, Jim, and have a drink."

Carlyle approached warily. "I don't want a drink. Wilson, you gonna surrender or not?"

Rudabaugh pulled his pistol. "Have a drink, Jimmie."

Carlyle watched Wilson pour him a shot, then both of the outlaws grinning as he downed it. He had to. There was a gun on him, and he no longer trusted in the honor of thieves.

For hours, the three men sat at the bar. Every time Rudabaugh and Wilson took a drink, they made Carlyle take one, too. They told stories and jokes and taunted him with his predicament, until finally they all passed out. Hours later, Carlyle was the first to wake up. The shadows

outside the windows were long, the day nearly gone. He sat up and saw
the Kid watching him from the far end of the room.

"Afternoon, Jimmie," he said. "I was jus' thinking of getting some
supper. You hungry?"

Carlyle shook his head.

The Kid smiled. "You best eat. These boys'll start drinking again as
soon as they're awake. You got an empty stomach, it's apt to kill you."

Carlyle stood up and staggered in front of him to the kitchen.

"Fix us something," the Kid said, sitting down.

"What?" Carlyle asked, his mind stupid. "What do you want?"

"I ain't particular."

Carlyle found a pot of beans and lit the fire under it, then poured
cornmeal into a bowl for bread. He'd made cornbread in a skillet a thousand times, but couldn't remember what came next.

"You put the milk and eggs in now," the Kid said.

Carlyle nodded woodenly, found the pantry, and came back with a
pitcher of milk and a basket of eggs. Beginning to revive as he whipped
the batter, he realized Steck was gone. "What's gonna happen here,
Kid?"

"What do you want to happen?"

"I'd like to walk out and ride away."

The Kid laughed. "I'd like that, too. Especially if you took the posse
along. But I don't think it's likely, do you?"

"I guess not." As he put the lid on the skillet of cornbread, Carlyle
wondered if there were any guns in the kitchen.

"Tell you what I want," the Kid said. "I want to ride out with you as
a hostage. When we get clear of the posse, we'll let you go."

"We could do that," Carlyle said.

"I'm jus' one man. There's two more in there and a lot more outside."

"Why don't you tell Hudgens your plan?"

"We don't have anyone to send with the message," the Kid said.
Then he smiled. "You're gonna burn them beans. I hate burnt beans,
amigo."

As they were eating the unburnt beans and the dry, flat cornbread,
the others came in, sour and surly. They ate, too, then they all sat watching the sky turn red outside the windows. When it fell into dark, Rudabaugh and Wilson made the move back to the tavern. The Kid followed
them all with a sardonic grin.

As before, they made Carlyle match drinks. Rudabaugh loomed on
one side, his breath foul, his gun in his hand half the time. Wilson was
maudlin, whimpering how his mother would be shamed to see him in a

house surrounded by a posse. She would cry, he said, she would cry her eyes out.

The clock on the wall marked the hours as the evening wore on. The Kid went into the kitchen and came back with a cup of coffee. The stimulating aroma teased Carlyle, but when he asked for some, Rudabaugh laughed and said there was plenty of whiskey, poured him another shot, and made him drink it.

Leaning heavily against the bar, Carlyle kept glancing at the Kid. Suddenly he saw the Kid spin around and draw his gun. Only then did Carlyle realize the kitchen door had opened and closed. Watching the Kid, Carlyle wondered, What if it's the whole damn posse? Will he just stand there and shoot until they kill him?

Steck boomed a hello from the kitchen, then appeared in the tavern door. He looked at the Kid. "They say if you don't let Carlyle go by midnight, they'll kill Greathouse." Steck turned away to leave.

"Wait up, pard," the Kid said, still holding his gun. "Why don'cha stay here with us? I bet it's colder'n hell out there."

Steck nodded. "The posse's near froze and haven't eaten since yesterday. They want to go home."

The Kid laughed. "Nobody's stopping 'em."

"They won't go without Carlyle," Steck said.

The clock read five minutes to midnight. Billy didn't believe the posse would shoot Greathouse; he was known to fence stolen stock, but that wasn't a hanging offense. Besides, if the posse killed him, Carlyle was done for. It was a stupid play all the way around. Billy figured if he waited them out, they would go home just for food and a fire.

Suddenly a gun fired outside. Thinking Greathouse was dead and he would be, too, in no more time than it took the Kid to raise his pistol, Carlyle dove for the window. He hurtled himself past three feet of windowbox to hit the sash with the full force of his body, taking the wood frame with him as he fell on the snow in a shower of glass.

"Sonofabitch," Billy whispered, watching his ticket out crawl away.

The posse fired. Carlyle lurched. Again the posse fired and he crawled on his belly another few inches, then collapsed and lay still.

"Sonofabitch!" Billy said again, knowing his hope for a fresh start was as dead as the hostage. In rage, he emptied his six-shooter at the posse.

Rudabaugh and Wilson opened fire as Steck dropped to the safety of the floor. For several minutes, gunfire exploded from both sides, then silence fell. Carlyle's body lay there all night, slowly freezing in the sprawled form of his last effort to move.

From his vantage at the empty window, Billy couldn't see or hear anything of the posse. Figuring they'd realized it was Carlyle dead in the snow, he took advantage of what he thought was the posse's shame at dropping their own man. "Let's go," he said, taking his gloves off the table as he walked toward the kitchen.

Rudabaugh and Wilson followed him, ready to fight their way to the corral. But the posse had withdrawn, taking every horse on the place. Seeing the empty corral and hearing the silence all around him, Billy started walking across the prairie. The others fell in behind.

After hours of laboring on foot through the deep snow, they reached Spencer's ranch. He took them in and fed them, but when Billy asked the old man if he had any horses to spare, Spencer said they were all out with his herders checking the stock after the storm. Thanking the old man for his food, Billy trudged into the snow again. Rudabaugh and Wilson followed him, walking through the night and reaching Puerto de Luna the next day. In front of the same *tendejón* where they'd met, they saw three horses standing tethered to the rail. Billy walked inside to get warm and scout out the situation.

The men who owned the horses were drifters heading south to the warmer clime of El Paso. Over a friendly drink, they all stood around the bar and swapped stories about being caught on the range when a blizzard hit. Billy told about one time he'd sheltered in a cave only to find his horse gone in the morning. One of the strangers agreed it was a bitch to be afoot in snow, or any other time for that matter. He told how their horses had caught distemper and died from the epidemic raging along the Pecos.

"What'd you do?" Billy asked.

"We took the next horses we saw," the man boasted.

"Those tied out front?"

"Good-looking horses, ain't they?"

"I was thinking that on my way in," Billy said. "They sure put ours to shame."

He waited until everyone finished their drinks, then ordered a fresh round and asked Rudabaugh and Wilson to come outside for a minute. Back in the cold, Billy untied a long-legged pinto. "I ain't stealing this horse," he said. "I'm jus' taking it."

He swung on and the other two followed, quietly walking the horses away. Once out of earshot of the men inside, the outlaws cut distance fast, heading for Yerby's.

44

In Fort Sumner, Garrett left two prisoners under guard in the old stockade and walked over to his father-in-law's house for supper. To his surprise, Barney Mason was sitting in the kitchen.

"You weren't in the Oaks long," Garrett said, joining him at the table.

"I saw the Kid!" Barney crowed. "He's riding with Dave Rudabaugh and Billie Wilson."

"You talk to him?" Garrett asked, wondering why the Kid had hooked up with scum like Rudabaugh.

"Yeah, and he was madder'n spit. But not as mad as later, I bet."

Garrett smiled at Señora Gutierrez setting a cup of coffee in front of him. As he sipped at it, he could see Barney was bursting with news. Setting his cup down, Garrett asked impatiently, "You gonna tell me?"

"I sent a posse after 'em."

"From the Oaks?"

"Yeah. Hudgens tracked 'em to the Greathouse ranch and had 'em under siege for twenty-four hours."

Garrett knew if the Kid had been caught, Barney would have blurted it out, so he waited, watching the man gloat.

"Jimmie Carlyle volunteered to go in and parley," Barney said, "and the Kid killed 'im."

"In the house?"

Barney shook his head. "Carlyle jumped through a window trying to escape. The Kid opened fire and dropped him in the snow."

Garrett smiled. He'd needed Billy to commit a crime that was both heinous and indisputably his. "Then what happened?"

"The posse was near froze so they rode into the Oaks to get warm. When they went back, the Kid was gone, so they burnt the ranch. Greathouse threw a fit but couldn't stop 'em. They were pissed over the Kid killing Carlyle." Barney leaned back with a grin. "That ain't all."

"What else?" Garrett asked, feeling a nudge of dread.

"The plains were drifted with snow so the posse had no trouble tracking the Kid to Spencer's ranch. They burnt it, too."

"The posse did?"

Barney nodded. "Now there ain't no place the Kid can hide! Who's gonna risk getting burnt out?"

"*¿Quiénes son los hombres malos?*" Señora Gutierrez muttered as she set a plate of supper in front of the sheriff.

Garrett watched her trudge back to the stove, knowing most people would agree with her and see the posse as the troublemakers. It fell into his hand, though, and he liked the new deal. If he acted fast, he could catch the Kid before he caught his breath.

"Where do you think he is now?" he asked, digging into his chile.

"Yerby's, most likely."

Garrett nodded. "O'Folliard's up there with Bowdre."

Leaving Barney to guard the prisoners in the stockade, Garrett gathered his posse and rode north to Yerby's ranch. Since he'd stopped in Sumner only long enough to eat and change horses, he figured he had a good chance of surprising the Kid. When the posse reined up on a plateau overlooking the southern valley of Yerby's range, the sheriff saw a rider heading in the direction of the line camp. Through his field glasses, Garrett recognized Tom O'Folliard.

Garrett remembered a pass he'd found by accident one day when he was lost. It was rough, but if they were quick they could intercept O'Folliard before he reached the camp, then there would be one less gun to defend the Kid. Garrett told his men, "This is going to be hard riding and it's every man for himself. If you can't make it, meet us at Sumner."

He galloped back down the ridge, found the pass and forced his horse to take it fast. Boulders blocked the trail and the horses had to jump or squeeze through, bruising their knees as they floundered and fell, scrambling up the mountain. The decline was the same, loose stones skittering out from under their hooves. The horses slid on their haunches, stumbled to run a few steps then slid again, but as they neared the mouth of the canyon, Garrett still had five men with him. He spurred onto the prairie and came out within three hundred yards of O'Folliard.

He had been loping along, looking forward to seeing the Kid again, taking him the latest newspapers and a couple boxes of ammunition. Tom had no warning of the posse until he saw them bolt out of an arroyo a few hundred yards away. Pulling his carbine, he got off some quick shots, then wheeled his horse into a dead run.

The outlaw rode a well-rested, fine animal that cut distance as if the posse were standing still. Garrett admired Tom's horse, his riding, and his quick reaction with his gun. But even as he admired him, Garrett cursed him, knowing Tom would beat them to the camp in time for the outlaws to escape.

Garrett was right. When he rode into the yard, the corral held only two mules braying with excitement. He pounded on the door of the hut. When it wasn't opened, he kicked it down and walked in on a sobbing Manuelita Bowdre. He threw her out into the slush of the yard. "Where'd they go?" he yelled.

"I don't know," she cried.

He bent low and slapped her. "Where'd they go, Manuelita?"

She spit in his face.

Garrett admired Mrs. Bowdre for protecting her husband, knowing he'd want his own wife to do the same. He turned away and swung onto his horse, telling McKinney to get the mules out of the corral.

"You can't take those mules!" Manuelita shouted, jumping to her feet. "Those are our mules!"

"All property belonging to outlaws is to be confiscated," Garrett answered, reining his horse away.

On the trail back, he met the rest of the posse, their horses battered almost beyond use. Watching Bob Olinger take his anger out on his mount, which crippled the animal further, Garrett shook his head at the company he was forced to keep. Then he led his already exhausted posse toward Wilcox's ranch, halfway between Yerby's and Sumner.

Wilcox's drovers were all out riding herd, so he was alone. And nervous, the sheriff thought, sitting at the table drinking coffee. "Have you seen the Kid?" Garrett asked.

"Not since the Carlyle tragedy."

"Do you think he's around?"

"I don't know. He ain't been here." Wilcox looked out the window at the posse. Knowing he didn't want his spread burned, he turned back to Garrett. "Bowdre wants to meet with you. I don't want it to happen here, though. You got to arrange it somewhere else."

"Meet about what?" Garrett asked.

"He wants the indictment against him dismissed. Says it ain't fair he can't claim the amnesty just 'cause he was indicted 'fore the war was over. He has a point, you know. Many men did worse and pled the amnesty."

"That's true," Garrett said, wondering if Bowdre would trade clearing his name for betraying the Kid. "Tell him to meet me at the fork north of Sumner, nine o'clock tomorrow morning. I'll come alone and hear what he has to say." He stood up and crossed to the door, then turned back. "Next time you see the Kid, tell him I said hello."

When Wilcox didn't answer, Garrett smiled, then walked out to his horse and led his posse into the hills to camp for the night. In the morning, he rode alone to see if Bowdre would show.

Even though it was cold, Garrett sat his horse in the shadow of a cottonwood, not wanting to be an easy target for a sniper. He'd been there only a few minutes when Bowdre came, cautiously ambling his horse toward the sheriff. Garrett let himself smile a friendly greeting. "So what's on your mind?" he asked when they were a few yards apart.

"I'm tired of this life," Bowdre said. "I want that indictment wiped clean so I can live straight again. I got a wife now, maybe children soon. I gotta think of them."

"That's smart, Charlie. Captain Lea has promised leniency to any of the Kid's gang that defects."

"I've heard about promises," Bowdre muttered.

"It's up to you. We could work out a deal where you get the amnesty if we get the Kid."

"Fuck you, Garrett!"

He flinched at the curse, but kept his voice calm. "If you don't quit the Kid, you'll get the same as him."

"I've already quit. I don't ride with him anymore."

"He spends a lot of time at your house."

"I can't refuse to feed him when he shows up."

"You're gonna have to. If you're with him when I get there, you'll be captured or killed and that's the truth."

Bowdre glared at him. "I'll think about it," he finally said. Reining his horse around, he galloped away.

In a melancholy mood, Garrett gathered his men and led them back to Sumner. The posse looked battered as they rode into town, half their horses lame. The men were cold and tired, and except for the mules, empty-handed. Keenly aware of the people smirking as they watched him return from his first foray against the Kid, Garrett tried not to care, telling himself he'd be hailed as a hero when the job was done. Maybe not here in the Kid's stronghold, but everywhere else in the territory. And no matter what their inclinations, the people could be forced to cooperate because Wild had appointed him a deputy U.S. marshal. Aside from Sherman, that meant Garrett outranked every lawman in New Mexico.

His prisoners were still waiting in the stockade to be picked up by the sheriff of San Miguel County. Not wanting to pay their keep, Garrett decided to take them to Vegas himself. Before leaving, he wired Wild in Lincoln, saying the posse's horses had come down with distemper and he needed funds to remount them. He asked that the money be sent care of Beaver Smith, then taking Barney Mason to guard the prisoners, Garrett commandeered a buggy for the hundred-mile trip to Vegas.

It was early December and the roads were crusted with ice. Despite that, Garrett kept the team moving fast, aggravated at having to interrupt his hunt for the Kid to deliver men he'd already arrested.

John Webb and George Davis were bellyaching about making the trip. They'd been dragged a hundred miles up the Pecos, they complained, then kept in a hovel not fit for a pig. Now they were being dragged another hundred miles to God only knew what. Garrett stood it as long as he could, then drew the team up sharp and turned in his seat to glare back at them. "Maybe I should kill you right now and not bother."

Barney cocked his Winchester to give weight to the threat. When Garrett turned back around and slapped the reins, Webb and Davis kept quiet so at least he could think.

The Kid wouldn't go back to Yerby's. Maybe Wilcox's, maybe the cave at the Portales. Right now he was probably cooling his heels in Sumner. Garrett wondered if Pete Maxwell had heard the rumors about Billy and Paulita. He couldn't imagine that Pete approved of the romance. Liking the Kid wasn't the same as taking him into your family. But Billy had free run of the Maxwell house and was often seen eating supper at their table. Even Luz Maxwell, widow of old Lucien himself, was supposedly fond of the Kid. Garrett would bet money that if Lucien were still alive, the Maxwells would extend a less hearty welcome to the outlaw.

But Pete had a personal antipathy for Garrett, stemming from when he'd fired him for rustling. That would have been ancient history if it wasn't making his job harder now. It was one thing to track a public enemy with the support of the populace; another altogether to track a man half the people protected. As powerful as they were, the Maxwells set a bad example to the *pobres.*

Ahead Garrett saw a herd of riders, fifteen, maybe twenty, coming fast. He reined up and drew his gun as Barney half-twisted on the flip-over seat to watch their approach. They were all Mexican, heavily armed and well mounted. With relief Garrett recognized Desiderio Romero, the sheriff of San Miguel County.

As the posse surrounded the carriage, Garrett and Romero shouted greetings, then agreed to exchange the prisoners in Puerto de Luna.

In the plaza, Garrett relinquished his prisoners by yanking them out of the carriage and shoving them into the midst of the posse. Then he walked over to Padrino's tavern and ordered whiskey. Padrino was a friend of the Kid's and Garrett's both. As he set a new bottle of his best stock in front of the sheriff, they exchanged wry smiles.

Garrett was just finishing his second drink when he heard someone come in behind him. Twisting on his stool, he eyed the burly Mexican wearing a belligerent scowl.

The Mexican came closer and shouted, "I am Juanito Mes. There are warrants against me for murder and thievery. I wish to surrender."

"I don't know you," Garrett said. "I've no warrant for you and I don't want you. Go away."

The man stalked back out and Garrett poured himself another drink. He could hear Mes shouting in the street that he'd challenged the sheriff to arrest him and Garrett had been afraid. Then Barney Mason came in carrying his Winchester. He sat down at a corner table and laid the rifle across his lap.

Garrett took his time trimming and lighting a fresh cigar. He was puffing with contentment when a man stomped into the room behind him. Garrett turned around again to see another Mexican, this one holding his hand only inches from the pistol on his hip.

"My name is Mariano Leiva," he announced. "I'd like to see the gringo who can arrest me."

Garrett blew smoke at the man. "Go away and don't annoy me."

Leiva wheeled and stalked back onto the porch where he cursed Garrett, calling the sheriff a coward for not arresting him when he had the chance. Garrett threw his cigar on the floor and strode onto the porch so fast Leiva stepped back and shut up.

"I've got no papers on you and I don't want you," Garrett said. "When I do, you won't have to find me."

"Chingada su madre," Leiva growled, aiming his fist.

Garrett slapped him off the porch. Leiva landed on his feet, drew his pistol and fired. He missed. Garrett pulled his gun and fired at Leiva, winging him in the shoulder. With a howl of pain, he dropped his gun and ran away.

Back inside, Garrett had barely poured himself another drink when Sheriff Romero came in. "I have to arrest you for shooting Leiva," Romero said. "Hand over your gun."

Garrett looked at him with disgust. "I have no intention of surrendering my arms. I've already been shot at and I aim to protect myself."

Padrino strode between the two lawmen. *"Madre de Dios,* Romero, can't you just go away?"

Romero looked at Barney with his rifle, then back at Garrett. "I will file charges and notify you of your appearance."

"You do that," Garrett said, watching him leave. Then Pat retrieved his cigar from where he'd thrown it on the floor, brushed it off and relit it. "Guess we'll go back to Sumner," he told Barney.

"Webb wants to see you first."

Garrett finished his drink. "Let's get it over with," he said, walking out into the cold of late afternoon.

The prisoners were in the back room of a *tendejón* crowded with the boisterous posse. Garrett pushed past the deputy guarding the door and stood glaring down at the men shackled hand and foot on the floor. "What do you want, Webb?"

"This posse's a mob," he implored, past pride. "You arrested us, we're your responsibility. You can't turn us over to be lynched."

Garrett cursed under his breath. "I'll stay with them into Vegas, that suit you?" he growled. Not waiting for an answer he left, angry because he'd hoped to be shut of the posse himself.

The next morning he went to the *alcalde*'s office, explained the shooting of Leiva, and the charges were dropped, so he rode north with the posse. With the prisoners now on horseback, Garrett and Barney were alone in the carriage. Surrounded by the posse, Garrett listened to the ludicrous boasting of the deputies.

The sheriff's brother, Isidro Romero, bragged he had once arrested the Kid. When Garrett grinned at the lie, Romero said, "I could arrest the Kid without any weapons, even. It's all in the eyes, *hombre.* You have to overpower a man with your eyes."

Garrett laughed. "I'd bet a night with a hot whore that you'd ride through a blizzard just to avoid being within ten miles of one of the Kid's old camps."

Romero growled a curse and reined his horse away.

When the noisy posse stopped at an isolated *tendejón* to slake their thirst, Garrett waited until they were all inside, then clucked to his team and made his escape. If he'd come across the Kid while in their company, Pat thought he might have been embarrassed enough to change sides.

In a *tendejón* in Anton Chico, he felt relieved to meet up with his own kind. Frank Stewart was there, heading a posse of Texans to replevin a herd from White Oaks. In a private back room, Garrett learned the ranchers Stewart represented were convinced the Kid had stolen the cattle and sold them to the Dedricks.

"I don't know," Garrett said. "We've kept Billy running pretty good lately. But it seems to me, you and I should join forces."

"Not a bad idea," Stewart said, refilling their glasses. "Did you know the governor's offered a reward?"

"What brought that on?"

"The *Gazette* ran an editorial accusing the Kid of being captain of a band of fifty cattle thieves," Stewart said, digging into his saddlebags for a copy of the December 12 issue. It was folded open to a block of print he pointed out as he handed the paper over. "Mr. Bonney chose to reply."

With an eager laugh, Garrett read the letter:

Open Letter to Governor Wallace
from Billy Bonney

I noticed in the Las Vegas Gazette a piece which stated that
Billy "the" Kid, the name by which I am known in the country,
was the captain of a band of outlaws who hold Forth at the Portales. There is no such organization in existence. So the gentleman must have drawn very heavily on his imagination. My
business at the Oaks the time I was waylaid and my horse killed
was to see Judge Leonard. he had written to me to come up, that
he thought he could get everything straightened out. I did not
find him at the Oaks and should have gone to Lincoln if I had
met with no accident. After my horse was killed we made our
way to a station, forty miles from the Oaks kept by Mr. Greathouse. When I got up next morning the house was surrounded
by an outfit led by one Carlyle, who came into the house and
demanded a surrender. I asked for their papers and they had
none. So I concluded it amounted to nothing more than a mob
and told Carlyle that he would have to stay in the house and lead
the way out that night. Soon after a message was brought in stating that if Carlyle did not come out inside of five minutes they
would kill the station keeper (Greathouse) who had left the
house and was with them. in a short time a shot was fired on the
outside and Carlyle thinking Greathouse was killed jumped
through the window breaking the sash as he went and was killed
by his own Party they thinking it was me trying to make my
escape. the Party then withdrew.

They returned the next day and burned an old man Spencer's
house and Greathouses also. I made my way to this place afoot
and During my absence Deputy Sheriff Garrett acting under
Chisums orders went to Portales and found nothing. on his way
back he went by Mr. Yerbys ranch and took a pair of mules
which I had left with Mr. Bowdre who is in charge of Mr. Yerbys
cattle he (Garrett) claimed that he had a right to confiscate any
outlaws property.

I have been at Sumner since I left Lincoln making my living
gambling. The mules were bought by me the truth of which I
can prove by the best citizens around Sumner. J. S. Chisum is the
man who got me into trouble and was benefited Thousands by it
and is now doing all he can against me There is no Doubt but
what there is a great deal of stealing going on in the Territory

and a great deal of the property is taken across the Plains as it is a good outlet but so far as my being at the head of a band there is nothing of it in several instances I have recovered stolen property when there was no chance to get an officer to do it.

One instance for Hugo Zuber post office Puerto de Luna another for Pablo Analla same place

if some impartial party were to investigate this matter they would find it far different from the impression put out by Chisum and his tools.

Garrett leaned back in his chair and laughed. "Should have gone to Lincoln, my ass." He paused to light his cigar, rereading the letter as he smoked. "Taking orders from Chisum, I don't like that and Chisum won't either." He puffed. "These best citizens around Sumner must be the Maxwells. But this part about the posse killing Carlyle," he looked up at Stewart, "that's the stupidest lie I ever heard."

"Except I never heard the Kid was stupid."

Garrett squinted at him through the smoke. "The posse wouldn't be that inept."

"Come on, Pat. They'd been standing in snow for twenty-four hours without even a cup of coffee. I bet they sure as hell wanted to shoot something, maybe Carlyle was just the first thing that moved. If that's the way it happened, you can be damn sure no man on that posse will ever admit it."

Garrett grunted, realizing the truth would never be known, but he didn't like people doubting the guilt of his prey. "So where's the part about the governor's reward?"

"Unfold the page," Stewart said.

He did and saw the black-edged box:

$500 REWARD

NOTICE IS HEREBY GIVEN
THAT FIVE HUNDRED DOLLARS WILL BE PAID
FOR THE DELIVERY OF BONNEY ALIAS "KID"
TO THE SHERIFF OF LINCOLN COUNTY.

LEW WALLACE
GOVERNOR OF NEW MEXICO

"He can't want the Kid very bad if that's all he's offering," Garrett said.

Stewart shrugged. "The Panhandle Association's offering eighteen hundred."

Garrett puffed on his cigar. "If we work together, Frank, we can have it in a month."

"You know his stomping grounds and how he thinks. I'll accept your help."

"Uh-uh. I'm heading this manhunt. Anyone comes along is under my direction."

Stewart sipped his whiskey. "All right. You know how famous he's getting? I hear they're writing about him in the big eastern papers, in Philadelphia and Boston and cities like that."

"That means we'll be famous for catching him," Garrett said. "What's your plan?"

"I was gonna ride into the Oaks and look for him there."

"I'm pretty sure he's in Sumner right now. If we move fast, we can catch him before he knows we're coming."

"Let's go," Stewart said.

When they walked into the saloon, the men quieted and looked up expectantly. Stewart raised his voice: "The sheriff says the Kid moved the cattle to Sumner. I've decided to look for them there."

There was a silence, then a man grumbled, "How could he move the herd? We all know he was afoot after the Carlyle killing."

"Yeah!" someone else shouted. "You're just after the reward and don't give a damn about the herd anymore."

"Suit yourself," Stewart said. "I want no man with me who'll hesitate when the shooting starts." He and Garrett walked outside and prepared to leave.

Six men followed them out of the saloon along with Barney Mason: Lon Chambers, Lee Hall, Jim East, Tom Emory, and two men known only as Animal and Tenderfoot Bob. Just before they were ready to leave, Juan Roibal walked up and volunteered to join the chase.

Garrett took an immediate liking to the young Mexican and allowed him to come. That night, when the posse camped a few miles above Sumner, Garrett sent Roibal into town alone.

He was seventeen years old, a sheepherder by profession, and unknown in Sumner. Walking into Beaver Smith's saloon and up to the bar, Roibal asked for a beer. The room was so dim he had to wait a long time before he could see the men in the shadows. None matched the description Garrett had given him, so he turned back to the Mexican beside him and said in Spanish, "I am Juan Roibal from Puerto de Luna looking for stray sheep. Have you heard of a rancher finding a flock on his land?"

"If a rancher did find such a flock," the old man answered, "he would shoot it."

"A man from Santa Fe took Charles Goodnight to court for that and won a lot of money."

"Santa Fe is a long way from Sumner. We have our own law here."

"I've heard it's called *el Chivato*," Roibal murmured.

The old man smiled. "When he's in town, nobody shits for fear of breaking the quiet."

"Is he here now?"

"Do you hear anything?"

"Have you ever herded sheep?" Roibal asked, sipping his beer.

It turned out the old man had, on land where Roibal himself had been a shepherd the summer before, so it was easy to pass another half hour and pretend regret at leaving his new friend. Shivering with the importance of his news, Roibal swung onto his horse and trotted quickly out of town. As soon as he was away from the lights, however, two riders emerged from the shadows and blocked the road.

"Evening," a Texan on a flashy palomino said. "Ain't seen you around before."

"My name is Juan Roibal," he said carefully. "I came down from Puerto de Luna to find some sheep for my employer."

"Who's that?" the Texan asked.

"Padrino, señor. Who are you, may I ask? In Puerto de Luna, we do not stop travelers and demand to know their business."

The Texan laughed. "Sorry, but around here we jus' can't be too careful." He pulled his horse out of the road. "Good luck finding your flock."

O'Folliard sat there watching the sheepherder disappear in the darkness. "I don't like it," he told Pickett, turning his horse and galloping down the avenue to the Maxwell home. Tom handed his reins to Pickett and walked across the yard to the back door, seeing the Kid through the kitchen window.

Paulita and her mother and Deluvina sat around the table laughing at a story Billy was telling. There were empty plates and a half-eaten chocolate cake in front of them. It reminded Tom of his mother's kitchen. He knocked on the door, but the Kid was already halfway across the room, smiling back an apology to the ladies.

In the shadows outside, Tom said, "A sheepherder was here asking whether you were in town. Said he was Juan Roibal from Puerto de Luna. Garrett was in Luna yesterday."

"Which direction did Roibal ride out?"

"North. And he wasn't in any hurry, so I don't think he was going far."

"Good work, Tom," the Kid said. "I'll jus' tell Paulita I'm leaving."

"I'll get your horse," he said.

Billy went back inside but stayed by the door. "Sorry, ladies, I got a little business to attend to."

"So soon?" Paulita asked softly.

"*Que te vayas bien, Chivato,*" Deluvina said, rising to clear the plates from the table.

Mrs. Maxwell stood, too. "Come again soon, Billy." Starting to leave the room, she turned back and stood by the window, watching Paulita walk out with him.

By the time Luz Maxwell had discovered her daughter was in love with the outlaw, she was too late to stop it. Now she hoped to postpone her daughter's disappointment when someday the young man didn't return, which is what Luz expected to happen. The Kid would wander on, and Paulita would be heartbroken for a time. But because of her youthful love for a dangerous young man, her life would be enriched over the long years of matrimony and motherhood, so Luz allowed the romance to flower.

She trusted the Kid. The evidence for her faith unfolded before her eyes as she stood in the shadows behind the window and watched them walk to the gate. She saw Paulita put her arms around his neck and kiss him passionately, his arms slowly encircling her waist as he kissed her back. Watching him break the embrace and give Paulita a scolding smile, Luz Maxwell smiled, too, and walked away from the window.

Billy had hoped for some time alone with Paulita. Now his time was up and he hadn't told her his plan. With the law so hot after him, a little distance made sense. He'd decided to ride up to the Nations and visit Fred. That's about as far as his plan went but it had been firm in his mind—until he saw Paulita again.

When he heard the horses coming up the street, he pulled his pistol and checked the chambers, then dropped the gun back in its holster and looked at her.

"Garrett's coming, isn't he?" she murmured.

Billy wouldn't lie to her. "I'll be back soon as he's gone. A day or two, no longer, I bet."

"You promise?" she asked, trying to smile.

"Sure," he said, taking his horse from Tom. "We'll find some time to be alone."

"Where will you go?"

Gathering his reins, he smiled down at her. "If you don't know, you can't tell, Paulita. It's better like this. See you real soon."

She watched him and Tom ride away at a brisk trot. They were met by four other men, then they all rode into the darkness together. From the distance, their laughter made her feel lonesome.

She couldn't understand why he was always leaving with his friends. It was true he went regretfully, but it was usually on no more than a moment's notice, and she was always left tantalized, never fulfilled. She yearned for him as perhaps only a young woman can yearn for her beloved, as if all the joys of life would be confirmed in union with the one she chose.

She knew Billy didn't see it that way. Yet when he was with her, she could tell he was torn between his desire to possess her and his wish to protect her. She didn't think she needed protection from him, and with each visit she could feel his resistance weakening. Now she had to wait for Garrett to come and go before Billy could return.

45

The posse spent a cold night on their blankets in the snow just north of Sumner. With Barney Mason, Garrett rode into town the next morning. They went first to the stables and saw that the outlaws' horses were gone. Not surprised that Roibal's visit had tipped the Kid off, Garrett didn't mind. All he had to do was pull the rope a little tighter and the Kid would be caught.

Leaving Mason in the stable, Garrett walked out alone. On the plaza, a boy nine or ten years old watched him from across the snowy expanse. As Garrett approached, the boy turned to run. Garrett caught up and grabbed him by the collar of his coat, lifting him off the ground.

"Let me loose!" he hollered, kicking as he dangled.

Garrett lowered the boy enough to get his footing. "You're Juan Gallegos."

"So?"

"You're a friend of the Kid's, aren't you?"

"What's it to you?" the urchin sassed.

"Yeah, you sound just like him. The church ladies would love you." He scanned the perimeter of the plaza. "What we're looking for here is another friend of the Kid's, someone he'd trust if they said I left town."

"I ain't gonna help you," Juan said.

"Yes, you are, sooner or later. But you'll be a lot more sore later, so you make up your mind." In the distance, he saw José Valdez. "He'll do," Garrett said, dragging the boy toward him.

Valdez knew the sheriff meant trouble, but he'd already been spotted and couldn't get away now. Garrett had a gun, and from what Valdez had heard happened in Puerto de Luna, he could use it whenever he wanted.

The sheriff towered over the shorter man. "You got a place we can talk private, Valdez?" Garrett asked pleasantly.

Valdez knew it wouldn't be pleasant. Leading the way back to his quarters, he watched the sheriff come in and close the door, still holding the boy. Garrett pulled handcuffs from his pocket, snapped them tight around one of Juan's ankles and shackled him to the table, then faced Valdez. "I want you to write me a note."

Valdez looked at Juan, then back at Garrett. "Can't you write?"

"Yeah," the sheriff said, smiling between the wings of his sweeping black moustache, "but I don't think the Kid would believe me like he will you."

"You can't ask me to betray the Kid," Valdez whispered.

The sheriff hit him and Valdez went down. He came to, staring into the dark end of Garrett's gun.

The sheriff smiled. "Like I said, I want you to write a note."

"I won't do it."

Garrett's boot hit Valdez in the face, breaking his nose. He howled and skittered away, holding his face with blood pouring through his fingers. Garrett found a towel and threw it at him. "You ready yet?"

Valdez nodded over the towel.

"Go wash up," the sheriff said. "We don't want blood on the paper." He turned to Juan. "Now, what I want you to do is deliver the note. You gonna do it?"

Juan looked at Valdez, spitting and coughing into the washbowl, and he nodded.

"Good," Garrett said, slapping him hard.

Juan cried out and ducked, but Garrett hit him again.

"That's just a taste of what'll happen if you let me down. Understand?"

Juan nodded, sucking blood off the inside of his cheek.

"Good," Garrett said again. "Hurry up, Valdez. We haven't got all day."

Valdez sat at the table, holding the towel to his face as he wrote what Garrett dictated: that the sheriff and his men had gone south to hole up in Roswell until the weather broke. When Valdez was done, Garrett took the pen and another piece of paper, then looked at him. "They're at Wilcox's ranch, aren't they?"

Holding his throbbing nose, Valdez nodded.

So Garrett addressed his note to Wilcox, saying he was determined to capture the Kid and hoped for cooperation. He asked Wilcox to send word when the Kid left, and to keep an ear open to where the outlaws were going. Then he folded both notes and held them up in front of the boy. "Can you read?"

Juan shook his head.

Garrett put the note from Valdez in the right pocket of the boy's coat. "This one goes to the Kid," he said, straight into the boy's earnest eyes. "And this one's for Wilcox," Garrett said, stuffing it into the left pocket. "If you mix them up, you and Wilcox will be murdered by the Kid and his gang. Do you understand?"

Juan nodded, believing Garrett.

He unlocked the handcuffs, drew his pistol and wagged it at the door. "Let's go," he said. The three of them walked back across the plaza to the stable. Juan was put on a horse and instructed again as to the importance of getting the right note to the right man. Juan said he understood and left.

Garrett sent Barney Mason to bring the rest of the posse into town. They left their horses in the isolated Navajo corral and occupied the old hospital building on the Texas Road east of the plaza. Manuelita Bowdre was living there now, and Garrett felt certain her room would be the outlaws' first stop. He sequestered his posse inside before the town was awake, giving orders that anyone who saw them was to be arrested and confined. Half a dozen men sat silently with the moaning Valdez, having had the bad luck of seeing the lawmen laying their trap.

A deputy sat with Manuelita. She was tied into a chair, gagged, and guarded at gunpoint. Garrett was taking no chances the gang would be warned. The sheriff himself was in an empty room, chosen because several pieces of harness hung from the portal as camouflage. He was playing poker with Barney Mason and Lee Hall on a blanket spread on the floor, passing the time until their sentry gave warning.

At eight o'clock that night, Lon Chambers poked his head in the door. "Riders coming," he whispered.

"It's them," Garrett said, blowing out the candle. "No one else would be riding this late."

The lawmen crept onto the portal and stood in the dark behind the loops of harness throwing a pattern of shadows from the full moon. A foot of fresh snow gleamed on the ground, and the posse could see three hundred yards across its glistening surface. When they heard the muffled patter of hooves, they raised their guns.

Billy had believed Valdez's note. It was just like Garrett to rest up at home and wait for a thaw, and Billy had been eager to believe it, happy at the thought of seeing Paulita one last time before leaving the territory.

Lately he'd felt on the defensive everywhere he went, always moving, always posting a guard. It was like in the war, except he never got the exhilaration of attack; he was always running. Up in the Nations he could sit in Fred's tepee, or whatever he had, and catch his breath for a while, make a plan for his future maybe. He looked at Tom riding beside him. "You gonna come up to the Nations with me?"

"I was thinking of visiting my mother," Tom said with an embarrassed smile.

"Give me her address before you go. I'll write you from Fred's."

"Maybe we can ride together again," Tom said hopefully.

"I don't see why not," Billy answered, "if we both stay alive."

Looking up the empty road, bright with snow, he felt a suspicion of something amiss. The old hospital building was completely dark and that wasn't right; somebody should have been awake. "Think I'll bum a smoke from Wilson," Billy said, reining his horse to the rear of the riders. But he didn't ask Wilson for any tobacco.

Watching the outlaws come, Garrett couldn't spot the Kid. It was bitter cold and the riders were hunched beneath coats and scarves, their hats low over their eyes. Only the sound of the hooves crunching snow broke the silence, the bridles like coins dancing in a bowl.

O'Folliard rode his horse straight toward the posse, coming so close Garrett could feel the heat of the animal's breath.

"Throw up your hands!" he barked.

Tom snapped to attention. His gun was outside his coat, just a second away. He had it in his hand the instant Garrett fired a bullet into his chest.

All the posse fired, a thunder of death exploding the quiet. Garrett shifted his aim to Pickett, but the horse reared and Garrett missed. He cocked the rifle and fired at the others galloping away, but missed.

O'Folliard's horse whinnied in panic, running in circles. As he whirled past, Tom cried, "Don't shoot, Pat, I'm killed."

Garrett saw three of the outlaws stop just out of range. He fired, knowing they were too far but guessing the Kid was one of them. At the fresh assault, they galloped away.

Tom couldn't understand why he couldn't control his horse. He felt stupid not being able to stop the animal, but it spun and his head spun with it. He could barely see through the haze falling over his eyes, something else he couldn't understand. The snow was brilliant in the moonlight, but the men were just smudges walking toward him. Finally he managed to pull back on the reins and his palomino pawed at the snow, impatient to be gone. Tom hung on with all his might, determined to control his horse.

"Be careful," Garrett called. "He might take revenge."

"Easy," Jim East said, coming forward in a crouch, his pistol aimed.

"Don't shoot," Tom moaned. "I'm killed."

"Drop your gun, then," Garrett ordered.

Tom couldn't loosen his grip. "I can't."

East came up and pried the pistol from Tom's hand. Two other men lifted him off the horse. They carried him inside and laid him on the floor.

Barney Mason squatted beside him, unbuttoning Tom's coat and ripping his shirt open to examine the wound. "It's jus' below the heart," he said. "He don't have long."

Tom focused on Garrett towering above him. "It hurts more'n I can bear, Pat. If you're a friend, kill me and make an end of it."

"I'm no friend to men of your kind," Garrett answered, "and I don't shoot my friends." He returned to his card game on the blanket.

Jim East sat by O'Folliard, watching the blood soak his shirt, the agony on his face. When Tom asked for water, East gave him some from a canteen.

Tom lurched and cried out, "My God, is it possible I'm dying?"

Barney Mason called from across the room, "Take your medicine, boy." To Garrett he muttered, "I'll raise you two-bits."

Tom clutched East's arm. "Write my ma, will you? Tell her I'm dead? San Antone. Mrs. Joseph O'Folliard. Will you?"

"Sure," he mumbled.

Jim East sat with Tom, giving as much comfort as he could though he'd never seen the man before. It took O'Folliard forty-five minutes to die. When it happened, East looked across at Garrett, who'd once claimed the outlaw as his friend, and watched incredulously as Garrett didn't pause in his deal of the next hand.

But Garrett knew that if he allowed himself to feel remorse for killing Tom, he couldn't pursue the Kid with pure intention. That's what it took, along with a lot of luck, and Garrett wasn't wasting energy on the past.

He figured the Kid would go back to the Wilcox ranch, hole up and shoot it out, or make a run from there. It would be child's play to track him in the snow, and there was no sense spending the night freezing as the Carlyle posse had. Garrett intended to give the Kid just enough respite to think he wasn't being followed, then hit him hard with everything he had.

As soon as he was out of range, Billy turned his mare and reined in sharp. Two of the others stopped but he didn't look to see who they were. He was watching Tom's horse circle a wild loop through the snow, thinking Tom must already be dead to lose control like that.

Billy heard him say, "Don't shoot, Pat. I'm killed." When the posse opened fire again, Billy turned his horse and kicked in his spurs, passing Bowdre and Pickett, hearing their horses fall in behind.

He couldn't help believing if he hadn't said that to Tom just before sensing something wrong, hadn't made that joke about one of them dying, Tom wouldn't be dead. The thought stuck in Billy's throat. He should have nudged Tom and beckoned him to fall back, as he had so many times before: just met his eyes without words and told him what to do. He should have. He had not. He saw blood on the snow in front of him.

Rudabaugh's horse was shot and the idiot hadn't even noticed. Or maybe he had and was going to run the animal until it dropped. He and Wilson were in the lead, riding hard toward Wilcox's. Billy knew they were scared shitless and he despised them for it.

His mare smelled the blood and snorted nervously, but he murmured comforting sounds close to her ears and she kept the pace. They'd almost caught up with the others when Rudabaugh's horse went down. Billy's mare shied, half-rearing and twisting off the road as Rudabaugh hit the ground running, jumped up behind Wilson and took off again.

Billy reined his mare skittering in a meadow, kicking up snow to sparkle in the moonlight. He cursed his companions, then fell in beside Bowdre and Pickett as they all ran hell-bent for Wilcox's ranch. His mare quickly outdistanced the others and he rode into the yard alone, walking her slowly to catch her breath.

Wilson's horse stood dripping sweat in front of the porch. The kitchen door was wide open, the room so brightly lit Billy could have shot both Rudabaugh and Wilson dead with his Winchester before they knew he was there. They were too interested in plundering Wilcox's cupboards, stuffing food into burlap bags. Billy walked his mare in a circle around the yard.

Bowdre galloped in, seeing Billy walking his mare and the men ransacking the kitchen. Charlie dumped his saddle in the snow and rubbed the lather of sweat off his horse's hide. Pickett came in and did the same, both of them listening to Wilson's horse wheezing, windbroke and useless.

Billy circled the yard, came back by Bowdre and Pickett, reined in and swung down. He did what they were doing, rubbing the strong legs of his mare who would have to give so much for him that night.

"I'm outlawed now," Bowdre muttered.

"What're we gonna do?" Pickett asked.

"Run," Billy said.

Rudabaugh and Wilson came scurrying out of the house carrying their provisions.

"Where we going, Kid?" Rudabaugh demanded.

"I ain't sure we're going anywhere together," he said, tossing his saddle onto his mare's back.

"You can't leave us!" Wilson whined. "We don't know these parts. You got to get us outta here."

"It's you Garrett's after," Rudabaugh growled. "None of this would've come down on us if we hadn't been with you."

"Don't be with me," Billy said, pulling the cinch tight.

"We got to," Wilson cried. "You can't leave us now, Kid."

"I'm leaving pretty quick," he said, tying the knot. "I can't see that you two got a horse."

"Wait for us," Wilson said, dropping his food and running for the stable. Rudabaugh lumbered after him.

Billy swung into his saddle and headed east with Bowdre and Pickett. He would have taken the food if he thought he was rid of the others, but he knew they'd catch up. It was an idiot's task to follow a trail through snow under a full moon. No less so for Garrett.

Billy forced his mare to plow through the deep drifts, wanting Tom's death in the past, scarred over, healed and forgotten most of the time. He ached with regret, concentrating on the rhythm of his mare cutting distance from the girl whose never-spoken good-bye had cost Tom's life.

When they reached the abandoned house at Stinking Springs, Rudabaugh declared he was staying the night. The five fugitives sat their horses and looked at each other, bonded in a way none of them liked but all recognized. Billy said, "We should keep moving, Dave."

"It's miserable cold, Kid. Garrett won't want to be out in it any more'n we do."

"I thought that once."

"Well hell, think it again," the fat man muttered, swinging down and tying his horse to the viga over the door. He took his bags of food and blankets inside. Wilson followed him. Bowdre and Pickett waited for Billy.

"I stopped to rest my horse," he said, swinging down and leading his mare inside.

"What the fuck!" Rudabaugh complained. "I'm sleeping in here!"

Billy laughed. "Watch out for hooves in the dark. My mare kicks when she's spooked."

"Goddamn, Kid," Wilson muttered from a far corner.

There were no windows in the hut, no door to close, and the air felt no warmer inside its stone walls. A strip of dazzling snow beyond the doorway was the only source of light. Billy hung the nosebag on his mare, then sheltered in the mist of her sweat as Bowdre and Pickett came in and spread their blankets away from the mare's hooves. Billy hunkered by her head, listening to her munch oats as the men began to snore. When she finished, he took the feedbag off, unrolled his blanket and settled himself, then stared out at the strip of snow, seeing Tom's horse spin out of control.

Billy didn't want to die like that. He wanted to call the shots till the end. He remembered the warmth of Tunstall's smile, the irony of Dick Brewer's, the swagger of McNab's, the forgiveness of McSween's, the sweetness of Tom's. The most the law had on Tom were a few warrants for rustling. That wasn't a hanging offense, yet they'd shot him down from ambush. Billy couldn't see that much had changed since the war. The killers still wore badges and rode in posses. They had different names but the Regulators were still their target. Billy and Charlie were the only two left.

The posse was ten strong. They'd slept in a warm room, eaten a big breakfast, and were now riding with blood on their hands. Halfway to the Wilcox ranch, they met the old man coming toward Sumner. He told Garrett the outlaws had taken provisions and headed east.

Garrett knew exactly where they were going: Stinking Springs. Abandoned and isolated, it was a perfect way station for men on the run. He led his posse across country, picked up the trail four miles from the hut, and approached just before dawn.

Leaving Roibal with the horses and sending Stewart and the others around back, Garrett kept Hall, Emory, and East. They crept along a shallow arroyo in front of the hut, spread their blankets, and bellied down in the snow with their rifles. Four horses stood tethered to the overhanging viga, their coats white with frost in the pale light of dawn.

Garrett whispered, "The Kid wears a gray hat with a green band. When I raise my gun, shoot to kill. Get the Kid and the rest'll surrender."

Lee Hall, Tom Emory, and Jim East dug into their blankets trying to stay warm, unsure only of the cost of their victory.

The sky turned pink, the horizon gold. Steam rose from the hides of the horses as Garrett heard the men inside the hut waking up. He listened for Billy's voice. Not hearing it, he still knew the Kid was there. They'd tracked five horses through the snow and only four stood tied to the viga. One of the men had taken his inside. The Kid was there, Garrett could feel him.

The horses nickered as a shadowy figure came into view, his back to the door. He turned but his head was down. He wore a gray hat and was taking a nosebag to one of the horses. When he stepped through the door, Garrett and his men fired.

Billy had been collecting himself to move. He moved now, pulling his gun as he rolled under the belly of his mare and came up on the other side.

Coughing blood, Bowdre crawled on his hands and knees back into the hut. Billy helped him lean against the wall, then looked at his wounds, one in the thigh, two in the chest. He met Charlie's eyes.

"Sonofabitch," Charlie said, bubbling blood.

Billy pulled Bowdre's gun and pressed it into his hand, then helped him to his feet. Giving him a nudge out the door, Billy said, "Go kill some of 'em before you die, Charlie."

The posse heard the Kid's words. They watched Bowdre stagger out of the hut, his gun halfway into position. His eyes were glazed, his progress meandering, and they knew he was no threat. He walked a crooked course to Garrett.

"I wish," Charlie mumbled through the blood in his mouth. "I wish, I wish . . ." Then he fell across Lee Hall. When Hall laid him down, Bowdre was dead.

Garrett stared at him for a long moment. Charlie could have lived if he'd quit the Kid, and he'd been close to quitting. Garrett had hoped he would. He thought of Manuelita, and that made him think of Apolinaria, and he felt lonesome suddenly and had to look away from the corpse.

"That you out there, Pat?" the Kid called from inside the hut.

Marveling at how chipper Billy sounded, Garrett answered, "Yes," as he reloaded his rifle.

"Why don'cha meet me like a man in a fair fight?"

"I don't aim to do that," he said, squinting through the sight of his gun.

The Kid laughed. "That's what I figured."

Hoping he'd come in range of the door, Garrett waited a moment, then called, "Why don't you surrender?"

"Go to hell!"

Garrett smiled, knowing the Kid's anger might give the posse an edge.

Billy hunkered inside the hut, holding the reins of his saddled mare. If he'd been alone, he would have ridden out shooting and taken his chances. He whispered to Pickett, "See if you can get your horse in here."

Pickett stood up flat against the wall, his fingers creeping along beneath the roof, out the door to the viga. He got the knot loose and un-wound the rope, then gently tugged the horse toward him.

Garrett saw the rope pull taut. "Hold your fire," he murmured to his men, his cheek against the stock of his rifle. "I got it."

The horse's head was through the door, Billy's mare was nickering a welcome. Then bam! Pickett's horse went down, blood spurting from its temple as it sprawled across the threshold.

"Sonofabitch," Billy muttered. "We'll never ride outta here now."

Three rifle shots cracked the silence. The horses outside jerked as their tethers were shot in half, then shied away.

Billy laughed at the grim faces around him. "You fellows too scared to look on the bright side?"

"It's pretty hard to see right now," Pickett answered.

"I don't know," Billy said. "We got nothing to do but lay around for a while. Least we ain't out there plowing through snow with a posse on our tail."

"But out there," Rudabaugh muttered, "we weren't caught yet."

"We're not caught now," Billy said. "It's a standoff. Anything can happen."

"You don't believe that," Rudabaugh scoffed.

"Sure, I do. We got plenty of ammo and food. We don't have to be in a hurry."

"So what's your plan?" Wilson asked eagerly.

"That's it." Billy laughed. "Break out some of that chow, Dave."

"We ain't got wood for a fire."

"Didn't you bring any canned goods with you?"

"Nah, just flour and raw beans and stuff to cook," Rudabaugh mumbled.

Billy bit his tongue, knowing he had to keep the men together or they didn't have a chance. "When I get outta here," he said, leaning back to cross an ankle on his knee and jangle his spur so it sang the way he liked it, "I'm going to Dodge City and get me the prettiest whore there. You ever think about all the things a whore can do for a man, all in one night?"

"I fucked a one-legged whore in Kansas City once," Rudabaugh said with a ribald laugh.

"All right! What'd it feel like, Dave?"

He grinned. "Sort of like fucking a bony cow."

The outlaws' laughter was heard by the posse outside. All day they listened to the Kid's voice, too low for them to catch the words but always followed by the others laughing at his jokes, while the posse lay shivering in the snow. At times, they envied the outlaws.

Garrett didn't. He'd enjoyed the Kid's fun enough times. It was the cold way he'd shoved Bowdre out the door that Garrett dwelt on. Late in the afternoon, he sent Stewart to Wilcox's ranch for a chuckwagon, then crawled out of range, stood up and walked over to his horse.

He brought a bottle of whiskey back and laid it in the snow beside him. Without looking at the other men, he said, "Put a blanket over Charlie, will you?"

"Which one?" Jim East asked. "I mean, which one of us do you want to lay in the snow?"

Garrett looked at the men, then at the corpse staring blind at the sky. "Forget it," he said, opening his bottle and taking a swig. He passed the whiskey around but watched till it came back, then took another swig and laid it in the snow again. When a fresh round of laughter burst from the hut, Garrett muttered, "Doesn't he ever shut up?"

The posse was from Texas and had never met the Kid. Listening to his constant banter, they knew he was keeping his men stirred up, and that meant a fight. He didn't have a chance in hell but the Texans figured he'd take some of them with him when he died. What he'd done to Bowdre proved that.

It was nearly dusk when the chuckwagon arrived. Garrett sent the posse in shifts to warm themselves around the fire and watch the side of beef drip fat into the flames. Garrett stayed on his blanket, nipping at his whiskey.

He knew the smell of cooking meat would encourage a mutiny, that the outlaws were hungry and the Kid must be restless. Garrett had seen him pace when confined inside, and he knew Billy didn't like the waiting any more than he did. He wondered if the Kid was crazy enough to ride out over the dead horse in the door. Most likely his mare would spook, rear back and knock his head on the lintel. He might be killed or just knocked out. Either way he'd be caught, so Garrett didn't think he'd try it. But what else was left? To come out shooting and be cut down? Would the Kid do that?

Garrett took another swig of whiskey. He was tired of killing men, and felt angry with himself for killing the wrong two, plowing his way like a bull instead of catching the Kid with finesse. Billy was caught now, but it was messy—anything could happen.

When the beef had dripped its grease into the flames for nearly an hour, Garrett noticed the outlaws had fallen quiet. "Hey, Kid," he called. "How are you fixed in there?"

"Pretty good," he called back. "But we ain't got any wood to cook supper."

"Why don't you come out and get some? Be a little sociable?"

The Kid laughed. "Can't do it, Pat. Business is too confining right now."

Garrett reached for his bottle again.

Billy looked at his companions. He could see they wouldn't be any good in a fight. With a subtle bending of his intentions, he relinquished control. "So what do you want to do?"

"We gotta surrender," Rudabaugh said. "I'm starving."

Billy looked at Wilson, who said, "They'll cut us down if we run for it."

Billy looked at Pickett.

He shrugged. "Can't see we have much choice."

"I'll go along," Billy said.

"Now you're talking, Kid," Rudabaugh crowed. "But you gotta lay down some conditions."

"I said I'd go along. I ain't negotiating the surrender."

The other three looked at each other. Finally Pickett said, "You're the one wants the conditions, Dave. You should go."

Rudabaugh looked at the Kid but he gave no indication of an opinion. "All right," the fat man said. He pulled a dirty handkerchief from his pocket, tied it to the barrel of his rifle, and crawled across to poke it out the door.

Billy retreated back beside his mare. Knowing he'd lose her, he balked at going through with it. He'd regretted the other times he let his enemies take him and couldn't see how this would be different. Then he remembered what Atanacio Martínez had said when they'd gone into Dolan's store to arrest Tunstall's killers. *"Hay un otro día, Chivato,"* the constable had said, and Billy clung to that advice.

When Garrett saw the handkerchief on the rifle, he almost let himself smile.

"I want to surrender," Rudabaugh called. "I want your word you won't shoot me down."

"You got it," Garrett said.

Slowly the fat man emerged from the hut. He'd left his guns behind and walked with his hands in the air. Halfway between, he stopped and asked, "Where are you gonna take me?"

"The nearest marshal's office is in Vegas."

"They'll lynch me in Vegas."

"Where do you want to go?"

"If you promise to take us to Santa Fe, we'll surrender."

"The Kid said he'll go along with it?"

"Yeah."

"I'll take you to Santa Fe." Garrett raised his voice. "Come on out,

Kid. The rest of you, too. You won't be harmed. Leave your guns behind and come out with your hands up."

Billy patted his mare's neck in farewell. Then he dropped his gunbelt and walked into the red sunset reflecting off the snow. He walked with his arms spread wide, watching Garrett come over the rise to meet him. Garrett was smiling, carrying a shiny new Winchester. They stopped a few yards apart, the one with the gun, the other with his palms lifted to catch the last of the sun.

Garrett grinned. "Look at the fix you're in now, Kid."

"I'm alive," Billy said.

They both laughed, holding each other's eyes as the posse milled around them. Lee Hall pulled the Kid's hands together in front, tying them with rope.

"Damn, this is low class, Pat," Billy said. "I expected steel shackles."

"You'll get them. You want to eat first?"

"What'cha got? I'm particular about my food, you know."

"I bet." Garrett chuckled, leading the captives to the ravine sheltering the chuckwagon.

The posse were all there, watching the Kid with curiosity. One by one each man introduced himself and shook the Kid's hand, though it was tied with rope. Billy got into it after a while, seeing in their eyes that it meant a lot to them. He couldn't quite figure it out, but he decided this brief period of captivity might be an interesting experience.

Sitting on someone's blanket, he ate a big plate of beef and beans, chatting with the men around the fire, asking where they were from and what they were doing in the territory. After he'd asked everyone, he looked at Garrett, then back at the men. "You mean you *all* came over here from Texas jus' to get me?"

They murmured a general assent.

Billy laughed. "If I'd known I was so famous, I would've sold tickets."

Garrett shook his head, realizing the Kid didn't know the extent of his own reputation. For a moment, Garrett balked, certain that once the Kid was in the hands of the judiciary he'd be sacrificed to appease the bloodlust of the Ring. But like Brady before him, the sheriff of Lincoln County knew that to back out now would be suicide.

Garrett put the Kid on a scrawny nag that couldn't outrun a burro, and gave his mare to Stewart for helping with the capture. Watching Stewart's face gleam, Billy spit into the snow with disgust. But by the time they were on their way, he was joking again, keeping a ripple of chuckles bouncing through the posse as they rode into Sumner.

This time the reception was different. No one snickered as Garrett

rode in with the Kid and his gang, captured and tied. They rode right
through the plaza, and it was the sheriff's turn to smirk at the faces of
hostility watching from under the portals.

He took his prisoners to the blacksmith shop and ordered shackles
hand and foot. Then he left Stewart in charge, walked over to the telegraph office, and wired the sheriff in Vegas and the marshal in Santa Fe,
saying who he was bringing and when. Satisfied, he walked to the home
of his father-in-law for a meal and a bath. He was halfway through supper when Lee Hall came in.

"What is it?" Garrett asked, his heart sinking.

"There's an Indian woman with the Kid. She says Mrs. Maxwell sent
her to ask if he could call at their house and say good-bye. Stewart wants
to know if he should do it."

Garrett had learned Pete wasn't home, and he didn't think the
women were a threat, so he decided there was no need to antagonize the
Maxwells by refusing. "Take him shackled to Rudabaugh. That fat pig
couldn't run a hundred yards and the Kid won't either, towing him. But
don't leave him unguarded for the blink of an eye. You got that?"

"Yes, sir," Hall said, leaving to deliver the message to Stewart.

Billy listened, then winked at Deluvina. He wasn't really keen on
seeing Paulita while chained to Rudabaugh, but none of these Panhandle
Texans spoke Spanish, and Deluvina had told him there were guns in the
house. Billy didn't think the Texans would be stupid enough to let him
anywhere near a gun, but a long shot was always worth the try.

46

Shackled to Rudabaugh, the Kid was escorted through the plaza by two
deputies carrying rifles. The portals were lined with villagers who
watched in solemn silence as *el Chivato* was led by in chains.

He felt humiliated to be seeing Paulita while wearing shackles, but
he covered his discomfort with playful banter. Much more nimble than
Rudabaugh, Billy often outstrode him only to be caught by the chain.
Joking that he hadn't been trained to harness, the Kid laughed at his
own clumsiness. The deputies laughed, too, marveling at his ability to
make walking through snow wearing chains an adventure with its own
special challenges. Climbing stairs was even more tricky, and standing
on an icy porch could take a man down in no time. He kept it up until he
saw Paulita surrounded by her ancient ancestors watching him enter
their parlor shackled to the dirty, stinking Rudabaugh.

Mrs. Maxwell stood regally erect beside her daughter. When Deluvina joined them, Billy could hardly bear to look at their faces of grief.

Mrs. Maxwell said to Lee Hall, "Thank you for bringing him, Sheriff."

"Garrett's the sheriff," he answered, thinking surely she knew that. "We're special deputies."

"Thank you anyway," she said.

"Just following orders, ma'am," he replied, wanting to add that it was worth it to see such handsome women.

"I wonder, gentlemen," Mrs. Maxwell said, "if you would allow Billy to go into another room with my daughter so they might share a private farewell. It's just right here and has only one door."

"We can't do that, ma'am," Jim East said, exchanging a smile with Lee Hall. "All the world loves a lover, but I just don't think that would be wise."

Paulita hadn't expected her plan to work but felt compelled to try. Now she approached close to Billy. Ignoring the horrible man he was chained to and the deputies holding guns, she touched the front of Billy's shirt and looked into his eyes. "Where will they take you?"

"Santa Fe, is what they said." He smiled. "I'm all right, Paulita. Don't worry about me."

"I love you," she whispered.

"Yeah," he said softly, leaning to give her a quick kiss.

She clung to him, kissed him a long time, then held him tight until a deputy cleared his throat and she stepped away.

"*Adiós,*" Billy said, raising his manacled hands to tip his hat at Mrs. Maxwell and Deluvina.

Luz Maxwell watched him leave, thinking he was out of their lives. She believed the Kid would be sentenced to prison for a long time, long enough for Paulita to marry and become a mother. Even if he escaped, he'd be a fool to come back, and Luz knew the Kid was no fool. She remained standing in the parlor, waiting for her daughter to cry. But Paulita only excused herself and went to her room.

Luz found her sitting on the bed, tatting lace. She sat down in the window seat and studied her daughter. Paulita seemed intent on her silver needle, tying knots to follow the curve of the collar she was making. Gently, Luz asked, "Are you all right, Paulita?"

"Yes," she replied, not looking up from her work.

Luz chose her words carefully. "I would have thought you'd feel sad to see Billy like that."

"He'll get away."

"You sound certain."

"He always has."

"Because he had friends. Now Tom's gone. And Charlie. Anyone who shelters him risks being burned out. Who will help him?"

"God will," Paulita said. "Deluvina told me so."

Luz wouldn't have destroyed her daughter's courage for any reason. "I'm sure Deluvina's right," she answered. "You're doing a lovely job on that collar."

"I think so, too," Paulita said, examining it closely, "until I compare it to one Abrana has made. Then my work seems inferior."

"Abrana is especially talented. We're lucky to have her in the village."

Laying the collar aside, Paulita said, "I'm going to Charlie's funeral tomorrow."

"I don't think that's a good idea," Luz answered, surprised and thinking fast. "Billy won't be there. The posse is leaving tonight."

"I know."

"I don't think it's a good idea, Paulita. I certainly can't go. How would it look for Lucien Maxwell's widow to attend the funeral of an outlaw? And I won't have you going alone."

"Deluvina can go with me, so it'll be perfectly proper. I'll have a duenna, and I think it appropriate the family is represented when a villager dies. Manuelita comes often to the house."

"To sell her wares, as does everyone else."

"I'm going, Mother," Paulita said, picking up her lace again.

She wore a dove gray dress under a long black cloak with a hood to cover her head during prayers. Walking the mile down the road to the cemetery, she and Deluvina arrived before the procession from town. They stood near the wall, watching the pallbearers carry the casket through the gate, followed by the widow and mourners. Abrana was holding Manuelita's arm, watching her solicitously, and Paulita felt touched by their friendship.

No priest lived in Sumner so an alderman spoke. Listening to the drone of his mournful message, Paulita looked down the path to the granite stone over the grave of her father. Lucien Maxwell had been a powerful man in the territory. If he were alive, he could force the governor to bestow the pardon he'd promised. But Pete was not the man his father had been. The family fortune was diminished and their power nil away from the Pecos. Paulita had no one to intercede on her beloved's behalf. As modern as she considered herself, she lived in a patriarchal world, and like Sue McSween, could only petition power. In any other situation, the person she'd turn to would be Billy himself. Now she had no one, and she held to Deluvina for comfort.

Two dozen mourners stood in the cold wind praying for the soul of Charles Bowdre. Most of them were Mexicans, simple farmers who were also Billy's friends. They didn't linger; they tossed their clods of earth and walked quickly out of the graveyard. Manuelita stayed, the wind whipping her thin shawl as she watched the gravediggers bury her husband, waiting until the mound was patted smooth and a cross erected at his head.

Seeing how thin Manuelita's shawl was, Paulita felt guilty in her warm woolen cloak. Abrana looked snug in a long, green serape. Paulita knew green was Billy's favorite color, and she wondered if he'd given the serape to Abrana. She herself had received no gift to remember him by, hadn't even known him as Abrana had. It grieved her, and she started to leave.

At the same moment, Manuelita and Abrana turned away from the grave and saw Paulita for the first time. They shuttered their faces as they approached, not acknowledging her presence with any greeting.

When they were close, Paulita said, "Manuelita, I'm so sorry for your loss."

Manuelita's face softened as she started to speak, but Abrana interrupted her.

"That's not good enough," she snapped, then mimicked, " 'I'm so sorry.' Bullshit, Paulita. Did you think it was a game they were playing with Garrett? The Kid only came back to tell you he was leaving. He told me easy enough, but you were dense and he had to explain. So he came back and Tom was killed." Her voice wavered against crying. "Garrett tracked them through the snow, a child could have done it. Now Charlie's dead and because of you, Billy will hang!" Her tears broke and she sobbed, "Because of your stupidity, *niña!*"

It was the widow who pulled the distraught Abrana out of the graveyard. Paulita stood stunned, unable to reply as she watched them go. Then she looked at Charlie's grave, Tom's close beside it, almost as fresh. Could it be true their deaths were her fault? Because he loved her? Because he'd come back to tell her good-bye? Paulita stifled a sob, turning to Deluvina.

"Pay no attention to Abrana," Deluvina murmured. "She is jealous. *El Chivato* loves only you."

"Does he?" she whispered, letting the Navajo woman lead her through the gate and away from the graveyard.

"Believe in his strength," Deluvina said, "and he will make you strong."

"Yes," Paulita said as they walked along the road.

Deluvina sighed. "Poor Bilito, though. When I visited him before they took him away, he was shivering so in the cold. I asked what happened to his coat, and he said one of the possemen took it and called it a relic. I don't know what that means. But it was hard seeing him shiver while those men held guns, and him in chains like that. This will be a hard time for him, Paulita. Believe in his strength and you will make him strong."

"Thank you," Paulita said, kissing Deluvina's cheek as they entered the house.

Luz smiled with concern. "How are you, Paulita?"

"I'm fine, Mother," she answered, kissing her cheek, too.

Then she hurried up the stairs to her room where she closed and locked the door. Falling to her knees beneath the crucifix on the wall, Paulita prayed to God, not really knowing if she believed, but willing to believe if He would help. And because of Billy's strength, her prayers rose from the pure soul of a virgin.

Charlie Bowdre was buried on Christmas Day, 1880, while Garrett was taking his prisoners to Vegas to catch the train for Santa Fe. He had dismissed most of his posse. The four who remained rode horseback all around the prisoners, shackled together in the bed of a wagon. Garrett drove the team.

The Kid was cheerful, keeping up a joking banter with his guards and Rudabaugh, but Wilson was sour and Pickett looked worried. They stopped at Padrino's in Puerto de Luna for a change of horses, then drove all night to Hay's ranch, where they ate breakfast and traded teams again. In the middle of the afternoon, they pulled into Las Vegas.

News of their arrival had preceded them. The streets were packed with heavily armed men trying to catch sight of the prisoners. Garrett drove the team fast all the way into the yard of the jail, then whisked the men inside before their arrival could take hold with the crowd. Knowing they were after Rudabaugh for killing one of their lawmen, Garrett intended to make his stay brief. He left Stewart in charge of the prisoners, then walked over to the train depot to settle the reservations he'd made by wire.

Shackled to Wilson now, Billy stood in the large stone vestibule leading to the cells. Their iron door was open and he made Wilson shuffle over to take a look. Seeing an earthen pit, larger but otherwise identical to the jail in Lincoln, Billy shivered. He started to pace, but the chain jerked him short.

Wilson yelled, "Can't you just hold still?"

"Maybe you'd feel better if you moved once in a while," Billy said.

"Shut up!" Stewart shouted, seeing the hostility between them. "Bide your time. The smithy's coming to cut you loose for a while."

The Kid shrugged. Then he just stood there, kicking the toes of his boots against the floor.

The door opened, letting in the noise of the crowd with Lee Hall and the blacksmith. "There's a reporter outside from the *Gazette*," Hall told Stewart. "You want to let him in?"

Thinking he would be included in the write-up, Stewart said, "Sure, why not?"

Hall opened the door and shouted above the noise of the crowd, "Stewart says it's okay, Fitzpatrick."

The Kid watched him come through the door, a small man wearing a funny round hat and carrying a notepad and pencil, then shifted his attention to the blacksmith cutting the shackles. When the chains fell to the floor, the Kid laughed.

"You certainly seem to be chipper," Fitzpatrick said.

"What's the use of looking on the gloomy side?" the Kid answered, his eyes on the blacksmith cutting his manacles.

The door opened again and a group of men came in. Fitzpatrick knew they were the mayor and the city councilors, even the *mayordomo* of the *acequia madre,* accompanied by a reporter for the *Optic* and one for the Santa Fe *New Mexican,* who must have just arrived on the southbound train. They all stood staring at the Kid flexing his hands now that they were free.

He scanned the faces watching him. "Maybe now you've seen me, you'll think me half a man," he joked bitterly. "The way you write about me, you'd think I was some breed of animal."

"You don't look like an animal," Fitzpatrick answered. "I'd say you look like the hero of the Forty Thieves romance we're serializing in our paper. Have you read it?"

"No," the Kid said with a frown. "Don't go writing that shit, either. Though I can't imagine folks believe what you write anyway."

"Oh, I think they do, Mr. Bonney. We've built our reputation on veracity." Fitzpatrick was thinking he'd title his article "An Interview with the Best-Known Man in New Mexico."

"In yesterday's Extra," the Kid scoffed, "I jus' read where I called the men I ride with cowards. I would never say that."

Receiving the glare of the outlaw's pale eyes, Fitzpatrick suddenly felt uncomfortable. "I'll see that a retraction is printed."

The Kid shrugged and started to pace.

"Just stand still, Kid," Stewart said. "We'll have you outta here in a minute."

The shackles on Rudabaugh fell to the floor and Stewart stood up. "That's it," he said. "Let's go."

As the outlaws approached the cell, the Kid turned back to Fitzpatrick and laughed, then said, "They say a fool for luck and a poor man for trouble. Garrett gets 'em both."

The streets were rowdy with men carrying guns, and Garrett knew moving the prisoners would be tricky. When he walked back into the jail, Sheriff Romero was in the vestibule with half a dozen guards.

"Trouble, Stewart?" Garrett asked, expecting it.

"Romero says he won't release Rudabaugh," Stewart answered.

Garrett frowned down at the sheriff. "He's in my custody."

Romero nodded at one of his men. He opened the cell and pulled the Kid and Wilson out, handcuffed together, then slammed the door shut. Rudabaugh and Pickett watched from behind the iron bars.

"You can keep Pickett," Garrett said. "I wouldn't have arrested him if he hadn't been with the others. But I'm taking Rudabaugh."

"He killed one of my men," Romero argued. "I have a fair claim."

"That may be. But I arrested him under a federal warrant and I aim to deliver him to the territorial authorities in Santa Fe. You can negotiate with them to get him back."

"Why go to all that trouble?"

"It's the law and I say so!" Garrett jerked his head at Stewart. "Call the men in." Then to Romero, "I outrank you, Sheriff, and I'm leaving with my prisoners."

"Give him Rudabaugh," Romero muttered.

A deputy opened the cell and Rudabaugh came out, desperately watching Garrett. Pickett stood behind the bars as the cell was slammed shut again.

Barney Mason, Lee Hall, and Jim East came in from outside, their faces grim. Barney said, "It looks mean out there, Pat."

Romero smiled. "You should leave Rudabaugh here. The people will tear him apart before you get to the train."

"They'll have to get through us to do it," Garrett said. "Let's go."

Barney opened the door and they hustled for the wagon. Connected only with handcuffs, the Kid and Wilson easily hopped onto the tailgate and swung their feet over. Garrett watched Rudabaugh lumber aboard, then gave the Kid a shove deep into the bed. "Lay down and stay low," he ordered, climbing into the driver's seat. The deputies crouched with their rifles ready, bracing themselves as Garrett lashed the horses and the wagon bolted from the yard. The mob yelled, jumping out of the way as the horses galloped through the streets.

At the depot, Garrett slid the wagon broadside against the train. He leapt down and yanked the prisoners off and up the steps into the car. Four businessmen looked up with alarm as the chained captives and heavily armed lawmen walked down the aisle and claimed a block of seats.

The mob swarmed into the depot. They were all Mexicans, their faces rabid as they demanded the killer of one of their own. The train started to move, then abruptly stopped. As the mob raged against the car, Rudabaugh slid lower in his seat.

The Kid stood up and opened a window. Leaning out into the frenetic scene, he laughed with delight.

Garrett watched him with amazement, then turned around as the door to the next car opened. A burly man came in wearing the badge of a deputy U.S. marshal.

"I'm Tony Neis," he said, shaking Garrett's hand.

"What's holding us up?" he asked impatiently.

"Some Mexicans got guns on the engineer. It looks ugly. You aim to fight?"

"Damn straight. I'll arm the prisoners, if it comes to that."

The Kid laughed. "All right, Pat! All I want is a gun." Then he looked out the window again and said, "But these fellows won't fight."

Garrett wasn't so sure. He looked at the traveling salesmen watching him nervously. "There's likely to be a fight here, gentlemen. Anyone who doesn't want part of it better leave."

As the drummers scurried to escape, Garrett stepped onto the platform between cars and fired his Winchester into the air. "I order you to disperse. We're not giving you the man you want. If you try to take him, a lot of you will be killed. Go on home, all of you." Wanting to add a few choice profanities, he shut his mouth and stepped back inside the car.

The crowd howled, throwing stones. The Kid ducked to miss one, then went back to his window laughing. He saw Fitzpatrick in the crowd and shouted, "Come see me in Santa Fe sometime."

Rudabaugh was on the floor, staring with beseeching eyes at Garrett. Wilson was green, his hand shackled to the Kid's, who stood by the window enjoying himself. Stewart and the deputies were edgy. Garrett swore under his breath, wishing he had the Kid on his side. He turned to Neis. "Go on up to the engine and see if you can't move this damn machine."

Neis drew his pistol and crossed the platform to the next car. It was empty, its windows shattered by the wrath of the mob. Neis crouched low as he neared the platform to the wood car, then stepped out, looking for anyone who'd spotted him. But the crowd was all on the depot side of the tracks. He ran along the wood car and climbed the ladder into the locomotive. The engineer was gone, the cubicle empty. Neis stepped in, released the brake, and yanked the throttle.

The giant wheels spun on the tracks. Steam belched from the stack and cinders showered onto the crowd. The mob jumped away, screaming in fright. The wheels threw sparks as they spun, then the locomotive lurched forward, roaring out of the depot.

The men in the car were thrown to the floor. Garrett sat with his gun ready, watching through the open door as the mob swirled away, then swung back to yell and throw rocks, cursing the sheriff and Rudabaugh with the same evil threats. When their noise was left behind with the station, Garrett looked at the Kid. He smiled his congratulations as they both sat on the floor.

Inside the locomotive, Neis couldn't resist pulling the whistle long and loud. Then he wondered wryly if he could stop the contraption when they got to Santa Fe.

Billy had been in Santa Fe once before, when he was thirteen and new to the territory. He and his mother and his brother Joe had come to meet the man his mother would marry. Uncle Billy Antrim had found them in the plaza. Because Uncle Billy had been wearing his Sunday suit, Billy had thought him a dapper old dude with a dumb smile. A dupe, is what Billy had thought, to take on a sick woman and two nearly grown boys.

He could remember watching the ceremony, then signing his name as a witness. He'd felt as if he'd lied in church, though he hadn't said a word. He'd simply signed his name, which only meant he'd seen it happen, not that he approved. It wasn't really a lie, but Billy had never gone inside a church again.

That had been way back in 1873. It was New Year's Day of 1881 when Billy returned to Santa Fe. The train came as near as Lamy now. The marshal had a wagon ready with armed guards and his own set of shackles. His name was John Sherman and he was the highest-ranking law officer in the territory. Watching Sherman and Garrett shake hands inside the depot, Billy caught on that Garrett was going home. Sherman saw him watching and laughed.

"So this is the Kid, huh? Looks kind of small."

"Don't underestimate him," Garrett warned.

"No, that's one thing I won't do." He jerked his head at his deputies. The men came forward and put another pair of shackles between the Kid and Wilson.

Billy couldn't get Pat to meet his eyes.

"Heard you had some trouble in Vegas," Sherman said.

"We handled it," Garrett answered. "You'll probably find a transfer for Rudabaugh waiting in your office."

"Yeah, I'll send him down and he'll be hung." Sherman grinned at Rudabaugh, then said to Garrett, "Sometimes it seems like a waste of good effort to drag these bums through the courts. But that's our job, when you get down to it. We're just errand boys for the judge."

The Kid laughed and Sherman turned to him with a sneer. "He's another one we're dragging around the territory so they can decide where to hang him. I got orders to take him clear down to Mesilla." He turned back to Garrett. "I'm considering Neis. You think he can handle it?"

"From what I saw in Vegas, he's a capable man. I'm glad it won't be me. I've done my part."

"And you did it well, too," Sherman said. "I hear Catron raised the reward on the Kid to twenty-five hundred dollars. That'll buy a lot of petticoats for your wife."

Garrett looked at the Kid, who was surprised enough that he was letting it show. Defensively, the sheriff said, "What did you think, Kid, I was doing this for nothing?"

"No, I didn't think that," he answered softly. "I guess I thought you jus' like to be mean."

Garrett turned away and opened the door.

"Hey, Pat," Billy called. When the sheriff had stopped and was look-ing at him, Billy smiled and said, *"Adiós."*

"Good luck, Kid," Garrett grunted.

He was gone. The door closed and Billy looked at Sherman.

"Load 'em up," Sherman said to his deputies.

The prisoners were led out to the wagon. Chains were run through the shackles on their feet, then into brackets welded onto iron belts around the bed. When Billy realized no one ever sat on those boards ex-cept men who were chained to them, he fought to resurrect his mood.

They traveled up the Santa Fe Trail to the plaza. Billy recognized the

Palace of the Governors, a long adobe building festooned with ginger-bread. Inside those walls, Lew Wallace probably sat at his desk, not thinking of outlaws or pardons. But riding by in the prisoners' wagon, Billy thought about Lew Wallace.

As they traveled through the muddy town, people watched with hostility as the wagon rumbled by. The road ended at the imposing brick structure of the county jail. Sherman led the prisoners through a series of locked doors, each hall quieter and darker, farther from sunlight and heat. Finally the marshal pulled a cell door open, watched the prisoners walk in, then strode away, leaving two armed guards standing with the jailor.

The jailor yelled after him, "You want their chains left on?"

"Unhook the two of them, otherwise yes," Sherman called back, then the iron door slammed shut.

Looking at the shackles connecting the Kid and Wilson, the jailor said, "You sure got a heap of chains there."

Billy rattled them impatiently. "Sherman ain't taking any chances."

"He rarely does," the jailor said. "I'll have to come back with a lock-smith. Or a blacksmith. I'm not sure. But I'll be back." He closed the door and turned the huge key as he smiled at the men inside. "You'll like it here. The building is brand new."

"I didn't know that," Billy said. "When you come back, can you bring me stuff to write a letter?"

"I can do that," the jailor answered pleasantly. Followed by the two guards, he walked away, then the iron door at the end of the hall slammed shut again behind them.

Billy moved toward the wall of bars. When Wilson resisted, Billy yanked the shackles and made him follow. The hall was forty yards long, the doors to all the other cells standing open. "We're alone in here," he said.

"So what?" Rudabaugh growled.

"It's peculiar, that's all," he said, moving again.

"For Christ's sake, Kid!" Wilson complained.

Billy sat down on the floor. "What'll we do now?"

"Wait," Rudabaugh said.

It was an hour before the jailor returned with a blacksmith and a guard. Billy had spent the time studying the walls, looking for cracks in the mortar, soft spots in the seams. A new building, after all, might have flaws not yet discovered. Now he stood impatiently, watching the smithy sever the chains. As soon as he was free of Wilson, Billy sat down on the floor and wrote a letter to the governor:

January 1, 1881

Gov Lew Wallace
Dear Sir

I would like to see you for a few moments if you can spare
time.

Yours Respect.

W. H. Bonney

When he handed it over, the guard laughed at the name on the envelope. "You know how many of these the governor gets?"

"He'll get this one, won't he?"

The guard shrugged. "We'll send it to the Palace," he answered, then carried it away.

As soon as they were gone, Billy crawled under a bottom bunk, struck a match, and checked the masonry. He did the same with the other bunk, then crawled back out and sat on the floor.

"You lose something, Kid?" Rudabaugh asked.

He laughed. "You might say that. We're in the east wing, ain't we?"

"Yeah," Wilson answered, following his thoughts. "This is the outside wall, I'm sure of it."

"So?" Rudabaugh grumbled. "What're you gonna do, jus' walk through it?"

Billy pulled a large silver spoon from his sleeve and held it up.

"Where'd you get that?" Wilson whispered.

"Padrino's," Billy said. "He told me I could have anything in his store anytime I wanted, all I had to do was ask. I didn't ask, but it wasn't rightly stealing as I had permission."

"You ain't gonna dig through brick with no spoon," Rudabaugh scoffed.

"The floor's dirt," Billy said.

"A tunnel?" Wilson whispered.

"If this is the outside wall," Billy said, "we gotta have the bunks on top to hide our work. So first we'll move the beds, see if they notice, and if not," he grinned, "we'll dig our way out."

They moved the bunks, erased the trail in the dirt, then sat down to wait. The silence was greater than any Billy had ever experienced. On the prairie he was always hearing the wind, some critter calling to its mate, the ripple of water or hum of insects, cattle from far off, music maybe, people laughing, having fun.

They waited for supper as a break in the monotony, but it never came. After what seemed like an eon, Rudabaugh and Wilson fell asleep. Billy lay awake on his bunk, watching the light flicker in an unchanging pattern from the gas jets in the corridor. Knowing only that he was to be taken to Mesilla, he couldn't remember one good thing that had happened to him there. With any luck, they'd dig out and he'd never have to go.

He awoke to the same flickering pattern of light on the ceiling and the other men still snoring. Billy decided it was early morning only because they both woke up within minutes of each other, grumpy and complaining of hunger. Billy lay on his bed listening to them for a few minutes, then joked, "Maybe they're gonna starve us to death and save themselves the price of a rope."

"I ain't gonna be hung!" Wilson cried. "I'm just charged with passing counterfeit money, and I didn't even know it was phony. You gave me that hundred-dollar bill, Kid."

"Did I?" he asked, jumping down with a clatter of chains.

"Don'cha remember? The one with all them bitty pinholes in it?"

"Oh yeah," he said, stretching. "I knew you were gonna do some shopping at Dolan's store."

"So you used me to pass phony money on Dolan!" Wilson whined.

Billy shrugged. "I didn't want the damned thing. And it got you your supplies, didn't it?"

"It got me indicted!"

"Sorry about that." Billy laughed, winking at Rudabaugh. "You know what they say about bad comp'ny."

Rudabaugh guffawed. "You oughta know, Kid."

The iron door at the end of the corridor banged open. Billy walked to the bars and peered out, then laughed with pleasure. "Goddamn, Pat, jus' can't stay away, can you?"

Garrett was followed by two guards carrying rifles. "I was fixing to head south," he said, "and just wanted to make sure you boys are all right. Everything okay so far?"

"Sure, Pat," Billy said. "We're having a good time."

"Sounded like it when I came in," Garrett replied.

"We didn't get no supper," Rudabaugh complained. "No breakfast, neither."

Garrett looked at the Kid. "You've had nothing to eat?"

"Not even a drop of water," he said.

"I'll take care of it. Any other requests before I leave?"

With a suggestive grin, Billy said, "Say hello to Apolinaria for me."

Garrett turned around and walked away.

"I'd tell you to say hello to Tom," Billy yelled, pressing himself against the bars to watch the lawman's retreat, "but he ain't there no more, is he, Mis-tuh Patrick Garrett?"

The door slammed shut, leaving them in silence.

"You shouldn't get yourself all riled up, Kid," Rudabaugh said. "We're gonna be here a long time."

"Sonofabitch!" Billy said, tripping on his chain, falling and kicking at it tangled around his feet until he thought he'd explode. He let himself flop back on the floor and stared at the flickering pattern of light. The same flutter of shadows danced on the ceiling, falling in the same order at the same rhythm, over and over for hours, until the door opened and the jailor brought them supper.

They began excavating a tunnel, hoping to get at least into the yard if not outside the prison. At first they hid the dirt under the beds, then under their blankets, so they slept nestled on soft mounds of soil. The days passed, eking by to the rhythm of the scratching of the spoon and the Kid's chains as he paced. Twice a day food was brought, a thin gruel tasting vaguely of beans and onions. Once a day they were given a fresh pail of water and the slop bucket was emptied. Other than that they saw no one, and the cheerful jailor never noticed the change in the beds or the odd lumpiness under the blankets.

After the passage of weeks, Rudabaugh was taken for trial in the U.S. District Court. Found guilty of murder, he was sentenced to hang, then brought back to wait for his transfer to Vegas to stand trial there. The outlaws thought it a fine joke, since a man could only be hung once, but Marshal Sherman was in a sour mood when he came to tell the condemned man he'd be moved in the morning.

The prisoners were so chipper it made Sherman suspicious. He noticed the bunks were in a different position from those in every other cell on the block. Then he saw the lumps under the blankets and called the guards, shifting his eyes to the Kid.

Half a dozen guards came running down the corridor. They stood with their rifles ready as Sherman ordered the prisoners out. When he told two guards to move the bunk, the tunnel was exposed, shallow and pathetic for so much work, but criminal just the same. Sherman wheeled around and hit the Kid hard.

"I don't have to ask whose idea this was," Sherman growled, watching the Kid pick himself up. "Rudabaugh, you're going to Vegas tomorrow to be hung." He looked at Wilson and spit on the floor. "Put the other two in separate cells and don't feed 'em tonight. Bring the Kid with me."

A guard at each elbow, Billy was led along the corridor, through the iron door, down a flight of stairs he had to take slowly because of his shackles, along another corridor and down more stairs, to a wooden box five feet square furnished with only a stool. Sherman told the Kid to sit down. The guards chained him to both the stool and hardware in the floor, then left.

"A lot of folks have been asking to see you," Sherman said in a pleasant tone. "They want to bring you presents and sit and talk to help you pass the time, but I tell them I can't allow that. 'He's a dangerous man,' I say, 'and I won't be responsible for your safety.' So I send them away, with their pies and handknit scarves to keep *el Chivato* warm in prison. Sometimes I keep the food. Depends on how hungry I am." He grinned, then stepped back and closed the door.

47

Even the prairie on a moonless night when clouds hid the stars hadn't been as black as solitary in the jail of Santa Fe. Even that night they'd stolen Chisum's herd, stampeding through a darkness so inky Billy hadn't been able to see his mare beneath him. Tom had been leading that night, even though he could see no better than Billy could. Only at the end Tom couldn't see, couldn't control his horse or shoot his gun. He'd sat there spinning in the bright snow.

Billy started to get up but the chains held him down. He moved again to make them clatter, discovering the dark wasn't empty, the silence not quiet. He thought of Paulita kissing him good-bye. Cuffed together in front of him, his hands had pressed between her legs. Damn! if she didn't open them more, so that standing there in front of her mother and the lawmen, he'd had to fight getting hard. Damn! if she wasn't a tease. He tried to get up. The chains held him down. He told himself he wasn't stupid, he could get it through his head he was chained in place.

The weeks passed. It was February, though Billy didn't know it. The time spent chained to the stool felt like forever. Sometimes the door would open, flooding his cell with light, and he'd see people staring in at him. Normal people, not lawmen or guards. Women in fancy dresses and men in odd hats. Billy would squint through the sudden glare, then the door would close and he'd be left in the dark again. His mind spun, trying to latch on to a plan of escape.

One day when the jailor brought supper, Billy asked to write a letter. He was given paper, pencil, and a stub of a candle that gave him light for half an hour. The next day Sherman opened the door and stood in the light holding a plate of gruel. "I hear you have a letter to go out."

"So?" Billy asked, squinting at him.

"All mail going in or out is censored."

"I don't care, long as you deliver it."

The letter lay at Billy's feet. Sherman told him to hand it over as far as he could. Giving the Kid the plate of food, Sherman leaned against the wall and read the letter.

> Gov Lew Wallace
> Dear Sir
>
> I wrote you a little note the other day but have received no answer I expect you have forgotten what you promised me two years ago, but I have not; and I think you had ought to have come and see me as I have requested you to. I have done everything that I promised you I would and you have done nothing that you promised me I think when you think the matter over you will come down and see me, as I can explain everything to you.
>
> it looks to me like I am getting left in the cold. I am not treated right by Sherman. he lets every stranger that comes to see me through curiosity in to see me, but will not let a single one of my friends in, not even a lawyer. I guess they mean to send me up without giving me any show but they will have a nice time doing it. I am not without friends. I shall expect to see you some time soon.
>
> Patiently waiting
> I am very truly yours Respect.
>
> W. H. Bonney

Sherman refolded the letter, then slid it into his pocket. "I heard rumors the governor promised you a pardon, but I never heard Wallace mention it."

Billy made no reply as he kept shoveling the tasteless gruel into his mouth.

"The governor's been out of town, maybe that's why he didn't answer your first letter," Sherman said. "Always worth another try, isn't it? But saying bad things about your jailors isn't smart, Kid. You're gonna be with us a long time. You best learn what behooves you."

"I've heard that word before," Billy said.

Sherman chuckled. "Too bad you never listened."

"I listened enough to know I'm s'posed to have a trial. How long you gonna keep me here?"

"We're waiting for the papers from San Miguel so we can send them with you to Mesilla. The judge likes to have all the papers together so he knows who he's sentencing."

"Is it gonna be Bristol?" Billy asked, licking the plate.

"He's the only judge down there."

"I thought Wallace was gonna replace him with Leonard."

"He tried, but he failed." Sherman smiled. "I don't think there's another drop on that plate, Kid."

Billy tossed it to him. "Why do I get the feeling you enjoy this, Sherman?"

"Most of the men I deal with grunt when they want to say something. It's always a pleasure talking with you, Kid. I'll see that your letter gets delivered." He turned to go.

"What about a lawyer?"

Sherman looked back with a smile of condescension. "We'll see," he said, then he closed the door and it was dark again.

So the governor had been gone. That explained it. Surely he would come talk to him. Wallace had given his word. He was a gentleman, a goddamned general. Who kept their word if generals didn't? Dudley didn't. He was a colonel. Wallace had fired Dudley. Took him to court. Dudley was exonerated. Dolan was exonerated. Wallace had failed. Billy clattered his chains in raucous glee. He sure could pick allies, that's all he could think. Tunstall and Mac and now a governor who'd been gelded by the Ring. Billy had bet on the wrong horse every time out of the gate, and it was funny, if nothing else.

That was the fourth of March. Sherman was gone from Santa Fe and no one came even to taunt him. Just the daily supply of gruel and walk to the latrine. If not for that walk, Billy didn't think he could stay sane. Being able to move brought hope. His legs were still there, his feet still covered ground. They would do it again, free of chains.

He amused himself remembering when he'd been free, riding with Tom, or Brewer and the Regulators, the campfires and banter. He remembered the Jones family saying grace before dinner, when little Nib had been teething on John's six-shooter. Remembered being on his knees at John's grave, promising Ma'am not to go after Olinger. That was Billy's strongest regret. Now he created intricate fantasies of revenge, channeling his anger into hatred for Olinger, giving himself a reason to survive and keep himself strong.

There was a softer, more succulent reason, but he rarely let himself think about her. When he did, his loins burned with pain and he turned his thoughts to Abrana, memories of fucking Abrana. He realized that's what he'd done in the flesh, taken to Abrana what he felt for Paulita, and it was no wonder both women felt cheated. He tried to imagine what they were doing, and how Manuelita was getting along without Charlie. But remembering the quiet streets of Sumner shaded by cottonwoods along the river, and how he'd never even thought about having the freedom to walk down the street and see Paulita whenever he wanted, he shut those memories off fast.

That left him with memories of men, riding the country, fighting battles, tall tales he'd heard. He repeated them all aloud, thinking it was dangerous to talk to himself but he had to do something or he'd go crazy. The meals came, always the same gruel, the daily walks to the latrine, stretching his muscles, remembering freedom, then back in the dark, his mind wild with visions, memories ricocheting with repercussions.

Mrs. Mac in front of the fire telling them to kill Brewer; not Brewer—Brady; but Billy could see now that the one death had led to the other. Chisum laughing at Billy's gun, saying, "I know you won't shoot an unarmed man." Why hadn't he? Why did he follow some rules, break others? Why had he killed any of those men? They hadn't attacked him until he rode for Chisum. He'd thought it was for Tunstall and later Mac, but it was Chisum behind them. Except he hadn't been there when it came down. So Billy had killed for Chisum, a man he despised. When he grew weary of massacring Olinger, he throttled Chisum, and time passed, the darkness forever before him.

One day he had a visitor. A slight man wearing spectacles came into the cell and stared in shock at the small room and the prisoner cramped from sitting chained on the stool so long.

"I'm Edgar Caypless, a court-appointed attorney," the visitor said. "I understand you asked to see me."

"What does court-appointed mean? You gonna work for me or the judge?"

"For you, Mr. Bonney, if there's anything I can do here in Santa Fe. I can't travel to Mesilla and represent you there. I'm sorry."

"What I need, you can do here," Billy said. "Garrett stole my horse when he arrested me, said property belonging to outlaws was to be confiscated. Was that legal?"

"There's no law stipulating that. If he did indeed take your horse, you have the right of replevin."

Billy laughed. "I want to replevin her then. But I don't want my mare back, I want you to sell her and give me the money."

Caypless nodded. "The mare's in Las Vegas. Garrett gave her to

Frank Stewart and Stewart made a gift of her to Mrs. Scott Moore, who lives in that city."

"You seem to know all about it."

"It's been in the newspapers. Mrs. Moore renamed the mare Kid and shows her off to anyone who's curious."

"Sherman does the same to me," Billy said. "Can we get the mare back?"

"Is that what you wish? For me to draw up papers of replevin?"

"Yeah."

"I'll proceed immediately. Is there anything else?"

"No, jus' the money." Billy smiled. "You won't forget me, will you, Caypless?"

"Indeed not, Mr. Bonney. I'll be back in a few days to let you know how our case is proceeding."

But he didn't come back. Billy had liked Caypless, so he guessed it was Sherman making everything as hard as he could.

One day toward the end of March, the door opened again. Billy squinted into the light, recognizing first the silhouette of Sherman, then, slowly, the face of Henry Hoyt.

"Hey, Henry!" Billy laughed, standing up the few inches his chains allowed. "It's good to see you."

The doctor from Tascosa advanced slowly into the cell, horror plain on his face. "Are all these chains necessary, Marshal?"

"You bet," Sherman answered. "I had them specially forged of the strongest steel made. They weigh fifteen pounds, and that's a new lock. I'm taking no chances he gets away."

"I can see that," Hoyt said. "May we be alone?"

"Nope," the marshal said, leaning against the wall.

"Don't mind him," Billy said to Hoyt. "He's too dumb to follow an intelligent conversation anyway."

Hoyt chuckled. "How are you managing?"

"I'm all right, Doc. How about you? Still in Tascosa?"

"No, I have a practice in Bernalillo now." He smiled wryly. "Not so many gunshot wounds, more broken bones." Then he frowned. "Do they ever let you up from there?"

"Oh yeah, the marshal treats me like his brother. I got no complaints."

Hoyt nodded. "I'm to have dinner with the governor tonight."

Billy smiled. "Tell him hello for me, will you?"

"Is it true he promised you a pardon? We've heard rumors but the Palace is silent."

"Man makes a lot of promises," Billy said.

"I shall speak to him on your behalf."

"Thanks, Doc, but don't stick your neck out. I already wrote him two letters he didn't answer. So I took that for an answer, you know what I mean?"

"Write him again."

"Why bother? 'Sides, I kinda like aggravating ol' Sherman."

"You won't have long for that," the marshal said. "You go to Mesilla tomorrow."

"Write the governor again," Hoyt urged. "I'll take the letter to the Palace myself."

Billy knew once he was out of Santa Fe it would be all that easier for the governor to forget him, so he took the chance, the long shot again. "You got any paper?"

His note was brief, his sentiment succinct:

Gov Lew. Wallace
Dear Sir

For the last time I ask. Will you keep your promise. I start below tomorrow. send answer by bearer.

Yours Resp.

W. Bonney

He gave it to Hoyt, who started to put it in his pocket, but Sherman lifted it from his fingers. Hoyt turned in outrage to Billy.

The Kid laughed. "Rules of the house. Don't let it get to you."

"Good advice," Hoyt murmured. "Is there anything I can bring you?"

"I'd love to have a six-gun, but I don't think Sherman would let you bring it in."

"Visit's over," the marshal said. "Let's go, Hoyt."

The doctor leaned down to shake hands. "I hope to see you again, Billy. Good luck."

"Same to you, Doc. Hope you have a plum of a practice with those rich folks back East, like you said you wanted."

"Thank you," Hoyt answered, unable to think of anything to wish back.

Henry Hoyt had never seen a building less deserving of its name than the Palace of the Governors. It was true that the rulers of New Mexico had officiated from its rooms for over two centuries, but there was nothing palatial about the edifice. The adobe walls were crumbling away, and the floors creaked as Hoyt was escorted through a hall to the state dining room. During dinner, he had the disquieting experience of watching sand filter from the latillaed ceiling onto his plate. He wondered if he had an unfortunate seat, or if the governor had learned to accept sand in his food as a hardship of his post.

Rumor said that Lew Wallace would soon leave the territory since his novel had been published to high critical acclaim. Hoyt looked forward to reading it, a tale of the Christ, reportedly, called *Ben Hur*. Mrs. Wallace, who had only recently joined her husband, was a handsome woman with dark hair wound in two braided ovals over her ears. She wore a coral silk dress and a dozen silver bracelets from the Middle East.

Hoyt kept listening to her bracelets chime as she moved her hands in accompaniment to the story she was telling. The sound was familiar, reminding him of something he'd heard just recently though he couldn't place it. Her words pierced through his puzzle when she said, "And we were told terrible stories about Billy the Kid. How he intended to ride into the plaza and murder the governor. I worried so, with Mr. Wallace writing by the lamp before the window night after night, but he wouldn't heed my advice."

Remembering the chains on Billy, Hoyt looked down the table at the governor as Wallace laughed and said, "Well, I survived. Shall we, gentlemen?"

They crossed the drafty vestibule and entered a room facing the plaza. Wallace offered cigars, saying they were direct from Havana and a gift from President Hayes.

"The territory is changing so fast, gentlemen," he mused, staring into the fire as he puffed on his cigar. "When I first came, I traveled from Trinidad in a stagecoach, and only the forts were connected by telegraph. Now every village has its telegraphy office, and when I leave I'll depart on a train. Isn't that amazing progress to have been accomplished in only three years?"

The gentlemen murmured agreement. One asked, "Have you accepted another position, then, Governor?"

"I've just learned I'm to be appointed ambassador to Constantinople," he announced, smiling around his cigar.

The room of a dozen gentlemen, mostly travelers passing through the capital, all hurrahed their congratulations. Someone added that it seemed an especially apt appointment.

"Yes," Wallace said, knocking his ash into the fire. "I've always been fascinated with the Middle East."

"As proved by your novel," Hoyt said. When the governor looked up, eager to discuss his book, the doctor reminded him, "I'm Henry Hoyt, a physician from Bernalillo, though Minnesota is my home."

"Yes, I remember, Doctor," Wallace said. "Have you read *Ben Hur?*"

"Not yet, though I anticipate doing so with pleasure. I wonder, however, that you found time with all your pressing duties as governor. You must be a great manager of hours, sir."

"I try not to squander them." He smiled. "In truth, though, the territory practically runs itself, at least now that the violence has been quelled."

"Are you referring to the Lincoln County War?" a gentleman asked.

"Yes," Wallace said, his eyes nearly as bright as the coal gleaming on his cigar. "I met the Kid when I was in Lincoln."

"The ruthless outlaw who threatened your death?" an Easterner asked in awe.

Wallace smiled. "I had him demonstrate his shooting skill for me." He laughed and knocked his ash into the fire. "I was impressed, gentlemen, believe me."

They all chuckled politely, then one asked, "But weren't you afraid to be with him when he had a gun?"

Wallace shook his head with an amused smile. "He wouldn't have harmed me. I was the only one between him and his enemies, you see."

The gentlemen laughed, standing in the warm room smoking their presidential cigars.

"Excuse me, Governor," Hoyt said. "I'm a friend of Mr. Bonney's and I've brought you this letter."

Wallace took the envelope and slid it into his pocket. "Did you visit him in prison, then?"

"Yes, just today. Is there any hope for his case?"

"That depends on the expertise of his attorneys."

"We heard rumors, sir, of a pardon."

Wallace looked into the fire a long moment. "It's too late," he finally said. "Anyway, I don't know why a fellow like him should expect help from me."

Billy didn't think it was too late. As he sat in the dark after Hoyt's visit, he thought about the doctor and how different their lives were. Henry Hoyt would return to his world carrying his frontier adventures like luxuriant pelts to warm the cold nights of old age. A doctor who healed, he would never kill another man, and he'd been allowed that luxury by the luck of his birth.

Billy didn't begrudge him that, but he saw the difference. In Lincoln

County, Hoyt would have been the same as any of them: Dick Brewer or
George Coe, Fred Waite or Charlie Bowdre. Billy wondered what he'd be
like if he'd been born in Hoyt's place. Would he be strong enough to
walk through life, even on the frontier, even in Tascosa, without violence?

Strong enough? Strongarm, strongman, gun. Without weapons you
were McSween. Maybe Heiskell Jones, but his eight armed sons compensated for his pacifism. Yet Heiskell possessed a quiet strength that
brought out the best in men. Billy didn't think he did, except in battle.
He could ramrod fighters, he was good at that. But he'd never had the
religious awakening George Coe experienced on the mountain. Never
possessed the moral rectitude of Dick Brewer, drawing the line without
equivocation. It is who I am, Mac had said.

Billy knew that only with courage. He would never run, never surrender. He had done both. He regretted it and raged against the chains,
then remembered he was going to Mesilla in the morning. He'd be outside traveling across country, pass many strangers, sit close to men wearing guns, one of which would be his chance.

He thought of the guns he had owned. The Winchester given by
Tunstall then taken by Brady, retrieved from the sheriff's dead hand only
to be left behind in the burning McSween home. The Colt's Lightning
Action he'd surrendered coming in to try for the pardon. The forty-four
he'd left in the hut with his mare, all his belongings abandoned on the
dirt floor at Stinking Springs.

He tried to remember himself before his first gun. He'd bought it off
Sombrero Jack as a kid in Silver City. Now *there* was bad company. Billy
laughed, remembering the grizzled old drunk. Uncle Billy might have
bought him a gun if they'd been friends and gone hunting together. He
realized he hadn't given his stepfather a chance, hadn't even met him
halfway. He'd hated him from the first time he heard his name. As he
hated his father.

Billy had lied to Paulita when he told her he never knew his father.
He knew him. His name was "Dad" McCarty. That's the only name Billy
ever heard. Dad McCarty owned a fruitstand near the tenement where
Katherine McCarty, who wasn't related, had lived.

She must have been all of nineteen, working in a factory twelve hours
a day, stopping at the fruitstand on her way home in the evenings, buying an apple or a pear for her supper. Billy didn't know how long the
courtship had lasted, but he was a product of the consummation. He'd
grown up sleeping on the trundle bed in the parlor with his brother.
Except Billy didn't sleep.

On the nights the fruit vendor came, Billy would lie there as long as he could stand it, trying to shut out the sounds from the bedroom but hearing every nuance. His mother's little mewing noises, the man panting until it was over. Then it would start again. Her initial moan of protest followed by murmurs of acquiescence. The bedsprings, her small stifled cries, and Billy would get up and leave.

He discovered he liked prowling the streets at night. Never a great sleeper, he felt alert in the quiet hours before dawn. Randy with aggression and the rage he felt in defense of his mother's virtue, he began picking fights with the coppers on the beat, until he became known as a troublemaker and ended up sitting in the office of a welfare lady who pronounced him a bastard.

In the darkness of his cell in Santa Fe, Billy remembered that boy prowling the midnight streets of New York City looking for trouble. He'd come a long way but he'd found it. Good things, too. He'd found friends, shared good times. He wasn't hated like Jesse Evans, wasn't an unbathed stinking pig like Dave Rudabaugh, or a weakling like Wilson crying because he'd been duped with a bogus hundred-dollar bill. *El Chivato* didn't cry. He'd outwait his enemies, ready to pounce on his chance when it came.

Ready to pounce like a cougar calculating the best instant to leap. That's how he'd get Olinger. Billy would play with him like a cat, let him think he had a chance and watch him scramble as Frank Coe had when they'd killed McNab, running up arroyos toward the mountains. Every arroyo Olinger chose would be boxed in. Billy would let him run to the next one where the escape would be tighter, and Olinger would remember firing those slugs into the back of John Jones. Olinger hadn't known John was a friend of the Kid's. Now he knew, now as he scuttled through sand crumbling under his bulk. Billy would watch with a smile, waiting for that irrevocable moment.

On his knees beside John's grave, he'd promised Ma'am not to go after Olinger. Billy knew she wanted no more killing, and that was a good goal. But some people deserved to die. Certainly Bob Olinger. Certainly John Chisum. Garrett, now, too, for killing Tom and Charlie. Billy realized it would never stop, and that's what Ma'am had been talking about. The killer always deserved retribution, but at some point the war had to end.

Alone in a dark cell, without his gun that had made him so famous, without his friends who'd obscured the meaning of his acts, Billy saw he was the dupe. He'd looked at the world, seen violence was effective, and become skilled at destruction, then followed the whims of fate to a cauldron of murder called the Lincoln County War. It had been a real war. Only the generals sat in banks instead of offices in Washington, sending their commands down through the ranks. Billy had been where the buck stopped both ways: he executed the deed, and he bore the culpability before the law.

If he hadn't been so visible, if he hadn't taken his due from Chisum so outrageously, if the people didn't talk about him so much, serenade him in jail and shelter him from soldiers, then his enemies might have left him alone. But that's who he was. More than his gun, not only his gun, he was *el Chivato,* whom the people loved. Billy found peace with that thought. He decided that when his chance came he'd go to Mexico and live among the *pobres.* Maybe he wouldn't even tell them who he was. He'd be just a stray gringo wanting to make friends.

The door of his cell opened and Billy blinked in the sudden light, seeing Sherman's silhouette as the jailor came in to unlock the chains. Slowly Billy stood up, easing his muscles, stretching them gently, watching Sherman as the chains rattled free from the pins in the floor. The marshal beckoned him out. Billy moved awkwardly, dragging the fifteen pounds of shackles. He shuffled into the corridor and saw the men who would take him to Mesilla: Deputy U.S. Marshal Tony Neis, the burly man he'd seen on the train in Vegas, and standing like a bear beside him, Lincoln County Deputy Sheriff Bob Olinger.

Billy smiled, thinking life was a bitch but she sure was a hot one. "Howdy, Bob," he said. "That's a lot of guns you got. You know how to use 'em?"

"Just make a break, Kid, and I'll prove it," he snarled.

Sherman laughed, then said to Neis, "If you don't get him there alive, nobody's gonna cry. But do your best."

48

Billie Wilson traveled south with them, having been indicted for more than the counterfeit money after all. The grand jury had ordered him arraigned for the murder of Carlyle. The Kid and Rudabaugh were included on the indictment but that didn't make Wilson any happier. He was poor company, silent and glum most of the journey. Neis was friendly enough, but taciturn. So that left Billy with Olinger.

He watched the deputy constantly and enjoyed seeing him start when their eyes met. Olinger would shroud his fright with an ugly insult, keeping up a steady flow of curses without being goaded. Billy just smiled, waiting for the stupid man to slip up.

They rode the same prisoner wagon back to the train, then traveled in a coach with other passengers to Bernalillo, where the train stopped in the depot for half an hour. Billy sat looking out the window, imagining himself free again. When he saw Henry Hoyt in the crowd, he stood up and yelled, "Hey, Henry!"

"Sit down," Olinger barked.

Hoyt entered the far end of the car with two other men. He was smiling and Billy half stood up, calling hello. As he shook the doctor's hand, Billy laughed and said, "I didn't think I'd get to see you again, Henry."

"No," Hoyt answered with a puzzled frown at the men who'd come with him. They were quickly retreating back down the aisle. "I was going to introduce you," he said, embarrassed.

"Don't worry about it," Billy said with a wink. "They're prob'ly scared of all the guns these guys have."

Hoyt looked down at the deputies, then back at Billy. "I spoke to Wallace. Did you hear from him?"

Billy shook his head. "That's come and gone, Doc."

Hoyt remembered the governor had said the same. "Is there anything I can do for you?"

"You can get me a pistol," Billy answered. "I'd love to face ol' Bob here in a fair fight."

"You ain't gonna get that chance," Olinger sneered.

Hoyt looked at the lawmen again, then at Billy shackled hand and foot, and it sank in that the young desperado was en route to his execution.

Billy grinned, guessing his thoughts. "Don't worry, Doc. There's many a slip 'twixt the cup and the lip. A judge told me that once and damn! if it didn't come true."

"Won't be no slip this time," Olinger growled.

Billy laughed and Hoyt marveled at his spirits. When the train started to move, they shook hands, then Hoyt jumped off and stood waving on the platform. Billy waved back until he couldn't see him anymore.

The countryside was beautiful, the air fresh through the open window, the snow-covered mountains looming into a blue sky vibrant with sunshine. Billy whistled as he listened to the wheels carrying him closer to Lincoln and his friends.

Rincon was the end of the line. From there, they continued their journey south in a wagon. The Kid and Wilson were shackled together in the bed, Neis drove the team, and Olinger rode horseback behind, his shotgun perched on his hefty thigh. They traveled on through the night, following the Rio Grande. The river valley was a flat desert stretching speckled with cactus all the way to the Jicarillas, the Capitans, and the Sacramentos—mountains Billy knew well.

They arrived in Mesilla in the middle of the afternoon. Among the crowd gathered outside the jail, Billy saw men with small cards reading PRESS stuck into the bands of their hats. Still shackled together, he and Wilson started their mincing shuffle toward the door. A man stepped forward and said, "I'm Oscar Pall from the Philadelphia *Times*. Which one of you is the Kid?"

"He is," Billy said, laying his hand on Wilson's shoulder.

"Mr. Bonney," Pall asked Wilson, "will you tell us your age?"

Wilson looked at Billy with silent disgust, sick to death of his jokes. The lawmen hustled them inside before any more questions were asked.

On March 30, 1881, before the Honorable Warren H. Bristol, Case No. 441, *The United States of America* v. *Charles Bowdre, et al.,* was called. Only one defendant was led into the courtroom, shackled and unbathed, to stand before the bench and enter a plea. The judge looked down and asked if the accused was represented by counsel. The clerk answered that he was not. When Bristol then asked if he had financial resources to hire an attorney, the clerk said the defendant was indigent.

Bristol had anticipated that. He asked Albert J. Fountain if he was available to take the case, listened to the affirmative reply, then pronounced: "The defendant is given until ten o'clock tomorrow morning to confer with his attorney and enter a plea to the indictment."

Billy was led from the court into a small room with a table and one chair. There was no window and he could hear the two guards chatting in Spanish outside the door. In the mincing steps allowed by his shackles, Billy paced the scant distance back and forth.

Albert Jennings Fountain was a dynamic man in the territory. His law practice flourished despite his opposition to the Ring, and his Mesilla newspaper, the *Independent,* had been a voice for McSween. Perhaps affection for his fallen ally inspired him to aid the cause of the last Regulator. He bustled into the room, sat down and pulled a sheaf of papers from his satchel, then looked up at the man watching him. "It's a difficult defense, Kid. I'll need your help."

"What do you want me to do?" he asked, taking in the lawyer's fancy clothes and soft hands, wondering if he and Fountain could pull together as a team.

"Tomorrow I'll interpose a plea on the Buckshot Roberts indictment. Blazer's Mill is not now and was not at the time of the crime, if any," he paused to smile, "part of the Mescalero Reservation. Therefore, the federal courts have no jurisdiction."

"What's that mean?"

"The charge will be dismissed. You'll be remanded into the custody of the Doña Ana authorities to stand trial for the murder of Brady."

"Will I get a dif'rent judge?"

"Same room, same judge. Just a change of names on the door."

"Is Rynerson gonna be prosecutor?"

"He retired. Filed on the old Tunstall ranch and is doing quite well running cattle, I hear."

"Prob'ly partners with Dolan," Billy scoffed.

"As a matter of fact, he is," Fountain said. "Nothing has changed since before the war, except the county lost many good men."

"Seems like the good ones are who we lost," Billy said.

"Yes. Well, let's try to save your life, shall we?"

"Sounds good."

"Is there anyone who could testify on your behalf?"

"To say what?"

"That you weren't behind the gate when the ambush occurred?"

He shook his head. "I was there."

"That you didn't fire a weapon at the sheriff and his men?"

"I fired it."

"That you didn't intend to kill Brady and Hindman?"

"I intended to kill more of 'em than we did."

Fountain frowned and shuffled his papers. "What about Fred Waite?" he asked, reading the name from the page. "Would he testify on your behalf?"

"He's up in the Nations. We could write and ask."

"We don't have time for that. We go to trial in three days. What about John Middleton, Hendry Brown, the Coes?"

"None of 'em could get here in three days."

"Is there anyone in Lincoln who could testify for you?"

"To say what? I ain't gonna ask my friends to lie and say I wasn't there. Everybody knows I was."

"Is there some extenuating circumstance as to why you shouldn't be held accountable for Brady's death?"

"I don't know that word."

"Were you following orders, did someone hire you to do it, ask you to as a favor? Was it because you wanted to impress your friends, did you go along because they were doing it?"

He shook his head.

Fountain frowned. "You must make yourself a victim, Kid. Throw yourself on the mercy of the court. Say you're sorry, that you were duped, and beg forgiveness."

"You gotta be shitting me."

"It's your only chance. If the jury believes you, they may come back with a second- or third-degree conviction carrying a sentence of ten to twenty years, as opposed to execution."

"I'll take execution."

"Do you want to plead guilty?"

"I didn't say that."

"Not guilty?"

"Yeah."

"On what defense?"

"Self-defense. The fucker was trying to kill us."

"Had he threatened your life?"

"You were here then, Fountain. What do you think?"

"I'm not on trial," he answered curtly. "Had you direct knowledge that Brady was acting to kill you?"

"I heard him say jus' before I fired that he was looking forward to hanging me."

"But at that point, you had already decided to kill him, you were in place, ready to do it. What sent you there?"

Billy remembered Mrs. Mac standing in front of the fire telling them to kill the sheriff, Chisum stepping from the shadows and offering blood money. If Billy told the truth, he might scratch the surface of Chisum's arrogance, but he would destroy Mrs. Mac.

"Kid?" Fountain asked, straining for patience. "Why did you kill Sheriff Brady?"

Billy smiled. "He took my Winchester. I wanted it back."

"You realize you're telling me we have no defense."

"I get the feeling it wouldn't do me any good if we had."

"You'll be convicted, no doubt," Fountain said, standing up and dropping his papers into his satchel. "We can always appeal. Perhaps before the territorial court in Santa Fe you'll have a better chance. I'll see you tomorrow."

On April 5, Billy listened to Fountain enter the plea on the jurisdiction of the Buckshot Roberts murder. Judge Bristol gave the defendants their freedom from further prosecution and ordered them to go thence without delay. Billy smiled bitterly, thinking Charlie would like to go thence. Then he laughed when Bristol droned on that William H. Bonney, alias Kid, was to be remanded into the custody of the sheriff of Doña Ana County and returned to court to plead to the charge of the murder of William Brady and George Hindman. The following day, Billy stood up and said, "Not guilty." Then he was taken back to jail.

His cell was a dirty, windowless room, stuffy and unfurnished except for a slop bucket in the corner. Billy sweated in the heat, thinking it would feel good to be clean again. He'd had neither a bath nor a change of clothes since the night just before Christmas when he'd ridden into Fort Sumner to say good-bye to Paulita.

On April 8, he was again taken to court. He had barely walked in when the clerk called, "The Territory of New Mexico versus John Middleton, Hendry Brown, Frederick Waite, and William H. Bonney, alias Kid, charged with the murders of Sheriff William Brady and Deputy George Hindman in the township of Lincoln on April first, 1878."

The jury was empaneled, Mexicans all, screened and offered by Simon B. Newcomb, the district attorney prosecuting the case. The territory called three witnesses: Isaac Ellis, Saturnino Baca, and Jacob Mathews. Only Ellis was uncomfortable performing his civic duty. Baca was vindictive, Mathews triumphant. They all answered the same questions with nearly the same words: that they knew the defendant had been behind the gate from which the ambush erupted, that he fired his weapon at Brady and his deputies from that place of concealment, that the bullets fired at that time from that place caused the death of Sheriff Brady and Deputy Hindman.

On the second day of the trial, Bristol instructed the jury. Fountain offered a motion that they be allowed to choose between conviction for first-degree murder or acquittal. He didn't want it that way, his client insisted. Bristol ignored the motion and instructed the jury that they could find the defendant guilty of first-, second-, or third-degree murder, but if they believed beyond a reasonable doubt that the defendant actually fired the shots causing the deaths of the deceased, or was present and assisted in firing the fatal shots, or assisted the parties who fired the same by his advice, encouragement, procurement, or command from a premeditated design to effect the deaths of the deceased, the defendant must be found guilty in the first degree.

The jury deliberated twenty minutes and returned with a verdict of guilty in the first degree.

On April 13 at five o'clock in the afternoon, the last Regulator was returned to court for sentencing. When Bristol looked down at the young outlaw and asked if he had anything to say, Billy shook his head. Bristol intoned: "The defendant shall be confined in prison in the County of Lincoln, by the sheriff of said county, until on Friday, the thirteenth day of May, in the year of Our Lord Eighteen Hundred and Eighty-one, between the hours of nine of the clock in the forenoon and three of the clock in the afternoon, when he, the said William Bonney, alias Kid, shall be taken from such prison to a suitable and convenient place of execution, and then and there the said William Bonney, alias Kid, shall be hanged by the neck until his body be dead."

Fountain walked with Billy out of the courtroom. "It's what we expected. Have you thought about the appeal?"

"I'd have to go back to the jail in Santa Fe?"

"For the interim, but with the possibility of being exonerated."

Billy laughed. "I've been fucked, I may as well be exonerated. What would an appeal cost?"

"I could begin with a small retainer," Fountain answered.

"I'll let you know," Billy said, shaking his hand.

Before being locked in his cell, he asked for paper to write a letter. The guard merely laughed and shut the door. On the fifteenth, Billy was given the stationery and told he would leave for Lincoln in a matter of hours. Billy sat on the floor and wrote Caypless in Santa Fe.

Dear Sir

I would have written before this but could get no paper. My United States case was thrown out of court and I was rushed to trial on my Territorial charge. Was convicted of murder in the first degree and am to be hanged on the 13th day of May. Mr. A. J. Fountain was appointed to defend me and has done the best he could for me. He is willing to carry the case further if I can raise the money to bear his expense. The mare is about all I can depend on at present, so hope you will settle the case right away and give him the money you get for her. If you do not settle the matter with Scott Moore and have to go to court about it, either give Fountain the mare or sell her at auction and give him the money. Please do as he wishes in the matter. I know you will do the best you can for me in this. I shall be taken to Lincoln tomorrow. Please write and direct care of Garrett, sheriff. Excuse bad writing. I have my handcuffs on. I remain as ever,

Yours respectfully

W. H. Bonney

At ten o'clock that night he was surrendered by the Doña Ana deputies into the custody of officers from Lincoln County. Deputy Sheriff Bob Olinger was in charge of the men chosen to transport the prisoner. Billy's old nemesis Jake Mathews was among the guard, as was John Kinney, the notorious outlaw and rapist who had been reinstated as a deputy. They both grinned as they watched the Kid shuffle toward them in shackles. The other men, Tom Williams, Dave Reade, and Wes Lockhart, didn't know the Kid. They were surprised at how young he was, how agile despite the chains, how sharp and pale his eyes were, how calmly he stood in the cool of the night while they exchanged documentation.

Moving the Kid was supposed to be secret, but a small crowd had gathered outside the jail. They were nonthreatening and the lawmen ignored them, until a man stepped forward. The guards all pulled their guns, but when they saw it was only Hawkins from the *News* they relaxed and let him approach.

"Mr. Bonney," the journalist asked with the utmost politeness, "how do you feel about traveling with these men?"

The Kid laughed. "I'll stay with 'em till their whiskey runs out."

"Do you think you have anything to fear from them?"

The Kid's eyes sparkled as if he considered the question a fine joke. "I don't think they'll hurt me," he finally said, "unless someone tries a rescue. They've said if that happens, they'll kill me first and deal with my friends later."

"Do you expect a pardon from the governor?"

The Kid kicked his boots into the dirt, his chains rattling. "Considering the promise he made, I think he should pardon me. Don't know that he'll do it. I think it hard that I should be the only one to suffer the extreme penalty of the law."

"Do you have anything to say in your defense?"

He stood stock still, meeting the reporter's eyes. "I don't intend to say a word on my own behalf 'cause everybody'll jus' say I lied. The editor of the *Semi-Weekly* has been trying to incite a mob to lynch me. He sent me a paper which showed it. It's like the fuckers are never satisfied, but I suppose he thought to give me a kick downhill. If bastard law is gonna rule, better dismiss judge and sheriff and let everyone take their chances alike. Advise persons never to engage in killing for nobody."

The reporter looked up from where he'd been scribbling the Kid's words as fast as he could write. He watched as the outlaw dragged his shackles into the wagon and was chained to the seat.

Olinger sat facing the Kid, Kinney beside him, Mathews facing Kinney. Lockhart drove the team. Reade and Williams rode on horseback. They had one hundred fifty miles to travel to Lincoln, a trip of three days, through San Agustín Pass and across the white sands to La Luz, then up the Tularosa Canyon into the mountains Billy knew and loved. He whistled as they drove along, admiring the land as the wagon took him closer to the domain of his friends.

Angelita Sedillos rode her grandfather's burro down the trail alongside Eagle Creek, then east into the lower Hondo Valley to save the Kid. Billy had been in Lincoln a week now. Many people had tried to visit him but all had been turned away. They whispered among themselves how he was held in Murphy's old bedroom. The jail wasn't strong enough to hold a cripple, they said, and the county had bought the Big Store and made it the courthouse. The sheriff's office was there, too, and *el Chivato* was held in an upstairs room, chained to the floor.

The little burro picked its way slowly toward the ranch of Widow Casey, recently returned from Texas. Angelita had heard that the daughter was engaged to the deputy guarding Billy, and that the deputy would be visiting today. When she came near the house, she saw a huge man and a thin woman sitting on the porch swing, and suddenly Angelita felt so afraid she stopped.

Lily Casey had seen the girl when she first came into view. Watching the slow ambling of the burro, Lily was unhappy to be interrupted from reveling in the rare presence of her beloved. Bob was on full-time duty guarding the Kid, and Lily was impatient for his duty to be done.

She didn't, however, think the young woman riding the burro so shyly toward the house had anything to do with the Kid or even Bob. Lily didn't know what to think. That's why she kept looking up from relishing Bob's kisses. There was something odd about the girl's approach, as if she were afraid, and finally Lily said, "Bob, look there."

Olinger sat up and squinted at the girl. She was dressed poorly in a common brown frock, homespun and worn out. Her saddle was Apache but she sat it sideways, her thin skirt rippling to reveal the flounce of an eyelet petticoat catching the sun. A pretty girl, she seemed well seasoned and compliant. Olinger stood up, adjusting his gunbelt on his broad hips.

When Angelita saw them watching her, she wanted to run. She reminded herself that Billy had fought these people at risk of his life. She could risk humiliation to free him. She kicked her burro to move again, ambling forward to stop in front of the steps.

"What can I do for you, honey?" the man asked, stepping down and coming closer. His hair was long and amber red, like trickles of oil down his shirt, and his small eyes were scummed with lust above his smile.

She forgot her English. *"Me llamo Angelita Sedillos. Vengo a hablar con Señor Olinger."*

"I'm him," he said. "But I don't speak your lingo."

"I do," the woman said, standing up and walking to the edge of the porch. She was bony, her face pinched, her hair thin and dull. Angelita had never seen such ugly people. *¿Qué quieres?"* the woman asked, using the familiar, as if Angelita were a child or a servant.

"I have come," she said softly in Spanish, looking at the man, hoping for mercy from his lust, "to see the deputy who is guarding *el Chivato.*"

"*El es,*" Lily answered impatiently. She wanted the girl gone, not appreciating the way her fiancé was drooling all over her. The little twit wasn't fighting it, either. She looked as if she would trade her life for what she was about to ask, to say nothing of her virtue, if she had any.

"*Mi abuelo me dijo que en México,*" Angelita said slowly, pleading with her eyes as she addressed the man in Spanish, "there is a law that says if a woman marries a man who is condemned to die, he will be pardoned. Is there such a law here, señor?"

The woman's eyes snapped with ridicule as she translated the question. Olinger guffawed, laughing so hard he held his belly as he took a step backward, his eyes squeezed shut. Angelita wished she had a gun to smash his laughter down his throat with a bullet, but she said nothing, trying not to show her hatred.

Finally he was quiet, wiping his eyes as he grinned. He gave his *novia* a quick glance, then said, "Tell the señorita there ain't no such law in the territory, and there ain't nothing in heaven or hell that'll save the Kid."

Lily translated quickly, wanting to add an order for the girl to go away.

"*Perdoneme, señor,*" Angelita persisted. "*¿Está seguro?*"

"*Sí, él está seguro,*" Lily answered for him. "I don't know what you want with the Kid anyway. He always had an aversion to work when I knew him."

"Perhaps he did not wish to work with you," Angelita replied, turning the head of her burro and ambling away. As soon as she was out of their sight she let herself cry, yet she felt proud, too. Her power was slight and she had failed, but she hadn't let Billy down.

Pat Garrett was riding back to Lincoln from the Oaks where he'd been collecting taxes, one of his duties as sheriff. His business wasn't finished and he would have to return, but he'd promised Olinger he could visit his sweetheart, so Garrett was riding in to take the deputy's shift of standing guard.

The Kid was handling the situation with his usual high spirits. He was a model prisoner, always smiling and friendly, doing as he was told. Even Jim Bell, who'd been a friend of Carlyle's, had fallen for Billy's charm, which disappointed Garrett. But Bell was alert and competent; if he was a bit soft, Olinger more than compensated for it. Sometimes Garrett wished Olinger would lay off. He didn't want his deputy driving the prisoner so mad he'd do anything to escape. So Garrett had sent Olinger to see Lily Casey, hoping if he raked his ashes he'd come back with a little more compassion.

Except for a brief glance from the door, Garrett hadn't seen the Kid since he'd been brought from Mesilla. Now they were to spend four hours together, and the fact that Garrett was the man who stood between the Kid and freedom would be the physical truth for that span of time.

Garrett rode his horse into the yard of the courthouse and handed his reins to Old Man Gauss, the caretaker who'd once worked for Tunstall. Garrett entered through the west door, then climbed the narrow staircase to the second-floor hall, flooded with morning sun from the south window. He turned left, then right into his office. It was furnished with a desk, shelves cluttered with the absurd amount of paperwork his job demanded, a bed specially built to accommodate his stretch, and a rack holding a dozen Winchesters locked with a key that Garrett always kept on him. He walked through the room and opened the door on his prisoner.

The Kid was sitting astride a chair facing the open window overlooking the yard, the chain from his shackles stretched taut. His arms were folded on the back of the chair, his chin resting on the sleeves of the same shirt he'd been wearing when Garrett arrested him. Watching the Kid turn with the lethargic curiosity of a confined animal, Garrett smiled at his torpor.

When the night guard handed the sheriff his rifle, then left, the Kid stood up and smiled. "You get the honors today, Pat?"

Garrett nodded. Leaning the rifle against the wall near the door, he carried a chair over to sit at the table. "Cigar?" he asked, taking one from his vest pocket.

"No, thanks. I gave 'em up."

"Why's that?" he asked, trimming, then lighting his stogy with a matchstick from a pile beside a deck of cards on the table.

The Kid swung his chair around to face the sheriff, sat back down and said, "Gotta keep my wind up."

"You aim to do some running?"

"Man makes a lot of plans."

"Yours shouldn't go past May thirteenth."

"It ain't here yet."

"It will be," Garrett said, taking a deep drag on his cigar.

"You gonna be glad?"

"Relieved, is the word."

The Kid looked over his shoulder out the window a moment, then turned back with a smile. "Want to play some poker?"

"Sure," Garrett said, sticking his cigar in his mouth and shuffling the cards.

"We gotta play for matchsticks," the Kid said. "It's all I got."

Garrett smiled. "And you don't even smoke."

"I know it," he agreed. "I could always burn the building down, but I think I'd rather be hung than burnt alive, wouldn't you?"

"I wouldn't choose either one," Garrett said, dealing five-card stud.

Billy picked up his cards. Seeing he had two one-eyed jacks, he thought it was a shame they weren't playing for possession of the Winchester by the door.

As the deals came and went, Garrett had to borrow matchsticks to stay in the game. He was having such a good time, he went back to his office for a bottle of whiskey and two glasses, then let them sit on the table. He thought it would be interesting to get the Kid drunk and listen to him ramble. But Billy outwaited him. Finally Garrett opened the bottle and held a glass of whiskey up in a silent gesture of invitation.

The Kid leaned back with a puzzled smile. "Do you think, Pat, that by putting chains on a man you change who he is?"

Garrett sipped his whiskey. "If that were true, we could take the chains off and he'd be safe in society again."

"Safe in society? I've got more friends than Dolan has."

Garrett relit his cigar, then said through the smoke, "In the grand scheme of politics, Kid, your friends don't count."

He shrugged. "I thought we was playing poker."

Garrett continued to work on the bottle, relaxed because he was unarmed. Even in the unlikely case that he was overpowered, the Kid still wouldn't have access to a gun. That was a rule of Garrett's: no guns within the confines of the chain. Besides, he felt sharp and was having fun. He laughed when he had to borrow more matchsticks and the Kid said he was going to start charging interest.

When he'd been cleaned out again, Garrett stopped to relight his cigar, then puffed on it a moment as he studied the Kid. "You know, I could excuse the killing of Brady. That was war and I don't think you should be held accountable for it. But the murder of James Carlyle was a detestable act."

"I told my side of that," the Kid answered, his eyes guarded.

"Maybe you should tell it again," Garrett said. "Maybe it'll be more believable if you insist it's the truth."

"Why should I? Everybody'll think I'd say anything to get outta being hung."

"Maybe if you inspire enough doubt, you'll generate compassion. We'll soon have a new governor."

The Kid laughed. "Deal the cards, Pat."

At one o'clock, they were still playing when they heard Bell coming up the stairs to relieve the sheriff.

"That ain't Pecos Bob," the Kid said. "What'd he do, fall off his horse and hurt himself?"

Garrett listened to the light footsteps coming down the hall. Thinking Billy hadn't lost his acuity, he told himself he should warn the guards again of the Kid's slyness. "Bob took the day off to visit his fiancée," Garrett answered.

"Some woman's gonna marry that sonofabitch?"

"Lily Casey," Garrett said, smiling around his cigar as Bell came through the door.

The Kid shook his head. "She must be hard up to want him nuzzling her in bed."

Garrett rose and stood looking down at him. "I thought I'd bring you a whore for your last night, Billy. Sort of a going-away present." He was surprised to see the fight blaze in the Kid's eyes.

"I can get my own women, thanks."

Garrett laughed. "You're right about one thing. Wearing chains hasn't changed you at all." He walked out and closed the door.

Billy turned his chair to straddle it again and look out the window. The trees were bright with new leaves that bounced and rustled in the breeze. Squirrels chattered on the branches, batting their tails when they caught him watching. He could see down the street to the charred hole of the McSween house, and beyond that, Tunstall's store, now Dolan's. People rode horses and wagons or walked up and down the street, busy with errands. Billy marveled at their freedom, how they took for granted the ability to change direction in the middle of the road.

When Mrs. Mac had her dress splashed by a wagon, she went into the millinery to wash it off. While she was inside, Dolan came riding a smart chestnut gelding up the street, his back to Billy in the window. Dolan had barely passed when Mrs. Mac came out again, her dress wet. She walked to the doctor's office but he wasn't there. Billy watched a buggy stop alongside her, and a gentleman step down and hand her in.

If her dress hadn't been splashed, she would have seen Dolan and her mood would've been spoiled. If the doctor had been in, she wouldn't be driving off with this new man and laughing so pleased with herself. All of life was a quirk, no one controlled it. They could manipulate the bejesus out of it and get their way some of the time, but no man—not Chisum, not Dolan, not even Sheriff Garrett—controlled Billy's fate. Not even he himself, he recognized that. He needed help. Whether it came through the action of a friend or the mistake of a guard, it would be a quirk however it happened. He stood up and turned his chair around. "Hey, Bell, you want to play some poker?"

Jim Bell looked up from his newspaper. He was a tall, lanky man with a religious bent that he kept to himself most of the time. When he'd first taken the job, he stated flat out that he wouldn't pull the trap on the gallows. He wondered how Garrett could do it, hang his old friend, and Bell hadn't been surprised to learn Olinger had volunteered. Bell despised the noisy braggart. To put up with his taunting of the Kid was almost more than he could bear. It was watching the Kid take it that made Bell stick with the job. He was afraid if he quit Garrett would find another Olinger, and no man deserved that kind of punishment.

Bell had gone along with the posse to the Greathouse ranch because Carlyle asked him to. When the shooting happened, Bell had been squatting in the bushes. He'd believed the posse's version until reading the Kid's letter in the *Gazette*. It threw enough doubt in his mind that as far as he was concerned proof of guilt hadn't been established, and he bore no grudge for the death.

It was a risk inherent in being any kind of lawman, even standing guard in jail, which was simple enough if you kept your wits and stuck to the rules. Riding in posses, there were no rules and bad luck could fall on anyone. So Bell played cards with the Kid and talked with him as if they were friends, trying to make at least part of his last days pleasant.

They played all through the afternoon, until the shadows were long in the street below and the sky was red above the mountains. Then the night guard brought the Kid's supper and Bell went off duty. Billy was left alone. There was a guard outside his door and one beneath his window, but he was alone in his room with the clinking of chains every time he moved.

He ate the food before it got cold, then dragged his chains back to the window and stood there watching night settle on the village. Squire Wilson trundled by, getting along nimbly for such a fat man on crutches. Sam Corbet walked down the street with one of the Baca daughters. As they passed in front of a lighted window, she smiled up at Sam and he blushed. Billy grinned, wondering if he'd looked so obvious walking through Sumner with Paulita, if the people had smiled behind their hands at the smitten young man he'd been.

It would be warm in Sumner now, the riverbank humming with insects, the bees swarming in the orchards. She'd be wearing her summer dresses already, her arms and neck bare, so delicate in the sunlight he'd be tempted to kiss the damp warmth between her breasts. He wished he had.

Fewer and fewer people were out. He watched a lamp lit in Mrs.

Mac's house and wondered if it was Sebrian or the widow wanting more light. Billy hadn't seen her come back from her drive with the gentleman, and he wondered if she was thinking of getting married again. Wondered, too, why she didn't help him now when he needed it. But if she paid a lawyer to pursue Billy's appeal, people would know she was guilty of complicity to murder, and he didn't guess that would bode well for her future. He didn't begrudge her, knowing he wouldn't go out of his way to help her again either.

The room grew dark around him, the town silent. Still he stood with the chain stretched as close to the window as he could get, inhaling the scent of pines on the evening breeze as he listened to the animals up and down the valley, a burro braying, the long plaintive bawl of a cow. Coyotes yipped in the distance as the moon rose higher, flooding the valley with a silver light, the ruts in the road like ribbons of milk, the mud puddles a filigree of jewels. Somewhere nearby a horse nickered. Billy yearned to catch that horse and escape through the night, free of the chains and the consequences of his past. He was twenty-one years old. He figured he deserved another chance, and he was determined to win it.

49

In the morning, Olinger returned. Billy lay on his bunk listening to the big man thump up the stairs, down the hall, across Garrett's office, then through the door. Rolling over to watch the deputy holding his shotgun as he slid the breakfast tray on the table, Billy smiled. He got up from his bunk, clanked over to the table and started eating, though the eggs were cold. He ate to stay strong, to be quick when his chance came.

Olinger retreated back to the chair. He proceeded to open his shotgun and load it, which made Billy realize the deputy hadn't been careless after all since the breech had been empty. Leering at the Kid watching him load the weapon, Olinger said, "I got a piece of pussy last night. Bet you'd like to have some."

"Not the piece you had," Billy said, shoveling the cold eggs into his mouth, hoping to finish before Pecos Bob hit him.

"How would you know?" the deputy scoffed.

"You were with Lily Casey, right?" he asked, leaning back and pushing his empty plate away.

"She's told me all about'cha." Olinger sneered. "She doesn't think much of you and I ain't gonna believe anything you say."

Billy shrugged. "I didn't say nothing 'cept I wouldn't want to fuck her."

Olinger snapped his shotgun closed and stood up, aiming it at the Kid. "Whoever gets both loads of this'll feel it," he predicted.

"Ain't gonna be me." Billy smiled. "Garrett would chew your ass clean off."

Olinger lowered the gun. "I get to pull the trap. That's gonna feel good, Kid, watching your boots kicking for ground and not finding none."

"Don't stand too close. I might mistake you for thin air."

"It'd be worth it to feel the life kicking outta you."

Billy laughed. "It amazes me what some men do for pleasure. But anyone who'd fuck Lily Casey has gotta be strange."

"That so?" Olinger snarled, setting the shotgun down and stalking into the circle. "A little whore of yours came to see me yesterday. Angelita Sedillos. Remember her?"

"Never heard of her," Billy said, getting up and walking the length of his chains away.

"She came begging to save your life. Said there was a law in Mexico that if she married you, you'd be pardoned. She offered herself in the deal."

Billy turned slowly to face the ugly man.

"Course I took her up on the offer, and she was a sweet little ass, I'll tell you. I go in through the back door, you know what I mean? Then when I was done, I had to tell her there weren't no such law in the territory."

"You sonofabitch," Billy said, wishing the fat man would come closer with his guns.

Olinger laughed. "Thought you didn't know her." He retreated to drop his gunbelt on the chair, then returned. "Angelita. Oooh, she was sweet." He came right up to Billy, who was backed as far as his chain would reach. "I had to rough her up a little at the end. She wanted to kill me when I told her there weren't no such law. But she'll be all right soon as the bruises heal."

Billy hit him. He had to use both hands and his reach was only a foot from his waist, but he gave it all he had and felt his fists sink into the fat man's belly.

Olinger retaliated, dropping the Kid to his knees and flattening him with a hook to the jaw, then turned around to see Sam Corbet standing in the door. "What the fuck do you want?" Olinger growled, stomping toward him.

"I came to visit the Kid," Corbet answered, watching him pull himself to his feet.

"He ain't allowed no visitors," Olinger barked.

"I can see why, if this is the sort of treatment a visitor might witness."

Billy shook the dizziness out of his head, then managed a smile. "Don't mind him, Sam. He jus' has to get it out of his craw first thing every morning. It's damn good to see you."

Buckling on his gunbelt again, Olinger asked, "How'd you get up here anyway?"

"Sheriff Garrett gave me permission," Corbet said, looking at the Kid. "I have to go to Mesilla on business and won't be back before. I wanted to say good-bye."

"That's right nice of you, Sam," Billy said, approaching the length of his chain.

Corbet reached out to shake hands with the Kid. Their palms clasped and their eyes met as the small square of paper was exchanged.

Billy smiled. "Good luck to you, Sam. You've been a good friend."

"Godspeed," he murmured.

"His death's gonna be a lot faster'n this good-bye," Olinger said, grabbing Corbet's arm and yanking him toward the door. "Out! Now!" He pushed him across the threshold and followed him through Garrett's office.

Billy hurried to the light near the window and opened the note. One word: PRIVY. He smiled, knowing his chance had come. Wadding the paper into a tight ball, he swallowed it, then stood smiling down at the sun in the yard until he heard Olinger clumping back. Billy lay down on his bunk, hoping Pecos Bob would leave him alone to think for a while.

Pecos Bob didn't. "You hear Corbet is gonna marry one of the Baca daughters?" he asked incredulously as he settled his bulk into the chair. "How anybody can marry a Mexican is beyond me. They make good whores, but who wants their children half brown?"

"You're half Cherokee, ain't you, Bob?"

"Quarter, and it ain't the same."

"I had a Cherokee whore once. She smelled funny. The same stink I pick up off you. I don't know, Bob, if I was a Mexican woman I wouldn't want my babies coming out smelling like you."

Through the hours of the morning the insults continued, Billy always coming back with a low blow that kept the big man so angry the stock of his shotgun glistened with sweat.

At one o'clock, Bell took over. Seeing the Kid deep in thought on his bunk, Bell thought the inevitability of his execution was finally sinking in. Olinger had left his shotgun leaning against the wall, but Bell didn't touch it. He sat down and unfolded his newspaper as he listened to the heavy deputy herd the other prisoners down the stairs to Wortley's for their midday meal. A few minutes later, the Kid asked to visit the privy. Bell went into the sheriff's office and took the key from the wall. He came back and told Billy to stand near the window. Garrett had said to make sure the Kid was far enough away, and to watch him with one eye while turning the key in the lock. Maybe Garrett could watch him with one eye and get the key in with the other, but Bell couldn't. He always had to take his eyes off the Kid for a second. Billy had never threatened him, though, and Bell guessed when you had to take a crap you weren't looking for any delays.

Bell pulled the chain free of the shackles, stood up, drew his gun and wagged it for the Kid to precede him. They walked through Garrett's office, as Billy had every day he'd been there, lusting after the Winchesters in the rack. Then into the corridor, the doors on the north porch open to the breeze, the light from the south window flooding the floor with sunshine.

With the deputy right behind him, Billy hobbled down the narrow staircase. Around the landing and down a few more stairs, then the short distance to the side door and the jump over the threshold onto dirt.

He crossed the corral, the mountains towering with their fragrance of pines like the sweet scent of freedom. Through the gate and into the privy, a wooden box over a hole of shit. Beside the hole was a pile of newspapers, crumpled and misfolded. Billy searched hungrily, found the cold metal grip of the gun and pulled its long black nose from under the papers. He smiled and kissed it, restraining himself from laughing in joy. Silently he opened the chamber. Six live shells. Six chances to stay alive.

Unbuttoning his shirt, he stuck the gun behind his belt, regretting to relinquish it even that much. He wanted to burst out of the privy and blast his way to freedom, but he held back, calculating his best chance, and the armory upstairs was included in that. Six shells might get him out of town but not much farther.

Bell yelled, "You okay in there, Kid?"

"Yeah," he said. "Coming." He buttoned his shirt, pulled it loose to conceal the gun, crumpled some paper and dropped it down the hole, clumping his boots as if he were pulling up his pants. Then he opened the door and grinned at Bell. "Pretty day, ain't it?"

"Yeah, it is," he said, feeling sorry that the Kid didn't have many days left.

Old Man Gauss was just coming out of the caretaker's cottage, his pipe smoking in his mouth. He smiled at the Kid as he and Bell crossed the yard. Corbet lived with Gauss, and Billy gave him a wink to let him know the gift had been found. At the last minute, Gauss called to Bell, "Garrett took the two bays to the Oaks. The only horse we got is Burt's." "Damn!" Bell stopped to answer. "I hate that black devil."

Billy kept going, across the threshold and up the few steps to the landing, then hopping up the stairs, pulling the gun so he wouldn't drop it or shoot his foot off, bouncing against the walls as he ricocheted up the narrow passage. He gained the top, turned, and held the gun cocked and ready, breathing hard as he waited.

Bell came skipping up the stairs watching his feet, not even looking for the Kid. Then he looked. Seeing the gun, Bell's eyes shone with fear. "I don't want to kill you," Billy warned.

Bell turned and ran. Billy fired and the bullet ricocheted off the wall into Bell's side. He stumbled down the stairs, opened the door, and fell into the arms of Godfrey Gauss, who hadn't expected the Kid to kill Bell.

Billy hadn't either, but now wasn't the time for regret. He shoved against the armory door until it swung open. Feasting his eyes on the weapons and cases of ammunition, he grabbed a Winchester, made sure it was loaded, then hobbled back through Garrett's office to the room of imprisonment. Olinger's shotgun was leaning against the wall. Billy laughed as he picked it up, tossing the Winchester on his bed as he shuffled by. Going straight to the window open on the yard below, he primed the shotgun and leaned out.

Olinger was crossing the street from Wortley's, still chewing his last mouthful of food. He couldn't see the window behind the tree. Gauss ran out from behind the courthouse and shouted, "The Kid's killed Bell!"

Olinger was directly below the window. He looked up, saw the Kid and said, "He's got me, too."

Billy smiled. "Howdy, Bob," he said, exploding eighteen grain of buckshot into the deputy's face.

Laughing in triumph, Billy hobbled back through Garrett's office and out the door onto the balcony to look up and down the street. It was empty. Shuffling to the end of the porch, he leaned over the railing and shouted at Olinger's corpse, "Here, take these, too, damn you to hell!" He emptied the other barrel into the body, broke the breech and threw the shells at the bloody mess, then the whole gun, expelling the fury of his hatred.

He hobbled back to the armory, buckled two full cartridge belts around his waist and a holster with a forty-four. He stuck another pistol in his belt, grabbed a saddlebag and packed it with boxes of bullets, hundreds of cartridges, all forty-fours to fit both the pistols and the Winchester. Then he went back to the porch and yelled for Gauss.

Timidly, the old German approached from behind the building.

"Don't be afraid," Billy said. "I won't hurt you and there ain't nobody to stop me."

"What do you want I should do?"

"Bring me a pick for my shackles. Fetch it first and throw it up here."

As Gauss hurried away, Billy stalked up and down the porch. The people were coming out now, standing under the portals and watching him. He saw no guns in the crowd, no angry faces. The people simply watched. He laughed. He was free!

Gauss came back and threw him a small miner's pick. Billy caught it deftly and laughed at his success. "Now I want a horse, some water, and a blanket. Can you manage that?"

"Reckon," Gauss answered, turning away again.

Billy sat on the porch working at his shackles for an hour, glancing up and down the street at the people watching in silence. Finally Gauss came back with a prancing black horse. He held it at the east door and yelled up to the Kid. Billy only had one foot loose, but it was enough to sit a horse. He tied the chain to his belt and walked back to his room, picked up the Winchester and his deck of cards, then walked back through Garrett's office and down the hall, the sunlight beckoning with freedom.

He descended the stairs easily now, his stride restored. Seeing the gouge in the wall where his bullet had ricocheted into Bell, Billy thought it was a damn poor shot but had done the job.

He stepped out the door, seeing the shadows from the trees bounce on the dirt as he rounded the corner. When he saw Bell's body, he paused with regret. "If you hadn't run," he murmured, "I wouldn't have hurt you."

He turned the last corner and saw Gauss holding a skittish black horse on the other side of Olinger's corpse. Billy walked straight to the hated deputy, looked down at the bloody pulp of his face, and kicked him hard in the gut. "That's from John Jones," he said with a smile.

He slid the Winchester into the empty saddle scabbard, then took the reins, not even drawing his pistol because the people looked so peaceful. He smiled at them and turned to pull the horse close as it shied away from the sound of his chains. Then he noticed Gauss had forgotten something.

"I ain't got no blanket," Billy said. "You want I should freeze to death after escaping being hung?"

"No, Kid," Gauss answered, scurrying back to his cottage.

Billy looked at the people across the street, at the other prisoners in a chain gang in the yard of the Wortley, everyone watching him as if they were hypnotized. "Goddamn!" he shouted. "I'm free!"

"We're glad," a man called, coming forward. "Can I shake your hand? It'd be something to tell my grandchildren I shook Billy the Kid's hand."

"Sure you can!" Billy laughed, taking a few steps to meet the man. "Excuse the bracelets. I ain't had time to take 'em off yet."

Another man came forward, and then another, until a line had formed. Billy knew some of the men, others were strangers. All of them were friendly, their eyes glowing with respect, the women smiling beneath their rebozos under the portals.

When Gauss returned with a red blanket, Billy begged their forgiveness and turned to go. He draped the blanket behind the saddle, put his foot in the stirrup, and hefted the additional weight of fifteen pounds of chains into the leather. The horse didn't like the chains. It skittered sideways, then bucked before Billy had the other stirrup. He went flying through the air. Pulling the pistol out of his belt, he landed surprised in the dirt, then watched the horse run toward a boy standing in the middle of the road.

"Catch that horse, pardie!" Billy yelled. He watched with satisfaction as the boy jumped for the reins and dug in his heels, stopping the animal. Proudly, he led it back to the Kid, who was standing up now.

"If you hadn't caught that horse," Billy teased, "I would've killed you. I'm fighting for my life."

The boy laughed and said, *"Sí, Chivato."*

Billy took the reins and approached the nervous horse. In a voice like honey he said, "We're hightailing it outta here, *amigo.*" As he stuck his boot in the stirrup, he added, "And we're gonna do it right now." He swung into the saddle. The horse stomped and chafed at the bit as Billy looked at the people watching him.

They saw *El Chivato,* the happy young victor of his own resurrection, astride a dancing black horse draped with a blanket as red as the blood of human sacrifice, and the people knew him for a hero and were pleased.

"Adiós," he said, laughing and turning the horse, loping down the street of Lincoln, heading west, into freedom.

Hijenio Salazar was just finishing supper when he heard the Kid's whistle. He smiled and stepped outside. The whistle came again and he followed it until he found his friend standing in the forest, holding a horse so black only the silver of its bridle was visible in the dark. Hijenio enclosed the Kid in a hug, hearing the chains clatter as he squeezed back tears.

"I am happy to see you, *amigo,*" Hijenio whispered. "I spoke with Sam Corbet. He told me he had a plan and I was waiting, not wanting to interfere. But I would have done something if his plan didn't work."

"*Gracias, amigo. Ayúdame ahora.*"

"Come into my home."

Billy shook his head. "I don't want to bring the law down on you. This way, I can slip off before they get here. Bring me some food, will you? And something to cut their fucking chains?"

"*Con gusto,*" Hijenio answered, turning to go.

Billy waited beneath the trees, wondering if they'd be able to track him. Garrett was in the Oaks. It would take half a day before he reached Lincoln, another half to raise a posse. He'd be here before long, Billy was sure of that. Most likely, though, Garrett would expect him to head south to Mexico. The sheriffs along the way would be alerted. Everybody would be looking for him. Better to go north, east toward the Pecos. The deception was the beauty of it.

Hijenio returned with a bowl of beans, half a dozen tortillas, and a small, sharp pick. Billy used the tortillas as a scoop to shovel the beans into his mouth while his friend worked on the shackles. Each blow sent a jar up Billy's spine, but he ignored it and kept eating. Finally the shackles fell off. He jumped up and kicked his feet, laughing in joy.

"Four fucking months I wore those chains," he said, dancing in the shadows. He spooked the horse and it whinnied, stomped and bucked. Billy sidled up slowly, talking softly to calm the animal, then he turned back to Hijenio. "This horse is a pain in the butt. Think I'll send it back."

"I have a horse, *Chivato,*" his friend said. "I have been saving it for you."

"All right, *hombre!* Let's get these manacles off."

They sat in a patch of moonlight as Hijenio bent over his work. The manacles had been forged without a lock so he could only break the steel itself and his progress was slow. After a while, Hijenio rested. "I suppose you had to do some shooting," he said.

Billy dropped back on the fragrant pine needles and watched the stars peeking through the branches. "I had to kill Bell and I'm sorry for it. He shouldn't have run. Can't believe he'd think I'd hurt him."

"And the other? Was he there?"

"Yeah." Billy smiled. "But he ain't no more!"

Hijenio laughed. "*Pinche cabrón!*"

"*Andale,*" Billy said. "Let's get rid of their shit."

The cuffs were too tight for Hijenio to buffer Billy's wrists from the blows, and the final strike that broke the steel gouged a deep crescent in his flesh. It bled profusely. Using Hijenio's handkerchief to staunch the flow, Billy pressed the cloth against the wound with his knee while Hijenio worked on his other hand, again gouging the wrist when the manacle fell free. Hijenio went to the house and returned with alcohol to clean the wounds. "Will you sleep here in the forest?" he asked when he'd finished.

"With pleasure," Billy said, lying back on the pine needles again. "It feels good to be outside."

"You must be tired," Hijenio said, picking up the chains. "I will bury these and come back in the morning with breakfast."

Billy reached to shake his hand. It felt so good, he jumped to his feet and did it again. "Goddamn! I can move!"

Hijenio smiled. "Try to sleep," he said. "I will keep watch and warn you with our whistle."

"Gracias, amigo. Buenas noches."

"Buenas noches."

Billy lay back down, savoring the beauties of the forest. An owl hooting, the wind rustling in the trees, the stars playing peek-a-boo with the leaves like a woman's eyes behind her fan. He touched his guns, felt safe, and slept.

In the morning, Hijenio returned with a plate of eggs, fresh tortillas, and coffee. After eating, Billy shifted the saddle onto the horse Hijenio gave him, looped the rope around the black's neck, and let it go. The lean dark horse kicked up its heels in the sudden freedom and Billy laughed, watching it disappear in the trees.

"Where will you go?" Hijenio asked.

"Haven't decided," he said, swinging onto the tall bay.

"You should get out of the territory *pronto, amigo.*"

"Yeah, I reckon."

"Don't be *loco, Chivato.* There is no place safe for you here."

Billy looked around at the mountains he loved. "But if I jus' vamoose, that means Dolan won."

Hijenio snorted with disbelief. "There is no doubt he won. You should go to save your life."

Billy smiled slyly. "The dance ain't over yet," he said, leaning down to shake his friend's hand.

As he traveled across the mountains, Billy thought the world was beautiful, and he felt sorry to see it spoiled by a few men's greed. The county had been named for the president who freed the slaves. Recognizing the irony of that, Billy thought if he refused to submit, he could strike a blow for freedom that would outlive even the Santa Fe Ring.

He didn't stop until he found an oasis shimmering in the moonlight. Reining in beside the pool, he listened to his horse nicker with thirst. He walked it in a circle once, twice, dismounted and unsaddled before letting it drink. Hobbling the horse to graze, he stripped and took his clothes with him into the water. It was tepid from the warm sun of the prairie, alkaline with the caliche of the soil, but he hadn't bathed in four months, hadn't changed his clothes, and he knew where he was going now. He'd allowed it to come clear in his mind, and he wouldn't see her dirty.

He stopped first at the west line camp of the XIX, pleased to see Pete Maxwell saddling a horse in front of the shack. Billy slowed to a walk as he approached, giving Maxwell time to decide how to greet him. Pete came forward eagerly, reaching up to shake hands.

Billy smiled. "Howdy, Pete. Good to see you."

"Didn't think I would. I'm glad, Kid, though I suspect it cost a lot."

Billy swung down and ran his hand along the sweaty neck of his horse. "I've ridden this fellow too hard. Will you put him out to pasture for me and never sell him? He's earned a long rest."

"I'll do it," Pete said, "and give you another when you're ready to leave. Will you stay for breakfast?"

Billy shook his head. "Gotta keep moving."

"Then take this mare," Pete said, walking back to his horse, pulling his saddle off and leading her over.

"You're a good friend, Pete," Billy said, tossing his damp blanket and saddle onto the sorrel's back. He switched the bridle, then turned to shake hands. "I'll prob'ly be around Sumner awhile. Thought I'd stay with some of your herders, if you don't mind."

"I don't mind, Kid. But don't tarry long. Garrett'll be ripping the country apart looking for you. Unless . . . You didn't have to kill him, did you?"

"No, but I did my guards. Garrett will come looking but I'll be gone by then. See you around, Pete. *Gracias por todo.*"

"*De nada,*" he murmured, watching him ride away, thinking no one would believe the Kid had come back to Sumner.

Billy was counting on that. This was his stronghold, nearly everyone his ally. He could move around the line camps for weeks and not wear out his welcome, trusting his friends not to betray him. He felt good. He was clean, riding a fresh, fast horse, and he was free, returning to his lady love without a dime in his pocket but happier than the richest man on earth. He laughed with the gladness of redemption as he forded the Pecos, then ambled his sorrel under the cottonwoods along the avenue into Sumner.

The people stopped and watched, smiling shyly when he caught their eye. They felt they were seeing a ghost, a phantom of a better time, a memory of courage they had believed defeated. Yet he was there, smiling at them as if they were beautiful. The people turned and watched after him, and they felt important again because *El Chivato* had returned.

He rode right into the Maxwells' yard and tied the horse in the shade, knowing no one would think anything of seeing Pete's horse tied behind his house. Billy walked to the back door, opened it and stepped into the kitchen.

Deluvina was doing dishes at the sink. She turned with soap on her hands and stared at him a moment, crossed herself, then laughed with joy. "Bilito, Bilito, I prayed for you!" She laughed again, hugging him close, then held him at arm's length. "I see you now and I can hardly believe it. You have come back! God is good, He has freed you. It has made me a Christian again. I will light candles and say rosaries on my knees forever because you are free." She stopped, tears running down her cheeks as she smiled up at him.

He laughed. "It's good to see you, too, Deluvina. Is Paulita home?"

"*Sí*, in her room."

"Where's her mother?"

"In the market."

"If she comes home, keep her downstairs, will you?"

"*Sí*, Bilito."

He kissed her cheek, then climbed the stairs to Paulita's room where he knocked on the door.

"*Pasa*," she called.

He opened the door and watched joy light up her face.

"Billy!" she cried, jumping from the bed where she'd been cutting squares to make a quilt. She ran and threw her arms around him, laughing with tears.

He pushed the door closed and locked it, then held her in his arms, inhaling the scent of her hair and the moist fragrance of her cheeks, tasting the succulent flavor of her mouth. For a long time they stood melded together, one breathing reunion of love.

Paulita laughed. "Come sit down, Billy," she said, leading him toward the bed.

He let loose of her hand and watched her collecting the bright swatches of cloth, admiring the lean curves of her body as she stretched to gather the far pieces. She set them on the table and climbed onto the bed, sitting cross-legged near the pillow. He smiled at her. "I've thought of you a lot, looking jus' like that."

She smiled back. "And I of you, standing by my bed so pleased with yourself."

He laughed. "Do I look like that?" He began pacing the floor trying to collect his thoughts, as she had gathered the cloth, to arrange the chaos of the last four months into a neat stack of experience that would tell her who he was now. But he was unable to articulate what he wanted to say; the words didn't add up. He was free, he felt happy, he wanted to love her every way he knew how. Yet he came to her with two more killings behind him and she had a right to know that. Before he took what she could never regain, he wanted her to understand there was no future in loving him. But the words weren't there. With a self-deprecating laugh, he asked, "So what have you been doing?"

"Waiting for you, dreaming of you, remembering you, hoping and praying for you, longing and dying for you."

He smiled. "All that?"

"I'm glad you're free."

"Doesn't it matter how I did it?"

She shook her head.

"I thought about a lot of things, Paulita," he said, pacing again. "They shut me up in solitary in Santa Fe and there wasn't any light." He realized his footsteps were announcing to anyone below that there was a man in Paulita's bedroom, so he sat down, facing her across the expanse of her bed. "I haven't decided what I'm gonna do yet. I oughta go down to Mexico and change my name. Thing of it is, my name's all I got." He looked into her eyes so full of love. "I know one thing: I want you with me. I was sorry I hadn't loved you, but I ain't now. I'm free and it's better. I won't be around long, though. I want you to understand that."

She stood up and moved to the windows, freeing the tasseled cords and shutting out the light. Then she returned to stand in front of him. Her frock buttoned up the front and his fingers moved deftly down the row of tiny pearls, all the way to the floor.

She had longed for this moment since she'd first seen him on the porch illuminated by the light falling through the stained glass window. Smiling at his adeptness with her many petticoats and the intricate lacing of her corset, she held her breath as he unlaced her camisole and she felt the cool air on her breasts. He kissed them, and she marveled at this new pleasure, the joy of his love after yearning so long.

He stood up and smiled at her. "Get in bed, Paulita," he said.

She obeyed him with a laugh, slithering under the covers and shivering in anticipation, watching him undress. He stood there a moment to let her get a good look at him, then lifted the covers and slid in beside her, pressing his body the length of hers, giving his hands free rein to do as they pleased.

He was gentle, knowing no man had touched her before, and he wanted to take his time, to savor loving her, but it had been too long and he knew he'd be quick. Hearing her moan with pleasure, he smiled with his mouth against her belly, then slid between her legs and pushed against her resistance.

She stiffened, she couldn't help it. She was hungry to be filled by him, yet her body balked, her hips rose against him, and she bit her lip to keep from crying a protest.

"It always hurts the first time, Paulie," he murmured against her ear.

"I know," she said. "Do it."

He thrust through, heard her cry and felt her ripple beneath him. She was wet now with blood and he dove deep, starved for consummation.

They lay unmoving, listening to the sounds of their mingled breath. Finally he looked at her and brushed her hair away from her face, seeing tiny tears in her eyes.

"I'm so happy," she whispered.

"Are you? I am, too." He moved inside her again, saw her wince, pulled out and lay beside her, holding her in his arms as he fell asleep watching the rosy sunlight through the drapes.

When he awoke, he saw with a start that the sun was close to the horizon. She was watching him with a satisfied smile. He shook his head. "That's never happened to me before."

She laughed. "What hasn't?"

"Falling asleep with a woman, when she was still awake, I mean." He sat up. "What time do you think it is?"

"Nearly four. Mama has gone out again to visit Mrs. Rudolph in Sunnyside. She won't be back until late. Deluvina came in and told me she'd gone."

"Holy shit," he said, moving out from under the covers and reaching for his trousers.

"What's the matter, Billy?" she asked, worried.

"I gotta get moving," he said, standing up to button his pants. "I can't believe I slept through someone walking in like that."

"You were tired," she said, puzzled. "How long has it been since you'd slept? You're safe here. Mama won't be back for hours and Pete not until the day after tomorrow."

"I seen Pete," he said, sitting on the bed and picking up a boot. He looked at her then, the creamy skin of her breasts beneath the curls of her long black hair, the light of love in her eyes. "Lord Jesus," he murmured. "I don't think I can leave you, Paulita."

"Then don't," she said.

He let the boot fall, took his trousers off, and pulled her back beneath the covers. "We shouldn't be doing this," he said as he claimed her again.

"Why not?" she asked, holding him close.

"There's no future in it."

"Only now," she said.

Burying his face in her hair, he whispered, "Move with me, Paulie."

She wasn't sure what he meant but her instinct was strong. As she lifted herself to meet him, she felt a twinge of pleasure and she smiled, knowing there had to be more than the initial, painful shedding of blood.

" 'Attagirl," he murmured in her ear. "Now you got it, Paulie."

50

To no one's surprise, cattle rustling continued unabated during the Kid's four-month captivity. The Panhandle Stockmen's Association sent a new man into the troublesome territory to try and alleviate their losses. His name was John Poe. He went first to the sheriff of Lincoln County and asked for advice.

Garrett commissioned him a deputy and sent him to the Oaks because the booming mining town was host to a constantly changing collection of outlaws. When Garrett received news of the Kid's escape, Poe was there. He watched the sheriff's face as he read the telegram, saw his lip twitch beneath his moustache, then met his cobalt blue eyes, cold with anger.

"Now I'll have to do it all over again," Garrett said, handing the telegram to Poe.

Together they rode back to Lincoln and saw the bodies of Olinger and Bell laid out in a shed. Garrett was silent a long time, then softly cursed and walked out the door to call for a posse.

For a week they searched the surrounding country without picking up the Kid's trail. They rode to Las Tablas, San Patricio, and Tularosa. No one had seen the escaped outlaw. The Kid had disappeared.

Garrett returned the death warrant, written in Governor Wallace's own hand, with the notation that he was unable to execute same because the said William Bonney had escaped. That seemed to end it for Garrett. He stayed home in Roswell most of the time, regularly visiting his office in Lincoln and continuing his duties as sheriff in all other particulars, but making no effort to track the Kid.

The Ring-controlled newspapers crucified Garrett. The man they had feted only months before as the savior of law and order was now chastised as lazy, irresponsible, and timid for not pursuing the outlaw who had thwarted the courts and humiliated the power of the law, then ridden out of Lincoln in broad daylight and disappeared. They wanted the Kid's blood, and that Garrett did nothing was intolerable.

Garrett explained that he had his spies out gathering information. Eventually he began saying the Kid had left New Mexico, that he'd be a fool to stay in the territory with a death warrant and two new murders on his head, and everyone knew the Kid was no fool.

Billy was staying with shepherds only a few miles from Sumner. The young Mexicans working for Pete Maxwell welcomed the fugitive, shared their suppers of beans and tortillas, and talked with him late into the night.

During the days, Billy stayed in camp while the shepherds tended the flock, practicing with his gun to hone his edge after four months of captivity. His plan was only that he'd go to Mexico. Something would fall in his lap and net him a few dollars, then he'd vamoose. Garrett would never find him in Sumner. The people would never betray him.

One night while Billy was enjoying a convivial conversation around the shepherds' fire, he forgot for the moment who he was. Then he heard horses approaching the camp, and he became himself again. Grabbing his Winchester, the Kid rolled into the shadows, alert with defense.

"I will see who it is," Julio said, walking away from the fire toward the place in the darkness where two riders waited.

One of them said they were looking for stray horses and wondered if the shepherds had seen any. Julio said they hadn't, and they themselves had no horses. The rider was quiet, studying the men sitting around the fire, the two empty blankets, the horse tethered to the wagon. "Who else is in your camp?" he asked softly.

"No one," Julio answered.

The man's saddle creaked as he thought. "Goddamn," he finally whispered. "Wouldn't be the Kid, would it?"

"There is no one here, señor," the shepherd said again.

"Well, we ain't messing with the nobody that ain't there. We'll be moving along." He turned his horse and the other rider followed.

Billy stood up and watched them leave. When he was sure they were gone, he returned to the fire and hunkered down next to his friend. "How'd they know it was me, Julio?"

He shrugged. "Who else would we hide?"

Billy thanked the shepherds for their hospitality, saddled his horse, and headed southwest into the mountains.

Sheriff Pat Garrett had been doing paperwork in his office in Lincoln for three days. Sometimes when he looked through the open door to where the Kid had been kept, he knew how Billy had felt day after day. It made Garrett wonder who was the victor and who had been caught, since he was perennially doing work he'd rather not while Billy was off having fun. Wherever he was, the one certainty about the Kid was that he always enjoyed himself.

Garrett remembered a time in Sumner when the Kid had met three Mexicans spoiling for a fight. Billy obliged them, unbuckling his gunbelt and laughing as he said he didn't want to kill anyone but could beat them all with his fists. Thinking it was a good joke, the Mexicans attacked him individually at first. When that didn't work, they attacked him en masse. The Kid dropped all three in the dust. Then, wiping his bloody nose on his sleeve, he offered to buy them a drink. By the end of the night, they were pledging their undying loyalty and Garrett had congratulated the Kid on bringing enemies into his fold. He laughed and said, "They was never enemies, Pat. They was jus' looking for something worth doing."

Confined in his office laboring over paperwork, Garrett thought about how his goal had been to capture the Kid. But Billy had escaped. It was Pat who was caught.

On a small homestead near the Rio Peñasco, the Kid was eating supper with John Meadows and Tom Norris.

"How'd you get out of that fix in Lincoln?" Meadows asked.

Billy finished buttering a biscuit as he considered his answer. Not wanting to implicate Corbet, he lied. "I got Bell's gun away from him. When he ran, I had to shoot him."

Meadows nodded. "How do you feel about Garrett now?"

"He treated me decent," Billy said with a smile. "I wouldn't shoot if he was riding by and didn't know I was there."

"What about Olinger?" Norris asked.

"I proved my feelings toward him a few days ago."

Meadows stared for a moment, then said, "We hadn't heard. He's no loss to the world, that's for damn sure."

"What'll you do now, Kid?" Norris asked, bringing the bean pot and refilling their bowls.

"I'd like to stay here a few days, if you don't mind."

"Glad to have you," he said.

"We've had no comp'ny since winter," Meadows said. "Gets lonesome, and you're welcome to stay long as you want."

"Thanks," Billy said, reaching for another biscuit.

He stayed a week, doing chores and practicing with his gun, keeping his friends laughing at his jokes. One morning Norris asked Meadows if the first summer *baile* in Fort Sumner wasn't coming up soon. They studied the calendar tacked to the wall, not even knowing the day of the week. Billy said quietly, "It's the tenth of May. I've been free thirteen days."

"So tomorrow's the eleventh!" Norris cheered. "That's the night of the dance!"

Billy laughed. "Let's go kick up our heels."

The dance hall was across from the row of quarters where Charlie Bowdre had once lived. His widow didn't attend the *baile,* having been in mourning only five months. Nearly everyone else in the village and countryside came, and they all murmured with pride to see *El Chivato* walk through the door.

The *pobres* claimed him as their own. Marveling at the miracle of his escape, they closed around him with a seemingly invincible shelter of protection. When he started the dancing with Señorita Maxwell, the people thought she'd never looked so beautiful, as if she'd suddenly blossomed at the touch of a man who had defied death when all odds were against him.

The *baile* lasted well into the night, the musicians trading off so the people could dance without stopping. Celebrating the end of spring planting and the coming of the long summer days waiting for harvest, the people whispered among themselves that the resurrection of *El Chivato* was a good omen for the bounty of their fields. When they saw him leave early with Señorita Maxwell, they smiled in understanding of her fecund bloom.

The feted couple had talked and laughed as they danced for hours. They were silent now, not even touching as they walked through the warm night, fragrant with peach trees flowering in the orchard. Passing through the dimly lit kitchen, they climbed the stairs to her bedroom, where they fell into each other's arms with hungry passion. This time they knew each other, and were in no hurry.

It was midnight when he rose to leave. She watched him in the moonlight falling through the window. "Must you always go?"

He laughed. "What would your mother say if I came down for breakfast with you?"

"I'm willing to find out."

"I bet you are." He smiled, taking his gunbelt from her headboard and buckling it on as he watched her.

"Don't you know someplace," she asked, "where we could stay all night and wake up together in the morning?"

"What would you tell your mother?"

"I stay with friends occasionally. I can arrange it."

"Don't tell your friend what you're doing."

She shook her head. "Do you know of a place then?"

"I could prob'ly get a sheepherder's wagon for a night. Would that do?"

"Ooh, yes." She laughed. "We'd be like gypsies. When, Billy?"

"I'll let you know," he said, then kissed her and walked out, as if it were the easiest thing he'd ever done. Skipping quietly down the stairs, he listened at the bottom to be sure the house was still empty, then stole quickly outside and into the shadows.

The more he was with her, the more he thought it might work, being married. But they couldn't go away because he didn't have any money. Since nothing had fallen into his lap, he figured he had to do a little poking around and decided to visit Manuelita Bowdre.

Her room was still lit when he knocked on the door. It took her a moment to open it, then she stood staring at him with a mixture of joy and grief on her face.

"Evening, Manuelita," he said. "I jus' come by to see how you're doing."

When she invited him in and closed the door, the room felt haunted with memories. She put her arms around him and held tight. "I prayed for you, Billy. I prayed they wouldn't kill all of you."

He laughed. "They didn't kill any of me."

"Would you like some coffee?" she asked with a smile.

"Yeah, thanks." He dropped into the chair where he'd sat so many times waiting for Charlie. It felt too strange and he got up and started to pace.

"Still the same Billy," she said from the kitchen, "always moving."

"Wish I had somewhere to go," he answered.

"The world is a big place."

"Have you seen Tom Pickett around?"

She stared a moment, then whispered, "Don't, Billy."

"What?" he asked, all innocence.

"Whatever you're thinking of doing with Tom Pickett."

He shrugged. "Prob'ly wouldn't ride with me anyway. Prob'ly figures I'm a jinx after last time."

Her silence made him suspect the idea wasn't new to her.

"Is that what you think?" he asked. "That it's my fault, what happened to Charlie?"

She shook her head. "I know it was because of the war, and things he did before we fell in love."

"Charlie was a good man," he said, watching her carry the cups in and set them on the table.

"I miss him very much." She turned away to pull a handkerchief from the sleeve of her dress.

"Hey, don't cry, Manuelita. Did you hear the indictment was thrown out against him? He's been exonerated, you know?"

"I wish I could tell him," she whimpered.

He took her in his arms and held her close.

The door opened and Abrana stood staring at them. Her face crumpled with hurt, then she stepped back and closed the door.

He looked down at Manuelita. "You gonna be all right?"

She nodded.

"Sorry I can't stay for the coffee," he said, kissing her cheek.

"Que te vayas bien, Chivato," she murmured.

He ran after Abrana, worried she would hold what she'd seen against Charlie's widow. Catching up, he turned her to face him. "That was nothing," he said. "We was talking about Charlie."

Tears glistened on her cheeks. "Oh Billy, I love you so much."

He could have kicked himself for looking toward the Maxwell house.

"I'm going to have your child," Abrana whispered.

"Sonofabitch," he said, looking away again, this time toward the corral and the prairie beyond.

She cried out and ran down the portal, her bare feet slapping in the dust. He caught her just inside her door. "I didn't mean it," he said, holding her close. "I'm glad, I swear it. Jus' don't cry, Abrana."

Finally she was quiet. Raising her eyes and seeing that he was impatient to leave, she leaned against the wall in defeat. They looked at each other a moment, then he touched her cheek and was gone.

Toward the end of June, John Poe left the Oaks and rode over to Lincoln. Finding Garrett in his office, Poe passed along the news that he'd heard the Kid was in Sumner. Garrett laughed. "I've been told he's in El Paso, Mesilla, Las Vegas, and Santa Fe. I'd bet my last drink he's nowhere near Sumner, of all places."

"I got it on good information," Poe said.

"From who?"

"Ol' Man Pritchard."

"He's a drunk and a bum."

"He sleeps in the Dedricks' stables. Says he overheard 'em say the Kid's in Sumner." Poe shrugged. "It's worth checking out."

"Might be, if you like riding through hundred-degree days and being eaten alive by mosquitoes at night."

Poe laughed. "We could spend the Fourth in Roswell, have us some fun before we take that ride."

Garrett did want to see Apolinaria and the baby, and it was true there would be festivities in Roswell for the Fourth of July. Maybe someone there would tell Poe the Kid had been seen in Montana, and they could forget about riding to Sumner.

It was almost July when Billy took Paulita to stay overnight in the camp of Sebastiano Anaya, a shepherd visiting his wife and new baby at home. His wagon was a small prairie schooner, the bed just big enough for a mattress and trunk, with a kitchen of cubbyholes along the outside. Billy slid off his horse and lifted Paulita down. "This is it," he said. "Hope you ain't disappointed."

"It's lovely," she answered, looking at the empty prairie stretching flat in all directions.

She carried her satchel to the back of the wagon and set it inside. Seeing the bed covered with a red and white checkerboard quilt, she smiled in anticipation of their pleasure, then watched him unsaddle his horse and hobble it to graze. She admired the quickness of his agility, his taut awareness of every nuance around him.

The first stars were faint, the moon not yet risen as she walked a few steps into the prairie. From a distance she listened to him building the fire, and she told herself it would feel like this if they were married. She would take him for granted and not even think about the sounds he made working. It never occurred to her that he had no work. When she returned to the fire, he had a cauldron hung over the flames and a skillet nestled among the coals.

"Sebastiano left us supper," he said. "Was nice of him, wasn't it?"

"Yes," she said, sitting down and hugging her knees. "Have you eaten many meals in the open like this?"

He laughed. "Quite a few," he said, handing her a large wooden spoon. "Stir the pot once in a while, will you?" He walked to the wagon and began searching through the cubbyholes.

She lifted the lid off the pot and looked in: black beans speckled with green chile. Carefully she stirred them and replaced the lid. He came back and handed her two metal bowls and spoons, then pushed the coffeepot in at the edge of the coals. When he lifted the lid off the skillet, she saw it was full of baking biscuits. He put the lid back, apparently satisfied with their progress, then sat down and leaned with his elbow against his saddle. "Did you stir the beans?" he asked. "I hate burnt beans."

"Yes, sir," she said, leaning to stir them again. "They smell delicious."

"Sebastiano's are the best. That's why I asked him to make us a pot."

She nodded and stirred them again, worried now that they'd burn. When the coffee boiled over, she used the hem of her skirt for a hotpad and managed to slide the pot out without catching her dress on fire.

He laughed softly. "I get the feeling you don't cook much, Paulita."

"Deluvina does it for us," she said.

He nodded. "You know how to make biscuits?"

"No," she answered contritely.

"I can teach you," he said. "Cornbread. Lots of stuff. Beans, steak. I know how to cook a good steak."

She laughed. "We won't starve."

It hung there between them, the idea of going away together. He pulled the skillet from the fire and flipped the biscuits out with his knife as she dished up the beans, then they ate without talking. When they'd finished, the flames were dancing on embers. "Can I do the dishes?" she asked, because she thought she should.

"Jus' drop 'em in that bucket by the wagon," he said, handing her his. "We'll do 'em in the morning."

She came back and sat down, snuggling against his chest as she looked at the stars.

After a moment, he asked, "You got a good horse, Paulie?"

"Yes. Pete gave me a three-year-old mare a few months ago."

"Think you could ride all day, for a coupla weeks maybe?"

"Tell me what it would be like," she said dreamily.

"We'd eat only food we could carry, sleep out even if it was raining. Maybe we'd find a cave, but prob'ly not. If we crossed a river you might get a bath, if it didn't have snakes in it. We'd have to move fast, stay away from towns at first. I don't know, Paulie, it'll be a tough ride for a man."

She sat up and met his eyes. "I can sit a horse all day, and it won't hurt me to go without a bath. Just because I'm small doesn't mean I'm fragile."

He laughed and gave her a hug, then stood up and walked over to check on his horse. She watched him scan the horizon, and she thought he was beautiful. When he returned, he sat down on the other side of the fire, poured himself another cup of coffee and smiled at her across the soft glow of the coals. "What'll you take with you?" he asked playfully.

"Oh," she said, considering her wardrobe. "My brown serge riding habit. I'd wear that, of course. Let's see. My blue frock, and the dove gray—that's suitable for so many occasions. And the yellow, do you remember it? It's not bright but a real soft maize, and I always feel so happy when I wear it. And then my green velvet for parties in the winter, and my black for really formal occasions. And I'd need fifteen petticoats, and . . ."

"We ain't taking a fucking wagon train, Paulie."

She was startled by his profanity, then laughed at it. "You've never used that word with me."

"You've heard it before, though, haven't you?"

"Yes. Sallie Chisum and I discussed it once."

He laughed. "How can you discuss a word?"

"Neither one of us knew what it meant at the time." She studied him coyly. "Sallie told me you kissed her." When he said nothing, she asked, "Did you?"

"That's what I thought I was doing, but I was really kissing Chisum's ass and didn't know it."

She recoiled away from him. "My, that was crude."

"All of life ain't pretty, Paulita. I want you to know who I am 'fore you leave with me."

"So this is a test," she said slowly.

"Ain't it for both of us? Ain't you here 'cause you want to find out how you'll feel waking up next to me? See if it's something you want to do more'n once?"

"I suppose," she answered. "But I have no doubt I will want it, that I do want you. Do you doubt you want me?"

"No. But I can't see how you're gonna be happy bumming around dragging a packtrain loaded with your dresses and petticoats."

"Will we always bum around?" she asked, not having considered it. "Won't we have a home?"

He shrugged. "I ain't had one since my mother died."

"Never had a house? A cabin you rented or an abandoned one you claimed as your own for a while?"

He shook his head. "I sleep outside, stay with friends when it's cold, if I'm lucky."

She thought about that, then said, "When I'm twenty-one, I'll have my trust fund."

He laughed. "I knew a doc up in Tascosa who told me to choose a rich girl when I made up my mind to get married."

He hadn't used that word since the first time, and she felt happy to hear him say it again. "That's three years away," she teased. "I hope you don't wait to marry me for my money."

He stood up and held his hand to help her, then slid his arm around her waist as he led her toward the wagon, whispering close to her ear, "I'll show you what I'm gonna marry you for."

It was nine o'clock the next morning when he took her home. Still on his horse, he smiled down at her standing on the kitchen steps, and he thought to make her happy was a joy, to see her smile, the sparkle in her eyes, knowing they were meant for him.

Her love gave him something to honor in life, but only if he could keep her as she was, not drag her into poverty and early old age like the wives of homesteaders he'd known. They were worn out by the time they were thirty. Usually they died, and the homesteader found another young wife and bred another brood of offspring. Billy didn't want Paulita to die, didn't care if they never had children. He wanted her the way she was: young and in the bloom of health forever. Leaning from his saddle, he kissed her with love.

Coming from the market where he'd met with a man about harvesting his wild wheat in the fall, Pete Maxwell turned the corner to see his sister kissing the Kid in the bright light of morning.

Pete froze. Remembering a thousand smiles he'd ignored, a thousand times he'd seen them together and thought they were childhood friends, he realized his error with an irrevocable rejection of the Kid and an instinctive and violent repossession of his sister.

Too prudent to attack the Kid directly, Pete stepped back around the corner and sank onto the front steps, holding his head in his hands as he tried to stop berating himself for letting it happen, encouraging it even. How many times had he told the Kid he was welcome? And Pete had meant it, but his invitation hadn't included his sister. He didn't need to see the satchel to know she'd been out all night. The Kid was obviously kissing her good-bye, saying thanks for the good time, see you again soon—after he'd visited the whores, and someone had seen him knocking on Manuelita Bowdre's door, and Pete himself had seen the Kid come out of Abrana García's room.

That had been the night of the first summer *baile*. Paulita had said she danced with Billy all night, and even then Pete hadn't caught on. Had the Kid brought her home, taken what he wanted, then gone to Abrana for more? Pete squeezed his head between his hands, trying to stop the pain of knowing Paulita was ruined. He'd have to marry her off quickly. Who would accept a soiled wife to gain the prestige of the Maxwell name? His mind sorted through young bachelors he knew, frantically looking for a solution, anything to ease the pain of betrayal. He'd trusted the Kid, befriended him when the entire legal machinery of the Ring was set against him. In return, he had ruined Paulita.

Pete Maxwell stood up and walked quietly back through the gate, down to the stable where he saddled a fast horse and rode out to the north range looking for a man named Henry Porter. Porter had worked for Pete for years, and Pete trusted him completely. He found him at the camp, playing a harmonica with his chair tilted against the hut.

Porter's song was sorrowful as he watched Pete dismount and walk toward him. When Pete crossed the light falling from the door, Porter saw a scowl of anger such as he'd never seen on the face of his boss, and he broke off his song abruptly.

"I need your help," Pete said.

"I'll do anything for you, Pete. You know that."

"You mustn't tell anyone. Ever. I mean exactly that. If Paulita finds out what I'm doing, she'll never forgive me. You'll be the only one to know. Swear you'll never tell."

"I swear it."

"The Kid has seduced her. I want him gone."

"I'm sorry to hear it," Porter mumbled. "What do you want *me* to do?"

"Ride down to Roswell. Tell Garrett to come get him."

51

One evening in early July, while John Poe and Pat Garrett were sitting on the veranda of Garrett's house, a small boy approached shyly and stopped just outside the gate. Reminded of Juan Gallegos, the urchin who'd carried his messages in Sumner, Garrett stood up and walked toward the boy with curiosity.

"*Buenas tardes,* Señor Sheriff," the boy said softly. "I was sent by a man who wants to see you in secret."

"Did he tell you his name?"

"No, señor. Only that he has information and you must come alone. No one must know."

"Where is he?"

"I will take you."

Garrett called to Poe that he'd be right back, then followed the boy along a dry, crusted road leading into the marshes along the river. In the warm still air preceding a thunderstorm, the trees drooped beneath the overcast sky. The sheriff saw a horseman under one of the trees, then heard the boy running away. Slowly Garrett walked toward the man who had sent for him. He dismounted in the deep shadow of a cottonwood, a hanging tree people called it, because of its strong low branches.

When Garrett recognized Pete Maxwell's righthand man, he turned away to hide his smile as he struck a match and lit his cigar. Puffing, he turned back around and asked, "What can I do for you, Porter?"

"I've been sent with a message," he answered nervously, "but first you gotta promise you'll never let on who told."

"I generally keep my sources confidential."

"There ain't nothing general about this," Porter argued. "We're talking about someone innocent getting hurt bad."

"Your boss send you?" Garrett asked, feeling pleased.

"Swear you'll never tell."

"All right. I swear never to reveal where I learned what you're about to tell me."

Porter looked around, then whispered, "The Kid's in Sumner."

Garrett stared at him hard. "You sure?"

"He'll be at the *baile* on the fourteenth. Meet my boss in his bedroom at midnight."

Not waiting for Garrett's answer, Porter mounted his horse and dug in his spurs. He'd owed it to Pete, but for no other man would he have betrayed the Kid.

The sheriff stood watching him ride away, then turned and slowly walked home, puffing on his cigar, deep in thought. There could be no doubt of the information's veracity: Pete had finally caught on to the Kid and Paulita and had acted to protect his sister. All that was clear enough. The incredible part was that Billy was there at all.

It had been two months since his escape. Why wasn't he in Mexico, the Nations, anywhere but his old stomping grounds? Garrett didn't want to chase him again. Like Pete Maxwell, Pat just wanted him gone. But unlike everyone else in the territory, it was Garrett's job to see it accomplished. He knew the Kid would never again be taken alive, so he'd have to kill him. There was no other way. If the Kid would just get out of New Mexico, Garrett wouldn't have to. But Billy wouldn't leave, and Pat couldn't understand why.

With Poe and Tip McKinney, Garrett left Roswell on the night of the tenth. They rode north on back trails where they wouldn't be spotted, and on the night of the thirteenth, they camped in the sand hills five miles south of Sumner. The next morning, Garrett sent Poe in to reconnoiter, arranging a rendezvous for just after dark at the fork north of town.

Poe had never been in Sumner. He felt eyes from all directions as he ambled beneath the shade of the towering cottonwoods along the river. When he swung down in front of Beaver Smith's saloon, three men surrounded him.

"Who are you?" one asked.

"My name's John Poe," he answered, tying his reins to the hitching rail.

"What'cha doing here?" another asked.

"I've been mining in the Oaks," Poe replied, allowing only a trace of indignation in his voice. "I'm on my way back to the Panhandle where I used to live."

The men looked him over, then the third one said, "That's all right. Whyn't you come inside for a drink?"

Poe followed them into the long, narrow room and up to the bar. His eyes took a few minutes to adjust from the bright light outside. When he saw half a dozen hardcases lounging in the corners watching him, he turned back to his companions at the bar. One of them bought a round of whiskey, and they stood leaning on their elbows talking mining until Poe realized they were waiting for him to finish his drink and buy the next round. He obliged and they stood awhile longer, talking about cattle and horses and even sheepdogs for a time. After three drinks, Poe pretended to leave his friends with regret.

He walked over to a café and ordered a meal. As he ate at a table by the open window, he admired the pretty little plaza. It was clean and quiet, the air sweet from the peach orchards, the people pausing on their errands to spend a few minutes in pleasant conversation with their neighbors. Without exception, when they stopped and chatted, the people looked at him before going on their way. Wondering if they could all be protecting the Kid, he could think of no other reason to account for their surveillance.

Poe left the restaurant feeling lazy. He sat on a wooden bench in the shade of a tree. After a few minutes a young, pregnant woman came and sat down on the bench on the other side of the tree. Poe admired her high cheekbones and silken ebony hair tied up off her neck in the heat. She sat cooling her face with a wooden fan, not even looking at him.

"Terrible hot, isn't it?" he asked pleasantly.

Her dark eyes flashed with scorn. "I don't know you."

"No, ma'am. Name's John Poe."

She turned away.

"You get many travelers through here? I ask 'cause it seems you folks don't cotton to strangers much."

"We don't like trouble," she said, fanning her face with a tight, rapid rhythm.

He laughed easily. "All strangers aren't trouble, are they?"

Her eyes flashed again. "It only takes one, señor."

Someone across the plaza called her and she rose and walked away from him. He thought Abrana was a pretty name, the woman herself pretty in an exotic way, but his mood hadn't been lightened by the few moments spent chatting with a pretty woman as it usually was. There was something mean about this town, as peaceful and somnolent as it appeared. An edge of defense lay right under the surface, and it was sharp and struck back when touched.

He moseyed up and down the avenue, falling into conversations when he could. Not once did anyone mention the Kid or his escape, though it was still the talk of the territory everywhere else. Poe rode out of Sumner feeling certain the Kid was in town. When he reached the dead cottonwood hovering over the crossroad, he saw Garrett and McKinney coming from the opposite direction. They all reined up together in the jagged pattern of moonlight falling through the bare branches.

Garrett looked up, remembering when he'd sat there waiting for Charlie Bowdre. The tree had since been struck by lightning and destroyed, as Charlie had. Garrett nudged his horse out from under the shadow and led his men the back way into town.

After leaving their horses under a stand of willow trees by the river, Poe and McKinney followed Garrett into the orchard. The air was sultry with the sweetness of rotting peaches squishing under their boots in the weeds, and the music from the *baile* drifted on the breeze. They walked through the alternating shadows and patches of moonlight, the deputies thinking they were following Garrett to the door of the Kid's sweetheart.

The sheriff was stalling. "Come at midnight," the messenger had said, and Garrett merely intended to wait in the orchard. Knowing everyone would be at the *baile,* he figured he could slip in under the trees and find a place to hide. But he'd forgotten that the orchard was a trysting place for lovers, and he almost interrupted a couple in the tall grass. He retreated quickly, beckoned his men the other way, and led them back toward the road where he settled down in the darkness beneath an overladen tree.

So intent on each other that they hadn't heard the stealth of the lawmen's approach, it was Billy and Paulita lying in the grass. They continued their pleasure unaware they'd been seen, stealing love in the orchard because Pete was home. Neither of them minded making love beneath the humid perfume of the peaches, the heat heavy on their naked skin so slick with sweat they eased into everything without resistance. They knew as long as the *baile* was still going no one would be walking through the orchard. When the music stopped at midnight, they rose to go.

She picked up the blanket while he buckled on his gunbelt, then they stood smiling at each other, not wanting to part. Lifting the blanket from her hands, he draped it over her head.

"That's the way I first seen you," he whispered. "I mean, really seen who you are in my life."

Paulita smiled. "I asked, 'If I make myself into a squaw, will you take me with you?' "

He laughed. "That's right."

She stepped closer and touched his face. He had grown a beard now. It was soft, a sandy color, and she loved to touch it as she looked into his eyes. She felt happy, the days passing as if in a dream. The people treated her like a madonna, and once a week they danced at the *baile* while she and Billy made love. It was a magical time and she felt little impetus to hurry it. She stood on tiptoe to kiss him good-bye.

"You want me to walk you home?" he asked.

She shook her head. "Pete hasn't been sleeping lately. It seems he's always awake, prowling the house. You go along first, I'll be all right."

He leaned to kiss her again. *"Buenas noches."*

"Buenas noches," she murmured. *"Duerme bien."*

"Pretty good, Paulie. By the time we go to Mexico, you'll be talking like a native."

She looked at him with the question, silent.

"Shhh," he said, kissing her again quickly. *"Que te vayas bien."*

She watched him cross the orchard's dapple of shadow and moonlight, gracefully leap the fence, and disappear in the dark. Folding their blanket, she walked home smiling as she remembered the hours just passed.

Garrett and his deputies had watched the Kid emerge from the shadows, jump the fence, and jog up the road. They'd heard the voices murmuring in Spanish, guessed they were the lovers they'd nearly stumbled across earlier, and watched the young Don Juan go on his way without suspecting who he was. The woman whose house they were watching came home alone, and no one visited before her lamp went out. They waited in the orchard a few minutes more, then Garrett said he had one more place to check before giving up.

They walked along the edge of the plaza where clusters of men stood talking before going home. Garrett kept to the shadows, knowing his height would pin his identity. He led his men along the edge of the flower gardens, sickening with scent, and toward the picket fence around the Maxwell house.

Billy walked toward the home of a friend who was out of town, though his wife would be there. In no hurry, he stopped to talk with the scattered groups of men on the plaza. They all welcomed a few minutes of his attention, enjoying his fluid Spanish as he talked of crops and the weather as if he were one of them. When he reached his friend's room, the door was open.

Celsa was slapping out tortillas for his meal when he came in. He gave her a kiss on the cheek, then sat down on the settee to read the newspaper. Her hands made quiet sounds shaping the tortillas, pat, pat, pat, flattening the round balls of dough, laying them on the griddle where they hissed as they rose and puffed, then fell just before she flipped them with her fingertips. Pat, pat, pat, the dough for the next one, the singe of heat again, and pat, pat, pat. The sound was somnolent, the fragrance enticing.

Billy put his newspaper down. He pulled off his boots, took off his coat and gunbelt and dropped them on the end of the settee, then stretched out with his gun beneath his jacket as a pillow.

Celsa worked in the kitchen, making many tortillas because her husband would return before dawn. And men were always hungry, hungry and horny; feed them and fuck them and they gave you their money. All except the Kid. He never had any money, and Celsa was amused that Paulita Maxwell thought she could be happy as his wife. Abrana was right: the rich girl wasn't playing with a full deck and her luck was doomed to die as soon as she got pregnant. Then her family would whisk her off to some Rio Grande rancher, and the Kid would go back to Abrana.

Celsa liked Abrana. The Kid was blind not to see that she had the strength and fortitude to be an outlaw's wife. He wanted the delicate, spoiled rich girl who couldn't cook or sew or find medicine in the wild herbs. Paulita possessed none of the skills needed to carve a home out of nothing. That's what the Kid had, charm and grace and the pleasure of his company, but his woman would have to fend for herself otherwise.

Celsa hummed as she patted the tortillas. When she lifted the lid off the pot of beans to stir them, the fragrance of chile mingled with the toasting bread, and the Kid sat up. She smiled at him from where she patted dough in the kitchen.

"What else you got to eat, Celsa?" he asked.

"Beans," she said with a shrug. "When Saval comes home, we will have money again."

"Pete butchered a steer today. Think I'll walk over and cut me a steak."

"Okay," she said, then smiled. "I will cook it for you."

"Thanks," he said, walking out as he was, in his stocking feet and shirtsleeves, without his gun.

The moon was bright, the village asleep around him. He walked down the portal to the corner, then cut along the edge of the plaza toward the white picket fence around the Maxwell house.

Garrett left his deputies outside without telling them where they were or what he was doing. The door to Maxwell's bedroom was open in the stifling warmth. "Pete?" Pat whispered.

"Garrett?" came the dry reply.

"Yes," he said, moving slowly through the dark as his eyes adjusted. He sat near the pillow on Pete's bed.

Poe sat down on the top of the wide steps leading to the front door, shadowed by a pillar. McKinney leaned against the fence in the dapple of moonlight falling through the trees.

Billy opened the gate and walked into the yard. Knowing the beef was hanging on the back porch, he pulled his knife from his belt as he started to skip up the steps, nearly colliding with a man sitting in the shadows. Billy leapt into the deeper darkness of the porch. "¿Quién es?" he whispered.

"Don't be afraid," Poe said, thinking he was a Mexican who worked for the owner of the house. Knowing the man could see how heavily armed they were, Poe added, "We won't hurt you."

Billy backed toward Pete's open door, watching the men, not knowing who they were. He stood silhouetted on the threshold a moment, then ducked inside and across the dark room. His knife glinted in the moonlight as he leaned with both hands on the bed, his left an inch from Garrett's knee, and asked, "Pete, who are those men outside?"

Like the croak of a toad, Pete whispered, "That's him."

Garrett pulled his pistol.

Hearing the sound and realizing someone besides Pete was in the bed, Billy backed away. He thought of throwing his knife, but he didn't know who was there; a friend of Pete's, maybe, a woman even. "¿Quién es? ¿Quién es?"

Garrett aimed for the voice and pulled the trigger, slid onto the floor, shot again, then jumped to his feet and ran from the room. Pete ran after him.

Billy felt himself fall. Blood in his throat, a bullet in his heart. Who was it? he wondered. Wanted to yell, "Pat, is that you out there?" Wished it was, wished he would come in and say good-bye. Billy coughed, strangling on the blood, then laughed, knowing this time the joke was on him. There was too much blood. He couldn't catch another breath.

"I got the Kid!" Garrett said, yanking Poe into the shadows as Pete came running from the room. Poe raised his gun but Garrett batted it down. "Don't shoot Maxwell."

"Maxwell?" Poe whispered. "You've made a mistake, Pat. The Kid wouldn't come here."

"I heard his voice."

"He may only be wounded," Pete said.

They all stared at each other on the dark porch, then Garrett asked, "Which one of us is gonna find out?"

The front door banged open and bare feet pounded along the veranda. Deluvina turned the corner, holding a shawl closed over her nightgown, looking frantically at the men. "What happened?"

"Garrett killed the Kid," Pete said. "At least we think he did. He's in there." He nodded at the open door.

Deluvina spun on her heel and walked into the room. She crossed to the table, found the matches and lit the candle, then turned around to see the Kid had been killed.

In a torment of rage she catapulted herself onto the porch, attacking Garrett with the full force of her fists. "You pisspot! You didn't have the courage to face him in a fair fight! You shot him down in the dark, unarmed! Damn your soul to eternal hell, you cowardly long-legged sonofabitch!"

"Deluvina!" Pete shouted, dragging her off the sheriff.

Garrett walked into the room, lit now by the flickering candle, and closed the door. The Kid was lying on his back, shot through the heart, with only a hunting knife in his hand. Garrett marveled that Billy had felt so safe among the people of Sumner he would walk its streets unarmed, that finally in his life he had found that kind of freedom. Garrett had not, and knew now he never would.

Outside, Deluvina was screaming curses. Then she broke off and cried, "No, Paulita, don't come here." Garrett reached into his pocket for his flask and took a deep swig of the bitter brew.

Poe came in, followed by McKinney.

"There's a crowd gathering," Poe said, looking at the outlaw for the first time.

"How do they seem?" Garrett asked.

"Quiet," Poe said. "Sad."

"He didn't have a gun," Garrett said.

The deputies looked carefully and saw he was right.

"Find out where he was staying," Garrett said. "Bring me his gun. And don't either one of you ever tell that I shot him unarmed. You hear me?"

"Yes, sir," they both said.

"I want that gun in his hand before anyone else comes in here."

Garrett waited alone, thinking once again that Billy had escaped but he was caught. He remembered the Kid's infectious enjoyment of life, and how when they first met he'd thought Billy was simply a rambunctious youth who'd wandered into the wrong side of a war and acquitted himself honorably. Garrett felt no honor for having killed him. The Ring had won. Garrett had lost. Remembering Billy's smile, Garrett knew he'd never again share the Kid's inordinate pleasure at being alive. Now and for the rest of his life, Pat would be known as the man who killed the Kid.

Finally the deputies returned and Garrett placed the gun in Billy's dead hand, then let the family back in. Deluvina had the Kid carried to a nearby carpenter's shop where he was laid on a bench, his body draped with a red blanket and his head resting on a lace pillow from Señorita Maxwell's bed. Candles were lit all around him. The women of the village knelt and prayed as the men stood with their hats in their hands, solemn with sorrow. Paulita did not attend. Only Deluvina represented the family in the long night of grief.

In the morning, the man the *pobres* called *El Chivato* was carried to the *camposanto* and buried beside his friends Charlie Bowdre and Tom O'Folliard. Everyone in the village walked in the procession and stood around the grave, their silence broken only by the crying of women and a lonely wind blowing across the empty prairie. The bare earth was covered with flowers, and the people went home.

EPILOGUE

In 1884, Juan Patrón was killed in Puerto de Luna by a paid assassin of the Ring. In 1896, A. J. Fountain and his three-year-old son were murdered in the White Sands, disappearing without a trace along with documents the lawyer carried that were potentially injurious to the Ring. Pat Garrett, cantankerous in old age and vociferous in his criticism of the Ring, was shot in the back in 1908 by men who pleaded self-defense. In 1928, the writer Emerson Hough investigated Garrett's murder until advised by persons in high places to desist for the sake of his health.

Jimmie Dolan drank himself to death in 1898 on the Rio Feliz; he was lauded by Roswell as a pillar of the county. Lily Casey spent a term in prison for rustling cattle; after a failed marriage, she died in Ruidoso in 1946, leaving a manuscript praising John Chisum. Chisum had died of cancer in Eureka Springs in 1884. Sue McSween, raising stock given to her by Chisum, achieved fame as the Cattle Queen of New Mexico, but died bitter and alone in the ghost town of White Oaks in 1934. George and Frank Coe returned to their farms, where their descendants live today. George's fine red barn is still standing. Lincoln survives as Billy the Kid's town. Fort Sumner was swept away when the Pecos flooded in 1937. The *camposanto* is all that remains. Paulita is buried near her father. It is not believed she ever learned of her brother's treachery.

She married José Jaramillo when she was eight months pregnant, and lived long and apparently happily as his wife. It was a condition of the engagement that she never confess her child was not fathered by her husband. Paulita kept that promise, except to the son himself.

The story around Sumner was that José had been impetuous to enjoy his fiancée and was now so deep in Mexico buying cattle for his father's ranch that he couldn't come home soon enough to rectify his haste. Everyone accepted the story, though they'd never seen José Jaramillo in their village and Paulita wasn't known to travel far. She would live in Las Cruces after her marriage, and few there knew the history of her romance. Those who did kept quiet to protect the honor of the family she joined.

One cool autumn evening while Paulita was waiting for her fiancé to come home and claim her, she sat on the porch swing and talked with some cowboys visiting her brother.

They had been told of the overeager José and couldn't blame him, Paulita was so pretty in the moonlight. They were new to the territory and hadn't heard the rumors about her and the Kid, the stories now so thoroughly squelched by Mexican propriety. As they sat along the wall on a horsehide settee, Paulita moved the swing gently with her foot against the floor. One of the cowboys was named Gus, and the other Sylvester though they called him Sly. They were talking about nothing in particular when suddenly Gus said, "Billy the Kid was killed on this porch, wasn't he?"

The swing stopped a moment and Paulita's smile became melancholy. "In Pete's bedroom around the corner there," she answered. Then the swing creaked as it moved and her skirt lifted in the breeze.

"They say folks who die violent deaths haunt the place they was killed," Sly said. "You ever hear his ghost walking around?"

Paulita laughed, a gay silver song like the jingle of a fine spur. "No," she said. "I never have."

They sat a few minutes in silence, watching the lightning bugs in the flower garden. The stalks were all withered now, the blossoms brown on the ground.

"I heard tell," Gus said, "he was in his stocking feet and didn't die with his boots on, like they say fighters always want to. Is that true?"

"I don't think fighters ever want to die," she answered.

"No, I s'pose not," he said.

The village was dark around them, the house silent. Gus heard a soft prowling footstep. When he heard it again, his ears pricked to attention. "You hear that?" he whispered.

"It's him," Sly whispered back. "It's the Kid returning to where he was killed."

Impatiently Paulita rose from the swing, walked around the corner and picked up the black cat she'd seen prowling the yard every night for

weeks now. She carried it back to the men and sat down in the swing.
"Here's your ghost," she said with a smile. "Just a lost critter looking for
a home." She stroked the lush fur and the cat purred with contentment.

"You don't believe in ghosts a'tall?" Gus asked.

She shook her head.

"Ain't you never heard stories that made you wonder?"

"I was very close to my father," she said, "and other people who have
died. If communication with the dead were possible, I would know. So,
no, gentlemen, I don't believe in ghosts."

"Not even a teeny, little bit?" Sly teased. "Ain't you never been
afraid when you heard something odd in the night?"

She shook her head, smiling.

"I bet you're afraid to walk by a graveyard on a night like this, with a
full moon, all by yourself. I bet you're afraid then."

"How much do you want to bet?"

He laughed. "Two-bits."

"Remember that *camposanto* you passed riding into town?"

"Sure, that's where the Kid's buried. We stopped and looked at his
grave."

"I'll bet you two-bits I walk down there and back right now."

"You're on."

Gus grinned. "I'll add another two-bits."

Gently she lifted the cat and set it in the swing beside her, then rose
and walked down the steps, through the gate and along the road toward
the *camposanto.*

Gus said, "You think we should've let her go? I've heard it's bad luck
for a pregnant woman to pass anywhere near a graveyard."

"Aw, she won't go," Sly answered. "She'll walk down the road and
wait awhile, then come back and tell us she went. We'll believe her, a'-
course."

"That ain't fair," Gus protested.

Sly shrugged. "What is?"

Paulita walked in the warm midnight beneath the full moon, happy
to be away from the silly cowboys and their thoughtless banter. Of
course, they didn't know. No one would ever know. She had agreed to
that when she'd seen the fear in her mother's eyes on learning of the
child. Paulita had been given a daguerreotype of José Jaramillo; he had a
kind and serious face, and she thought she could be a good wife to him.
She knew she would never love another, so it remained only to find a
comfortable husband, and she felt she had as much chance of that as most
girls marrying for love.

She stopped in the gate to the *camposanto,* looking at the graves among the prairie grasses, dry and withered. Keeping her eyes on his, she walked thirty steps down the path, turned and walked three feet west, then stood a moment before the three sinking mounds, the three wooden crosses, Billy's on the right.

With a moan she lay facedown on the earth and poured her love into the soil, creating by her wish and her will a moment of sharing her life with him again. Her hand reached up to clasp the cross and clutch it in agony as she trembled with the power of her loss, then she lay peaceful and acquiescent, then she laughed.

"Sorry, Billy," she whispered into the earth, "but I have to win my bet."

Yanking the cross from the ground, she held it silhouetted against the harvest moon.

"Eternal life," she prayed.

Then she carried the cross back to the astonished cowboys.

AUTHOR'S NOTE

No one writing of the events and people described in this novel can fail to acknowledge a tremendous debt to the historians who salvaged the facts. Principal among them is Colonel Maurice Garland Fulton, whose work is substantially responsible for saving the story for posterity. He was followed by William Keleher, who brought a lawyer's mind to the tangle of legal documentation. Among their more contemporary successors, Frederick Nolan made an important contribution with his biography of Tunstall, and Eve Ball deserves high praise for giving us both the story of the Jones family and finding and bringing to publication the manuscript of Lily Casey. Noteworthy among newcomers to the field is Jerry Weddle, who finally solved the mystery of Billy's activities in Arizona.

Other writers have recently added to the literature of Bonneyana, but in most cases I disagree with their conclusions. One author went so far as to imply that the Lincoln County War was fought because Sue McSween wanted new furniture, and another, though a qualified historian, could see no more significance in the war and Billy's continuing fame than an expression of America's penchant for violence.

I have been faithful to the truth in my reconstruction of historical reality but admit my treatise was based from inception on the belief that folk heroes do not attain public adulation without cause. Billy Bonney was "the" kid, charming and ebullient, a vagabond who lived without a home or a job. Embracing elements of both Robin Hood and Peter Pan, he used his skills of aggression to defend the poor and antagonize the rich, and because he never grew old, he remains forever young. The story of the Lincoln County War, however, is more important than any one person.

Psychoanalyst Alfred Adler was the first to note the totemic symbolism of Billy's name among the Hispanic *pobres* who were his true public. They called him *el Chivato,* colloquial Spanish for a young goat or kid. A scapegoat for the sins of his Anglo contemporaries, Billy was sacrificed because he refused to submit to the political and social order of his time. As such, he was a freedom fighter on the western frontier, and the Lincoln County War was a battle for individual rights against the machine of big business. The war was lost, and is continuing to be lost in America today.

—ELIZABETH FACKLER
El Paso, Texas